The Belfast Anthology

The Belfast Anthology

edited by
Patricia Craig

THE
BLACKSTAFF
PRESS

BELFAST

First published in 1999 by
The Blackstaff Press Limited
Blackstaff House, Wildflower Way,
Apollo Road, Belfast BT12 6TA, Northern Ireland

Supported by the National Lottery
through the Arts Council of Northern Ireland

ARTS
COUNCIL
of Northern Ireland
NATIONAL
LOTTERY
FUND

The acknowledgements on pages 429–37 constitute
an extension of this copyright page

Typeset by Techniset Typesetters, Newton-le-Willows, Merseyside

Printed in England by Biddles Limited

A CIP catalogue record for this book
is available from the British Library

ISBN 0-85640-651-1

Contents

Introduction

'Belfast is really a wonder,' wrote the journalist F. Frankfort Moore in 1914, before going on to marvel at the city's expansion during the previous seventy years, and singling out, in an amiably sardonic tone, the 'stupendous statistics' in the areas of employment, production and so forth, that face you at every turn. Belfast is a wonder, a cynosure, a big noise in the world, however you look at it – and many, it must be said, have looked in a spirit less admiring than F. Frankfort Moore's. The first thing many observers noticed about Belfast was its mercantile drive, which suggested either a go-ahead attitude, at odds with the fecklessness of the rest of Ireland, or out-and-out philistinism: you could take your pick. Belfast has always had its upholders, and its detractors.

There are several distinct phases in its existence. First a castle and virtually nothing else, then a minuscule plantation town 'plotted out' by Sir Arthur Chichester, Belfast still didn't amount to much more than five or so streets at the end of the seventeenth century. It wasn't advanced in outlook either. 'A barbarous nook of Ireland': this was John Milton's memorable and exasperated tag for the place in 1649. Even though his outburst was occasioned by a particular doctrinal controversy, when the Belfast Presbytery came out against religious toleration, his phrase struck a chord with hearers at the time and since – whether they believed he'd got it horribly right, or simply smiled at his miscalling of the place.

Barbarous and out of the way, Belfast remained more or less at a standstill, as far as a building programme was concerned, until the middle of the eighteenth century; then came a period of seventy-odd years, during which time the town acquired something of a reputation for elegance and enlightenment, qualities not associated with it before or since. This was the era of the 'streets broad and strait' commended by a succession of travel writers, of the shapely Old White Linen Hall and the founding of 'Inst', of the United Irish movement and concomitant egalitarianism – though it's true that counterforces were massing at the time and didn't take long to gain the upper hand. The Frenchman de Latocnaye, for example, had his equanimity disturbed by the 'troubles' of 1796, when soldiers ran through the streets of Belfast smashing windows as they went. Within five years, and in the aftermath of the 'United Irish' Rising of 1798, the Union of Great Britain and Ireland had taken place, and a gradual change of heart was overtaking the radical, forward-looking town. There are complex reasons for this, which have been well documented by historians such as A.T.Q. Stewart, Marianne Elliott and Jonathan Bardon, but chief among them were a repudiation of revolutionary tactics, once republicanism in action was seen to have failed, and a hardening of sectarian attitudes – the latter in response to the increasingly emphatic demands for Catholic emancipation.

Catholics at the time were converging on Belfast from all over the province as industrialisation got under way; and confrontation between factions became inevitable. Sectarian riots in Belfast stretch all the way back to 1813, when two men were shot dead in North Street. Further outbreaks, complete with bludgeons, broken heads and party tunes, occurred in 1832 and 1833; however, as Jonathan Bardon notes in his *Belfast: An Illustrated History*, these were nothing to what happened later in the century, when the place had grown into a great industrial city. The years 1857, 1864, 1872, 1886, 1893 and 1898 all afforded opportunities for the bulk of the populace to become adept in the tactics of street-fighting, and led to the city's getting a name for unruliness, a reputation which has stayed with it.

It was also becoming notorious for immoderation in its religious views: the two things are indeed intertwined. 'The clash of broken glass was a familiar sound in the streets of Bigotsborough,' states the author James Douglas in 1907, making no bones about descriptively renaming his native city. And Mrs Tonna: 'Parties run very high in Belfast,' she writes in her *Letters from Ireland* (1838). One more recent reporter, the journalist T.J. Campbell, attributes all the riots mentioned above, directly or indirectly, to the Reverend Henry Cooke, 'the framer of sectarianism in the politics of Ulster'. Cooke's abominations were, as he put it himself, 'fierce democracy on the one hand, and more terrible Popery on the other'; it's a peculiarity of the city that it throws up, or draws in, from time to time, these demonic clerics who see no merit in ecumenism.

The great Belfast industries – ships, linen, tobacco, rope-making and so forth – burgeoned in the nineteenth century and contributed enormously to the character of the city (or the incipient city; it remained officially a town until 1888), conferring on it prosperity, expanding suburbs and a business-like outlook. William Makepeace Thackeray, on a visit in 1842, found it hearty and thriving, and looking as if it enjoyed roast beef for dinner. That is one view; another comes from the Reverend W.M. O'Hanlon, minister of the Congregationalist Church in Upper Donegall Street, who's reduced to outrage by the twenty-two public houses he counts in the vicinity of North Queen Street. O'Hanlon, originally from Lancashire, spent a lot of his time in Belfast venturing into hovels in the slums ('We advanced along Durham Street, peering ... into all manner of courts and entries'), and reporting his findings in a series of heartfelt letters to the *Northern Whig*. (*Walks Among the Poor of Belfast* was published in book form in 1853.) He was greatly provoked by what he saw as the connection between destitution and debauchery, and wanted nothing more than to effect a cleaning up of morals along with living quarters. Whiskey drinking, and the lewd songs he heard issuing from the slums, made his hair stand on end. His Belfast is a more lurid place than the pious, decorous, pig-headed, mushrooming, belligerent or quotidian locale of other commentators, but his letters have a value in putting forward a strong image of the reeking Victorian city.

Belfast has never been easy with sex, treating it always as something lurid, seedy or unspeakable: the puritanical ethos of both Catholicism and Protestantism, on top of a certain provincial uncouthness, must have gone a long way towards atrophying the erotic instinct in more than the hero of Brian Moore's novel *The Feast of Lupercal* (1958) – though the virgin schoolmaster Diarmuid Devine, in that book, seems a pretty typical victim of ignorance, ineptitude and priestly browbeating. The farce and horror surrounding poor Mr Devine's one attempt to achieve unchastity puts him off the activity for life. This novel is an energetic indictment of the repressive *mores* saturating mid-twentieth-century Belfast. Some people native to the city, succumbing to despair over its obduracy, inurbanity and atavistic thinking, took themselves away from it as quickly as they were able, only to find, like Brian Moore, that its hold on their imaginations was ineradicable. Growing up in Belfast, if it does nothing else, gives you something to react against; few writers could refer to a childhood there, as Philip Larkin famously did with Coventry, as a 'forgotten boredom'.

You can take it or leave it, but it makes an impression. 'Belfast was detestable' (V.S. Pritchett); 'I knew at once that Belfast was an awful city' (Paul Theroux); 'Belfast! Belfast! The city of smoke and dust' (Louis MacNeice). Caroline Blackwood remembered the 'backwaterishness . . . bigotry and . . . tedium' of the whole benighted province, and never got over the amazement she experienced, around 1970, on seeing it thrust into the face of the world on innumerable television screens. 'Can there be,' she wondered, thinking of the grimy dockyards, the musty parlours and chained Sunday swings, 'a boredom so powerful that it finally acts like an explosive?' – a viewpoint others might consider frivolous, preferring to point a finger at injustice, ghettoism, misgovernment over a period of fifty years; the rottenness of its foundations finally bringing the whole show down.

Still, Caroline Blackwood's perception of Belfast as the ultimate place where nothing happened can't be judged askew: in the years between 1921 and the late 1960s, Belfast was going about its ordinary business, keeping out of the headlines, putting on a face of respectability and behaving, for the most part, in a law-abiding way. You could, with justice, have called it provincial or dull (though many didn't: Stephen Rynne, for example, referred in 1956 to 'this dynamic place', and Kate O'Brien, in 1960, shows a good deal of affection for the 'perverse and awkward city' in which she found herself). It was only in odd corners, in Campbell's Café opposite the City Hall, in the Elbow Room on the Dublin Road, around Smithfield Market and in an *avant-garde* bookshop or two, that enlightened social criticism got itself expressed, and slowly began to produce an effect. The advocates of an equitable future might have seemed to be coming into their own in the 1960s, the civil rights era, before the noise and drums, the ranting and ruination, started up again – this time devastatingly. Whatever liberal impulse existed in the city, it wasn't a match for ancestral incompatibilities.

Since 1969 and its acquisition of 'troublespot' status, Belfast has been endlessly scrutinised and analysed – in the light of socialism, sociology, psychopathy and what-have-you. Outsiders have poured into the place in search of a *frisson* of danger or repulsion (the horror of it all). Paul Theroux is a case in point, though his comments on Belfast are framed in a pungent and comic manner, which is thoroughly bracing. And alongside those agog at extremes of unrest are others – mostly local – at pains to show that violence and destruction aren't the whole of the picture, that blight and buoyancy of spirit can coexist.

This is an anthology, not a history of Belfast, or a travel guide, or a sociological survey. It's arranged thematically, not chronologically, in seventeen sections, and contains material stretching from early 1600s to the present (the bulk of it coming from the nineteenth and twentieth centuries). It aims to build up a composite picture of the city, its atmosphere, exigencies and eccentricities. This material is drawn from most available sources, and includes memoirs, poetry, fiction, history, local history, travel writing, letters, social studies (but not drama: I had to draw a line somewhere). Most of the extracts are fairly short, though one or two may extend over a couple of pages – I am thinking, for example, of F. Frankfort Moore's very lively account of a riot he witnessed in 1857, as a spellbound infant in the charge of a nursemaid; or of Ciaran Carson's superb poem 'Hamlet' – the last word on the Falls – which defies abbreviation. (As far as recent poetry is concerned, I was very much spoiled for choice, given the remarkable outbreak of talent which hit the north around 1969 and after.)

Fiction is the area in which it's most problematic to remove a segment from its context; the one thing an anthology cannot do is appease the appetite for narrative momentum. Of its nature, it is meant to be dipped into, or taken bit by bit. For this reason – although you will find a number of set-pieces scattered throughout this collection – I've scoured novels and stories on the look-out for moments of description or reflection, rather than episodes requiring knowledge of the plot to make a proper impact. This hasn't been a hardship: there are a few classic Belfast novels – *Call My Brother Back, Judith Hearne, The Red Hand of Ulster* are titles that spring to mind; but on the whole, before the 1960s, Belfast fiction is pretty dismal and lightweight stuff – although careful reading will nearly always yield up an instructive, vivid or intriguing passage or two. Since the 1960s, novels about Belfast have proliferated, and these too are frequently of a quality to be deplored. I can recall an instance of someone spending a weekend in Ballymurphy or somewhere similar, and subsequently basing a work of fiction there. Belfast's notoriety has endeared it to the thriller writer, but resulting thrillers all too often present a characterless city, populated solely by hoods and hardliners. Only Brian Moore's *Lies of Silence* – his eventual return to a Belfast setting – stands out as an exemplary entertainment along these lines. Good straight novels set in Belfast do exist, however, and I hope I have included a sufficiency of these, and succeeded in extracting passages which indicate their flavour.

As well as the qualities which everyone, rightly or wrongly, ascribes to Belfast – tenacity of purpose, egregiousness, a hand-me-down fanaticism in religion and politics, grim northernness, indifference to the arts and, in recent years, resilience – certain landmarks stand out in the city's past, and somehow adumbrate its character: the Home Rule crisis of 1912, for instance, the building and sinking of the *Titanic*, the inauguration of Stormont, the United Irishmen's pledge to republicanism on top of the Cave Hill, the hanging at Cornmarket of Henry Joy McCracken, the civic confidence displayed at the turn of the twentieth century in the construction of the City Hall. In the recent past, such landmarks are apt to be more baneful: the burning of Bombay Street, the Ulster Workers' strike, and the sorry catalogue of atrocities whose names – the Abercorn Restaurant, Oxford Street Bus Station, McGurk's Bar – still resound with chilling power.

All these elements of Belfast are touched on in the following pages, the last particularly in the section entitled 'Bloody Hand'; it would be perverse, indeed, to try to exclude them from an anthology which aims to be as comprehensive as possible, as well as putting its finger on the quality of life in the city, at any given moment. However, when it comes to writing about present-day terrorism, I have chosen to be extremely selective, for a number of reasons. In the first place, the sheer weight of words on this topic – through journalism, fiction, reportage, political analysis and so on – militates against any attempt to sort out the most illuminating portions from all the rest. And then, the thirty-year impasse is still to be definitively resolved, despite all the optimism engendered by the IRA and loyalist ceasefires of 1994, and the Good Friday Agreement of 1998, which is still, as we go to press, awaiting enactment. A line remains to be drawn under violence, or the threat of violence. It is time that old moulds were broken in the north, but they're not quite broken yet. What you should pick up (among other things) from this anthology is a sense of continuity in the city's patterns of disruptiveness – right down to the use of paving-stones in street-fighting.

But the necessity for discrimination with regard to the present is dictated most strongly by the main aim I've had in mind while compiling *The Belfast Anthology*: to provide a record of the kind of place that Belfast used to be, at whatever period you care to name. It should, if I've done the job properly, get to grips with the idea of Belfast (like any city), as a palimpsest, with each age superimposing its own predilections, for good or ill, over those of its predecessors. It's a far cry, indeed, from the careful planning of the late eighteenth century – the neat, orderly streets and befitting buildings ('A very well built town of brick,' wrote Arthur Young in 1780, a mite dutifully – he was really more interested in jotting down the price of provisions – 'potatoes, 9d a bushel, pigeons, 6d a couple ...', and in noting the dimensions of Lord Donegall's card room, than in giving an overall impression of the place) – a far cry from such pleasing homogeneity to the current policy of decimation: sweep away the whole architectural heritage of Belfast, and stick up replacements as repellent as you can make them. Accretion is one thing, agglomeration another. It's true that the Housing Executive has done its bit, since 1971, to ensure that a certain standard is kept up in the field of new domestic architecture; and the Ulster Architectural Heritage Society has alerted people (well, some people) to the riches in danger of going the way of the Queen's Elms on University Road, and the Ulster Club in Castle Place. But the rot continues. Change is inevitable, but it doesn't have to be indefensible.

The upsurge of interest in local history testifies to the sense of loss (however subliminal) occasioned by incontinent rearranging of the city's contours, and lends a timely aspect to an anthology such as this one. I suppose you could class this compendium as an enterprise akin to the one engaged in by the group of Belfast-Australians in Ciaran Carson's poem 'The Exiles' Club', who meet every Thursday in the Wollongong Bar to reassemble the old Falls Road, not omitting 'the effects of the 1941 Blitz, the entire contents of Paddy Lavery's pawnshop'. But I would hope – for all its homing in on details, the sound of goods trains in the night, horse-trams, a tern on a pond in Botanic Gardens – it presents a wider perspective than this might suggest. It's not just about loss, but should remind us of all kinds of enduring indigenous graces, from the city's mountainy backdrop to a special kind of urban élan, along with psychic inheritances both salutary and oppressive. It would serve no purpose whatever to indulge one emotion to the exclusion of all others; and although I am sometimes assailed by rage and depression when I consider the destruction of the city I grew up in (not to mention its earlier incarnations – the period between 1880 and the 1920s or 1930s, for example, when Belfast, it seems to me, projected the strongest possible self-image), I wouldn't want to minimise the horrors, poverty, disaffection, areas of injustice, even the architectural infelicities, that prevailed then as now.

As for the really distant past – I defy anyone with an interest in Belfast not to be intrigued by allusions to such unfamiliarities as the rural beauties of Peter's Hill, sinister-looking resurrection men making a beeline for Friars' Bush, or travel about the streets by means of sedan chair. It's a poignant exercise to envisage cows and buttercups in the fields behind Inst, or skating in winter on the lake at Ballydrain ... To pursue this line any further is to risk quaintness: thatched houses off York Street, benignant heads under castor hats, picturesque localities going by the names of Tea Lane and Cripples Row ... right down to thon wee, wee, crickety sweetie-shop beloved of the poet Padraig Gregory. There's a thin line between relishing the more blatant constituents of bygone local colour and out-and-out regressiveness, and I'd like to think I hadn't overstepped it. I have, however, quite deliberately, included the odd touch of populism and blether – not only a selection from the *Belfast Telegraph* pieces about Ballymacarrett written by St John Ervine in the 1940s, but Richard Rowley's 'Oul' Kate in Heaven' (too long, unfortunately, to print in full), such anonymous party-pieces as 'My Aunt Jane', 'The Cruise of the Calabar' and 'Carson's Cat', and Raymond Calvert's 'Ballad of William Bloat'. These are in because I'm as susceptible as anyone to high-grade Belfast aplomb, and because I believe that no anthology purporting to distil the flavour of the city would be complete without them. And I think you will find sufficient seriousness, astringency and scintillation elsewhere in the following pages to offset the appearance of a frivolous item or two.

In his paper entitled 'Belfast in Literature', delivered in 1955 to the Belfast Natural History and Philosophical Society, John Bebbington identified five recurrent themes: the shipyards, Smithfield Market, Cave Hill and the other mountains, religion and politics. The last two have since been fused together under the heading of 'the Troubles', and the shipyards no longer loom large, but the mountains are still in place, despite improvident quarrying and the incursion of newer and newer housing estates. As for Smithfield – as everyone knows, that market and marvel went up in smoke nearly a quarter of a century ago: black was the night. Most of the pieces about Smithfield are gathered under the heading 'Labyrinthine Alleyways, Obliterated Streets': this section includes both recollections of places no longer in existence at the time of writing, and evocations of places remote from us.

All Bebbington's themes, and much else, receive a good airing here, though I have drawn the line at religious tosh: the kind of thing that comes with a title like *The Sandy Row Convert: A Tale of the Belfast Revival.* (Not that tosh is altogether missing: for example, you'll find a passage or two from a long-forgotten work called *The Pool of Garmoyle.*) And, although I was tempted by curiosities such as the nineteenth-century French author Joseph Méry's 'The Scientist and the Crocodile', which refers to Belfast and the 'science [which] runs through its streets as wit through ours', I decided I had to stick to those pieces which truly illuminated some facet of the place. By the same token, I've omitted G.K. Chesterton's strange poem 'Me Heart', which has a line about 'the folk who live in black Belfast' without displaying any insight into them or it.

When it comes to Belfast life and the way it's been lived over the past two hundred years, there are certain works which suggest themselves immediately as primary sources: George Benn's *History of the Town of Belfast* (1880), Thomas Gaffikin's *Belfast Fifty Years Ago* (a lecture delivered in 1875 and subsequently published), F. Frankfort Moore's *The Truth About Ulster* (1914), Thomas Carnduff's *Life and Writings* (drafted, I think, in 1954, but not published until thirty years later – and a jolly sight more interesting than his verse), Denis Ireland's volumes of evocative jottings, some autobiographical fiction (for example, Robert Harbinson), a lot of autobiographies (for example, Robert Graecen, John Boyd), one verse autobiography (John Hewitt's *Kites in Spring*). I have immersed myself in all these and come up, I hope, with many telling passages. I would also hope – in common with all anthologists – that there's a sufficiency of unexpected material here not to rule out the element of surprise for even the most knowledgeable aficionado of Belfast writing.

At one point I found I had accumulated an enormous number of travellers' comments – mostly nineteenth-century – and quickly decided that only the most striking should stay. Some people – this is true until well into the twentieth century – took the view that Belfast was an Irish city, others that it wasn't. (I'd align myself with the former.) An amazing number kept going into raptures over the countryside between Lisburn and Belfast, while others complained about a want of picturesqueness in the city itself (for example, Madame de Boret in 1891). Outsiders' impressions of a place can, indeed, be extremely revealing; however, I think it's to those native to the city that I'd turn for the most compelling, resonant, astute and spot-on appraisals. 'A strange, tough, hybrid town, with a forest of factory chimneys on both banks of the Lagan' – Denis Ireland describing his birthplace in the 1890s; 'strange city, god-fearing, far-faring, devil-may-caring' – thus W.R. Rodgers in exuberant mood. Hugh Shearman looks out at industrial Belfast on a grey winter's day and can't think of anywhere he'd rather be (he also commends the bulk of its inhabitants – this is in 1949 – for retaining their virginity as long as they stay unmarried). For Robert Johnstone, the place remains mysterious, 'like an incorrigible extra parent or shady uncle, who shaped one's life but whose doings only filter through in reports or rumours'. Sean O'Faolain – not a Belfastman — allows himself to relish, just for a moment, Belfast's old Burke-and-Hare atmosphere, 'the evening dusk and the fogs up from the Lagan'. You can't ask for anything more heady than this.

O'Faolain really preferred the countryside, which he was entitled to do; for others of a more suggestible temperament, though, a preference for rural simplicities was tied up with that old commonplace in full flower around the turn of the century which equated hills and fields with integrity, and streets with iniquity. Some of Belfast's ill-repute can be traced back to this notion. At its highest level, I suppose, it found expression in the novels of Forrest Reid, who consistently viewed Belfast with distaste – think of the affronted young hero of *Peter Waring*, who finds himself in lodgings in a spot with 'the gas works and a public lavatory hardly ten yards away' – and only relented towards it when he focused on its outskirts, well back in the past – a time when 'Molly Ward's cottage, not a vulcanite factory, guarded the approach to the river …' I am all for vulcanite factories, as it happens, and Molly Ward's cottage (or its equivalent) – but not Windsor House, almost any church erected since 1930, or the Europa Hotel. People who dislike Belfast ('Who then is it that dislikes Belfast?' thundered the *Northern Star* in 1794, going on to answer its own question: 'a gang of corrupt courtiers … base mercenaries … dissolute Bishops … tax-gatherers, pensioners and syco-phants … guzzling corporations … old, idle, card-playing tabbies …', and making a vigorous list) – those who dislike Belfast will not be at a loss to find some indigenous enormity to bolster their aversion; and an anthology that took no account of the strong critical strain running through the mass of writing about the city would end up bland and unbalanced. However – and with full acknowledgement of its defects – I would hope that this an-thology presents a place of the utmost interest, singularity, contrariness, spir-it, and one endowed with a good measure of abrasive charm to boot.

Perhaps I should say a word about my own credentials. Certainly anyone as attached to Belfast as I am, by birth and affinity, would have jumped at the chance to put together a collection such as this – and it is, of course, a personal selection, dictated no doubt by all kinds of crotchets, biases and *idées fixes*. I was born in Belfast near the junction of the Donegall Road with the Falls Road (on what I take to be the old Blackstaff Lane, long gone, alas, by the time I appeared) and lived there for twenty years until the merest chance took me to London, where I stayed until 1999, when I returned to Northern Ireland. My world as a child was bounded by Celtic Park and the Bog Meadows, the Globe Laundry and the patch of waste ground in front of it, the top of the Whiterock Road where it met the Mountain Loanin, and the Falls Park bus depot – not the most enticing or glamorous of home territories, indeed, but perfectly satisfactory as a playground to me and my friends.

I soon learned to distinguish other areas of the city – Andersonstown where my cousins lived, with its multitude of newly built houses and smell of damp concrete, suburban Windsor Park where I went to school (Aquinas Hall), Upper Malone and the end of Dunmurry Lane, where I used to be taken every Sunday, no doubt wearing some kind of horrid little puff-sleeved dress, to visit the gate lodge inhabited by my grandparents. I count myself lucky in my ancestry, in so far as it is half Protestant and half Catholic, enabling each strain in me to cancel out the other as far as belief is concerned; and also – as in Fleur Adcock's poem 'Please Identify Yourself' – causing one form of atavistic allegiance or the other to assert itself whenever its counter-part comes on too strongly. Or perhaps I was just born irreligious; though it's true that I was got by nuns – Dominican nuns – at an impressionable age, and consequently had any possible spiritual leanings quashed at the start. But I don't believe that these would have flourished in any case. If ever there was a natural atheist, I am sure I am it.

Some of the material in this anthology I know I have read in totally the wrong spirit. The section on Belfast, for instance, in Robert McLiam Wilson's *The Dispossessed* (1992) has a lot about current varieties of hardship, disaffection and so on, and one of the case histories he presents concerns an ex-prostitute, barmaid and battered single mother (whom he calls Moira) living wretchedly in Clonard. The point, the *only* point, for me, is that Moira was educated at the Dominican Convent on the Falls Road, and I am overtaken by malicious glee to think that the school that expelled me after an exiguous sexual escapade in the Gaeltacht should now number prostitutes among its past pupils.

One of the ways in which I grew to know districts outside my own had to do with the pursuit of light reading; once I'd exhausted the juvenile resources of the Donegall Road and Falls Road libraries, at the age of eleven or so, I took to travelling by bus to all the far-flung libraries about the city: Ligoniel, Ormeau, Oldpark Road, Shankill Road. I remember being terribly disappointed when I took out a novel by Richmal Crompton from the Ligoniel branch, only to find that it didn't bear the slightest resemblance to her 'William' stories. I remember the Donegall Road librarian taking my mother to one side to warn her that I'd likely become retarded if she didn't get me off Enid Blyton, quickly. I remember, I remember ... When I was sixteen, my best friend lived in Derby Street, and I got into the habit of catching a bus down there every evening, when we'd go to an Irish class, to the pictures, or just to sit in a coffee bar in the city centre, invariably to be picked up by boys. Later, after I'd become an art student at the College of Technology, in the 1960s, I used to go around unconsciously in the footsteps of the Reverend O'Hanlon, 'peering ... into all manner of courts and entries', only with a sketch-book instead of a programme for moral and social reform. I think I caught a glimpse of the one-storey dwellings at Upper Library Street, or Carrick Hill, just before the bulldozers moved in. And Smithfield ... well, enough has been written about Smithfield, as you will see. What is equally regretted by me, and not often mentioned by anyone, is Maggie Moore's old-clothes shop in Sandy Row: a soot-encrusted, cobweb-infested, stone-floored double room opening off the street, from which you might – gingerly – pick out some absolute treasure of an antique dress. You had to bear it off at once to the nearest dry cleaners, hoping the moths hadn't had too much of a heyday.

If I never succeeded in acquiring what John Morrow has graphically called 'an up-the-entry sex education', it was because (a) I was still clinging to the last remnants of convent teaching, and (b) I don't think I ever ended up with anyone qualified to provide the right kind of instruction: we were all more or less inept. But dingy entries, as I recall, did play a part in this kind of essential experimentation, though a more wholesome site of all our unproductive erotic impulses was the back of the Falls Park, especially on a winter evening when there weren't many potential voyeurs about. One of the sights of Belfast that has stayed with me (a recurrent sight) is the Falls Road alive with people along its entire length, all emptying out of the side streets and streaming towards the park, whole families from grandmothers to toddlers, carrying buns and lemonade and bent on securing a sunny patch of grass on which to settle themselves for the whole afternoon. I could mention particular cinemas, and walks up the mountain, sectarian anomalies and complexities, bygone social customs, local peculiarities . . . but you will find all these, and more, and more, in the anthology itself.

I have ended on this autobiographical note just to make it clear that I have been shaped almost entirely *by* Belfast – and that this seems a kind of justification for the following attempt to impose a shape *on* Belfast. And, as I have found immense pleasure, knowledge, odd bits of illumination and elation in the process, so I hope that readers will gain an equal amount of stimulation and exhilaration.

I should like to thank the Authors' Foundation and the Arts Council of Northern Ireland for financial assistance, and the following for help and advice of various kinds: Jeffrey Morgan, Gerry Keenan, Nora T. Craig, Michael and Edna Longley, Douglas and Marie Carson, Nigel and Naomi May, Robert Johnstone, Derek Mahon, Gerald Dawe, Val Warner, Anne Christopherson, the late Bill McCulloch, John Kennedy Melling, Gwendoline Butler, Maureen Murphy, Anne Tannahill, Patricia Horton and everyone at Blackstaff, the librarian and staff of the Linen Hall Library, Belfast, the librarian and staff of the London Library, and the librarian of St McNissi's College, Garron Tower.

PATRICIA CRAIG
ANTRIM
JUNE 1999

The Pale Light of
That Provincial Town

I lived there as a boy and know the coal
Glittering in its shed, late-afternoon
Lambency informing the deal table,
The ceiling cradled in a radiant spoon.
I must be lying low in a room there,
A strange child with a taste for verse,
While my hard-nosed companions dream of war
On parched veldt and fields of rain-swept gorse.

DEREK MAHON, 'Courtyards in Delft'

When the sun does shine, or is only partly obscured by
fleecy clouds fleeing across the lough, Belfast enjoys a
sparkling light. It is a light which casts the brilliant
highlights and sharp shadows which makes, for instance,
Copenhagen assume that unique crispness of cities by
water. Although in some ways Belfast resembles industrial
towns in the Midlands and North of England none of these
enjoys the pellucid atmosphere which, in spring and
summer at least, Belfast does.

ROBIN BRYANS, *Ulster: A Journey Through the Six Counties*

AT NOON IN BELFAST, EVEN IN BAD WINTER, one seems to be in
presence of the full light of the sky, and all the inexcusable buildings around and including the City Hall stand leisurely back from
the wide, white-gleaming pavements so that you can mock them at your

ease. And the flower-barrows on the kerbsides are radiant and the women in charge of them witty and friendly to match. There often is wind blowing, salty from the Lough – and hats fly off and newspapers flap, and cornerboys make soft local jokes. I was looking one day at the gentle Palladian façade of a small building which still calmly turns its polite eighteenth-century face towards the unappealing south flank of the City Hall. Looking in wonder that the quiet little edifice should still be there. And a lady passing said to me:

'Go in if you like. I'm sure you'll be very welcome – and they'll give you some nice coffee and cakes.'

It was a meeting house of some Christian sect. I thanked the passing lady. I thought it sweet of her, and – as I was to learn – *very* Belfast. That friendliness in passage, the bright word on the wing – a kind of unheeding grace. And I think it would be wrong to decide that this pleasantness that runs the streets, this uncalculated quality of charm that the people have – and 'charm' is almost the word, though not sufficiently loose, sufficiently accidental – this attractiveness is not, as it might be, a civic quality developed against the grain of industrial, pedestrian and money-making life; rather maybe it comes paradoxically out of the very texture of that life; is not perceptibly a contradiction of Belfast and it is as little wry or deprecatory as it is bumptious. Perhaps it is just an expression of energy and love of life. It is in any case a happy corrective against the clanking ugliness of industrial success. And come to think of it, it has always enriched and sweetened Belfast writing, the best of which has usually been strongly regional, and because of that, laced with a peculiar humaneness and good sense, qualities not primary ever in the best writing of Dublin or Munster.

KATE O'BRIEN, My Ireland, 1962

THE BELFAST REGION despite rapid urbanisation is still at one with the rest of the Province in largely preserving old Gaelic nomenclature with minimum corruption. The Gaelic *Béal Feirsde* is first mentioned in Irish records in the fifteenth century in connection with a castle located at the centre of the city. It has undergone a series of regular phonetic changes in the mouths of Gael and planter to give locally *B'al-fast*, notwithstanding stabilisation of the spelling *Belfast* by the Ordnance Survey a century ago. The name literally means 'the mouth of (= approach to) the sandbank (or crossing)', – not 'the mouth of the (river) Farset', since *béal* is never used in this sense. Farset rather takes its name from the sandbank or crossing. The original *fertas* (metathesised to *fersa(i)t*) is a derivative of *fert(ae)* and was applied to any raised bank of earth or sand, mound or tumulus. 'Sandbank', 'sandbar', hence 'crossing-place', 'ford', are well-attested secondary meanings.

Many of the better-known divisions and suburbs of the city still take their names from its rural past. Malone and Falls are abbreviations of names for petty territories formerly known as *Tuath (Ó) Maoil Eóin* and *Tuath na bhFál*. *Tuath* ('people', 'territory', 'state') is a descendant of Celtic *teut ā*, which was borrowed into Germanic to give (with suffix) *Deutsch*. *Mael Eóin* ('devotee of St John') is a personal name, and with *Ó* and the genitive, a family name. *Tuath na bhFál* meant perhaps, 'the territory of the fences'. Shankill ('old church') was otherwise formerly 'the white church of the crossing' (*ecclesia alba de vado*), and was dedicated to St Patrick. Stranmillis has the attractive Gaelic equivalent *sruthán milis*, 'sweet stream' – a tributary of the Lagan. Stormont, Holywood, etc., are exceptional, the former being a wholly Scottish importation, for it is otherwise the name for a part of Perthshire. According to Watson (*History of the Celtic Placenames of Scotland*, p. 120) the original *Stormont* is a corruption of Scottish Gaelic *stair mònadh*, 'stepping-stones moor'.

JOHN B. ARTHURS, *Belfast in its Regional Setting*, 1952

from THE OTHER VOICE

I make that crossing again
And catch the salt freshness
Of early light on Queen's Island.

I lay claim to those marshes,
The Lagan, the shipyards,
The Ormeau Road in winter.

That back room off Donegall Pass,
Remember, where the cell met?
That cupboard of books, tracts and poems?

Plekhanov flares like a firework,
Trotsky crosses Serbia
Turning the pages of Homer,

Raskolnikov wears a long coat
And the end justifies the means.
'Soon the rosewood *meubles*

'Will shake in the drawing-rooms
On the Malone Road.
After the long marches

'There will be shares for us all
In the means of production.
Songs of a new society

'Will grow like flowers
From the barrel of a gun.
It's easy. It's easy.

'*Love is all you need.*'
The record sticks and the party
Spins on forever.

TOM PAULIN, The Strange Museum, 1980

I AM ATTACHED TO BELFAST by my lifelong familiarity with its sights and sounds – by the narrow back streets and ubiquitous corner shops in the east, by a few suburban avenues in the south, by the River Lagan at the Queen's Bridge, the Albert Bridge, the Ormeau Bridge, the King's Bridge, the Governor's Bridge, each encompassing a different segment or circle of the city, like rings of a cut-down tree, the inner rings beginning to rot. All the bridges – with the exception of Ormeau – are unimaginatively named, like the plethora of Belfast streets called after Queen Victoria. Belfast is a Victorian, mainly Protestant city which protests its Protestantism loudly and too often for its own moral good. I am also detached and distanced from my native place and its dominant tradition, and estranged from its materialistic values and its raucous bigotry. All the same I have found it no hardship to stay, unlike some of my friends, particularly writers. John Hewitt, though, was one who, on his retirement, chose to return home and soon found himself recognised as the father-figure of the younger poets such as Seamus Heaney, James Simmons, Derek Mahon – all the nestlings nurtured by a young, energetic academic from Queen's called Philip Hobsbaum who not only wrote poetry himself but tried to turn everybody he met into a poet. If Philip did not always succeed he at least implanted in the heads of many young people an understanding that poetry lived outside text books and was an enduring activity not to be neglected if their lives were to be worth living. But Philip left Belfast for academic preferment in Glasgow and left his nestlings to grow up, and a few flew away to America or London or Dublin.

JOHN BOYD, The Middle of My Journey, 1990

THE DOUBLE-ENDED TRAM

I heard about but truly never knew
the old horse-trams with trace-boys for the hills,
though sometimes now and then my father'd show
the warning boards still left by certain sills.
Our trams were trolley-roped, electrical,
sparking at corner-points, and double-ended;
and at the terminus they'd swing and haul
the trolley round from which its rope depended.

The driver like the pilot of a ship
stood up in front and cranked his handle round;
the conductor punched the ticket for your fare;
but you would always try to make the trip
upstairs, where you could change the seat-backs round
and watch the whole town pass below you there.

JOHN HEWITT, Kites in Spring, 1980

THE CITY HAS OVERLAPPED ITS BOUNDARY POSTS to such an extent that its former green belt, which was fairly extensive in 1900–1, has now completely disappeared. Stranmillis, Upper Malone, Beechmount, Bally-gomartin, Ardoyne, Ballysillan, Skegoniel, Whiterock, Cregagh and Knockbreda were outlying districts in my youthful days and only fre-quented as lovers' lanes. The Cave Hill was accessible by way of the quarries or the Sheep's Path. The Shaftesbury estate wall ran the entire length of the Antrim Road from the Old Cavehill to the Sheep's Path. There was no Hazelwood or Bellevue in those days.

There were no electric trams, buses or taxi cabs. The old Irish jaunting car and hackney cab were always available at their stands around the city. The horse tram system, inaugurated less than thirty years previous to 1900, was a cumbersome and nerve-racking mode of travelling. The tramcars were hauled around the city by a pair of powerful horses, supplemented by a tracer, ridden by a boy where a difficult hill had to be negotiated . . .

Kitchen houses were easily obtainable at half-a-crown a week; parlour houses were four and sixpence. Kitchenettes were unknown fifty years ago, and Devon grates had yet to be invented. Household bins were unknown, and the refuse of the 'middens' was, in the case of streets where there were no entries, often moved through the living-room to the street. Middens lay for weeks before being attended to, and how the health authorities stalled off disease is still a mystery to me.

Working-class food in those days was plain and, of necessity, cheap.

Porridge, broth, stew, potatoes and buttermilk, without variation, was the daily subsistence. Cooking was done on the open grate, and the immense iron pots and kettles used then have disappeared. Home-baked soda scones and potato bread on the family griddle was the custom in every household. Coal wouldn't be more than a shilling a bag, perhaps cheaper. There were few gas ovens.

The younger generation fifty years ago read *Buffalo Bill, Dick Turpin, Comic Cuts, Pluck,* and the *Marvel.* Our elders were reading *The Redeemer* by Hall Caine; *Sherlock Holmes* by Conan Doyle; *She* by Rider Haggard. Evenings at home, we entertained by Edison Bell records on phonograph. The gramophone had not yet superseded this form of amusement. The phonograph records were, I admit, a bit scratchy, owing to the continuous playing.

Men wore bowler hats and caps in winter, straw hats and soft Panama hats in summer. Bare heads were not fashionable for men or women. Beards and mutton-chop whiskers were still retained by elderly people, but the rising generation were gradually breaking away from tradition and adopting the moustache alone as a facial ornament. Well-starched collars, three inches in breadth, kept the chin in position and made it almost a sacrifice to swallow.

THOMAS CARNDUFF (1954), *Life and Writings*, 1994

HERE HE WAS, OVER SEVENTEEN, and the cheap seats at the pictures was a thrill and a fish-and-chip supper a treat. And, oh, those long penniless Sunday walks along the Lagan towpath or up the Malone Road with Boney in pursuit of girls! The brazen impudence you had to have to walk beside a couple of silent girls a hundred yards or more, trying to think up a joke that would strike a spark from them. And even when you knew that your one would like to strike up, the other one would pluck at her coat, which is only what you might expect when your pal has a face and dumb tongue like Boney's. Well, all that nonsense and misery would stop. He had better things than that in him. From tomorrow he would start watching the Situations Vacant in the paper.

SAM HANNA BELL, *The Hollow Ball*, 1961

IT WAS HALF PAST FIVE when she walked up Camden Street, wet with the rain in her shoes and her hair tossed by the blustery rainy wind. She let herself in as quietly as possible, hoping Mrs Henry Rice would think she had come home later, after having dinner out somewhere. She took her shoes off as she went up the creaky stairs.

The bed-sitting-room was cold and musty. She lit the gas fire and the lamps and drew the grey curtains across the bay window. Her wet raincoat she put over a chair with a part of the *Irish News* underneath to catch the drops. Then she took off her wet stockings and hung her dress up. In her old wool dressing-gown she felt warmer, more comfortable. She put her rings away in the jewel box and set a little kettle of water on the gas ring. It boiled quickly and she found only enough cocoa for one cup.

The rain began to patter again on the windows, growing heavier, soft persistent Irish rain, coming up Belfast Lough, caught in the shadow of Cave Hill. It settled on the city, a night blanket of wetness. Miss Hearne ate her biscuits, cheese, and apple, found her spectacles and opened a library book by Mazo de la Roche. She toasted her bare toes at the gas fire and leaned back in the armchair, waiting like a prisoner for the long night hours.

BRIAN MOORE, *Judith Hearne*, 1955

I FIRST MET HIM [James Boyce] on St Patrick's day of 1951, and until his death, he was the closest friend I had. He was then a school-master, shortly to throw up his safe but stifling job for the perilous life of a freelance broadcaster. His house in University Street was a meeting place for people of the most diverse interests and talents, where conversation and all the ephemeral arts flourished. There and at various literary and journalistic pubs, it was possible to meet interesting people who by no means belonged to the conventional Unionist world: established actors, authors, playwrights, and painters: but also, odd men out such as Sam Thompson, shipyard playwright; Markey Robinson, boilermaker turned artist; George McCann, at once military man and sculptor; Fiddler Moore, tram-conductor turned linguist and entertainer; Ralph Bossence, newspaper columnist and glass-in-hand-philosopher.

I had apprehensively feared to find Belfast a black, boring, provincial city, and life there a dreary come-down after Oxford and Paris. I was quite wrong: below the grimy and conventional surface, it was a city bursting with a stimulating life of its own, fed by the conflicts hidden not far below the surface. No doubt, from the plateau of middle age, or the trough of the continuing Troubles, I tend to look back to some extent to a lost golden age; but I still think that in the 1950s and 60s life in Belfast was probably more invigorating and rewarding than in Dublin, Glasgow, or any other provincial city of the British Isles.

C.E.B. BRETT, *Long Shadows Cast Before*, 1978

HISTORY

Where and when exactly did we first have sex?
Do you remember? Was it Fitzroy Avenue,
Or Cromwell Road, or Notting Hill?
Your place or mine? Marseilles or Aix?
Or as long ago as that Thursday evening
When you and I climbed through the bay window
On the ground floor of Aquinas Hall
And into the room where MacNeice wrote 'Snow',
Or the room where they say he wrote 'Snow'.

PAUL MULDOON, *Why Brownlee Left*, 1980

THE MALONE ROAD is one of the most attractive and picturesque of the
roads out of Belfast. It runs almost due south, through a slightly undulating district, with many big houses and a lot of trees. It generally
counts as our 'West End' in Belfast, for it is a very middle-class district,
inhabited by business people, professional people, surgeons, professors,
senior civil servants and people with four-figure incomes. It is even accused
of having an accent of its own. But I have found too much good broad
Belfast spoken there to believe that the Malone suburb is dominated by its
alleged accent, and it is certainly not the only part of Belfast in which one can
encounter the thing known as the Malone Road accent. The Malone Road
runs roughly parallel to the much less attractive Lisburn Road, a long, bleak
road with terraces of brick houses, which depresses visitors coming in by
road from Dublin.

From the end of the Malone Road I made many excursions along the
Lagan and through the neighbouring countryside. The contrast between
that district south of Belfast, which is low, gently undulating, wooded,
cultivated and rather English in its atmosphere, and the district on the
north side, which is hilly, bare, wild and rather Scottish in its atmosphere,
represents the difference between County Down and County Antrim and
gives a good hint as to the composition of the population of Belfast.

HUGH SHEARMAN, *Ulster*, 1949

'CAME BY A STRONG FORT built upon a passage on the plains of Moylon,
with a strong palisade and a drawbridge, called Hilsborowe.
Within it is a fair timber house, walled with bricks, and a tower slated.
Some other houses are built without it, wherein are some families of
English and Irish settled. This fort was built by Moyses Hill, who hath a

8

lease for sixty-one years of the same, with a good scope of land, from Sir Arthur Chichester.'

'Within about a mile of Hilsborowe, by the river of Lagan, where the sea ebbs and flows, in a place called Strandmellis, we found the said Moyses Hill in hand with building of a strong house of stone, fifty-six feet long; and he intends to make it two stories and a half high, it being already about the height of one story, and to build a good bawn of lime and stone about; which lands are held by like lease as Hilsborowe aforesaid.'

Commissioners' Report, 1611

In upper Malone
They dwell alone
In their fine suburban houses,
Where at half past three
They meet for tea,
The fierce old female fossils of the town.

JAMES SCOTT, *Interest*, 1960

A ND DAY AFTER DAY – post-war, just as they had pre-war – in the wealthy suburbs of Belfast the wives of industrialists went on reading the Bible, drinking their sherry and eating scones.

CAROLINE BLACKWOOD, *For All That I Found There*, 1973

I T IS CURIOUS NOW TO REFLECT that Belfast was one of the great centres of disaffection and opposition to the union a century ago. Its population, mainly Presbyterian, was strongly touched with democratic views. The French Revolution appealed to them and they were in close sympathy with the American States. The famous Society of United Irishmen was organised in Belfast; but that town has always had a genius for keeping out of harm's way. Neither in 1642 nor in 1689 did it emulate the heroism of Derry or share its sacrifices; and in 1798 the rebellion that broke out in consequence of the United Irishmen's conspiracy did not affect the place where the plot was hatched.

Since 1800 Belfast has been a stronghold of the Protestant ascendency; the gulf which separated Nonconformists from Churchmen in political sympathies has been bridged over. And Belfast certainly has reason to bless the union, for she is the one Irish town which has won a share in the great access of industrial wealth produced by Free Trade. Between 1861 and 1871 the population rose from 119,242 to 207,671. Since then the great shipbuilding industry has developed at an extraordinary pace. The Victoria Channel from the quays direct to the sea has been cut at great cost, and there is no better example of a great port that has been created in spite of natural difficulties.

As for the general appearance of the place, it is one of the cleanest among manufacturing towns. Its situation, too, on Belfast Lough is picturesque, and there are fine views of the Great Cave Hill, which overhangs the town and silhouettes against the sky a strange likeness of Napoleon's profile.

STEPHEN GWYNN, *Highways and Byways in Donegal and Antrim*, 1899

ALTHOUGH MODERN MEN have found the likeness of notabilities, varying from Napoleon to Lord Carson, portrayed by the rugged outline of Ben Madighan, their ancient forefathers sought their gods elsewhere. It has its place in history, however, for on its summit Wolfe Tone, before going into exile, vowed to dedicate his life to the cause of Irish freedom.

The raven nested up there on the steep cliffs and in the owl-light or 'dayligone' – to use the lovely Ulster word – the woodcock would go roding, bat-winged, along the skirts of the forest which mantled the hill-slopes. Although this gigantic escarpment behind the house cut off our view of so many fine sunsets it yielded ample compensation in other ways; as the year wore on we watched expectantly for the changing beauties which never failed to adorn cliffs, woods, and slanting meadows, though the degree of their splendour varied delightfully from year to year.

In the winter its shoulder would often be white though in our milder garden not a snowflake had fallen; and when the snow lay deep the trees were clothed in ermine and the ridges glittered with silver tinsel. In spring when the larches tufted their dark twigs, the woods burst into vivid green, and there would follow weeks when the clearings were yellow with primroses, blue with wood-hyacinths or white with hawthorn blossom. From far below we could look up and see these patches of colour plainly. The year faded in quiet beauty, for after the heather had flared forth in purple glory on the hill-tops the withering bracken laid its snug russet covering over the flanks of the mountain.

EDWARD ALLWORTHY ARMSTRONG, *Birds of the Grey Wind*, 1940

THIS TOWN, WITHIN THE LAST TEN YEARS, has been reputed to contain nearly 4,000 houses (inclusive of the suburbs), and a population of 30,000 souls, which, with the exception of a few private families and professional individuals, is composed of persons in the numerous walks of trade; all of whom, from the brogue maker to the banker, stand, like the men of England, on a level with their business, attend assiduously to it, and seem to think of nothing else, until the sabbath-day (which they hold in great veneration) arrives, when they drop, like a hot potatoe, all the small concerns of this lower world, and assemble, *shaved and white-washed*, some to chaunt a Latin hymn to the music of the holy Pope; others, a psalm in English, to the more modern notes of the English bishops; others to the most barbarous broad Scotch slang that ever disgraced a conventicle in the mountains; a few to our dear brother Smith's 'sacred harmony', which flows back upon him, from the tuneful sisters, in melting responses; and lastly, a select number of wise men assemble, who say nothing, and, therefore, do not leave it in your power to offer a criticism upon their compositions; or, if they speak, it is in the rough cough of uneasy silence, or in humiliation's soft still sigh, which borne upon echo's gentle wing, may reach the heart, but in that impenetrable fortress, cannot be assailed by the shafts of criticism. – The men of Belfast, with all this character of trade, are, however, very attentive to the public institutions of their town, and are said to be very liberal in making provision for them. In former periods of their history, they were also eminently distinguished by a spirit of political independence, which, subsequently to our union with England, appears to have taken a long *repose*.

A. ATKINSON, *Ireland Exhibited to England*, 1823

CLOP-CLOP-CLOP-CLOP... we are in a four-wheeler rattling over the uneven squaresets of the Belfast streets through the damp twilight of a September evening, 1908; my father, my brother, and I. I am going to school for the first time. We are in low spirits. My brother, who has most reason to be so, for he alone knows what we are going to, shows his feelings least. He is already a veteran. I perhaps am buoyed up by a little excitement, but very little. The most important fact at the moment is the horrible clothes I have been made to put on. Only this morning – only two hours ago – I was running wild in shorts and blazer and sandshoes. Now I am choking and sweating, itching too, in thick dark stuff, throttled by an Eton collar, my feet already aching with unaccustomed boots. I am wearing knickerbockers that button at the knee.

C.S. LEWIS, *Surprised by Joy*, 1955

THE WHITE LINEN HALL, as it was called, and the Flags – meaning Donegall Place – was the great promenade in fine weather, especially on Sunday evenings. The great attraction was the military band, which, on the space in front of the present archway or entrance to the hall, gave a two hours' performance. The main walk round the Hall was enclosed from this space by an iron railing on each side, with small gates for ingress and egress. The most respectable of the persons listening to the music were distributed on both sides, and it was the practice to turn and walk round between each piece, which rendered at times the presence of great crowds at the rear of the hall, changing sides in succession. During this ceremony the democrats stood their ground, with the bandsmen in the centre. Oil lamps distributed at distances of about twenty yards all round the Hall – some of the standards are still to be seen in the railing – made it a pleasant walk even in the winter evenings.

THOMAS GAFFIKEN, *Belfast Fifty Years Ago*, 1894

IT IS SAID THAT THE MILITARY in any town infuses into it a life and gaiety not to be otherwise obtained. If this be so with occasional visitants, what must Belfast have been during the many years in which regular regiments, volunteers, and yeomanry had possession of it. To be sure, the most of them were but carpet-knights, who had never seen service; still they had uniforms, swords, guns, and drums. These they kept constantly in service, and the ladies and gentlemen of the town paraded Donegall Place, then the only flagged street in the town, listening to the delicious strains. The yeomen approached nearest to civilians. We remember admiring the playing of a fifer, one Sunday morning, as being particularly shrill and piercing. The fifer took our measure for a pair of boots the next day, having doffed for another week his military trappings.

But the country residences were not obtained all at once by our rich town inhabitants.

The borders of our famous bay were most in favour, though not always. We once heard an old man, from whom we were inquiring about these and other matters connected with Belfast, say that it was considered very strange that Mr Lyons should have built his house of Old Park 'on the top of a whinny hill at the foot of the mountain'. This, not at all a correct description of Old Park, proceeded from one of the *profanum vulgus*, but people of that class generally convey popular sentiment as well as any other, and sometimes in more vigorous and plain-spoken language. He was incorrect in this instance, for though Old Park, built a century ago, may have been an unimproved land, and probably whins growing therein, it was, sixty years ago, a beautiful rural home, with fine gardens and trees, and a convenient distance from 'the madding crowd'. Now, in our time, the forty-two acres of which the demesne consists are advertised to be let in lots for villas or streets, which will doubtless be the case in due time.

GEORGE BENN, *A History of the Town of Belfast*, 1880

HE WENT DOWN THE ROAD, and when he came to the Antrim Road he crossed it and walked along one of the streets which run at right angles to it. When he had walked some time, and had crossed York Street, and had penetrated into the little slums that lie on the south of it, he found himself at the harbour. Rain began to fall, and he stood in the porch of a public-house for shelter. The sheds into which the cargo of the cross-Channel steamers was discharged had a dreary, dreepy look, and the carters and stevedores, who had covered their shoulders with sacking as a protection from the rain, had a cold, moist appearance that made him feel cold, too, when he saw them. A keen air came blowing down the quays, and when he thrust his head out to see what the sky was like, it caught hold of him and caused him to shiver.

'It's damn coul'!' he muttered to himself, thrusting his hands deeply into his pockets, and stamping his feet on the tiles in the porch.

ST JOHN ERVINE, *Mrs Martin's Man*, 1913

PRESENTLY SHE ROSE and went across to the window, and stood looking out. The morning was clear and bright. Across the Lough wisps of white mist still clung to the folds in the Antrim hills, but the sun would soon have them. The Lough was still, and almost empty of traffic. The cross-channel steamers would be past long ago, and their passengers in Belfast by this time. Laura was well acquainted with the times and seasons of the steamers. In the isolated life she had led their coming and going was a welcome contact with the outside world. She was comforted to watch the rows of moving lights going down the Lough on winter evenings, and was always up in time to greet the incoming boats in the morning. There were other people in the world beside herself and Mildred. Now there was only herself, and the boats had gone by. But there was George; he had come yesterday, and he would come again. He would surely come again, and when Mr McAlister and Miss Parks were not there. The sun shone in at the window and she felt the warmth of it on her bare feet, and turned at last to dress and meet the day.

JANET McNEILL, *Tea at Four O'Clock*, 1956

GATHERED AROUND THE LINEN MILLS are the streets of red-brick houses divided by hidden barriers of religion. The strongly Protestant areas of Shankill and Sandy Row are separated by a solid wedge of Roman Catholic Ireland in the Falls Road. The social geography of Belfast is a fascinating subject but one on which the visitor should beware of making hasty judgments. The docks area has attracted newer industries such as tobacco and flour-milling, dependent on imports, and to the east of the river, in the old, weaving suburb of Ballymacarrett, is the great ropeworks which, historically, links the textiles to the shipyards. Marine engineering, too, grew after 1850 out of the older manufacture of textile machinery. The marriage of iron ships and Ulster flax meant economic bliss for some decades, for they were mainly dependent one on male, the other on female labour. But both industries flourished only when world conditions were favourable, and there have been times of depression and serious unemployment. There are of course countless other activities, and many new industries have been attracted in recent years to support a population which is approaching half a million. Two other industries we must mention: deep beneath the city is a bountiful supply of pure water in the New Red Sandstones, and it supports, with fine impartiality, the production of both whiskey and mineral-waters.

E. ESTYN EVANS, *Northern Ireland*, 1951

THE LEADING EMPORIUM OF FASHION for the ladies was Miss M'Elroy's little shop in Castle Place, next to the Donegall Arms. The fashions have altered in fifty years almost as much as the town. Gentlemen wore high hats (much higher than at present), yellow topped boots, and buckskin breeches. These inexpressibles cost two guineas, but a man in Hercules Place made a cheaper sort (of sheepskin) at 7s. 7d., or a seven thirteen-piece, as they called it, being the third of a guinea. These were called crackers, because they expanded when wet, but when drying they cracked and shrivelled up to more than a skin fit. A buff vest, a swallow tailed coat, with bright buttons, a frilled shirt, with ruffled cuffs, and a large gold seal hanging from the fob, completed the costume of a dandy. I cannot describe the ladies' dress with any minuteness, but its tone seemed to me more severe and forbidding than later styles. The coal scuttle bonnet kept the gentlemen at a respectful distance from their faces, while in fine weather they might admire their slender waists, and sandal shoes with ankle ties, but in wet and wintry weather the ladies took their airing in sedan chairs or muffled up and mounted on pat-tens. The sedan chairs were kept in entries off High Street, and the measured tramp of the bearers could be heard going to and from the theatre, evening parties, or the church on Sundays. The ladies' pattens were heard even more distinctly, and on Sundays in winter the porch of the parish church would be lined during the time of Divine service with beautiful pattens of various sizes and colours.

THOMAS GAFFIKEN, *Belfast Fifty Years Ago*, 1894

WHEN THE CARSON MOVEMENT BEGAN it was taken for granted that women, as always in the past, would be content to remain in the background. The organisers had framed their plans solely with an eye to the male population. There was no place for women in the Ulster Volunteers or the Unionist Clubs, and they were expressly excluded from the Ulster Covenant. But women were not satisfied thus to be cold-shouldered. Before many weeks they were squibbing miniature rifles on the ranges, battalions of women signallers were flag-wagging from dawn to dusk, and if they were not permitted to sign the Covenant they made amends by drawing up an equally vehement declaration of their own. The enthusiasm was genuine beyond a doubt, but some old-fashioned Tories, however much they welcomed it in theory, were inclined to look askance at it in practice. They discerned behind this departure not only the driving force of Unionism, but the mailed fist of militant Feminism; and cynics who remembered the variegated abuse that had been hurled at Suffragist crusaders in Ulster found rich entertainment in the spectacle of these champions of the 'ladylike' woman taking to their bosoms legions of armed amazons.

Since the war women in Belfast, as elsewhere, have been marching fast and far towards new horizons. Munition work, in particular, has taught them more about Labour than they could have gleaned from a lifelong attendance at political meetings. Women who have encountered foremen at first hand, and learned by hard experience the manoeuvres by which employers keep down wages to a proper level, can be heard to-day using language which not so long ago they would have denounced as the blasphemous heresies of Syndicalism. It remains to be seen whether women of this type will be willing to return to their old groove, and accept with the same unquestioning faith the orthodox formulas of their class. Personally I have a suspicion that however thoroughly the problem of demobilisation may be carried out in a material sense, intellectually there will be no reversion to the old standard. Women have tasted the sweets of liberty of action and liberty of thought, and the shocked, if muffled, protests that are beginning to be heard from the dowagers and duennas of the old tradition are to me the best proof that the youthful generation will not readily abandon its new privileges.

JAMES WINDER GOOD, *Ulster and Ireland*, 1919

TO-DAY I WATCHED A TERN ALIGHT on the pond in the Botanical Gardens. Settling, he folded his wings with a gesture that was like a benediction over the waters. The trees surrounding the pond shivered in the wind, and the tern, sailing to and fro, lunged disdainfully with his beak among the ripples. Then, neglecting several sodden fragments of bread that floated within easy reach, he suddenly unfolded his wings again, and rose, flicking the surface in farewell. For a moment or two he floated round the pond, his white streamlined body outlined against the trees, his hard, beady eyes intent upon the water ... then he soared suddenly on a freshening breeze, side-slipped like a white flash over the tree-tops and disappeared ... as if he had just remembered that this was no place for a real fisherman, and that, after all, not so many wing beats away beyond the smoke and filth of the city was the wide, fish-inhabited expanse of the sea.

A suburban tennis club. In the distance there is a *popping* sound, like the drawing of distant corks. No one takes any notice; the white-clad figures weave and rearrange, as if in a combined maze, upon the green; water continues to fall with a subdued roaring over the weir. The *poppings* begin again, this time in a kind of pattern. Somebody says something about a machine gun. Well, who cares? *Deuce, vantage* ... If people like to murder one another in the streets of Belfast, let them – it has nothing to do with us ... The tea interval arrives, and we drift over to the pavilion. The *poppings* continue. But now nobody discusses them. They are *vieux jeu*, and the conversation is all about the latest scores from Wimbledon.

An hotel lounge. In the street outside the aftermath of the riots can be seen in the form of smashed windows and knots of police stationed at corners with rifles. A green-uniformed inspector of constabulary snores exhausted in an arm-chair; another, too strung-up to sleep, drinks a whiskey-and-soda with the rapid jerky motions of a marionette. They have the job of cleaning up something that began before they were born, the impact of forces released by politicians long dead ...

DENIS IRELAND, *From the Irish Shore*, 1936

from AUTUMN JOURNAL: XVI

And the North, where I was a boy,
   Is still the North, veneered with the grime of Glasgow,
Thousands of men whom nobody will employ
   Standing at the corners, coughing.
And the street-children play on the wet
   Pavement – hopscotch or marbles;
And each rich family boasts a sagging tennis-net
   On a spongy lawn beside a dripping shrubbery.
The smoking chimneys hint
   At prosperity round the corner
But they make their Ulster linen from foreign lint
   And the money that comes in goes out to make more money.

A city built upon mud;
　　A culture built upon profit;
Free speech nipped in the bud,
　　The minority always guilty.

LOUIS MacNEICE (1938), Collected Poems, 1966

IMAGINE A SUNNY MORNING IN CAMPBELL'S during the Second World War. Belfast has been gashed by the Nazi bombers, khaki–clad figures and their War Department vehicles are everywhere. Civil Defence workers are no longer laughed at for their inactivity. Like London, Belfast is learning to 'take it'. The Yanks are here, some said 'over–paid, over–sexed and over here'. They have started dating local girls – 'Say, whaddya do about sex?' Through the windows of Campbell's, one looks across at the City Hall erected in the full flush of Victorian prosperity by the Protestant bourgeoisie. Its statues and gardens I have known from childhood. The City Hall indeed, like the poor and the war profiteer, is something one puts up with. After the war, perhaps, change may come . . . but will the war *ever* end?

ROBERT GREACEN, The Sash My Father Wore, 1997

IN CAMPBELL'S CAFÉ opposite Belfast's grandiose City Hall, Denis [Ireland] was often the centre of an admiring circle who relished his anecdotes. Indeed oral storytelling was an art that he perfected, perhaps because he spent a good deal of his time practising it. He loved an audience and told his stories deftly. Belfast humour greatly appealed to him, but occasionally one of his stories about the mores of the working class grated on me. Perhaps I was being too sensitive, too conscious that I myself was working class and resentful when middle-class raconteurs raised loud laughs at the accent and attitudes of the class I belonged to. Yet Denis was no snob and, unlike many of his class, made no attempt to overlay his own distinctive Belfast accent with what was our local caricature of an English accent. Like most of us he possessed a streak of vanity, though the form it took was perfectly harmless. He used to tell a story of how once when he was attending the Abbey Theatre someone called out, 'Surely to God that's W.B. Yeats's ghost!' Denis indeed looked remarkably like Yeats: tall and distinguished, with a lock of white hair across his forehead. This resemblance to Ireland's famous poet gave him great pleasure and he was fond of telling that little story. He was equally fond of telling the story of the boxing bout in the Chapel Fields at which the two boxers had exhausted themselves and were resting with their arms entwined around each other's necks until a wag in the crowd shouted, 'Referee, wud ye favour us wi' a song?' I used to attend these bouts myself, as much for the wit displayed by the spectators as for the excitement of the actual contests, but I doubt very much whether Denis ever attended the Chapel Fields. He was more of a collector of stories at second hand, stories remembered to gain the plaudits of the coffee drinkers round the table upstairs in Campbell's where literary aspirants like myself and Sam Hanna Bell congregated.

JOHN BOYD, *The Middle of My Journey*, 1990

THE READING-ROOM OF THE CLUB is on the first floor, and the window commands an excellent view of Donegall Place, one of the principal thoroughfares of Belfast. The club stands right across the eastern end of the street, and the traffic is diverted to right and left along Royal Avenue and High Street. At the far, the western end, of Donegall Place stands the new City Hall, with the statue of Queen Victoria in front of it. There again the traffic is split at right angles. Some of the best shops in the town lie on either side of this street. A continuous stream of trams passes up and down it, to and from the junction, which is directly under the club windows, and is the centre of the whole Belfast tramway system. It is always pleasant to stand at the reading-room window and watch the very busy and strenuous traffic of this street. As a view point on that particular morning the window was as good as possible. Donegall Place is the chief and most obvious way from the northern and eastern parts of the city to the place where the meeting was to be held.

Between eleven o'clock and twelve the volunteers began to appear in considerable numbers. I saw at once that I had been wrong in supposing that they meant to spend the day in bed. One company after another came up Royal Avenue or swung round the corner from High Street, and marched before my eyes along Donegall Place towards the scene of the meeting. Small bodies of police appeared here and there, heading in the same direction. Now and then a few mounted police trotted by, making nearly as much jangle as if they had been regular soldiers. The hour fixed for the meeting was one o'clock, but at noon the number of men in the street was so great that ordinary traffic was stopped. A long line of trams, unable to force their way along, blocked the centre of the thoroughfare. The drivers and conductors left them and went away. Crowds of women and children collected on the roofs of these trams and cheered the men as they marched along.

GEORGE A. BIRMINGHAM, *The Red Hand of Ulster*, 1912

THE BELFAST OF MY CHILDHOOD differed considerably from the Belfast of today. It was, I think, spiritually closer to that surrounding country. Then, as now, perhaps, it was not particularly well educated, it possessed no cultured and no leisured class (the sons of even the wealthiest families leaving school at fifteen or sixteen to enter their fathers' offices); but it did not, as I remember it at any rate, bear nearly so marked a resemblance to the larger English manufacturing towns.

The change I seem to see has, of course, brought it closer to its own ideal. For some not very intelligible reason, a hankering after things English – even what is believed to be an English accent – and a distrust of things Irish, have always characterised the more well-to-do citizens of Belfast. But in the days of my childhood this was not so apparent, while the whole town was more homely, more unpretentious. A breath of rusticity still sweetened its air; the few horse trams, their destinations indicated by the colour of their curtains, did little to disturb the quiet of the streets; the Malone Road was still an almost rural walk; Molly Ward's cottage, not a vulcanite factory, guarded the approach to the river; and there were no brick works, no mill chimneys, no King's Bridge to make ugly blots on the green landscape of the Lagan Valley. The town itself, as I have said, was more attractive, with plenty of open spaces, to which the names of certain districts – the Plains, the Bog Meadows – bear witness. Queen's University was not a mere mass of unrelated, shapeless buildings; the Technical Institute did not sprawl in unsightly fashion across half the grounds of my old school. Gone is the Linen Hall, that was once the very heart of the town in its hours of ease. A brand new City Hall, all marble staircases and inlaid floors, garnished with statues and portraits of Lord Mayors and town councillors, and fronted with wooden benches on which rows of our less successful citizens doze and scratch the languid hours away, flaunts its expensive dullness where that old mellow ivy-creepered building once stood, with its low, arched entrance, its line of trees that shut out the town bustle and dust. The Linen Hall Library, transported to another building, still exists, but, as with the city, expansion has robbed it of its individuality. The old Linen Hall Library, with the sparrows flying in and out of the ivy all day long, fluttering and squabbling, was a charming place. It was very like a club. Its membership was comparatively small; its tone was old-fashioned; it belonged to the era of the two and three-volume novel; it had about it an atmosphere of quiet and leisure.

FORREST REID, *Apostate*, 1926

THE PRINCIPAL LIBRARY is in one of the rooms of the linen hall. I spend some hours every day in it – solitary hours; for the bustling inhabitants of this great commercial town have little leisure (I do not know that they have little inclination) for reading. Round the hall there is a public walk, prettily laid out with flowers and shrubs. I meet with as few people here, as in the library. Young women appear to walk as little as the men read. I know not whether this is a restraint of Presbyterianism, or of education; but let the cause be what it may, it is a very cruel one – young women have few enjoyments; it is a pity, therefore, to deprive them of so innocent a one as that of walking. I have conversed with them at parties, and generally found them rational and unassuming. To an Englishman, as may be easily conceived, the rusticity of their accent would at first be unpleasant. But his ear would soon accommodate itself to it, and even find beauties in it – the greatest of all beauties in a female, an apparent freedom from affectation and assumption. They seldom played cards, nor did the elderly people seem to be particularly fond of them. Music was the favourite recreation, and many were no mean proficients in it. They are probably indebted for this to Mr Bunting, a man well known in the musical world. He has an extensive school here, and is organist to one of the meeting-houses; for so little fanaticism have now the Presbyterians of Belfast, that they have admitted organs into their places of worship. At no very distant period this would have been reckoned as high a profanation as to have erected a crucifix. I was highly gratified with Mr Bunting's execution on the piano-forte – nor was I less so with the voice of a gentleman of the name of Ross. He is, I think, one of the finest private singers I ever heard. Mr Bunting is a large jolly-looking man; that he should fail to be so is hardly possible, for Belfast concerts are never mere music meetings – they are always followed by a good supper, and store of wine and punch. Mr Bunting is accused of being at times capricious, and unwilling to gratify curiosity. But musicians, poets, and ladies have ever been privileged to be so. I went to the meeting-house at which he performs, to hear him on the organ, but as it was only a common psalm he accompanied, I had no opportunity of judging of his powers.

JOHN GAMBLE, *A View of Society and Manners in the North of Ireland*, 1813

DOMESTIC CARES AND THE OFFICE WORK filled up most of the day, and then in the long evenings, when James was from home – these absences had always been fairly frequent and tended to become more so – there was the inexhaustible delight of books, and with a fine catholic taste she made the acquaintance of nearly every new volume that the inestimable local library in the Linen Hall added to its shelves. James, on his return home, would find her awaiting him, always in the same pose, book and candle at elbow, and marvelled greatly at her passion for print. Blind to her requirements he did not recognise that books supplied what was lacking in her life – excitement, distraction, and a familiarity with thoughts and aspirations that far outwent the parochial intelligences of those among whom her lines had fallen.

JOHN HERON LEPPER, *The North-East Corner*, 1917

Gas is first mentioned about 1810, as having been partially introduced into Glasgow and London. It was nearly a dozen more years before Belfast obtained it. As in other places, small experiments preceded its general introduction. Though stepping out of bounds, we may mention here that we first saw a series of experiments on gas in Rosemary Street, about the year 1820. It was in a shop or house near Winecellar Entry. Great crowds assembled to witness it. The illumination was very great, produced by a small or temporary Retort in the back part of the house. From the appearance of the light, the universal opinion was that the old oil lamps in the streets were doomed to eternal extinction. At the same time, many of the boys in the town of a scientific turn were making *improvised* gaslight. They accomplished this by means of a tobacco pipe, the bowl of which was filled with pounded coal, then covered with clay, and inserted between the bars of a grate, where the fire was burning. Smoke issued from the mouth-piece, which lighted, on the application of a match, and of course burned brightly so long as the coal dust lasted. The discussions on the subject, exactly similar to those now heard about the electric light, were continued here for some time, till the pipes were laid down in the streets, and all doubts as to the inestimable advantages of gas ended.

GEORGE BENN, *A History of the Town of Belfast*, 1880

ON DUNMORE'S WASTE

We had our cricket team, our football team;
our jerseys blue, our heroes, I should say,
were Glasgow Rangers, Linfield. Like a dream,
McCandless passed once, home on holiday.
On Dunmore's waste we strove with small success,
our goalposts bundled coats, all penalties
disputed – with no whitewash to express
the limits which the book of rules supplies.

At cricket every summer, on those fields
balls bounced or shot erratic on bare clay.
No word or mention any record yields

of our excitement every Saturday:
remembered names these syllables deploy,
McClean, MacManus, Maxwell, Dillon, Foy.

JOHN HEWITT, *Kites in Spring*, 1980

SOME SHOPS WERE CONSPICUOUS from the nature of the business. The establishment immediately adjoining Grattan & Co.'s Medical Hall was kept by a certain Mrs M'Callum, who had ever a kind word for all the children in the neighbourhood. There was a step down from the street to the earthen floor of her shop – and an ordinary sized person could have reached down a bundle of sawdust balls, skeleton dolls, or tin whistles, from the ceiling. Besides toys, her shop contained a variety of common household requirements – such as coal, turf, pot sticks, pot lids, and wooden dishes, earthenware and tinder boxes – the latter a commodity unknown now that lucifer matches are to be had. Barber's shops were most frequented on Sundays, and in some of them drink was supplied to the customers. Mary Street could boast of a female barber who did a good business. On Sundays, too, the apothecaries and confectioners, as well as the fruiterers, had their places of business open. The principal clothes shops or warehouses in High Street were M'Clean's, Smith's, Reid's, Day & Bottomley's. Wier's and Halliday's were wholesale woollen warehouses in other parts of the town. Hardy's British Woollen Hall was the first place which exhibited any great improvement in the matter of shop fronts, and was very attractive and much admired. Then followed MacLurcan's, and adjoining it was Lennon's with the 'Golden wool pack'.

THOMAS GAFFIKEN, *Belfast Fifty Years Ago*, 1894

PORTSTEWART, UNLIKE CASTLEROCK, has grown almost out of recognition in the last thirty years, and makes a good second to the populous resort of Portrush (*Port ruis*, the landing place of the peninsula) three miles further east; indeed, it will soon be the western end of Portrush if the intervening tract continues to be built over – and no doubt it will do so, for this rocky coast, all open Atlantic in front, is an extraordinarily invigorating place. Wherefore Portrush is especially beloved of the people of Belfast, and thither they troop in thousands in July and August. When I first came to Dublin from the north, over forty years ago, I remember being struck by the different conception in the two cities as to the venue for the annual holiday. Belfast people turned out *en masse* to Portrush and Newcastle, where they bathed and played golf and tennis with all the people with whom they consorted at home. Dublin folk, on the other hand, got their passports into order and bolted to Switzerland or Tyrol or Italy or Germany. It is true that Dublin has attractive places around it, but they have remained to some extent undeveloped – with the exception of Bray, which is to Dublin merely what Bangor is to Belfast – and probably that is to some extent accountable for the difference in procedure: but it is no doubt mainly due to the fact that Dublin was a capital city with many cosmopolitan interests while Belfast was still to all intents a market-town. It has still a weekly market-day like the little towns around it, and until a few years ago a flock of leisurely geese waddled among the parked motors in Cromac Square, and camped on its barren concrete – possibly a survival of the days when grass grew there; but they are all gone now. Belfast is now a city, larger I believe than Dublin: yet I am inclined to think that this difference as to holidays persists to a great extent, and that many more foreign travel tickets are issued in the southern capital than in the northern. Which is a pity, for the great business community of Belfast, absorbed in office work for forty-eight or fifty weeks out of each fifty-two, stands to gain more from a complete change of environment – new people, new languages, new ideas, new customs – than the more varied, more pro-fessional and more leisurely groups that make up the same class in Dublin.

ROBERT LLOYD PRAEGER, *The Way That I Went*, 1937

PAINTINGS IN THE CORRIDORS AND ROOMS record events and visits of royalty and other important guests. My favourite story about the City Hall's VIP visitors concerns Lady Lavery, the legendary London hostess of the 1920s. Her husband was the Belfast-born Sir John Lavery whose paintings were one of the Royal Academy's main attractions at Burlington House for many years. Belfast always fêted the Laverys, although Hazel lent her extraordinary beauty as model for the colleen on the Irish Free State banknotes and was a close friend of Michael Collins. On her first visit to Belfast after her husband's knighthood a civic banquet was given in their honour. She swept up the marble stairs. At the top landing before the banqueting room, she paused.

'Lady Lavery,' she said proudly to the lackey announcing names.

Embarrassed, he whispered in her ear, 'Second door on the right, by the Lady Mayoress's retiring room.'

ROBIN BRYANS, *Ulster: A Journey Through the Six Counties*, 1964

IN THE SPRING OR SUMMER OF 1846 I gladly took leave of discount ledgers and current accounts, and went to Belfast for two months' instruction in the duties of Principal Coast Officer of Customs, a tolerably well-sounding title, but which carried with it a salary of but £80 a year. I put up at a Temperance Hotel in Waring Street, slept soundly (O Youth!) in a small front room in that narrow noisy thoroughfare, trudged daily about the docks and timber yards learning to measure logs, piles of planks, and, more troublesome, ships for tonnage: indoors part of time practised Customs book-keeping, and talked to the clerks about literature and poetry in a way that excited some astonishment, but, on the whole, as I found at parting, a certain degree of curiosity and respect.

WILLIAM ALLINGHAM, *William Allingham: A Diary*, 1907

I AM SEVENTEEN-AND-A-HALF. I have begun work in the office of a morning newspaper in Belfast. The *Northern Whig* was founded in 1824 as 'a political journal devoted to the advocacy of Liberal principles'. F.D. Finlay, the first editor, suffered two terms of imprisonment in 1826 and 1832 in the course of his struggle for various reforms, including that of Catholic emancipation. After 100 years the newspaper has changed its character, is hardly Whig any more. It submits to the prevailing political line, which is Conservative and Unionist (the word Unionist meaning unity with England, not with the rest of Ireland). I can't say that I'm in favour of its now changed politics. What I'm there for is to gain newspaper experience. Every evening from 7 p.m. to 2 a.m. I work in the office near the docks, not far from the Albert Clock. What late hours! On leaving the office I am obliged to walk nervously to my distant digs through a city under curfew.

Shots ... buildings on fire ... this is night-time in Belfast during the Troubles.

For centuries Ireland was a subjugated colony of England. The resistance movement against the occupying Power, stimulated by the attempted coup d'état of 1916 in Dublin, grew in force, and by 1920 had won a partial independence for the country, under the terms of which the island was divided into two parts. At the time of which I am writing – in the Southern part dissatisfied nationalists are still continuing their fight against England. But in the Northern part a loyalist (loyal to England) government has been established, and has been greeted with outbreaks of violence from nationalist opponents. This violence leads in turn to widespread reprisals from the loyalists. To deal with the disorders British troops have come in; and Belfast is almost continuously under curfew.

At night the streets are empty and are patrolled by armoured cars, as I go home. Sometimes a sentry lets me walk past him for 50 yards and then recalls me, for the pleasure of making me come back to show my permit. He is a B Special. He has his own way of enjoying night duty.

When I arrive and am about to open the door of the house where I lodge, I imagine gunmen waiting, perhaps behind the gable or inside in the hall. I say to myself: 'You must control these fears.' And next day quite likely I read that an hour before or an hour after my passing some 'outrage' has been committed in one of the streets: perhaps a family has been lined up and shot by raiders. I am only a few minutes or a few steps, it seems, from the raging murder.

In this respect the *Northern Whig* isn't innocent. Leading articles refer to reprisals and may appear to suggest them, articles written by a greybearded Englishman who wouldn't hurt a fly. He is disgusted, for example, at James Joyce calling the sea 'snot-green' in the first chapter of *Ulysses*. As a comment on our climate he walks about the office wearing gumboots.

GEORGE BUCHANAN, *Morning Papers*, 1965

HE [FORREST REID] WAS A FRIEND OF YEATS AND E.M. FORSTER and his few novels have an element of pagan symbolism that is present also in Forster's early short stories, and reflect something of Yeats's mysticism. The idea of the ghost or revenant, some shade of a lost culture or a guilt appearing out of the past is often found in Irish literature. Reid's autobiography, *Apostate*, describes his upbringing in Belfast. It is a minor classic, and it will stand beside Gosse's *Father and Son*. He was indeed an apostate in that awful, rainy and smoky Presbyterian city: he was a genuine pagan. He stayed there as if in hiding, I used to think. He lived alone on the top floor of a sour house, shaken by industrial traffic, and opposite a linen mill. The smoke hung low and blew into his windows, so that he had been obliged to bind his thousands of books in white paper covers: not very practical in that place for the smuts stood out on them. One passed old bicycles in the hall, then climbed stairs of torn linoleum to his bare room on the table of which there was usually a pile of novels for review from the *Manchester Guardian*, and a bone of cold mutton pushed to the other side of it. He was the first book reviewer I ever saw. He was a thin fellow and he had a strange nose, very long and thin, that tipped up suddenly like a small hook at the end. He had A.E.'s habit of poking the soot off the back of his little fireplace as if looking for secret intimations. After sniffing out politics in mills and newspaper offices, or coming back from some Orange beano at which an English politician would be trying to beat the Orangemen down before they all started singing (of all songs), 'Oft in the Stilly Night' by Tom Moore – I would make for Forrest Reid's room to hear softer and more civilised accents. It was a relief after a day with a shipyard owner. There was one to whom I spoke about Forrest Reid.

'Wratin' poetry don't drave no rivets, yoong man,' he said.

I may exaggerate Reid's isolation, for there is a decent university in Belfast and the Belfast playwright who wrote that biting farce *Thompson of Tir-na-Nog* must have been worth knowing; but it was odd to find a mystic, deep in

Blake and Yeats, among the linen mills. Why didn't he go South? Perhaps because of some core of Ulster obstinacy or of family chains that are so powerful in all Ireland.

V.S. PRITCHETT, *Midnight Oil*, 1971

ON APPROACHING THE CAR his fingers searched absently for the keys. Fast cars had been his one extravagance and the Aston Martin, which Catherine was not allowed to drive, was the reminder of his bachelor freedom. The keys were missing. He scrutinised the ground, thinking he had dropped them, and was about to turn back to his office when he realised that he had left them throughout the day in the car itself. The hood was down and he vaulted over the door into the driving seat, then noisily revved up the engine. In what other city could one leave a car unlocked ready for any thief to drive off? He thought of the English buyer he had entertained over lunch and the man's astonishment when he told him that even in the centre of Belfast people left their houses open and the car parked at the front door with the keys inside. Northern Ireland was fifty years behind the times: there were few divorces, the suicide rate was the lowest in Europe, and there was practically no serious crime. It was boring to be a policeman because the Ulsterman, John had insisted, was naturally law-abiding – it was a dull little country!

There was little traffic because most people were at home having their tea. Under a mild summer sky the Victorian buildings looked rosy and pleasant and, when he entered the main square to circle the City Hall, he slowed down to admire that late imperial extravagance with its vast dome and white encrusted pillars. The lavish architecture boasted the wealth and success of a city which, a hundred years earlier, had been an insignificant little town in a country that elsewhere remained impoverished.

NAOMI MAY, *Troubles*, 1976

BELFAST HAS ESCAPED the worst extremes of social instability. On the one hand it has escaped many of the vices of a more leisured and conventionally sociable city. For example, one is very rarely accosted by a prostitute in Belfast, not at all as often as in certain other cities. Belfast's prostitutes tend to serve distinct and restricted clienteles and do not range widely through the life of the city. Probably on account of this restriction of range, they seem be a less varied and more uniformly coarse-grained element than their more frequently encountered equivalents in Dublin. They have some amateur competition in Belfast, but probably a considerably larger proportion of unmarried people in Ulster retain their virginity than is the case in most other communities. Drink consumption in Northern Ireland is also relatively low, compared with England or with southern Ireland. Horses and dogs have their followers in the province, and football pools have given heavy burdens to Ulster postmen; but for the most part there remains a strong tradition in Ulster which regards anything in the nature of a bet or a gamble as a mug's game.

On the other hand, conditions in industrial Belfast were never so unattractive and frustrating as to drive working people in large numbers into vicious forms of escape. Much of the emotional rebound in the nineteenth century, which might have found vent in less desirable ways, found its outlet in religious revivals in Belfast, of which the biggest was in 1859. Such events are not so characteristic of Ulster today, for, though there is always a good deal of rather spectatorial interest in efforts to start them, they have not gathered a big momentum in recent decades.

There has thus been a certain balance in industrial Ulster, and the tone of society has been relatively healthy and pleasant. Ulster people are creative and they have a capacity for finding suitable outlets and modes of expression for themselves. For example, there is a great deal of handiwork and mechanical ingenuity put into Belfast houses by the menfolk. And when they are not creative in ways like this, Belfast people are contemplative. It is remarkable how many of them like to go out for walks into the country and the hills. In the old days of long hours and early rising, people in the suburbs used to hear the clatter of boots before six o'clock on any fine Sunday morning, as factory and shipyard workers went out singly or in little groups for rambles over the Belfast hills. And, though people keep later hours now, the same urge to go out of the city continues to manifest itself.

HUGH SHEARMAN, *Ulster*, 1949

I STILL FEEL SURPRISED whenever I hear Ulster mentioned in the news. It always used to seem like the archetypal place where nothing would, or could, ever happen. For as long as I can remember, boredom has seemed to be hanging over Northern Ireland like the grey mists that linger over her loughs. Boredom has seemed to be sweating out of the blackened Victorian buildings of Belfast, running down every tram-line of her dismal streets. Now, when Northern Ireland is mentioned, the word 'internment' rattles through every sentence like the shots of a repeating rifle. And yet for years and years so many Ulster people, both Catholic and Protestant, have felt that they were 'interned' in Ulster – interned by the gloom of her industrialised provinciality, by her backwaterishness, her bigotry and her tedium.

CAROLINE BLACKWOOD, *For All That I Found There*, 1973

THE BELFAST HE LEFT, the Belfast the Ex-Pats forswore, was a city dying on its feet: cratered sites and hunger strikes; atrophied, self-abased. But the Belfast he had heard reports of this past while, the Belfast he had seen with his own eyes last month, was a city in the process of recasting itself entirely. The army had long since departed from the Grand Central Hotel, on whose levelled remains an even grander shopping complex was now nearing completion. Restaurants, bars and takeaways proliferated along the lately coined Golden Mile, running south from the refurbished Opera House, and new names had appeared in the shopping streets: Next, Body Shop, Tie Rack, Principles. And his own firm, of course, Bookstore.

GLENN PATTERSON, *Fat Lad*, 1992

HIS HOUSE WAS IN THE NORTH END OF BELFAST, part of that much larger city which surrounded the central ghettos, a quiet, unpublicised, middle-class Belfast where Protestants and Catholics lived side by side, joined by class, by economic ties, even by intermarriage, in a way the poor could never be.

BRIAN MOORE, *Lies of Silence*, 1990

THERE MUST HAVE BEEN OTHER YOUNG MEN AND WOMEN suffering from cultural isolation though we were unaware of them. The university, to us, was incredibly provincial and bourgeois: a degree-giving institution, and so we scorned it. Isolation was preferable to assimilation by such an institution, and we had before us the example of Joyce in exile from Dublin's paralysis. Our *quartier* remained Davy McLean's bookshop, the second-hand bookshops in Smithfield and the Royal Avenue library.

On the verge of the *quartier* was the Labour Hall in York Street which we attended for political lectures and debates, especially during the period of the Spanish Civil War. The most memorable evening we had there was an amateur production of *Waiting for Lefty*, the once famous propagandist play about a strike of New York taximen. This short play by Clifford Odets and the lengthy novels of Theodore Dreiser made a great impression on us, and Bob [Davidson] ransacked the public library for all sorts of books by American writers. But despite our absorption in literature and politics we felt asphyxiated in the city and cycled to youth hostels all over the north to breathe fresh air and look at mountains instead of mills.

JOHN BOYD, *Out of My Class*, 1985

LEAVING BELFAST
for Craig Raine

Driving at dusk on the steep road
north to the airport, *Look back,*
you say, *The finest view of Belfast,*
and point, proud of your choice to stay.

How clear the rows of streetlamps show
which way we came. I trace them slope
by slope through marshlands slipping down
to lanes, and find the roofs again,

their stern geographies of punishment
and love where silence deepens under rain.
Each sudden gust of light explains itself
as flames, but neither they, nor even

bombs redoubled on the hills tonight
can quite include me in their fear.
What does remains invisible, is lost
in curt societies whose deaths become

revenge by morning, and whose homes
are nothing more than all they pity most.
I watch the moon above them, filling rooms
with shadow politics, though whether

voices there pronounce me an intruder,
traitor, or a friend, I leave them now
as much a stranger as I came, and turn
to listen in the twilight for their griefs,

but hear instead the promise of conclusion
echoing towards me through these miles
of stubborn gorse, until it disappears
at last in darkness, out beyond the coast.

ANDREW MOTION, *Dangerous Play: Poems 1974–1984*, 1985

THE MIST GRADUALLY FADED from the corners of the window and there could be seen the closed doors on the opposite side and a cat sheltering on one of the window-sills. The rain streaked the red brick under the eaves and fell pattering on a sodden newspaper that stuck to the wet road. Drops formed on the arms of the lamp-posts and were quickly blown off again. Holes in the street filled up with rain water and when the wind rippled across them it made waves as tiny as the markings on a bird's wing.

MICHAEL McLAVERTY, *Lost Fields*, 1942

Bog Meadow
and
Surrounding Hills

The Belfast hills enter into many city scenes. No matter how urban the centre of Belfast may be, you can never quite forget the hills. Sometimes at night, too, you can hear curlews flying overhead, reminding you that every road out of the city leads towards a wild and romantic beyond.

HUGH SHEARMAN, *Ulster*

And the imagination fills
Bog-meadow and surrounding hills . . .

MICHAEL LONGLEY, 'Letters'

LOOKING UP FROM THE TRAMWAY JUNCTION I saw the Cave Hill blocking the end of the street. And my family's house lay under the Black Mountain – not black, but a luminous grey-blue. There was no speck of wetness on the streets. The macabre elements seemed to have vanished – no El Greco faces under shawls, no torn feet of newsboys leaping on racing trams.

The house was full of azaleas and the long greenhouse of geraniums. Built in the last century by a tea merchant, it was a hideous house, but very comfortable – run by five maids who slept in a wing over the garage. The walls stiff with heavy anaglypta wallpapers, plaster vine-leaves grossly choking the cornices. The wooden panelling on the stairs ended at the turn to the second floor.

LOUIS MacNEICE, *Zoo*, 1938

F INAGHY IS A JUNCTION ON THE LISBURN ROAD, between Upper Malone and Andersonstown. When I was born it was an outpost of the suburbs, and in fact my mother could have wheeled my pram in any of three directions to reach 'the country' in minutes. Walking south-east you were quickly into the gentle landscape of the Lagan Valley. The cars along the Malone Road provided a diversion rather than an irritant, and you could measure your walk by turning at the cottage on the corner of Dunmurry Lane. Its garden always seemed to be overflowing with the colours of flowers. Walking north-west towards the mountains – hills really, but they were always called mountains – you crossed over a rustic railway bridge which the trains would blast black on both sides, leaving a smoke-ring enveloping the road. There was a little station, complete with ticket office and waiting room. The houses grew more sparse from there until you got into the more severe upland scenery, where there were the wilds of Collin Glen and all the promise of what lay over the other side. In the third direction, down the Lisburn Road towards Dunmurry and Lambeg, there were thick woods and low marshy fields.

In some ways it was better just to look at the mountains from our kitchen window and think of their names: Black Mountain, Divis, Cave Hill. They had an infinite variety of colour and incident, innumerable subtle shades of blue and purple, grey, a hint of green. The buildings were laid in a carpet before you, petering out as the slope grew. At night car headlights would mark romantic journeys across their face. There was excitement as the BBC and ITV television masts were erected, with their little ladders of red lights and one lamp at the top of each, winking for the planes coming in and out of Nutts Corner. Sometimes the mountains would smoulder like Sertsey when farmers burned gorse, and swathes of steely smoke would sweep across their tops. And the quarries – there was an active quarry where the mountains dipped at the southern end, its huge machinery silhouetted against the skyline. Blasting at the quarries could be heard distinctly where I lived, and I think you could hear the rock tumbling and see the smoke of the dynamite and the stone dust billowing. I remember that just beyond that quarry, in a niche of the horizon, was the shape of a single tree. Sunsets could be dramatic affairs, as the disc sank behind the mountains or lit up vivid clouds like a vast theatre, golden light transforming the ordinary roofs of our neighbours. I would not like to live in a place without mountains.

ROBERT JOHNSTONE, *Images of Belfast*, 1983

P OLEGLASS, TWINBROOK, THE FALLS, Andersonstown, Clonard, Ballymurphy, Turf Lodge. These areas form a rind around the lean meat of the city centre and the commerce of Boucher Road. The area is not quite a satellite of the city but it forms a restless scrub land that fades away from central Belfast into the very foot of the Black Mountain.

Although this forms a region economically depressed on a scale it is hard to describe, the area can still be beautiful. The sky can quickly grow awe-inspiring. The first ten years of my own life were spent in the radius of Turf Lodge, the very end of the city, the elbow of the arm of West Belfast as it turns alongside the mountains. The estate seemed radiant to me as a child. The pebbledash and pale brick of Turf Lodge lent it the air of a dusty *pueblo* like the ones in which my favourite television cowboys strode their manful. There seemed no want of glamour and resonance in Turf Lodge's rubble and trouble.

ROBERT McLIAM WILSON, The Dispossessed, 1992

THE ROWS OF HOUSES DID NOT GO ON FOR EVER. Beyond them lay the Bog Meadows' marshy steppes where refuse heaps broke the flatness, and where the narrow, shallow Blackstaff River meandered, colourless and unmusical. Near its banks the tinkers camped. We at least held hopes in our heart – who knew, one day we might even have the chance of a council house. But the tinkers could not warm themselves with such a comfort but only over reluctant fires that hissed in the drizzle outside their tents of rags.

God ordained that even the Bog Meadows should end and had set a great hill at their limit, which we called the Mickeys' Mountain. Among a knot of trees half-way up the flank a small cottage sheltered, and near by two fields were cultivated. Seen from the Bog Meadows they stood out amongst the bracken and heather like a giant hatchet. In terms of miles the mountain was not far, and I always longed to explore it. Somewhere, or in the hidden hills behind, lay the boot stuffed with goldpieces buried by Neeshy Haughan, who once upon a time robbed the rich to pay the poor, kindnesses ended by a hanging at Carrickfergus. What things might be bought with the highwayman's long boot of gold! But the mountain was inaccessible because to reach it we had to cross territory held by the Mickeys. Being children of the staunch Protestant quarter, to go near the Catholic idolators was more than we dared, for fear of having one of our members cut off.

ROBERT HARBINSON, No Surrender, 1960

THE BOG MEADOWS was a favourite meeting place for the working class people of Belfast at weekends. The geographical layout with the Black Mountain, the Castlereagh Hills and the River Lagan and smaller rivers created this large wild life sanctuary. In former times the Bog Meadows had been used as a hunting ground for game and wild fowl by the gentry. In the 1930s it was only one fifth its original size as with the growth of

Belfast land had been reclaimed. But nevertheless it provided an area where the lower classes would meet, play pitch and toss, have cock fights and the odd dog fight was known to have taken place. All these forms of entertainment were gambling-related and prohibited by law. Lookouts had to keep their eyes open for the police. If they were spotted, the Bog had many escape routes to accommodate those who were breaking the law.

Local tough men, such as Barney Ross and Silver McKee from the Markets area, Stormy Weather and Buck Alec, from the Shankill and Dock area of the City, earned their living as scrap metal merchants, cattle herders, minders, bouncers and dock hands. They helped and assisted with the gambling and made sure any rules were not broken. No one paid any attention to the official law anyway, except Sergeant Fitzpatrick and Pig Meneelly. To add to all these goings on Buck Alec had a pet lion with no teeth. He had legal documentation to own this cat which was fearsome looking until it opened its mouth. Buck would carry on an act, much to all the children's enjoyment, of sticking his head in between its jaws. Anyone who could pay gave a ha'penny, which went to help feed the lion. He also gave the children a ride on its back for the same price. Buck also travelled round all the working class areas through the week performing the same act.

GEORGE FLEMING, *Magennis VC*, 1998

ON THE WHOLE, SANDY-ROW agreeably disappoints one who, like myself, had been prepared to find its external aspects in keeping with certain notable deeds of its inhabitants. Its suburban situation is greatly in its favour. Many of its people are, doubtless, very poor, and their domestic and sanitary condition capable of great improvement. But they are not shut up within walls which debar the entrance of the pure air and light of heaven. The mountain breezes play upon their dwellings, and they have only to look around to catch some glimpses of the country, not yet quite eaten up by the insatiable appetite of our monster town.

THE REVEREND W.M. O'HANLON, *Walks Among the Poor of Belfast*, 1853

FORTUNATELY BELFAST IS NOT MODERN to the exclusion of nature; as in Edinburgh, the country dominates the town. From its busiest streets one has only to lift one's eyes to rejoice in hills and heather; a penny tram journey will bring the traveller into a region as wild as Donegal and as lonely as the Irish midlands. If Belfast children are city born, it is their good luck not to be street-bred. They have the key of the fields, and the least adventurous of them roam far and wide.

JAMES WINDER GOOD, *Ulster and Ireland*, 1919

BELFAST IS BEAUTIFULLY SITUATED. Surrounded by a rim of soft, glaciated hills – the Black Mountain, Carrick Hill, Divis – opening out onto the lough, it lies like a puddle of cold tea in a saucer. Much of the town was built on marsh and bog. Like my secondary school, St Catherine's Girls' Convent School. The Sisters of Charity. The Brown Bombers. It rose out of the bog meadows, with the cemetery on one side and the Protestants just over the Peace Line to the east. For years we held fast to the hope that the school was sinking into the bog. But even at an inch a year it wouldn't be fast enough.

MARY COSTELLO, *Titanic Town*, 1992

THEY STARTED IN THE COLD BRIGHT OCTOBER WEATHER, after giving Bessie repeated instructions concerning the kitchen fire. Autumn was well advanced. The scarlet creeper that covered Mrs Wilberforce's house had already lost some of its leaves, though there were still a few yellow roses in the garden, and next door Professor Lanyon's dahlias and purple clematis were magnificent. Mrs Seawright and her companions – one on either side of her – walked briskly, for the air was sharp. They made directly for the cemetery, which was situated on an open stretch of rising ground at the foot of the Black Mountain. They crossed the dreary expanse of the bog meadows, passed the Cats' and Dogs' Home and the huge football-ground, with its hideous walls of corrugated iron, emerging on the upper road at a spot directly opposite the cemetery gates. Here the ground rose steeply, its green surface broken by innumerable white and grey monuments, and threaded with dark trim paths. The hard silhouettes of a few cypresses, and the softer outlines of the trees in the park alongside, stood out against a pale blue sky; while beyond, yet quite close, was a dark low range of hills, the air from which blew down, fresh and cold.

FORREST REID, *At the Door of the Gate*, 1915

HE TIED THE LACES OF HIS BOOTS TOGETHER, and then swung his boots round his neck, and walked on through the fields in the direction, as he thought, of the Malone Road, but it was a long while before he came to any road, and then he did not know what road it was. He deliberated for a few minutes, hoping that some one would appear who could direct him towards the town, but no one did, and he continued his walk. He came presently to a field without a gate through which he walked until he found himself in the strangest place he had ever seen. He gazed about him in astonishment, for the field had a singular shape. It was made like a great horse-shoe; its grassy banks seemed to have been built for spectators at some sort of performance.

In the middle of it was a heap of stones, with a long heavy stone on top of them. They seemed to have been set there. 'You would near think you were in a circus,' he said to himself, as he gazed about him. He walked in the centre of the ring and stood there, silent and unaccountably afraid. In front of him, he could see the high, dark humps of the Antrim Mountains, and seeing them, he realised that he must have come away from the town when he meant to go towards it. He was puzzled by the sense of alarm he had. The field was a queer one, indeed, but what was there to be afraid of? He moved away from the centre of the ring and climbed on to the bank and looked about him. That place over there, reaching out to the mountains, must be the Bog Meadows, where there was great skating in the wintertime. He had heard of them many times, but had never seen them before. And this place, what sort of a place was it at all? Who in the wide, earthly world would ever think of making a field this shape? Men had made it – of that he felt certain – unless it was like the Giant's Causeway that looked as if it had been made, but, according to all accounts, was not made at all. He walked round the ring until he found himself again at the place where he had entered the field. An old man approached him.

'That's a brave day!' Robert said.

The old man paused and looked at him. 'Aye,' he said, 'it is!'

'What kind of a place is this at all?' Robert asked, turning to survey the field.

The old man gazed at him in astonishment. 'D'you mane t'say you never heard tell of it?' he exclaimed incredulously.

'I wouldn't be askin' you about it if I had!'

'But you have the sound of a Belfast fella!' the old man persisted.

'That's just what I am – a Belfast fella. I was born in this place,' said Robert.

'An' yit you never heard tell of the Giant's Ring! Well, man dear, that bates all I ever was toul!'

ST JOHN ERVINE, *The Wayward Man*, 1926

ABOUT FOUR MILES FROM BELFAST, in the parish of Drumbo, stands the Giant's Ring, one of the most stupendous and extraordinary monuments of antiquity in Ireland. It consists of an enormous circle, perfectly level, about five hundred and eighty feet in diameter, or nearly one-third of an Irish mile in circumference, comprising an area of eight plantation or nearly thirteen statute acres. This vast ring is enclosed by an earthen mound or outwork, upwards of eighty feet in breadth at the base; and though it is probable, in the lapse of nearly two thousand years, the height of this bank must have much decreased, it is still so great as to hide the surrounding country, except the tops of the mountains, entirely from the view; and in its original state there is scarcely a doubt but they too were invisible, so that a person standing near the centre could only see the enclosure and the sky. Near the centre of the circle stands one of those Cromlechs, or rude stone altars, so common throughout Ireland, and which have been so much the subject of antiquarian disquisition.

JAMES ADAIR PILSON, History of the Rise and Progress of Belfast, 1846

from PATCHWORK

Snags of greyish wool remind me of the mountain that we
    climbed that day –
Nearly at the summit, we could see the map of Belfast. My
    father stopped
For a cigarette, and pointed out the landmarks: Gallaher's
    tobacco factory,
Clonard Monastery, the invisible speck of our house, lost in all
    the rows
And terraces and furrows, like this one sheep that's strayed
    into the rags
And bandages that flock the holy well. A little stack of ball-
    point pens,
Some broken spectacles, a walking-stick, two hearing-aids:
    prayers
Repeated and repeated until granted.

CIARAN CARSON, The Irish for No, 1987

FOUR WEEKS OF COLM'S HOLIDAYS had passed before peace came to the city and hovered over it like a spring cloud. Women wheeled out their prams and went up to the park; and one Saturday afternoon Alec, Colm, Jamesy, and Rover went up the fields to the mountain. Jamesy had a long pair of flannel trousers on him, tubular and oil-stained, and carried in one of the pockets a bottle of milk which was corked with a wad of twisted paper. Colm had sandwiches made from tinned meat, and Alec had bought apples and a packet of cigarettes for himself.

It was a lovely day with the sun shining and people stretched in the fields. Up past the brickyard they went, looking down at the deep pit, and clay hard and caked, the bogie lines shining. Into the wide open fields they raced where Rover rolled over and over with delight and barked teasingly at Colm and Jamesy. They jumped a little stream and came out of the fields on to the Whiterock Road. At the top of it an ice-cream man was sitting on the shaft of his red-painted barrow. Alec bought three sliders from him and they sucked them as they climbed the white stony lonin that led to the mountain's foot.

Banks and hedges were at each side and filled the lonin with leaf-shadow and a dewy coolness. Here and there were crumpled newspapers where lovers had crushed into the banks the previous night. On big boulders there was printed in white paint: WHAT THINK YE OF CHRIST? ALL HAVE SINNED.

At gaps in the hedges they stood to look down at the city and felt the blood hammering in their heads. Alec loosed his belt, and Rover lay in a stream that swirled over stones at the side of the lonin. They passed a lake with a line of pines, and a tin church – so small and so diminutive that it looked like a child's toy. And then they reached the foot of the mountain, Alec puffing and blowing: 'Thank God, we're here at last!'

He sat down on the bank near the drinking pool and fanned himself with his cap. 'I'll have a quare slug of that in a few minutes,' he said to himself as he watched Colm and Jamesy put their mouths to the cold spurt of water that gushed into the pool. Rover rolled his liver-and-white body in it while Colm and Jamesy splashed it around their hot faces and plastered their hair.

Their path cut diagonally up the mountain. It was loose and stony, and the heat struck up from it in thick waves. Colm and Jamesy led the way, and Alec stopped often to admire the view. Jamesy hurled a stone down the side and heard it bumping until it fell and broke in pieces at the bottom. Colm lifted a brown caterpillar that was crossing the path and placed it on the palm of his hand, counting the rings on its back whenever it stretched itself.

At the top of the mountain they lay in the heather and gazed at Belfast spread out in the flat hollow below them, its lean mill chimneys stretched above the haze of smoke. Rows of red-bricked houses radiated on all sides and above them rose blocks of factories with many of their windows catching the sunlight.

They saw their own street and could make out the splash of whitewash on the wall that Alec had daubed there as a mark for his pigeons; it was all very far away like a street seen through the wrong end of a telescope.

'I can see my mother standing at the back-door throwing a crust to the fowl and Biddy McAteer hanging out her curtains,' joked Jamesy.

'And look at Mrs O'Brien cleaning her ear with a knitting needle,' answered Colm.

Alec gave a loud sniff: 'Man dear, I can smell the sausages frying for our tea.'

Their eyes ranged over the whole city to the low ridge of the Castlereagh Hills, netted with lovely fields and skimming cloud-shadows, to the blue U-shaped lough covered with yachts as small as paper boats, and steamers moving up towards the docks where the gantries stood like poised aeroplanes.

They shouted out to each other the names of all the churches that they knew: there were the green spires of Ardoyne where the sinners brought their great sins to the Passionists, there was the stumpy spire of the Monastery, and farther along in the heart of the city, sticking high above the smoke, were the sharp spires of St Peter's – the church that was always crowded with shawled factory workers saying their beads. Near their own street was the Dominican Convent, its fields very green and its hockey posts very white. And when Jamesy asked was it true that the nuns dug a bit of their graves each day and slept in their coffins at night Alec laughed: 'It'd be a queer deep grave some of them ladies would have for they're as ould as the hills.'

MICHAEL McLAVERTY, Call My Brother Back, 1939

IN THE SUMMER AS WE GREW OLDER, walks up to the Divis and Black Mountains became more and more frequent and whole days were spent exploring the caves or the forests. Looking back, the 'caves' were rather humble efforts and the 'forests' were far from grandiose affairs but even jaundiced hindsight cannot minimise the fun we had dodging and yelling through thick bushes or along little mountainy trails. On Sundays whole families made their way up the mountain lonnan, past the wee tin church, stopping for a drink at the river and away on up the windy track to the waterfall, where the real mountain started. The mountain lonnan meets the Ballygomartin Road at this point and a small whitewashed cottage sits at the junction. There are two paths, the lower skirting the base of the mountain and branching upwards at a number of points while the upper path reaches directly for 'the hatchet field' and 'the gully'.

A hundred yards above the whitewashed cottage, a huge jagged rock face stands the height of several stories of a building. We called it 'the riddley rock' and frightened ourselves by daring each other to scale it. Above were acres and acres of bracken and heather specially laid out for us to tumble through headlong, screaming and whooping with the sheer joy of being alive. We found wild strawberries once away towards Ligoniel and called the mountainy road 'strawberry path' ever afterwards. Likewise with 'running path', because of our inability to stop once we set off downwards. Behind 'the hatchet field', so called because of its shape, was 'the bottle field', which also got its name from its distinctive shape. Between them an acre of bluebells raised their heads amid heather and whin bushes.

GERRY ADAMS, Falls Memories, 1982

FROM OUR FRONT DOOR we looked down over wide fields to Belfast Lough and across it to the long mountain line of the Antrim shore – Divis, Colin, Cave Hill. This was in the far-off days when Britain was the world's carrier and the Lough was full of shipping; a delight to both us boys, but most to my brother. The sound of a steamer's horn at night still conjures up my whole boyhood. Behind the house, greener, lower, and nearer than the Antrim mountains, were the Holywood Hills, but it was not till much later that they won my attention. The north-western prospect was what mattered at first; the interminable summer sunsets behind the blue ridges, and the rooks flying home.

C.S. LEWIS, *Surprised by Joy*, 1955

IN THOSE DAYS Belfast was bounded by the Holywood Arches, the Botanic Gardens (where I saw a balloon ascend every Easter Monday), the Waterworks and the City Cemetery. It seems to have no bounds now. Beyond the Arches, one was in the country. Ballyhackamore was truly a village then, savoury with the smell of turf smoke. I once stayed at a farm at The Knock. (I'm told that it is no longer called The Knock, but simply Knock. Why?) There was a far distant country place called Ligoniel – Oh, what a long way off for a little lad, away, away beyond the tramlines. You got very tired when you went that far. But I seldom went north of the Junction. I was a Ballymacarrett boy, and we Ballymacarrett people were very particular about where we went.

Belfast could think itself lucky to be part of Ballymacarrett, we thought. We had all we needed within our boundaries, though I never knew what those boundaries were, and had no need to go searching for things elsewhere. We were industrialised, and yet we had the country practically on our doorsteps. I remember fields and hedges almost the whole length of the Albertbridge Road from the Methodist Church at Templemore Avenue to the Newtownards Road. I remember when 'Glentum' football club had its ground in Madrid Street. I remember when you could smell the country in Castlereagh Street, by the Beersbridge Road, smell the mingled odours of whin blossoms, and crops and cattle and seaweed, the lovely smells of Down, full of turf smoke.

ST JOHN ERVINE, *Belfast Telegraph*, 1945

MY EARLIEST RECOLLECTIONS OF THE CITY OF MY BIRTH, though somewhat obscured and hazy because of my tender years, are of the old White Linen Hall in the glory of a summer's day, with its cool and shady grounds festooned with stately foliage, jealously watching the inevitable destruction of what was at one time the aristocratic residential quarter of the city. I lived in Little May Street then, and we children had fun and frolics round the railed enclosure of the old building. The Chapel Fields, too, were our playground. The Fields were bordered by Ormeau Avenue and stretched from Joy Street to Linen Hall Street. For many years they were used as a fair ground at Christmas and Easter holidays.

I spent a few nights in what had been my grandparents' home in Sandy Row, a small, single-storied white-washed cottage with its half door, which stood, one of a row of similar dwellings right on the corner of Hope Street. The Brewery Buildings, with its fine, ornamental entrance, often held me spellbound. Even in my childhood days I could never discover any Sandy Row man who remembered the brewery working.

The Bog Meadows stretched from Broadway across to the GNR embankment with Roden Street, then half built, its southern boundary. Ballynafeigh was a straggling suburb, with Ravenhill a wilderness beyond My Lady's Road. The Stranmillis, Stockman's Lane and Finaghy were lovers' lanes. Ligoniel was 'a brave wee dander' from Ardoyne Chapel through picturesque country scenery.

THOMAS CARNDUFF (1954), *Life and Writings*, 1994

INSIDE HIS BARS the tiger reclined on the crest of the rise, startling and immaculate. He was enjoying the fine day and the view of Belfast Lough spread out below him, trees, hills and water whose surface was criss-crossed by dark unaccountable liquid ribbons, a checkboard of fields on the hills rising from the further shore, spires, chimneys, roof-tops, a housing estate sedate as children's bricks, a mill dam throwing back the sky's colour, the cemetery to the left with memorial stones white like bones, and far up the Lough the angles and heights of the shipyards.

There was a crowd round the cage, admiring, exclaiming, taking photographs, holding up their children. The animal stared steadfastly over their heads, superbly indifferent, and pulled a casual growl out of nowhere with barely a movement of his throat.

JANET McNEILL, *The Maiden Dinosaur*, 1964

'AWAY, AWAY, FROM MEN AND TOWNS.' From the modern city of Belfast, with its modern history and modern buildings and modern factories and shipyards, we turn to the beautiful and attractive area which surrounds it. Not that any slight to Belfast is implied. But what does the Belfast business-man himself do (and in Belfast almost every man is a business-man) but get away from it as soon as ever his business is done – to

Balmoral or Knock or Bangor: and I may claim the same privilege, and leave the guide-book to do justice to Belfast. Dublin is beautifully situated, with mountains rising only a few miles beyond its southern suburbs, and the richly wooded Liffey vale, the bold headlands of Howth and Bray, and the broad sands of Dublin Bay. Cork can make a good bid too: but to my mind Belfast stands pre-eminent in Ireland for the beauty and variety of its environment. To north and west the high scarp of the basalts rises nobly. The City Hall, standing at sea-level, is distant only two and a half miles from the thousand-foot contour-line; and the lofty cliffs of the Cave Hill are a conspicuous feature from Castle Junction, the central point of the city. On a volcanic vent at Carrickfergus (*Carraig Fhearghusa*, Fergus's rock) ten miles down the lough, the great castle which John de Courcy built in 1177 stands intact, now a local museum, its stirring military days long past. A significant feature near by is the pit-heads of the Duncrue salt-mines – one of the very few of the many Irish mining enterprises that are not now abandoned. Beds of salt up to eighty-eight feet in thickness occur here among the marls of the New Red Sandstone. In mining, half of the bed is left to form a roof, and the other half is cut away except for massive pillars to support the overlying strata. The mineral is often very pure, containing up to 98 per cent of salt. Beyond, where the coast turns northward, are the Chalk and basalt cliffs of White Head and Black Head. South-west of Belfast lies the valley of the Lagan, richly-wooded. South-east, the undulating lands of County Down stretch far – fertile and smiling, but supplying less variety than any other part of Belfast's environment. The Down side of Belfast Lough, however, compensates for this, being well-wooded, varied, with a rocky shore. Then a little further off is the long island-studded lough of Strangford, anciently *Loch Cuan*, the *Strang Fiord* of the Norsemen, full of archaeological and natural history interest. Only twelve miles west of Belfast, across the hills, lies Lough Neagh, the largest sheet of water in Ireland and larger also than any in Great Britain; and beyond White Head is Larne Lough. So delightful a combination of land and water within a few miles of a great city is surely unique; and the variety of rocks which occurs also is striking, representing a remarkable span of world history.

ROBERT LLOYD PRAEGER, *The Way That I Went*, 1937

ON CAVE HILL I saw that there is one thing to be said in favour of Belfast – you can get out of it quickly: and, accordingly, all around the Lough are little settlements of commuters who wisely use the city for their affairs, and leave it in the evening. The beanstalk growth of Belfast compels this flight. Unlike Dublin, which was a great fashionable and residential centre, and catered for itself with grace and wisdom, Belfast has not given itself a single public park within the city. It has none of those lovely city-squares that the Georgians have bestowed on Dublin and London. Indeed what charm it offers is the charm of its most workaday quarters – such as the shipyards with their great cranes and gantries, painted by Paul Henry from away up-river, or the colour and variety of the market-stalls on Chichester Street, or the bird-fanciers in Gresham Street of a Saturday night, or the second-hand stalls in Smithfield, eerie with their fluttering gibbets of cast-off old clothes. As for buildings, there are only two worth while – the new Stormont House of Parliament, with the fine statue of Carson by Merryfield, and the Custom House on the river; though it may be that I am here thinking less of the architecture – the building cannot hold a candle to Gandon's magnificent Custom House in Dublin – than of the argumentative groups who once made 'the Custom House steps' as famous for oratory as Hyde Park.

SEAN O'FAOLAIN, *An Irish Journey*, 1940

HAYSEEDS AND THE HILLS, ships and the sea, meet in Belfast, and encroach at every street's end. Not only after church or chapel on Sunday, but after a day in the shipyard or on the loom the men and women of Belfast can take their greyhounds or their lovers out to the Black Mountain, Cave Hill, McArt's Fort, Squire's Hill, and out to the alluring groves of Carr's Glen and Shaw's Bridge, and on up to the majestic sweep of Divis – the Mountain of Tears. Here, on this highest of the Belfast Hills, they have the city and its lough before them as though in the palm of their hand. Up there, nearly sixteen hundred feet above the sea, the Storm God of the ancient Druids was said to have his throne. And there too the pagan priests called on their gods to defend them from the new Christians whose symbol of power was impudently nothing more than two bits of a rough tree trunk fashioned into a cross.

ROBIN BRYANS, *Ulster: A Journey Through the Six Counties*, 1964

THE SCENERY OF THIS DISTRICT OF THE SHORE IS BEAUTIFUL. Towards the inland side, a chain of high hills extends from nearly one extremity of the parish of Hollywood to the other. The sloping country, between these and the bay of Belfast, is beautifully diversified, and being richly cultivated, planted, and decorated with gentlemen's seats, has a most picturesque effect. This effect is greatly heightened by the prospect of the bay, terminated by the town of Belfast at its upper extremity, and bounded on the opposite side by that magnificent chain of mountains usually denominated the Belfast

43

mountains. These extend along the shore from Carrickfergus to Belfast, and fade from the eye in the internal country.

A. ATKINSON, *Ireland Exhibited to England*, 1823

I WAS DELIGHTED WITH MY EVENING'S WALK. I met crowds of people re-turning homewards, their hooks on their shoulders, and women and children by their side. They all bade me good e'en as they passed. Several were smoking. I was not sorry to see this. Men will intoxicate themselves some way or other, and smoking is a better way than drinking. I do not think I met a single wheel-car beween Lisburn and Belfast. The vehicles for the conveyance of goods were all waggons and carts. Every step, indeed, I advanced, I felt more forcibly I was in the neighbourhood of a great town. Had it not been for the lofty ridge of mountain on my left hand, which seemed to move along with and accompany me, I should have thought myself in the environs of London. The country was in the highest state of cultivation – it looked like one continued garden, shadowed with trees, in-terspersed with thickets, and neat white-washed houses, smiling in beauty, scented with fragrance, thrilling with harmony, delightful to the eye, ear, and smell. I looked into one or two of those cottages. I saw nothing to heighten the delusion certainly, nor did I see any thing greater than might be expected, to lessen it. Wherever, or whenever we see human nature close, we see it to disadvantage. A man finds in a house food and repose; if he wishes for enthusiasm, he must keep out of doors. The evening shades came fast upon me in the latter part of my journey, nor could I at length distinguish more than the soft repose of the green vale by my side – yet the indescribable noise, the faint hum, told me I was approaching the habitations of men.

JOHN GAMBLE, *A View of Society and Manners in the North of Ireland*, 1813

THE COUNTRY AROUND LISBURN is highly improved; but in the direction of Belfast, it is one continued chain of plantation beauty. 'We think it is scarcely possible,' says Mr Atkinson, 'to bring any country to a state of higher perfection than this district of Antrim. A minute description of all the works of art and nature which combine to produce this perfection is incompatible with the limits of a sheet, but when the reader presents to his imagination a magnificent landscape, bounded in front by the Belfast mountains, watered by the river Lagan, besprinkled with beautiful villas, bleach-yards upon the mountain sides, glistening in the dancing ray; cottages white as snow, with cropped hedges enclosing gardens bending under the weight of their productions; valleys teeming with the gifts of

Ceres, and all in full view of the traveller, over a charming road, which passes through domains and villas of incomparable beauty; forming one continued chain of rich plantation from Lisburn to Belfast, – he will have formed some idea of the country to whose natural and artificial history we have here introduced him.'

JAMES ADAIR PILSON, *History of the Rise and Progress of Belfast*, 1846

THE LOUGH OF BELFAST has a reputation for beauty, almost as great as that of the Bay of Dublin; but though, on the day I left Belfast for Larne, the morning was fine, and the sky clear and blue above, an envious mist lay on the water, which hid all its beauties from the dozen of passengers on the Larne coach. All we could see were ghostly-looking silhouettes of ships gliding here and there through the clouds; and I am sure the coachman's remark was quite correct, that it was a pity the day was so misty. I found myself, before I was aware, entrapped into a theological controversy with two grave gentlemen outside the coach – another fog, which did not subside much before we reached Carrickfergus. The road from the Ulster capital to that little town seemed meanwhile to be extremely lively; cars and omnibuses passed thickly peopled. For some miles along the road is a string of handsome country-houses, belonging to the rich citizens of the town; and we passed by neat-looking churches and chapels, factories and rows of cottages clustered round them, like villages of old at the foot of feudal castles. Furthermore it was hard to see, for the mist which lay on the water had enveloped the mountains too, and we only had a glimpse or two of smiling comfortable fields and gardens.

WILLIAM MAKEPEACE THACKERAY, *The Irish Sketch Book*, 1842

SEE, AS WE REST ON THE BRAE that leads from Sandymount to Stranmillis, and look on the river, how the opposite fields rise from its reeds, with a gentle curve, that reminds one of the line of beauty; and rich woods, grounds, and mansions fill the distance – and there, a long, black lighter is gliding down, drawn by a reeking horse, and guided by the sluggish figure that leans on the rudder's arm, and puffs at the soothing weed.

We now descend, and make for the first lock of the canal, inhaling the sweet scent of surrounding crops; leaping on the bent sally tree, whose model is the tower of Pisa; or starting little birds from the hedges of the lane. And when the lock is left behind, and the boatman's cottage, with its wild roses and creeping honey-suckle, fairly passed; there is an instinctive pause at 'Molly Ward's' – that fountain of curds and cream, and grave of urchin's pocket-money. By the by, I could never learn whether or not the same Molly was a mere *myth*, or ever clothed in solid flesh; and a learned pundit, who will certainly be a Bishop one of these days, maintains to this hour, that the *unde derivatur* is to be found in – a *moily* cow; however, it was the firm conviction of a school-fellow, whose ears had been well boxed by a solemn matron, for some mischievous prank, that none save the real Molly herself could have lent him such an astounding blow.

And thus, we may proceed from lock to lock, and bridge to bridge, each suggestive of its own incidents – the river now verging from the canal, then seeking it again with varied bends; here, by bordering woods, drooping willows reflected in the water, or tall sedges rustling on the brink, and wily coots dodging under; with houses greeting us at every angle; gay daffodils turning their yellow blossoms to the sun, or the modest daisy peeping from the grass – there, by flat marshes, green meads, or springing corn; and, finally, by the old bleach-green, its beetling mills, and shining cloth.

ANONYMOUS, 'The Banks of the Lagan', *Northern Magazine*, April 1852

from BELFAST: A POEM

The eye now tranquilly surveys
That vale which Nature's charms pourtrays
Contiguous to the mountain's base,
Where goat, sheep, deer, in sportive chace,
And maids and lads, midst toil and play,
Were wont to cheat the passing day;
Where Lodges rise, red, gray, and white,
Whose splendid beauty charms the sight,
Where now the yellow vies with green,
And crossing fences intervene,
Calling to mind Life's checker'd scene.
Where York-street's opening frees the mind
From noise and labour more confined,
When Pleasure smooths the wrinkling frown,
That clouds the brow for cares of town,
And the glad cits with speed repair
T' imbibe the sweets of rural air,
And chief to enjoy with fuller glee
The cooler breezes of the sea, –
There old MOUNT COLLYER stately stands,
The seat of hospitality;
Whose ancient plantings, aspect free,
The passing vision first command.

SAM LYONS, 1822

THE AIR OF THIS REGION is reputed colder and more moist than in the more southern districts. The difference of temperature in the atmosphere, even at the distance of a degree, is said to be sensible to every observer. The vicinity of the county of Antrim mountains, which are ranged on the opposite shore of the Belfast lough, with Lough Neagh upon the one side, and Strangford lough, which lies at the distance of about five miles, in the opposite direction, may cause the district of Belfast to be more moist and inclement, than its latitude would otherwise indicate. The summers are tempered by cool refreshing breezes, which render the air peculiarly salubrious at that season; but the whole line of country on one side of the lough, lying exposed to the N.W. winds, so prevalent here in winter and spring, the temperature at these seasons is more strikingly severe, and is hurtful to vegetation. The inhabitants, nevertheless, do not give any proofs of its insalubrity, being generally healthy and robust.

A. ATKINSON, *Ireland Exhibited to England*, 1823

THE PROXIMITY OF THE CAVE HILL TO BELFAST, like Arthur's seat at Edinburgh, is associated with the town, commanding an extensive view of land and water. On the evening of the Prince of Wales's wedding day, a hundred tar barrels were carried to the top of the hill, and when lighted, the effect, even in the streets of Holywood, was very great. At this time the white duck trousers appeared to be indispensable for the Cave Hill on Easter Monday. The principal tailors were – Watt, Marshall, Talbet, Henry, Robb, and Tim Leeson, from Dublin. In Galway's cloth shop, in Bridge Street, M'Neight or Billy Nocher might be seen measuring a person with a long tape like a piece of paper, nipping it in different places with a pair of scissors. This operation succeeded the choice by the customer of the cloth. Merchant tailors were then unknown in Belfast. The shops in Castle Place and Corn Market began to improve; but Mr Galway and the Misses Officer in Bridge Street, at the *Belfast News-Letter* Office, retained the old bow windows with the small panes for a longer period than any of their townspeople.

In Adam M'Clean's shop, near the corner of Bridge Street, I stood by whilst the great-grandfather of the present Marquis of Downshire purchased from Mr M'Clean the material for making some buff vests, which he carried himself to the carriage on the street.

THOMAS GAFFIKEN, *Belfast Fifty Years Ago*, 1894

ON THE EXTREME EDGE OF THE CITY opposite McArt's Fort, from the front-room windows of the houses along the Lower Braniel Road where the Castlereagh Hills begin to rise, there is a panorama [which is] breathtaking. But since it is from gentle County Down, the viewpoint seems a more protective one. On the right, near Dundonald, the white classical parliament building of Stormont stands in its grand setting at the top of a mile-long hill, shining out its wholly compromised idea of a Protestant parliament for a Protestant people. You can see all the areas of Belfast: from Gilnahirk and Tullycarnet, the Short Strand and Ballynafeigh, to Carnmoney Hill, apart from the rest; you can see the gap up to Glengormley, where terriers are tamed, to Wolf Hill, where the last wolf was killed, and Divis with the head of the waters, one stream flowing north and west to the Bann and Lough Neagh, the other east to Belfast Lough. Then the Black Mountain. In between, out of the haze of the city centre, the shipyard's cranes rise, you see the great cylindrical oil containers, the reclaimed land thrusting into the lough, the green dome of the City Hall and the few tall buildings here and there, the white arch of the King's Hall, Balmoral. Within the city boundary the land rises from soft mud at sea level to black basalt at 1,500 feet. Looking across you have the compulsion to identify and name each place you recognise, to comprehend it, to understand the delights and hurts it had the power to inflict.

ROBERT JOHNSTONE, *Belfast: Portraits of a City*, 1990

PARTIES AND EXCURSIONS were planned for our amusement; and certainly the whole of our deportment and reception at Belfast very little resembled those of a man who escaped with his life only by a miracle, and who was driven into exile to avoid a more disgraceful fate. I remember particularly two days that we passed on the Cave Hill. On the first Russell, Neilson, Simms, McCracken, and one or two more of us, on the summit of McArt's fort took a solemn obligation – which I think I may say I have on my part endeavoured to fulfil – never to desist in our efforts until we had subverted the authority of England over our country and asserted her independence. Another day we had the tent of the first regiment pitched in the Deer Park, and a company of thirty of us, including the family of the Simms, Neilsons, McCrackens, and my own, dined and spent the day together deliciously.

THEOBALD WOLFE TONE, *Diary*, 1795

A FRIEND OF MINE IN THE WEST ONCE SIGHED, after a fortnight among the primitive beatitudes, for a cigar and a cathedral. Belfast makes me sigh for a touch of lyricism and a romantic folly. When I had been there three days I bethought me of Mac Art's Castle up on Cave Hill where Wolfe Tone swore his oath of loyalty to Ireland and enmity to England, and for comfort I went out there on the tram. I climbed through a pleasure-garden with a zoo attached, called Bellevue, and so by a long winding path to the summit. It was not a good day for the view, but the Lough was wide and brave, and the sea lost itself in the mist, and far, far below was the smoke of the city to the south and south-east. I was a little disappointed at first. My idea of Wolfe Tone does not fit in with his idea that the best place to take an oath is on top of a mountain. But then I remembered the date, the Gothic eighteenth century, and I was touched by the youthful romanticism of the man – so quickly to be snuffed out by his innate realism, and mocked away by his readiness to see the ridiculous in everything. Still, would that a few Belfast men of his creed and class would do something as hotly, frivolously, high-heartedly, enthusiastic to-day.

SEAN O'FAOLAIN, *An Irish Journey*, 1940

SOMETIMES I AM IN RELIGIOUS AWE OF THE POWER OF NAMES. Milltown is a banal enough example, but it carries for me a recollection of the tiny mill-village adjacent to the cemetery, which you approached by a steeply-descending chalk-and-dirt loaney that took you off the broad thoroughfare of the Falls Road into a time-warped zone of half-occupied ancient staggered dwellings and a derelict mill that had once been powered by one of the many streams that emanated from Black Mountain, flowing beyond the mill into the misty fen of the Bog Meadows. There was a disused sandstone quarry nearby, carved out by artifice and weathering into a microcosmic Grand Canyon, which I used to explore in detail in my early teens, imagining brick-kilns, tunnels, chambered galleries and mausoleums within its compass. Then, St Gall's Gaelic Athletic Club maintained its HQ in the rear of the moribund Milltown Industrial School, a grim-looking building which might formerly have been the mill-owner's residence, and was taken over by the De la Salle Brothers who managed St Gall's Public Elementary School. I am a past-pupil of the school, and an erstwhile member of the club, which acquired some ground on the verge of the Bog Meadows, which was made, by dint of some voluntary and moonlighted labour, into a hurling and football field. In my day, it was rough, slanted and bumpy, with baldy patches on it; now, when I perceive it, driving on the M1 through the remnants of the Meadows, it has been ironed out into a broad green flat sward; and there, just beside it, is the tiny red pit of the quarry.

CIARAN CARSON, *The Star Factory*, 1997

JUBILEE NIGHT. A bonfire on Collin mountain. This is the mountain I used to see standing mistily blue through the apple blossom in our orchard, the orchard that we mistakenly cut down in order to utilise the space for a vegetable garden. Now beside the bonfire a scoutmaster in *pince-nez* calls for hearty British cheers . . .

Far-away bonfires twinkle on the surrounding hills: Scrabo, Castlereagh, the Sperrin mountains beyond Lough Neagh. Then the heat mist comes down, obscuring everything except the lights in the valley below. Belfast glows like a jewel in the darkness, the long glittering lines of street-lamps radiating from the centre, set here and there with the red and green blaze of advertisement sky-signs, like the filigree of a diadem, with the floodlit dome of the City Hall floating triumphantly above what appears from the mountain-side to be a sparkling spider's web. Beyond all this illumination the lough lies dark and unresponsive, while from somewhere on the hills beside the Parliament House at Stormont the long white finger of a searchlight stretches up to sweep the skies. But there is no sign of the bonfires on the Scottish coast; we strain our eyes in vain towards where in daylight the Mull of Galloway sometimes appears as a smudge on the skyline beyond the opening of the lough; a sea mist has come down and we are shut off here alone in our island in the Atlantic. Perhaps the mist is symbolical . . .

DENIS IRELAND, *From the Irish Shore*, 1936

No Pope,
No Priest,
No Surrender,
Hurrah!

One of my earliest recollections is of a lesson I received from a very aged but still indomitable clergyman, Dr Drew, who in his day was the leader of the North of Ireland Orangemen. He was in my father's study when I was brought to him, a tiny boy with long yellow curls, in which my mother rejoiced, but of which I was bitterly ashamed, dressed as small boys were in those days in petticoats. Dr Drew took me on his knee and taught me to say over and over again: 'No Pope, no Priest, no surrender, Hurrah.' . . .

I was never an Orangeman and for a great part of my life have been in opposition to the political opinions held so firmly by my fellow Protestants of Northern Ireland, but the spirit of defiance and detestation of authority which inspired them has remained with me.

GEORGE A. BIRMINGHAM, *Pleasant Places*

I DID NOT LEARN THE PROTESTANT VERSION OF HISTORY FROM BOOKS, but by word of mouth passed on from generation to generation. The 'quality', who had education and leisure, knew the details and the dates, but ordinary folk like ourselves carried the facts – or alleged facts – of history in our very bones and in our hearts. We were the people who had never surrendered and would never surrender. As each Twelfth of July came round, Protestant fervour would rise again and be reaffirmed.

In Sandy Row and the Shankill and the Newtownards Road, street would vie with street in putting up decorative arches tricked out with the symbols we knew and loved: the open Bible, William crossing the Boyne on his white horse, a black servant kneeling at the feet of his sovereign lady, Queen Victoria. Even the name Victoria – Victory – had a triumphalist tone. Crude but emotive paintings of scenes from history would appear on gables in working-class streets. So would slogans such as 'No Surrender', 'Remember 1690' and 'Ulster is not for sale'.

ROBERT GREACEN, The Sash My Father Wore, 1997

THE MUSICIANS' UNION

While over the lintels on Lenaderg Terrace
The Red Hand ruffles in the tea-time breeze,
Off carpets, chairs and Chesterfield suites,
The idle are stirring from *Scene Around Six*:
For thunder is rumbling round 'Coole cul-de-sacs
And along the side entries of Executive houses;
It's shaking new windows in puttyless frames;
And startling infants, sticky with sweeties,
In their pavement prams – with two big drums
And a fleet of flutes, here comes the band.

In scruffy school uniform or funeral gear
(Fashionable fatigues for the marching season)
And Oxford brogues or black Doc Martens,
The band hits the street in a steady rhythm.
On hands and on arms, they're tattooed to a man,
With slogans and symbols for today and tomorrow
From the tattoo-template of their forefathers' skin:
There's a covenant signed with both God and Ulster;
UDA, UVF, No Surrender – and Mother,
And crimson hearts punctured by arrows.

With the bold Prince of Orange soon on the horizon,
The street is the scene for the evening drill,
But tonight the band's out on official parade.
It's canvassing time in the local election,
When bigots and brethren court doorstep opinion;
It's a chance for a band to come into its own,
So long as it carries a tuneful selection

For the voters' riposte to the Pope and the bomb –
Partisan ditties that in booths they will whistle,
Where X marks the spot and completes the charade.

ADRIAN RICE, *Impediments*, 1997

IN MY YOUNG DAYS the Orange Institution was generally regarded in Ulster as an unmitigated nuisance – a perpetual menace to the peace and comfort of people who only wanted to be let alone. The Fenian troubles were making the South and West of Ireland unfit for respectable people to live in; but they did not oppress us in Ulster; Fenianism and flax do not thrive in the same soil. But the summer evenings in certain districts of Down and Antrim were made hideous with the thumping of big drums and the cackling of the ear-piercing fifes in the hands of the Orangemen, and that constituted a distinct nuisance.

Then in the month of July there were Orange celebrations in several parts of the Province, and these were regarded as the crescendo of nuisance; for the Orange anniversaries were not at that time recognised as universal holidays, and the absence for some days of fifty or sixty men from their work in the shipbuilding yards was a serious thing to their employers. In those days the celebration of one of the anniversaries meant, if not quite an orgy of drinking, at any rate an intake of much more drink than was consistent with the peace and comfort of the neighbours. In Irish Police Court parlance, those Orangemen who were not drunk had 'drink taken', the result being that those who had not heads broken had heads aching.

The Orange Institution was not taken very seriously by any of the population except the Orangemen, and they took it very seriously. Peace is the greatest enemy to patriotism, and Orangeism (in the opinion of Orangemen) is only another word for patriotism, so that it is not surprising that in those good years there was a disposition to treat the 'loyal Order' pretty much as one treats a noisy child – a shake of the head – a compassionate shrug – a suggestion that the members knew no better, and that we must only put up with them.

But with the menace of Home Rule, which was regarded in Ulster as equivalent to Rome Rule as well as to Home Ruin, people awoke to the fact that the Orange Institution would bear to be accepted as a force instead of a farce, since it had its feet resting on the very foundations of the Colony in Ulster – since the note that had come from every Orange fife at every celebration sounded the key to which Protestant Ulster was to be attuned, if it meant to hold its own against its enemies; and so for the past twenty-five years I fancy that the Orange Institution has been more highly respected than it was since the first glow of its inauguration was upon it.

F. FRANKFORT MOORE, *The Truth About Ulster*, 1914

SOME EIGHT HUNDRED VOLUNTEERS paraded in St George's Market where Colonel Chichester proposed we join forces with the UVF, threatening to resign on the spot if the majority refused. The vote was practically unanimous and the Young Citizens ceased to be an independent force.

A Special Service brigade had been organised from amongst the rank and file of the UVF members and the Young Citizens were attached to this body because of their standard of training. The Special Service brigade were to be ready for hazardous work if the occasion should arise. By now, most of the UVF were uniformed in khaki, with slouch hats and cavalry bandoliers slung across their shoulders.

Carson inspected the brigade at the Balmoral Show grounds and promised we should be armed and equipped in a few weeks. I noticed my two brothers in the ranks of the South Belfast regiment as the Young Citizens swung through the gates of the show grounds.

The men themselves were settled in regard to the outcome of the whole affair that only force of arms could determine the issue. The politicians and businessmen weren't just as enthusiastic towards this eventuality as the UVF. The conception of the business was that the Liberal government would drop the Home Rule Bill rather than face a civil war.

But the rank and file trusted Carson. None of us wished to clash with the military or police, yet the spirit of the Volunteers was such that even if a collision with the military was considered inevitable, there was no way out for the service brigade.

Some time later, the Young Citizens had an emergency order delivered at all their homes to parade at Ormiston House, the residence of Colonel Chichester. In pitch dark, we paraded on the lawn facing the house to listen to the Colonel instructing us what to do in the event of a certain plan being put into operation. We dismissed and returned to our various homes knowing we were on the brink of a crisis.

Meanwhile, out at sea, Major Crawford was steaming a cargo of guns and ammunition up and down the coast, waiting his opportunity to run into Donaghadee. In Ulster, the high-ups were wrangling amongst themselves as to the likelihood of a government coup and the consequences to them of such a catastrophe. The rank and file of the UVF were eagerly watching from the shores of Belfast Lough for the signal that was to herald the arrival of the guns.

In Belfast and the surrounding towns, we were standing by, ready and poised for action.

THOMAS CARNDUFF (1954), *Life and Writings*, 1994

SETTLERS

They cross from Glasgow to a black city
Of gantries, mills and steeples. They begin to belong.
He manages the Iceworks, is an elder of the Kirk;
She becomes, briefly, a cook in Carson's Army.
Some mornings, walking through the company gate,

He touches the bonnet of a brown lorry.
It is warm. The men watch and say nothing.
'Queer, how it runs off in the night,'
He says to McCullough, then climbs to his office.
He stores a warm knowledge on his palm.

Nightlandings on the Antrim coast, the movement of guns
Now snug in their oiled paper below the floors
Of sundry kirks and tabernacles in that county.

TOM PAULIN, *A State of Justice*, 1977

THERE ARE CERTAIN MAIN THREADS that run through the texture of life in Belfast. Protestant Puritanism is one of them. The Puritan is hard to define. There are adverse definitions and favourable ones, and both might find scope for application in Belfast. At the best, the Puritan is one who shapes his means to his end and pursues a straight, honest and simple path towards his objective. There is much Puritanism of that kind in Belfast. And, in looking for the best in the Ulster Puritan tradition, we have to remember that Belfast Puritanism has long been a very freethinking Puritanism. It has long had an independent and speculative tradition running through it. It has not been a Puritanism of conformity. In Ulster Calvinism, for instance, there has been a tradition, not wide but strong, of a trend towards a freethinking Unitarianism which caused opponents, outraged by its sceptical though philanthropic atmosphere, to declare that it was not even Christian. In Ulster theological history, this freethinking Puritanism has been a powerful element, but it is of significance, not merely for itself, but for the temperamental attitude from which it has sprung. For, while the serious theologians of Ulster have often found temperamentally congenial an attitude which was 'advanced' and highly 'unorthodox', the ordinary man in the street in Belfast has similarly tended to adopt quite unusual and unorthodox lines of behaviour without for a moment imagining that they are unusual in the least. Indeed, Ulster Puritanism has sometimes shown a tendency to end up, with a disconcerting lack of self-consciousness, in an attitude that is calmly pagan.

HUGH SHEARMAN, *Ulster*, 1949

IN REGARD TO THE DIFFICULTIES AND DANGERS that threatened Protestant-ism, he said – 'But if we must constitutionally strive for our civil and religious liberties, 'tis not five years will tire either our patience or our exertions, nor ten times five, nor ten times ten. And if within that period we be all gathered to our fathers, by the blessing of God we shall leave those behind us who know the worth of British liberty – who feel that if it be worth the having it is also worth the holding – an inheritance of which the threatener is unable to deprive us, and we will not, in five years of hopeless endurance, resign; but which we will maintain with the indomitable spirit of our fathers in the perennial fee-simple that lies in 'No Surrender'. We have sound Protestant principles, we have true Protestant hearts; above all, we have humble and secure dependence upon the mighty God of Protestant-ism; and whatever threats, whether of legal prosecutions or brutal force, may be hoarsely thundered from the high walls of Derrynane, or sweetly squeaked from the shrill and discordant sparrow-pipe that chirrups in the groves of Tipperary – still will the spirit of Irish Protestantism remain with heart unaffrighted, with arm untired, with faith unsubdued, with loyalty unchanged, with ranks unshaken, adopting as its motto of patient endurance of injuries, and ardent hope of redress, the words of Luther when arraigned before the Diet of Worms:– "Here I take my stand; I can do nothing else, and God be my help." From Protestantism alone does our civil constitution derive its power of perpetual renovation. It flourishes alike in the sunshine and in the shade; it blooms in the brightness of the parterre, and it ripens in the gloom of the dungeon; it repays the hand that protects it by its loveliness and its fruitfulness; and, like a medical plant of our gardens, it defies the foot that tramples it, and grows the more vigorously the more it is depressed . . .'

J.L. PORTER, *Life and Times of Dr Henry Cooke*, 1871

CARSON'S CAT

Sir Edward Carson has a cat,
It sits upon the fender
And every time a mouse it gets,
It shouts out 'No Surrender!'

He left it by the fireside,
Whene'er he went away
On his return he always found
It singing 'Dolly's Brae'.

The traitors grew indignant,
At hearing such a noise

But Carson made the cat sit up,
And sing the 'Protestant Boys'.

The traitors then decided
To hang it with a rope
But every time they tried the rope,
It yelled 'Hell roast the Pope!'

The people came from far and near,
To hear the pussy sing
Good old 'Britannia Rules the Waves',
And may 'God Save the King!'

A few said 'What a pity,
The cat is such a fool',
But Carson's Cat yelled out the more,
'WE WILL NOT HAVE HOME RULE!'

ANONYMOUS

THE GREATEST PHYSICAL TRIAL in connection with Mission work arose from the filthy habits of the people and the vermin with which they were infested. Robert found it necessary to wear a special suit when visiting, which he took off as soon as he got home. Fleas were always terrible to Robert, he was extremely susceptible to them and they worried him night and day.

Not only the dirt was trying, but the intermittent riots diversified his life. One day in Sandy Row he heard a volley of musketry, on hastening to the spot, he saw a pool of blood, where a man had been shot dead a few moments before, and the marks of many bullets on the neighbouring house. Passing through Castle Place on another occasion, he noticed the shopkeepers hurrying to put up their shutters; a minute or two afterwards a dense mob came rushing down Castle Street, waving their bludgeons above their heads and stones rising in the air above them. They came on with a roar, sweeping everything before them, and naturally created great alarm. Again a large part of North Street was covered with feathers from the feather beds, taken from the houses that had been sacked. It was at this time that the opposing parties would chalk on walls 'No Pope' and 'No Cooke'. Even after they were settled in Newtownbreda, there were terrible riots in Belfast and at night they would be kept awake with the sound of musket shots. Most of the firing was not aimed at any object, people who lived in a disturbed district spent the night in dread of an attack and kept up firing to let their opponents know that they were on the alert and prepared to meet them.

MARGARET A.K. GARNER, *Robert Workman of Newtownbreda, 1835–1921*, 1969

I AM SORRY WE DID NOT GO TO CHURCH next morning, for the pulpits of Belfast were thundering against Home Rule, as we saw by the Monday papers. Instead, we walked down to the river, for a look at the harbour and custom house, and then about the streets to the city hall, with its dome and corner towers oddly reminiscent of St Paul's Cathedral; and then we took a tram to the Botanical Gardens. The tram ran along a tree-embowered street, lined on either side with villas set in the midst of grounds so beautiful that any of them might have been the gardens; but when we reached the end of the line, we found we had come too far. The conductor was greatly chagrined that he had forgot to tell us where to get off, and sternly refused to accept any fare for the return trip.

The gardens, which we finally reached, are very attractively laid out, but far more interesting than the flowers and the shrubs was the crowd which was coming home from church. There seems to be a church on every square in Belfast, and I judge they were all full that day – as they no doubt are every Sunday, for church-going is still fashionable in the British Isles; and the crowd which poured along the walks of the gardens was as well-dressed and handsome as could be seen anywhere. It was a crowd made up of people evidently and consciously well-to-do, and one distinctive characteristic was a certain severity of aspect, a certain prevalence of that black-coated, side-whiskered, stern-lipped type which was much more common in America thirty years ago than it is now. Our type has changed – has softened and grown more urbane; but I should judge that the cold steel of Calvinism is as sharp and merciless as ever in Belfast.

The men walked slowly along in twos and threes, talking over the sermons they had just listened to; and the sermons, judging from the newspapers, were all cast in the same mould; and that mould gives so clearly the Orange attitude toward Home Rule, that I shall try to outline it here, quoting literally from the newspaper accounts.

Home Rule, then, according to the Belfast preachers, is a Papal-inspired movement, whose object is 'to thrust out of their birthright over one million enterprising, industrious, and peaceable citizens, whose only crime was their loyalty to Crown and Constitution, and to put them under that Papal yoke from which their sires had purchased their liberty. Their beloved island home had never been more prosperous. They were grateful and they were satisfied, but their Roman Catholic fellow countrymen seemed to have no sense of satisfaction or gratitude. The Irish Nationalists had entered into a movement to sacrifice Protestantism upon the altar of Home Rule, but Orangemen and Protestants had entered into a covenant the object of which was the maintenance of their rightful heritage of British citizenship, of their commercial and industrial progress, and of their freedom. In the same spirit of patriotic Protestantism as was displayed at the siege of Derry, they would go forth to combat the onslaughts of Rome, and they would show that the same spirit lived in them as in their illustrious sires.' Some of the services concluded with singing a new version of the National Anthem:

> Ulster will never yield;
> God is our strength and shield,
> On Him we lean.
> Free, loyal, true and brave,
> Our liberties we'll save.
> Home Rule we'll never have.
> God save the King.

That last line is so perfunctory that it provokes a smile.

BURTON E. STEVENSON, *The Charm of Ireland*, 1915

A QUESTION OF COVENANTS
28 September 1913

> The *Patriotic* turns to face
> an invisible sea. From Castle Place
> thousands swarm through side-streets
> and along the unprotected quays just
> to glimpse Carson, gaunt as usual,
> who watches the surge of people
> call, '*Don't leave us. You mustn't leave us*',
> and in the searchlight's beam,
> his figure arched across the upper deck,
> he shouts he will come back
> and, if necessary, fight this time.
>
> It is what they came to hear
> in the dark September night.
> As the *Patriotic* sails out
> Union colours burst in rockets
> and bonfires scar the hills
> he departs from, a stranger to both sides
> of the lough's widening mouth
> and the crowd's distant singing
> 'Auld Lang Syne' and 'God Save the King'.

GERALD DAWE, *The Lundys Letter*, 1985

ONE IS OFTEN TOLD that Paisleyism is as old as Protestant Ulster, or as Scottish Calvinism. But nowadays its effects are more harmful than ever before. In its Free Presbyterian manifestation, the emphasis is as much on anti-ecumenism as on anti-popery; and Paisley's determination to maintain Northern Ireland's traditional level of bigotry and discrimination has so far proved the strongest single force on the Northern political scene. Throughout his career he has fostered an atmosphere in which authority is belittled and mob-law becomes possible. The psychological effects of his successful campaign in 1967, to block the then Anglican Bishop of Ripon's visit to Belfast, have proved long-lasting. Letting Paisley have his way during the sixties was one of Stormont's worst mistakes. If Yorkshire were threatened by cholera the government would not hesitate to enforce laws against the spread of infection, even if the liberty of the individual had in some cases to be curtailed. Why are similar precautions not taken against infectious emotional diseases?

It is generally believed in Belfast that Paisley's zenith has passed. The observations I took in the Martyrs' Memorial over the next year showed a steady decline in attendance and one shrewd Belfast shopkeeper summed it up thus: 'His own people are turning against him because violence is spreading in all the Protestant areas. It was OK before – sectarian killing was confined to the slums and only poor nameless Taigs were being thrown in the Lagan. But now that the Provos are retaliating, and the violence is extending to the businesses and homes and lives of middle-class Protestants, the picture is changing.' However, there remains a vast reservoir of hate in the Orange ghettos – and can that terrible accumulation somehow be rendered harmless or will it be like those indestructable deposits of nuclear waste that threaten future generations? I put this question to an elderly Protestant woman who runs a little café and in her spare time does voluntary work for the Alliance Party. 'Cheer up, love,' she said, 'and listen to this one! Mrs Paisley was getting into bed when she stubbed her toe hard and cried out "Oh God!" So Paisley says, "It's all right, dear, you don't have to call me that when we're alone."'

It is impossible to be gloomy for long in Belfast. I was feeling rather depressed one afternoon when I turned a corner and saw on a gable-end the familiar NO POPE HERE. And underneath, in different coloured paint, LUCKY OLD POPE!

DERVLA MURPHY, A Place Apart, 1978

B ELFAST JOKE: A man goes into a bar on the Shankill Road, leading a crocodile on a chain. 'Hey, barman! Do ye serve Roman Catholics?' 'Yeah, OK.' 'Good, will ye please serve one to my crocodile?' Har-har.

CAL McCRYSTAL, Reflections on a Quiet Rebel, 1997

JUNE 14 [1689], BEING SATURDAY, King William landed at Carrickfergus about four o'clock in the afternoon. The account of his entry into Belfast is thus related by an eye witness – 'Notice being given to the general (who had prepared Sir William Franklin's house at Belfast for his Majesty's reception, and was there attending his landing) his Grace went in his coach with all speed, to wait upon the King. Major General Kirk, and several officers that were there, expecting the King's landing, attended the Duke; his Majesty was met by them near the Whitehouse, and received them all very kindly, coming in the Duke's coach to Belfast; he was met also without the town by a great concourse of people, who at first could do nothing but stare, never having seen a king before in that part of the world; but after a while, some of them beginning to *huzza*, the rest all took to it and followed the coach through several regiments of foot that were drawn up in town towards his Majesty's lodgings, and happy were they that they could get but a sight of him.'

Historical Collections Relative to the Town of Belfast, 1817

JOHN'S GRANDFATHER had bequeathed to his son a tiny lozenge of silk which had once been part of a French flag taken at the siege of Derry. He had seen rebels hanged from lamp-posts in the streets of Bigotsborough. The tradition of loyalty was alive in the Gordon family. They had drunk fear and hatred of the Roman Catholic religion with their mother's milk. To them the Pope was a symbol of cruelty and treachery, oppression and wrong.

JAMES DOUGLAS, *The Unpardonable Sin*, 1907

THE ORANGEMAN

A ginger-faced man
With a walrus moustache
His eyes, like his soul,
Of the colour of ash

With the fire gone out of it:
Breaking to flame
Of a sulphurous glare
At the touch of the name

William. For Billy
Of Orange, he knows,
Saved him and his seed

From the devil's own woes!
His faith, 'Sixteen-Ninety;
His love, none; his hope,
That hell may one day
Get the soul of the Pope.

Damnation writ large
On the walls of his home –
Red brick in a back street;
While the Ogre of Rome

Lives in beauty, with Venus
And Psyche in white,
And the Trojan Laocoön
For his spirit's delight.

Not that the aesthete
In him is dumb:
There's the flap of his banner,
The tap of his drum.

Straussian discords,
For peace, and – revolt?
The crash of the paver,
The crack of the bolt.

A monster! Not quite,
As you guess from my song;
But clay marred in the mixing –
God's image gone wrong.

JOSEPH CAMPBELL (1913), The Poems of Joseph Campbell, 1963

D R KANE WAS ... A COMPLEX PERSONALITY. Standing well over six feet, straight as a lance, he resembled, when arrayed in his trappings as Grand Master he headed his legions on the Twelfth of July, rather a mediaeval bishop going forth to war than a meek Protestant pastor. No man raged more loudly against priestly domination; no man practised it more thoroughly at the expense of his parishioners. It was a common sight to see him driving with his blackthorn into church a mob of loafers whom he had culled from publichouse corners; and while his face would flush past red into purple as he denounced the iniquities of Catholic priests who dragged politics into religion, his own sermons were better fitted for an Orange platform than for a Christian pulpit. To do him justice, he did not fly at small game; and I remember him bearding to his face a Tory Lord Lieutenant who had ventured to remonstrate with Belfast Orangemen. Dr Kane had his own quarrels with his official leaders, and in his later years his line of development was a sore trial to his associates. He joined the Gaelic League at a time when many Nationalists looked askance at the movement. 'My Orangeism,' he said, 'does not make me less proud to be an O'Cahan.' I have heard him boast that his ancestors were with the rebels in '98, and that had he lived then he was not at all certain on which side he would have fought. Unlike the new school of Orangemen, Dr Kane had no great opinion of the inherent wisdom and beneficence of the English rulers of Ireland. His part in the campaign against over-taxation in the early nineties brought him into contact with strange allies, and had he been a smaller man he would have been denounced for 'trafficking with traitors'. Not that this would have troubled him overmuch. He could always be relied on to give as good as he got, and were he alive to-day I am certain he would have fought tooth and nail as an Irishman against Sir Edward Carson's scheme for making the north-eastern counties English shireland.

JAMES WINDER GOOD, Ulster and Ireland, 1919

I DO NOT KNOW how many Orange societies there are at Belfast, but we saw at least a dozen march past that night, each of them headed by a band or drum-corps, and each with a bright new Orange banner flaunting proudly in the breeze. Each banner bore a painted representation of some Orange victory; King Billy on his white horse fording the Boyne being a favourite subject; and the banners were very large and fringed with gold lace and most expensive-looking; and before them and beside them and behind them trailed a mob of shrieking girls and women and ragamuffin boys, locked arm and arm half across the street, breaking into a clumsy dance now and then, or shouting the lines of some Orange ditty. There were many men in line, marching along more or less soberly; but these bacchantes out-numbered them two to one. They blocked the street from side to side, stopped traffic, and conducted themselves as though they had suddenly gone mad.

Presently all the societies, which had been collecting at some rendezvous, marched back together, with the mob augmented a hundred-fold, so that, looking down from our window, we could see nothing but a mass of heads filling the street from side to side – thousands and thousands of women and girls and boys, all vociferous with a frenzied intoxication – and in the midst of them the thin stream of Orangemen trudging along behind their banners.

I went down into the street to view this demonstration more closely, for it was evident that here at last was the spirit of Ulster unveiled for all to see; but at close quarters much of its impressiveness vanished, for the mob was composed largely of boys and girls out for a good time, and rejoicing in the unaccustomed privilege of yelling and hooting to their hearts' content. A few policemen would have been quite capable of dealing with that portion of it. But the men marching grimly along behind their banners were of different stuff; they were ready, apparently, for any emergency, ready for a holy war; and I wondered if their leaders, who had sown the wind so blithely as part of the game of politics, were quite prepared to reap the whirlwind which might follow.

A man with whom I fell into talk said there would be a procession like this every evening until the twelfth; but I should think the drummers would be exhausted long before that. I have described the contortions of the Dublin drummers, but they are nowhere as compared with the drummers of Belfast. And, though about a fourth of Belfast's population is Catholic, you would never have suspected it that night, for there was no disorder of any kind, except the wild disorder of the Orangemen and their adherents. I suspect that, in Belfast, wise Catholics spend the early evenings of July at home.

BURTON E. STEVENSON, *The Charm of Ireland*, 1915

'I HAVE BEEN A CONSISTENT SUPPORTER OF THE UNION,' said Babberly, 'for twenty years. In season and out of season I have upheld the cause we have at heart on English platforms and in the House of Commons. I know better than you do, gentlemen, what the temper of the English people is. I know that we shall sacrifice their friendship and alienate their sympathy if we resort to the argument of lawlessness and violence.'

'It's the only argument they ever listen to,' said McNeice. 'Look at the Nationalists. What arguments did they use?'

'Gentlemen,' said Babberly, 'are you going to ask Ulstermen to fire on the King's troops?'

'I reckon,' said Conroy, 'that we mean to use our guns now we've got them.'

Babberly made a curious gesture with his hands. He flung them out from him with the palms upwards and then sat down. McNeice rose next.

'For the last two years,' he said, 'we've been boasting that we meant to resist Home Rule with force if necessary. That's so, isn't it?'

Malcolmson growled an assent.

'English politicians and Irish rebels said we were bluffing. Our own people – the men outside there in the street – thought we were in earnest. The English went on with their Bill. Our people drilled and got rifles. Which of the two was right about us? Were we bluffing or were we in earnest? We've got to answer that question to-morrow, and we'll never get another chance. If we don't fight now, we'll never fight, for there won't be a man left in Ulster that will believe in us again. I don't know that there's any more to be said. I propose that Lord Moyne puts the question to the meeting and takes a vote.'

Then Cahoon rose to his feet.

'Before you do that, my lord,' he said, 'I'd like to say a word. I'm a business man. I've as much at stake as any one in this room. My fortune, gentlemen, is in bricks and mortar, in machinery and plant not ten miles from this city. I've thought this matter out, and I came to a conclusion years ago. Home Rule won't do for Belfast, and Belfast isn't going to have it. If I saw any way of stopping it but the one I'd take it. There are thousands, yes, gentlemen, thousands of men, women, and children depending on my business for their living. Home Rule means ruining it and starving them. I don't like fighting, but, by God, I'll fight before I submit to Home Rule.'

GEORGE A. BIRMINGHAM, *The Red Hand of Ulster*, 1912

THE CUSTOM HOUSE STEPS in Belfast is a famous place for meetings. Militant Catholics call it an infamous place. Orange apostles of a certain type regard it as sacred ground. The Salvation Army generals look upon it as of primary strategic value. It is the Sunday forum of the city. It is also the storm centre of ranting aggressiveness. There is a fine open space in front of the Custom House. Steps lead from this space or square up to the flagged esplanade, which is a few feet over the level of the pavement. Around the esplanade, separating it from the square, is a balustrade. The orators hold forth from the steps, or they lean over the balustrade.

It is an ideal place for open air meetings. The steps and balustraded esplanade constitute a splendid platform. The space in front affords standing room for thousands of people. The speakers are in full view of their audience, and it is their own fault if they are not heard by a good many hundreds of the crowds who assemble to listen to them.

The Pope is dethroned, scalped, roasted and consigned to eternal perdition every Sunday afternoon during busy times from this platform. Popery with its works and pomps is denounced, menaced, and torn to pieces. Orange demagogues expatiate on the creed and politics of Papists and call forth thunders of applause. All things national and Catholic are thickly coated with mud, and the green flag is flittered into shreds.

Sometimes the oratory is so drastic that the audience becomes infuriated and goes up town on the war trail looking for battle. Perhaps they fall in with a Catholic procession or manifestation, and then there is sure to be trouble. At other times a few hundred or a few thousand disciples of the Custom House prophets, well loaded with whiskey and other fire water, and headed by a brass band, will march up town with colours flying.

When they come to a Catholic church they will sing Orange chorus songs and beat the big drum at a pressure of several tons to the square inch. When they burst a drum they get another one. When one drummer drums himself into a fit they get a new man. No procession starts without a good set of drummers. An energetic Orange drummer in Belfast is like the big hundred ton guns – he can only be used a limited number of times. He batters his elbows to pieces and breaks his wind. He lives at high pressure for a season and then succumbs. During his periods of activity, to use a volcanic expression, he knocks the ends out of several drums. After an exciting day it is necessary to take precautions in regard to him, because he is likely to drum in his sleep. I heard of a drummer of Belfast who drummed so terrifically in his dreams that he killed his wife and broke nearly everything in the room that could be broken by a twelve inch shell. If I were a Belfast undertaker I do not think I would be safe in coffining one of those dead drummers without first putting him in handcuffs.

WILLIAM BULFIN, *Rambles in Eirinn*, 1907

I HAVE READ, with some amusement (it is like sitting in heaven, twangling a harp and reading one's own obituary), an academic thesis on the rise and fall of the Northern Ireland Labour Party that describes me as one of the Party's 'political ideologues'. There is truth in this; but it did not absolve me from the more down-to-earth obligations of membership. I learned, not without difficulty, to speak in public and in the open air; though I was always, I think, too much of a highbrow to appeal much to my audience. I spoke on the Custom House Steps, traditional rendezvous of the left wing in Belfast. On May Day I spoke on the blitzed ground in High Street (long since built over) from the traditional platform, Billy Maginness's cart: Billy was a street trader of very left-wing views who boasted that his horse and cart had provided a platform for every leading politician of the left since the earliest days of the Spanish Civil War. In these attempts at speechifying, the good advice of David Bleakley was invaluable to me. And they were not wholly unsuccessful: on those early May Days, a part of our audience always comprised special branch policemen, sent along by Lord Brookeborough's government to report whether we were, as was expected by the Unionist establishment, preaching both republicanism and treason; I well remember the day when one of these plain-clothes policemen, whose faces we had got to know well, came over to me at the end of the meeting and confided that he and 'all the boys at the barracks' had been convinced, and were on our side.

But I was more at home in a committee-room than on the back of a cart or a lorry.

C.E.B. BRETT, *Long Shadows Cast Before*, 1978

A S I CONTINUED MY WALK HOMEWARD, first through the broad thoroughfares of the city and then through the broad highway of the southern suburbs, I met scores of the same class of the population who had left their houses in the side streets, and especially in the ultra-Protestant Sandy Row, the scene of many a fierce encounter between the two religious factions, to put to me in their own idiom and staccato pronunciation the burning question:

'Is them 'uns bate?'

And when I assured them that the unspeakable Nationalists had been beaten by a good majority, once more cheers were raised. I was slapped familiarly on the back by half-dressed 'Islandmen' (the shipwrights) with shouts of 'Bully wee fella!' as though the defeat of the measure was due to my personal exertions; and I remember how the blinds of the bedrooms of many of the best houses on the road were pulled to one side, while the sunshine of the early morning disclosed white figures beyond thrusting a head forward to see what was happening. Some way further on, where the villas of the suburb began, I was surprised to hear myself hailed by name by someone at a window beyond the shrubbery of a carriage-drive. I found myself responding to the director of one of the chief banks. He told me he had been unable to sleep during the night, and he had risen and sat at his open window to await my passing with news. At two other houses of the same type I found gentlemen awaiting my arrival, and at one of these it was with difficulty that I managed to get away without drinking the health of the majority who had caused the Bill to be thrown out – that was the penalty which the wealthy damask merchant suggested I should pay for having lifted a great weight from his mind. A tumbler of whiskey at 4.30 on a lovely summer morning! Only the hospitable impulses of a Belfast man would have been equal to such a suggestion.

The next night, however, the streets were full of an excited people. The Roman Catholic clergy had issued strict commands to their flocks to remain within their houses, or within the boundaries of their own localities, so that they might not be tempted to respond to the insults which they would be certain to receive from 'the other side'. This advice had been accepted, though not without grumbling; but it was undoubtedly the best that could have been offered to the people. The high spirits of 'the other side' might have been displayed through a medium familiar to both. As it was, the music of the Unionist bands of Sandy Row and the Shankill Road began playing as early as six o'clock, and there were processions and noise and excitement in the principal thoroughfares until long past midnight. In several directions bonfires had been lighted within half-an-hour after sunset, and some were still burning when I passed them at three o'clock in the morning, and boys were watching the expiring embers.

It is unnecessary to say that the Police Commissioner and his officers were extremely uneasy during these days. One of them, who afterwards rose to the highest command in the Force, told me that, in his opinion, if that Home Rule Bill had passed, all the Constabulary in the city would not have been able to prevent such a wrecking of the Roman Catholic quarters as would have changed the whole aspect of the municipality – 'wrecking and massacre', were his words; and before another fortnight had passed I agreed with him, for by that time fifteen hundred armed men were unable to drag the city out of the hands of the rioters, and for seven weeks there were daily fights, and these not confined, as previous outbreaks had been, to the usual area of disturbance between the Protestant Shankill and the Roman Catholic Falls, but on the Crumlin Road and the Antrim Road, in the very centre of the town, and through the mile length of York Street, excited mobs had passed, breaking windows and looting shops. They were charged by troops of Lancers, and by bayonets of Highlanders, and by fixed swords of the Constabulary; the hospitals were crowded with wounded men, women, and children, and there was not a newspaper in the city that had not on its staff a reporter who was limping in his walk, or with an arm in a sling, or a head bound up.

F. FRANKFORT MOORE, *The Truth About Ulster*, 1914

'WHAT ARE YOU?' As far as I remember, these were the first words ever spoken to me by an Ulsterman. Well, an Ulster child, actually. We would both have been about seven years old and it was my first day at school in the province. I'd previously attended a preparatory school in Cambridge and another in Dunfermline, but neither had prepared me for the question so abruptly shoved in my face that morning. In form it seemed grandiosely philosophical, a rhetorical gesture in the 'What is the stars, Joxer?' tradition. But the tone of voice – down-to-earth, menacing – belied that idea. I wasn't sure what the question meant, but I was left in no doubt that the wrong answer would have unpleasant consequences.

'I'm English,' I admitted grudgingly. My Scottish schoolmates had made the most of having a real live hostage to re-fight history with. You could see them thinking: 'This time, do we get to win?' Hell yes, and next time, and the time after that. I was just wondering how I could contrive to be ill for the rest of the year when the boy replied: 'Oh fair enough. You're one of us then.' His accent was so thick and gritty it was some time before I understood the words. The sense continued to elude me. One of them? Presumably he was being cruelly sarcastic.

About the same time, my mother was stopped in the street by a neighbour and asked: 'Is your husband a black man?' Not only were blacks as rare in Ulster as Albanians, but the neighbour in question was well-acquainted with my father's appearance. 'No, he's English, actually,' my mother replied, to which the neighbour returned: 'Is he walking the day?' 'No,' was the faint reply, 'he's gone by train.' They parted amicably, each thinking the other was crazy.

My mother's neighbour was asking whether my father was a Black Man – that is, a member of a Protestant Masonic Lodge (cf. Orangeman) whose ostensible purpose is to process up and down in fancy dress ('walking') accompanied by flute bands and seventeenth-century war drums, but which really exists to maintain the Protestant stranglehold on all financial and professional services within the province and to ensure that however high the rate of unemployment in their community, it's twice as bad for the Catholics. In Ulster we 'English' (i.e. mainland Brits) are not just any old foreigners. We're 'one of us'.

MICHAEL DIBDIN, *London Review of Books*, April 1988

I WAS ENROLLED at the new elementary school in Templemore Avenue, the biggest building but for the City Hall I had yet seen. It smelled of fresh paint, wood shavings and disinfectant. Unfortunately for me, it was solidly Protestant – so there would be no way of escape from morning assembly. I consoled myself with the fact that Protestants prayed less than Catholics. O bustling, rainy city with swings and slides in the children's playground at Scotch Row (locked up, of course, on Sundays when all good children were at home studying the Bible or at Sunday School).

But have I, by any chance, suggested that delights were hard to come by? Time took care of that. I discovered the solidarity and the intrigues of the back streets, the politics of children's leisure time. By politics I mean the little groupings and alliances, the fallings-out and the fights, all based on personal attractions and clashes. Mother gave strict instructions that I could not absent myself without permission given or refused at our business headquarters, the Kenilworth, where we lived over the shop. I often had to ask the question: 'Have you the right time, mister?'

Crowds of boys appeared on all sides – new potential friends, new potential enemies. Helpful, cheerful, tidy little boys roamed the streets, as did others who were double-faced, malicious, dirty. Yet they were all of the Protestant tribe. It was considered wrong, even dangerous, to tangle with the Catholic nationalist tribe. We thought of 'us' and 'them' – we were the good guys, they were the bad guys. Every boy jack of these new boys I began to meet was crammed with city lore. How did you straighten out the metal top of a lemonade bottle? Simple – just place it on a tram-line and wait for a tram to pass. How did you see part of a football match? Wait outside until half-time and then walk in. What did the sign 'FP' mean? Father's prick, of course.

ROBERT GREACEN, *The Sash My Father Wore*, 1997

THERE IS A PASSAGE somewhere in *Madame Bovary* to the effect that townsmen of peasant origin tend to carry in their hearts some of the hardness of the hands of their ancestors. Some such theory as this has gone to the building up of what may be called a stage Ulsterman or, more specifically, a stage Belfastman. According to this mythical interpretation of the Belfastman, he is a 'dour' person; he is wholly occupied with obtaining money; his religion consists in objecting to the religion of other people; he is devoid of 'culture', and Belfast has only two bookshops. One can think of various quarters where this myth might have been cultivated or received, but, before trying to understand Belfast people, it is necessary to lay the myth aside.

HUGH SHEARMAN, *Ulster*, 1949

I WENT OVER QUEEN'S BRIDGE ONE DAY – not only because I had seen Sam Thompson's play the night before, *Over the Bridge*, but all the more because of that. What a good, straight play – simple, fine, finely acted – and about real issues of conscience, courage and responsibilities; a play so much more illustrative of Irish life, it seemed to me, than some hysterical works now emerging from Ireland's 'deep South', and sweeping amateur actors into misjudgment throughout the country.

Queen's Island, over the Bridge, is where in the past hundred years Harland and Wolff have built their famous ships. It is, or at least has until recently been, I believe, the most important shipyard in the world. It is therefore a field of drama always, industrial and personal; yielding regular work for about twenty thousand souls – or suddenly not yielding it, or threatening uncertainty, or hinting at sudden marvels – it is forever a grey, hard centre of anxiety, great anxiety and great hope, for the poor man, and a theatre of stress and competition for tycoons. Wars, markets, trade routes, imperial and national ups and downs – these make the tides of good and bad fortune for Belfast.

So it catches the eye and the imagination. It builds great ships; it also overhauls and reconditions them. The cold day I looked around there was a great aircraft carrier on the stocks for India, a Pacific and Orient in progress, some tankers for Russia, a Swedish liner being modernised – a fierce, unpausing orchestration of hard labour. Good news for Belfast, all that swinging of cranes and gantries; blasts, flames and shrieking whistles, an immeasurable great throb of industry – fine news while it lasted; but they were murmuring that this winter did not promise to be good. And understandably, slack times in such a monstrous hive are to be dreaded, as long experience has taught.

I remembered the *Titanic*, pride of Queen's Island, and how some old crone of a mythmaker had told us children after it sank, that it had 'To hell with the Pope' stamped on its every piece of steel. That was indeed silly talk to be making up in faraway, sleepy Limerick; but in Queen's Island itself the traditional bigotry of 'Prot' against 'Papish' is always an especial difficulty – as Sam Thompson's play witnesses. It takes Ireland, I suppose, to have men still in 1959 opposing each other to the points of tragedy and death on an issue of religious belief; perhaps it marks our country's unmanageable originality. But the author of *Over the Bridge*, who so rightly found truth and drama in this tenacious individualism of the working men he knew at home, may have been startled that his play failed outright in London. The religious issue was obsolete, the critics and the small, few audiences seemed to think. Maybe that is so, though one pauses on the word 'obsolete'; perhaps 'out of fashion' would be a safer phrase, lacking arrogance. In any case, it will be long before a difference of opinion on religion will be obsolete in Belfast, or anywhere in Ireland. So much the worse for Ireland, the enlightened may say. But surveying the world which tolerance and enlightenment have brought to pass, some of us beg leave for indecision.

KATE O'BRIEN, *My Ireland*, 1962

B ELFAST. The town that gave the world the *Titanic*. The ship would have been the highlight of our achievement. We did it arseways. Belfast holds the real secret of the sinking of the *Titanic*. It was the serial number on the ship; they say that if you held it up to a mirror it read: NO POPE HERE.

MARY COSTELLO, *Titanic Town*, 1992

A HEAD OF THEM and slightly to their right they can see Napoleon's Nose, a cliff face dropping away for several hundred feet. Set back a little from the edge is a concrete beacon which from this distance looks like a wart on the nose. When they reach it Roy stands leaning against it, panting. It is covered in graffiti, the most prominent of which is a red 'No Surrender'. His father stands beside him shaking his head.

'Can you imagine carrying a spray can the whole way up here just to do that?'

'Shows Ulster determination, I suppose.'

His father goes over to the edge. A crow flaps across the space beneath him.

'You're high up when you can look down on the birds.'

'Careful,' says Roy. 'Don't stand so near the edge. In your condition one fart would propel you over.' Roy stands at a safe distance and takes out his camera. He snaps the panorama, moving a little to the right each time. The blue Lough lies like a wedge between the Holywood hills at the far side and the grey mass of the city at his feet and to his right. Spires and factory chimneys poke up in equal numbers. Soccer pitches appear as green squares with staples for goalposts.

The old man shouts over the wind. 'You could read registration plates in Carnmoney on a day like that.'

'But who'd want to be in Carnmoney?'

'Good one, Roy.' He laughs and comes over to his son who is crouching, threading a new film into his camera. He clicks the back shut and takes three quick exposures of his feet, each time winding on with a flick of his thumb.

He looks up at his father and says, 'This was the place the United Irishmen took an oath to overthrow the English. They were all Prods as well.'

'History, Roy. It's not the way things are now.'

BERNARD MacLAVERTY, from 'Some Surrender',
The Great Profundo and Other Stories, 1987

IN BELFAST

The years' lessons are written on the walls –
No Surrender – Ulster Says No.
I see in the sky a Presbyterian rainbow,

orange and unforgiving, woven of fire.
To tear apart what oneself owns!
The nun strides through the city like a whore.

The present seethes about the Holy Book.
And drums tap on the coffins of the slain.
The tanks will ride tall through Genesis: masked men stalk.

O Rose of Sharon, modest and demure,
when among broken stones will you bloom once more
into an ordinarily guilty future,

among the waste of broken iron, doors.
And men rather than angels greet across fences
the scoured tired eyes of pity and remorse.

IAIN CRICHTON SMITH, The Village and Other Poems, 1989

First
Impressions

We arrived safely at Belfast. We passed along a bridge over an arm of the sea. It is said to be an English mile in length. It consists of about twenty arches. The town is beautifully situated, but it is not very pretty itself . . .

We took a second breakfast here. Two Miss Pattersons of Comber visited Mrs Boyd. They were both pretty girls. The eldest was clever and like an Actress, and took my idle fancy. All this place belongs to Lord Donegall. I believe no subject of the three kingdoms has so large a town in property. There is a good Mall to walk in, but there is some standing water in a ditch that is offensive and spoils the pleasure of a grove of noble old trees.

Between Belfast and Lisburn there is the finest country I ever saw . . .

JAMES BOSWELL, *Jaunt to Ireland*

O N THE WAY TO COLERAINE AND THE COAST I was in a train with about ten other people, two in each car – and some got out at Botanic Station, a mile from Central. I had never imagined Europe could look so threadbare – such empty trains, such blackened buildings, such recent ruins: *Dangerous Building – Keep Clear*. And bellicose religion, and dirt, and poverty, and narrow-mindedness, and sneaky defiance, trickery and murder, and little brick terraces, and drink shops, and empty stores, and barricades, and boarded windows, and starved dogs, and dirty-faced children – it looked like the past in an old picture. And a crucifix like a dagger in one brute's lapel, and an *Orange Lodge Widows' Fund* badge in another's. They said that Ulster people were reticent. It seemed to me they did nothing but advertise. *God Save the Pope* painted on one ruin, and on another, *God Save the Queen*. And at Lisburn a large sign by the tracks said *Welcome to Provoland*. Everyone advertised, even urban guerillas.

Fifteen minutes outside Belfast we were in open country . . .

PAUL THEROUX, The Kingdom by the Sea, 1983

BELFAST: APRIL 12, 1949: Impossible to fathom why I like this city but I do. Admittedly a cold, ugly sort of place even in this radiant northern April, its setting of windy mountains and dark shipyards blotched with fin-de-siècle mansions and fussy streets full of plate-glass and cake shops and trams, but there is something about it all, its fantastic practicability, its bleak, bowler-hatted refusal of the inevitable.

MICHEÁL MacLIAMMÓIR, Put Money in Thy Purse, 1952

ALMOST ALL THE LITTLE TOWNS through which we drove that evening were lit up with gas. It is wonderful what progress this important new invention has made in these islands. In Germany, a great city is very proud of being distinguished by gas-lights, in the British islands scarcely a town can be pointed out which is without them.

At length we arrived at the central point of all the gas-lights of northern Ireland, the central point also of the great linen manufacture, – at the thick cluster of houses and inhabitants which Irish flax has knotted together at Belfast. I thought at first that it must be some great festival, for wherever I looked, on every side, I saw great houses, four, five, and six stories high, illuminated from top to bottom. There were even buildings, within which lights glittered from one hundred and two hundred windows. Yet all this was but the every-day, or rather every-night, appearance of a great manu-facturing city.

J.G. KOHL, Ireland, 1843

APRIL, 1762: 'Where to preach in Belfast I did not know. It was too wet to preach abroad, and a dancing-master was busily employed in the upper part of the market-house, till at twelve the sovereign put him out by holding his court there. While he was above, I began below to a very serious and attentive audience. But they were all poor; the rich of Belfast "cared for none of these things".'

July, 1771: 'I never saw so large a congregation there before, nor one so remarkably stupid and ill-mannered: yet a few should be excepted, even gentlemen who seemed to know sense from nonsense. I have found as sensible men at Dublin as at Belfast; but men so self-sufficient I have not found.'

June, 1778: 'The streets are well laid-out; are broad, straight and well-built.'

JOHN WESLEY, *The Journal of the Reverend John Wesley*, 1909

O N THE MORNING OF TUESDAY, THE THIRD OF AUGUST, I awoke early. The Liverpool to Belfast boat was thudding its way over the Irish Sea. It was five o'clock, and through the porthole I could see only a stream of light floating on water and the dim disappearing coast-line of the Isle of Man. In spite of the early hour there was that slight thrill and added movement which always makes itself felt on board ship when the land for which one is making comes in sight. It seemed astonishingly near and clear when I saw it for the first time shining green and yellow under the austere light of dawn. The silver breakers seemed to lick the edge of the round, verdant slopes of the hills. Scattered houses appeared, and churches, and villages, and now and again, far behind the lesser slopes, the summit of a mountain caught and reflected the early rays of the sun.

The chill mist and the distressing rain-clouds which had covered England for half the summer had gone. There was a transparency in the air by which every visible object gained a fine edge, and a kind of vast decorativeness in the delicately tinted scene as if Nature had bathed and come forth glittering. One after another white or grey residences on the shore floated into the line of vision like pleasure domes. And just as the wayfarer may chance to perceive through a window the intimacies of an unknown family, so there were revealed to us the intimacies of each house, backed by its green park, or its garden, or its field; but between lay the separating gulf of radiant, interminable water.

Most of my fellow-passengers were Irish people, and many of them may have sailed this way a dozen times before. But the panorama of habitations on the green hillocky shore drew their attention as it drew mine. We had a glimpse of the inland water of Strangford Lough; Donaghadee and Copeland Island and its neighbouring lighthouse appeared and disappeared; Bangor detached itself as a dark mass of houses and spires and filmy smoke against the horizon. The sight of land on our starboard side announced the fact that we were entering Belfast Lough, and the water of the narrowing channel was no longer blue and purple, but grey and clammy. Now, in the river Lagan, our ears were greeted with the clanging, discordant din of the beating of hammers, and on both sides masses of gaunt scaffolding and the ribs of half-built ships rose up like skeletons. The clamour of the beaten iron had sunk into the distance when we became absorbed in the ever-familiar sight of quays, the ridiculous bustle of the donkey-engine, the crowding of passengers, and the business of landing. We have reached Belfast, the real starting-point of our journey.

R.A. SCOTT-JAMES, An Englishman in Ireland, 1910

I SEEM TO RECALL lecturing to two surprisingly small classes of pass students, and having dealings with two individuals – a young man and a young woman – who were reading for honours. This latter fact seems so odd that I am inclined to wonder whether my memory is betraying me. But I think it isn't so. During my time in Belfast there were just those two individuals in that category. And the one was a Catholic and the other a Protestant.

So here I come to the only point of much general interest about my impressions of Belfast in the later 1940s. Whether those two young people were in any sense close friends, I don't know. But they did, apparently, get along perfectly well together. And it seemed to be so with Protestants and Catholics at large. I was conscious, indeed, that tensions existed. There were more Protestants than Catholics – although the birth rates suggested it wouldn't always be the case. The Protestants were much more prosperous than the Catholics, and commanded the best jobs. Of this the Catholics were naturally resentful, and testified to the fact by here and there chalking up on walls the injunction, 'Kick the Pope'. As robust demotic utterance goes, the exhortation seemed surprisingly mild. Once, I recall, I went to some sort of quasi-Anglican church, and was startled to hear a sermon consisting of a diatribe against the Church of Rome. But throughout the community as a whole, although a certain unease may have been diffused, there was no detectable sense of impending calamity. And at least among the sort of people I chiefly met, the dichotomy chiefly felt was not one within Ulster itself, but rather one between North and South. Writers in particular seemed very conscious of being unable to hold up a candle to their fellows across the border: a reasonable modesty with O'Casey still living and Yeats and Joyce not long dead. The cultural heritage of Northern Ireland, in fact, seemed a meagre affair indeed when compared with that of Eire. 'Is Liffey worth leaving?' Joyce had asked. One answer seemed to be, 'Certainly not for anywhere beyond the Boyne.'

J.I.M. STEWART, Myself and Michael Innes, 1987

I BELIEVE THAT the many gifted and cultivated individuals who are natives of Belfast, and love their perverse and awkward city are more sensitively aware than any stranger could possibly be of this curious indifference to beauty made by man, this clumsiness that thrusts it off, which has been allowed to become too fixed a characteristic. A temperament and an attitude grew unnoticed during the busy generations of money-making – and now they have proudly hardened.

Yet Belfast is not hard. It is not a city of brisk here-and-now: it is not spruce and forward-looking; it does not roar and rush night and day towards the 1970s, the 1980s. On the contrary, its pace is easy, and it trails its immediate past and Victorian haphazardry almost too indulgently. Walking about the streets alone, especially at evening, I have experienced a sharp, unlooked-for melancholy, and an inexplicable sympathy with the untidy streets and people. In that area which stretches from College Square and past the Railway Station on to Queen's University – Royal Terrace – University Road and the streets to left and right, with the slums of Falls Road and Sandy Row not far off to the west – in that region, which is early Victorian in plan, but has a straggling, unfinished character, and in so far as it is finished became so only belatedly and at the hands of *late* Victorians – a very special kind of people – I have wondered when Belfast will find its own true novelist.

KATE O'BRIEN, My Ireland, 1962

IT HAD BEEN ON A SATURDAY EVENING that we first saw Dublin, and it was on a Saturday evening that we reached Belfast; and we had thought the streets of Dublin crowded, but compared with those of Belfast, they were nowhere. Even in our first ride up from the station, along York Street and Royal Avenue, it was evident that here was a town where life was strenuous and eager; there was no mistaking its air of alert prosperity; and when, after dinner, we sallied forth on foot to see more of it, we found the sidewalks so crowded that it was possible to move along them only as the crowd moved.

It was a better-dressed crowd than the Dublin one, but I fancied its cheeks were paler and its bodies less robust. Indeed, I am inclined to think the average stature in Belfast an inch or so under the average elsewhere. Great numbers of the men and women we saw on the streets that night were obviously undersized. I am by no means tall; five feet eight inches is, here in America, about the average; but when I walked among that Belfast crowd, I overtopped it by half a head. It was this strange sensation – the sensation of being a tall man, which I had never before experienced – which first drew my attention to the stature of the crowd.

There must be several regiments of British troops stationed at Belfast, for soldiers were much in evidence that evening, and in a great diversity of uniform. They, too, for the most part, seemed undersized, in spite of their erect carriage; and they were, as is the way with soldiers everywhere, much interested in the girls; and the girls, after the fashion of girls everywhere, were much interested in the soldiers – and there was a great deal of flirting and coquetting and glancing over shoulders and stopping to talk, and walking about with clasped hands.

Next to the crowd, the most interesting feature of Belfast is the shops, which are very bright and attractive. The Scotch have a genius for fancy breads and cakes, and the bakers' shops here were extremely alluring. There seemed to be also an epidemic of auction sales and closing out sales and cut price sales, announced by great placards pasted all over the windows; but there were so many of them that I fancy most of them were fakes.

One notices also in Belfast the multiplicity of bands. It seemed to me that night that a band, playing doggedly away, was passing all the time. Sometimes the band would be followed by a body of marching men, sometimes by men and women together, sometimes it would be just playing itself along without any one behind it. Nobody in the crowd paid much attention, not even when a big company of boy scouts marched past, looking very clever in their broad hats with the little chin-straps, and grey flannel shirts and flapping short trousers showing their bare knees.

What I am setting down here are merely my first impressions of Belfast. I do not allege that they were correct impressions, or that they fairly describe the town, but, as we were fresh from many weeks in the south and west of Ireland, the sense of contrast we experienced that first evening is not without significance.

We went back to the hotel, finally, for we had had a strenuous day; but for long and long we could hear the bands passing in the street below; and then the martial rattle of drums and scream of fifes brought us to the window, and we saw a great crowd of children march past, with banners waving and tin buckets and shovels rattling. It was a Sunday School picnic, just back from a day at the seashore; and the air which the fifes and drums were playing with a vigour that made the windows rattle was 'Work, for the Night is Coming!' I had never before realised what a splendid marching tune it is!

BURTON E. STEVENSON, The Charm of Ireland, 1915

THEY CALL BELFAST THE IRISH LIVERPOOL; if people are for calling names, it would be better to call it the Irish London at once – the chief city of the kingdom, at any rate. It looks hearty, thriving, and prosperous, as if it had money in its pockets, and roast-beef for dinner: it has no pretensions to fashion, but looks mayhap better in its honest broadcloth than *some people* in their shabby brocade. The houses are as handsome as at Dublin, with this advantage, that the people seem to live in them. They have no attempt at ornament, for the most part, but are grave, stout, red-brick edifices, laid out at four angles in orderly streets and squares.

The stranger cannot fail to be struck (and haply a little frightened) by the great number of meeting-houses that decorate the town, and give evidence of great sermonising on Sundays. These buildings do not affect the Gothic, like many of the meagre edifices of the Established and the Roman Catholic churches, but have a physiognomy of their own – a thick-set citizen look. Porticoes have they, to be sure, and ornaments Doric, Ionic, and what not; but the meeting-house peeps through all these classical friezes and entablatures; and though one reads of 'Imitations of the Ionic Temple of Ilissus, near Athens', the classic temple is made to assume a bluff, down-right, Presbyterian air, which would astonish the original builder, doubtless. The churches of the Establishment are handsome and stately; – the Catholics are building a brick cathedral, no doubt of the Tudor style. The present chapel, flanked by the National Schools, is an exceedingly unprepossessing building of the Strawberry-Hill or Castle-of-Otranto Gothic: the keys and mitre figuring in the centre – 'the cross-keys and nightcap', as a hard-hearted Presbyterian called them to me, with his blunt humour.

WILLIAM MAKEPEACE THACKERAY, The Irish Sketch Book, 1842

I SPENT A DAY IN THE LIBRARY, which was instituted in 1788, and now contains 8000 volumes, without *one* of fiction. Is there another library on the globe that can say this? It speaks more for the good sense and correctness of principle in the people of Belfast than any comments or praise whatever *can* do. I felt, while sitting there, that here was an atmosphere of truth, entirely new. What would the reading community of all nations be, if youth had access to such libraries as these, and to no others?

From Belfast I went up the coast of Antrim, visited many beautiful towns and places, but all was saddened by the desolations of the Famine.

ASENATH NICHOLSON, Annals of the Famine in Ireland, 1851

WE REACHED BELFAST ABOUT 9.30 A.M. ON FRIDAY MORNING, August 11. Amid drenching rain the vessel arrived at her moorings. The captain is reported to have said that it always rains at Belfast, and even an Irish passenger thinks it won't clear up that day. The cars, which I see for the first time, look so dripping wet that it was difficult to imagine how any persons could find pleasure in riding on them. I shouldered my knapsack to the surprise and amusement of the passers-by, and having partaken of some breakfast at a restaurant took up my quarters at the Queen's Hotel. Ireland, I soon found, was not a country for knapsacks; but, at the same time, I was not the man who having once shouldered one was going to put it down again until my travels were over.

The prognostication as to the weather happily proved unfounded, and so I sallied forth to see the town. The first place I visited was the Museum, which contains a fine local collection of curiosities. Many of the fossils of the county Antrim have been recently added, but the specimens are apparently still incomplete. It would be much more interesting if a separate room were devoted to the fossils and stones of the Giant's Causeway district. One main fault of local museums generally is that the founders attempt to make them too universal. If each town which aspires to such an institution would collect the special remains or curiosities of the district, then such a museum might be established as would attract the attention of antiquarian visitors from all parts, and it would become a just cause of pride to the natives of the locality.

AN ENGLISHMAN [W.W. BARRY], *A Walking Tour Round Ireland in 1865*, 1867

TO PEOPLE WHO KNEW THE MANUFACTURING TOWNS of what is called the Black Country, and even of Lancashire, not excepting in some respects Liverpool and Manchester, the first appearance of Belfast a quarter of a century ago was more than prepossessing. It was in some degree a surprise. In more recent years, as the town, now a city, has extended, Royal Avenue has been made, through what was a very wretched district of old houses, and nearly every house and shop in High Street have been rebuilt without much regularity, but in a gay and even fantastic style, of which the effect is agreeable. Scottish excursionists come over on their holidays in large numbers to Belfast, and especially from Glasgow. In the early morning hours when the steamboats arrive, I have often witnessed the astonishment of some of these visitors as they first entered High Street from the quay. 'Belfast is very much like Glasgo, maun,' I have often heard said, as well as in some instances the rejoinder, 'I think it looks finer.'

THOMAS MacKNIGHT, *Ulster As It Is*, 1896

ONE MIGHT WELL VISIT THE MUSEUM AND ART GALLERY if one wants a sour laugh. Most of it is enough to make one believe that the Ulsterman has no sense of humour. For it is largely devoted to such things as Waterford Glass, Viking ornaments, the inauguration-chair of the O'Neills, reproductions of ancient Irish ornaments, a skeleton of the extinct Irish elk, a plaster-cast of a cross from Monasterboice, and such-like things, every one of which mocks at modern Belfast and the Six Counties with foreign jaws. So, one likewise will see there a statue of Wellington, who lived in and was educated in County Meath. The paintings in the art gallery make a pleasant collection, including a fine Paul Henry. Then come a dreary pile of casts. But as a whole the wretched place is a bitter commentary on the contempt of modern Belfast for culture and one is scarcely repaid the trouble of the visit.

But nobody knows better than I do how ridiculously inadequate any such picture as this is of Belfast as it must appear to those who are born in it, grow up in it, live in it, and doubtless form a queer divided kind of affection for it. Of that inner, intimate life I know nothing, and can never hope to know anything. I have just been reading Michael McLaverty's fine novel of Belfast life, *Call My Brother Back*, and its warmth and imagination would be enough to reprove me if I pretended to know anything about Belfast's inner life. I get there picture after picture of young lads to whom this rivalry of hate can become a rivalry of loyalties, and end as a kind of formless saga. I gather too how magical Belfast can look from the mountains, 'its lean mill-chimneys stretched above the haze of smoke . . . the Castlereagh Hills netted with lovely fields and skimming cloud-shadows, the blue U-shaped lough covered with yachts as small as paper boats, and steamers moving up towards the docks where the gantries stood like poised aeroplanes'. And then the spires, the convents, the Celtic and the Linfield football grounds, and more spires . . . though a sense of disease and confusion arises when one of the little fellows heaves his chest and cries, 'wouldn't you think now to see all the churches and all the factories and playgrounds that it was a Christian town?'

For those lads would also have seen the sky reddening with bonfire flames when the Orangemen celebrate the Boyne, heard the night shattered by rifle-fire, and not without feelings of dread and daring lit their own fires on the fifteenth of August to honour the Assumption of the Virgin Mary. I recommend the reader to go to such books as that for pictures of the intimate world of Belfast.

SEAN O'FAOLAIN, *An Irish Journey*, 1940

O N AND OFF, I have been a fan of Belfast for the last twenty years. I have a vivid memory of my first visit in July 1970 to see the Orange Order parade on the Lisburn Road. The crowd looked hostile, but I was proud to be there. After all, I could tell my students back in Paris that I had been surrounded by the sullen throng and seen the Orangemen marching, could describe the eleborate banners and sashes and the sound of the Lambeg drums. They would look admiringly at their brave professor who had been right in the thick of things. 'Weren't you afraid, sir?' they would ask. I have never been afraid in Belfast. The city loves its visitors: its problem is self-hatred.

Twenty years ago the streets at night were empty, the pubs deserted and the restaurants closed. I remember eating with a friend in a restaurant that could seat 200 people; there were just two of us dining there and the waiters were queuing up to serve us. The city was getting ready for twenty years of demonstrations, killings, hunger strikes, conferences, strikes, unemployment and the rest of the litany. During those years children were born and grew up in South, East and West Belfast, went to school, played in the streets and went to church or to Mass. People were killed and others were arrested, tried and imprisoned. Countless books and articles were written.

MAURICE GOLDRING, *Belfast: From Loyalty to Rebellion*, 1991

SHORT AS WAS MY STAY IN BELFAST, I shall not readily forget the impressions it left on my mind. I shall not forget that curious little hotel which serves as a sort of coffee-house for the broader-minded Nationalists of Belfast, nor its landlady who can respond to the wit of a party of casual roisterers, or initiate a discussion on European literature – she is one of the leaders of opinion amongst a small set of Belfast people who are as interested in art and humanism as they are in politics. I shall not forget my visit to the theatre, where an unsophisticated audience sat out three plays performed by the Irish National Theatre company without any of that pride of origination which puffed out the audiences of the Dublin Theatre, or the Repertory Theatre in London. Nor shall I forget the inner office of the Ulster Canal and Lagan Navigation Company, whose secretary evinced great interest in our canoe journey, and produced maps and guides and a magical passport which served us in good stead in our subsequent voyage. I remember with a feeling of personal gratitude which I do not remember to have felt for any London tradesmen, the grocer who packed us a box of provisions, the ironmonger who sold us a hatchet, the draper from whom we purchased dish-cloths, the boot-shop man from whom I bought boots, and the barber who shaved me. A town after all should be known by its tradespeople, and in no big city of England or Ireland have I come across tradespeople from whom it is so pleasant to make purchases as from the dealers of Belfast.

R.A. SCOTT-JAMES, *An Englishman in Ireland*, 1910

WALK THROUGH BELFAST'S MAIN STREETS and note the most frequent and characteristic names: MacDonnell, Baird, Sharman, Mayne, Erskine, Magill, Biggar, Lepper, Crawford, Hanna, Stewart, Dunlop, Sloan, Hamilton, Maxwell, Orr, MacCracken, Hope, Mahaffy, Munro, Neilson, Hazlett – they are the names of Highland and Lowland clans. The more rare names in Mac present a rich collection: MacConkey, MacIlhagga, MacCorquodale – and those who do not know Ulster often are surprised that a city so full of Macs is not bursting with Gaelic enthusiasm.

AODH DE BLÁCAM, *The Black North*, 1938

THE FIRST TIME I WENT TO BELFAST I drove right into the city centre and parked in High Street. Half a minute after slamming the door of the car, I found myself in a throng of lunch-goers. Corn Market and Castle Lane were packed with pretty, brightly dressed girls bubbling with pent-up high spirits. The pavements of Donegall Place were thronged with lunch-going men, guffawing and grinning. Was it an act they had put on, hearing of my arrival from Dublin? Where was the famed dourness? Beyond in an open place, and sun-bathing, was the City Hall. I knew all about it before I came: it is pretentious and swaggering; a three-tiered wedding cake; a stanza in stone from God Save the King. When the City Hall was built, the world wagged well for the British Empire and Belfast was on the crest of a wave. It is a monument to success and opulence. But the flower-beds shone in red and yellow, the pigeons strutted under the pedestal of the smudgy figure of Queen Victoria, or they perched on the heads of the Carrara marble nobodies. Where was the City Hall's famed ugliness? Was this another act?

The man who enters Belfast indoctrinated is in a sorry plight. Books and tongues poison the place; the less he reads and listens, the better. The unfortunate man, with no other idea except to enjoy himself will arrive in Belfast burdened with preconceived ideas. The city has no history; it is a fungoid growth. Money is its only god. Bigotry is rampant here; the Pope is thrown at the Queen and the Queen at the Pope (bolts and half-bricks sometimes being the vicarious missiles). The public buildings are atrocities, the monuments hideous. It has no aristocracy, no culture, no leisure. The greater part of the city is as drab as Glasgow. What a mass of lies and half-truths! What a descent into pessimism!

Those few writers and talkers who take on themselves the task of praising Belfast are poor propagandists; their laudations are almost depressing, their whitewashing often defacing things which look far better in the natural black. I know of only two men who have in some slight way successfully interpreted the city: William Conor the painter and Richard Rowley the poet.

> Terrible as an army with banners
> Through the dusk of a winter's eve,
> Over the Bridge
> The thousands tramp . . .

I, too, stood at the end of Queen's Bridge and watched the army of shipbuilders going home after the day's work. Most of the fifteen thousand leave the yards nowadays in special buses, but there were enough pedestrians to wear me down and send me back to my base before the end of the trek. I had seen what I had come to see: 'the faces of strong men'; stern old chaps who eyed me sharply; young fellows (a pair of them holding playing cards in their hands and going on with a game as they hastened homewards); the foremen wearing hats (whom the others refer to as 'The Hats'); the rank and file in caps and greasy dungarees. All honest bread-winners, 'rejoicing in the strength they daily prove against the strength of steel'; fine men, proud of their shipbuilding and proud of their city.

STEPHEN RYNNE, *All Ireland*, 1956

MY TOUR IN IRELAND embraced all but the county of Cavan. I have made no mention of the north, for want of room, but cannot close without saying that in Belfast the Protestants made me feel as if I were by a New England fireside, where I was neither worshipped as a goddess, nor made a second-hand article if I performed some domestic service suited to my sex. Their religion appeared, in many cases, that of the heart.

ASENATH NICHOLSON, *Lights and Shades of Ireland*, 1850

12 DECEMBER

INTO BELFAST. Little white lighthouses on stilts: a buoy that seems to have a table tied to it: a sunken ship right up in the dock. Cranes like skeleton foliage in a steely winter. The flicker of green flame in the bellies of building ships. Hundreds of dockyard workers stop altogether to see one small ship come in.

Endless impatient waiting for the immigration officer to come on board. Why the anxiety to get ashore in so dull a place? It is the cruise spirit perhaps. I thought it just as well to go to Confession before the Atlantic. The hideous Catholic church difficult to find in Protestant Belfast. At the Presbytery a towsled housekeeper tried to send me away when I asked for a confession. 'This is no time for confession', trying to shut the door in my face. The dreadful parlour hung with pious pictures as unlived in as a dentist's waiting-room, and then the quite nice young priest who called me 'son' and whose understanding was of the simplest. In the same street the pious repository selling Woodbines from under the counter to old women.

In the evening a dozen and a half Galway oysters and a pint and a half of draught Guinness at the Globe. Then back to the ship.

GRAHAM GREENE, *from* 'Convoy to West Africa' in *The Mint: A Miscellany*, 1946

ONE MORNING I was waiting for my *Northern Whig* in a crowded little shop. It was the rush hour, and the fat young woman behind the counter, flying up and down, was serving us all at lightning speed and with godlike accuracy. A small man beside me, who was a regular, I'd say, said gently every time she passed him: 'Ten Green Gallahers'. As we might say 'Ten Players'. About five times he said it. At the sixth she smiled: 'I'll give them to ye yet in spite of ye,' she said. At the ninth pass he got them. Often in memory I enjoy that gentle turn of wit. I call it wit.

I say nothing emphatic or informative about Belfast. A stranger chancing to follow me there will have had to fend for himself, with his own maps and histories. As elsewhere throughout my rovings. But I have not undertaken to guide any save only myself backward through impressions and memories and these I must suppose are pointless, except for me.

KATE O'BRIEN, *My Ireland*, 1962

'LIGHT, MISTER?'
Turning to the voice at his elbow, Sidney was confronted by one of the most astounding sights in a lifelong experience of party junkets to odd corners of the earth. A plump, pasty-faced girl of about thirteen was pointing to an unlit cigarette dangling from a mouth already shaded by an incipient moustache. The astounding thing was that on her head she wore a huge, emerald-green busby, looped with gold chains and held in place by a gold chinstrap. Her short tunic was of white (smudged) silk with emerald-green and gold facings; her shorter pleated skirt, of a spangled gold material, barely covered the crotch of her off-white knickers. But most astounding of all, her fat, puppy-mottled thighs billowed up out of shiny-black, knee-high boots! Sidney gaped. What was it? Was she part of some sort of anti-American-bad-taste tableau? – Disneyland and Reeperbahn; Wizard of Oz and Berlin beer cellar ... He was reminded of obscene pastiches involving well-known cartoon characters which he had seen when serving on a committee investigating London vice ...

'Have ye a light, Mister?' she asked impatiently, taking the cigarette from her lips and waving it at him. Her other hand was hooked by the thumb through a strap on her left shoulder, like a rifle sling. Looking around the field he saw, to his further astonishment, that dozens of her had appeared suddenly, lounging around in all manner of erotic poses. The thing strapped to her shoulder and slung behind was, he learnt, an accordion. There were also drums lying around; one big one, being lugged about by a teenager built to the proportions of a lady mud-wrestler, bore the inscription: 'The Little Flower Pioneer Accordion Band'.

'In the name of God are you deef or daft?' inquired his Little Flower venomously.

'Please forgive me,' he stammered ... 'I'm terribly sorry. I don't smoke.'

She glared at him for a moment with such livid intensity that he thought she might attack him. 'Well, you mighta said that,' she spat finally, 'steada stannin' there with yer face on ye.'

Leaving him to ponder this enigmatic rebuke, she stamped away to join a comrade who waited with fag ready. 'That friggin' spastic in the cowboy coat,' he heard her say. Both glared at him menacingly.

JOHN MORROW, The Essex Factor, 1982

BELFAST TODAY is often compared with London during the blitz. But at least the Londoners were united against an identifiable foreign foe and not exposed to the furtive exploits of members of their own society. It is the unpredictability rather than the frequency of Belfast's hazards that makes them so nerve-racking; and the seemingly elaborate security arrangements are a deterrent rather than a protection. The prim-looking young woman ahead of you on the pavement carrying a plastic bag just might be on her way to blow up Marks and Spencers. Or the neatly dressed, respectable elderly man carrying a tidy brown paper parcel just might be going to hide it in that pub towards which you are heading. Can people really get used to living with this sort of thing? After ten days I fancied that I had become reasonably immune to it. Then one evening as I was writing in a friend's empty house a door banged upstairs and for the next five minutes I could scarcely breathe, so violently was my heart hammering. Yet in any other part of the world I simply do not react to sudden loud noises.

DERVLA MURPHY, A Place Apart, 1978

AT FIRST I WAS SURPRISED at how little had changed. The Ben Tre school of urban planning ('It became necessary to destroy the town in order to save it') has of course left its mark here as elsewhere, notably in the form of one-way systems of the kind Birmingham recently took to their logical conclusion when the city was turned into a race-track. But despite all the free demolition work by the two rival firms, the Seventies have dealt relatively lightly with Belfast. Perhaps the planners feel the place has suffered enough. The worst eyesore is the Europa Hotel, a charmless tower block with precisely the air of prawn-cocktail-and-Mateus-rosé sophistication that the name suggests. For this, the stately GNR terminus was sacrificed. But the Crown Liquor Saloon opposite, the San Marco of pubs, is not only still there but protected by the National Trust. I was apprehensive of what I might find inside. *Diary of an Edwardian Country Lady* beer mats? A glass cover over the 'genuine' sawdust sweepings? But conversation in the massively intimate snugs was anything but hushed, and the punters (lurkers and late-risers every one) standing around in the polychromatic magnificence of the tiled bar had eyes only for the television suspended from the ceiling, relaying the 4.30 at Catterick.

Outside, the soft warm rain, as if the air had grown fur, proved itself still capable of soaking you to the bone in minutes, while the grey sky was in a class of its own, as far superior to the English model as those of Provence are to its blue. Because of the Emergency, vehicular access to the centre is strictly limited and any unattended parked car likely to be blown up. This drastic but extremely effective tactic has transformed the city centre into a *de facto* pedestrian precinct, and the broad Edwardian thoroughfares can be seen for the first time more or less as their builders intended. The place looks oddly prosperous, too, no doubt because of the extra money being pumped in for political reasons, and the local arts scene is healthier than in most mainland cities of its size. Belfast will never be the Athens of the north, but compared to Dublin, which is looking more like its Naples all the time, it seems trim and buoyant, with an almost manic optimism in the air, the irrational euphoria of the survivor. If our towns, like the French, adopted the custom of listing their attractions – *Son plan d'eau, sa piscine municipale* – then Belfast might well emulate the village I once saw whose sign, whether in defiance or desperation, read *Son futur.*

MICHAEL DIBDIN, *London Review of Books*, April 1988

YOU PROBABLY THINK BELFAST looks like those photographs of Belfast you always see. Not at all. It's a charming port, one of the world's great deep-water harbours, cupped in rolling downs on the bight of Belfast Lough. Cave Hill rises to the north like Sugar Loaf Mountain above Ipanema beach, causing some to go so far as to call Belfast 'an Hibernian Rio' (not that anybody really wants to see an Irish girl in a string bikini). The city is built in the best and earliest period of Victorian architecture with delicate brickwork on every humble warehouse and factory. Even the mill hand tenement houses have Palladio's proportions in a miniature way and slate roofs you couldn't buy for money now.

The Belfast pictured in *Time* magazine, the rubble and barbed wire, litter and graffiti Belfast is, in fact, a patch of highly photogenic impoverishment no more than a mile long and half a mile wide. It is as though *Architectural Digest* came to 'do' a house and took pictures of the closet in the teenager's bedroom. The rubble is from slum clearance not bombs (though which is worse may be argued by critics of the modern welfare state). And the barbed wire is on top of the 'Peace Wall', a kind of sociological toddler gate erected by the British to keep the ragamuffin Protestant homicidal maniacs of Shankill Road away from the tatterdemalion Catholic murderers in Falls Road two blocks over. The graffiti and litter are real.

P.J. O'ROURKE, *Holidays in Hell*, 1988

A
Barbarous Nook

But here, utterly forgetting to be ministers of the gospel, they presume to open their mouths, not in the spirit of meekness, as like dissemblers they pretend, but with as much devilish malice, impudence, and falsehood, as any Irish rebel could have uttered; and from *a barbarous nook of Ireland*, brand us with the extirpation of laws and liberties; things which they seem as little to understand as ought that belongs to good letters or humanity.

JOHN MILTON

BIGOTSBOROUGH IS A CITY WITH A SOUL. The fact that it is a turbulent soul ought to increase our interest in the problem. There is some reason for the strange fact that Bigotsborough is not as meek as Liverpool or as mild as Manchester. For generations it has been remarkable for two things, namely, revivals of religion and revivals of rioting. It is the city of riots and religions. It may seem absurd to suggest that there is any connection between its love of religion and its love of rioting, but I am sure that both are produced by the same cause. Bigotsborough is a city which suffers from unsatisfied aspirations and baffled aims. Its imagination is starved, and it is oppressed by an intolerably grey monotony. It is the loneliest city in the world. It would be happy if it were on the Clyde, for its blood is Scottish. But it lives in exile amid an alien race. It has ceased to be Scottish, and it is too proud to be Irish. It has the hunger of romance in its heart, for it has lost its own past, and it is groping blindly after its own future. It cannot identify itself with Ireland or with Scotland or with England, and it vehemently endeavours to give itself to each country in turn. It is like a woman who dallies with three lovers, and cannot make up her mind to marry any of them.

JAMES DOUGLAS, The Unpardonable Sin, 1907

THEN ONE MORNING HE WAS VERY LATE and Alec gave him the money for the tram. The tram-conductor was very excited and at every stop he shouted. 'We mightn't get down the road at all. There's sniping going on, all the morning.' Some people turned home again at his warning and the half-empty tram passed down the Falls Road. Nearing Conway Street shots rang out, and Colm and the other passengers lay flat on the corrugated floor. There was a crack like a stone through ice and when the tram stopped in the shelter of a mill a man stood up beside Colm with blood claw-streaming from a wound in his hand. 'I'm hit!' he said.

Colm ran down the stairs of the tram and on to the road. He turned to go home. The road was deserted and the sun shining. 'Cage' cars were racing up and down, the rifles peeping out. The tram had gone on its way at terrific speed.

Colm ran down a side-street. All the doors were closed. He saw a man in his shirt-sleeves firing a revolver towards the Protestant quarters. A dog was running up and down barking. Colm knocked at a door, but shots rang out close to him and he ran off, going from one side of the street to the other. At last he saw a door slightly open and he pushed it quickly and closed it behind him. He was standing in a sour-smelling kitchen, coke burning on the fire, and crusts of bread on the floor. A woman was sitting with a crying baby on her lap.

'Good God!' she said. 'I thought you were Harry. My man went out ten minutes ago for sweet milk and he's never back yet . . . Sure you shouldn't be out to school a morning like that! What was yer Ma thinkin' about?' Before Colm could reply somebody kicked the door impatiently and the woman ran with the child under her arm.

A man stumbled into the kitchen with an empty jug in his hand: 'What'd ye close the bloody door for? D'ye want me bloody well riddled?' he shouted; and then seeing Colm he lowered his voice. 'There's not a taste of milk to be had for love nor money. There hasn't been a milkman seen this morning.'

'What'll we give the child, Harry?'

'Boil him some water and sugar.'

'He'd no more look at it than he would at castor oil!'

'Try and get him to sleep. They'll hardly keep shootin' the whole bloody day.'

He turned to Colm; his black hair uncombed, his face unshaven, and a brass stud in his shirt. 'This is a damned town-and-a-half to be livin' in. No work in it and them that have work can't get down till it.'

'There was a man shot in the tram I was in,' said Colm.

'There was a woman shot stone dead on the other side of the street. There's a sniper on the mill all the mornin' and you daren't put your nose out the door.'

Shots cracked fiercely and the man instinctively ducked his head.

MICHAEL McLAVERTY, *Call My Brother Back*, 1939

A T THE FAR END OF THAT DISTRICT I cycled up a once attractive street past nine empty semi-detached houses from which Catholic families had recently been driven. Workmen were busy around some of them and by now I daresay all are occupied by Loyalist paramilitary supporters. But one Catholic was standing fast – a widower, recently retired from his profession and resolved not to move whatever the paramilitaries might do. 'I've lived here with it all my life,' said he. 'My father was shot dead by the Tans in '21 as he was standing in a city-centre pub having a pint. And I well remember going to school through holes in garden walls, from garden to garden, because the streets of Belfast were considered too dangerous for children. But y'know – maybe this will surprise you – I reckon we're over the worst. The modern world is going to be too much for Northern Ireland. What was acceptable in the twenties won't wash in the eighties. We just need a little more patience – we don't need to do anything. And I'll bet Britain sees this. The Brits may look stupid in Westminster but they've an awful lot of grey cells tucked away in Whitehall. If we all sit back and wait, the whole bigotry-based structure of Northern Ireland is bound to collapse. Simply because it's against European human nature towards the end of the twentieth century. Even in Spain, they wouldn't stand for it now. Moderation will overtake us whether we want it or not.'

DERVLA MURPHY, *A Place Apart*, 1978

'D O YOU COME FROM NORTHERN IRELAND?' I remember Foxy Falk barking the question at me years ago at an Oxford dinner. I was used to contemptuous responses from English people whenever I answered this question. 'The South of Ireland is very nice,' was all they would usually say. Or else, making one feel like some kind of mongrel impostor: 'Oh, then you are not even proper Irish at all.' But I felt that the question, when asked by Foxy Falk, was going to lead to something a little different. A collector of Ming vases, Cézannes and Persian carpets, he was a man who said that he believed in 'the rule of the élite and the artist'. He was tyrannical, reading

Keats's letters aloud to people who had little desire to hear them, forbidding anyone in his household to use the telephone because he felt that it had ruined the art of conversation – and thereby creating daily difficulties as to grocery orders etc. He would intimidate by his spluttering rages, which made one fear that the boil of his anger would crack his arteries. He was famous for the fact that he had once been Pavlova's lover.

'Do you come from Ulster?' I saw that the charge behind his question had already turned his whole face to a tomato-coloured balloon. Then his fist came smashing down on to the table so that the knives went shivering against the glasses. 'All I can say is that the place where you come from ought to be blown up! It ought to be blown skyhigh, and wiped from the face of this earth!' If he felt like that . . . I found myself staring blankly at his poor old turkey wattles, which were wobbling with agitation as they dripped down over his high Edwardian collar.

Then he calmed a little and explained that Pavlova at the height of her fame had danced in Belfast, and that the theatre had been totally empty except for two people. He claimed that she had never felt so insulted and distressed in her whole life – that Belfast was the only place in the world which had ever given her such a criminal reception.

Maybe because of the bombastic way the whole subject had been approached, and because I felt I was being personally blamed for the disastrous unsuccess of her visit, all I could feel was a sudden impatience with both Pavlova and her lover. Why were they so astounded by what to me seemed to be so very unastounding? What could have made them think that her dance could ever set the grimy dockyards of Belfast dancing? When had that most austere of cities ever pretended for one moment that its prime interest was the dance?

CAROLINE BLACKWOOD, *For All That I Found There*, 1963

I KNOW MANY TO WHOM the most fitting symbol of the town is the appalling chorus of steam-whistles, buzzers, and hooters that startles the stranger from sleep in the small hours of the morning. It is a Futurist fantasia that would delight Marinetti; to more sensitive folk it sounds as if factories and workshops were roaring, like lions at feeding time, for their daily tribute of human bodies.

JAMES WINDER GOOD, *Ulster and Ireland*, 1919

WHEN THE BELFAST SITE was first occupied or when a fortified place was first made there, we do not know, but the site has such an obvious strategic value that it must have been very early. The modern history of

Belfast begins in the twelfth century when John de Courcy took control of it. The subsequent history of the castle of Belfast is a chronicle of conflicts. The castle changed hands and was destroyed on various occasions. We need not trouble with these episodes until we reach Elizabethan times, when the merits of the site of Belfast seem to have been clearly recognised. Belfast was granted in 1573 to the Earl of Essex, who 'buildeth a forte neare Belfaste, whereby he commandeth the passages over certain rivers and waters and cutteth downe wood quyetly to the great discouragement of the Irish'. In 1574, the year in which Essex treacherously seized Sir Brian O'Neill and murdered many of his people at a banquet at the castle of Belfast, Essex wrote that the brewhouse, storehouse and mill of his new establishment were now completed. In 1575 he wrote: 'I resolve not to build but at one place; namelie at Belfast; and that of littel charge; a small towne there will keepe the passage, relieve Knockfergus with wood, and horsemen being laid there shall command the plains of Clandeboye, and with footmen may keep the passage open between that and the Newrie, and keepe those of Kilulto, Killmarlin and the Dufferin in obedience, and may be victualled at plear, by sea, without daunger of Scot or pirate.'

HUGH SHEARMAN, *Ulster*, 1949

1596

THE ENGLISH PALE which above 200 years before extended from Dunluce point to the southward of Dublin, and 'had in the midst of it Knockfergus, BELFAST, Armagh, and Carlingford', was now so considerably reduced, that these towns were in this year esteemed 'the most outbounds and abandoned places in the English pale, and indeed not counted of the English pale at all; for it stretcheth now no further than Dundalk towards the North'.

Historical Collections Relative to the Town of Belfast, 1817

IN THE YEAR FOLLOWING, 1708, on the 24th of April, the castle of Belfast was consumed, by the carelessness of a servant, who put on a large fire of wood to air a room she had washed, by which accident, Lady Jane, Lady Frances, and Lady Henrietta Chichester, daughters of Arthur, third earl of Donegall, were unfortunately burned to death.

Historical Collections Relative to the Town of Belfast, 1817

THE BOOK-SHOPS which I saw in this thriving town said much for the religious disposition of the Belfast public; there were numerous portraits of reverend gentlemen, and their works of every variety: – 'The Sinners' Friend', 'The Watchman on the Tower', 'The Peep of Day', 'Sermons delivered at Bethesda Chapel', by so-and-so; with hundreds of the neat little gilt books with bad prints, scriptural titles, and gilt edges, that come from one or two serious publishing houses in London, and in considerable numbers from the neighbouring Scotch shores. As for the Theatre, with such a public the drama can be expected to find but little favour; and the gentleman who accompanied me in my walk, and to whom I am indebted for many kindnesses during my stay, said not only that he had never been in the play-house, but that he never heard of any one going thither. I found out the place where the poor neglected dramatic Muse of Ulster hid herself; and was of a party of six in the boxes, the benches of the pit being dotted over with about a score more. Well, it was a comfort to see that the gallery was quite full, and exceedingly happy and noisy; they stamped, and stormed, and shouted, and clapped in a way that was pleasant to hear. One young god, between the acts, favoured the public with a song – extremely ill sung, certainly, but the intention was everything; and his brethren above stamped in chorus with roars of delight.

WILLIAM MAKEPEACE THACKERAY, The Irish Sketch Book, 1842

'A REPORT THAT THE DOCTOR WAS TO PREACH on the sin of theatricals drew me one evening to May Street Church. I was in attendance a little before the hour appointed, but found the immense place of worship quite full – every seat occupied, so that I with difficulty found standing-room in the aisle ... The streams of irony and eloquence and argument that flowed that evening from the pulpit of May Street, and blended altogether in one burning flood of fiery declamation, were as irresistible as a cataract from the hills. In the midst of the sermon all the gas-lights in the house were simultaneously extinguished, whether from design or accident is un-known to me; and for nearly fifteen minutes the church was in total dark-ness, with the exception of whatever light emanated from four candles that burned upon the pulpit, and that served only to make the darkness visible. But the preacher did not stop, nor even falter. Like a hurricane at midnight, on he thundered through the gloom; and when the gas-lamps were re-lighted, he concluded with a splendid peroration. That night is memorable to me, being the first time I ever was made to feel the power of eloquence; and it is memorable to more than me, for theatricals in Belfast received a shock that evening from which they have not yet recovered.'

PROFESSOR WITHEROW, quoted in J.L. Porter,
The Life and Times of Henry Cooke, 1871

from BELFAST: A POEM

Thy Chapels, too, whose well-taught flocks
Cleave to their ancient Orthodox,
With fervent hearts and due reserve,
Their forms of worship they preserve –
With all consent be freely given
To each his fav'rite road to Heaven;
And let each traveller know his own,
Lest wandering, he in sin be thrown.
And though by many a different road
We seek Felicity's abode,
Yet, when this pilgrimage is past,
May we all meet in heaven at last!
Where Rectors shall with peace prevail,
And the wild Thresher drop his flail;
Where Presbyterians too shall join
The angels of celestial line,
And honest Quakers' souls shall rest,
From ills of flesh securely blest;
And Methodists, with loud accord,
Shall chaunt the praises of the Lord.

SAM LYONS, 1822

I WILL NOT VENTURE TO ASSERT that the condition of the lowest poor of Belfast exhibits a picture of greater actual destitution and neglect than may be found in other parts of the empire – that is not likely – but I must say, that the contrasts which glare out upon the eye as it descends from the summit to the base of the social fabric here is stronger than I ever remember to have seen it in any other locality. Nor is this my testimony alone; for, having conversed on the subject with some whose duties have led them to explore the general state of the lower classes in many parts both of England and Ireland, fully and minutely, I find a coincidence of sentiment in relation to this matter, which confirms and corroborates my own impressions. Can that, then, let me ask, be a sound or even a safe state of things, in which the different grades of the community are not rising equally, and advancing *pari passu*, in the march of improvement and civilisation? Is it, indeed, true, that in this Northern Athens of ours, with its seats of learning, its collegiate and academic halls, its large and elegant temples of worship, its public edifices of various kinds not wanting in architectural ornament and beauty, and its commerce superior to that of any other port in the kingdom – greater than that of Dublin and Cork combined – is it true, that in this, one of the most flourishing, intellectual, and (shall I add?) religious towns of the united empire, we have in our back lanes and alleys, an amount of wretchedness – physical, social, moral – which, if not absolutely, is at least relatively, larger and more appalling than may probably be found beside, throughout the length and breadth of the land? Doubtless, the very prosperity of the town may have indirectly and in part contributed to all this, by drawing towards it, from various quarters, great numbers of the most destitute, with the hope of bettering their circumstances. But I have shown other causes at work much more potent in their influence, and affording a more satisfactory, though at the same time more melancholy, explanation of the phenomenon.

When the Representative of our gracious Queen lately made an almost Royal progress through our principal streets, and gazed at those proofs of opulence and prosperity which everywhere met his eye, how little could he or any of his distinguished *cortége* imagine the misery to be found in immediate proximity to the brilliant and joyous scene. If only some of those streets through which he passed could have opened, and disclosed what lay beyond, the effect would have been as that of a loathsome spectre at a feast, or as of the corruption of a charnel-house breaking in upon the gaiety and glitter of a bridal. It is perfectly right to deck ourselves in holiday attire, when called upon to receive and welcome the highest public functionary of the land, but it is not right to forget the abject condition of the vast numbers of our population who could only grimly smile at such a happy spectacle; nor is it right to overlook the fact that there are diseases at work beneath the surface – at the very core of the social body – which it will demand something widely different from a gala day and public *fête* to cure, or even mitigate.

THE REVEREND W.M. O'HANLON, *Walks Among the Poor of Belfast*, 1853

THE POLITICAL FEELING has greatly altered of late years. The party animosity has become, during the last twenty years, more marked, disgraceful, and disastrous than it was in the beginning of the century. We remember when, so far as we know, the first lives were lost by party collision. It was in 1813, when two men were shot in North Street. This excited wonderful consternation, and yet we know it was nothing compared with later events. About sixteen years ago, more than a dozen persons were killed in the streets of Belfast, and the town was for several days in possession of a riotous mob. This has given Belfast a bad name in England, and strangers from that country have landed at our quays with pistols in their pockets to defend themselves. We have never seen this, but can very well believe it. A little army is required to keep the town in order on the anniversaries of events that happened nearly two hundred years ago.

GEORGE BENN, *A History of the Town of Belfast*, 1880

I WAS GOING TO IRELAND AND TO ULSTER at a remarkable time. The Fenian organisation was believed to be growing in strength. Mr James Stephens was represented, and indeed represented himself, as the head of a great conspiracy which involved the whole country in a network, and which was supposed to be ready when the signal should be given to appeal openly to arms. Ireland was not thought to be the most agreeable country for an Englishman, devoted to the peace and the unity of the kingdom and the empire, to enter upon the duties of a public instructor. Five years before, indeed, when my predecessor in the same journalistic enterprise, Mr F.H. Hill, went to Belfast, a friend, as I was afterwards informed, presented him in a spirit of commiseration with a revolver. It was thought to be the most suitable gift for one going to be an Irish editor.

THOMAS MacKNIGHT, *Ulster As It Is*, 1896

A MAN TOLD ME IN NORTH-EAST ULSTER that he had heard a mother warning her children away from some pond, or similar place of danger, by saying, 'Don't you go there; there are wee popes there.' A country where that could be said is like Elfland as compared to England. If not exactly a land of fairies, it is at least a land of goblins. There is something charming in the fancy of a pool full of these peculiar elves, like so many efts, each with his tiny triple crown or crossed keys complete. That is the difference between this manufacturing district and an English manufacturing district, like that of Manchester. There are numbers of sturdy Nonconformists in Manchester, and doubtless they direct some of their educational warnings against the system represented by the Archbishop of Canterbury. But nobody in Manchester, however Nonconformist, tells even a child that a puddle is a sort of breeding place for Archbishops of Canterbury, little goblins in gaiters and aprons. It may be said that it is a very stagnant pool that breeds that sort of efts. But whatever view we take of it, it remains true, to begin with, that the paradox could be proved merely from superficial things like superstitions. Protestant Ulster reeks of superstition; it is the strong smell that really comes like a blast out of Belfast, as distinct from Birmingham or Brixton.

G.K. CHESTERTON, *Irish Impressions*, 1919

OLD STYLE

She was extremely small; not more
Than four-foot-six I guessed.
And she was also fabulously old,
A Queen Victoria in rusty black:

Commanding a café table, or
Clasping her books in Donegall Square West.

Held high, a babe in arms, she said
She'd witnessed Wellington's
State funeral. One of her forebears sat
In Grattan's Parliament at College Green.
    She'd peddled tea to pay her dues
And lived on air, to graduate from Queen's.

As later, when I knew her, she
    Lunched off a penny bun,
Saving a guinea for the library.
And, penny-pinching, resolutely skimped
    On tram-fares, and was seen to tramp
Enormous distances, shrunk in the rain.

Despite her foreign languages,
    She said demurely – Greek,
And French (and English) – nonetheless, she cried,
She was illiterate in her native tongue.
    Each day, at noon, she'd meditate
On Ireland, closed and still behind her book.

Descended from Ascendancy,
    She'd chosen to pursue
An unprotected path outside the pale.
Irish, not *Anglo-Irish*, she decreed.
    At noon today, compatriots,
One with a gun, gutted the library.

ROY McFADDEN, *Collected Poems (1943–1995)*, 1996

THE ARTICLES IN LIBERAL PAPERS oscillated between entreaties and threats. One of them, in a paper supposed to be more or less inspired by the Government, pleased me greatly. It began with a warm tribute to the loyalty which had always characterised the men of Ulster. Then it said that troops were being moved to Belfast in order to overcome a turbulent populace. It went on from that to argue that troops were entirely unnecessary, because Ulstermen, though pig-headed almost beyond belief in their opposition to Home Rule, would not hesitate for a moment when the choice was given them of obeying or defying the law. They would, of course, obey the law. But, so the article concluded, if they did not obey the law the resources of civilisation were by no means exhausted.

As no law had, up to that time, been made forbidding the holding of the Belfast demonstration, this article was perhaps premature in its attempt to impale Babberly and his friends on the horns of a dilemma.

GEORGE A. BIRMINGHAM, *The Red Hand of Ulster*, 1912

I SHALL NEVER FORGET a speech I once heard a Unionist member make to his constituents, after what was probably the rowdiest election modern Ulster has known. In the square where he spoke practically every window had been shattered by stones, and a couple of hundred yards away police with drawn batons were charging an Orange mob which had raided into Nationalist territory. Yet the burden of the new member's song was that the election would be an example to the South and West of the discipline and order that made Ulster irresistible. At the time I felt sure he was speaking with his tongue in his cheek; now I know that, however illogical he may have been, he was not consciously insincere.

JAMES WINDER GOOD, *Ulster and Ireland*, 1919

DURING THE DAYS WHEN I VISITED WITH MY FATHER on Sunday afternoons to see his 'poor people', as he called them, I saw some curious places, and some very queer people, but he never led me into those quarters where rioting might be met with at any street corner. Rioting was the popular pastime in those days amongst many members of Belfast's rapidly growing population. In those evil days it was an easy thing to start a riot. Even the whistling of what was called a 'party tune' had been known to cause a tumult which swept the town like a tornado from end to end. It was before the days of concrete, and paving stones were easily come by. Once you prised up two or three of these, the rest was as easy as shelling peas. Men, women, and children entered eagerly into the task of providing am-munition, and I have seen whole streets emptied of their paving stones which were piled up in readiness for the 'sport'.

It was during one of these lamentable orgies that my father did a very gallant thing. He wanted to set an example in tolerance towards the warring factions, and persuaded a friendly priest whom he knew to go with him. Together the two men walked through the now devastated area, stopping here and there to speak to a man or a woman. Unbelievably, not one uncivil word was spoken to either of them. It was a noble gesture, and, I fancy, quite useless.

PAUL HENRY, *Further Reminiscences*, 1973

W E PASSED HOLYWOOD and the large army depot, and then the gantries and cranes of the shipyard, which meant we were near Belfast, the old horror.

It was a city of drunks, of lurkers, of late-risers. It smelled of wet bricks and burning coal. It stank. It had a sort of nightmare charm. When the rain came down in Belfast it splashed through the roof and spattered through the window glass and poured into your soul. It was the blackest city in Britain, and the most damaged.

Belfast had a tourist bureau. Don't be afraid, was their message. I liked the blarney in their brochure:

> No coward soul is mine
> No trembler in the world's
> storm-troubled sphere

These lines by Emily Brontë (daughter of an Ulsterman) are often quoted to describe the spirit of Belfast. Visitors, having heard only news of the city's political troubles, are invariably surprised when they see the citizens' 'business as usual' briskness and the positive signs of achievement ...

But the Brontë poem ('Last Lines') was about the love of God and 'Heaven's glories' and faith 'arming me from fear'. Trust in God and you'll be safe in Belfast!

The achievement, I supposed, was that after such a battering the city still stood; after so many streets had been torn up, and so many bombs thrown, there were still buses running; after so many windows broken there were still windows intact. Life went on, how could it not? Forty per cent of the Ulster population lived in this city and most of the remaining industry was here. But the outlook was grim. The shipyard, Belfast's largest employer, was said to be laying off 4,000 men. 'That's when the real trouble will start,' a hard-faced man named Muncaster said to me. 'The British Government's been protecting their "workers". But what happens when they don't have any more workers?'

Muncaster – 'call me Jack' – was a real Belfast toughie. The city either destroyed a person or else it made him merciless. The people of Belfast – most of them – suffered from what journalists had begun calling 'compassion fatigue'. They had seen so much misery and heard so many explosions and cries for help they hardly blinked.

'What do I think of the bombers?' Muncaster said. 'I think they're boring. When I hear a bomb go off I just look at my watch. I look at the time – I don't know why – and then I walk away. And I feel a little safer after a bomb, because there probably won't be another one that day. But God, it's boring!'

PAUL THEROUX, *The Kingdom by the Sea*, 1983

BELFAST

The hard cold fire of the northerner
Frozen into his blood from the fire in his basalt
Glares from behind the mica of his eyes
And the salt carrion water brings him wealth.
Down there at the end of the melancholy lough
Against the lurid sky over the stained water
Where hammers clang murderously on the girders
Like crucifixes the gantries stand.

And in the marble stores rubber gloves like polyps
Cluster; celluloid, painted ware, glaring
Metal patents, parchment lampshades, harsh
Attempts at buyable beauty.

In the porch of the chapel before the garish Virgin
A shawled factory-woman as if shipwrecked there
Lies a bunch of limbs glimpsed in the cave of gloom
By us who walk in the street so buoyantly and glib.

Over which country of cowled and haunted faces
The sun goes down with a banging of Orange drums
While the male kind murders each its woman
To whose prayer for oblivion answers no Madonna.

LOUIS MacNEICE (1931), *Collected Poems*, 1966

'NO POPE HERE', 'Not an inch', 'God save the King', and 'Remember 1690' were signs we saw every day. They appeared in huge permanently painted letters on the gable ends of the streets round about. Although our street lay mid-way between Falls Road, the centre of every-thing Catholic in Belfast, and Sandy Row, the strongest Orange quarter, we were staunchly Protestant. Even ruder slogans against His Holiness decorated some gables; together with elaborate paint-ings, some twenty feet or more high, of coronation scenes complete with flowering robes, regalia, and recognisable portraits of King George V and Queen Mary. The crossing of Boyne Water by King Billy, with flying banners and flashing swords, was, however, the favourite topic for these vast outdoor murals.

We had a mural too in the backyard of our house, but only a painted crown on the whitewash under the window-sill. Higher up, only just visible, remained the fragments of King Billy's charger, the open Bible, a lurid eye through the clouds, Jacob's ladder, the rainbow, and Noah's ark, painted years before by my father while in a mood of patriotism. Whatever they represented religiously and politically, the pictures added a dash of colour and life to the drab mien of the streets.

We tried to reckon how much an ordinary Mickey would have to pay at confession for a week's sins. It was our firm belief that every sin had to be paid for in hard cash, and that was why so many Catholics were publicans – unlike so many others their tills were always full of cash.

For one particular crime we could never forgive the Mickeys; their hatred of the Bible. All Catholics were under orders, we were told, to burn any scripture they found, especially New Testaments. The old song supported us,

> *The intriguing Paypishes surround this loyal and ancient town*
> *They tried you know not long ago to pull the Bible down*
> *And to destroy it root and branch they often have combined*
> *But from Sandy Row we made them fly like chaff before the wind.*

What pride we enjoyed for living so near to Sandy Row – the Boys of Sandy Row, stalwarts of our Orange Order.

We imagined also that newly dead popes were embalmed like Takabuti in the museum, and then put on display as human money-boxes; and that when they were stuffed so full that not another penny would go in, they were canonised and became saints.

ROBERT HARBINSON, *No Surrender*, 1960

TERROR OVERPOWERED ROBERT. He turned to go back by the way he had come, and as he did so his arms were seized, he was whirled round, and he saw a gang of rough youths and heard a thick harsh voice shouting at him, 'Curse King William, you Protestant "get" you!' Then, because he did not reply a fist suddenly struck his face, and he could feel blood dribbling from his nose . . .

ST JOHN ERVINE, *The Wayward Man*, 1926

IMAGINE A LONDON in which the inhabitants of Kensington are afraid to visit old friends in Chelsea; in which nobody from Camden Town dares to drink in Hampstead pubs; in which a youth from Wimbledon would be risking his life by strolling through Green Park; in which a change of taxis is sometimes necessary between Putney and Richmond because few drivers are willing to venture outside their native borough. A London suffering from an acute housing shortage though row after row of solid, spacious dwellings stand empty with bricked-up doors and windows. A London where policemen are likely to be shot dead within moments of entering certain districts – and so never do enter them – and where large buildings are frequently razed by uncontrollable swarms of small boys. A London in which only the West End is comparatively safe for all Londoners to shop in, because it has been securely barricaded off from the rest of the capital and is constantly patrolled by large numbers of heavily armed troops. Such a London could happen only in science fiction – we hope. Yet all the world knows that one city in the United Kingdom has been reduced during the past decade to this almost unimaginable way of life.

DERVLA MURPHY, *A Place Apart*, 1978

IF THERE IS ONE QUALITY IN BELFAST AND ULSTER more outstanding than another, it is *common-sense* – in these days a very desirable asset – and everywhere you go you see the Johnsonian strong and sensible countenance, sometimes, indeed, too strong.

The Belfast man is often blamed for being rough and rugged in speech, brusque in manner, and for using country dialect and pronunciations not always fitting to city life, but defects in this direction, where there are such, are made up by heartiness, earnestness, goodwill and pump-handle handshake. There is no real brogue in Belfast, and one does not hear of a 'foine toime' as in Dublin, but the native has a somewhat Scotch-like accent, more or less staccato and not exactly musical, so much so that while there is nothing to be ashamed of, 'his speech betrayeth him' anywhere over the wide world. Thus independence of character has its own distinguishing marks. There are thousands of exceptions, of course, but for the most part early training and environment have left him plain, blunt and sometimes uncouth, yet on the other hand civil, honest and fair. Some defend the use of dialect in city speech, but surely the golden mean is to avoid farmyard language such as 'a brave, wee lump o' a hussey' on the one hand, or Piccadilly affectation such as 'living yeahs on the Malown Rowd', on the other.

JAMES LOGAN, *Ulster in the X-Rays*, 1922

IN BELFAST, WORKING-CLASS ACCENTS are all very similar. The main difference is between East and West Belfast, and it is quite a subtle difference. East Belfast speakers are rather more likely to say 'haun', 'maun' for *hand, man* and similar words and rather less likely to say 'kerrot', 'kebbage' for *carrot, cabbage* and similar words. West Belfast speakers (especially older ones) are more likely to say 'kyar' for *car* and similar words, and may occasionally have 'thet', 'hev', 'flet', 'trep' for *that, have, flat, trap*, whereas East Belfast speakers do not use these forms (as far as we have been able to check). We are dealing here not with two completely different accents, but with two similar ones that have slight and subtle degrees of difference between them. We are also dealing with probabilities, not certainties. Thus, if a youngish man says 'kyar' for *car*, he is *probably* not from East Belfast.

The question of ethnic difference in Belfast is again bound up with regional difference and other social factors. Working-class accents are tending to become more similar throughout the city, so that younger people are not easily identifiable on an accent basis. Older people, however, may show some differences. Within West Belfast, some older Shankill speakers show a tendency to retain some older Scots forms, such as 'wer' or 'wor' for *our* and, occasionally, 'gless' for *glass*. The use of *ky* and *k* in words like *car*, *cart* is heaviest amongst middle-aged and older men in West Belfast Catholic areas. Even so, the use of, for example, 'kyar' for *car* would certainly not prove that the speaker is a Catholic!

In general, older Catholic speakers in West Belfast may seem to have an accent that is somewhat closer to mid-Ulster rural speech than other Belfast accents are. However, it is obvious that younger people are avoiding these rural features, which are therefore dying out. The result is that clear 'ethnic' differences in speech are very difficult to pin down. Perhaps we should take encouragement from the fact that while people of the different religions cannot agree with each other on political matters, they do seem to be identifying in speech as a single community.

JAMES MILROY, Regional Accents of English: Belfast, 1981

PERHAPS THE MOST REMARKABLE FACT in the industrial history of Belfast is that no printing-press was ever brought into the city before the year 1696. In barbarous Russia, therefore, printing was used more early than in this British city. Yet Belfast was the town in which the first Bible ever printed in Ireland was published in 1714, and where the oldest Irish periodical, the 'Weekly Magazine', was originally established. Germany, therefore, has many older periodicals than Ireland. There are now seven newspapers published at Belfast, all more or less liberal in politics, and all hostile both to the Tories and the Church of England.

J.G. KOHL, Ireland, 1843

ENGLISH PEOPLE NEVER CAN UNDERSTAND that Ireland is peopled by two races – nay, by several races, as distinct from one another as the Cornishman or East Anglian is from the Northumbrian or the Lowland

Scot. So that *vox populi* by no means implies a combined voice, and the phrase 'So Irish!' – alas, too often an opprobrious adjective – includes types of character as opposite as the poles. Here, for instance, on this Antrim coast, which was populated almost entirely by immigration from Scotland, the faces, the manners, nay, the very accent, were so strongly Scotch that it was difficult to believe one's self on the western, rather than the eastern shore of the Irish Channel. Still more difficult – except when one thought of the Covenanters, whose blood, traceable through generations, yet lingers here – was it to realise that an industrious, well-to-do, thriving, peaceful population, should give way to such a Cain-and-Abel madness. Which yet had a sort of prudent method in it – for a friend told us, laughing at our fears, that Belfast was 'quite quiet in the daytime'; that the gentlemen went up to business, and the ladies to do their shopping, only taking care to come away before 6 p.m., 'when the fighting began'. It was extraordinary how little people living on the spot seemed to trouble themselves about a state of things which had seemed so dreadful to us at a distance.

MRS CRAIK, *An Unknown Country*, 1887

MY MOUNTAIN MUSINGS were sometimes conducted to a less soothing obbligato than the birds' melodies. I have been on those hills when machine-guns crackled in the city streets below and the larks' love-lyrics were accompanied by rifle-fire. It was an incongruous situation – roaming the quiet moorland in quest of birds when men were trying to shoot each other not far away. But during 'the troubles' folk grew accustomed to civil tumult and the chatter of machine-guns became almost commonplace. I am surprised now to find that in my nature notes I made so little comment on these disorders.

I can best give a description of a visit to these hills by transcribing a page or two of an old nature diary just as it was jotted down:

'On the hills yesterday. Going through one of the streets at 10.30 a.m. I saw a sparrow-hawk chasing a sparrow across the street to a tree, then around a baker's cart where the sparrow escaped by flying underneath. There were a good many unheeding people about at the time. The hawk flew away over the city. Weather fine but rather misty on the hills.'

EDWARD ALLWORTHY ARMSTRONG, *Birds of the Grey Wind*, 1940

from GATHERING MUSHROOMS

The pair of us
tripping through Barnett's fair demesne

like girls in long dresses
after a hail-storm.
We might have been thinking of the fire-bomb
that sent Malone House sky-high
and its priceless collection of linen
sky-high.
We might have wept with Elizabeth McCrum.
We were thinking only of psilocybin.

PAUL MULDOON, Quoof, 1983

A S WE APPROACHED THE ROAD JUNCTION at the Andersonstown Leisure Centre rain began to fall heavily.

'We'll duck in here for a minute,' said Thomas running under the porch of the leisure centre.

Already the road was littered with broken bottles, smashed paving stones and bricks. A rich collage against a bright mess of paint-bombs which had missed the mark and splattered brilliantly over the pavements, up the walls, across the shop-fronts and the parked cars. A bizarre gaiety in an otherwise desolate scene. The perpetrators could be seen milling on the waste ground behind a row of nearby shops: Hales Fruit and Vegetables, Cosgrove's Pharmaceuticals, etc.

At that moment four mammoth saracens battled heavily down the road and grated to a halt outside the leisure centre. Soldiers in full riot gear issued reluctantly from the vehicles and took up positions clustered behind the armoured doors or squatting beside the wheels. Nothing happened for a few minutes, then suddenly a wild and strangely playful cry went up from behind the shops. The soldiers exchanged glances. The split-second before panic. But professionalism asserts itself: they lowered their face shields and raised their guns.

Immediately a crowd of about two hundred boys burst from the waste ground armed with rocks, bricks, paint-bombs. They rushed exhilarated to within dangerous proximity of the riot squad and with a climactic choral yell let fly their improvised missiles. The next second, even before the weapons had found or missed their mark, they had turned and retreated as speedily as they attacked. And already the soldiers had released a round of the big, rocket-shaped rubber bullets which went bounding across the road after the disappearing crowd. Few reached the retreating throng. None lethally. The spent bullets were quickly captured by their enterprising targets. Rubber POWs – black gold. Worth a fiver to Yanks and visiting journalists.

We were still sheltering from the rain, unwilling to move on and miss the spectacle. A line of local traffic had begun to pile up not a hundred yards from the riot scene. Suddenly the commanding officer signalled retreat and the soldiers leapt into the saracens, banged the doors shut and took off down the road, almost ramming the queue of cars as they passed. A tactical retreat, more to do with wet thighs than the ferocity of the opposition.

We went on up the road. Outside the Busy Bee a hijacking was in full swing. A burnt-out bus smoked in the mouth of a sidestreet. A group of excited youths were using hurley sticks to remove the last windows from the extinct vehicle. Local cars manoeuvred nervously over the layers of broken glass. A hundred yards further on a huge ice-cream lorry had been parked across the road and was being quickly emptied of its contents by armies of children.

'Is there any Neapolitan?' inquired a passing woman.

I thought briefly of securing dessert, but it would be too cold to carry. I went on home empty-handed.

That night, Radio Ulster.

'There have been reports this evening of an outbreak of food poisoning in the Andersonstown area. Chiefly affected are children and young people, and it is believed that the outbreak could be related to the hijacking of a food transportation van in the area this afternoon. The van was carrying a quantity of ice-cream which had been condemned by a Technical Services health inspector, and was on its way to the city dump to be destroyed.'

MARY COSTELLO, *Titanic Town*, 1992

T HE SECOND TOWN IN IRELAND is commercial, Protestant and wealthy; that is to say, profoundly uninteresting. People who admire wide streets, well laid out and clean, with tramways in the middle, bordered by brick houses covered with stucco, and shops blazing with gas, will be delighted with Belfast. One feels that these large windows with their Venetian blinds belong to wealthy dwellings where people eat off massive plate, drink claret of the best brands, use fine solid furniture, and bore themselves horribly. Down to the hospitals and the prison everything is magnificent. Everything is also new. In 1612 the town consisted of about a hundred huts grouped round a castle of wood. English and Scottish colonists settled there, and a hundred years later it counted rather less than 8000 inhabitants. At the beginning of this century there were not more than 40,000, and to-day there are over 200,000. It is the least Irish of all Irish towns. One might fancy oneself at Glasgow or Bristol. Bare feet are rare even in the lower quarters, and there are few loungers, except on Sunday, when the men group themselves, pipe in mouth, around the taverns. Sunday is no joke in Belfast. As the hotels generally have a public bar, the door is locked during the hours of Divine service, and travellers are obliged to have it opened for each entry. Needless to say that every kind of spirituous liquor is freely supplied in the dining-room, or that drunkenness goes on at a great rate in the suburbs all Sunday evening. But the moral discipline of this very religious town forbids all entry into public-houses during service; I say entry, because those who are in can remain behind drawn blinds all the time of mass or sermon. This exterior rigidity of Sunday manners hardly exists to-day save under Protestant auspices. But Belfast, I repeat, is a Protestant town. The Episcopalians are in a minority, but the Presbyterians and the Methodists are prosperous. The third of the population which professes the Catholic faith is composed almost exclusively of the working classes and small shopkeepers. Belfast is the battle-ground of religions, a Protestant stronghold in the midst of Catholic and apostolic Erin, and the zeal of both sides is quickened by contact. This town is the headquarters of the Orange-men, bound together by a sort of Protestant freemasonry intended to counteract the action of the United Ireland associations. It is not easy to say whether political or religious animosity plays the greater part in the strife of these two factions. Five years ago, when Mr Gladstone's Home Rule Bill was rejected by the House of Commons, the Protestants of Belfast were loud in their demonstrations of delight, and the enraged Catholics fell upon them tooth and nail. The Protestants drowned a Catholic youth; the Catholics replied by killing some Protestants; and for three weeks there were riots in the streets. Might not the Catholic priests have repressed the zeal of the faithful? It would seem so in a country where ninety per cent are regular in their attendance at the confessional.

I have sought vainly for a picturesque corner in Belfast.

MADAME DE BORET, *Three Months' Tour in Ireland*, 1891

I WAS RECEIVED WITH MUCH KINDNESS by Mr Birch, whom I had seen on my first arrival, and I proceeded again to Belfast, where I arrived in time for the celebration of the King's birthday, and heard the volleys fired by the garrison in honour of His Majesty. The people of this town, who were represented some time ago as about to rise, appeared now in a sort of stupor hardly distinguishable from fear. In the evening the town was il-luminated, and the soldiers ran through the streets armed with sticks, breaking the windows of those who had not lit up their houses, and of a great number also who had done so. They went into all sorts of holes and corners breaking back-windows and the fanlights of doors. They seized their officers and bore them, in turn, on their shoulders through the streets. The yells, coming from the soldiers, and the huzzas were simply terrible. Three weeks earlier it was the people who assembled tumultuously and made a racket. If I may say it, I think a crowd of soldiers and a crowd of people differ very little in point of the danger to be expected; in the former case, however, if the officers have their soldiers well in hand there is less danger, as by the terror they inspire they are able to prevent the excess to which the populace might give way.

I imagine that the people of Belfast will not for long forget the terror in which I found them. General Lake, however, walked the streets the whole night and arrested some soldiers who were becoming unruly; he dispersed the crowd, too, as soon as the time fixed for the illumination was past. The row was so agreeable and entertaining to the soldiers that they would have been very glad to begin it again; a report was, indeed, circulated that there would be a second illumination next day. In every country soldiers are delighted with the chance of making a rumpus, than slashing and cutting they like nothing better, and it required all the activity of General Lake to keep them within bounds.

The next day, desiring to see the Sovereign, as the first Magistrate or Mayor is here called, his house was pointed out to me by a poor woman who was near the door. 'There it is,' said she, 'but he is not in, and I am waiting,' she added, 'to make him pay for my broken panes.'

On the same day a man with whom I dined, and who was in a state of alarm, said to me: 'France is in great trouble, Italy is ravaged, a revolution is coming in Spain, Germany is ruined, Switzerland is about to declare war, Holland no longer exists; here we are breaking our windows, and we shall finish, perhaps, with slaughter; – where is peace to be found?' 'Faith,' said I, 'I know one sovereign who has not been troubled, and to whom anyone can go very quickly.' 'And who is he? tell me, Sir.' 'The big Devil in hell,' I answered.

The troubles, however, having made Belfast a somewhat disagreeable resting-place, I provided myself with passports and started out. I was much surprised to see that the soldiers had taken the trouble to break windows as far as two or three miles from the town. I travelled by coach, thinking it not desirable to risk myself on foot, on the road, after what I had seen. I passed successively through Lisburn, Hillsborough, and Dromore; the two first-named are situated in beautiful and perfectly-cultivated country. Hillsborough, where is the castle of the Marquis of Downshire, is on a height dominating a most fertile and rich country.

CHEVALIER DE LATOCNAYE, *A Frenchman's Walk Through Ireland 1796–97*, 1917

AND IF WE MAY HAVE YOUR LORDSHIPS' CONSENTS, there is yet one other abbay, called the Market town, where we would place another band of footmen with some horsemen, which place being kept together with Glanarme, shall bring all these parties of the North as civil as the English Pale, as also to keep out the Scots for ever; the rest of the country between this and the English pale is in very good quietness. We have fortified Belfast, and have placed there 15 horsemen, so that in this town we live as quietly as in Dublin, and yet may it do more good that the two bands be here, although they tarry not, to give a greater terror unto those that be wicked or intend to be.

PIERS & MALBIE TO THE QUEEN, 1567

B ELFAST WAS DETESTABLE. The only 'decent' hotel at that time was grubby. The city is the most dreadful in Ireland. The Ulster accent, a bastard lowland Scots, is harsh, and is given a sort of comic bluster by the glottal stop imported from Glasgow. (It is strange to think that Henry James's Ulster ancestors may have spoken in this manner.) The humour is boisterous; the fanaticism is brutal and the relations between the Ulster employers and workers was rough; it was a simple matter to rouse national passions, so that social reforms were checked. The minority of the liberally minded were the merchants and middlemen; the manufacturers were more obdurate. Still, I have known genial Ulstermen. It is no good trying the southern Irish game of evasion, indirection and covert conspiracy with them, at least not with the Protestants; one has to stand firm and hit back hard. They understand that and, like plain-speakers in northern England, they grin.

V.S. PRITCHETT, *Midnight Oil*, 1971

W ITHOUT MUSIC AND LITERATURE our lives of quiet desperation would have been almost unbearable, and to strengthen our stoicism we attended a WEA course on philosophy given by Professor Alexander Macbeath of Queen's – a bald severe-looking Scot who delivered his lectures with clarity and precision but who failed to hold our attention. In dismay, we gave up; which was our fault more than the professor's, because as a speaker he could hardly have been bettered. Our failure was probably due to the nature of the course itself, for we were expected to bite off more from the corpus of philosophy than we could chew. So we retreated from the hard chairs in the chilly room in Bridge Street adjoining the *Whig* newspaper and relaxed in the plush seats of Du-Barry's bar near the docks, consoling ourselves that we would learn more about life there than sitting in a classroom where we hopelessly confused ourselves trying to make sense of the transcendental dialectic of Kant. We couldn't deny of course the importance of classical and modern philosophy, but reluctantly had to admit our intellectual limitations.

Much later, however, when I read Macbeath's pamphlet 'A Plea for Heretics' I learnt what this rather prim and puritanical Scottish professor stood for: the need for liberal values in the illiberal environment of Belfast.

His pamphlet is now forgotten – the fate of nearly all such pamphlets – and his *magnum opus*, *Experiments in Living*, a study of comparative ethics, may well have suffered the same fate. But perhaps Macbeath himself isn't entirely forgotten: he was one of the few professors who dared to speak out on social issues when professors were expected to keep silent and mind their own business.

JOHN BOYD, *Out of My Class*, 1985

IT IS 1.35 ON THURSDAY MORNING and my 16-year-old son gets home at last from the Limelight disco in downtown Belfast. I pour out a torrent of verbal venom until, finding a space, my son tells me to calm down – after all, it is half-term and the Limelight is comparatively safe. The danger is more than it was, I remind him. Only when I get to bed do I remember to be thankful he took a taxi home.

During break I sit with colleagues at Millfield, part of the city's further education institute. 'If I could go, I'd go now, to Spain or somewhere – my wife and I like the sun,' says a lecturer, calculating whether an early retirement package would enable him to live abroad. He has been teaching here since 1969, when rioting raged in the streets outside. Now, he says, the atmosphere is as tense as it was 20 years ago. Another stabs her finger at the *Sun*'s picture of Gerry Adams carrying the IRA man's coffin. She is outraged, and though we're from all parts of the city, no one disagrees. If anyone thinks John Hume should still be talking to Adams, they do not say so.

I seem to be the only one who does not know someone immediately affected by the killings of the past 10 days. One told of a neighbour in his eighties who rushed to help in the Shankill last Saturday: in his mind he was on campaign once more against Rommel, digging his mates out of the rubble, shouting warnings of a fresh German attack.

As I drive home in the late afternoon, I realise it is almost 30 years to the day since I arrived in Belfast from Dublin. I remember how I walked with a friend to the bottom of the Shankill Road, bought two folding iron beds for five shillings apiece and carried them two miles through the streets to our room in the Lower Ormeau Road district. In 1963 it was safe to walk anywhere at any time.

Thirty years ago Belfast still had the appearance of a great industrial city. The cranes and gantries on Queen's Island were to me both beautiful and exotic, and I was awed by the army of shipwrights pouring out of Harland and Wolff at 'dinner hour'. Sulphurous clouds from the tightly packed houses mingled with black smoke from the flax mills, which still gave employment to thousands.

In 1964 I began my first job in a school in east Belfast, my voice in the classroom intermittently drowned by a Short's aircraft on a test flight. The fathers of nearly all the boys seemed to be employed in Short's, the shipyard, the ropeworks (still the biggest in the world), British Oxygen or the Hughes Tool Company. None of them was a Catholic. Later that year I was knocked insensible when, out of idle curiosity, I wandered into the short-lived Divis Street riots. Back then, I was by no means alone in my certainty that sectarian tensions were fading into history. Many of the incoming firms employed both Catholics and Protestants; in the new housing estates there appeared to be a good deal of religious mixing; young people seemed to be united by a common enthusiasm for popular culture and the Prime Minister of Northern Ireland, Terence O'Neill, was intent on reform.

That was more than 3,000 violent deaths ago. Now, at 6.30 p.m. on Thursday 28 October 1993, I drive into the city centre with my driving licence on the dashboard ready to hand to police at the checkpoint by the City Hospital. I go through Bradbury Place and Shaftesbury Square, still bearing the scars of an IRA bomb 18 months ago; I pass the Europa Hotel, dozens of its windows boarded up, and the Grand Opera House, covered in scaffolding after a car bomb last May; and I park beside Windsor House, Belfast's tallest building, just back to normal after an 800 lb bomb in January 1992.

And yet we are not back where we were in the 1970s. Twenty years ago the city centre would have been deserted; the pubs closed early and the last bus left at 8 p.m. This evening, as every Thursday, there is late-night shopping and a good throng of people are out in Donegall Square with their Next and Marks & Spencer bags. M&S has its second busiest branch in the UK in Donegall Place.

This evening I wonder why there are so many rubbish bags outside the shops. Then I remember: there was no collection because council workers were paying their last respects to Jimmy Cameron and Mark Rodgers, murdered by the Ulster Freedom Fighters at their cleaning depot on Tuesday.

I skirt the City Hall, gleaming after a recent clean-up, to enter the Linen Hall Library. I am here for the opening of an exhibition by John McSorley, the Lisburn painter. The crowd is warm and welcoming.

In 1983 Padraig O'Malley, the American political scientist, described Belfast as 'ugly and sore to the eye, the will to go on gone ... a modern wasteland'. The following year, an *Observer* correspondent went so far as to compare the city to 'Berlin after a thousand-bomber raid'. Yet even as these impressions were being written, the transformation of Belfast had begun.

I see it as I walk back to my car: flower tubs, rows of trees, new paving and modern lamp standards adorn the main streets. Almost every British multiple store has a branch here. Of course, there are too many 'To Let' signs, but probably not as many in proportion as I saw last month in Manchester.

My car is parked opposite the Ulster Hall. Here in 1886 Randolph

Churchill warned that Home Rule could come like a thief in the night; in 1912 Edward Carson prayed before signing the Ulster Covenant defying the will of Westminster; and in 1941 Delia Murphy sang all night to an audience marooned during a German air raid. Now there are discos, pop concerts and, every Friday night, performances by the Ulster Orchestra. A season ticket holder I know disapproves of the way audiences 'carry on something shocking', greeting visiting soloists with cheers and rapturous stamping of feet.

As I make my way home, lights are blazing where restaurants and cafés have, until tonight perhaps, been attracting plenty of custom. There seem to be more taxis about than usual, their drivers running a greater risk of murder than anyone other than the security forces. Soon I am back in my south Belfast suburb. Here middle-class Catholics, Protestants and those of no religion live amicably together. It is not so in most of Belfast.

The city has perhaps the finest public housing in the UK, but in some estates male unemployment can be as high as 80 per cent. Deprivation, hopelessness, fear and resentment combine to make the deadly cocktail that fuels the violence. It was not always so. In the nineteenth century Belfast was in the most violent corner of Ireland, but the killings then amounted to no more than a few dozen for the whole period. Between 1923 and the late 1960s Northern Ireland was so quiet that Westminster almost forgot it.

I disconcert my friends by drawing parallels with Bosnia. I listen to the late news: in another loyalist revenge shooting Rory and Gerard Cairns have been murdered in front of their sister. Belfast is nowhere near as violent as Sarajevo and the deaths – terrible though each one is – are on a small scale by comparison with the former Yugoslavia. After the past 10 days, however, who will predict with confidence that Belfast will not some day resemble the killing fields of Bosnia?

JONATHAN BARDON, *Independent*, 31 October 1993

A S THE PROSPEROUS HEAT of Belfast's economic and industrial boom waned so drastically, I believe that the city found itself increasingly incapable of supporting the size of its population. That population had been created for and by the massive spurts of rapid industrial growth of the past. A large Belfast poor was thus inevitable and the worst dispossession occurred, predictably, among the Catholic minority. A situation as inequitable as this could not have been secure for long. As a growing population fought to reap the shrinking dividends from the declining city, conflict was ultimately predictable and widespread poverty even more assured.

ROBERT McLIAM WILSON, *The Dispossessed*, 1992

THE CAR WHICH HAD BEEN SENT OVER FROM MCAULEY'S, the car hire people, was a small, shiny Fiat with less than five hundred miles on the odometer. The motorway connecting Belfast with Lurgan was well-designed and well-signposted, a high-speed autoroute which provided occasional glimpses of new factories and neat farmhouses set in well-tilled fields. It was a reminder that this part of Ireland was a part of Great Britain, its roads and public services far superior to those in the Irish Republic, less than a hundred miles to the south. Driving on this road, Dillon might be in one of the English shires. But tonight, he was reminded of what, on a normal night, he would ignore. Visible on his right, looking like a factory in the late summer's light, was the notorious prison where, under British supervision, torture had been carried out, a place where Catholic and Protestant paramilitaries, demanding to be treated as political prisoners, had refused to wear prison garb, going about draped only in blankets, walking their excrement-smeared cells like bearded Christs. It was a place where the false martyrdom of IRA hunger strikers had come to world attention, the prison the British called the Maze and the Irish Long Kesh.

BRIAN MOORE, *Lies of Silence*, 1990

FLOODS

At high tide the sea is under the city,
A natural subversive. The Farset,
Forced underground, observes no curfew,
And, sleepless in their beds, the sullen drains
Move under manholes.

Blame fall on the builders, foolish men.
This strained civility of city, sea, breaks
Yearly, snapped by native rains,
Leaving in low streets the sandbagged doors,
The furnished pavements.

FRANK ORMSBY, *A Store of Candles*, 1977

IT MAY BE SAID that the popular places of amusement in Bigotsborough are public houses and churches. When Bigotsborough is not getting converted it is getting drunk. The poorer the district the more public houses it contains. It would be difficult to throw a stone in Bigotsborough without breaking a tavern window.

JAMES DOUGLAS, *The Unpardonable Sin*, 1907

THE COMBATIVENESS OF BELFAST is equalled only by its self-assertiveness. For many the name conjures up a flushed and vehement person, with a bowler hat crammed down on his ears, who resents a slight on his town as Cyrano resented a reflection on his nose.

JAMES WINDER GOOD, Ulster and Ireland, 1919

WHEN I OPEN THE WINDOW of my top-floor study here in south Belfast I often hear rifle-fire from the Falls. I also look down on the roof of the house next door where Anthony Powell was billeted in World War Two, a minor Horace exiled to the equivalent of Dalmatia or the Black Sea coast. The goat-mascot of his regiment was also billeted next door – in the shed at the bottom of the garden.

As far as Anthony Powell was concerned, what came of the exile was one of the series of novels called *The Music of Time:* one in which the music was jangled. This one was called *The Valley of the Bones*. It cast very little light on the province to which the novelist had been exiled; none at all on the red-brick Victorian terrace where the exile was endured.

Yet if more than a quarter of a century ago Anthony Powell was sitting there next door making notes for *The Music of Time*, what did he see when he looked out of the window? Possibly, if it was winter and the leaves were off the trees, he saw the outline of the Black Mountain, dark blue or sullen green according to the atmospheric mood of the moment. A dark blue or sullen green Irish mountain, but almost certainly not an Irish mountain as I – as an inhabitant of the island of Ireland – see it. When I think of an Irish mountain, I revert to Slieve Gullion. In my private Irish world Slieve Gullion has always been an historical symbol. Years ago, when I was an Irish senator travelling at intervals from Belfast to Dublin and back again, I watched Slieve Gullion in all its moods from the windows of the train – in those days a big handsome train headed by a handsome blue locomotive. I remembered the wooded flank of Slieve Gullion long after we had roared down from the high plateau of the Meigh (once Irish-speaking) to the wide cattle-rearing central plain of Ireland and the first blue-green vistas of the Irish Sea. I think that, sub-consciously, I carried a mental picture of that wooded flank of Slieve Gullion all the way into the gracious eighteenth-century interior of Seanad Eireann, past the voluminous bronze statue of Victoria that still, in those days, guarded the entrance to the Irish Parliament.

Once, not so long ago, shots had been fired in anger in those woods – shots still echoing in 1972 under the blue or sullen green of the Black Mountain, Belfast. The shots did not begin in Belfast; they reached Belfast from the background of Irish history, all the way back to the battle of Kinsale.

DENIS IRELAND, From the Jungle of Belfast, 1973

Born
in Belfast

I was born in Belfast between the mountains and gantries
To the hooting of lost sirens and the clang of trams.

LOUIS MacNEICE, 'Carrickfergus'

In some way Belfast remains a mysterious place. Its dark
hearts lie unexplored in my cognitive map like old charts
of Africa. Terrible and dramatic crimes occur obscurely in
places one has no reason to visit and often every reason to
avoid; civilised and measured lives carry on in unremarkable streets. Belfast is an incorrigible extra parent or shady
uncle, who shaped one's life but whose doings only filter
through in news reports or rumours. If asked, large numbers of its citizens will profess to love the place. They do so
with such alacrity that you begin to suspect they don't
think you believe them. The city remains a member of the
family, from whom you might at times want desperately
to escape, but with whom there is an unbreakable bond.

ROBERT JOHNSTONE, Images of Belfast

A HAPPY BOY

This is the story of a happy boy,
born in this place while yet the century
scarce offered hint we'd not by now enjoy
a tolerant and just society
through wise congruence of our people's choices;
the path seemed clear, and only for a time

would some, deflected by ancestral voices,
posture and mouth in bigot pantomime.

The map dissolves. Familiar town decays.
No man can ever walk these ways again,
blind to the brooding of the coming storm,
and pacing towards apocalyptic days;
and yet his boyish hope was never vain;
if it seems foolish now, it still stands firm.

JOHN HEWITT, *Kites in Spring*, 1980

A PLEASANT RECOLLECTION of these early days is our going to the milking, and drinking the milk 'warm and fresh and sweet and white' drawn foaming from the cow into the lid of the can. The meadows were quite near our house on the willowy banks of the Black Staff, and were our usual afternoon and evening resort in spring and early summer. I can well remember those sunny evenings of long ago – the slanting rays illuminating the peaceful scene, the cows wading among the long grass spangled with buttercups and waving gently in the breeze, the busy milkmaids with their pails, the quiet river sparkling in the sunset glow, the willows dipping in the stream, and we little children in the midst of all this sweetness and beauty, the happiest of the happy. The picture as it rises before me makes me happy still. These lovely meadows are all built over now, and bustling crowds hurry along the streets.

ELIZABETH THOMSON KING, *Lord Kelvin's Early Home*, 1909

FROM DONEGALL SQUARE, Wellington Place brings one to another building which is the subject of some controversy. This is the Royal Belfast Academical Institution, a sober Georgian building, rather spoilt by the fact that the governors of the school leased part of their grounds for the erection of a large technical college which is built in an inappropriately contrasting style. 'Inst.', however, retains a certain appearance of Georgian distinction, though it is rather a bleak building of its kind and has been compared by an unfriendly critic to a bonded store. Although this is an old part of the town, some of the adjacent buildings are relatively new. So countrified was the district round 'Inst.' that when my grandmother was a small child she got lost one day in a field of tall corn near the present site of the Great Northern Railway Station. In a house opposite 'Inst.' was born in 1824 William Thomson, later Lord Kelvin, the great physicist. He must be one of the very few great men whose birthplace has been indicated by his name on a neon sign; for his birthplace became converted into a cinema theatre called after him. Similarly, as the centre of the city became mainly a business area and population moved outwards to new suburbs, Sir Samuel Ferguson's birthplace became a hat shop.

HUGH SHEARMAN, Ulster, 1949

BALLYHACKAMORE

Only a step from childhood –
My mother crippled with baskets
Myself leafing *The Magnet*
Only a stoned crow's
Fright from the trees in Stringer's Field
Alight with the flash of trams
On the Upper Newtownards Road –

For Ballyhackamore
And the cottages
Still a townland
Went on regarding

Paddy Lambe's and its sawdust
Smart's Butchery with its sawdust
And the church with the iron bell –

Myself reading before eating:
It was the shop at the corner
Of Earlswood Road where my pennies
Tilled an exchange at noon
On Saturdays when Billy-Bunter-full
I stumbled home like the local drunk
Reluctant for the meal, head down –

I remember in my pram
A hard stare at me
I remember falling under
A dog's aggression –

I remember myself at school
Pee on the floor and the smell
Of rubbers and rulers and pine
Desks and sand in boxes,

And the clean
Plasticine smell of the teacher, blue trams
Flashing past windows and
The big boys who told you
Forbidden things –

Ballyhackamore:
Later my grief,
And my pocketed love.

ROY McFADDEN, Collected Poems (1943–1995), 1996

SCHOOL. The school stood on a main thoroughfare in Belfast, with the statue of a famous Presbyterian divine overshadowing its railings. Outstanding memory, the heating system. Hot air was delivered into the classrooms through huge pipes, and a dart cleverly thrown at the vent-holes would turn and sail above the heads of the class, descending from the most unexpected quarters – even, on red-letter days, from behind the master's desk.

Item. The playground was extremely muddy and covered with brickbats.

DENIS IRELAND, From the Irish Shore, 1936

DR COOKE WAS BY FAR the most popular Protestant clergyman in the north of Ireland; and he was one of the staunchest opponents of Rome. He was a noble-looking old man when I was a boy, and he died before I was old enough to appreciate a sermon lasting longer than forty-five minutes. In his day he was, I believe, a fine preacher, though, of course, there were people who called him rabid. He greatly distinguished himself some time in the forties – or perhaps it was the thirties – by a controversy which he had with Daniel O'Connell on some thoroughly controversial subject – it may have been 'Catholic Emancipation'. And there was no true Presbyterian in Ulster that was not ready to affirm that he did not leave O'Connell a leg to stand on. But the pamphlet which was published by his authority and was supposed to embody the eloquence that had swept the most brilliant debater in the Kingdom off the platform, made me feel that if the Presbyterian champion was able to accomplish his purpose by such an effort as that which was attributed to him, the Irish Liberator must have been in a singularly yielding mood. Dr Cooke got his statue within eight years of his death. The town in 1876 was singularly deficient in sites for statues to its eminent citizens, and the only way that the admirers of Dr Cooke could manage to get his memorial a place was by removing a statue that had occupied the most eligible position for twenty years: it represented a son of the Marquis of Donegall, whose courtesy title was Earl of Belfast. He had once been extremely popular in Ulster, but no one could be so unreasonable as to expect that his effigy would be allowed to block the way when Dr Cooke was coming along. So the poor young earl was unostentatiously removed to obscurity, and a procession of Orangemen a mile and a half long marched to the laying of the foundation stone of the great champion of the Institution. For several years the statue of the Earl was lost; but I believe that it was discovered, after some inquiry had been made, and given house room in the entrance hall to some public building. But the indignity done to it has been amply revenged; for no one knows anything of the statue of Dr Cooke; but if you ask for 'The Black Man', you will not find anyone in the city who cannot direct you to it – unless, indeed, Belfast has found a more stalwart hero still to occupy the site of honour, *vice* 'The Black Man', deposed.

F. FRANKFORT MOORE, *The Truth About Ulster*, 1914

NOBODY EVER CALLED IT the Royal Academical Institution. We called it 'Inst.' and worshipped it. You may think it unnatural in a boy without any great devotion to learning to look forward in this fashion to passing within the gates of an academical institution. But even the gates of learning have allurements for the inexperienced if within them heroic footballers subject themselves to the tyranny of masters. For years I had idolised the Inst. football team. For years I had regarded it as one of the dark hours of the spring if they were worsted in the fight for the Schools' Cup by the Methodist College. Long before I went to Inst. we small boys had already sorted ourselves under opposing loyalties, the one side jibing at the other as 'Methody gorbs', and the others retorting on us as 'Inst. skinnies'. You would have understood *Romeo and Juliet* better had you but seen a few novitiate Methody gorbs meeting a few novitiate Inst. skinnies and exchanging insults on the pavements, each side refusing the wall to the other.

No wonder, then, that, years before going to the school, I had already bought a yellow and black football jersey, and worn it, like an impostor, on lesser fields. It was from these colours that we became known to the vulgar by our other name of 'Inst. wasps'. To be an Inst. wasp seemed to me to be somthing finer than going on a Crusade. All the great men of the world were Inst. wasps.

ROBERT LYND, *The Orange Tree*, 1926

READING

I learned to use the Public Library,
that red-brick haven which Carnegie built.
In bed, at table, I read avidly,
for in our house there was no blame or guilt
because 'you stuck your nose in some old book'.
Upstairs the landing held a well-filled case,
and when my books were read I'd often poke
through those my parents scattered round the place.

I borrowed *Coral Island*, Ballantine,
but thought far more of Henty and Jules Verne,
loved Haggard, Conan Doyle and Stevenson;
but always prose; I never scanned a line
of any poem I had not to learn
save *Hiawatha*, that excepted one.

JOHN HEWITT, Kites in Spring, 1980

THE CONDUCTOR PUNCHES OUT the pink tuppeny ticket of Belfast Corporation Transport. Usually, I'd climb into the smoke-fogged Upper Saloon and occupy its front seat and pretend to drive, revolving my imaginary wheel and gazing down into the stream of Fords and Humbers, bikes, milk-carts, brewers' drays, linen emporia vans and mineral water lorries. The desultory red of an Inglis' bread-van, the yellow of a Hughes', illuminated the occasion. I'd float proud and high above it all, looking spaceman-like at these familiar Dinky aliens.

Or sometimes, going on down-town expeditions with my mother, we would take the lower Saloon, her faint rouge mingling with the red upholstered leather aroma. She would lean into me as the bus curved down the road, past Lemon Street and Peel Street, past Alma, Omar, Balaclava Street, until we disembarked at Castle Junction. Coming up to Christmas, four o'clock was nearly dark, and Royal Avenue was lit by tall, spaced lightpoles bearing glassy orchids of electric sapphire blue. The massive clock above the Bank Buildings shone like a Roman-numeralled moon. Snow and tinsel glittered in the shop windows. Salt crystals crackled under our feet.

CIARAN CARSON, The Star Factory, 1997

MOST OF OUR FRIENDS REMAINED in Belfast and it was a relief for us to leave the isolation of Ballymacash for weekend visits to

Ballymacarrett where my mother-in-law lived. The fresh air of the country was all very well but I could get too much of it and was glad to return to the stale air of the city. I was city-born and city-bred and more at home there. And I felt completely at home in the McCune house in Madrid Street, off Templemore Avenue, for Baskin Street, where I was born, and Chatsworth Street, where I had spent my childhood, were only a couple of hundred yards away. I circled round them like a homing pigeon. But my home ground had been battered by German bombs; worst of all, as far as I was concerned, was the destruction of Templemore Avenue public library. When I looked at the shell of the building where I had spent so much of my childhood and youth making literary discoveries, from the adventure tales of G.A. Henty to the masterpieces of Thomas Hardy, I felt that at last I had tangible proof of the barbarism of the Nazis, proof that shocked me more than their infamous burning of the books in Berlin.

JOHN BOYD, *The Middle of My Journey*, 1990

IT WAS THE BLITZ OF 1941 that chased us from our first north Belfast home in Baltic Avenue. The street had a pub, the Hole in the Wall, and – directly opposite, almost hidden from view by an air-raid shelter – an off-licence, Baltic Wine Stores, which dispensed whiskey in whatever receptacle the customer cared to produce. Beyond these modest Bacchic temples lay the Waterworks, across Antrim Road. The Waterworks provided much of Belfast with drinking water, but the Luftwaffe, knowing from their intelligence maps that they were bombing the *Wasserwerk*, and not the *Schiffswerft* of Harland & Wolff or the *Flugzeugwerk* of Short & Harland, let fly anyway on the buildings near by. Houses across the street from us were destroyed. When I drove down Baltic Avenue not long ago, the bombed site had been reoccupied by an electricity substation. A steel-mesh cage protected the Hole in the Wall from paramilitary ground attack. The Waterworks, partially filled in, was no longer a reservoir, but a park where old gentlemen took their ease.

Bits of memory flew at me like shrapnel: air-raid sirens, the growl of planes and the detonation of their cargoes; searchlights silvering a barrage balloon in the turbulent night sky; my father's flashlight finding Brendan's potty as we cowered beneath the stairs; a frantic banging on the front door and soldiers escorting us to the air-raid shelter. On the way there, Colm, clutched in the arms of a fire warden, pointed excitedly to an unexploded incendiary bomb beneath a waiting ambulance. In the shelter's fetid and fearful air, neighbours said rosaries aloud, over and over again, numbing the mind for the operation on the soul. To address the stomach, slices of dry soda-bread were passed around, though I cannot imagine anyone feeling hunger at such a time. In the yellow glow of candlelight, I was aware of my mother nursing an imperturbable Brendan and Colm's face all tightened up, despite the praise being heaped upon him for spotting the fire-bomb. I cannot remember if I was scared or exhilarated. Perhaps I was in shock. But in monitoring others I was, it seems reasonable to assume, seeking evidence – from flickering facial expressions, vocal cadences and nervous responses – that all was not as bad as it seemed. Mrs Keaney, whose husband owned Baltic Wine Stores, produced a whiskey bottle containing (to my father's profound disappointment) Holy Water, which she sprinkled over us all; a final ablution to prepare us, perhaps, for the blast heavenwards. When the siren confirmed the 'All Clear', I stood beside Colm, our day clothes over our pyjamas, both of us shivering in the acrid night, queuing for the bus that would remove us from the street for ever.

CAL McCRYSTAL, *Reflections on a Quiet Rebel*, 1997

THE WAR WAS THE CENTREPIECE IN OUR UPBRINGING. Its effects on the Belfast of my boyhood were clear. Behind our house, the Brickies – a derelict site; above us, the deserted US Army installation – a warren of outhouses and garages; away below us, *Prefabs* which housed hundreds of families whose homes had been destroyed when Belfast was blitzed in 1941.

And the stories of my great grandmother sitting through the Blitz under the stairs, giving out to the Jerries as an unexploded bomb lodged in the back wall; my grandmother working in an ammunitions factory, ducking IRA bullets; my mother's romance with a touring Army bandsman, and the men you could see and hear throughout the fifties and sixties, on the buses late at night, or stumbling home of an evening, regimental blazers and grey flannels, talking away to themselves or to their indignant yet knowing wives.

GERALD DAWE, *The Rest Is History*, 1998

WITH ITS DOZENS OF LITTLE SHOPS and the Regal Cinema where entrance to the front stalls cost threepence the Lisburn Road became my hinterland. The cinema was demolished not so long ago, and many of the shops have now been transformed into Chinese restaurants and fast food take-aways. But the rows of back-to-back houses remain, the homes of Herbie Smith, John McCluskey, Norman Hamilton, Sally Patterson, John Boland, Alan Gray, Helen Ferguson, Norma Gamble.

MICHAEL LONGLEY, *Tuppeny Stung*, 1994

MY AUNT JANE

My Aunt Jane, she called me in,
She gave me tuck outa her wee tin,
Half a bap, with sugar on the top,
And three black lumps, outa her wee shop.

My Aunt Jane, she's awful smart,
She bakes wee rings in an apple tart.
And when Hallowe'en comes round,
Fornenst that tart I'm always found.

My Aunt Jane has a bell on the door,
A big stone step, and a clean swept floor,
Candy apples, hard green pears,
Conversation lozengers.

ANONYMOUS

IN THOSE EARLY DAYS Belfast was rather like a large market town. Very early in the morning the market carts laden with country produce – butter, eggs and vegetables – clattered noisily over the cobble stones or the square sets into the sleeping city. To a small boy who loved the open air, this proximity to the country made Belfast a very desirable place to live in, for within a few minutes' walk it was literally open country. We had only to walk down Ulsterville Avenue to reach a little rise which we named for some reason Poverty Peak.

It looked across a wide stretch of the bog meadows where, a few years later, I made a drawing of a group of poplars mirrored in the bog water and where I reached my first magpie's nest after nearly breaking my neck. From this point I could see over the bog (for it really was a bog), over the upward sweep of Colin Mountain and the Cave Hill with its Napoleonic profile.

Directly opposite our modest house stood Queen's College, later to become the Queen's University, with its pleasant lawns shaded by chestnut trees: these I fancy had been badly planted because they never seemed to grow any bigger. Beyond this open space was the Botanic Gardens, a pleasant place to stroll in with its trees, glass houses, and ornamental lake. We had access, because my father was a subscriber to its upkeep. The Botanic Gardens was also a stopping place for the new horse trams. Hard by the gate and shaded by some fine elm trees, and as if to shame the arrogance and flamboyance of the Gardens with its top hatted and goldlaced commissionaire flaunting his medals and stripes from the Zulu war, stood a little cottage, tumble-down and disreputable. Cocks and hens strutted round it and there were geese in the yard, a haystack and a strawyard close by. A man curry-combing a horse, the rattle of pails and buckets, wooden pails at that, lent a pleasant air of the country. The old farmhouse was used as livery stables which were run by a man called Dillon. His noisy family were always quarrelling savagely among themselves, to the great disgust of their neighbours who were definitely of the Malone Road class.

PAUL HENRY, *Further Reminiscences*, 1973

from BELFAST: A POEM

How shall I style thee, famed BELFAST?
(On whom let none aspersions cast)
Wilt thou be styled imperial Rome?
Where wealth and splendour had their home,
Where mighty spirits loved to dwell,
Till super'bundance burst the swell,
And Fate, with dread decisive blow,
Laid Luxury and Faction low!

Or rather shall I Athens say,
Where Learning shed her milder ray,
Where Arts and Science walked apace,
The noble name of man to grace?
Or shall I thee great Tarsus call,
Where erst there dwelt th' Apostle Paul,
And where to heights of fame there grew
An Oppian and a Nestor too,
Philosophers and Poets more,
Who tower'd in scientific lore?

Whate'er yclept, all hail, sweet town!
Whose fate may every blessing crown,
Thee whom I call my *alma mater*
May no foul enemy bespatter;
Where oft I've chanced to roam at large,
Yea, even to danger's fatal verge,
And still have found each regulation
Conducive to a man's salvation,
Whose wandering spirit oft might draw
His steps beyond true Wisdom's law.

SAM LYONS, 1822

WHAT LITTLE RELIGION I HAVE SITS LIGHTLY ON ME, I am glad to say. I was not very deeply imprinted. From time to time we sat in our rented mahogany horse-box, with our name on it, in Rosemary Street Church, to see the minister emerge from a mysterious door behind his high, wide and solid pulpit, where he sat, like God, in his gown and bands, rising at intervals to preach and, at even greater length, pray. My father joined us very rarely in the horse-box. On one occasion when he did, I remember the minister expressing satisfaction, from the pulpit, at seeing him there. Sunday mornings were consecrated by my father to doing the rounds of his nursing homes, where the private patients formed, no doubt, the most lucrative part of his practice. My brother and I sometimes went sampling the rich variety of religious fare which Belfast had to offer: the Moravians who shook hands with you (which nowadays the Catholics do), or the half-built cathedral of the Episcopalians, or May Street, where the Reverend Wylie Blue, a large man with a large voice and a great deal of white hair, had a line in histrionic pulpitry with which, when not bombinating in Belfast, he used to stump the circuits of North America or Australia.

MAURICE JAMES CRAIG, *The Elephant and the Polish Question*, 1990

ALTHOUGH WE WERE FAR FROM BEING A WEALTHY FAMILY, we weathered the depression more comfortably than many of our friends and neighbours, thanks to the fact that my father had a war pension of fifteen shillings a week and a job with a modest regular wage of about thirty shillings a week. I can remember having his old army greatcoat over the bed in winter but we were much better off than other kids. We were never in our bare feet although our shoes leaked in heavy rain, and we had a set of Sunday-best clothes, unlike others who had to wear their single jersey and short pants every day until they wore out. My mother wouldn't let us go round the doors selling chopped sticks or papers, which most other kids had to do to eke out the small outdoor relief payments and help to pay the rent. Nevertheless, my mother's wedding ring and my father's Sunday suit were regularly in and out of the pawnbroker's as they struggled to make ends meet.

PADDY DEVLIN, *Straight Left*, 1993

FINALLY, and with the same suddenness as it had begun, the rioting ended. The authorities got round to erecting corrugated iron fences between the Catholic and Protestant halves of the streets.

But by now violence had seeped away from even the most belligerent.

The mean streets again became what they normally were, crawling ant heaps of people.

Bare-footed children with streaked mud on their legs or wearing big, heavy boots, began to run again in wild flurries along the pavements and up the foul back entries, kicking and banging at the bins; dogs began yapping in chorus; women placed themselves at their doors, bare arms folded across great bosoms, leaning on their mops and brushes, shouting at each other across the street; rag and bone carts came clattering over the cobbles; 'charryacters' – wooden boxes fixed on small metal wheels – squealed along the pavements; the herring-man came back shouting 'Ardglass herrings, Ardglass herrings!'; the street hobby-horses returned – 'A penny a ride or two jam jars'; then, in the evening light, the men came home from the shipyards; at nightfall, girls heavily made-up, went slinking out; later, drunken men stood singing under the lamplight; then arose the deep-night sounds, voices raised in angry inexplicable rows, the yelling and sobbing of hurt women; the wailing and girning of young children; the everlasting barking of dogs – the streets were themselves again.

And Catholic and Protestant still went on living uneasily, perforce side by side.

It was a pattern, it seemed, that nothing could change.

MAX CAULFIELD, The Black City, 1952

from AFTERLIVES

I am going home by sea
For the first time in years.
Somebody thumbs a guitar
On the dark deck, while a gull
Dreams at the masthead,
The moon-splashed waves exult.

At dawn the ship trembles, turns
In a wide arc to back
Shuddering up the grey lough
Past lightship and buoy,
Slipway and dry dock
Where a naked bulb burns;

And I step ashore in a fine rain
To a city so changed
By five years of war
I scarcely recognise

The places I grew up in,
The faces that try to explain.

But the hills are still the same
Grey-blue above Belfast.
Perhaps if I'd stayed behind
And lived it bomb by bomb
I might have grown up at last
And learnt what is meant by home.

DEREK MAHON, The Snow Party, 1975

'JESUS.' GAVIN STOPPED ON THE LANDING. 'WHAT'S THAT?'
Over the noise of footsteps and the giggling sounds of girls, a sudden cough of explosions.

'Bombs?'

'Guns,' Freddy said. 'Ack-ack, behind Cave Hill.'

'Let's get up on the roof and have a look.'

For a moment, coming up through the trap door onto the flat roof, they were blind mice, unsure in every direction. The first thing they discerned were two searchlights, circling across the semicircle of sky, intersecting, then falling, great white columns, down behind the black horizon. Tiny and sudden, flashes of light appeared on the far off hills, followed by the stammer of guns, which, like firecrackers, went off all around the perimeter of the city. Then, silence.

'Listen,' Freddy said. 'What's that? Do you hear?'

Did he? At first, Gavin could not be sure. But as he and Freddy approached the parapet of the roof, he heard it again, a disant grumble like the growl of a lion, a growl which grew to a loud, snarling roar: the sound of huge engines.

'Where are they?'

'Coming up from the Lough.'

'Going for the shipyards, I'll bet.'

The first bomb dropped. The explosion, far different from the harsh cough of the guns, preceded the faint red sheen which arose in the sky above the place of impact, then faded, leaving in the eye's retina a momentary afterimage of rooftops and church spires. The guns chattered like chickens.

'That was a bomb,' Freddy said, redundantly.

Two more explosions boomed on the far side of the city. The guns were silent. Then, beautiful, exploding with a faint pop in the sky above them, a magnesium flare floated up in the stillness, lighting the rooftops in a ghostly silver. Freddy was revealed, a few paces away from Gavin, his face uptilted, his glasses silvery opaque as they searched the sky. And in that moment, within Gavin there started an extraordinary elation, a tumult of joy. He felt like dancing a Cherokee war dance on the edge of the parapet. The world and the war had come to him at last. Tonight, in the Reichschancellery of Berlin, generals stood over illuminated maps, plotting Belfast's destruction. Hitler himself smiled in glee, watching the graphs of the planes' progress. Tonight, history had conferred the drama of war on this dull, dead town in which he had been born. And what about your parents? asked the White Angel. What about Kathy and Owen, down there in the darkness. And you. You too can be blown to smithereens.

But there, there was the joy. He had no fear: he did not care. He was actually smiling, impervious to his danger, enjoying the bombing as though it were a military tattoo, put on for his benefit.

'We'd better find some sandbags,' Freddy said. 'It looks as though they're dropping incendiaries.'

On a rooftop across the street, flames grew with startling suddenness, licking across the slates, exploding from an upper-storey window. In the reflected light of the flames, Gavin saw that Freddy seemed nervous.

'Hey, see over there.' His own voice was elated. 'Look. That one's on the Ormeau Road, I'll bet.'

'Maybe on Reverend Batshaw's house,' Freddy said. 'Go on. Blow up old Baldy Batshaw.'

The Reverend Batshaw, an archenemy of Freddy's, had once threatened to put the police on Freddy for going around with the Reverend's underage daughter.

'Do you hear me, Batshaw?' Freddy shouted. 'This is the bloody revolution, Batshaw, you praying mantis, you. It's the end of your whole bloody world. Come on, Hitler. Blow up his bloody church.'

'Yes, and blow up St Michan's,' Gavin shouted, prancing in his war dance on the roof.

'Blow up City Hall.'

'And Queen's University.'

'And Harland and Wolff's.'

'Blow up the Orange Hall.'

'And the cathedral and the dean.'

'Jesus, what a show.'

But the next bomb fell quite close. The roof shook. Gavin was thrown to his knees.

'Are you all right, Gav?'

'OK.'

'Let's find those sandbags.'

'I saw some behind you.'

A high, ominous whine sounded above them, and, instinctively, the heroes of a moment ago crouched down, hands over their necks. A second explosion shook the street, and they heard, in delicate counterpoint, the tinkling, rending smash of windows in their own building. They stood, ran to the parapet and looked over. 'Blew out every window in the place,' Freddy announced, triumphantly. 'That was close, let me tell you.'

'I wonder are all the nurses out?'

'Maybe we'd better look.'

Back down through the trapdoor to the sound of the ack-ack guns. The lights had gone out inside the building and, instead of the giggles and footsteps of ten minutes ago, there was the black silence of an empty loft.

'Hey, nursies,' Freddy shouted down the stairs. 'Nursies,' echoed back. A bomb fell. The staircase shook. 'Let's go back up,' Gavin suggested. Somehow it seemed safer on the roof than in here, in this black emptiness, knowing that bricks and marble and concrete could tumble down and bury you.

Up on the roof again, they had a clear, fire-lit view of the city. 'Flaming, by Jesus, all over the place,' as Freddy put it. 'Except here and in the Antrim Road.'

Gavin's house was in the Antrim Road.

'Blow up a few capitalists,' Freddy shouted, suddenly.

'And the Bishop of Down and Connor,' Gavin yelled.

'And Stormont Castle and Lord Carson's statue and the houses of bloody Parliament.'

'Not with a whimper, but a bang.'

They stood for a moment, drunk with the bombers' power. 'Say, Gavin, do you smell something funny?'

Smoke drifted over the parapet of the roof. 'Maybe the hospital's on fire. Let's have a look.' Gingerly, they approached the parapet. The hospital was invisible in the blackout. But two streets away, a house blazed with flames, illuminating smaller fires all along a row of working-class dwellings. The smoke, however, came from somewhere closer. They began to cough and choke. They moved to the other side of the roof. 'Hey, Freddy?'

'What?' Freddy's myopic eyes blinked and watered as he peered out across the city.

'Look down below. Do you see?'

Two floors beneath them, smoke and flames were coming from one of the windows of the Home.

'Christ, we're on fire.'

BRIAN MOORE, *The Emperor of Ice-Cream*, 1966

SLATE STREET SCHOOL

Back again. Day one. Fingers blue with cold. I joined the
lengthening queue.

Roll-call. Then inside: chalk-dust and iced milk, the smell of
   watered ink.
Roods, perches, acres, ounces, pounds, tons weighed
   imponderably in the darkening
Air. We had chanted the twelve-times table for the twelfth or
   thirteenth time
When it began to snow. Chalky numerals shimmered down; we
   crowded to the window –

These are the countless souls of purgatory, whose numbers constantly
   diminish
And increase; each flake as it brushes to the ground is yet another soul
   released.
And I am the avenging Archangel, stooping over mills and
   factories and barracks.
I will bury the dark city of Belfast forever under snow: inches,
   feet, yards, chains, miles.

CIARAN CARSON, The Irish for No, 1987

IT WAS VERY COLD IN THE PARK. I had a piercing pain in my ear because of
the wind. A tricolour hung at a jaunty angle from the top of the pensioner's bungalow, placed there by some lads. The army would take it
down tomorrow in the morning. The swings, the trees and grass banks
looked as thoroughly careworn as the surrounding streets.
   Lincoln, Leeson, Marchioness and Mary, Slate, Sorella and Ward.
   I used to name them in a skipping song.
   The park had been my playplace as a child, I used to go there in the
mornings and wait for someone to lead me across the road, to the first gate.

ANNE DEVLIN, from 'Naming the Names', The Way-Paver, 1986

NAN MOURNED A TIME when everyone she knew went home in the
evening to a small kitchen-house where the fire in the range never
went out, winter or summer. Children were bathed on Saturday nights
before its glow, in a bath that hung down from a nail in the coal-house the
rest of the week. People washed themselves at a thick brown sink in the
scullery; the water closet was out in the yard. Her father would say, 'Ten
o'clock, my girl, no later, or the door will be locked', and she would rush
out to put on lipstick before the mirror in the phone box. Four girls jostling,
giggling and sharing the same tube of Lucky Pink.

MAURICE LEITCH, Silver's City, 1981

MOIRA HAD ATTENDED ST DOMINIC'S, an excellent girls' grammar school on the Falls Road. She had eleven O levels, six of them Bs and above. That's a whole lot of O levels for a poverty-stricken, unmarried, ex-prostitute mother. Things had happened, she said. I'd learnt already that when women said 'things' they meant men happened. Men had obviously happened to Moira in a very big way. Of all the people I had met, Moira seemed the one whose situation was the most worthy of despair. Moira was well fucked into the next century. She had about half an hour before some evangelical arm of the caring state robbed her of her children. Her handful of excellence certificates wasn't going to cut much ice in the Clonard employment market. She would be caught defrauding the DSS in her tiny necessary way and the second volume of her criminal record would open.

ROBERT McLIAM WILSON, *The Dispossessed*, 1992

from VALEDICTION

See Belfast, devout and profane and hard,
Built on reclaimed mud, hammers playing in the shipyard,
Time punched with holes like a steel sheet, time
Hardening the faces, veneering with a grey and speckled rime
The faces under the shawls and caps:
This was my mother-city, these my paps.
Country of callous lava cooled to stone,
Of minute sodden haycocks, of ship-sirens' moan,
Of falling intonations – I would call you to book
I would say to you, Look;
I would say, This is what you have given me
Indifference and sentimentality
A metallic giggle, a fumbling hand,
A heart that leaps to a fife band:
Set these against your water-shafted air
Of amethyst and moonstone, the horses' feet like bells of hair
Shambling beneath the orange cart, the beer-brown spring
Guzzling between the heather, the green gush of Irish spring.

LOUIS MacNEICE (1935), *Collected Poems*, 1966

MY MOST VIVID CHILDHOOD MEMORIES relate to that house in Conway Street, one of three streets that formed an all-Catholic enclave on the Shankill Road side of the Falls. We were not really part of the Falls and by choice we were most definitely not part of the Shankill. Adjacent to the three streets was the 'back field', the traditional battleground for Catholics and Protestants. The area was one of Belfast's most dangerous sectarian flashpoints, and there was regular rioting even after what was called the 'big trouble' of the early 1920s had subsided. In my mind's eye I can still see the pockmarked pattern of bullet holes on the back wall of our bedroom. Apparently the man who lived there before us was a gunman who was always exchanging fire with the Protestants. At night when we were going to bed by candlelight you could clearly see the holes where the bullets fired at him had come in through the window and embedded themselves in the wall.

PADDY DEVLIN, Straight Left, 1993

OUR HOUSE was number forty-six Chatsworth Street, a parlour house with a kitchen and scullery at the back, a back yard with a water closet, and two bedrooms upstairs. It was known as a 'respectable' street, and the musty parlour, which was seldom used except on Sundays, was a symbol of that respectability. Unfortunately number forty-six was at the Lord Street end . . .

If we'd lived at the Templemore Avenue end father would have got a good day's sleep and, what was just as important, I'd have got peace to read and do my homework. But at the Lord Street end there was never any peace and quiet. Always neighbours gossiping, shouting and laughing; coal carts, milk carts, bread carts, carts of all kinds passing up and down; then, all day long, the out of work corner-boys in Lord Street playing football with a hanky ball, or playing a noisy game of marbles, or getting drunk on a Friday or Saturday night. Father said they were good for nothing, would neither work nor want and were always causing trouble. He told me not to go near them.

Now although our end of the street was the rowdy end I didn't mind the rowdiness all that much. At the kitchen table, where I did my homework, the noise disturbed me only because I was anxious to know what was going on outside. I was all for excitement – if a fight broke out in Lord Street I'd shut my exercise book and run outdoors without even bothering to let the ink dry or use my blotter.

JOHN BOYD, Out of My Class, 1985

JOHN HEWITT

Sports jacket, corduroys, red tie.
A voice in Belfast middle-class
Proclaims the Marxist line of '38.
A plump young man, moustached,
Defines the issue of the time.

'Some want conscription' – pause –
'But others are of military age.'
'Who's that?' I ask. Boyd whispers:
'Another John – surname's Hewitt.'

I'll pass him on Stranmillis Road.
'Hello,' he'll say, abrupt and shy,
Museum man not yet in Coventry.
One day he bids me call him John,
Asks me to his Mount Charles flat.
He's not a man who seeks
Confessions, drunk alliances,
The praise of coteries,
Lounge bar politics.

We rarely write or phone
To bridge the Irish Sea.
He and McFadden tried to break
The mould of bigotry.
Last met in '84, John bearded,
Frail, eye-troubled, stick in hand,
Snug in the *Châlet d'Or*.
We chat of friends, our craft,
The temper of the local streets.

Talk done, I watch him walk away,
Admire his stubborn gait.

ROBERT GREACEN, *Collected Poems 1944–1994*, 1995

FOR SEVERAL WEEKS IN 1971 the school was under siege by a rioting crowd from the Bone; there was a constant bombardment with bricks and stones, and the factory across the road was set on fire. Bursts of rifle fire now and then hit the old school building, and most of the windows of the classrooms in the senior corridor were smashed. This was before the army moved in; for a fortnight troops sent up to protect Finiston school slept under their Saracens in the Oldpark Road. Since then a thirty-foot-high sheet-steel-and-wire-mesh fence has been built alongside the senior playground, and windows are less frequently smashed. The school has been evacuated a dozen times because of bomb scares and excessive shooting. On these occasions, as when the rocket hit, there has been no alarm. Russell [the headmaster] has sent word down one corridor and taken it himself down the other for everyone to get to the infants' playground, behind the school. 'No panic, just an orderly retreat.' But he's of two minds as to whether forming up in the playground (at which no shots have been directed, so far) is safer than staying in the classrooms. Sometimes when firing is heard and a boy says, 'Miss, are we going to get shot?' he's told, 'You'll get shot if you don't get on with your spelling.' And they stay put.

ANTHONY BAILEY, *Acts of Union*, 1980

IN 1944, aged thirteen, I started work as a part-timer in a cardboard box factory, 'spoken for' by a lady boxmaker who Endeavoured For Christ's Sake with my Mother. For three hours daily after school (3s. 6d. per week) I was to keep the place tidy, maintain a supply of materials to the workers and do local deliveries with a two-wheeled handcart, roped between the shafts like a donkey. (Sounds wildly Dickensian, but it's the God's Truth – on many a winter's day, skidding like mad on a black icy incline, I'd have changed places with any warm, dry little chimney sweep.)

JOHN MORROW, *Northern Myths*, 1979

HE LEANT FOR A MOMENT OR TWO against the railings of the Orange Hall in Clifton Street, and looked about him with appealing eyes. 'Are you not well, son?' a woman, wearing a shawl about her head, said to him. 'I'm rightly, thank you, mem!' he answered quickly, and then walked on his way. He crossed the road at Carlisle Circus, and was almost knocked down by a tramcar coming from the Crumlin Road. 'Why the hell don't you look where you're goin', you gumph you!' the angry and startled driver shouted at him. He did not answer the driver, for he did not hear him.

ST JOHN ERVINE, *Mrs Martin's Man*, 1913

FIRST MOVEMENT

Low clouds, yellow in a mist wind
Sift on far-off Ards

134

Drift hazily . . .

I was born on such a morning
Smelling of the Bone Yards

The smoking chimneys over the slate roof tops
The wayward storm birds

And to the east where morning is, the sea
And to the west where evening is, the sea

Threatening with danger

And it would always darken suddenly.

PADRAIC FIACC, By the Black Stream, 1969

I WAS BORN IN A VILLAGE IN THE CITY OF BELFAST and I grew up in that village. I believe that nearly everybody who has lived in Belfast, or in any other large city, will discover, if he looks round and thinks about it, that the city is really divided internally into quite a number of little village communities. I am not referring to ancient survivals from the distant past, villages that have been surrounded or partially engulfed by the growth of the city, as is the case with the village of Ligoniel or the village of Ballyhackamore in Belfast. I am thinking of those distinct areas inside the city which come to have a separate, self-contained life of their own, through the common interests, activities and institutions of the people who live there. Such areas come to have much of the character of separate villages. Of course the village feeling is more vague and unprecise in those urban villages than it is in villages situated in the country; there are more people coming and going, and the more local village feeling constantly merges into the larger city outlook. Nevertheless, I feel that I was born in a village in Belfast, and I shall tell you about my village, not because it is a more important village than some of the other villages that make up the city of Belfast, but because it provides a very good example of its kind. After recognising one good example, we shall be able to discover others for ourselves, for I belive that some tendency towards this village feeling is something that we all encounter wherever human beings congregate together.

My village is the Cliftonville suburb on the north side of Belfast. Its main street and market place is the Cliftonville Road, a windy, open road, leading, as always, uncompromisingly up towards the open hills, between cheerful red brick houses and neat privet hedges, with discreet and more or less tidy gaps among some of the houses where bombs once fell. The Cliftonville Road itself is about a mile in length and it branches off from the Antrim Road, the main road running north out of Belfast, and merges into the Oldpark Road at its upper end. It is segregated from other districts by the Belfast Waterworks on one side and by a couple of sports grounds on the other. At the upper end of the Cliftonville Road, where it joins the Oldpark Road, some of us Cliftonville men feel that there is a portion of the Oldpark Road that ought really to belong to us – the piece of the road that runs from Cliftonville Circus as far as the thatched farmhouse and the place where the old sally trees stood before they were cut down in 1925 – but we are not too unreasonably aggressive in urging these irredentist claims of ours.

The growth of this village of mine is fairly recent, though it is certainly not the youngest or even one of the youngest of Belfast's many villages. About eight years ago there was no Cliftonville suburb. A little country road ran up a short distance to a remote rural place which used to be called Solitude. The oldest city houses on the Cliftonville Road were built about 1870. Since Ulster styles of architecture then lagged about forty years behind English practice, these houses have some late Regency features, with tall windows and deep cornices. In the grounds of these grave and formal old houses there are some very old trees, some of them very much older than the houses themselves. Old gardens run down behind these houses, with stables opening on to a lane at the back, like the lanes that run behind the older Dublin houses. When I was a child I used to be moved to a reverent curiosity about those mysterious old houses and their inaccessible gardens. Now I am actually living in one of them, and from where I am writing this I can look out over a formal old garden and across the tops of apple trees in blossom to large old trees beyond, with nothing at all to tell me that I am within a mile in a straight line from the very centre of a great industrial city. Inside these houses there are some very solid, old-fashioned fittings and woodwork, though the worms have got at some of them. In this house the joists under the floors run right through the house from front to rear, each a single, solid piece of timber over thirty-seven feet long, like the mast of a ship, brought in the 1860s from the Baltic provinces. And, of course, all the nails were hand-made, laboriously hammered out by a nailer.

HUGH SHEARMAN, *Ulster*, 1949

THERE WERE SEVERAL WAYS to the summit and I knew them all. There was the winding 'Sheep's Path' which led through shrubberies beloved of thrushes and past a gigantic cherry-tree which, in its season, was laden with blossom. By the wayside were little grassy glades where we learned to look out for the white rabbits which were sometimes to be seen there; and higher up beyond the beechwoods was a rugged scree where scrumptious raspberries could be picked at the cost of scratches on hands and knees. A little farther a vast amphitheatre came into view; we called it 'The Devil's Punchbowl'. Rising sheer from it were magnificent black cliffs. The caves in them had plentiful romantic associations for there were traces of their habitation by primitive man, and a subterranean passage connected two of them. Beneath a great crag was a recess in which ravens nested annually. Another path led past extensive quarries where a basalt dyke could be seen in the limestone, a geological object-lesson which stimulated a boy's imagination to visualise the terrific scene when boiling lava oozed up to create the plateau of Antrim. I dug out many fossils from an outcrop of greensand near by, and often hammered hopefully at the Liassic shale but never happened upon the ichthyosaurus which I so optimistically sought. The sight of a fine local specimen in Belfast museum always revived my hopes when they were inclined to flag.

I knew where the sundews grew in the bogs and the saxifrages in the cliffs, but the dwarf juniper which once, and only once, had been reported from these mountains eluded me. Nor was I lucky enough to happen upon the moschatel in its solitary Irish 'station' in the woods. I used to be puzzled by finding sea-pink and sea-campion on declivities amongst the heather but it was from these plants that I learned to notice how organisms adapt themselves to varying environments.

EDWARD ALLWORTHY ARMSTRONG, *Birds of the Grey Wind*, 1940

A T THIS TIME [1818] my father was engaged in building two houses in what afterwards became College Square. As soon as they were ready he let one and moved into the other; and this is the house in which my earliest personal recollections of life begin. They reach very far back into the dim past.

One winter night, when I was a little more than three and a quarter, Belfast was visited by an awful storm. Our house and the one adjoining it still stood alone, fronting the open plain with its blue encircling hills; and they were quite unsheltered from the blast, which swept down at times with tremendous force. On that dreadful night I well remember the howling of the wind, the rattling of the nursery windows, and at last the crash, when, in the midnight darkness, they were blown in, and a hurricane of wind and rain rushed fiercely into the room, and blew round about the beds. Every window in the front of the house was shattered. The kitchen, which was built out at the back, had a tall chimney of its own to carry the smoke up to the level of those of the main building. This great chimney was blown down and fell through the roof in ruins on the kitchen floor. The next day was Sunday, and I have the most distinct remembrance of my father carrying me in his arms, wrapped in a large shawl, from one darkened room to another; – for the shutters were all closely barred, and the storm was still raging, though with abated fury. First he took me to the door of the kitchen and let me see the mass of brick and slate on the floor, and bade me look up through the hole in the roof at the angry clouds scudding across the sky. Next he took me into the dining-room and showed me the mercury heaving in the tube of the barometer, telling me that the heaving was caused by the wind. Then he opened the instrument and showed me the cup of mercury in which the base of the tube was immersed.

ELIZABETH THOMSON KING, Lord Kelvin's Early Home, 1909

ENCOUNTER, NINETEEN TWENTY

Kicking a ragged ball from lamp to lamp,
in close November dusk, my head well down,
not yet aware the team had dribbled off,
I collided with a stiffly striding man.

He cursed. I stumbled, glimpsing his sharp face,
his coat brushed open and a rifle held
close to his side. That image has become
the shape of fear that waits each Irish child.

Shock sent each reeling from the light's pale cone;
in shadow since that man moves out to kill;
and I, with thumping heart, from lamp to lamp,
still race to score my sad unchallenged goal.

JOHN HEWITT, Kites in Spring, 1980

IT WAS USELESS TO LOOK AT HIS WATCH AGAIN: he had looked at it a few minutes ago. But he did. It was ten past five. No sense waiting any longer. But he did not move. There was no hope she would come now, it was far too late. But he peered from the doorway of Rosary Hall, watching each bus arrive and depart.

The sky cast a harsh, strange light as the afternoon died in a storm threat. Spatters of rain began to appear on the pavement. They grew thicker, beating on the corrugated iron roof of the hall with a noise like operatic thunder. For sure now, she would not come. But he waited.

Night fought its way up the street, isolating the street lamps. The rain died to infrequent gutter splashings. Shipyard workers came home from Queen's Island in straggles, throwing out snatches of talk about football and the dogs.

Six o'clock. Blinds were drawn in front parlours. People were eating their supper. What was the sense in waiting? His feet were cold and the shoulders of his raincoat were wet through. But a wee minute longer wouldn't make any difference. He paced a sentry beat outside the hall, watching another bus discharge its load on the corner. A woman got off, lowering a child to the pavement. She reached back to receive her parcels from the bus conductor. A tall, thin old man in a raincoat and a bowler hat hopped down, a copy of the *Belfast Telegraph* under his arm. The bus conductor touched the communication buzzer and the bus started again. And then, at the last moment, she rushed downstairs, jumping off, stumbling slightly, splashing her stockings in the gutter.

He ran across the street; she ran towards him and, running, they met, his hands catching the elbows of her grey tweed coat.

'Oh, you're here after all,' she said. 'I was sure you'd have gone.'

'No.'

'I'm awfully sorry. I telephoned your digs and your landlady said you'd gone. So I came on down, late and all.'

'Yes, yes.'

'What time is it, Dev?'

'After six.'

'Oh, that's awful. And I can only stay a few minutes. We won't really have time for a rehearsal.'

'Oh?'

'Let's have a cup of tea instead. Do you want to?'

'Yes, yes.' Hastily, he took her arm and they began to walk towards the teashop on the corner. The rain began again, a brutal shower that stung the pavements and sent people hurrying to doorways. They ran again, Mr Devine making an extra effort to reach the teashop door before her. As he jerked the handle, a little bell rang shrill and a fat woman looked up from the cash register.

Una's hair was plastered to her cheekbones, her tweed coat was sodden. When Mr Devine closed the door and took his hat off, a brimful of water dribbled to the floor. They smiled at each other.

'We're like something the tide washed up,' she said.

BRIAN MOORE, *The Feast of Lupercal*, 1958

GLENGORMLEY

'Wonders are many and none is more wonderful than man'
Who has tamed the terrier, trimmed the hedge
And grasped the principle of the watering-can.
Clothes-pegs litter the window ledge

And the long ships lie in clover. Washing lines
Shake out white linen over the chalk thanes.

Now we are safe from monsters, and the giants
Who tore up sods twelve miles by six
And hurled them out to sea to become islands
Can worry us no more. The sticks
And stones that once broke bones will not now harm
A generation of such sense and charm.

Only words hurt us now. No saint or hero,
Landing at night from the conspiring seas,
Brings dangerous tokens to the new era –
Their sad names linger in the histories.
The unreconciled, in their metaphysical pain,
Dangle from lamp-posts in the dawn rain;

And much dies with them. I should rather praise
A worldly time under this worldly sky –
The terrier-taming, garden-watering days
Those heroes pictured as they struggled through
The quick noose of their finite being. By
Necessity, if not choice, I live here too.

DEREK MAHON (1968), *Poems 1962–1978*, 1979

THEN THERE WAS THE CAPTAIN. He haunted High Street for the most part, walking up and down with a cudgelly looking stick in his hand, and seeming to be searching for something or someone. At intervals he would throw up both his arms and utter a loud and dismal cry. This man did not frighten me as some of the mentally bereft did. I thought him a romantic figure because of his history, as it was told to me by my relatives, though whether the history was true or false I do not know. The Captain – I never knew his name – had been on the bridge of his ship in a storm when his wife and child were washed overboard and drowned before his eyes. The calamity destroyed his mind. That was the story, and I never saw the unfortunate man without imagining that when he threw his arms up and uttered his terrible forlorn howl, his eyes were full of that frightful vision.

There were, of course, people who were not oddities at all, in any of the senses I have described, but who somehow excited derision in all they met. There was a man in Belfast then who could not appear in any street without instantly causing every boy within sight to shout Choke-the-Ducks at him. I have seen him in a fearful frenzy with the baiting he received, but I cannot think of any reason why he should have been baited. He was a harmless person, innocent, I should say, of any baleful intention towards the fowls of the air; but, unluckily for him, he had only to turn a corner and encounter a 'clan' of boys to scatter them all over the street shouting hard, 'Choke-the-Ducks! Choke-the-Ducks!'

ST JOHN ERVINE, Belfast Telegraph, 1944

IT WAS THE FRIGHTFUL WINTER YARNS told at Aunt Nin's wee house that really made my kidneys suffer, for even if I had to go under pain of embarrassing myself, wild horses couldn't have dragged me outside to Aunt Nin's water closet. She didn't have a bathroom like ours, just a little shed rather haphazardly tacked on to the back of the house like an afterthought. The seat was a long wooden board with a hole cut out over the lavatory, and I only flushed it in daylight since I had to stand up on the bench and grope about in the dark for the chain.

Aunt Nin's house was perfect for winter yarns. The Belfast Corporation deemed it too expensive to convert the old houses to electricity, so Aunt Nin's was lit by little gas lamps that cast a greenish glow on everything and enhanced the tales of the supernatural. A howling wind leaving draughts in its wake could play havoc with the nerves of even the stout-hearted as those gas lamps flickered and threatened to plunge us into darkness. There were at least twenty tales involving the peculiar baying of a dog or the queer whining lament of a child 'crying out' a member of its family from this world. The teller always gave his rendition of what the actual baying or whinging sounded like. 'God have mercy, you couldn't even look at that chile crooked but she was whimpering and crying – for nothing a'tall, mind you! But the minute her mother died – that was it – not another whine out of her!' Winter yarns covered a vast spectrum of the unexplainable; they told of curses and their aftermaths, of the dreadful meaning associated with wraiths, three thumps on your wall, a picture falling off its nail without earthly reason and of warning pinches from the friendly dead that someone close was on the way out. Anytime I couldn't account for the origin of a tiny bruise, I frantically sought Grandmother's diagnosis. How she was able to tell the difference between a normal earthly bruise and a dead nip was beyond me.

And the stories they told about Creswell's would have put the wind up anybody. Long ago the dairy had been a coaching inn, and the dark deeds of treachery and murder committed there had earned Creswell's second-place standing among the few ill-omened patches of earth in Greencastle. They said that the ghosts of everybody who'd ever died a violent death in Greencastle all ended up at Creswell's. And Grandmother maintained Old Coffey lit the lamps at the dairy first so he'd never be caught there in the dark. And the few lamps he lit, she said, only assured you of seeing what you didn't want to.

These stories were prefaced with the cryptic statement, 'Now, I wasn't there, but I know them that were', which lent credence to the unholy events being related.

MARJORY ALYN, *The Sound of Anthems*, 1983

'BET YE'RE AFEARD TO GO UP THE BIG TURN!' That was the gauntlet tossed. There was nothing to be lost by the punter – no cash, no marbles, not even cigarette cards. Only the challenged could lose, and what he lost would be face. To go up the Big Turn was a test of courage, a traditional tribal ritual, sorting out the boys from the kids. The Big Turn, the entry to Glentoran Street, was a long narrow one with a couple of sharp corners. In daylight it was about two hundred yards long; at night it was about a mile long and darker than a coal mine, still and eerie enough to strike terror in a small breast. Bats, rats, ghosties and ghoulies lurked in its inkiness. When my big brother took me for a walk at nights he teased me perpetually about the menace that might well be hiding in the black surroundings.

ROWEL FRIERS, *Drawn from Life*, 1994

JOHN REA ... LIKE SIR EDWARD CARSON, was a lawyer, but a lawyer with a difference. In the vivid Irish phrase, Rea was a 'playboy', whose foible it was to see good in both political parties, and who fought for that good with a persistence that amazed no less than it confounded narrow partisans. His favourite description of himself as 'her Orthodox Presbyterian Britannic Majesty's Orange-Fenian Attorney-General for Ulster' was not only a Gargantuan mouthful of words such as his soul loved, but was strictly true to the spirit of his chequered career. From the windows of his house Green and Orange flags flew side by side; and when he was released from jail – imprisonment for contempt of Court was so much the rule with him that he appeared to plead important cases with a bag packed with necessaries for a spell behind prison bars – Nationalist and Unionist bands joined in amity to play him home.

Clifford Lloyd, the notorious resident magistrate whose exploits in Land League days out-Zaberned Zabern, was first stationed at Belfast, where naturally he came into conflict with John Rea, whose Protean political activities would have staggered a much more sympathetic guardian of the peace. One of Lloyd's first duties was to enforce the suppression of an Orange demonstration, which had been summoned to overawe a

Nationalist meeting held in Nationalist territory. Despite the proclamation the Orangemen assembled, and, headed by John Rea, strove to force their way through the ranks of the constabulary, in order, as they said, to assert the right of public meeting and free speech. A few weeks later Clifford Lloyd was called on to protect an Orange meeting against which the Nationalists had threatened reprisals. To his amazement, when the attackers appeared, John Rea, mounted on a horse and carrying a green flag, led them into action. The third encounter between the two took place in a Belfast theatre, where Rea, rising between the acts, pointed out Clifford Lloyd to the mob in the gallery, and denounced him with such eloquence that the unlucky magistrate, assailed by Nationalist and Unionist partisans alike, was forced to beat a hasty retreat. Rea's originality was not confined to politics. He tramped about Belfast attended always by a couple of Irish water-spaniels, believed by some of his clients to be his familiars, and, like most men of his generation, he made Byron the god of his idolatry. When he was approaching his grand climacteric he announced his intention of swimming Bangor Bay in imitation of his hero's feat in swimming the Hellespont, and the special trains which an enterprising railway company ran to the scene were wholly insufficient to accommodate the thousands of Belfast people who were determined to witness the exploit.

JAMES WINDER GOOD, *Ulster and Ireland*, 1919

BELFAST WAS THE SCENE OF SOME WEEKS' FIGHTING ... in 1864, and then I was at a boys' school and fully capable, I thought, of appreciating the merits of the quarrel. I have since come to the conclusion that circumstances prevented my taking a perfectly unprejudiced view of the situation, the fact being that there were not half a dozen Roman Catholic boys in the school, and the first thing the Protestant majority, numbering about three hundred, learned, was to shun the others. We looked on them as curiosities, and only spoke to them now and again, as the Burney family spoke to Omai, the young South Sea Islander who had come to England with Captain Cook. We wanted to hear from them what it felt like to be a Catholic, and if they worshipped idols – which they could hardly deny – what particular idol they were worshipping at the moment the inquiry was put; and also was it true that they had to wash in Holy Water every Sunday, and did it burn like the sulphuric acid in the school laboratory. Also we wanted to know why it was a sin to eat meat on a Friday, and if they had ever been told by anyone competent to pronounce an opinion that they would all go to hell? These innocent inquiries were constantly being put to the Roman Catholic boys during school hours, and I have since thought that we expected too much information from them, and that some of our questions were of too intimate a character to be strictly polite; at any rate, I know that we invariably cut the Catholics when we met in the street; and the general idea that prevailed through the town was that it was a pity that the terms of the foundation of the school were so loosely worded as to admit of Roman Catholics being 'on the strength'. The founder was, however, a man of a broad mind, and it was his aim in etablishing the school to bring about a more friendly feeling between Protestants and Romanists than existed in his day, which was early in the nineteenth century. It is greatly to be feared that his intelligent ambition was not realised. It is said that the pall-bearers at his funeral were three Protestants and three Roman Catholics; but I doubt very much if the *rapprochement* between the two denominations survived the discharge of the melancholy duty. Be that as it may, so far from creating a good feeling between the younger generation of Protestants and Romanists, the school seems to me, looking back at the years I spent within its walls, to have contributed largely to the widening of the breach between the two, though I am quite certain that the masters – who, by the way, were all Protestants and Presbyterians – treated the boys with perfect equality.

F. FRANKFORT MOORE, *The Truth About Ulster*, 1914

AFTER THE FIRE

After a night when sky was lit with fire,
we wandered down familiar Agnes Street,
and at each side street corner we would meet
the frequent public houses, each a pyre
of smoking rafters, charred, the floors a mass
of smouldering debris, sideboard, table, bed,
smashed counters, empty bottles, shards of glass,
the Catholic landlord and his family fled.

I walked that day with Willie Morrissey;
while I still feared all priests he was my friend.
Though clearly in the wrong, I would defend
his right to his own dark mythology.
You must give freedom if you would be free,
for only friendship matters in the end.

JOHN HEWITT, *Kites in Spring*, 1980

AND AS I AM AN IRISHMAN, so are the others of my kind up here in Belfast, and I am a Sandy Row-born Protestant, who passed through all the normal organisations of my kind, including membership of the Special

Constabulary. Our advice to the Roman Catholic politicians in the north, who are so insistent that they speak for the nationalists, would be to go out on to the highways and byways of Ireland and paint on all the dead walls a truth that is yet hidden from the people. That Belfast is an Irish city: that the Protestants of Belfast are as Irish as the Catholics. The shock might help the nationalists, north and south, to grow up and realise that the country has a minority problem, which is religious not racial in character, however much British interference in the matter has made it an issue between the two countries.

THOMAS CARNDUFF (1954), *Life and Writings*, 1994

from OUL' KATE IN HEAVEN

Oul' Kate was a washer till her trade
In a laundry in Bedford Street,
Day in, day out, stooped over her tub,
She worked till she died on her feet.

Nigh sixty years she had rubbed and scrubbed,
She was bent and twisted and grey,
And the day they stretched her out for her grave
Was her first holiday.

'A body must work if a body would live'
Was a wise word she often said;
She took her first rest in a coffin of deal,
For a body can't work that's dead.

A decent, quiet old soul was Kate,
So, when she found her way
Up the steep road to the Heavenly Gate,
Saint Peter had naught to say.

He drew the bolts and he loosed the bars,
And he swung the great gates wide;
Oul' Kate she swithered a minute or two
Before she slipped inside.

Then, with a welcoming grace to her
Came golden angels three,
'Now what is your will, Oul' Kate?' they asked.
Said Kate, 'Just let me be.

'Just let me be for a bit,' she said,
'It's awful quare an' strange,
For till this from Sandy Row, Belfast,
I can tell ye's a tar'ble change.

'Just let me be till I get my breath,
An' mebbe I'll settle down,
For here is so shiny and bright,' said she,
'An' Belfast's a smoky town.'

RICHARD ROWLEY, *The Old Gods*, 1925

OUR FIRST TOPIC IN HISTORY was England from 1066. In literature we read Kipling, the bard of imperialism, while geography beyond the British Isles concentrated not on Europe but the countries of the Commonwealth. It was not until the later years that we came to Irish history (which was soon enough, as it was an incomprehensible tangle of warring factions) and Irish literature – Yeats, O'Casey, Synge and Frank O'Connor: plenty about Dublin and the West of Ireland, nothing about Belfast. Our education confirmed a suspicion gained elsewhere that our state and our home town were not suitable topics for study. History happened elsewhere, in London or the streets of Dublin, and Lord Brookeborough and his party of upper-class Ulster Tories saw to it that it kept well away from Stormont. The effect was to stimulate a distaste for our people and place along with a recalcitrant and contradictory pride.

ROBERT JOHNSTONE, *Images of Belfast*, 1983

NOR IS THE BELFAST MAN'S 'guid conceit' of himself merely a piece of arrogance. He is conscious of having created something unique of its kind in Ireland, and any attempt to belittle that achievement brings him into the field, horse, foot, and artillery, ready and panting for battle. Strange as it may seem to outsiders, the Ulsterman is firmly convinced that to have woven better linen and built bigger liners than his rivals is a proof not merely of his economic superiority but of the soundness of his politics and the truth of his religion.

JAMES WINDER GOOD, *Ulster and Ireland*, 1919

I WAS BORN IN BELFAST and brought up to believe that, like St Paul, I am a citizen of no mean city. I am still of that opinion, though my experiences of men and cities has taught me that the rest of the world has not nearly such a high opinion of Belfast, as Belfast has of itself. Yet, even after many wanderings in other lands, I cannot help thinking that Belfast's self-confidence is justifiable and that the rest of the world is wrong in the estimate it forms of us. We used to boast and I daresay still do boast, that we possessed the largest ship-building yard, the largest spinning mill, the largest tobacco factory, and the longest rope walk in the United Kingdom, perhaps even in the world. These things are surely legitimate sources of pride. Dublin, which we despised as well as disliked, has nothing to show for itself except Guinness's Brewery, and, grievous as would be the loss of that famous drink, the world would get on better without it than it would without the ships, linen, tobacco, and rope. We also believe, and I think with justice, that we walked about our streets with an air of purpose and eager swiftness, very different from the leisurely amble of Dublin people. They, we thought, walked as men stroll who have nothing of any importance to do, and are in no hurry to do it. We were eager about our work and never had a minute to waste when getting to it. If our eagerness resulted in our hustling each other, that was simply a defect of our high qualities and a sign of business energy. If our manners were bad – and we would have admitted a certain abruptness – that was a sign of our sincerity and contempt for affectation. After all, very suave manners must be insincere and, probably, a waste of time. God had in fact given us that good conceit of ourselves for which some Scotchman is supposed to have prayed.

GEORGE A. BIRMINGHAM, *Pleasant Places*, 1934

FROM THE WINDOWS OF THE ROOM IN WHICH I AM WRITING, I look due south across the three-mile width of Belfast Lough to the little town of Holywood. There I was born, there my great-grandfather lies buried, there I shall no doubt in due season be buried myself. It is an ancient town, though there is not much sign of its antiquity today. King John spent the night there in 1210, and left a tip of 60 shillings for the sailors of a ship from Bayonne that had ferried him over the Lough from Carrickfergus. The Franciscan Monastery, which stood in the holy wood, was burned down in 1572 by the O'Neill of Clannaboy lest it furnish a refuge to Thomas Smith's expedition, of which Lieutenant Jerome Brett was a member. The big ships slide past here now, a mile and a half from my window, on their way in and out of Belfast docks.

To the east, I can see the mouth of the Lough, and beyond, on clear days, the hills of the Mull of Galloway: the nearest point of Scotland is less than thirty miles from my window. On the southern shore of the Lough is Bangor Bay. From the great monastery here, St Colombanus and his twelve companions set out in 575 as missionaries to Gaul, Germany, and

Switzerland. Into this bay, in 882, the Viking long-ships slid, burning, plundering, and murdering. In the old castle of Bangor my great-great-great-grandfather Charles Brett was born in 1758; and from Bangor quay he set out for Bordeaux, in hot pursuit of a colleague who had swindled him, in 1790. As a schoolboy, I watched the American fleet assemble there in preparation for the Normandy landings of 1944.

Closer at hand, on the northern shore of the Lough, is the grey bulk of Carrickfergus Castle, built by John de Courcy in the 1180s; besieged and captured by King John in 1210; besieged and captured by Edward Bruce in 1316; besieged and captured in 1760 by Thurot with his three French frigates. At Carrickfergus quay William III landed in 1690. Here the poet Louis MacNeice spent his childhood. The enormous chimney of the power station at Kilroot, towering over the town, stands almost on the site of the thatched house in which Jonathan Swift lived for a year in 1695.

To the south-west, beyond Sydenham airport, lie the Castlereagh hills, in a fold of which still stands Charleville, the family home of Charles Brett for fifty years at the turn of the eighteenth and nineteenth centuries. Beyond lie the steeper slopes of Slieve Croob, where many of the rebels took refuge after the battle of Ballynahinch in 1798; and, further again, visible only on clear days, the Mountains of Mourne – some forty miles away – looking down on the barony of Lecale, where my family struck its roots in Ulster three centuries ago.

At the head of the Lough lies Belfast, its skyline dominated by the Goliath cranes of the shipyard; the bulk of a supertanker fitting out; the slim flame-tipped chimney of the oil refinery; the smoke-tipped chimneys of mills, factories, and chemical works. Just visible from my window too is the Cave Hill, its escarpment overhanging the city. The notch at the summit is Mac Art's Fort, an ancient though waterless fortification. Here Henry Joy McCracken sought refuge in 1798 after the battle of Antrim, and watched, vainly, for a ship to take him to America.

I belong to all I see from my window: and, in the same sense, it belongs to me. Has any republican the right to take from me my share in this heritage of Ulster? Has any loyalist the right to take from me my share in this heritage of Ireland?

C.E.B. BRETT, *Long Shadows Cast Before*, 1978

Linen Town,
Titanic Town

I am a good old working man,
Each day I carry a wee tin can,
A large penny bap and a clipe of ham,
I am a good old working man.

ANONYMOUS, 'The Wee Falorie Man'

... But the sheet was Irish linen.

RAYMOND CALVERT,
'The Ballad of William Bloat'

I N THE TOWNLAND OF BALLYNAHATTY. Looking down from Terrace
Hill on the serpentine reaches of the Lagan above Shaw's Bridge.
Below, hidden in thick woods, beyond more bends in the Lagan,
Edenderry House, Georgian red brick fronting an ancient rath and a grove
of beech-trees, with attendant whitewashed linen mill, foundation for the
fortune of the red-brick mansion, murmuring beyond the beech grove. In
the reign of Victoria my father and mother, not long married, drove six
miles from a red-brick terrace in the political jungle of Belfast to attend a
ball in Edenderry House, down there beyond the plantation, at the bend of
the river. They drove in a four-wheeler, through the freezing winter night,
my father clutching his white gloves for the Sir Roger de Coverley and the
schottische, his feet buried in the straw on the floor. It was the golden era of
the Irish linen trade that followed the American Civil War and the blockade
of American cotton. Nursing his white gloves, feet buried in odoriferous
straw, he was on his way to become manufacturer as well as merchant, to

own a small factory in the county Armagh and hand out yarn to farmer-weavers working hand-looms in whitewashed cottages.

Yet something escaped the double-entry, the day-books recording how much yarn had been handed out to which hand-loom weaver. Yesterday, looking down from Terrace Hill at the red-brick mansion and the grove of beech-trees, I evoked Victorian ghosts dancing to nineteenth-century dance music; to-day, in bomb-blasted Belfast that looks like Ypres in the 1914–18 war, I found a *memento mori* for their way of life. It was a desolation, a vast open space, a wasteland littered with half-bricks: the site, and nothing but the site, of the towering warehouse and offices that were the pride and property of the family with the whitewashed linen mill beyond the rath and the plantation of beeches at the thickly-wooded bend of the Lagan.

DENIS IRELAND, *From the Jungle of Belfast*, 1973

THE LINEN-HALL IS AN EXTREMELY BEAUTIFUL BUILDING, and one of the handsomest walks in the vicinity of the town is in view of it, and of the new college. – This building was opened for the sale of white linen cloth in 1785, since which there has been a regular and constant market.

A. ATKINSON, *Ireland Exhibited to England*, 1823

LINEN TOWN
High Street, Belfast, 1786

It's twenty to four
By the public clock. A cloaked rider
Clops off into an entry

Coming perhaps from the Linen Hall
Or Cornmarket
Where, the civic print unfrozen,

In twelve years' time
They hanged young McCracken –
This lownecked belle and tricorned fop's

Still flourish undisturbed
By the swinging tongue of his body.
Pen and ink, water tint

Fence and fetch us in
Under bracketed tavern signs,
The edged gloom of arcades.

It's twenty to four
On one of the last afternoons
Of reasonable light.

Smell the tidal Lagan:
Take a last turn
In the tang of possibility.

SEAMUS HEANEY, Wintering Out, 1972

AND STRANGELY, by a conspiracy of history and accident and geography, the river Farset, this hidden stream, is all these things: it is the axis of the opposed Catholic Falls Road and the Protestant Shankill, as we follow it through the old Shankill Graveyard – now a municipal park – till it disappears beneath the Shankill Road and surfaces in Bombay Street (burned down in the '68 Troubles), sidles along the back of Cupar Street, following almost precisely the line of the Peace-Line, this thirty-foot-high wall of graffiticised corrugated iron, the interface, the deadline, lost in what survives of Belfast's industrial Venice – for water, after all, was power – a maze of dams, reservoirs, sluices, sinks, footbridges that I remember in my dreams as walled-in by Titanic mills, gouts of steam breaking intermittently through the grit and smog, as it sinks and surfaces finally in Millfield and then is lost in its final culvert under High Street. It remembers spindles, arms, the songs of mill-girls. It remembers nothing: no one steps in the same river twice. Or, as some wag has it, no one steps in the same river once.

CIARAN CARSON, from 'Farset', Belfast Confetti, 1989

THREE STRANDS ARE WOVEN into the human fabric of this city of linen and ropes, and indeed enter into the composition of the Province as a whole. Two strands, the English and the Scottish – most easily recognised by their surnames and by their adherence to the Episcopalian (and Methodist) and Presbyterian churches – are now united in the common bond of Protestantism and political Unionism. The third strand, more colourful and elastic than the others, is old Irish, predominantly Roman Catholic in faith and broadly speaking not reconciled to the new political regime. These diverse elements, with their differing social and religious traditions, contribute to the variety and virility of life in Belfast.

Founded as a market-town for English settlers in the early seventeenth century, Belfast inherited a Gaelic name and soon became a magnet to immigrant Scots seeking new opportunities. From the sea beaches of western Scotland were brought the cobblestones which paved its streets. Of its two major industries, linen and shipbuilding, one grew out of Ulster soil, the other out of raw materials and skills imported from England and Scotland. Despite the wide distribution of the linen industry in Northern Ireland, 85 per cent of the spindles are in Belfast. Linen gave the city its best public building, the White Linen Hall (1783), which was replaced by the more imposing City Hall in 1906. In fact few eighteenth-century buildings have survived the rapid expansion of the nineteenth and twentieth centuries; the most notable is the Charitable Institution (1771). In the early nineteenth century the town was laid out on a grid-plan which, though soon out-grown, still gives dignity to the city-centre, whose hub, 'Castle' Junction, commemorates the first English strong-point on the little Farset river which now flows under High Street. Much of this central part is built on a level floor of mud ('sleech') which was under the sea 5000 years ago, and the lough front has been steadily pushed forward by reclamation during the last two centuries. Ease of excavation and a small tidal range have helped the port, which handles nearly 90 per cent of Ulster's overseas trade. Thanks partly to unstable foundations, the city-centre has few tall buildings, but the absence of large blocks of flats is due rather to the Ulsterman's hostility towards anything that he thinks threatens his independence. The country-man's ideal – and most Belfast people are no more than a generation or two off the land – is to live 'where he cannot be overlooked'.

E. ESTYN EVANS, *Northern Ireland*, 1951

AS FOR LINEN, that is Ulster's own incomparable fabric. The fine damasks, with 400 threads to an inch, the delicate fabric still made on handlooms as when Jemmy Hope worked at Downpatrick, these are the pride of the trade; but there are the great sheets of snowy napery, or the gold-tinted cloths that delight housewives, and the white, white linen that is made for God's altar. You cannot enter Belfast without seeing its noble linen in some form, for shop after shop exhibits the white folds and ornamented pieces; while you cannot but note the smart, starched collars that Belfastmen wear when the rest of the world has grown slovenly. So much linen is displayed that you know yourself instantly in the Linen World, and you think of old-world cleanliness and austerity. The day will come, let us hope, when every Irish woman in all Ireland and the Irish world overseas will have dresses for herself and playing-clothes for her children in this excellent washable fabric.

AODH DE BLÁCAM, *The Black North*, 1938

IN MY YOUTH hacklers and roughers, doffers and carders, spinners and weavers, and the tiny tots known as 'half-timers', could be seen hurrying to the mills and factories at the peep of day. The working hours were 6 a.m. or 6.30 a.m. to 6 p.m., or 7 a.m. to 7 p.m. and on Saturday from 7 a.m. to 12.30 or 1 p.m., with intervals for breakfast and dinner. Theirs was a hard life, a brief life, and a niggard wage. Mill-hands fell easy victims to pulmonary tuberculosis – 'decline' was the name for it in the vernacular. Their vitality was sapped by the conditions under which they worked. When they fell ill, death was hovering near their uneasy pallets. To so many of them death was a happy and blessed release. Their reserve of resistance to sickness was poor. Many mills and factories were raised on their toil and sweat. If a carder got a card at 18 years her life generally terminated at 30, so extremely unhealthy was the employment. Chest diseases were rife among weavers, winders and reelers. Often mills were ill-ventilated, processes were unhealthy, and the temperature was high. Chest affections arose in a great measure from inhaling the dust and from un-sanitary conditions. Flax dust called 'Pouce' floated thick in the heated atmosphere. The moisture and temperature of the rooms frequently caused spinners to faint. Phthisis was induced or aggravated by the poor garments of spinners and doffers being soaked by the spray thrown off from the spindles and by the operatives then going out into the cold air on their homeward journey at night. Bread, tea and sugar three or four times a day was the staple diet of the mill workers. What heroic types were these humble folk! How they helped one another! In those days there was no health insurance, no old-age pension, no unemployment benefit or assistance, no workmen's compensation.

Little mites worked on a system of morning and afternoon sets, or of alternate days, and attended school in the intervals. These were the 'half-timers'. Up to the year 1893 children could be employed in factories and mills under the age of 11 years. Their race of life was often run when it had hardly begun. The wages on beginning employment were 3s. 2d. a fortnight.

T.J. CAMPBELL, *Fifty Years of Ulster 1890–1940*, 1941

THE 1920S AND 1930S, when I was growing up, were grim times in Belfast. There was little work for men. The great shipyards, then among the finest in the world, and the ancillary engineering firms in the Lagan Valley were all in chronic depression. World trade was in steep decline. No shipping orders were on the horizon. Belfast's other great industry, linen, was equally badly affected, with the mills either closing down or on half-time. One in four was out of work, and thousands of skilled and unskilled workers dug trenches in the streets for grocery chits of token value. There were no wages being earned and little actual cash around, so rent went unpaid. For a time the bailiffs were rampant, until the unemployed workers organised resistance to them.

PADDY DEVLIN, *Straight Left*, 1993

THE STREETSCAPES ARE FAMILIAR to anyone who has lived in a provincial industrial city. East Belfast in particular was defined by that industrial past since shipbuilding physically dominated the horizon. In a literal and imaginative sense the gantries, sirens, workers' houses and buses; the very sounds and sights of post-war Belfast were determined by the ups and downs of shipbuilding orders at the two great industrial sites of Harland & Wolff and Workman Clark.

GERALD DAWE, *The Rest Is History*, 1998

WHENEVER HIS SHIP TIED UP my father followed a strict ritual. As soon as he had finished wiping down the engines he came up on deck from the engine room and collected a bucket of hot water from the galley. He carried this up on to the fo'c'sle head, stepping over the two-foot-high breakwater that ran slantwise across the deck. Then he descended into the port side of the fo'c'sle, where the engine room crew had their quarters. There he undressed and scrubbed himself pink-clean.

Dressed in his shore-going navy blue suit, white shirt and black tie, he hoisted his long, seaman's bag on to his shoulder and went down the gangway, out into Whitla Street, and into Phil Maguire's pub nearby. With him usually were his pals the bo'sun and lamptrimmer. In Phil Maguire's they bevied for a couple of hours.

Around about this time, his family were in a fine state of excitement, back in Cosgrave Street. This street was built on a steep hill that looked straight down on the docks, where the ocean-going ships tied up. Often it was possible to see from our street Dad's ship move slowly into view as she berthed. Her outline was unmistakable – all the Head Line ships carried the emblem of the Ulster Steamship Company, the Red Hand of Ulster on a white shield. The funnel and hull were painted black, and the upper works were white and yellow.

The shipping news in the *Belfast Telegraph* would have alerted us the day before the ship was due in any case, but all the way across the last leg of her journey I would have been following her course. Pinned up in the reading room of the Belfast Public Library was a copy of Lloyd's *Shipping Gazette*, and the noon position of Dad's ship was there. It was only a matter, for a school kid like me, of standing on tiptoe and looking for it.

'*Dunaff Head*, noon 25 January. Bar 40, vis. 15, NW Force 3, bound Belfast', it would say, giving the ship's position. I would sit on the hot pipes in the reading room, get my atlas out of my schoolbag, and check the noon position myself.

SAM McAUGHTRY, The Sinking of the Kenbane Head, 1977

THE STITCHER

What time is that? It's strikin' four.
My God, to think there's two hours more!
The needles go leapin' along the hem,
And my eyes is dizzy wi' watchin' them.
My back aches cruel, as I lean
An' feed the cloth to the machine,
An' I hate the noise, an' I hate the toil,
An' the glarin' lights, an' the stink of oil;
An' yet, it's only strikin' four,
Two hours more, two long hours more!

Well, there's another dozen done,
An' here's another lot begun;
When these are finished there are more,
My God, it's only just struck four!
An' all day long, an' every day,
I'll sit an' stitch the same oul' way,
An' what's the good? I might ha' been
Born just a part o' my machine,
An' not livin' woman at all;
A wooden figure or a doll
Has just as much o' life as me,
Tied till a bench, an' never free.

Monday morning till Saturday,
I sit an' stitch my life away,
I work an' sleep an' draw my pay,
An' every hour I'm growin' older,
My cheek is paler, my heart is colder,
An' what have ever I done or been,
But just a hand at a sewing-machine?
The needles go leapin' along the hem,
An' my eyes is sore wi' watchin' them;

Och! every time they leap an' start,
They pierce my heart – they pierce my heart!

RICHARD ROWLEY, *City Songs and Others*, 1918

A N EVEN MORE FAMOUS PUBLIC DISASTER than that of the R101 left a small trace on my childhood memories. In about 1926 or 1927 when I was seven or eight, a man came to dinner with my parents, and at the time I remember being told that he was Mr Wilding and was a naval architect, by then, I think, living in Liverpool or it may have been Glasgow. I believe that it was not until many years later that I identified him as Edward Wilding the assistant chief designer, under Thomas Andrews, of the *Titanic*. It is, of course, possible that I remember his name because I was told at the time of the *Titanic* connexion: but I think not. My parents used to relate how my father saw her sail down Belfast Lough on her way to Southampton, and my mother saw her sail down Southampton Water on her way to Cherbourg, Queenstown and points West.

MAURICE JAMES CRAIG, *The Elephant and the Polish Question*, 1990

F ROM THE CREST OF THE HILL there was a magnificent view of the lough and the city of Belfast at its head, perennially clouded with a blue pall of smoke. Toy steamers and microscopic sailing-craft crawled over its wrinkled surface, and at night cottage windows blinked across the water to the friendly lights of passing ships, and ribbons of street lamps rambled in fantasies of diminishing, twinkling sparks into the distance. Man's artificial galaxies of stars and clustering constellations vied impudently with the milder brilliance of the heavens.

The lough, fourteen miles in length, was a great source of interest to me and I can still imagine I hear the din of the shipyards, a diffused clangour carried for miles on warm summer-morning breezes. I was a little boy when my father took me on board the *Titanic*, then the greatest ship that had ever been built, as she lay in dock. I mischievously cut off a sliver of woodwork from the gangway as a memento, though I could not know then that a few months later she would lie at the bottom of the sea, having carried fifteen hundred men, women, and children to their doom on her maiden trip. Huge paddlings of wigeon, scaup, golden-eye, and other kinds of duck were to be seen on the lough in winter, and geese sometimes appeared, but in diminishing numbers. To a boy the coming and going of the ships and birds opened glimpses of a wide and wonderful world.

EDWARD ALLWORTHY ARMSTRONG, *Birds of the Grey Wind*, 1940

ONE RECALLS A DAY, not long ago, spent most of it in tramping over the Island Works, guided by two men who had worked for many years with Andrews and who, like others we saw and thousands we did not see, held his memory almost in reverence. In and out, up and down we went, through heat and rain, over cobble stones and tram lines; now stepping on planks right down the double bottom, three hundred yards long, from which was soon to rise the *Titanic*'s successor; now crouching amongst the shores sustaining the huge bulk of another half-plated giant; now passing in silent wonder along the huge cradles and ways above which another monster stood ready for launching. Then into shop after shop in endless succession, each needing a day's journey to traverse, each wonderfully clean and order-ed, and all full of wonders. Boilers as tall as houses, shafts a boy's height in diameter, enormous propellers hanging like some monstrous sea animal in chains, turbine motors on which workmen clambered as upon a cliff, huge lathes, pneumatic hammers, and quiet slow-moving machines that dealt with cold steel, shearing it, punching it, planing it, as if it had been so much dinner cheese. Then up into the Moulding Loft, large enough for a football ground, and its floor a beautiful maze of frame lines; on through the Joiner's shops, with their tools that can do everything but speak; through the Smiths' shops, with their long rows of helmet-capped hearths, and on into the great airy building, so full of interest that one could linger in it for a week, where an army of Cabinetmakers are fashioning all kinds of ship's furniture. Then across into the Central power station, daily generating enough electricity to light Belfast. On through the fine arched Drawing hall, where the spirit of Tom Andrews seemed still to linger, and into his office where often he sat drafting those reports, so exhaustively minute, so methodical and neatly penned, which now have such pathetic and revealing interest. Lastly, after such long journeying, out to a wharf and over a great ship, full of stir and clamour, and as thronged with workmen as soon it would be with passengers.

And often, as one went, hour after hour, one kept asking, 'Had Mr Andrews knowledge of this, and this, and that?'

'Yes, of everything – he knew everything,' would be the patient answer.

SHAN F. BULLOCK, *Thomas Andrews, Shipbuilder*, 1912

WHEN THE SERIES OF ANCIENT *Belfast News-letters* begins to be available, it presents a picture of a town of merchants engaged not merely in the linen trade, but in other branches of commerce, notably the trade in salt provisions, then flourishing all over Ireland. Though Belfast had built its first Linen Hall in 1739, even 45 years later it was by no means the most important centre for the disposal of linen, being surpassed by Lurgan (which sold more than twice as much cloth), by Lisburn, and Armagh. The linen turnover of Belfast was equalled by that of Ballymena, Cootehill, Newry, and Derry.

The port of Belfast was at this time not in a state to attract traffic. There was no natural deep water near the town. The earliest extant chart shows that for three miles below the site of the present Queen's Bridge there was at most $1^1/_2$ feet of water in the Lagan at low tide. It was said that in some places a hen could cross at low water without wetting her feathers. Only vessels of low tonnage could enter, and these had to lie on the sand or mud at each tide, causing difficulty and delay in unloading. In addition, the channel was so intricate and dangerous that many captains, rather than risk running aground, preferred to anchor outside at Garmoyle or Whitehouse and discharge by lighter. However, geography was now beginning to work strongly in favour of the port.

The North of England and South of Scotland were beginning to develop industrially. Towards the end of the eighteenth century Lancashire was fast growing, Liverpool was a rising port, also Glasgow, and the increasing American trade was fostering the growth of all the Western ports of Great Britain. Belfast lay not far from the middle of this developing area and close to some of the leading cities. It was also in the midst of the linen-producing districts, which stretched, roughly speaking, through the counties of Armagh, Down, Antrim, and Londonderry. Possible rival ports were Newry, Derry, and Coleraine, but these were on the borders of the linen districts, not close to the centre. Two days' journey would convey the linen from almost any Northern weaver's door to the quays at Belfast.

D.A. CHART, *A History of Northern Ireland*, 1927

FROM ALECK ROBERTSON'S EARLIEST INFANCY he had been bred to the mill, as his father had been by his father before him. It is a small, compact building, off the Falls Road, the Robertson mill is, harbouring not more than four hundred employees. But their fame is not in Belfast alone. Many the Royal house in Europe before the war had its bride's linen from the Robertson factory. It is a small mill, as it should be, with a small door, and on a by-street is the lintel with the name 'Robert Robertson and His Son, Founded 1803'.

A queer family, these Robertsons of Belfast, very solid, very stubborn. In five generations there has been but one son to the family, and no daughters. 'The Scottish weaver-bird, laying but one egg,' some dry doctor dubbed them. So they be. They are a tall, solid dynasty, marrying toward middle age a bride as solid as themselves. Young Aleck, red-bearded and rangy, could remember his father, as tall and rangy as he, and bearded, too, as his grandfather was, both silent, speculative men, students of the Shorter Catechism, and shrewd observers of life, possessors of the trust of glossy linen. They had their duties: to mind their own business; to take care of the mill, and to make fine cloth.

'They can see the linen in the flax, they Robertsons!' a workman of theirs once boasted, and it was true.

DONN BYRNE, *from* 'Belfasters', *Changeling and Other Stories*, 1931

NARRATOR:

Outside in the roadway stood the Black Man, a statue of a Presbyterian divine who had once notably confuted the errors of Arianism. And, not a beagle's gowl away, we crossed the Falls Road. Here the Scarlet Woman reigned, and the Adversary held open court.

My mother hurried me on into no-man's-land and Smithfield, past Mr Love's shop. 'What does H-Y-G-I-E-N-E- spell?' I asked her. She took my hand and dragged me grimly on.

MOTHER:

Never you go lookin' into *that* shop, Tommy. There's nothin' but bad goes on there.

NARRATOR:

Women and girls in black shawls were streaming out of the linen-mills, the girls hurrying to get home to get out again.

VOICE:

Oh, you'd easy know a doffer
When she goes down the town
With her long yellow hair
And her ringlets hanging down,
And her rubber tied before her,
And her pickers in her hand,
You'd easy know a doffer,
She'll always get a man.
Ay, she'll always get a man, always get a man,
Oh, you'd easy know a doffer,
She'll always get a man.

NARRATOR:

A nightfall of newsboys was crying the papers over the city, as we went home.

W.R. RODGERS, *The Return Room*, 1955

As the huge façade of Greeves's Mill is washed in a Niagara of
    flame
The riot fizzles out. Still smouldering as the troops march in,
    this welcome,
Singing, dancing on the streets. Confetti drifts across the city:
Charred receipts and bills-of-lading, contracts, dockets, pay-
    slips.
The weave is set: a melt of bobbins, spindles, shuttles.

Happy days, my mother claims, the mill-girls chattering,
    linking arms.
But then, it all changed when I met your father. The flicker of a
    smile.
It lights again on this creased photograph, a weekend
    honeymoon.
She is crossing the Liffey, the indelible ink of *Dublin*
    September 1944.

CIARAN CARSON, *The Irish for No*, 1987

THE LITTLE HOUSES OF THE NEIGHBOURHOOD were kept in immaculate
condition – every floor regularly scrubbed, every pan scoured. The
gleaming fenders around the fire where the cooking was done were
examples of the elbow-grease expended. One local resident described how
the chamber pots were kept clean by regularly scouring with spirit salts.
Those who managed to carefully save what little was left over from their
small wages bought furniture and ornaments to decorate their homes.
Dove-tail cabinets, delicately engraved with inlaid wood, were very
popular, as were china dogs and brass fittings. Hire-purchase was severely
frowned upon. Everything had to be paid for over the counter, in cash.

Despite this careful outlook, a substantial amount was spent on drink.
There were plenty of public houses in the Loney, usually on the corner of
two streets to draw extra custom, Kivlahan's in Cinnamon Street,
Murphy's in English Street, Blinksin's in Albert Street and McCurry's in
Baker Street to name a few. Of course the women were totally excluded
from bars. To drink, smoke or wear too much make-up was frowned upon!

The Loney had plenty of shops, also built on the corners of streets,
supplying the neighbourhoods' needs, as well as two chemist shops in
Albert Street and Dr Kennedy's Surgery on the Grosvenor Road. It was, in
every sense, a self-sufficient community.

The Doffers went to, and returned from, work in large groups. It was quite usual to see them descending from the Mills, barefooted, 'pickers' dangling from their waists, playing mouth organs and singing.

CARMEL GALLAGHER, *All Around the Loney-O*, 1978

J UST AS THE WEARING OF THE SHAWL and going barefoot were associated with the spinners and low status, so the singing of those girls and women acquired the same significance. A weaver might sing to herself, despite noise in the weaving shop; the individual winder or warper, working where there were fewer distractions, might also now and then break out in song. But the songs were the come-all-ye variety, songs of the day – war hits were popular – and, especially in country firms, hymns. Not for the factory girls the kind of rollicking, boisterous, simple worksongs which pervaded the typical mill during working hours and before, at meal breaks, and at party times. And, when leaving the factory and walking home, the majority did not emulate the daily arm-in-arm group singing which characterised the doffers and spinners. The 'residential' weavers in one section of Belfast did not appreciate either having their hats knocked off almost daily by the passing doffers, the 'roughs' who lived 'at the other [bottom] end of the street', or the kinds of songs those young girls sang, in this case one about the 'leader' of the boisterous group, newly married:

> Sara Murray
> Was a fool,
> She married a man,
> Without a tool.

BETTY MESSENGER, *Picking Up the Linen Threads*, 1975

from MACHINERY

At fourteen years of age
I started in a laundry. The first day
A wee girl caught her han' in a calender.
I mind her unearthly scream, an' how she groaned
While the machine was stopped an' the roller raised
To let her hand out – flattened an' crushed an' bruised,
The fingers pulped together in one piece,

Smothered wi' blood. And another day
A fine wee lass wi' a lovely head o' hair

Got tangled in a beltin', an' her scalp
Near han' tore off her . . .

RICHARD ROWLEY, *Workers*, 1923

WHERE, HOWEVER, A STRICTLY UTILITARIAN AIM HAS BEEN PURSUED, as in the city's cliff-like mills and factories, one gets an impression of naked power, that if not pleasant, is markedly impressive. Only those for whom aesthetics ended with Ruskin will deny beauty to Belfast Harbour and to the miles of shipyards that line the banks of the Lagan. The intricate steel tracery of the gantries that straddle over enormous liners makes an appeal to the imagination stronger than that of crumbling mediaeval castles, and the exquisite proportions and harmonious rhythm of the whole fabric would have delighted a Greek, even if it is despised by some who rave over the fretted stonework of Gothic cathedrals.

JAMES WINDER GOOD, *Ulster and Ireland*, 1919

I SUPPOSE TO SOME BELFAST IS UGLY AND SORDID. I never found it so. I never run short of subjects with which to illustrate its industry and the beauty it has for me.

WILLIAM CONOR, quoted in Judith C. Wilson, *Conor 1861–1968*, 1981

BELFAST. WALK ON THE CASTLEREAGH HILLS. A sunny day, the city, with its red tentacles of suburbs, sprawled below on the green floor of the Lagan valley, with the dome of the City Hall and the gantries of the shipyards rearing themselves above the smoke haze. Behind all this rises the Cave Hill, evoking memories of Wolfe Tone and Napoleon, or perhaps, for twentieth-century inhabitants, only of Napoleon, since they prefer, for the most part, not to think of Tone. And yet Tone once walked those streets, as large as life – the same streets where the worthy citizens whose sons and grandsons were to become the pillars of Victorian commercialism in Ireland were carrying Republicanism to the point of parading in uniforms fashioned on those of the French Republican Guard, and celebrating the downfall of the Bastille by the waving of tricolours and the firing of cannon. But all this happened in the last decades of the eighteenth century, and with the coming of the Union in 1800, Belfast's history was changed. Tone had come to a bloody end in the Provost's prison of Dublin barracks, and Ulster Presbyterianism, perhaps by force of example, had stopped fishing in the troubled waters of the French Revolution and had become respectable; the uniforms fashioned on those of the French Republican Guard disappeared from the wardrobes of prominent merchants, and no one thought any more of firing off cannon to celebrate the fall of the Bastille – so much so that by the middle of the new century it had become impossible to tell where a Presbyterian left off and a Churchman began. At the same time steam began to replace water power in the spinning and weaving of cotton and linen, and the stage was set for the appearance of that Belfast of the nineties where I was born – a strange, tough, hybrid town, with a forest of factory chimneys on both banks of the Lagan; a town which, paradoxically enough, regularly reared (and then promptly expelled) a host of writers, artists, and unpractical 'dreamers' of all kinds, spreading them with lavish generosity over the face of the earth and not being particularly kind to them when they made any attempt to return.

DENIS IRELAND, *From the Irish Shore*, 1936

W E WENT OUT, NEXT MORNING, to Ardoyne village, to see one of the few establishments where linen is still woven by hand. A beautiful old factory it is, with the work-rooms grouped around an open court which reminded us of the Plantin-Moretus at Antwerp; and the Scotchman in charge of it took us through from top to bottom. I have forgotten how many looms there are – some thirty or forty; and it was most interesting to watch the weavers as they shot the shuttle swiftly back and forth with one hand and worked the heavy beam with the other, while with their feet they controlled the pattern. Nearly all the weavers were old men, and our guide told us it was growing more and more difficult to replace them, because hand-weaving had been so largely displaced by machine-work that it was rapidly becoming a lost art. Few young men were willing to undertake the long apprenticeship which was necessary before they could become expert weavers, and he foresaw the time when hand-weaving would cease altogether.

Then we went upstairs, where the pattern mechanism is mounted above each loom; and though I understood it, in a way, after long and careful explanation, I am quite incapable of explaining it to anybody else, except to say that the threads which run down to the loom below are governed by a lot of stiff cards laced together into a long roll, and cut with many perforations, so that the roll looks something like the music-rolls used in mechanical piano-players.

Last of all we were shown some of the finished product, and very beautiful it was, strong as iron – far stronger than machine-woven linen, for the shuttle can be thrown by hand more often to the inch than is possible by machine; and some of the patterns, too, were very lovely; one, in especial, from the Book of Kells, the interwoven Celtic ornamentation, the symbol of eternity.

Of course we talked about Home Rule, and our Scotch host, who was evidently a devoted Orangeman, was very certain Ulster would fight before she would acquiesce. If the fight went against her, he prophesied that no Protestant industry which could get out of Ireland would stay to be taxed out of existence by a Dublin Parliament, and he said that many of the great factories had already secured options on English sites, and were prepared to move at any time.

I remarked that it seemed to me the wiser plan would be to wait and see how Home Rule worked before plunging into revolution; then, if it was found that Ulster was really oppressed, it would be time enough for her army to take the field. And I told him something of what I had seen and heard in the south and west of Ireland – that, among all the people I had talked with, not one had expressed himself with any bitterness toward Ulster, and that many had said frankly that the leaders of the Irish people would be largely Protestant in the future, just as they had been in the past. But he was unconvinced, and very gloomy over the outlook.

We came away finally, and took a last look about Belfast – at the busy streets, the bright shops, the humming factories, the clattering foundries; and then the hour of departure came.

BURTON E. STEVENSON, *The Charm of Ireland*, 1915

A FINE NIGHT-EXHIBITION IN THE TOWN is that of the huge spinning-mills which surround it, and of which the thousand windows are lighted up at nightfall, and may be seen from almost all quarters of the city.

A gentleman to whom I had brought an introduction good-naturedly left his work to walk with me to one of these mills, and stated by whom he had been introduced to me to the mill-proprietor, Mr Mulholland. '*That* recommendation,' said Mr Mulholland gallantly, 'is welcome anywhere.' It was from my kind friend Mr Lever. What a privilege some men have, who can sit quietly in their studies, and make friends all the world over! . . .

There are nearly five hundred girls employed in it. They work in huge long chambers, lighted by numbers of windows, hot with steam, buzzing and humming with hundreds of thousands of whirling wheels that all take their motion from a steam-engine which lives apart in a hot cast-iron temple of its own, from which it communicates with the innumerable machines that the five hundred girls preside over. They have seemingly but to take away the work when done – the enormous monster in the cast-iron room does it all. He cards the flax, and combs it, and spins it, and beats it, and twists it; the five hundred girls stand by to feed him, or take the material from him, when he has had his will of it. There is something frightful in the vastness as in the minuteness of this power. Every thread writhes and twirls as the steam-fate orders it, – every thread, of which it would take a hundred to make the thickness of a hair.

I have seldom, I think, seen more good looks than amongst the young women employed in this place. They work for twelve hours daily, in rooms of which the heat is intolerable to a stranger; but in spite of it they look gay, stout, and healthy; nor were their forms much concealed by the very simple clothes they wear while in the mill.

The stranger will be struck by the good looks not only of these spinsters, but of almost all the young women in the streets. I never saw a town where so many women are to be met – so many and so pretty: with and without bonnets, with good figures, in neat homely shawls and dresses; the *grisettes* of Belfast are among the handsomest ornaments of it, and as good, no doubt, and irreproachable in morals as their sisters in the rest of Ireland.

WILLIAM MAKEPEACE THACKERAY, *The Irish Sketch Book*, 1842

The hand-loom turns to lumber and the wheel
Becomes a thing to win a tourist's glance
When far from field and bird the factories rise,
A myriad spindles and a maze of looms
Cradled within four walls. On every side
Thin streets of small brick houses spawn and sprawl
Though none could give its neighbour elbow-room.
Sleep flies each morning at the siren's shout
And women hurry, shapeless in their shawls,
In multitudes made nameless, to the mill,
Some young, some old, and many great with child:
All wage slaves of the new industrial age,
All temple vestals of the linen god.
Some will put off their shoes from off their feet
And barefoot serve the spindles all day long,
Some will keep constant vigil where the looms
Like giant nightmare spiders pounce and crawl
With spider skill across the tethered web
While captive shuttles darting to and fro
Will weave, not hare and hounds, but shamrock sprays
To tempt nostalgic exiles. None may rest
Till day ends and the siren sets them free.
Even the children, sad as wilting flowers
Plucked in the bud, must give their days to toil,
Their nights to weariness and never know
How morning comes with laughter to a child.

But linen prospers and the linen lords
Build fine town mansions for their families
And plan a city hall whose splendid dome
Will soar above the long lean streets and look
Beyond them to the green encircling hills.

Back and forth
Warp and woof:
Wing of angel,
Devil's hoof:

MAY MORTON, *Sung to the Spinning Wheel*, 1952

THE 'ISLAND MEN' AS THEY ARE CALLED, that is the workers in the Queen's Island Shipbuilding Yards, are men of strong character and grit. It is said that all men get like their occupations, so that one may conclude that these ship-yard workers have qualities that wear, and are iron-clad in character. The Northern Iron has entered their spirit. They are excellent men to have as friends but the very opposite as enemies; in other words they are good lovers and strong haters, and when they choose a hero, as they did Sir Edward Carson some years ago, they stop short of nothing in support of him. They sometimes distrust their Roman Catholic countrymen and blame them all for being Sinn Feiners, just as the latter in turn rank all Protestants as Orangemen. To the English reader we may say, and it should be unnecessary to say so, that all Ulstermen are not Orangemen, probably not one-tenth of the adult male population, and even if they were, there would be nothing to be ashamed of in this, for so far as I know, the moral principles of Orangeism are based on Scripture and are void of offence to any man. Moreover, these men are loyal citizens, law-abiding and worthy of respect; they are not to be judged by a very small group of followers, who, by drunkenness or brawling or perhaps ignorance, bring disgrace and discredit to the Orange cause on the 12th of July, a circumstance which is always seized on by some English journalists who make a point of slandering and traducing Ulster on every possible occasion. (It might be well, however, if all kinds of party processions were suppressed, on whatever side.) Whatever mistakes may be in this book, let us, at all consequences, be fair. The 'Island Men' are rough and ready, staunch and determined, loyal and enthusiastic, hard-working and industrious.

JAMES LOGAN, *Ulster in the X-Rays*, 1922

B Y A PLEASANT PATH I came down from the heather-scented summit of the hills and passed some of the pretty whitewashed cottages which I was to find everywhere in rural Ireland; and by a sudden transition, came among the red-brick suburbs with which the new prosperity has thickly and dingily invested the town. I joined the long straight road which leads almost from the foot of the mountain direct to Donegall Square. It was late afternoon, and the great electric trams swung jingling past, with increasing loads of passengers. It was the time when the factories were closing and letting forth their stream of workers. In the space of a few minutes the hitherto scantily peopled road had become densely thronged with a crowd of women, bare-headed, or with their brown shawls wrapped hoodwise over their heads. Most of them wore broad, heavy boots, but many, from custom, I suppose, rather than from poverty, had feet and ankles bare. There were dark women and fair women, but it was the dark type which predominated – the woman with the black hair neatly tied in a plait or hanging mattedly round her cheeks, with broad brows, with large, round, as it seemed endless eyes. Here was no looseness of feature such as is characteristic of our English factory girls; no flabby mouths, no flaunted feather in the hat, or decorative, useless shoes. It was strange to find so many faces which bore the marks of distinctive character, so many indeed which were strikingly beautiful. And one noticed that most of these poorly clad women moved with a graceful swing from their hips, with a dignity of which they were unconscious. All these people, many of rustic origin and temperament, are becoming slowly acclimatised to the industrial conditions which in England we know so well.

R.A. SCOTT-JAMES, *An Englishman in Ireland*, 1910

from BELFAST: A POEM

And shall the Muse refuse the call
From theme so fair as LINEN HALL,
Where old RESPECTABLES resort,
Reviewing many a past report;
Men of fair fame, and high degree,
From toils of common bus'ness free.
Shall the impartial mental eye
O'erlook those names which ne'er shall die,
Whose honours, truly great, can't fade,
Prime guardians of your STAPLE TRADE –
SINCLAIR, whose ancient name survives,
And fresh in countless memories lives,
For public deeds in former days,

Beyond the meed of Poet's lays –
Where FERGUSON presides; than whom
No better man e'er held his room
In country, city, church or court,
Beyond the power of bad report,
Or wicked spleen his fame to blast,
Of honest, sober, polished cast –
Where ASHMORES, STEWART, and ANDREWS join
To grace this formidable line –
Where SMYTH and STEV'NSONS and M'CANCE
The fame of Linen Trade advance –
And NELSONS, ANNESLEY, ORR, MAGEE
Aid this alert society; –
Where RUSSELS, WILLIAMSONS, and BATT
Have oft in staple council sate,
Whose honest fame and sterling worth
Are not excelled from South to North; –
Where LYONS, too, of former days,
Was cheered by Fortune's splendid rays,
And by a fair perspective sense
'Gainst tides of fate had reared a fence,
And left a name from blemish free,
An honour to posterity.
To this thy far-extended trade
An ENSOR lends his learned aid,
And HANCOCK oft his will records
In honest well-directed words.

Such, too, are men who strongly claim
The merit of your high-raised fame;
Most men whom every one admires,
Except whom spite or malice fires;
And such thy works of public use,
Which health, wealth, learning, all produce.

SAM LYONS, 1822

THE WORLD OF COMMERCE AND FINANCE was all around me from the very beginning, I suppose, but I had no understanding of it and was not really aware of its presence. To this day, however, I waken while it is still dark, sometime around four a.m., at that hour when, long ago, the Island whistles blew, and all over Belfast the tramcars started taking the

Islandmen to work. On Sunday mornings we climbed up to the top of Cave Hill and looked down at the big ships which the Islandmen were building. We were very proud of the number of great and famous ships that had been built at Harland & Wolff's in Belfast and we knew a song about it although we didn't really understand it (at least I didn't). There was a lot in it about Thor and Odin and Britannia, who seemed to be banging away on an anvil somewhere or hiding in the shadows and spying on one another. It went:

> Clang, clang, clang on the anvil
> In the smithy by the dark North Sea.
> Is it Odin that is watching in the shadows?
> Is it Thor where the sparks fly free?
> Clang, clang, clang on the anvil –
> There are stee–eel shi–ips wanted on the sea.

We knew about the need for ships, they carried cargoes back and forth across the seven seas, and our father taught us a grace:

> For what we are about to eat
> We bless and thank the British fleet.

I was also aware of the linen trade; Irish linen was familiar from my babyhood:

> When I go to bed at night
> I lay my head on linen white.
> Of linen too the snowy sheet,
> Furzy scented, cool and sweet.

ALICE KANE, *Songs and Sayings of an Ulster Childhood*, 1983

THE BALLAD OF WILLIAM BLOAT

> In a mean abode on the Shankill Road,
> Lived a man called William Bloat,
> He had a wife, the curse of his life,
> Who continually got his goat.
> So one day at dawn with her nightdress on,
> He cut her b - - - - - throat,
>
> With a razor gash he settled her hash,
> Oh never was crime so quick,
> But the steady drip on the pillow slip,

Of her lifeblood made him sick,
And the pool of gore on the bedroom floor,
Grew clotted, cold and thick.

And yet he was glad that he had done what he had,
When she lay there stiff and still
But a sudden awe of the angry law,
Struck his soul with an icy chill.
So to finish the fun so well begun,
He resolved himself to kill.

Then he took the sheet off his wife's cold feet,
And twisted it into a rope,
And he hanged himself from the pantry shelf,
Twas an easy end, let's hope,
In the face of death with his latest breath,
He solemnly cursed the Pope.

But the strangest turn to the whole concern,
Is only just beginning,
He went to H - - - but his wife got well,
And she's still alive and sinning,
For the razor blade was German made,
But the sheet was Irish linen.

RAYMOND CALVERT

APPROACH BELFAST ON A GREY MORNING by the Channel boat which steams slowly through miles of docks and shipyards, when the black bones of fleets a-building are all about you, and you will gain another impression of the sombre strength which is the mark of industrial Belfast. Every ton of metal must be imported for the building of the iron ships, and the lough was too shallow for them when the old wooden ships went out: the Belfastmen, determined to excel in this trade of human Vulcans, simply built the yards out into the deep water and made land where none had been.

Nearly the largest ship in the world has been built here, in the iron forest, to the rattle and ring of the riveting, the roaring of the blow-lamps and furnaces, the clangour of the engines at work and the strange, broken echo of human voices. At night, the flares on the tangle of girders, the glowing windows of workshops, the glare of industrial fires, make these Titanic yards mysterious and terrifying to him who has not risen with Belfast's poet to a vision of the grandeur of this dark creative work of Ulster's hands and brains.

> *Splendid the ships they build, more splendid far*
> *The hearts that dare conceive such vastness and such power.*

AODH DE BLÁCAM, The Black North, 1938

WHEN HE WAS SIXTEEN, on the 1st May, 1889, Tom left school, and as a premium apprentice entered the shipyard of Messrs Harland & Wolff. In one important respect the date of his entry may be accounted fortunate, for about that time, chiefly through the enterprise of the White Star Company in the matter of constructing a fleet of giant ships for the Atlantic service, great developments were imminent, if not already begun, in the shipping world. To a boy of sixteen, however, the change from the comforts of home and the comparative freedom of school-life to the stern discipline of the yards must have been exacting. It was work now, and plenty of it, summer and winter, day in day out, the hardest he could do at the hardest could be given him. He was to be tested to the full. With characteristic wisdom, Mr Pirrie had decided that no favour whatever was to be shown the boy on the score of relationship. By his own efforts and abilities he must make his way, profiting by no more than the inspiration of his uncle's example: and if he failed, well, that too was a way many another had gone before him.

But Tom was not of the breed that fails. He took to his work instantly and with enthusiasm. Distance from home necessitated his living through the workaday week in Belfast. Every morning he rose at ten minutes to five and was at work in the Yard punctually by six o'clock. His first three months were spent in the Joiner's shop, the next month with the Cabinet makers, the two following months working in ships. There followed two months in the Main store; then five with the Shipwrights, two in the Moulding loft, two with the Painters, eight with the iron Shipwrights, six with the Fitters, three with the Pattern-makers, eight with the Smiths. A long spell of eighteen months in the Drawing office completed his term of five years as an apprentice.

Throughout that long ordeal Tom inspired everyone who saw him, workmen, foremen, managers, and those in higher authority, as much by the force of his personal character as by his qualities of industry. Without doubt here was one destined to success. He was thorough to the smallest detail. He mastered everything with the ease of one in love with his task. We have a picture of him drawn by a comrade, in his moleskin trousers and linen jacket, and instinctively regarded by his fellow-apprentices as their leader, friend and adviser in all matters of shipyard lore and tradition.

'He was some steps ahead of me in his progress through the Yard,' the account goes on, 'so I saw him only at the breakfast and luncheon hours, but I can remember how encouraging his cheery optimism and unfailing friendship were to one who found the path at times far from easy and the demands on one's patience almost more than could be endured.'

SHAN F. BULLOCK, *Thomas Andrews, Shipbuilder*, 1912

MEN OF BELFAST

O city of sound and motion!
  O city of endless stir!
From the dawn of a misty morning,
  To the fall of the evening air;
From the night of moving shadows
  To the sound of the shipyard horn;
We hail thee Queen of the Northland,
  We who are Belfast born.

Hark to the ring of the anvil!
  Hark to the song of the loom!
And the syren-call of the steamers
  Passing the harbour boom;
The spiral curve of the smokecloud
  Weaving a hazy screen,
The rattle of horse and vehicle,
  In one un-ending stream.

We gaze from the Cavehill's summit,
  The pride in our eyes aglow
As we look on a slumberless city,
  That stretches her arms below;
The dull red glow of the sunset
  Fades in a purple haze,
And the gloom of darkened valley
  Is bright with a thousand rays.

We are the men of Belfast,
  Her sinew, marrow, and bone,
By the graft of our brain and muscle
  We fashioned for her a throne;
And people, or lord, or parson,
  Class, or creed, or clan,

It's little we care for the title,
 If they play the part of a man.

With jealousy, cant, and rancour,
 They would crush her wide-world fame;
They would damp the flame of her furnace,
 To render her commerce lame;
But her ships will traverse the ocean,
 Her sons will ply at their trade,
Till the sheen of her glory will vanish,
 And the faith of her sons shall fade.

THOMAS CARNDUFF, *Songs from the Shipyards*, 1924

M ANY OF THE BELFAST FLAX-MILLS have a linen-weaving establishment connected with them, and the two together are called a Linen-yarn factory. During the last forty years many cotton factories have also sprung up in different parts of Belfast, which now contains in all twenty-one great cotton and linen-yarn factories, some of which employ two thousand labourers, and are carried on in immense buildings eight stories high.

A great deal of the Belfast linen is still woven at hand-looms in the cottages of the peasantry, but power-loom weaving, or that of machinery, is more and more trenching on their domains. The melancholy struggle between the hand-loom and the power-loom, which in England has already terminated in favour of the latter, is still going on at Belfast.

The spinning of flax by machinery was long a difficult problem to the inventive heads of English mechanicians. This process was much more difficult than that of wool and cotton spinning, because the flax consisted of a number of long single smooth fibres, which were not so easily spun into usable materials, as the shorter and more connected threads of cotton and wool. At length it was proposed to pass the flax through warm water previous to spinning it. This process splits, curls, and entangles the fibres, which are then easily spun into a long connected thread. Thus, by warm water, the manufacturers are enabled to do without the busy and delicate hand of the spinning-girl, and one spinner can now, alas! superintend machines which do the work of fifty-four spinning-wheels at once. Thus all the merry, whirring little spinning-wheels, which once enlivened the cottage firesides of Ulster, are absorbed into a few gigantic, noisy, senseless machines, and the hundreds of snug, cozy little spinning-rooms, enlivened by the cheerful voices of the singing spinners, are turned into vast factory halls, lighted up with long rows of gas, within which the watchful eye of the inspector maintains perpetual dreary silence and cheerless activity.

J.G. KOHL, *Ireland*, 1843

from THE NORTHERN ATHENS: A SATIRICAL POEM

Where'er the stranger, wrapt in wonder, roves,
The eye fond lingers on th' excursive view,
Where Taste the soul to admiration moves,
For ever various and for ever new –
Lo! yon fine pile – the LINEN HALL – where loves
Are in its arbours form'd, and lovers coo
'Midst groves outvieing VALLAMBROSA'S groves,
And all the groves of sweet *ould* IRELAND too:
Its fine, green foliage throws a rich, deep shade,
Where bales on bales of linen overtop;
At once a store-house and a fairy glade,
The green ARCADIA and a weaver's shop;
Where lone Retirement, *urbs in rure*, roams
'Midst vistas, alcoves, traddles, webs, and thrums.

ANONYMOUS, 1826

ANNE BOYLE TELLS OF THE PEOPLE IN SANDY ROW:
'They were very poor, but enterprising and hard working. They made the mill girls tea at lunch-time for a penny, or a penny bowl of soup or a penny bowl of rice. When I worked in the Linfield mill, all I had with me was two pennies for my tram fare, so, if I bought the tea, I had to walk to or from work. People were selling things from their homes: apple pies, soda bread, hot peas, pigs' feet, candy apples, candy. There was no relief at all and people were helping themselves. It was a great thing for fellows in their teens if their mother could buy them a pony and cart to go round with fish or vegetables. I think the saddest thing was the teenage fellows; they had nothing, no hope. They were young and they wanted things.'

Leo Boyle, likewise, remembers how:

'Every street had its shoe mender. They charged a shilling, one and six, for soling. Everybody that I can think of was doing something to help their homes. I remember people going out during the snow with yard brushes on their shoulders and going to the big houses up the Antrim Road and Cliftonville Road and cleaning their snow away for a shilling. There was great jealousy among the men over this, how many houses they got in a day.'

Here we see how the 'world of work' merges with the world of the jobless – it is a grey area of part work, part unemployment.

RONNIE MUNCK and BILL ROLSTON, *Belfast in the Thirties*, 1987

Having walked to Belfast one day, and back to Donaghadee the next, we left Ireland with a fair breeze. We slept last night at Port Patrick, when I was gratified by a letter from you. On our walk in Ireland, we had too much opportunity to see the worse than nakedness, the rags, the dirt and misery of the poor common Irish. A Scotch cottage, though in that sometimes the smoke has no exit but at the door, is a palace to an Irish one. We could observe that impetuosity in Man and Woman. We had the pleasure of finding our way through a Peat-bog, three miles long at least – dreary, flat, dank, black, and spongy – here and there were poor dirty Creatures, and a few strong men cutting or carting Peat. We heard on passing into Belfast through a most wretched suburb, that most disgusting of all noises, worse than the Bagpipes – the laugh of a monkey – the chatter of women – the scream of a Macaw – I mean the sound of the Shuttle. What a tremendous difficulty is the improvement of such people. I cannot conceive how a mind 'with child' of philanthropy could grasp at its possibility – with me it is absolute despair.

At a miserable house of entertainment, half-way between Donaghadee and Belfast, were two men sitting at Whisky – one a labourer, and the other I took to be a drunken weaver – the labourer took me to be a Frenchman, and the other hinted at bounty-money; saying he was ready to take it. On calling for the letters at Port Patrick, the man snapped out 'what regiment?' On our return from Belfast we met a sedan – the Duchess of Dunghill. It is no laughing matter though. Imagine the worst dog-kennel you ever saw, placed upon two poles from a mouldy fencing. In such a wretched thing sat a squalid old woman, squat like an ape half-starved, from a scarcity of biscuit in its passage from Madagascar to the Cape, with a pipe in her mouth, and looking out with a round-eyed, skinny-lidded inanity; with a sort of horizontal idiotic movement of her head – squat and lean she sat, and puffed out the smoke, while two ragged, tattered girls carried her along. What a thing would be a history of her life and sensations; I shall endeavour when I have thought a little more, to give you my idea of the difference between the Scotch and Irish. The two Irishmen I mentioned were speaking of their treatment in England, when the weaver said – 'Ah! you were a civil man, but I was a drinker.'

Till further notice, you must direct to Inverness.

YOUR MOST AFFECTIONATE BROTHER
JOHN

JOHN KEATS, *Letters*, July 1818

AN IDYLL OF THE RED CITY
The Awakening

Do you remember how, before dawn,
We were awakened by pealing notes,
By sudden outcry as of Titan voices,
Shrill, prolonged, shrieking together?

Or like chords on a vast organ
Flinging a wild chant to heaven,
Crashed in strange varying discords,
In rare, grand harmonies.

At that sounding, that summons,
Thousands in the city rose,
Groping in darkness, stumbling,
Making ready in eager haste.

We rose not for going forth,
But to watch the slowly brightening dawn,
Its fading stars – and on wet pavements
The long shine of the lamps;

On every side descending
The roof-ridges of many streets,
The chimneys like battlements
Serrated everywhere around,

Gulfs, channels, glens of gloom,
Between cliff-like walls of buildings;
In the distance greater darkness
And confusion of shapes.

Only above the crowded town,
Roofs' lines like waves below it,
Heaving its prow among stars,
The shape of a ship.

And here and there clearly outlined,
Slender, tall, chimney towers,
No smoke from them yet,
Or freshly out-curling.

Then we watched as in every quarter
The flat-roofed mills many-windowed,
Outshining brightest constellations,
Were suddenly laced with light.

Still the notes crying, pealing
Like startled 'trumpets' before battle,
Summoning in wild alarm
The help of a host.

We heard the host then coming,
The tramp, tramp of heavy feet
Of men in dingy multitudes,
Hurrying lough-ward.

Girls, women, came in groups,
In confused swift procession,
Head-shawled, gliding without talk
Towards the light of the mills.

Then the day-sun brightening,
Showed red streets in vivid glare,
Soon emptying of that crowd,
And the summoning notes ceased.

Another sounding then,
All day I overheard it,
As I strolled idly here and there,
Or read by open window.

From behind immense, trembling walls
The live-like hum where there were spinners,
And from that ship high in air
The sound of the smiting.

ALICE MILLIGAN, *Collected Poems*, 1954

IT MUST BE MOVING, troubling, to see the 20,000 go over Queen's Bridge in the morning at eight and again in the evening at five. But at any hour of weekday or sabbath the whole great functional prospect of the shipyard offers itself touchingly and disturbingly to contemplation. It is, after all, the terrible heart and entrails of Belfast: unashamed, and unselfconscious vitals. Beautiful, admonitory, alarming; yet one can be sure it rings from eight to five with that easy, fluent chat and humour, that response to plain life which is the characteristic of Belfast. No airs and graces hereabouts – but an overflow of all the other lively parts of human nature, and, let drill and siren do their damnedest, no downing or hurrying of the casual Ulster voice, or the individual Ulster opinion.

Cold, cruel field, steel-shafted, furnaced, thundering; a place for only mechanised giants to antic in, de-humanised, one would say; yet it is wholly inhabited, filled and emptied, by ordinary flesh and blood.

KATE O'BRIEN, *My Ireland*, 1962

from ISLANDMEN

Terrible as an army with banners
The legions of labour,
The builders of ships,
Tramp thro' the winter eve.

RICHARD ROWLEY, *City of Refuge*, 1917

THE HARNESSING OF THE POWER OF THE FARSET RIVER to drive the first grist mills early in the seventeenth century was the starting point of the growth of the industrial sector which is west Belfast. It subsequently developed into a distinctive landscape of small houses, peopled by thousands of families whose lives are regulated by mills and shipyards and whose existence largely centres on and is confined by the crowded and endlessly repeated streets. West Belfast is remarkably homogeneous, physically, and even socially, in spite of a fundamental religious division.

EMRYS JONES, *A Social Geography of Belfast*, 1960

The spinner and the weaver in the mill
Now earn a living and have time to live,
Children whose mothers were half-timers once
Untouchables in factory and school
May learn to play and even play to learn
And think of spindle as a word to spell.
Mill-girls have shed their shawl-cocoons and shine
Brighter than butterflies. With gleaming hair
And ankles neat in nylon each can look
Into her mirror with a practised smile
And see herself the reigning linen queen.

The great domed hall four-square in stubborn stone
With polished marble floors magnificent
As any Rajah's palace has stood now
For nearly half a century. Strange how
The little laurel hedge that hems its lawns
Reveals we still are country-folk at heart
Deep-rooted in the fields our fathers tilled.

MAY MORTON, *Sung to the Spinning Wheel*, 1952

TIME WAS WHEN MILLFIELD, Carrick Hill (now Upper Library Street), Pound Street and the 'Loney' (Cullingtree Road) were peopled by ancient families long connected with Belfast, and when the sound of the shuttle was heard in almost every house around Peter's Hill and Sandy Row.

Fifty years ago one could walk from Balmoral Show Grounds to Dunmurry and pass only a couple of roadside houses, and so from Ardoyne to Ligoniel. No streets abutted on the Falls beyond the Springfield Road, except at Broadway. Then and much later the old Asylum stood where the Royal Victoria and the Children's Hospital stand to-day.

T.J. CAMPBELL, *Fifty Years of Ulster 1890–1940*, 1941

I WISH TO RESCUE FOR THE RECORD the local dialect of modernism, the dialect of my childhood in Belfast. That dialect has been drowned out by the Romantic tones of Irish ruralism, behind which sound occasionally the harsher tones of Irish nationalism.

But this dialect was drowned out too by a century-old educational curriculum to which I was given access as a scholarship boy when the Butler Education Act came into force in Northern Ireland after 1947 (after 1944 in Britain). My newly-minted inheritance was Matthew Arnold's mid-Victorian distinction between the sciences and the arts (the Two Cultures, as they came to be called) and his awarding of the palm to the arts. I was educated into a disdain and distaste for the scientific culture, especially the applied science culture. It was this culture to which my relatives, particularly on my father's side, belonged. Harland & Wolff, Short Bros & Harland, Musgrave's, Sirocco Works, Mackie's, Workman, Clark – names that once filled me with a kind of effete dread now, too late, ring with the sound of Larkin's metallic and rough-tongued bell. My father and uncles did a hard day's work when young, then put themselves through technical and mechanical institutes in a hard day's night. I imagined I was getting a better view of things than they: if I was, it was their shoulders I stood on to get it.

JOHN WILSON FOSTER, *The Titanic Complex*, 1997

THE POPULATION BEGAN TO GROW RAPIDLY as the spinning mills and weaving factories increased. The districts of Millfield, Carrick Hill, and the Pound were thickly populated by old families long connected with Belfast, and strangers coming amongst them were looked upon with suspicion for some time. In these localities the cock fights and dog fights generally originated. The principal occupation of the people was weaving, but many of them wrought at the production of various articles exposed for sale in the stalls of Smithfield. Ballymacarrett, Sandy Row, and Brown Square were the greatest weaving localities. The sound of the shuttle was heard almost in every house.

THOMAS GAFFIKEN, *Belfast Fifty Years Ago*, 1894

Horrid
Homesteads

... what indescribable scenes of poverty, filth, and
wretchedness everywhere meet the eye!

THE REVEREND W.M. O'HANLON

ROM THE COUNTLESS NUMBER OF HOMELESS WANDERERS that is seen
every day in the streets, but particularly in Poultry Square, every
morning, a stranger would imagine that there are no charitable
institutions in Belfast for the reception of the poor. He could not think that
we have a Workhouse and Day Asylum capable of accommodating
thousands. But we have a Workhouse and a Day Asylum, and yet the
influx of paupers in the streets is beyond parallel. The Night Asylum is the
cause of Poultry Square being so much filled with wretched creatures. When
this place opens its gates in the morning, out rush batches of the most
miserable human beings that ever breathed, and instead of separating, the
majority of them squat themselves on the pathway on each side of the
Square and remain there for hours under the heat of the sun. Old and
young, the sick and the hale, the pickpocket, the burglar, the gambler, are
all huddled together like as many inferior animals in their lairs. Hunger, or
their respective avocations, at length rouse them, and they scatter themselves
over the streets in all directions. In the evening they return again to the
Asylum and take up their places for the night. Those who cannot get
admission stop out in the cold. As many as thirty often lie on the damp
ground overnight, and they do not stir until a thorough evaporation of the
dew from their garments has been effected by the sun in the morning. Thus
does one section of the Belfast community drag out its wretched existence.
Those who reside in Poultry Square are suffering the most painful

annoyance from the poverty, disease and destitution that invariably accompany the Night Asylum.

Belfast Weekly Vindicator, 24 July 1847

B UT LET US NOW PROCEED TO CARRICK-HILL, and its adjuncts. Campbell-court, named after the proprietress, contains as thick a population as can be packed into its twenty-one houses, and is left in such a state of neglect that, as we were told by persons on the spot, its accumulated refuse, especially in warm weather, is enough to poison the whole of its inhabitants. Plunket's-court, also named after one of the owners, is the resort of miserable women and pickpockets, who find a fit asylum amid its dark and filthy receptacles. Drummond's-court, which is visited, as we learned, by the scavengers but once a-week, has two or three families, in the usual style, in each house, and sleeping often in the same apartment – parents and children, of all ages and both sexes – strangers and relatives – all huddled together, without the slightest regard to decency or order. To compare their condition with that of the beasts of the field would be paying but an indifferent compliment to the lower animals, which assured-ly are, in this respect, in far more enviable circumstances. Pepper-hill-court presents a somewhat similar aspect, and affords similar revelations as to domestic arrangements, while whiskey-drinking and lewd singing relieve the monotony of the scene, and the lazy and laden atmosphere is duly stirred at times by the frantic shouts of low bacchanalian orgies. It was from one of the doors in this vicinity that the fever-car had just departed on our arrival, bearing away to the hospital some wretched victim of miasma and foulness. When told this fact, I could not help thinking that hospitals, like jails – magnificent buildings, raised and supported by large public funds – would be in little request, if half the money expended upon them were well and wisely employed in the work of prevention – proverbially easier than cure. Even the common maxims of worldly prudence, a due regard to our selfish interests, and to the laws of political economy – to say nothing of far higher and holier principles – should teach us to adopt a different course.

THE REVEREND W.M. O'HANLON, *Walks Among the Poor of Belfast*, 1853

AMELIA STREET

My feet fall in step with absent whores
Whose crippled legs and sallow faces haunt
The pavements here, whose perfume hangs in doors,
A fading spoor that taunts me, will not let

Me dwell on Siren voices, golden hearts.
Across the main street the railway looms –
Right that this slum of blackened brick should start
Beyond a terminus, unscheduled stop

For randy travellers, right that its boom
Was war time, the brief years of rootless Yanks
Welcomed with open legs in dingy rooms,
With stretched palms and loveless pelvic shuttle.

Disease and bastardy, the lurid past,
Still stalk Amelia Street its pores the sum
Of lasting miseries. The pox outlasts
The glands that bred it, rampant in the drains,

Or nesting, hostile virus, on the air,
The brick its victim. Simply walking here
Cancels immunity, allots a share.
Some taint by proxy prickles on my skin.

FRANK ORMSBY, *Business as Usual*, 1973

MILL CHIMNEYS, caked under their black lichen of smoke, phallic obelisks pointing in mockery up at heaven; the streets where lived thousands of sweated labourers, ranged in fearful geometry, row upon wretched stillborn row, and an outcrop of crude civic buildings, bloated into ugliness by the so-called city fathers of the last century; these were the core of Belfast. To decaying Protestantism, Belfast was a place of pilgrimage, a Mecca of Orangemen. Misery and darkness for the many; quick money for the few. Unloved children, old women rotting in dirt under their shawls, I knew as Keats and Hippolyte Taine knew. Since they wrote of the city's horrors times had changed little. Festering scab are words which described it well enough.

Mercifully, this was only a sore in our otherwise green land. Where its walls stopped, the fields began, running almost as if bricks and mortar chased them, to the mountains, and there reared up defeating even the omnipotent mill chimneys. The majestic, purple presence of the hills could be felt, and every dismal chasm of a street gave glimpses of a rounded hump or a blue, distant shoulder. Sometimes smoke or rain blotted the mountains out, drawing a drab pall over the city. And then, when the clouds cleared, they would reappear, comfortingly near, suggestive of wild cotton moors that stretched on the uplands behind them.

ROBERT HARBINSON, *No Surrender*, 1960

WHILE HE WAS IN THE TRAIN he felt exalted by his flight from his father's presence, but his spirits fell when he reached Belfast. The day was grey, and there was a drizzling rain falling when he arrived. He had given up his labour of thinking and thinking as he approached the city, and had contented himself with looking idly out of the carriage window ...

'Them houses is despert dirty-lookin'!' he said aloud in the middle of his recurring thoughts as the train passed by the back of Island Street; and a farmer's wife in the carriage turned to him and said, 'Beg your pardon!'

'Ah, nothin',' he replied. 'I was just thinkin' to myself!'

It was odd, he thought, that he had never before noticed the miserable look of those houses. He had travelled that way every week for several years, but it had not occurred to him that the houses were unfit for anything but destruction. 'I'm not near myself,' he thought to himself in explanation of his sudden perception. There was a poorly painted picture of King William the Third on the back of one of the houses ... He remembered that there was an agitation against Home Rule. 'They're makin' a quare cod of theirselves!' he murmured, and then he began to laugh aloud, for a workman had scrawled in whitewash on his wall, against a bedroom window:

OUR TRUST IS IN GOD

and underneath in chalk:

TO HELL WITH THE POPE

ST JOHN ERVINE, *Mrs Martin's Man*, 1913

MILLS LINED THE RIGHT HAND SIDE OF THE FALLS ROAD and the road itself was developed as a main route for traffic bringing raw and finished material to and from the mills.

The houses provided for the residents of this area, in keeping with the general conditions of working people, were miserable in the extreme. They were as small as possible, their yards had no exits or alleyways at the rear and there were no toilets, all sewage and refuse having to come through the front door. In 1852, 7,000 out of 10,000 houses had to rely for water on public fountains, pumps or water carts. The small overcrowded houses and the insanitary and polluted water supply earned Belfast the highest death rate from typhoid in both Ireland and Britain until 1898. There were also recurrent epidemics of cholera and typhus which claimed the lives of thousands.

In 1865 a bye-law was passed that all new streets were to be properly paved and sewered before occupation but even this basic necessity was a long time being implemented, and by the time regulations governing the structural quality and size of the houses were passed in 1889 the vast majority of houses in the old Falls area were already built. All were without inside toilets, hot water or baths. The Falls Baths, opened in 1894, provided such necessities. Insult was added to injury when Dunville Park was presented to the citizens of Belfast by the Belfast whiskey family Dunville in memory of their sister. It was complete with toilets and washrooms – 'where the working class may learn the art of cleanliness'. This situation remained unchanged until recent times when home improvements were made, not by the housing authorities but by the residents themselves. In fact, domestic electric lighting did not come to many parts of the area until the 1950s. I vividly recall our next door neighbour getting her electricity put in and can remember other houses, like hers, which were dependent on gas mantles or paraffin lamps for their lighting.

GERRY ADAMS, Falls Memories, 1982

FAMILIAR FROM A DREAM, perhaps, or from a film of an occupied town in Europe, 1944, the road is dirty, treeless, lined with small grey-brown terraced houses. At a street junction it opens out in an empty, melancholy space – the width emphasised by a lack of cars, parked or moving, and a lack of people. The shadow of a solitary man appears, then disappears, around a corner. A dog, careless of vehicles or gunfire, ambles across the road, sniffing at litter. Many of the shops are closed, as if because of strict rationing or depopulation. The windows of the corner pub are bricked up, and the building itself appears hazy behind a high wire-mesh fence, one section of which juts out from the pavement into the road toward a similar fence projecting from the butcher's shop on the other side, a few yards farther along. From a car, weaving through the gap between the fences, slowly negotiating the steep asphalt ramps that have been laid in order to make all vehicles slow down, one can see that these buildings have had to be protected. Anyone with a gun or rocket launcher has a long line of sight down the road.

To the left can be seen several streets borrowed from a sepia-tinted textbook illustration of the Industrial Revolution. The streets to the right are a shade less mean. The road itself feels like a dividing line. Now come several blitzed sites covered with rubble; a house with its roof gone; houses whose windows are filled with grey cinder blocks; a burned-out factory; an anonymous filling station, its forecourt lacking pumps, weeds sprouting through the shattered concrete. Up ahead, the stranded-whale shape of a derelict cinema. To the left, an open stretch – green fields of an empty municipal sports ground built over former brick fields (shapes of slag heaps like burial mounds), and sloping down to old mill buildings, silhouetted factories, lines of grey-slate-roofed houses running southwest, and then, abruptly, only a mile and a half away, a dark wall of hills. One is conscious of being on a patch of the earth roughened to cinders, which can be blown away. One is conscious – a sudden prickly feeling – of being watched.

ANTHONY BAILEY, *Acts of Union*, 1980

BELFAST, IN THOSE DAYS, was a very dirty city. Street cleaning was then in its infancy. On a dry windy day there were blinding dust storms, and on wet days the rain made pools of water on the uneven streets. Once you left the town proper, you had to walk willy nilly through a morass. When you passed the Malone Road, the pavement ended at the entrance to the Botanic Gardens and was succeeded by only a few inches of kerb which petered out at Notting Hill. From there on it was an open country road – mud and more mud. From the Botanic Gardens and up the Malone Road, the roads were kept clean by the clumsy contrivances known as scrapers: the mud which had been allowed to accumulate was put into carts and taken off to any depression in the fields and there dumped to form the ground work and foundations for the new houses which were springing up everywhere.

For Belfast was growing up. It is true that on some of the streets in the centre of the town asphalt was occasionally, but very occasionally, used: on others 'square sets', square blocks of granite, were replacing the 'kidney stones' – oval stones of more or less equal size – 'smooth stones from the brook'. There were very large deposits of the red loam from which bricks are made in the neighbourhood of Belfast; and there were limestone quarries of considerable extent on the Cave Hill. In my childhood days there was no more familiar sight than the unending procession of carts of bricks with which Belfast was feverishly built.

PAUL HENRY, *Further Reminiscences*, 1973

SOME SPRINGS WERE FOUND TO HAVE AN ABUNDANT SUPPLY. The water from Mundy's well in Sandy Row was brought into Fountain Street, and three fountains stood there for the use of poor people. Crowds of women and children were to be seen waiting for their turn at the fountains to fill their buckets and carry home the household supply. Water carts carried Cromac water to the better class houses, where it was sold at a penny for two pails full, and the tinkle of the water bells was heard through the streets. Hot and cold baths were *not* in great demand.

MARY LOWRY, *The Story of Belfast and Its Surroundings*, 1912

A T THE OTHER END I was met by my cousin George, a big-boned, red-haired hobbledehoy of seventeen, with a curiously small face, small, glinting, squirrel's eyes, and a freckled skin. George, I remembered, could be amusing, in a broad and vulgar fashion: he could at any rate make me laugh, and when I saw him standing on the platform my spirits rose a little. I proposed that I should send on my luggage and that we ourselves should walk. I saw nothing unusual in this arrangement, which was common enough at home. George, it is true, seemed surprised, but after the railway journey I wanted to stretch my legs. Besides, town itself was a comparative novelty to me, and I was interested in the streets.

Just now, it being Saturday afternoon, in spite of a drizzling rain they were full of people, and at the end of Queen's Bridge some kind of noisy meeting – religious or political – was in full swing. We did not stop to listen, but soon afterwards, turning to the left, entered a long straight dingy-looking street lined with unattractive shops. There was a liberal sprinkling of public houses, cheap clothiers, grocers, and second-hand furniture dealers, while here and there the gilded sign of a pawnbroker hung out over the greasy pavement. We walked on, and I was on the point of asking why he had chosen such a disagreeable route when George touched my arm and announced cheerfully: 'Here we are.'

'Here!' I echoed in unconcealed dismay.

'Yes; we live over the shop,' George explained. But he had noticed my momentary recoil and had coloured.

I pretended to have been astonished that we had reached our journey's end so quickly, but I don't think George was deceived. Inwardly I was furious with my father for arranging for me to come to live in such a place, with the gas works and a public lavatory hardly ten yards away. The narrow street, the mean drab houses, the mean drab people, the noise and rattle of lorries and trams – all were far more unpleasant even than I had anticipated. It wasn't quite a slum perhaps, but it was little better.

'We haven't been here long,' George continued. 'We used to be round the corner in Donegall Pass.' Then, as I stood motionless on the pavement: 'Aren't you coming in?'

He had pushed open the door, and a bell had instantly responded with a clear decisive ring. Inside, the shop was divided into two compartments – one stocked with pipes, tobacco, cigarettes, and sweets; the other with newspapers, magazines, stationery, and cheap novels in paper bindings.

FORREST REID, *Peter Waring*, 1937

L ORD STREET MARKED THE BOUNDARY between the 'respectable' parlour houses such as ours, and the slummy kitchen houses of Constance Street and the even more slummy Edith Street, known as 'The Gut'. In these streets many of the women wore brown or black shawls round their shoulders, and the men – most of them permanently out of work – slouched in and out of the pubs or stood chatting at the gable walls in their duncher caps, with mufflers instead of collars and ties, and shabby jackets with tattered worn sleeves. The younger men played game after game of marbles, called 'bulking', in the middle of the road, or in the 'wee field' when the ground was dry. On Fridays and Saturdays these corner-boys, as father called them, disappeared into the two pubs and only reappeared at closing time, sometimes so drunk they could hardly stagger out; then they would lie stretched on the pavement in front of the pubs and bawl out songs such as 'Nellie Dean' and 'I'll Be Your Sweetheart' when they were in sentimental mood, or Orange ballads such as 'The Orange Lily O!' when they were feeling aggressive; and their aggressiveness often ended in a street fight. Fists and feet would fly and women would join in, with screams of rage, to protect their men, and the police would arrive – usually after the violence had been quelled. These fights I wasn't allowed to witness at close quarters. As soon as one broke out I'd be called indoors, and would stand with my nose pressed against our parlour window, my heart thumping with fear when a head was bashed against a wall.

This corner, bisected by Lord Street, centred on the 'wee field', Constance Street, and our end of Chatsworth Street. According to father, it was the worst spot in the whole of Ballymacarrett, with its pubs, a bookie's office, an almost derelict shop which had once been a spirit grocer's, and Pilsen's shop, which displayed a crime magazine called *Police News* in its window. Pilsen's had an acrid smell so powerful that I would try not to breathe in when I was buying a poke of sweets for myself, or a packet of cigarettes for my father.

JOHN BOYD, *Out of My Class*, 1985

THE 1920S WAS A TIME OF GREAT UNEMPLOYMENT. There were no social services then and it was quite a task for parents to feed, clothe and rear their families with money so hard to come by. Cotton flour bags sewn together were used as sheets and pillowcases. On top of the bed were multicoloured patchwork quilts made from scraps of material brought home from the mills and clothing factories. In the winter many old coats were piled on the bed for warmth.

GEORGE FLEMING, *Magennis VC*, 1998

THE MILL STOOD in a narrow side-street in the heart of a district characterised by squalor and the numerous streets of a similar sort, as well as by the number of houses crammed in those streets and the multitude of human beings herded in those drab dwellings. It was the third largest linen factory in the world, and it rose like the awful, sheer wall of a canyon along the entire length of one side of the street. Towering above the houses opposite, it confronted the rays of afternoon sunlight which shone in reflection from its upper windows and which gave a rosy hue to the brickwork. That pink blush seemed to pour down the walls and permeate the air between the mill and the row of tiny houses on the opposite side of the street. It was the reflected glory of a sinking sun on a November afternoon, and for a little while it gave a splendid light to that place of murk.

F.L. GREEN, *Odd Man Out*, 1945

IT WAS AN ESTATE like a hundred others at the time. Cul-de-sacs miles from anywhere, no transport, the beginnings of pebbledash. But a damn sight better than Benares Street where the pokey little houses had been flung up around the great linen mills a hundred years before, arseways, and the streets named to commemorate Britain's colonial triumphs. Benares Street and Clonard were 'down the Falls' while Andersonstown was 'up the Falls' – the Falls Road being the central spine, thoroughfare and, according to the media, 'nationalist heartland' of Catholic Belfast, bound by mountains on one side and bogs on the other.

MARY COSTELLO, *Titanic Town*, 1992

MARY LIVED IN A SMALL, DIRTY TERRACE, its two windows blinded by hessian spud bags. When you passed, if the door was open, the stink of old dog and paraffin oil was overwhelming, for Mary would have no truck with anything as new-fangled as piped gas. But neither dirt, stink or gloom deterred her clientele. Her main source of income was the girls from the local mill who paraded down every pay night for a glance into their romantic futures. They queued up the hallway with ready-used cups clutched in their hands, the queue sometimes spilling onto the street. After being done, they deposited a coin in a big soup plate on the hallstand beside which crouched Scamp, Mary's mangy dog, watching. And woe betide the ankles of any girl who didn't make sure that Scamp saw the flash of a silver sixpence.

The girls said that Mary at work spoke in a deep voice, almost like a man's, with a trace of a Charles Boyer accent. Otherwise the only sound ever heard from her was a high-pitched screech, whether it was calling Scamp, cursing children or performing in the small hours, when it could carry three streets away even above the nightshift clattering in the nearby foundry or a passing cattle train on the Central railway line.

Her prologue varied little ... 'Oh, yis needn't think I don't know yis are all there with yer lugs cocked ... Oh aye, I know yis – nice God-fearin' folk all tucked up after sayin' yer prayers ... But I'm the one that knows the other side of yis, y'load of durty, two-faced gather-ups yis ...' Here there'd be a short pause, nerve-racking for those with something to hide, for all knew that nothing was safe from Mary. You could guard against the ordinary gossip, but against Savage Mary, who had never been known to speak a civil word to anyone, let alone gossip, there was no protection. All of which lent an aura of the occult to her revelations. And it could be anyone, any night ... 'Are ye listenin', Ellie Smith? Gittin' to be a big girl, aren't ye ... Yi'll soon have to let out a seam or two in that sausage skin you've bin wrigglin' about in. Eh? An' you needn't tell me it's because you've bin atein' fresh bread, for I'm the one that knows who you've bin goin' down the railway with ...' Ellie was on the first train to her aunt's in Lurgan the following morning. Mr and Mrs Smith didn't need a second opinion: Savage Mary had spoken. She had a particular down on the righteous ... '...oul skinny-ma-link McNabney, the select vestryman. Oh yer there all right, Wullie John. Butter wudn't melt in yer mouth. Mister Holy Joe McNabney, the master plumber that niver served an hour to the trade. Eh, Wullie John? They give you a quare groundin' up in Borstal that time you robbed the widda's gas meter in 1919...'

JOHN MORROW, *Northern Myths*, 1979

WE ENTERED ONE WRETCHED HOVEL occupied by three families. The windows of the lower part of the house were blocked up. We had not the most remote idea that such a den of darkness and squalor could be the abode of human beings, until we heard a voice issuing from the further corner of it. It was some time before our eyes could so adapt themselves to the gloom as to detect any object; but at length we discovered a woman sitting upon a bundle of straw, without a particle of furniture, and amidst a scene of desolation which it would wholly baffle my pen to describe. She had been living here for upwards of two years; yet, destitute and miserable as this woman is, she seemed unwilling to go to the workhouse. She thinks liberty a 'thrice glorious goddess', though in such a shrine. All we could do was to relieve her immediate wants, for she was starving. I suppose she will still be found in Dickey's-entry.

THE REVEREND W.M. O'HANLON, *Walks Among the Poor of Belfast*, 1853

DOCTOR THOMPSON FROM COLERAINE lies ill in a ... fever, got in his attendance on the fever hospital, where the patients are crowded and the attendants all ill; yet crowds and families rejected every day. The town subscribes above 200 guineas a month to *one* charity – the soup house – and yet our streets and the habitations of our lanes present scenes of vice and wretchedness unequalled in former times; a habitation which I visited yesterday, filled by 4 generations of females, two confined on their straw by sickness, without a remnant of linen, a chair, stool, or board to sit on, the [spinning] wheel at the pawnbroker's, and all they once possessed, for once they were decent. This scene has suggested to me the idea of charitable *dry* drums once a week, where opened cards are to be played with, and the usual card money go to the poor. The lady, at whose house the party is, to have the distributing of the money, *provided* she enters in a book for that purpose the names, circumstances and places of abode of those she relieves.

MRS McTIER TO WILLIAM DRENNAN (1801), Drennan Letters, 1931

BEFORE THE ONSET OF THE MOST RECENT 'TROUBLES', in 1969, the Oldpark Road formed a fairly effective and peaceful dividing line between working-class Protestants, to the northeast, and working-class Catholics, to the southwest (though for the latter there was almost always less work to be had). On both sides of the Oldpark, many houses have no garden; toilets are in the back yards; paved entries run between the houses; the women seem to wear bedroom slippers all day long. The sort of slums, still common in Belfast, that have been eradicated from just about every other British city. However, whatever is bad in the Protestant streets is generally a touch worse in the Catholic streets – greater poverty, greater despair, and eventually a greater potential for violence. The Catholic streets are called the Marrowbone (or Bone), from the shape they form between Oldpark and Crumlin roads, bounded on the northwest by the Ardoyne district. The Bone has its own Catholic schools, the closest of which to the Oldpark Road is St Colmban's Boys' Primary . . .

On both sides of the Oldpark, the troubles have caused families to move away, fleeing out of fear, intimidation, or panic. Many have moved to supposedly safer areas. (Around Finiston, a hundred out of three hundred houses are bricked up.) A number of families are squatting. Some streets that were once slightly mixed are now firmly segregated, as co–religionists bunch together for mutual protection. Two years ago, after several empty houses were set on fire and burned out, perhaps by vandals, the Protestant population of six small streets not far from Finiston packed up and moved out, and Catholic families from across the Oldpark moved in. Houses built for Protestant artisans in the 1890s were better than the slum dwellings in the Marrowbone. The new Catholic section is now called the Ballybone, since all its streets have the prefix *Bally* (Ballyclare, Ballynure, Ballycastle, Ballymena, Ballymoney, and Ballycarry); the section forms a wedge extending the Catholic ghetto into the staunchly Protestant neighbourhood. It is ... three hundreds yards of absolute bitterness. The move breached the so–called Peace Line of the Oldpark Road, running between the communities.

ANTHONY BAILEY, Acts of Union, 1980

A GLITTERING SUN GLIDED through the window, shone on the wet sod of grass, and made shadows with the husks that floated on the white drinking vessel. It was only a blink of sun, for a coat of clouds soon covered it, and rain fell again, combing its cold way through the sooty air. A milk-cart rattled up the street, its wheels crushing the sodden newspaper and leaving shadow-tracks on the road. At the backs of the houses the rain rattled on the bin lids, formed pools on the waste ground, hung files of trembling drops on the clothes–lines, and filled up the square patch where Johnny had cut his sod.

He had cut it at the top of a shelving river bank where patches of green had not yet been scuffed by the boys who played football or the children who had dug caves and covered them with rusty corrugated tin. The river this morning was the colour of clay. It was in flood, and piles of tin cans with loose labels were carried under the arch near the brick fields; it flowed down past the backs of more houses, under arches, past football grounds with tin advertisements and away under roads to the sewage of the city and the open sea. In the summer the same river would be almost dry, its big stones encrusted with clay, and here and there under the arches black sluggish pools that stank when stirred by children who came to shout and listen to their echoes sharpening from the curved walls. The river itself came from the mountain that overlooked the backs of the houses. At one time it had been contaminated by the soapy outflow from a bleach works and a steamy exudation from a cotton mill. But these were closed down now and there was nothing to discolour the river except the natural clay from the banks or the dregs that came from the empty tins that were tossed into it.

MICHAEL MCLAVERTY, Lost Fields, 1942

I HATED SUNDAYS. IT WAS A MATTER OF GEOGRAPHY.
Greencastle sits in the lap of land that sweeps down from the Cave Hill to the shores of Belfast Lough, split in two by the Shore Road, which runs parallel with the lough all the way to Belfast. On the lough side of the Shore Road, where Aunt Nin lived, the land is flat, its sandy soil support-ing lanes of tiny whitewashed row houses and four pubs (the Donegall Arms being far and away the most popular). Grandmother said publicans knew

what side of the Shore Road their bread was buttered on. Aunt Nin's house had windows little bigger than postage stamps and walls two feet thick that, Grandmother said, did bugger all to keep the damp out. They'd been built over a hundred years ago, before the great famine.

Across the road, on the Cave Hill side, the land rises immediately, and rows of brick terrace houses straggle up the hill, gradually giving way to semi-detached and single dwellings off the Whitewell Road, then on up to the grand estates adjacent to the Castle grounds at the base of the Cave Hill itself.

There were three clubs: the British Legion was ensconced in a solid brick building on the Shore Road; the Orange Lodge was situated in indomitable stone block quarters near the bottom of the Whitewell Road; and the Wolfe Tone Gaelic Athletic Club was housed in a variegated tin hut pitched at the side of a field near the top of the Whitewell. Few people remembered that the great Irish patriot had been so honoured since it was never referred to as anything but the Gaelic Hut.

Greencastle had four houses of worship: Methodist, Church of Ireland, Presbyterian, and Catholic. The latter, St Mary's Star of the Sea, had the most important vantage point since its gates were firmly implanted on the Shore Road; the chapel path curved up the first steep incline, and the chapel itself, an ancient, mossy edifice, looked down on the tiny whitewashed row houses inhabited by most of its flock.

But we didn't live in the shadow of the chapel. Grandmother, Aunt Madge, and I were stuck upon Serpentine Parade, about halfway between the village proper and the Cave Hill, and Sunday afternoons found me bereft of companions since Bobby, Pam, and the other children on our street spent every Sunday afternoon in Sunday School. Protestants took their Sundays seriously; adults didn't do any servile work that could wait until Monday, and children didn't play on the Sabbath day.

As I said, I hated Sundays.

MARJORY ALYN, *The Sound of Anthems*, 1983

IT WOULD NOT BE FAIR to ascribe the drunkenness of Bigotsborough to its natural depravity. It is not thirstier than any other city, but when it wishes to amuse itself it drinks. If you want to know why it drinks you should inspect its elementary schools. Many of them are cesspools of poverty – ovens in summer and ice-houses in winter. The children in them are under-sized, under-fed, and under-clothed, and many of them go barefoot all the year round. It is out of these children that rioters are made. They have no recreations when they are young, and no recreations when they are old. The children of the poor in Bigotsborough sharpen their wits on the kerbstones. Anarchy in the schools breeds anarchy in the streets, and the community which shirks its duty to its citizens when they are young cannot complain if they shirk their duty to it when they are old. A city without a civic conscience produces citizens without a civic conscience. Lawlessness is the revenge of poverty.

JAMES DOUGLAS, The Unpardonable Sin, 1907

THE SMELLS OF THE FOOD THEY HAD BEEN EATING hung heavily in the kitchen and dinette, so that they, too, seemed swollen and gorged. Mrs Martin opened the kitchen door like you would a notch on a belt. The television was on in the living room and, in exchange for the smell of fried cabbage, a newscaster's voice drifted through, telling them about the trouble. Rioting had gone on throughout Sunday and into the early hours of that day; it had been worst around the Unity Flats complex, at the junction of Peter's Hill and Upper Library Street, and in the Ardoyne area, north of the city. The newscaster had a pleasant, consoling sort of voice, even when talking about violence; polite too.

GLENN PATTERSON, Burning Your Own, 1988

CHATSWORTH STREET WAS NOISY when traffic was passing up and down; the street was cobbled with what we called 'pavers', and the noise created by the iron-rimmed wheels of the carts and vans would make the windows shake. We youngsters kept a sharp look-out for vans that we could 'hop' – that is, we'd let them pass without taking any apparent notice of them, then we'd crouch double, race after them, and hop on the back without being noticed. Sometimes we'd get hops as far as the Castlereagh or Bloomfield Road without being detected, then we'd jump off with a shout of triumph which would make the driver turn round and shake his whip at us. Some drivers were furious at being tricked into giving us a free ride; others were amused and didn't seem to mind our company at all; they would let us stay on board until we tired of the bumpy ride and began thinking of our long walk home.

When the 'slummage' carts with their horrible smell appeared in the street we held our noses and pretended to vomit. I was told that slummage was what was left over when whiskey was manufactured, and I could well believe that. Anyway, I detested the sight and smell of it; for it reminded me of the sour smell from the two public-houses in Lord Street, one in front of our house, and the other at the back, both with swinging doors that when opened gave off a stench that always made me wrinkle up my nose. As bad as the slummage carts were the carts that collected refuse: these were small grimy affairs, with a sad donkey or mule between the shafts. I liked the dirty coal carts because of the big patient horses that would let you approach so close that you could count the hairs on their noses; some were so friendly that they let you caress them. I also liked to watch the grimy-faced coal men, hoisting their big black lumpy bags onto their backs and tramping up our hallway into the kitchen, then throwing off their loads, amid a cloud of dust, into our coal hole.

JOHN BOYD, Out of My Class, 1985

IN ADDITION TO THE HEAT AND BREATHLESSNESS of the atmosphere in the little shop, where one or other sat nine hours of the day, its situation was too near the unsavoury river channel which, bricked over in the upper half of High Street, yet lay open to the sun in the lower half, and was little else than an open sewer, whose presence poisoned all the air in that part of the town in the hot weather. Then, when the daily vigil was over, there was no garden for spending the cool of the evening, no privacy in the wretched little fenced-in space which served as back yard, no repose from the incessant clamour of children playing in the street, no dignity in the surroundings, little sweetness or grace in life itself.

JOHN HERON LEPPER, The North-East Corner, 1917

Red Brick
in the Suburbs

Sir Arthur Chichester was the real founder of modern Belfast. He was Lord Deputy from 1604 and held the position until 1614. Though he was not often present in Belfast on account of his official duties, his strong, ruthless but intelligent character had a large influence upon the locality. One industry which he organised in Belfast was brick-making. Near Belfast there is a lack of good building stone; but the abundant clay has helped to make Belfast a city of red bricks, and in past times it made mud-walled farmsteads the characteristic style of architecture in the Lagan valley. Sir Arthur, in the course of his own building operations, caused over 1,200,000 good bricks to be made, 'whereof, after finishing the castle, there will be a good proportion left for the building of other tenements within the saide towne of Belfast'.

HUGH SHEARMAN, *Ulster*

BELFAST. AN INDUSTRIAL CITY at the mouth of the Lagan. Described by a French journalist who visited it during the troubles as *une ville sanglante* – referring, of course, to its red-brick villas, its (then) red tramcars, and the blood then running in its streets. Literal translation difficult. A red-brick city, with a forest of factory chimneys vomiting smoke, and sea-gulls screaming about its harbour gantries; forbidding for the stranger or the theatrical in third-rate lodgings; a *bleeding* city, perhaps.

Anyhow, at least in its own estimation, a thorn in the flesh of the Vatican.

DENIS IRELAND, *From the Irish Shore*, 1936

BALLAD TO A TRADITIONAL REFRAIN

Red brick in the suburbs, white horse on the wall,
Eyetalian marbles in the City Hall:
O stranger from England, why stand so aghast?
May the Lord in His mercy be kind to Belfast.

This jewel that houses our hopes and our fears
Was knocked up from the swamp in the last hundred years;
But the last shall be first and the first shall be last;
May the Lord in His mercy be kind to Belfast.

We swore by King William there'd never be seen
An all-Irish Parliament at College Green,
So at Stormont we're nailing the flag to the mast:
May the Lord in His mercy be kind to Belfast.

O the bricks they will bleed and the rain it will weep,
And the damp Lagan fog lull the city to sleep;
It's to hell with the future and live on the past:
May the Lord in His mercy be kind to Belfast.

MAURICE JAMES CRAIG, *Some Way for Reason*, 1948

A NEWCOMER APPROACHING BELFAST from the sea cannot fail to be aware of its striking setting. The contrast between the black, forbidding cliffs of the Antrim coast and the pleasant green hills of Down is dramatic; and it may be with disappointment that the modern traveller sees in the valley ahead, not the level expanse of woodland which completed the natural landscape until relatively recently, but a haze of smoke, discreetly covering man's use of the scene, and only dimly revealing the countless factory chimneys and the shipyard gantries which are life and livelihood to many thousands of people. But even in the city, however dominating the man-made landscape, however impelling the bricks and mortar and the asphalt and steel, there are still vistas which reveal Cave Hill and the Castlereagh Hills: even the most casual observer cannot entirely ignore the very fine physical setting. Belfast has also in one sense become a part of the environment, because it is in part made of it. Local marls have been fashioned into millions of bricks; the plateau face has been scarred to provide metalling, limestone and building stone, and the streams which flow into the Lagan and which have cut back the scarp face have also supplied the water power which was one of the bases of the city's growth.

EMRYS JONES, *A Social Geography of Belfast*, 1960

RICHARD SAT DOWN ON ONE OF THE BENCHES. Below the cemetery, and beyond the bog meadows, the town, laid out in uniform streets of little red houses, had in the clear air a quaint appearance that reminded him of the towns he used, not so very long ago, to build out of toy bricks; but farther to the left, above the city proper, hung a blue cloud of smoke, through which tall mill chimneys and the grey spires of churches pierced, slender and dark. Farther still, over Belfast Lough, the atmosphere cleared again, and the clouds, streaked with silver, drifted like fantastic birds, the swan-maidens of fairyland. The boy saw beauty in all this, but he could see none in the marble angel with the broken harp that his mother called upon Grace and himself to admire.

FORREST REID, *At the Door of the Gate*, 1915

SATURDAY AFTERNOONS AMONG THE BELFAST WORKERS are as often given up to political demonstrations as to games. Only the middle and upper middle classes clothe themselves in white and board the trams that take them to the cricket-grounds and tennis-courts.

And at 3 p.m. on the afternoon of May 7th, great numbers of working men might have been seen congregating in the neighbourhood of Carlisle Circus. It was the occasion of the first Elections for the Northern Parliament. At the corner of the side-street in which the procession was forming up, numbers of women, girls, and children stood. Every few minutes a brass or a drum-and-fife band marched up, and by degrees three large banners were unfurled on which were emblazoned the names of the candidates for North Belfast, together with such exhortations as:

'Vote for Union, Home, and Empire! Ex-soldiers, don't betray your comrades who shed their blood!'

When the procession set off along Antrim Road, it was to the strains of a rousing march and to facetious enjoinders down a column nearly a quarter of a mile in length to 'Keep step – left, right, left, right!' and 'March by the left there!' These men had served in the British Army, most of them in the Great War – that was evident.

Crowds, or rather clouds, of women, children, and youths accompanied the march, which encompassed the whole electoral district. Through innumerable side-streets of red-brick tenement-houses exactly and meticulously alike, with glimpses of washing and washing apparatus up alleyways, along the Shankill Road, scene of so many fierce encounters, past gasworks, past stretches of blank brick wall, and warehouses and factories – so back to Clifton Street and Peter's Hill. There were no untoward incidents.

'Up Dublin!' chalked in yellow on a wall roused no comment. The rain which began to fall steadily could damp neither bands nor enthusiasm.

WILFRED EWART, *A Journey in Ireland 1921*, 1922

IN BELFAST

In Belfast when the latest 'troubles' seemed
No more than beefs about job-hogging Prods,

I joked among the lawyers and bureaucrats
I'd gone to meet; thought nothing of the stiff

Response. Then not much later I was chilled
To see, on visits for the BBC,

Khaki and guns in red-brick, peacetime streets
That brought my boyhood Oldham back to me,

Mixed with the ghastly endlessness of war.
Once more the relationship of man and art . . .

The foolish male behaviour in the rut!
Some lessons from Rachmaninov and Yeats:

The melody's extension is the thing;
The patience and nerve to drop a rhyme, and choose

A different scheme; or find the inspiration
To flatter a theme with every variation.

You've got to try as long as possible
To keep work secret, for it's never done;

Though in the end one drops it in the stream.
It's said the tunes that go with children's games

Are usually in the major key; unlike
The compositions of Rachmaninov.

ROY FULLER, *Last Poems*, 1993

I TURN INTO DRAB STREETS where the red bricks and the red and blue advertisements glow in the afternoon sunshine. From many view-points the gauzy shoulder of Cave Hill rises against the sky: it is (according to your fancy) a huge but affable beast, a Landseer lion, Napoleon's Face, the Rock of Gibraltar, Arthur's Seat, or just Belfast's own presiding hill. I cross York Street, long and dull as suet-pudding, neither quite dead nor yet wholly alive, and enter a network of mean streets. The churches do a little, trickling business; a foursome of boys play cards on the pavement; there is a sad absence of cooking smells. The Sabbatarian siesta is in full swing.

St Anne's Cathedral is one of the most successful Irish architectural achievements of this century. Externally the portals are deep and impressive; internally the nave is wide, the clerestory high and the proportions grand. In this Protestant church a man, standing enveloped in heather-honey hues, feels clothed and protected. The Catholic St Patrick's is ruddy and not unpleasing externally; the inside is rather a jumble of curios. A side-chapel is decorated with Lavery's work: a feeble trio of disembodied spirits, the pigments gone sooty and greenish; Burne-Jones at his least inspiring. But mine is the supercilious view. No doubt the old woman swathed in the black shawl, resting soul and body at the end of a bench, finds the church tranquillising and companionating.

Belfast is thoroughly Irish. I cannot see English or Scottish industrial cities in its streets; I cannot see un-Irish character in its faces. Belfast is geared differently from Dublin and Cork, but there its un-Irishness ends. Coming up from the south with eyes sharpened to note 'foreignness', I can find nothing convincing. To the Irish, Belfast and Belfast people are Irish, hard-working, hustling, flag-waving, but Irish none the less. One does not have to be long in this great city before one discovers oneself saying, 'Belfast is a homely place'.

STEPHEN RYNNE, *All Ireland*, 1956

THE ALBERTBRIDGE ROAD was a busy shopping area and the windows of the many different stores presented great visual adventures to a young observer. Two shops I was to get to know well were the Maypole and Dunlop's: the Maypole, next door to Dunlop's, was all green, with its name in gold paint; Dunlop's was dark red with its name also in gold. Both shops faced Mount Street and it was when I was about seven, after my father's death, that I started going to Dunlop's for 'a pound and a half of Danish butter and a pound of Red Label tea'. Why I was unable to get these products in my own territory remained a mystery. Through the years I beat a track from the Ravenhill Road, up Shamrock Street, along Lower Mount Street, across the Woodstock Road, into Upper Mount Street and over the Albertbridge Road to the 'quality shops', as my mother termed them, and the proprietors concurred. There were times when I was on one of these errands when I forgot what I had been sent for, and had to return home to check. Too many other things would catch my interest *en route*, and the dreamer took over. There were also those times when I would mistakenly enter the green Maypole instead of the red Dunlop's, and ask for 'Green Label tea', at the same time testing them with 'Spanish butter'.

Memories can play tricks and mine was one of the trickiest. By then, of course, I was a loner, with no fatherly guide.

Past these two shops was The Mount, an area of distinction, where large Victorian houses climbed a hill to look snootily down their drainpipes on the three busy arteries below – the Albertbridge Road, Castlereagh Street, and the Mountpottinger Road. Robert Lynd, the great essayist, lived there, and off the Mountpottinger Road, in Madrid Street, was the residence of St John Ervine, the famous playwright. There, at the corner of Castlereagh Street, was a mounting stone, which, so I was informed, had been used by people of an earlier time to get on their horses.

ROWEL FRIERS, *Drawn from Life*, 1994

THE HOUSE WAS OLD. Once it had been inhabited by a single well-to-do family and its servants. Then the continuity had been broken for good with its conversion into 'flats' – some were mere hutches under the eaves, where the skivvies used to sleep. There were twelve bell-pushes now beside the front door. Outwardly the villa looked unchanged, red brick, sandstone facings, set generously back from the road behind glossy rhododendrons, but those tiny white and luminous buttons, each with its owner's name beside it in smudged script, gave the game away. They always reminded her of what a cold, unnatural home life they all had of it, each in their tiny partitioned-off existence, listening to one another's coughs and creaks. She thought of the terraced house in which she had been born, the street, the neighbours and their neighbourliness. That had come to be cloying eventually, but now she mourned the passing of all those comings and goings.

MAURICE LEITCH, *Silver's City*, 1981

THE WARMTH OF THE SUMMER DAY still hung in the air and the residents of Colinvista Street, who wouldn't have been caught dead lounging in their doorways, stood their doors ajar in the hope that a cooler air might percolate through the houses. It was different in Majestic Street. There the heat had sucked the people into the open. The dwellings were so honey-combed together that the numbers seemed to mount in tens as he stepped adroitly over the sprawling children. Their fathers and mothers, a day's work or idleness over, roosted on the window-sills and shook their heads, bosoms, bellies, fingers across the street at each other. Old men and women with quilts over their knees sat in the doorways, chuckling, scowling, dozing, or staring out with wide eyes as if they had been plucked back from a long journey. Men gave him the slow nod for the stranger, fat women winked, girls laughed as he passed. A surf of laughter and talk lapped and slapped backwards and forwards across the narrow, bent street.

SAM HANNA BELL, The Hollow Ball, 1961

A S TO SIGHTS, the City is not especially renowned for the beauty of its buildings. It is, for the most part, a place of harsh red brick, dour slate roofs, and (for variety) dreary grey rendering. There is a sprinkling of buildings of stone, always imported. Such architectural showpieces as it possessed have, in large measure, been either destroyed by the greedy merchants, or nimbly mangled by fire, bullet, bomb. Gaunt hulks, shells, and steel frameworks, obtrude upon the eye. Over broad hectares of cleared ground, weeds compete with rubbish for a livelihood.

But all this is partially redeemed by the fondness of the citizens for paint. As previously remarked, each faction has its own identifying colours, and provided the observer has been trained to interpret the colour-coding, there are few places in the City where he need be long in doubt as to the sympathies of the locality. At the appropriate seasons of festival, gaily painted banners (their poles sometimes surmounted by wreaths of emblematic flowers) are escorted through the streets. Flags, gonfalons and pennants are hung from the house-fronts. Ornate and elaborate wooden archways are erected. These rites derive something perhaps from Renaissance masques, something from the fiestas of hotter climates. At all seasons, there are to be seen crudely painted kerb-stones, cabbalistic signs and exhortations on the carriageways, ritual emblems painted on gable walls.

Some of these paintings are tribal – their iconography, like their execution, is primitive and unsophisticated; but they are vigorous, colourful, and within the compass of a passably competent house-painter equipped with a sufficient number of tins of the primary colours. Others, however, are the work of more skilled hands – usually, art students; and represent, with embattled realism, scenes from local mythology, hagiography, or military history. The artwork is often supplemented by letterpress – exhortation, abuse, piety, vindictiveness; threats, aspirations, objurgations, manifestos. Many of these messages reappear as aerosol-brushed or crudely scrawled slogans on whatever vacant surfaces may offer themselves throughout the City.

Its square miles are none too rich in greenery, despite the best efforts of the municipal gardeners. There is always, of course, the ever-present green-grey-blue scrubby backdrop of the surrounding hills. Trees there are, though they pay a heavy tribute to each summer's bonfire season. Flowers there are, in the parks, in occasional window-boxes, in the florists' tubs; but few elsewhere – unless one may call in aid the ubiquitous dandelion, and the mysterious herbs which somehow flourish on bombed sites. The aspidistra population has dwindled sharply in recent years; but survivors may still be found; castor-oil plants, and rubber-plants, live a pampered life in the flashier office buildings. There is a bird-fruit tree in a populous thoroughfare, where at night small globular passerines try to imitate oranges and lemons. Although the climate is unfavourable, it is believed that occasional plants of oriental poppy and cannabis sprout indelicately in sheltered suburban back gardens.

One thing the City has in common with other places: the night sky. A low-slung winter moon may sometimes be seen hanging by a thread from the beak of a dockside crane. Stars, planets, satellites, meteors, comets, flying saucers, the Leonids and Perseids, all inch and etch their way across the darkness of the City, as they do all other places on earth, with utter neutrality, impartiality, and abstraction.

ALBERT RECHTS, *Handbook to a Hypothetical City*, 1986

BELFAST, AS ALL MEN OF AFFAIRS KNOW, stands no nonsense and lies at the head of Belfast Lough. One slides up to it at dawn through mists and past the clangor of shipyards. Unreal yet squalid, its streets lack either picturesqueness or plan, and manage to exclude all prospect of the mountains that neighbour them. A clammy ooze clings to the pavements, to the dark red bricks, the air is full of the rawness though not of the freshness of the sea, and the numerous Protestant places of worship stand sentinel over huddled slums and over dour little residences whose staircases are covered with linoleum and whose windows seem always to face the east. Foursquare amid the confusion, like a wardrobe in a warehouse, rises the immense City Hall. It is a costly Renaissance pile, which shouts 'Dublin can't beat me' from all its pediments and domes, but it does not succeed in saying anything else. Near the City Hall, at the junction of three small thoroughfares, is 'The Junction', where all life congregates and where a motor-car containing Mr Winston Churchill was once nearly tipped over. Here, too, are the principal shops. The bookshops of Belfast are instructive. They are not only small, but incredibly provincial, and breathe Samuel Smiles when they are respectable and 'Aristotle' when they are not, 'Aristotle' being in these parts the compiler of a pornographic manual who is bound in red and gold and usually tied up with string. Yes; in all our far-flung Empire one could scarcely find a city which stood nonsense less. And yet she is haunted by a ghost, by some exile from the realms of the ideal who has slipped into her commonsense, much as the sea and the dispossessed fields, avenging nature, have re-emerged as dampness and as weeds in her streets.

E.M. FORSTER, *Abinger Harvest*, 1936

THE CITY OF BELFAST has now become like the City of London in regard to its inhabitants. Few of them live within the mile and a half radius from the Post Office in Royal Avenue. Why should they, when villas by the row await them in every direction? The suburbs of Belfast are sufficiently various to suit all tastes. Such people as like the bold scenery of the northern mountain range can go to the Antrim Road or the Crumlin Road; those who prefer more pastoral slopes can live along the base of the Castlereagh Hills; and lovers of the woodland will have plenty of choice on the Malone Road or the Stranmillis Road, the latter affording a beautiful view of the River Lagan. In a southern direction the road to Lisburn is now almost covered with villas and gardens of the prosperous business men of this marvellous city.

But more important than this tale of 'eligible building sites' is the knowledge of the fact that the housing of the tens of thousands of workers is such as few manufacturing centres can equal. Within easy reach of their daily work are streets and streets of workmen's cottages; and as most of them are modern buildings, they possess all the conveniences detailed in the agents' lists. Wealth is not essential to comfort in Belfast. I have good reason to know that one can live more cheaply in a Belfast suburb than in almost any part of England or Ireland. Moreover, so admirable is the administration of municipal affairs and so vigilant are the inspectors of the various departments, that food adulteration, the curse of so many industrial towns, is practically unknown. It should also be mentioned that the valuation for rateable purposes is extremely moderate, and that the rates are reasonably low.

F. FRANKFORT MOORE, *The Truth About Ulster*, 1914

THE HOUSE WE CAME BACK TO IN BELFAST was in Ponsonby Avenue, three streets away from Baltic Avenue and one street away from Holy Family School. Among our neighbours were salesmen, teachers, a carpenter, a post office official, a fruit-market wholesaler, a journalist, a sausage-skin salesman, an insurance salesman, a newsagent/confectioner. It was, by and large, a fairly quiet street in which every householder seemed to be gainfully employed. Some years after we moved there, a widow down the street, a Mrs Magowan, was battered to death by the man she hired to paint her house. He was set free, it was murmured, because he was a Protestant and his victim was a Catholic. Other than that, the neighbourhood generated no misconduct, waste, unnecessary drudgery, unnecessary quarrels, or the spectre of new wars. The art of living fairly comfortably and harmoniously seemed achievable. Children old enough to play on the street did so without fear of being molested or run over. They were in bed by eight, or at the latest nine. Discipline was tight.

CAL McCRYSTAL, *Reflections on a Quiet Rebel*, 1997

204

THE HOUSE WAS SMALL, the corner house in a row of red-brick workingmen's dwellings in a street sown with children who played chalk games on the pavements, wound ropes around street lamps to make Maypoles, and scrawled NO POPE HERE and UP THE PRODS in its narrow back entries. It was a street to which cloth-capped, collarless men returned heavy with porter when the pubs shut, a street in which husbands slapped pinafored wives, wives slapped small children, and grandmothers screamed imprecations at grandfathers who urinated too near the weekly wash in the back yard.

But this house, the corner house, had been transformed into Crummick Street First Aid Post 106. It had been chosen because it was only three blocks away from a large Catholic hospital.

BRIAN MOORE, *The Emperor of Ice-Cream*, 1966

I LIVE IN A VICTORIAN BACKWATER, a small terrace now surrounded by mountains of Belfast brick, once buried in green parkland. Shadowed by a towering lime-tree – a relic of the parkland – we've got as far as electricity, but electricity disguised, shut in crystal chandeliers and tablelamps that look vaguely Victorian, if not positively Regency. In the small square dining-room with its single low-set window that overlooks a patch of sooty lawn and in spring time the green explosion of the lime-tree, we've hung grand-uncle's portrait over the sideboard. He looks comfortably at home, sur-rounded by furniture not much altered since the charge of the Light Brigade; fits in perfectly with the ornate cornices, the elegantly-proportioned rooms, the gentle post-Regency curve of the staircase, the plaster archway in the hall that collects dust but maintains its mutely-eloquent protest against life in the twentieth century.

DENIS IRELAND, *From the Jungle of Belfast*, 1973

THE LAGAN VILLAGE had not completely vanished when I was a child. A row of dark brown brick houses adjoined the Royal Bakery, on the opposite side of the road to our house. Its gleaming window panes reflected the Old Crow distillery and the schoolhouse opposite. The footpath outside each house door was scrubbed in a clean semi-circle. Opposite the shop where I was born sat 'wee white houses', as they were termed – history on my doorstep but, to me as a child, just part of my playground.

ROWEL FRIERS, *Drawn from Life*, 1994

HE LEFT AT TEN MINUTES TO TEN to roar down the Lisburn Road. The morning was cold and cheerless with a steady drip of wetness from the roof-eaves. A watery sun, white through the great blanket of cloudy damp that enveloped the city, struggled in vain to impose itself. There was no wind, and the noise from his exhaust ricocheted heavily from the house-fronts.

He turned right at Windsor Avenue and in a moment had drawn up outside her house with the tall stripped hedge of the tennis club to his left. No play today; the courts were dark red and soaking. He sounded the high-pitched horn.

She came down in a moment, dressed in a heavy purple overcoat of some chunky woollen material, with a broad collar that buttoned up before the chin. The colour showed off her glossy hair in a breathtaking way; it flowed like a jet-black liquid against the bulky material. But it made her look pale and brought out the uneasiness of her eyes.

They smiled to each other, too embarrassed to say much, and Colin thought: The car will do the trick. With the bravado of the inexperienced he swung it out into Malone Road, heading south. Then left along Stranmillis, a plunge down a street of red-brick houses built on a hillside, across a bridge and along the Lagan embankment until in a moment they had debouched on to another narrower artery that overlooked a cemetery and a golf course, twin monuments of suburbia. The road was choked with traffic even at ten in the morning; he had to amble a good five miles until the semi-detached villas dwindled out. Then he gave the car its head and forged directly south, through a few frowning villages where women walked with shopping baskets and idlers stood cold at windy street corners, towards Newcastle and the mountain country of Mourne.

VICTOR PRICE, The Other Kingdom, 1964

KING WILLIAM PARK

The mountains must have watched it, the startled eyes
of swamp-life and the long-shinned estuary birds:
that tidal glitter curling out to sea
for the last time, abandoning its mud.
Then centuries of minute adjustments, rivers
changing their beds,
the shifting work of sloblands under the sky
and fibrous growths toughening, holding their own.

Fowlers, fishers and settlers, intricate drains,
channels and cargoes, chimneys, streetlamps and trams;
but always the brickwork tilting, buildings on stilts,

the tide-swell echoes creeping out of the ground
yearly to meet the rainfall and shaping themselves
to crests and troughs in the tarmac, undulant cobbles.
Or pouring their excess out of sudden wounds
in streets miles inland.

Here, where the park is, breakers found a shore
to bury shells, jetsam a place to lie.
Daily the winos spend their bleary rage
in squabbles among the benches,
or sing their hearts out searching for a song
on a green patch with trees beside a junction.
And knee-capped boys on crutches raise their heads
to follow us past the railings,

wintry eyes asking how far we have come
and where we are going. A terraced marsh away,
sludge-pumps have sucked a resting-place for stone:
the blocks of a new hospital are hauled
through scaffolding, past windows where the sun
flames in the evening gloriously, or the rain
drifts into soundless networks on its way
to the earth-clogged ears in the groundwork, the listening shells.

FRANK ORMSBY, *A Northern Spring*, 1986

THERE IS A SIMILARITY between the Shankill and Sandy Row in that both districts have been built up by working-class citizens.

Gentry and well-to-do merchants, even from the earliest days of the town's growth, gave both these thoroughfares a wide berth. Probably the great mills and factories, which sprang up between the Falls and the Shankill during the industrial progress of Belfast, were the chief cause of this.

Six hundred years ago, the Shankill was a barren wasteland with a rough track leading to the ford across the Lagan and an ancient church inviting the wayfarer to worship at its shrine as he passed on his way. A bare hundred years ago, it comprised a few cottages and farms here and there along its broadened carriageway.

Today, it is a densely populated district with its inhabitants feeding the mills, factories and shipyards with skilled labour. The ancient track has developed through the centuries into a great thoroughfare and banks, business offices and thriving merchants have made it one of the most progressive centres of Belfast.

There is a certain glamour attached to the Shankill, if one has the observant eye. As one approaches the rise of Peter's Hill on a clear summer afternoon, and casts an eye beyond to where the Shankill disappears over the steep incline of Bower's Hill into its Woodvale suburb, there is a grand view of Divis Mountain with its varied colours of golden corn, green field and purple heather, and an occasional white-washed cottage or farmhouse mirrored in the sunshine.

THOMAS CARNDUFF (1954), *Life and Writings*, 1994

BELFAST LOUGH AND THE LAGAN VALLEY ABOVE IT have in fact been excavated in the Triassic sandstones. During the Ice Age these soft rocks suffered severely, and the bright colour of the Boulder-clay about here shows how the red material of the marls and sandstones has been ground up and scattered. When the ice was in process of withdrawal, the Lagan valley was left clear, while the adjoining lough and the sea outside were still choked. This ice formed a dam, behind which, over and around the site of Belfast, a great lake was produced. Into this lake turbid streams brought much sediment, which settled as red sand or fine red clay. Thus are derived the sands of Malone and Knock, which form a dry and excellent foundation in those suburbs, and also the brick-clays out of which most of Belfast is built. In later times, when Neolithic man roamed the country, the land around Belfast stood lower than at present; the sea lay over the site of the future city, and the tide flowed far up the valley. In the calm waters, sediments accumulated. Deep excavations in Belfast Harbour give us glimpses of this post-Glacial history. Overlying the red sands is a bed of peat, now no less than twenty-seven feet below high-water mark, pointing to a much higher land-level than at present, and a surface on which woods of Scotch Fir, Oak, Alder, Willow and Hazel grew, and in these woods Red Deer, Wild Boar and other large animals roamed at will, while insects crawled among the herbage or flitted among the trees. The forerunner of the Belfast-man was no doubt present in those days, but his traces have not as yet been found in this deposit. Then the land began to sink, and this continued till the old land-surface was buried fifty or sixty feet under the sea, which covered the site of the future city and flowed up the valley as far as Balmoral. While Neolithic man was busy with his flint-implement factories at Larne and Kilroot, deposits of fine grey mud accumulated in Belfast Lough and elsewhere, burying deeply the old peat-bed. Then at last the land rose again, leaving a flat plain of soft clay from which the sea had retreated, and around it the scarps that told of the old land-edge on which the waves had beaten, and which still stand out boldly, as in the steep bluff at Tillysburn and the sudden little hill at the back of York Street and Royal Avenue in Belfast. Old Belfast, as around High Street, arose on this former sea-bottom, and it was only as the town spread that buildings began to be erected on the firmer foundations furnished by the red Glacial clays and sands – the deltas and sediments of 'Lake Belfast'. Below, on the flat, light buildings were possible; but when taller structures were planned, a firm foundation was necessary, which could only be obtained by piling – by hammering long balks of timber down through the soft silts to the red sands or hard clays far below. So the Belfast of today is essentially a city on stilts.

ROBERT LLOYD PRAEGER, *The Way That I Went*, 1937

Black Belfast

The week-end was all sunshine. I could not remember
Belfast like this, and the continuous sunshine delighted but
outraged me. My conception of Belfast, built up since early
childhood, demanded that it should always be grey, wet,
repellent and its inhabitants dour, rude and callous.

LOUIS MacNEICE, *Zoo*

IN BELFAST

Walking among my own this windy morning
In a tide of sunlight between shower and shower,
I resume my old conspiracy with the wet
Stone and the unwieldy images of the squinting heart.
Once more, as before, I remember not to forget.

There is a perverse pride in being on the side
Of the fallen angels and refusing to get up.
We could *all* be saved by keeping an eye on the hill
At the top of every street, for there it is –
Eternally, if irrelevantly, visible –

But yield instead to the humorous formulae,
The spurious mystery in the knowing nod.
Or we keep sullen silence in light and shade,
Rehearsing our astute salvations under
The cold gaze of a sanctimonious God.

One part of my mind must learn to know its place –
The things that happen in the kitchen-houses

And echoing back-streets of this desperate city
Should engage more than my casual interest,
Exact more interest than my casual pity.

DEREK MAHON, Night-Crossing, 1968

WALK UP DONEGALL PLACE any night about seven, passing the strolling poor, factory-hands, clerks, mill-workers, shipyard workers, domestics, and go into the big hotel a few hundred yards up, where you find the higher executives and employers enjoying themselves in the best eat-and-swill manner of an English industrial town. You have before you an outline of Belfast's social structure. There is no aristocracy – no culture – no grace – no leisure worthy of the name. It all boils down to mixed grills, double whiskeys, dividends, movies, and these strolling, homeless, hate-driven poor.

It is a brutal and a brutalising society. The worst of it all is that it works from the cradle up: from the time when little Protestant boys are sworn into the Orange Youth Movement, and little Catholic boys race home in groups from school lest they be attacked by their fellows. It is a germ in the blood. It is in the very air which grows heavy and ugly as the anniversary of the Boyne comes around every 12th July. A good government could alter the aura of Belfast. No 'Orange' Government ever can, or will. Neither, *as things are*, could (if that impossible became a possible) a Catholic Government. Britain supports the whole structure, morally and financially, and until she clears up the dirty mess she has made here, the Six Counties will remain one of her shameful failures.

SEAN O'FAOLAIN, An Irish Journey, 1940

I KNEW AT ONCE that Belfast was an awful city. It had a bad face – mouldering buildings, tough-looking people, a visible smell, too many fences. Every building that was worth blowing up was guarded by a man with a metal detector, who frisked people entering and checked their bags. It happened everywhere, even at dingy entrances, at buildings that were not worth blowing up, and again and again, at the bus station, the railway station. Like the bombs themselves, the routine was frightening, then fascinating, then maddening, and then a bore – but it went on and became a part of the great waste-motion of Ulster life. And security looked like parody, because the whole place was already scorched and broken with bomb blasts.

It was so awful I wanted to stay. It was one of those cities which was so demented and sick some aliens mistook its desperate frenzy for a sign of health, never knowing it was a death agony. It had always been a hated city. 'There is no aristocracy – no culture – no grace – no leisure worthy of the name,' Sean O'Faolain wrote in his *Irish Journey*. 'It all boils down to mixed grills, double whiskies, dividends, movies, and these strolling, homeless, hate-driven poor.' But if what people said was true, that it really was one of the nastiest cities in the world, surely then it was worth spending some time in, for horror-interest?

I lingered a few days marvelling at its decrepitude and then vowed to come back the following week. I had never seen anything like it. There was a high steel fence around the city centre, and that part of Belfast was intact because, to enter it, one had to pass through a checkpoint – a turnstile for people, a barrier for cars and buses. More metal detectors, bag searches and questions: lines of people waited to be examined, so that they could shop, play bingo or go to a movie.

PAUL THEROUX, *The Kingdom by the Sea*, 1983

WHEN I WAS A LITTLE BOY and my sister and I had to go to Belfast, we would sit in the train returning home, swinging our legs and chanting 'Belfast! Belfast! The city of smoke and dust!' Belfast was essentially evil – largely because it was new. Living in a town of Norman remains, I had held the doctrine that oldness was in itself a merit and new things *ipso facto* bad. This doctrine I no longer hold, so I must absolve Belfast on that score. For the rest I consider that Belfast politics are deplorable and the outlook of her citizens much too narrow. But that is not good enough reason for hating her citizens. If I hate, I only make them more hateable. And even if I had adequate grounds for hating them, I still ought to make sure that I am not hating them mainly because I identify them with the nightmares of my childhood.

LOUIS MacNEICE, *Zoo*, 1938

YOUR HORIZON FROM HERE is the Antrim Mountains, probably a uniform mass of greyish blue, though if it is a sunny day you may just trace on the Cave Hill the distinction between the green slopes that climb two-thirds of the way to the summit and the cliff wall that perpendicularly accomplishes the rest. That is one beauty; and here where you stand is another, quite different and even more dearly loved – sunlight and grass and dew, crowing cocks and gaggling ducks. In between them, on the flat floor of the Valley at your feet, a forest of factory chimneys, gantries, and giant cranes rising out of a welter of mist, lies Belfast. Noises come up from it continually, whining and screeching of trams, clatter of horse traffic on uneven sets, and, dominating all else, the continual throb and stammer of the great shipyards. And because we have heard this all our lives it does not, for us, violate the peace of the hill-top; rather, it emphasises it, enriches the contrast, sharpens the dualism. Down in that 'smoke and stir' is the hated office to which Arthur, less fortunate than I, must return to-morrow: for it is only one of his rare holidays that allows us to stand here together on a weekday morning. And down there too are the barefoot old women, the drunken men stumbling in and out of the 'spirit grocers' (Ireland's horrible substitute for the kindly English 'pub'), the straining, overdriven horses, the hard-faced rich women – all the world which Alberich created when he cursed love and twisted the gold into a ring.

C.S. LEWIS, Surprised by Joy, 1955

from THE ROUGH FIELD

Catching a bus at Victoria Station,
Symbol of Belfast in its iron bleakness,
We ride through narrow huckster streets
(Small lamps bright before the Sacred Heart
Bunting tagged for some religious feast)
To where Cavehill and Divis, stern presences,
Brood over a wilderness of cinemas and shops,
Victorian red-brick villas, framed with aerials,
Bushmill hoardings, Orange and Legion Halls.
A fringe of trees affords some ease at last
From all this dour, despoiled inheritance,
The shabby through-otherness of outskirts:
'God is Love', chalked on a grimy wall
Mocks a culture where constraint is all.

JOHN MONTAGUE, The Rough Field, 1972

'MY GOD!' LUKEY EXCLAIMED. 'It is about Johnny . . . they are talking about Johnny! They are waiting to see if he will come this way. They are waiting to see the Police lift him.'

And when he muttered that it seemed to him that the night itself with its icy wind and its furious voices stirred darkly over the city and probed the streets and the alleys and noisome entries. Its bitter fingers fumbled and tore at the darkness, to dispel the shadows, to rip wide the black curtains which might conceal Johnny. Its voices mumbled across the cobbles and whispered along the faces of huge, silent buildings. At corners, they broke into shrill chatter; and parting, they sped off to dart into deserted entrances or to pour wildly into the gutters or the dank foundations of walls oozing with slime and guarding a hollow silence into which the incessant breathing roar of the city dropped occasionally as the wind veered. Elsewhere, the greater currents drove harshly, never at rest, menacing and ominous, snatching words from the lips of people and merging them into a single sound.

'They are hunting him!' Lukey muttered. 'They are getting the trail of him and yelling at his heels!'

F.L. GREEN, *Odd Man Out*, 1945

FATHER QUIGLEY laid the announcement book on the edge of the pulpit and sighted the clock underneath the organ loft. It began to rain outside and the stained glass windows grew dark, darkening the whole church as though it were evening and the sun had sunk out of sight. In this gloom, this sombre preliminary lighting, the priest's white and gold vestments shone brightly out of the murk above his congregation. He lifted his long white hand and made the Sign of the Cross. Then he began:

'I had in mind to say a few words about the Gospel of today, which you have all read, or at least the good people have read, the ones that bring their Missals and prayer-books to Mass of a Sunday morning and try to follow the Holy Sacrifice. But I'm not going to talk about the Gospel, because this Gospel doesn't deal with the subject which has to be settled in this Church today, before this kind of hooliganism goes any further.'

He paused, stared hollow-cheeked at the crowded gallery. Then pointed a long spatulate finger at the people sitting above.

'You know what I mean, you people up there,' he shouted in hard flat Ulster tones. 'You that's jiggling your feet and rubbing the backs of your heads along the fresh paint that was put on the walls. I mean the disrespect to the Holy Tabernacle and the Blessed Body of Our Lord here in it. I mean coming in late for Holy Mass. I mean inattention, young boys giggling with young girls, I mean running out at the Last Gospel before the Mass is over, I mean dirtying up the seats with big bloothers of boots, I mean the shocking attitude of people in this parish that won't give half an hour to God of a Sunday morning but that can give the whole week to the devil without the slightest discomfort. I mean the young people, and a few of the older ones too, some of them that should know better but don't because ignorance and cheekiness is something that they pride in and the House of God is just a place they want to get in and out of as fast as possible and without any more respect for it than if it was a picture house, aye, not half as much, for you can see those same people of a Saturday night, or any night they have a couple of shillings in their pockets, you can see them lining up two deep outside a picture house. But I'll ask you one thing now, and I want you to examine your conscience and tell me if it isn't true. Have you ever seen the young men of this parish queuing up to get into a sodality meeting? Or have you ever seen the girls and women of this parish lining up to get into the Children of Mary devotions? You have not, and I'll tell any man he's a liar if he says he has. Because I haven't and I'm not at cinemas or dog tracks or dance halls during the week, I'm here, that's where I am, here in the Church, with a few good souls listening to me and the benches empty, the sodalities, just a few good men stuck in the front benches and the House of God empty, aye, empty.

'But the dog tracks aren't empty, are they now? Celtic Park or Dunmore Park on the nights the dogs run, they're not empty. Oh-ho no! No, no, the trams are full of young men and old men, and the buses too, and those that don't have the price of the tram after the races are over as thick as flies on the pavement. And the taxis are kept running full blast too. Aye, there are dogs in those taxis, dogs sitting up like human beings while human beings walk. And there are men in those taxis too. Men with bags of money on their knees and bookmakers' boards stuck on top of the taxis on the luggage racks. Aye, dogs ride home in taxis while Irishmen of this parish walk home without a penny piece in their pockets after giving it all away without a murmur. But let me ask for the money tomorrow for a new coat of paint for those walls that the young people of this parish seem to take a delight in dirtying up, and see the story I get. O Father, times has been very hard. Ah, yes, very hard. But not too hard to give that week's wages to the dogs. No, never that hard. And not too hard for the young bits of girls nowadays to have plenty of money for powder and paint and silk stockings and chewing gum and cigarettes and all kinds of clothes which you wouldn't see on a certain kind of woman in the old days. And not too hard to slap down a couple of shillings any night in the week to go into the cinema and look at a lot of people who're a moral disgrace to the whole wide world gallivanting half naked in glorious technicolour. No, no, there's always plenty of money for that.'

He paused, breathing heavily. Looking up at him, Miss Hearne saw his nostrils flare like a horse that has run a race. Such a powerful speaker, she thought, so very direct. Not the old style of priest at all, doesn't mince words, does he? But the young people, well, I think he's right, goodness knows, those young girls I saw at . . .

'Plenty of money!' Father Quigley roared. 'Plenty of money! Plenty of time! Plenty of time! Yes, the people of this parish have both of those things. Time and money. But they don't have it for their church! They don't even have an hour of a Sunday to get down on their bended knees before Our Blessed Lord and ask for forgiveness for the rotten things they did during the week. They've got time for sin, time for naked dancing girls in the cinema, time to get drunk, time to fill the publicans' pockets and drink the pubs dry, time to run half way across the town and stand in the rain watching a bunch of dogs race around a track, time to go to see the football matches, time to spend hours making up their football pools, time to spend in beauty parlours, time to go to foreign dances instead of *ceilidhes*, time to dance the tango and the foxtrot and the jitterbugging, time to read trashy books and indecent magazines, time to do any blessed thing you could care to mention. Except one.

'They – don't – have – time – for – God.'

He leaned forward, grabbing the edge of the pulpit as though he were going to jump over it.

'Well,' he said quietly. 'I just want to tell those people one thing. One thing. If you don't have time for God, *God will have no time for you.*'

BRIAN MOORE, *Judith Hearne*, 1955

WHEN I ARRIVED IN BELFAST an academic colleague, an Englishman, told me frightening stories of discrimination practised against Roman Catholics and thus prepared me for a visit to Bellevue, where, he assured me, some paths were actually reserved for Presbyterians. Incredibly I saw at the entrance to one path – it was a misty evening – a notice which I read as 'Presbyterians Only'. It took me some time to recover from the shock. It was a new experience for me to live in a town divided in this way by religion, and in looking for explanations I prepared maps, published in the *Ulster Journal of Archaeology* in 1944, showing the percentage of adherents to the three main religious groups in each ward of the city, using statistics published in the 1937 census. More recently Professor Emrys Jones, using the data for 1951, and breaking down the statistics into small enumeration districts, has published a much more detailed analysis. One explanation of the uneven distribution and of the regional concentrations relates to the sources of the immigrant population. Thus the predominance of Presbyterians in north Belfast and in most of east Belfast is linked with their easy access from strongly Scots-settled areas in mid-Antrim and north Down, while the greatest concentration of Episcopalians is in the Sandy Row and University areas which are linked with the English-settled Lagan valley. They are also stronger than average in the Shankill area (where Roman Catholics number less than 5 per cent of the total population) and in Ballymacarrett. The high concentration of Roman Catholics (over 90 per cent) in the Falls district is also partly explained by its links with the hill slopes towards Derriaghy and with the Irish hinterland beyond the hills, and historically with the first industrial suburb of the original town – as the name Mill Street indicates – which seems from the beginning to have attracted the native population.

E. ESTYN EVANS (1963), in *Ireland and the Atlantic Heritage, Selected Writings*, 1996

A T THE JUNCTION OF THE OLD AND NEW DUBLIN ROADS was the old
Blackstaff Lane, extending to the Falls and crossing the Blackwater
River, which is the proper name of this now celebrated stream. The term
Blackstaff was only known as referring to this lane, which was a country
road between the Falls and Lower Malone in the last century. The site of
Mountcharles and University Street was Mr Lindsay's nursery ground, and
where his son built a yacht, rigged and finished her completely. He had her
drawn into town, and launched at the slip at Donegall Quay. She was
considered a rare specimen of naval architecture, and was a well-known
craft in Belfast Lough for many years. The Botanic Gardens were then Mr
M'Dowell's farm and country seat. Friar's Bush graveyard was an uninclosed circular mound, occupying about an acre of ground, where the inhabitants of all creeds buried their dead. The Marquis of Donegall afterwards
gave ground to increase it to its present dimensions. It was then walled in,
and is now almost exclusively a Roman Catholic burial place. About this
time considerable excitement prevailed with respect to burials. Subjects, as
they were called, were in great demand, and our graveyards (with the exception of the new burying ground), being uninclosed and unprotected, it
was customary for the friends of the deceased to watch their graves for
several nights after the interments.

THOMAS GAFFIKEN, *Belfast Fifty Years Ago*, 1894

from THE NORTHERN ATHENS: A SATIRICAL POEM

Vile resurrection-men one holds in dread,
Whose occupation chills the blood's warm gush,
Not for their harm, but outrage, to the dead,
That puts each tender feeling to the blush; –
Yet sadder 'tis to see the lowly head
By rats devoured or gnawed at FRIAR'S-BUSH,
Whose venom'd fangs or prowling forms are hid
'Midst forms we lov'd: affections rush
Along the loathsome mysteries of the grave,
That fain would rescue from foul vermin's cranch
The cheek once lovely, and the heart once brave –
The wither'd cedar and the fallen branch –
Laid low in FRIAR'S-BUSH, where Horror squats
'Midst *wooden* tomb-*stones*, robbery, and rats.

ANONYMOUS, 1826

C HOLERA, which had been steadily travelling westward from India,
reached our islands in the early summer [1832]. It was the first visit of

the scourge, and very solemn and awful it was. We remained in town to be near the doctors; and I remember the dreadful dead-cart passing at all hours, with bodies to be interred in heaps at Friar's Bush, the Catholic burying ground, near Belfast.

ELIZABETH THOMSON KING, *Lord Kelvin's Early Home*, 1909

16TH MAY 1818

A WRETCHED OBJECT IN A BARROW was left at the Gate on Sunday evening where he remained until Wednesday morning when with the advice of Mr Munfoad I ordered him to be put into a waste house until the Committee determine what they will do with him. I would recommend that a Car shou'd be hired & the object sent to his native Parish which I understand to be Hillsborough.

JAS. FERGUSON,
ORDERLY.

R.W.M. STRAIN, *Belfast and Its Charitable Scoiety*, 1961

L ET ME ... DIRECT YOUR EYE to some of the purlieus of North Queen-street. Every one must have noticed the close affinity existing between intemperance and the grosser forms of sensuality; and this quarter exhibits, in immediate juxtaposition, facilities for the indulgence of both these classes of vice. How far the idle, and, in general, dissolute habits of the soldier life in barracks may have to do specially with the case, I must leave your readers to judge. But it is a fact, that no region of the town seems to be more fully furnished with the elements and means of immorality than this. In that very limited space of North Queen-street, which lies between the head of Great George and Frederick-streets, we reckoned about twenty-two public-houses, including a few at the angles formed by these latter streets with the former one ...

We learned that some of the public-houses referred to are used as music-saloons, where vice, under the garb of pleasure, is so cheapened down that, in the expressive words of Dr Cooke, at a recent meeting, the young of both sexes can purchase even 'a pennyworth of blackguardism'. Whether the same remark applies to the six or seven spirit-shops which we found vigorously plying their profitable trade in the upper part of Lancaster-street, in the immediate vicinity, or to the three which bless that miserable lane called Alexander-street, I am unable to determinate.

THE REVEREND W.M. O'HANLON, *Walks Among the Poor of Belfast*, 1853

SOME FOLK SEEM TO THINK that one should not procreate when one is poor. It is part of a lubricious and unwholesome idea that the private or sexual lives of the deprived are open to the investigation and interference of society's other classes. It conjures up an image of a sexually incontinent underclass in which the males repeatedly impregnate their females without due thought to income or future provision for their offspring. A myth persists that the 'lower classes' are somehow more promiscuous than their betters. Generalisations are always worthless and seductive in equal measure. I hesitate to make one, but my experience of sexual behaviour differences between classes certainly does not bear out this nightmare of the libidinous proletariat. I was born and brought up in working-class Belfast. When I was nineteen, I went to Cambridge University. Up until then my experience of promiscuity had been theoretical or literary. At Cambridge, I was privileged to see the youth of Britain's upper-middle-class conduct its sexual business. I was astounded by what I encountered. Sex seemed an easy seamless thing. Youth of both sexes had notched up a greater aggregate of sexual partners by the end of their first year than most people in working-class Belfast would have managed in a lifetime's striving.

ROBERT McLIAM WILSON, *The Dispossessed*, 1992

from THE NORTHERN ATHENS: A SATIRICAL POEM

' 'Tis true, 'tis pity, and 'tis pity, true,'
Half ATHENS' denizens are half-bred Scotch,
Like mongrel-curs upon a view-halloo,
Or sort of salmagundi, or hotch-potch.
At once in wealth the mighty ATHENS grew,
Like golden fruit at some enchanter's touch,
Scotch MAC's and brimstone, bannocks and bargoo,
Supplanting Irish O's and Irish itch.
This crossing of the breed, and transplantation
Of Adam's race, one cannot quite commend,
Since various manners mark each various nation, –
The Turk to tyrannise, – and Slave to bend; –
Hence Nature gave to PADDY bulls and brogue,
And made her SCOT philosopher and rogue.

ANONYMOUS, 1826

TWO MEN WERE HANGED in front of Bank Buildings in 1816, for burglary. Our prison was at that time the House of Correction, which was built in 1803, in Howard Street. It stood then among green fields, and on the stone over the front door was carved this warning – 'Within amend,

Without beware'. Serious offenders were sent to Carrickfergus Gaol, until our County Prison was built on the Crumlin Road. In the early days, one stipendiary Magistrate sat every second day in the Police Court, and there were two constables. The Police Office was in Rosemary Street. The old fashion of carving on the front of a prison was revived recently when the new Bridewell was built in Dublin. It bears across the front this polite apology, 'Fiat justitia, ruat cœlum', which translated means 'Let Justice be done, though the heavens should fall'.

MARY LOWRY, The Story of Belfast and Its Surroundings, 1912

A DELUGE OF SUMMER RAIN was sweeping the Belfast streets clean. Dawn had appeared, clad in delicate gray wrappings of sad misty cloud, and it is only fair to say the fulfilment of day did not belie the promise of morn. The sun remained resolutely ought of sight, the heavens were leaden, the earth was sodden; Devis, the Cave Hill, and the Black Mountain had not merely 'put their nightcaps on', but retired altogether from view.

A good stream, swift as a mountain torrent, was running down each filthy gutter. On Lettuce and Carrick Hills rosy, curly-headed, barefooted children were in the turbid water which rushed to flush the sewers, disporting themselves like ducklings. Upon the Crumlin Road, past the Courthouse, where Justice – her eyes bandaged with a stone fillet – sits high aloft, holding her scales, utterly crooked, car-drivers, with shout and whip, urged fast horses recklessly; Hercules Street, then lined with butchers' shops, was foul with garbage, borne onward to the gullies; in Sandy Row peace reigned; the weather was so bad the Orangemen had not a thought to spare for their friend Pious William or their foe the Pope; at the Docks wretched-ness unspeakable prevailed, miserable cattle awaiting shipment were penned together in sheds open to the wind and rain; in the air there was that raw, moist chilliness which makes the Irish climate so trying; the Lough re-sembled a sea of liquid mud, where white-crested billows tossed restlessly; the soft green slopes of Down and the bold scenery of Antrim were alike impartially hidden from mortal eye. Belfast was looking its worst – and that worst can be very bad indeed.

MRS J.H. RIDDELL, Berna Boyle, 1884

A N AIR OF CHEERFUL CONFIDENCE … proved at first not easy to sustain. Belfast, grimly utilitarian and shrouded in rain, was very little evocative of any gateway to the holiday spirit; it suggested rather a various detritus from the less appealing parts of Glasgow washed across the Irish Sea during the darker years of the nineteenth century. But this may have been an unfairly coloured view, since no city looks at its best when observed on a wet morning from a four-wheeler cab the progress of which irresistibly hints at a destination not in a railway station but in a municipal cemetery. Nor did Humphrey help in any ready uplifting of the heart, since he was silent, withdrawn, and apparently indisposed to favour his sceptical guardian with further fantasies... Mr Thewless, feeling the first stirrings of obscure doubt rising in him once more, jumped hastily from the cab and contrived his customary efficient capture of a porter. Humphrey followed. The railway station spread before them a classical portico nicely painted to look like milk chocolate. On one side stood an immobile policeman of gigantic size proportionately armed with truncheon and revolver. On the other a placard, equally generously conceived, announced

LIFE IS SHORT

DEATH IS COMING

ETERNITY — WHERE?

And upon this brief glimpse of the cultural life of Belfast their train received them and they were presently hurtling west.

MICHAEL INNES, *The Journeying Boy*, 1949

M ANY PERSONS have heard their fathers speak of the two bad seasons immediately following the Rebellion. They were the two most calamitous years Belfast ever endured. Cold was complained of in April, 1799, and in that month a heavy snow-storm happened, a most unusual occurrence. Incessant rain followed; August and September had no autumnal weather. The newspaper records state that the floods in the Lagan exceeded anything that had ever before been known. The usual consequences resulted. The corn crops were utterly destroyed. At this period the people had to depend for their food entirely on home-grown produce; and in October, the inhabitants of Belfast foresaw a dear and scarce winter, and famine at their very doors. The first notice that has been observed is the following, almost applicable in its terms and objects to the Belfast of 1878. 'We are happy to state that the means for alleviating the distress of the poor by means of a Public Kitchen has at last been attended to. Subscriptions have been going on for some time, and we will shortly communicate something interesting.' This was the first Belfast movement to meet the expected scarcity.

GEORGE BENN, *A History of the Town of Belfast*, 1880

THE PROTESTANT LIBERALS OF ULSTER, whose fathers and grandfathers were United Irishmen, had generally become warm supporters of the Liberal party as it had been led by Charles Earl Grey, Lord Melbourne, Lord John Russell, and recently by Lord Palmerston. Though the descendants of the United Irishmen, they were not at all disposed themselves to become rebels; but they were rather proud than otherwise of their ancestors for having been rebels. The events of that time, two years before the Act of Union, were vividly present to the descendants of those who had suffered in that dreadful insurrection, or rather series of insurrections. The wounds, though healed, left scars still visible. The scenes of the battles, as at Ballynahinch, and of the executions, as of McCracken in Belfast, were still pointed out. The High Street, then mean and small, and with a river running through it, was the theatre of McCracken's execution and several similar tragedies. The grandson of the Rev. Mr Porter, a Presbyterian clergyman, hanged by the ruling powers, was a merchant, an Ulster Liberal of great intelligence and ability. At a dinner this gentleman gave, during a Christmas visit of the late Mr Alexander Russel, for so many years the very clever and popular editor of the *Scotsman*, he said to another guest, a neighbouring country gentleman, 'Your grandfather hanged my grandfather.' 'Dear me,' said Mr Russel, 'this is coming very near.'

THOMAS MacKNIGHT, *Ulster As It Is*, 1896

IT WAS THE EVE OF ST PATRICK'S DAY, and all Bigotsborough was in the streets. The leaders of the Papist party had arranged to celebrate the day with more than the usual fervour and defiance. The walls of the town had been covered with green posters calling upon all true patriots to assemble in their thousands at Smithfield and march from that rendezvous through the Roman Catholic quarter along the Falls Road and past The Brickfields to Milltown. At the head of the posters flared the seditious emblem – the harp without the crown – and at the foot of the posters were the no less seditious words, 'God save Ireland'. In the dead of night some of these posters had been pasted on the walls of the Orange quarter, an outrage which filled its inhabitants with fury. The popular excitement was increased by the news that the Papists had savagely attacked the Islandmen on their way home from the ship-building-yard on the other side of the river Lagan.

Several hundreds of the ship-carpenters and riveters employed on the Island resided in the small streets leading off the Shankill Road. It was their custom when the party spirit was inflamed to march in military order, as it was necessary to traverse a portion of the Papist quarter on their way home. As they swung in a compact body along North Street, a shower of stones and bottles, flung by invisible assailants, came over the roofs of the houses.

As the street was narrow, the Islandmen suffered severely. In the pockets of their blue linen jackets they carried a supply of missiles – heavy iron bolts, nuts, and rivets. As they could not hurl these at their hidden antagonists, they vented their anger upon the plate-glass windows of Papist taverns and Papist shops. The crash of broken glass was a familiar sound in the streets of Bigotsborough, and it reached the ears of the Orange crowd at the top of the hill where North Street debouched into the Shankill Road. This crowd was composed largely of women and children, who were looking with some anxiety for the safe return of husbands and fathers, sons and brothers.

JAMES DOUGLAS, *The Unpardonable Sin*, 1907

IN BELFAST THAT 12 JULY [1969] the first ominous signs came, ironically, around a block of flats called Unity Walk.

Unity Walk is an isolated Catholic citadel at the mouth of the Protestant stronghold of Shankill Road. This Catholic presence at the entrance to the city's major loyalist ghetto – the legacy, as its name suggests, of an optimistic piece of town-planning – had long been an irritant. Even before breakfast on 12 July, Orange bands coming down the Shankill Road dallied at Unity Walk for ostentatious sectarian fanfares. Despite protests from residents the bands were not moved on; some police were afterwards alleged to have said that the Twelfth was the Orangemen's day and if the residents didn't like it they could go down south.

In the evening, as the bands were returning, trouble flared. Unity Walk's residents were on the forecourt of the flats, and missiles were exchanged with the bands' followers. A boy taking part in the parade with his father was hit by a bottle and quite badly hurt. The RUC occupied the balconies and forecourt of the flats, but apparently did little – possibly, could do little – to break up the Orange crowd. The affair was trivial, but the residents took it as evidence of police partiality. More important was the belief it instilled in Protestant minds that the Orange parade had been 'attacked' from the flats.

SUNDAY TIMES INSIGHT TEAM, *Ulster*, 1972

HE DROVE INTO DONEGALL STREET, then turned left into Millfield and drove across town until he reached the Falls Road. He turned up to the right.

The rain was falling in long blue slips before his headlights. The streets were deserted, but now and then a brilliantly lit-up tram would loom out of the watery darkness, racket past noisily, then vanish into the night like a ghost ship.

The road began to curve between great black cliffs that were the walls of linen mills, past huckster shops, pawnbrokers, pubs, fluttering hoardings, all flowing by in a rumpled depressed line, past narrow side streets whose labyrinthine depths formed the stronghold of the IRA. Flynn smiled to himself, as he drove through an area near the Public Baths, remembering that no policeman dared go in there alone.

The van rattled at every rivet. Flynn, caged solitary against the drenching night, was offered a rare moment for reflection. Even the excitements his life dangled before him would, he knew, over a length of time, fall into a pattern that amounted to little more than heightened routine. Would it be better if he went away, if he left the Black City altogether? Here the great stories to report were bombs up the Falls or priests' funerals – if you could call a long list of names a story.

The van seemed to lack springs entirely. It was a boneshaking ride. Yet it brought him quickly up the rain-streaming road. Suburban villas with gardens began to show up beside the street lamps, yellow islands in a drowning world. He had reached the City Cemetery – where they buried the Protestants. He had not far to go now.

There was a police car parked outside Milltown Cemetery. Flynn felt a soft gnaw gather behind his navel. It was a sensation he always got when about to tackle a difficult job.

Two policemen stood outside the arched sandstone gateways. They were young men, with florid, country faces. Flynn drew up opposite them, knowing they would become inquisitive. Sure enough, one came over.

'You can't park here.'

'Hello, officer, I'm Flynn of the *Telegram* –'

'What do you want?'

'I heard there was an explosion up here.'

'I know nothing about that. You'll have to ask the D.I.'

Flynn got out.

'Can I go in?'

'No.'

He argued for a moment, then gave it up and got back into the van, where it was warm and dry. The rain crackling in wild flurries on the pavement made him long for his warm bed, with the glowing light above his head, the smell of clean linen pillows in his nostrils and a book in his hands. Hurry, Monahan, he thought, you're slow the night.

MAX CAULFIELD, *The Black City*, 1952

ECCLESIASTES

God, you could grow to love it, God-fearing, God-
    chosen purist little puritan that,
for all your wiles and smiles, you are (the
    dank churches, the empty streets,
the shipyard silence, the tied-up swings) and
    shelter your cold heart from the heat
of the world, from woman-inquisition, from the
    bright eyes of children. Yes you could
wear black, drink water, nourish a fierce zeal
    with locusts and wild honey, and not
feel called upon to understand and forgive
    but only to speak with a bleak
afflatus, and love the January rains when they
    darken the dark doors and sink hard
into the Antrim hills, the bog meadows, the heaped
    graves of your fathers. Bury that red
bandana and stick, that banjo; this is your
    country, close one eye and be king.
Your people await you, their heavy washing
    flaps for you in the housing estates –
a credulous people. God you could do it, God
    help you, stand on a corner stiff
with rhetoric, promising nothing under the sun.

DEREK MAHON (1972), *Poems 1962–1978*, 1979

IN THOSE DAYS – more than thirty years before the most enduring Ulster Troubles broke out in 1969 – Belfast's tuberculosis death rate was the highest in the British Isles. The mortality rate for mothers had risen significantly since the First World War. The city's housing policy, in so far as it affected the poor, was nonexistent. Corruption on the corporation (later to be called Belfast City Council) seemed ineradicable. A world trade decline dealt Belfast's exports a crippling blow. One shipyard closed in 1934, and the other was greatly understretched. In the linen industry – a production line that had given Belfast the label 'Linenopolis' only a few decades earlier – more than 20,000 were out of work.

United in their misery and anger, the Belfast poor pushed their bigotry aside and marched together behind bands playing 'Yes, We Have No Bananas' to protest the Poor Law Guardians' refusal of adequate relief payments. It must have elated my father to see Protestant and Catholic working men and women, together, raging against a common foe – capitalist employers and their 'lickspittles' (a favourite epithet of his) in the Unionist government and in the Orange and Masonic lodges. But his elation was short-lived. It required only a couple of political speeches, carefully laced with sectarian poison, to divide the protesters and set them at one another's throats again.

CAL McCRYSTAL, *Reflections on a Quiet Rebel*, 1997

'PEOPLE WENT DOWN TO THE TIP HEAD AT DUNCRUE ROAD with buckets and went through the garbage for cinders and anything else that would burn. What was very common was men with patches on their clothes and boots. People patched their coats, trousers, boots. These had to be sewn on; there were no stick-on patches. The women had to sew them on. The women made pillow-cases and sheets from flour bags. They could have bought flour bags in Rank's or Andrews's flour mills for sixpence each. You washed and bleached the flour bags, sewed four of them together and binded them. That only cost two shillings or half a crown for a beautiful sheet that would last for ages. I remember once some of them made underwear for a girl getting married. It was made out of flour bags and covered with little pieces of lace.'

ANNE BOYLE, quoted in Ronnie Munck and Bill Rolston,
Belfast in the Thirties, 1987

TWO OLD WOMEN with black shawls over their heads and buckets in their hands passed wearily across the waste ground and paid no heed when the dog barked at them. In a weak, hoarse voice the granny called to the dog, but the old women walked on without looking to right or left, the tassels of their shawls shaking in the wind, their thin shoes sinking in the wet cart-ruts. She saw them go over to the dumps, push back the shawls from their grey heads and hoke amongst the rubbish for cinders and empty bottles. Blue smoke from burning rags rose from the dumps and fouled the air with a damp sweetish smell.

MICHAEL McLAVERTY, *Lost Fields*, 1942

from VALEDICTION

See Belfast, devout and profane and hard,
Built on reclaimed mud, hammers playing in the shipyard,
Time punched with holes like a steel sheet, time
Hardening the faces, veneering with a grey and speckled rime
The faces under the shawls and caps:
This was my mother-city, these my paps.

LOUIS MacNEICE (1933), Collected Poems, 1966

TURF LODGE, BALLYMURPHY, CLONARD, Andersonstown, the Falls, Twinbrook, Poleglass. It reads like a roll call of the seditious, factious Irish. Two steps away from the mountain's edge, these areas are tucked away from the city's sight with less success than elsewhere. They haven't managed to circumnavigate West Belfast entirely. That's one of the things about Belfast, its class divisions are shaky and flimsy. Folk from the Malone Road (Belfast's Kensington) aren't ignorant of the poverty of their dispossessed neighbours. This is mostly because these neighbours are only about five minutes down the road. Another reason, however, is that any journey in or out of the city takes you through some kind of poor area. You can't blink and miss it.

ROBERT McLIAM WILSON, The Dispossessed, 1992

WHEN HE TURNED ON TO THE ANTRIM ROAD, the white Ford was following him. His route would take him from North to South Belfast, through streets little changed since his childhood. He would skirt the boundaries of poor working-class areas and drive past the large monuments and buildings at the city's centre. It was a route which on a normal day was far too familiar to evoke in him any thought of what he was passing. But this morning, in a car which was a moving bomb, followed by terrorists who could radio in an order to kill his wife, he was driving for what might be the last time through this ugly, troubled place which held for him implacable memories of his past life. Now, in ironic procession, he would pass the house where he had been born, the boarding school in which he had been a pupil, and the university where he had written poetry, edited a student magazine, and dreamed of another life.

The house came first, at a turn in the road, not half a mile from where he now lived. It was larger than the houses which adjoined it, aloof in its own grounds with, at the back, a tennis court, a lawn, a vegetable garden, the whole surrounded by a high hedge which hid it from the surrounding streets.

It had been his grandfather's house, his grandfather who had started the family tradition of running hotels, his grandfather who had begun down on the docks with a pub and rooms to let above it and who, from that beginning, had made himself into A.D. Dillon, Importer of Wines & Spirits, owning two small hotels and supplying drink to a dozen pubs. His grandfather, who had died before Dillon was born, was known to him only as a figure in a family photograph. Bearded and broad-beamed like Edward VII, he was shown standing by a large Daimler car, on the running board of which sat his three children, dressed in sailor suits.

The house was called Ardath. Dillon's father had moved back into it in 1947, the year his grandfather died. Dillon was born there five years later and lived in the house until he was ten, when his feckless father sold it to buy Kinsallagh, a large country house in Donegal, which he turned into a hotel. He remembered his father playing tennis in long white trousers on the old grass court: he remembered the greenhouse which was always warm and where he watched frogspawn turn into frogs. Now, as he drove past, he could still see the old name 'ARDATH' on a stone plinth at the right-hand side of the gate. But a newer sign on the left read 'Sisters of Mercy: School for Girls'.

He drove on, passing the cinema where as a boy he had watched films in which men fired revolvers at other men and bombs blew up forts and other buildings, but where, always, in the end, the bad men paid for their crimes. It was now a quarter to eight. What if the bomb went off too soon?

He stopped the car at a pedestrian crossing. A young woman, pushing her baby in a pram, moved on to the crossing, and, halfway across, turned and smiled at him. At once, irrationally, he felt a sense of panic. Hurry up. Get away from me. He looked in his rear-view mirror but a heavy lorry loaded with aluminium milk cans had moved in behind him, so that he could not see the white Ford. When the girl and her baby reached the other side of the street, he drove on and at that moment saw the white Ford move up, passing the lorry, to pull in again at his rear.

Suddenly, three little boys, whirling their school satchels in the air as if to attack each other, ran across the street, shouting and laughing in the middle of traffic. They wore navy blazers and white shirts, with the tie of his school knotted like frayed rope-ends around their necks. Ignoring the squealing brakes around them, they gained the opposite pavement and continued their helter-skelter chase. Ahead, to his right, he could see the ornamental iron gates, the long tree-lined avenue and, at its end, the red brick façade of the Catholic school where for eleven years he had been a boarder, a school where teaching was carried on by bullying and corporal punishment and learning by rote, a school run by priests whose narrow sectarian views perfectly propagated the divisive bitterness which had led to the events of last night.

Look at me, look at me, he wanted to shout as he drove past those hated gates. See this car on its way to kill innocent people, see my wife in a room with a gun at her head, and then ask your Cardinal if he can still say of these killers that he can see their point of view.

BRIAN MOORE, *Lies of Silence*, 1990

R ELIGION WAS TO THE PEOPLE OF BIGOTSBOROUGH a kind of politics. Popery took the place of sin in their consciousness. They regarded Protestantism as synonymous with Christianity. They conceived God as being the Grand Master of an Orange Lodge, and Christ as a meritorious prototype of William the Third. They read the Bible as if it were an 'Orange Soldier's Pocketbook'. They identified their Roman Catholic fellow-countrymen with the Philistines, the Amalekites, the Hittites, the Sadducees, and the Pharisees. The emblem of the 'Open Bible' inspired their worst passions. It figured in the centre of their street arches, garlanded with Orange lilies and flanked by portraits of truculent Orange divines. They bore it on the peaks of their flagstaffs. They painted it on their banners. Round it they rallied in their riots, and many a drunken blackguard was carried to the police station with a ferocious text on his lips.

JAMES DOUGLAS, *The Unpardonable Sin*, 1907

M R JAMES DOUGLAS, the well-known London writer, satirises his native city as '*Bigotsborough*' in a novel of some fame, and draws some lurid pictures of former Belfast scenes. For bigotry, it might be wiser to use the word *prejudice*, and undoubtedly there is in some districts a great deal of this, due to lack of education, mutual distrust, historic feuds and narrowness of vision. This prejudice is not confined to any one class or religion, for there is a prejudice in the Roman Catholic Falls Road against Protestant Sandy Row, just as there is in Sandy Row against the Falls Road. With the spread of education, increase in reading and travel, and mixing together, this bias is on the decline, and visitors to Belfast are not to judge the city by offensive remarks on house gables here and there which are not exactly polite to the Pope or the King, but which no one takes seriously! Surely it must be conceded that no side or class holds a monopoly of either virtue or vice, and in the recent regrettable disturbances there were faults on both sides, but let sleeping dogs lie. The sooner this prejudice dies out the better, but it is not so venomous as some English papers (short of copy) would make out, and people who live out of Ireland and know next to nothing of the circumstances leading up to this prejudice have little claim to comment upon it.

JAMES LOGAN, *Ulster in the X-Rays*, 1922

'PROTESTANT OR PAPIST?' said the officer in command.
'Neither,' said Bland, 'I'm a high caste Brahmin.'

Fortunately I recognised the officer's voice. It was Crossan who commanded this particular regiment. It never was safe, even in the quietest times, to be flippant with Crossan. On a night like that and under the existing circumstances, Bland might very well have been knocked on the head for his joke if I had not come to his rescue.

'Crossan,' I said, 'don't make a fuss. Mr Bland and I are simply taking a walk round the streets.'

'If he's a Papist,' said Crossan, 'he'll have to go home to his bed. Them's my orders. We don't want rioting in the streets to-night.'

I turned to Bland.

'What is your religion?' I asked.

'Haven't any,' he said. 'I haven't believed any doctrine taught by any Church since I was six years old. Will that satisfy you?'

'I was afeard,' said Crossan, 'that you might be a Papist. You can go on.'

This shows, I think, that the charges of bigotry and intolerance brought against our Northern Protestants are quite unfounded, Crossan had no wish to persecute even a professed atheist.

We did not go very far though we were out for nearly two hours. The streets were filled with armed men and everybody we met challenged us. The police were the hardest to get rid of. They were no doubt soured by the treatment they received in Belfast. Accustomed to be regarded with awe by rural malefactors and denounced in flaming periods, of a kind highly gratifying to their self-importance, by political leaders, they could not understand a people who did not mention them in speeches but threatened their lives with paving stones. This had been their previous experience of Belfast and they were naturally suspicious of any stray wayfarers whom they met. They were not impressed when Bland said he was a newspaper reporter. They did not seem to care whether he believed or disbelieved the Apostles' Creed. One party of them actually arrested us and only a ready lie of Bland's saved us from spending an uncomfortable night. He said, to my absolute amazement, that we were officials of an exalted kind, sent down by the Local Government Board to hold a sworn inquiry into the condition of Belfast. This struck me at the time as an outrageously silly story, but it was really a rather good one to tell. The Irish police are accustomed to sworn inquiries as one of the last resorts of harassed

Governments. It seemed to the sergeant quite natural that somebody should be in Belfast to hold one.

GEORGE A. BIRMINGHAM, *The Red Hand of Ulster*, 1912

I TOOK OUT MY CAMERA AND BEGAN TAKING PICTURES. A girl, about sixteen years old, turned and screamed.

'He's a Taig!' she shouted.

I lowered my camera immediately. Given that night, that place, and those passions, it was a killing accusation. I had no idea how the girl reached her conclusion, unless perhaps she assumed I was Catholic because I had come over from that side of the road. She was drunk, bold, and very loud. A small group turned away from the fire to examine me, and others turned when they saw the beginnings of a new commotion. My accuser stepped forward, clutching a can of beer.

'Are you a Taig?' she asked.

'I'm an American,' I said. The answer had always worked in the past.

'American Catholic or American Protestant?'

'Just American.'

'American what?' she demanded. 'Catholic or Protestant?'

I was raised a Catholic, but by 1980 I hadn't practised for many years. I disagreed with many of the Church's teachings. I had no great fondness for the pope. In short, I didn't think I qualified as Catholic. I was being offered an opportunity many believers would have envied, a chance to stand up for the faith in the face of persecution. I was not enthusiastic. I was scared by the crowd and by the mean spirit I had seen on the Shankill, embarrassed by my uncertainty, and angry that a mob of drunken arsonists, led by a teenage girl, threatened to get the best of me.

I have since decided that I should have claimed Catholicism and solidarity in one breath, admitting that I had been raised a Catholic, but hastily adding that I worked for a living just as the people stoking the fire did, that I ate the same food, that I lived in the same sort of house, that in fact the only difference between us was that I didn't go to a different church than the one that they didn't go to. Belfast Protestants and Catholics would do well to receive strong doses of reality to dispel their myths about each other, and my claims of practising non-Catholicism would have been a small contribution.

Instead, I lied. I claimed I was a Jew. It was probably one of the few times in the recent history of Europe that someone has claimed to be a Jew in order to avoid religious persecution.

JOHN CONROY, *War as a Way of Life*, 1988

HIS IMAGINATION HAD CONSTRUCTED AN ORDERED SCENE of Sunday peace, a neat terrace of houses, each with a coat of fresh paintwork and a concave step scrubbed as a matter of habit. He knew such streets well; nothing had dimmed their image from the past. They existed out there reassuringly, whenever he had cared to think about them in that other alien world of wire mesh and dog patrols. But this was the true terrain of nightmare, fixed in its horrible aftermath. A vista of bricked-up doorways and windows stretched for as far as the eye could travel, for it was one of those immensely long, slightly curving streets, artery for all those little side streets which, together on the map, went to make up a defined city-area with its own nickname and loyalties. But all that was dead and done, merely a memory now. They picked their way through sodden debris and drifts of wind-blown rubbish, past the brutal breeze-block facings in the older brick. There was a reek of soot, damp and escaping gas.

MAURICE LEITCH, *Silver's City*, 1981

from THE PREACHER

Among old iron, cinders, sizzling dumps,
A world castrated, amputated, trepanned,
He walked in the lost acres crying 'Repent
For the Kingdom of Death is at hand'.

He took the books of pagan art and read
Between the lines or worked them out to prove
Humanism a palimpsest and God's
Anger a more primal fact than love.

And in the city at night where drunken song
Climbed the air like tendrils of vine
He bared a knife and slashed the roots and laid
Another curse on Cain. The sign

Of the cross between his eyes, his mouth drawn down,
He passed the flower-sellers and all
The roses reeked of an abattoir, the gardenias
Became the décor of a funeral.

LOUIS MacNEICE (1941), *Collected Poems*, 1966

I CROSSED SHAFTESBURY SQUARE. Though early, the Lavery's overspill was already out on the street. Groups of unusually dirty youths lounged on the pavement with beer glasses in their hands. As I passed the bar, stepping over their outstretched legs, a warm, urinous waft hung in the air outside the doorway. I hated Lavery's. It had to be the dirtiest, most crowded, least likeable bar in Western Europe. Consequently, it was enormously popular. Very Belfast. Einstein got it wrong. The Theory of Relativity didn't apply to Lavery's. Lavery's time was different time. You went into Lavery's one night at the age of eighteen and you stumbled out, pissed, to find you were in your thirties already. People drank their lives away there. Lavery's was for failures. I was working as a tile layer and I couldn't get into Lavery's because I was too successful.

I walked up the Lisburn Road and passed the Anabaptist Church – or double-duckers as we called them – the South Belfast Gospel Hall, the Windsor Tabernacle, the Elim Pentecostal, the Methodist Mission, the Presbyterian Presbytery, and the Unitarian Church of Protestant Mnemonists or something like that. At the door of all the adjacent rectories, broken pastors stood, staring at me with grim expressions. To the old law, they were true. You crap on my grandfather, you crap on me. I found these guys infinitely more frightening than Crab, Hally or Ronnie Clay. I tried not to look like a Catholic. I tightened my Bible belt. I thought they were convinced.

ROBERT McLIAM WILSON, *Eureka Street*, 1996

A THUNDERSTORM, which extinguished the electric-light supply from Larne, and went rolling and echoing down the glens all night long, flashing green strips of light between the curtains, and evoking for me uncomfortable pictures of greasy bogs and waterfalls in spate, warned me that I had dallied too long over my journey. I made for Belfast, which had begun to seem less and less desirable the nearer I came to it. I think I saw it, this time, under the worst possible conditions – war-conditions; sandbags; concrete shelters – pathetically futile; general gloom. Only at night, in the black-out, when every street was a gully of darkness, and a sense of eerie mystery lurked at every corner, did I feel the least stir of my imagination. Donegall Place suggested *The Murders of the Rue Morgue*. Grosvenor Road might have been a brothel quarter.

I was reminded of what a Northern woman once said to me about Belfast, that it has a Burke and Hare atmosphere, like old, murky Edinburgh. She made me imagine it before it developed grand notions about itself – warning me not to forget that Belfast was not made a city until as late as 1888 – drowsing in a Sunday sleep, behind heavy curtains, with tasselled pelmets, and the Bible open on the table. Outside the greyness of its older buildings and the redness of its newer red-bricked streets fading into the evening dusk and the fogs up from the Lagan, would reflect its grey industrialist outlook and the very dim glow of its Protestant heart. I could see what she was driving at. Places like the Falls Road or the district about Carlisle Circus are glum enough to-day: what must they have been like before Trade Unionism got going properly? I wish somebody would recreate that old Belfast in a play.

SEAN O'FAOLAIN, An Irish Journey, 1940

Versions
of the Falls

Osman, Serbia, Sultan, Raglan, Bosnia, Belgrade, Rumania, Sebastopol.

The names roll off my tongue like a litany.

'Has that something to do with Gladstone's foreign policy?' he used to laugh and ask.

'No. Those are the streets of West Belfast.'

Alma, Omar, Conway and Dunlewey, Dunville, Lady and McDonnell.

Pray for us. (I used to say, just to please my grand-mother.)

Now and at the hour.

ANNE DEVLIN, 'Naming the Names'

I GET ON MY BIKE, AND TURN, AND GO DOWN THE FALLS, past vanished public houses – The Clock Bar, The Celtic, Daly's, The Gladstone, The Arkle, The Old House – past drapers, bakers, fishmongers, boot shops, chemists, pawnshops, picture houses, confectioners and churches, all swallowed in the maw of time and trouble, clearances; feeling shaky, nervous, remembering how a few moments ago I was *there*, in my mind's eye, one foot in the grave of that Falls Road of thirty years ago, inhaling its gritty smoggy air as I lolled outside the door of 100 Raglan Street, staring down through the comforting gloom to the soot-encrusted spires of St Peter's, or gazing at the blank brick gable walls of Balaclava Street, Cape Street, Frere Street, Milton Street, saying their names over to myself.

CIARAN CARSON, *from* 'Question Time', *Belfast Confetti*, 1989

THE PRESENT FALLS ROAD met the old road at Maryburn Lane, a little way above Milltown, it then turned across what is now the cemetery crossing in front of the Industrial School and passing the workshops to the present road. A high ridge once crossed Falls Road at this point, as will be seen by the deep cutting just inside the Falls Park on the high ground of which the bus depot is built. To avoid this height, the road makers followed the line of least resistance by bringing the road round by the school. Lake Glen in the old days contained a lake with a crannog in the centre, and the old fort in the vicinity gave its name to the townland of Ballydownfine.

Leaving the Industrial School, the old road cut off a corner of the Park to the high ground of the City Cemetery, and through Glenalina, crossing the Whiterock Road above MacRory Park. A little portion of the old road still exists at this place, running between Whiterock and Dan O'Neill's Loney. The old road then made its way across what is now the Brickfields – some time ago we saw part of a wooden pathway unearthed here – then on by the great Fort that gave its name to the Forth River, on the site of which the old cotton mill now stands. The road then passed through Springfield village, recently demolished and rebuilt, and on to Shankill.

In the long ago Whiterock was known as Kill Piper's Hill, and a little fort on the north side of MacRory Park is said to be the Fort of the Pipers.

A little over a hundred years ago the City Cemetery was covered with linen cloth. It was the bleach green of the Glenalina Bleach Works, the proprietor of which, William Sinclair, was known as 'Sinclair of the Hawks'. His hounds were kept at the rear of his house in Donegall Place, where he also kept his hawks and his falcons, and when he rode out to Whiterock – with his falcon at his wrist – the streets of the old town were loud with the baying of his hounds and the unusual and colourful stir caused by his hawking parties.

CATHAL O'BYRNE, *As I Roved Out*, 1946

MY BIRTHPLACE WAS AT 54 DIVIS STREET, BELFAST, demolished in recent years, almost within sight and sound of the city centre – Castle Junction, and my birthday was 14th December, 1871. It has been said that one ought to be careful in the choice of one's parents. I was fortunate in mine – in my father, Joseph Campbell, in business a stationer, who hailed from Maghery, County Armagh, on the shores of Lough Neagh; and in my mother, Sarah Campbell (née Morrow), a native of Ballynaris, Dromore, County Down. So I can claim to be Ulster of the Ulster. My father saw Queen Victoria drive through Belfast in 1849, and saw often on her journeyings through the city Mary M'Cracken, sister of Henry Joy M'Cracken, who outlived her patriot brother well nigh 70 years. How

M'Cracken died was long told by Belfast firesides. Nationalist processions were wont to lower flags when passing the place of execution at Corn Market. Divis Street is as old and storied a street as any in Belfast. Running off Divis Street is Barrack Street, where military were first stationed as long as two centuries ago. This barrack was used in my childhood for what was popularly called a ragged school for poor lads from the Shankill, between whom and lads from the neighbourhood skirmishing with stones was not unknown about the Twelfth of July.

T.J. CAMPBELL, *Fifty Years of Ulster 1890–1940*, 1941

THE POOR LAW RATE BOOK FOR 1860 lists only two shops on the Falls Road, yet by the turn of the century, the area possessed a very well-developed shopping structure. There were shops along the road supplying almost every human need, from every day necessities to luxury goods.

There were generally two types of shops. The smaller of the two was called a Parlour Shop because the ground floor, or perhaps only the front room, was converted into a business premises, while the family lived at the back or upstairs. These were seldom structurally altered, that is, the little house remained as it was, and the ordinary front window was used to display the goods.

To make larger shops structural modifications had to be made to give greater space. Perhaps the wall between the two downstairs rooms would be taken away or an extra bit built on. We can tell which were the parlour type and which were the larger shops from their rateable values. The larger premises would be charged higher rates. The best possible situation for a business was on the corner of two streets, attracting custom from both.

CARMEL GALLAGHER, *All Around the Loney-O*, 1978

WHEN I WAS BORN AT THE FAMILY HOME in 46 Lady Street on the Falls Road on 8 March 1925, the new Northern Ireland was still coming to terms with partition. It was hoped this was the final solution to reconcile the conflicting objectives of unionists and nationalists in Ireland . . .

My earliest memories are . . . of Lady Street, which ran parallel to Albert Street, off the Pound Loney. It was a cobble-stoned, terraced street of small houses, each with a kitchen and livingroom downstairs and two small bedrooms upstairs. Water came from a single cold tap in a stone sink behind the door; there was a pit in the back yard for refuse and an outside lavatory. Every Saturday night we were taken into the small room off the kitchen one at a time to have a bath with water that had been boiled on the stove during the day.

Our daily lives were governed by the bells of St Peter's, which as the crow flies was only a couple of hundred yards away from the house. The chimes every fifteen minutes were a constant reminder of our routine, dictating where we should be or what we should be doing. Attendance at one church ceremony or another was virtually an everyday commitment, with regular mass, confession and communion every week, and a midweek confraternity meeting. For a time, under pressure from my aunts who wanted me to emulate the boy next door, I reluctantly trained to be an altar boy but I dropped out before being finally accepted. Another unwelcome involvement came when the family pushed me into playing the cymbals with the West Belfast Accordion Band for a few months.

PADDY DEVLIN, *Straight Left*, 1993

from LETTER TO DEREK MAHON

And did we come into our own
When, minus muse and lexicon,
We traced in August sixty-nine
Our imaginary Peace Line
Around the burnt-out houses of
The Catholics we'd scarcely loved,
Two Sisyphuses come to budge
The sticks and stones of an old grudge,

Two poetic conservatives
In the city of guns and long knives,
Our ears receiving then and there
The stereophonic nightmare
Of the Shankill and the Falls,
Our matches struck on crumbling walls
To light us as we moved at last
Through the back alleys of Belfast?

MICHAEL LONGLEY, *An Exploded View*, 1973

BETWEEN THE YEARS 1870 AND 1886 there were several outbreaks in the seismic area of the city – that part in which the streaks of disagreement lie in parallel lines running northward. On the Shankill Road are the dwellings of Protestants, only the publicans and pawnbrokers being Romanists. Not far from being parallel to this road is the Falls, inhabited almost entirely by Romanists. Between these two chief arteries leading out of the city and into a picturesque region of hills and meadows and water-brooks, are countless streets of workmen's houses, some rows occupied by Protestants and others by Romanists. Now, anyone passing through these localities will perceive, on being made aware of the respective creeds of the inhabitants and of the spirit of animosity which is inhaled by all from their earliest years, how easy it is for a riot to be started.

F. FRANKFORT MOORE, The Truth About Ulster, 1914

HAMLET

As usual, the clock in The Clock Bar was a good few minutes
    fast:
A fiction no one really bothered to maintain, unlike the story
The comrade on my left was telling, which no one knew for
    certain truth:
Back in 1922, a sergeant, I forget his name, was shot outside the
    National Bank . . .
Ah yes, what year was it that they knocked it down? Yet, its
    memory's as fresh
As the inky smell of new pound notes – which interferes with
    the beer-and-whiskey
Tang of now, like two dogs meeting in the revolutionary 69 of
    a long sniff,
Or cattle jostling shit-stained flanks in the Pound. For *pound*, as
    some wag
Interrupted, was an off-shoot of the Falls, from the Irish, *fál*,
    a hedge;
Hence, *any kind of enclosed thing*, its twigs and branches
    commemorated
By the soldiers' drab and olive camouflage, as they try to melt
Into a brick wall; red coats might be better, after all. *At any rate,*
This sergeant's number came up; not a winning one. The bullet had
    his name on it.
Though Sergeant X, as we'll call him, doesn't really feature
    in the story:
The nub of it is, *This tin can which was heard that night,*
    trundling down
From the bank, down Balaclava Street. Which thousands heard, and
    no one ever

Saw. Which was heard for years, any night that trouble might be
Round the corner . . . and when it skittered to a halt, you knew

That someone else had snuffed it: a name drifting like an afterthought,

A scribbled wisp of smoke you try and grasp, as it becomes diminuendo, then

Vanishes. For *fál*, is also *frontier, boundary*, as in *the undiscovered country*

From whose bourne no traveller returns, the illegible, thorny hedge of time itself –

Heartstopping moments, measured not by the pulse of a wrist-watch, nor

The archaic anarchists' alarm-clock, but a mercury tilt device

Which 'only connects' on any given bump on the road. So, by this wingèd messenger

The promise 'to pay the bearer' is fulfilled:

As someone buys another round, an Allied Irish Banks £10 note drowns in

The slops of the counter; a Guinness stain blooms on the artist's impression

Of the sinking of the *Girona*; a tiny foam hisses round the salamander brooch

Dredged up to show how love and money endure, beyond death and the Armada,

Like the bomb-disposal expert in his suit of salamander-cloth.

Shielded against the blast of time by a strangely-mediaeval visor,

He's been outmoded by this jerky robot whose various attachments include

A large hook for turning over corpses that may be booby-trapped;

But I still have this picture of his hands held up to avert the future

In a final act of *No surrender*, as, twisting through the murky fathoms

Of what might have been, he is washed ashore as pearl and coral.

This *strange eruption to our state* is seen in other versions of the Falls:

A no-go area, a ghetto, a demolition zone. For the ghost, as it turns out –

All this according to your man, and I can well believe it – this tin ghost,

Since the streets it haunted were abolished, was never heard again.

The sleeve of Raglan Street has been unravelled; the helmet of
    Balaclava
Is torn away from the mouth. The dim glow of Garnet has gone
    out,
And with it, all but the memory of where I lived. I, too, heard
    the ghost:
A roulette trickle, or the hesitant annunciation of a downpour,
    ricocheting
Off the window; a goods train shunting distantly into a siding,
Then groaning to a halt; the rainy cries of children after dusk.
For the voice from the grave reverberates in others' mouths, as
    the sails
Of the whitethorn hedge swell up in a little breeze, and tremble
Like the spiral blossom of Andromeda: so suddenly are shrouds
    and branches
Hung with street-lights, celebrating all that's lost, as fields are
    reclaimed
By the Starry Plough. So we name the constellations, to put a
    shape
On what was there; so, the storyteller picks his way between
    the isolated stars.

But, *Was it really like that?* And, *Is the story true?*
You might as well tear off the iron mask, and find that no one,
    after all,
Is there: nothing but a cry, a summons, clanking out from the
    smoke
Of demolition. Like some son looking for his father, or the
    father for his son,
We try to piece together the exploded fragments. Let these
    broken spars
Stand for the Armada and its proud full sails, for even if
The clock is put to rights, everyone will still believe it's fast:
The barman's shouts of *time* will be ignored in any case, since
    time
Is conversation; it is the hedge that flits incessantly into the
    present,
As words blossom from the speakers' mouths, and the flotilla
    returns to harbour,
Long after hours.

CIARAN CARSON, *Belfast Confetti*, 1989

UP ALONG HIGH STREET THEY WENT, Colm seeing their reflections in the blinds of the big shop windows as they passed. They turned into the Falls Road. Here there was life. An ice-cream man was standing between the shafts of his barrow rattling the lid. Loads of children, returning from a day in the Park, were shouting from the tops of trams; boys held aloft empty bottles that had held watery milk, the girls waved rags of handkerchiefs, all their faces smeared from the jammed pieces devoured in the cool of the trees. But the MacNeills were too tired, too cross, for their hearts to leap with joy, Clare alone of them envious and lagging behind. Then she'd run and catching up with them say, her voice quivering with vexation, 'Take the tram, Mammie. Take the tram. I'm tired.' They paid no heed to her as they trudged on with the sweat breaking on them.

Away in front the sun was sinking behind Divis, its evening light flowing into the tram lines and dusting with gold the sooty spires of St Peter's. Around them the mills were strangely silent, the flock on the wire-guarded window disturbed by no draught, the brick walls oozing out the heat held captive during the day.

'Och, such a day,' would come from the mother, as she dragged her feet. 'To think that twopence ha'penny would take us home in comfort and me without a fluke!'

And when she got into the house she stirred up the fire under the kettle, made tea, and sent Colm off to bed early as he had to rise for school in the morning.

MICHAEL McLAVERTY, *Call My Brother Back*, 1979

THE TRAMCAR WAS FULL. Inside, there were men and women from the day-shifts in the factories and shipyards, together with housewives returning from an afternoon in the cinemas or late shopping. Besides these, there were youths and girls going to dance halls or cinemas in the locality.

Seamus was inside, standing between two girls styled fantastically in the manner of screen actresses and a stout man smelling of spirits. The air was putrid, for ever since the car had left the shed earlier in the day, and perhaps as long ago as a week or even a month, the tiny windows and little ventilation shafts had remained closed. Sometimes passengers who were almost overcome by the acrid atmosphere would attempt to open one of the little flaps, but at once some stout man or woman would complain.

'Sure, the draught is terr'ble! Do you want us all destroyed with the influenza?'

'This tram stinks!' the passengers asserted.

'Och, away out o' that!' someone retorted. 'Stop lettin' in the draughts on us!'

Or the little conductor would heed the complaint about the atmosphere of his car and come in and try to open the ventilators.

'Some people,' he muttered, closing his eyes and slightly jerking his head upwards, 'you would think some people lives in fields! This window has come stuck!'

About every hundred yards the tram halted at the stops. A few passengers alighted. Many more pushed and scrambled aboard. Somebody on the platform tugged the bell-rope and the vehicle jerked forward, jostling the passengers violently together. The little conductor came clattering down from upstairs; and pushing aside the passengers who were crowded on the platform, he seized his way bill and began to enter the particulars of his takings. When the car stopped he returned the bill to its place and regulated the outflow and inflow of passengers. His voice was crisp and authoritative, and all the actions of his little limbs and body were vigorous; yet nobody seemed to take any notice of him, imagining him to be only a person who collected fares and gave them a ticket which, at the end of the journey, the majority of them dropped in the roadway. Swarms of boisterous, vigorous youths stormed the vehicle, pushing the alighting passengers roughly aside, shouting, laughing, filling the stairs, the platform, and the doorway. One of them tugged the bell-rope. Then again the car jerked forward, flinging everybody about. The imperturbable conductor rattled the coins in his hand and shouted:

'Fares! All fares! Fares, please!'

F.L. GREEN, Odd Man Out, 1945

THERE'S A GOOD PUB IN SANDY ROW, the 'Bluebell', and a former proprietor refused to allow the Duke of Edinburgh to play the Orange Drum there – on the grounds that he wasn't a member of the Orange Order and that playing the drum was too serious a business for even the Duke to be permitted to do it. A lot of royal visits to the North take place. The Catholic upper and middle class rather fancy them, but they are afraid to say so. The Protestants treat them as a joke, but look on them as a sort of a guarantee that the Six Counties are not going to be handed over to the Republic, for the present, anyhow. The Unionists in the North use the Royal Show as a kind of Conservative Party circus to pull in the votes – just as it does in England. I was never a one for the Show myself, preferring the Victoria Palace to Buckingham Palace.

The Falls Road area is the main Catholic area. I've been there frequently but I remember it mainly for an incident that happened to me round there during the war. I was trying to make an impression on a girl. I was about eighteen, and another fellow and the girl and myself were sitting in a house on the Falls Road drinking tea. The other fellow remarked on the enormous wages being earned by the workers in the shipyard and in the aircraft factory. He referred to one family, in particular, and while I wasn't trying to make the girl think that my people were millionaires, I certainly did not expect him to say: 'And there's the MacSweeneys. Do you know thon crowd, Brendan, have a piano, and before the war, they were the same as ourselves – they had nothing!'

BRENDAN BEHAN, *Brendan Behan's Island*, 1962

MATTERS CAME TO A HEAD in 1932 when the poor buried their religious differences and jointly challenged Craig's government on its failure to reform the system and make relief payments on a scale comparable with those in other major British cities. For the first time people from both the Falls and the Shankill areas made common cause. Indeed, nearly 60,000 people from both religions throughout the city marched by torchlight to the Custom House steps to protest. They were led by bands from both traditions, which played the tune 'Yes, we have no bananas' over and over again in case the traditional party tunes would give offence. But it was only after several days of serious rioting that the shaken government was finally forced to increase the relief payments by 50 per cent. Thereafter, payments were made in cash, instead of by the grocery chits from which unscrupulous shopkeepers siphoned off as much as 25 per cent of the value in commission.

PADDY DEVLIN, *Straight Left*, 1993

POUND ROAD WAS THE APPROACH to the Pound through Cripple Row from the Falls, and was an early populated district. The Pound and Dog Kennel were situated on the north side of Barrack Street, and its junction with our Pound Street and Durham Street. It is now occupied by houses, and by that portion of Durham Street which has been continued up to Divis Street. You were supposed to be on the Dublin Road when you turned out of Barrack Street into what is now called Durham Street. The Pound was lower than the road, and was enclosed by a stone wall, on which all the idlers of the neighbourhood used to rest. A clear stream of water ran through the Pound, and the keeper was strictly bound to preserve it carefully for the use of the cattle that might be committed to his charge. This stream ran through gardens and orchards until it joined the Blackwater River, and it is even now known as the Pound Burn. I remember pulling gooseberries in one of these gardens: it was just where the Messrs Hinds' mill now stands. There was a cotton mill in Millfield, and tobacco pipes were made in Pipe Lane.

THOMAS GAFFIKEN, *Belfast Fifty Years Ago*, 1894

O FF THE MIDDLE FALLS ROAD at that time [1967] was a broad stoney lane which led to the Whiterock Road housing estate – by and large a decent, settled working-class red brick housing estate built in the late 1920s. The broad lane was known as the Giant's Foot. It was about 300 metres long and was so named because it resulted in a long curving instep. About half-way up, two old pen-knifed telegraph poles held sickly yellow lights. They flickered rather than burned. At right angles to the Giant's Foot was a long dark road with a large gate at the end, which led to Our Lady's Hospice – a hospital for old people, run by nuns. It was forbidden and screened by large thickets of laurel and tall Scots pines. It was imaginatively named, but no-body ever knew by whom. No plate ever endorsed its name.

Girls were afraid to walk that way at night because it was wild with tall nettles, and a bump in the slushy pebble-dashed wall was supposed to have been a nun's head. That's all we ever knew. Also, because of the depression of the 1950s and official neglect, a smattering of localised crime was evident. Unemployment was always chronic and the railings turned year after year to rusted husks.

BRENDAN HAMILL, *Krino*, 1995

C ASTLE STREET AND ITS CONTINUATION by Mill Street and Divis Street outwards into the Falls Road is certainly one of the most unromantic thoroughfares in Belfast, and undoubtedly looks it. There are heavy currents of carts, alternating with funerals, and men and women streaming continually all day – industrial workers and those who know too well the seamy side of life. Even its myriad shops with no great pretence at prominence have a bored and jaded appearance. Castle Street is narrow, so narrow that the car must come to a halt now and then to let some heavy dray pass, and Mill Street, its continuation, is dull and drab. There is Barrack Street to the left, with some little tinge of history, for through it the Dublin Mail Coach entered Belfast, and its name comes from the old military depot once here. We are soon in the midst of the many Mills. There on the right is Bath Place Spinning Mill and on the left a huge flour mill. A little higher up the road is a somewhat dilapidated brick building within its railings, the Model Schools – once a 'sight of the city', and a reminder of one of the best systems of elementary non-sectarian education ever given to Ireland, yet spurned because sectarian management was ignored. A little higher up the road and we are in the midst of big weaving and spinning factories almost burying up a branch Municipal Baths. We begin to see now where some of the linen comes from. Industry and religion predominate on the Falls Road. It is the Roman Catholic quarter of the city, just as a few hundred yards away, across any of those parallel streets stretching to the right, *i.e.*, to the Shankill Road, we find the people

245

intensely devoted to the memory of the Prince of Orange. So here convents and monasteries with imposing RC churches abound.

The car comes to a halt at Springfield Road in front of a neat square, about $4^1/_2$ acres in extent, known as Dunville Park, and presented (with its Doulton fountain) to the city by R.G. Dunville, the distiller. In this bald looking enclosed area old men sit of summer evenings smoking drowsily or reading their newspapers, weedy young men who live and work in these parts dally there with their sweethearts, and unwashed, pale-faced children – the small ones nursing smaller ones – wrangle and weep and build sand castles together, happy without knowing it; whilst across the road in the big Hospital are sufferers tossing to and fro, speculating on the toss up that means life or death. At the corner we get just a peep at the Victoria Hospital, Belfast's chief hospital, built on exceedingly up-to-date principles. Then as the car goes onward we see on the left clearly Divis Mountain and on its slope somewhat the City Cemetery, about 45 acres in extent, and from its elevation giving good views of Belfast – not that its many silent residents avail themselves of this advantage. Further along the road and adjoining it is a public pleasure ground, Falls Park (44 acres), with a charm in its naturalness in contrast to stiff walks and stereotyped flower beds. In Belfast the sectarian differences are allowed to prevail even after death, for there across the road is another necropolis, Milltown Cemetery, endowed by a grant from the rates to satisfy the Roman Catholic hierarchy, who demanded a separate resting-place for their people from the Protestant. How they will commingle at the Resurrection is an open question. And now we wheel to the left and go between flowery hawthorn hedges with leafy gardens and farm plots. It is the country and an escape from brickdom.

When the car finally stops we have a choice of routes for returning. We may proceed a few yards and, turning to the left, traverse Stockman's Lane to come out – 15 minutes or so later – and board the Lisburn Road car.

But we elect to return again by the Falls Road, *telling the conductor we wish to alight at Springfield Road.* Here we board a Springfield Road car going to the city. We pass the front of the splendid Victoria Hospital, owing its existence to Lady Pirrie and opened by the King in 1903. Then come the gates of the Lunatic Asylum, and now we have a long wide straight thoroughfare before us. It extends right from the base of the mountains to the river almost, for away in the dim distance that white clock dial surmounts the Fish Markets by the river. If uninteresting it is nevertheless a fairly busy road, and when we emerge at the Hippodrome and the Assembly Buildings we see now our geographical location, for five minutes later, after circumventing two sides of the City Hall, we are again in Donegall Place and back at Castle Junction.

A. MOORE, *Belfast Today*, c. 1910

'FREE-MAN! FREE-MAN! EARLY SIXTH! EARLY SIXTH!'

The newsboys shouted, the trams clanked, the bells clanged. Was there ever such a place for trams? Crowds ambulating along High Street, shopping crowds and business crowds colliding all day long at the junction of Royal Avenue and Donegall Place – the pivot of Belfast.

And at night – what a crush at the junction! 'Antrim Road – Shankill Road – Falls Road – Belmont.' On the stroke of ten-thirty – silence . . .

I took a tram to the Falls Road terminus. Row upon row of newish brick tenement-houses, of squalid shops, picture palaces innumerable, youths playing football in waste spaces, and near the end of the long road a small, quiet park overlooked by Squire's Mountain. A feature of the journey was the names above the shops – Murphy, Ryan, Connor, Mahoney, Keogh, Molloy. And they, in turn, accounted for inscriptions on blank walls such as: 'Up Dublin! Your hour is come! Beware! Shoot on sight! Up the rebels!'

If Belfast's characteristic sound is the clangour of the tramcar bells, her characteristic hour is 5.30 p.m. Then the shipyard workers crowd out of the docks until Waring Street and High Street are blocked with them. A similar scene may be witnessed near the gates of the West India Docks, London – crowds of brawny men with grimy faces in caps and blue overalls and shirts without collars, carrying small wicker baskets. In Belfast you have the spectacle of special trams labelled 'Workers only', crowded from roof to floor and passing in procession at this hour down High Street.

WILFRED EWART, *A Journey in Ireland 1921*, 1922

IN THE SUMMER we made guiders or had them made for us, pressing pram wheels and planks into service for the mad rush down Dunville Street. Ball-bearings were much in demand. Short-planked guiders, big wheels to the front with a single or double ball-bearing at the rear ensured a real weeker of a guider. We also had a hoop and cleek season, the hoop improvised from the spokeless rim of an old bicycle wheel, the cleek made from bull wire, looped to make a handle at one end with a U-shaped cleek by which the hoop was guided at the other. The real test of skill was in one's ability to make the hoop reverse its flight and come back to its owner.

Our elders must have had infinite patience because the small back streets reverberated to the hum of ball-bearing guiders and the clatter of hoops for the few months that these noisy playthings remained in season. Mossycock, cribby, kick-the-tin, and rally-oh were less noisy games. We also played rounders with a hurling stick, until the Christian Brothers taught us the merits and skills of hurling itself. Marbles, or marleys, was perhaps the most regularised of our pastimes. For some reason unknown even yet to me, all of a sudden everybody seemed to know that it was marley season. In the summer time old men played it in a little marley-pitch in the Dunville Park but we played it everywhere, along the pavements and on the street itself. There were bewlers and dinkies, shooters and ballies. The bewlers were large 'knuckle busters', dinkies were small highly prized miniatures; shooters, favourite scarred and proven score getters; and ballies were the sometimes illegal ball bearings. There were various ways of playing marleys. In one, the object was to knock your opponent or opponent's man out of the chalked circle; in another, to hit him from a measured distance; and in yet another, to succeed in dribbling into a hole in the ground. Some boys were expert at bunking, others at dribbling, most at spanning. Ricochets were often disputed but cheating was difficult and as most games were evenly contested, being completely 'cleaned out' was a rare occurrence. When wet days prevented outdoor sessions we played an indoor game by cutting holes in the base of a shoe or sweetie box and endeavoured to shoot directly into them.

We rarely mixed with wee girls, who minded their own business even when we interrupted their games of hop-scotch; one, two, three red lights, swings, queenie-oh or skips. They played house with dolls, sometimes dressing up and chalking out a kitchen which stretched from the front hall out into the pavement. They also played 'two balls' or 'three balls' against a wall much more expertly than any of us could have, though we would not have admitted it in those days. Anyway, for any boy to have been caught competing would have made for much slagging and reddeners all round.

Swings, simply made by looping rope and tightening it around a lamp post, were particularly favoured by girls. They also played with spinning tops or peeries, a game which we enjoyed as well. In the summer days both sexes converged in separate groups upon Dunville Park where swings, see-saws, slides and a witch's hat were much abused. Playing in the bushes with the added thrill of a chase by the wackey was strictly a boys' province, as were cheesers which we collected from the chestnut trees at the Falls Park.

GERRY ADAMS, *Falls Memories*, 1982

GERRY ADAMS'S *Falls Memories* arises from a sense of community. It is a local and partly personal history of West Belfast, mainly of that part I could not get to past the concrete blocks. The distant past is compiled from the history books, but written, interestingly, from the point of view of an outsider, of the Catholics pushed out towards the mountains by the exclusively Protestant town. I can see that perspective now, imagine the feeling of being shut out by the huge silver wall. I even think of Conn O'Neill, standing on the Castlereagh Hills and looking across at the city growing on the land he sold off piece by piece. I have lived on the main arteries – the Lisburn Road, the Ormeau Road, just below the Malone Road – so that coming down the New Lodge or Andersonstown feels somehow like being behind the face of my imagined city.

Thinking of the little group of Celtic enthusiasts who have established their own Gaeltacht in the area, remembering the Adams election posters, I envisage West Belfast plunged in a different mental universe. The religion, strange to me, even more enthusiastically observed than the Protestant ones, although after fourteen years of violence the young boys are beginning to stay away; the preoccupation with the Army in their great forts, and with faraway, foreign Dublin; even the language is struggling to be different. A poster down in Castle Street exhorts Catholics to use Irish: 'Speak your own language,' it says, in English.

And yet the few scenes Adams describes from his own childhood are not so different from my own. Being egged on by a bolder schoolmate to sneak into the pictures without paying is something I was equally reluctant to submit to at the Tivoli; I took just as much care to avoid the bad boys in their gangs looking for an excuse to start a fight; and we found a little of nature in the fields and vacant ground while Gerry Adams was up on the mountains. The green spaces around Finaghy may have been built upon, but it seems that even the still-available mountains are not made use of by so many children nowadays.

But of course it must have been very different, and it seems more so now. People look on a different past, they see the city from different angles, they think about it with a different armoury of ideas, and they look to a different future, if Gerry Adams's vision of a 'united Gaelic Ireland' (for 'Gaelic' one is tempted to read 'Catholic') is shared by many. The image of the Falls that stays in my mind is not from *Falls Memories* but from a television programme. A little boy of about ten or less is dandering up the road. An Army pig goes by. He stoops to pick up a stone and throws it cheerfully at the soldiers. I think he is walking past the Sinn Féin offices at the time.

ROBERT JOHNSTONE, Images of Belfast, 1983

THE EXILES' CLUB

> Every Thursday in the upstairs lounge of the Wollongong Bar, they make
> Themselves at home with Red Heart Stout, Park Drive cigarettes and Dunville's whiskey,
> A slightly-mouldy batch of soda farls. Eventually, they get down to business.
> After years they have reconstructed the whole of the Falls Road, and now
> Are working on the back streets: Lemon, Peel and Omar, Balaclava, Alma.

They just about keep up with the news of bombings and
    demolition, and are
Struggling with the finer details: the names and dates carved
    out
On the back bench of the Leavers' Class in Slate Street School;
    the Nemo Café menu;
The effects of the 1941 Blitz, the entire contents of Paddy
    Lavery's pawnshop.

CIARAN CARSON, The Irish for No, 1987

ONE THING I NOTICED if I was in a crowd at that time in Belfast – you'd never see any nice-looking men or boys. The girls looked all right but if the men had nice faces they were small and squat or if they were tall their faces were uncouth. So I wasn't expecting to meet anybody handsome at the class and Dermot Hughes didn't look much really – mousy hair, greyish eyes, not tall. But he had a clean collar even though it was a Tuesday. Most people that I knew in those days did with one clean shirt a week, starting on Sunday. One pair of socks too, it must be admitted. He was wearing a lovely soft shirt with green and white checks and a dark green wool tie. His clothes were shabby enough apart from that so I knew he couldn't be rich. Most of the people in the class were from around the Falls Road, some from away up at the top of it where the houses were far better than Mary Brigid's. They were nearly all in pairs or groups talking and laughing. I was alone. When I said to the girls at work would they come to learn Irish they said, 'Is your head cut, Martha Murtagh? Are you mad?' Dermot Hughes was on his own too and when I smiled at him he came over and sat beside me. When I asked him why he had come to the class he said, 'My mammy told me,' making fun.

    The teacher was an old man in a tweed suit and a little gold ring in his lapel to tell people he would like to talk to them in Irish. The cloth round the ring was all pricked and plucked because he kept pulling the ring in and out on its long pin. He spoke in Irish the whole time so I understood very little and he had old charts with pictures on them of a man or a woman or a child or a table with writing in Irish underneath. He'd point to the picture and say the words over and over and then he'd ask somebody, 'Caidé sin?' and we were expected to say 'Is tabla é' or 'Is bean í'. I couldn't see how I'd ever learn to read a book in Irish but Dermot kept me laughing with the remarks he passed about the pictures. At home-time it turned out that he lived about ten minutes away from our house, in the next parish. It was a warm September night with a half moon and stars so we walked home and I told him about the Yeats plays and he didn't make fun of me. He asked where I worked and he said he was out of a job. 'But I'll get one soon. I'm bound to. I can drive a van. There's always work for anybody that can drive a van.'

MARY BECKETT, Give Them Stones, 1990

WHAT I LIKED ABOUT THE ULSTER LIBERAL PARTY was the free for all discussion that followed the address. If you were in favour of retaining the British connection you were afforded every facility to state your view. The nationalist members who visited us were of a different type than the present. The church did not control them to the same extent as today. I can imagine what would happen if three orange lodges on the 12th July morning passed by St Paul's on the Falls Road and down the Grosvenor Road headed by a band and Father Convery, PP, standing at his manse looking on. Yet for years this route was insisted on by Father Convery. I had lived in Rockville Street on the Falls Road and the street was mixed but religion was never mentioned at any time. My Roman Catholic friends are legion, but it was the invitation to Winston Churchill who was in the Liberal cabinet that smashed the Ulster Liberal party.

I made my protest against him coming to Belfast and I resigned. I had been Secretary of the South Belfast branch which had been gaining strength every month. It is my conviction that Ireland would have remained under the union and that a plan would have been formed that would have satisfied North and South. The Irish MPs North and South at that time could have made as good an agreement as we have at present without any blood being shed, but bringing over an Englishman who had no knowledge of Ireland, it was a big blunder and it was the finish of my taking part in political parties. When I look back on them, I believe the Liberal party was wrecked on the Irish question.

ROBERT McELBOROUGH, The Autobiography of a Belfast Working Man, 1974

WHEN THE CHICHESTER FAMILY occupied the town of Belfast in the seventeenth century, they saw to it that no Irish place name would survive their overlordship. Tradition is hard to obliterate, and the inhabitants of the surrounding countryside held grimly to the ancient titles of their native townlands. So we have the oldest and central part of the city ornamented with the Christian and surnames of titled gentry and local merchants, whose pedigrees are as doubtful as their contributions to the progress of the town itself.

Still, it is a consolation to the Belfast citizen that we still retain such ancient titles as Stranmillis, Malone, Ormeau, Cromac, Shankill and the Falls. The influence of the Donegall family upon the Town Council during the seventeenth and eighteenth centuries encouraged their servitors to obliterate as far as possible all reference to the early origin of the various districts comprising the town.

Most of the earlier maps of Belfast refer to the Shankill as the Antrim Road, but once the new road to Antrim was constructed in the 1830s, the inhabitants insisted, by word of mouth, which has more authenticity than maps, in returning the district to its ancient origin. The Falls, which was the old highway to Dunmurry and Crumlin, never lost its traditional title in any single generation.

The powers that be at that period were satisfied to refer to the Falls simply as the road from Crumlin. To this day it remains the road from Crumlin.

Up till the early half of last century, the Falls had no real existence as a populated district. True, there were a few farms and labourers' cottages scattered about the hillsides where the mountainy people struggled hopelessly to earn a living on the poor and stony soil. With the exception of Andersonstown, where there was a small cluster of houses, the road was a bleak, unfrequented highway.

During the 1830s, the Falls Road commenced at Barrack Street and here a distillery was erected. Further along, where Dover Street now stands, a cotton factory was established and, a short distance above that, a flour mill commenced operations. The Falls had become industrialised! Barrack Street was still the limit of the town boundary and accommodation was limited outside this for workers, so that most of the employees of these new undertakings were recruited from Castle Street and Smithfield.

Hoping to include the new industries into a proposed extended boundary of the town, the Council pushed the Falls further into the countryside and re-named the thoroughfare Mill Street. Later, they again changed the name to Divis Street, giving the Falls a further push back, this time to where Northumberland Street now stands. Then the Town Fathers ran out of names and were forced to allow the ancient Falls to retain its original meaning.

THOMAS CARNDUFF (1954), *Life and Writings*, 1994

HE HAD ARRANGED TO MEET EILEEN IN THE DUNVILLE PARK — a square patch of ground with high railings which islanded it from the trams and the traffic. He was early and he sat on one of the round-backed seats, his shadow lengthening in front of him. Squads of children paddled their feet in the basin of the fountain and above them the lowering sun made a rainbow with the sparkling jets of water. A group of workless men came near him and one of them tied a dog by the leash to the seat, and another took out a marble and pressed it into the ground with the heel of his boot. He made three holes, swept the dust away with his cap, and marked them with chalk rings. Hugh got up and moved towards the quiet summer house, but there he saw the floor covered with spits and two old men hunched in carven attitudes over a game of draughts. He left them to their game and sat on a vacant seat amongst shiny laurel bushes.

Eileen came in through a side gate and waved to him. He sat sideways, his legs crossed, one arm drooped over the back of the seat. She was dressed in a light grey costume, a scarlet bag under her arm, her patent shoes catching the sunlight. To embarrass her he stared at her feet, and smiled when she walked ungainly. She sat beside him, her face assuming an expression of affront.

'Well?' he said.

'Well, yourself, that's a trick to play on people – staring at them like that' – she hoped that he would admire her costume, but he said nothing and she knew that something had annoyed him. 'Are you here long?'

'I've just arrived,' and he flicked a pebble into a laurel bush, and a leaf shook. 'I had a row with my mother.'

'Another one?' and she fluffed out her fair hair.

'I don't want any codding!'

She became grave and stretched out a hand to his: 'Hugh, I'm only joking. Don't worry about the row and everything will turn out all right.'

At the fountain two barefooted boys began to fight and their followers gathered round, encouraging them with shouts and pushes. Little girls wheeled their go-cars to the side and a dripping terrier ran around with a stick in his mouth. The parkranger approached and the boys scattered and shouted nicknames at him.

'Wee fellas are always fighting, Hugh.'

He combed his black hair with his fingers and lit a cigarette. The parkranger moved off, and in ones and twos the children slunk back and splashed in the fountain as if nothing had happened. Hugh moved closer to Eileen and told her about the row and how he had mentioned to his mother about marriage.

MICHAEL McLAVERTY, *Lost Fields*, 1942

PLEASE IDENTIFY YOURSELF

British, more or less; Anglican, of a kind.
In Cookstown I dodge the less urgent question
when a friendly Ulsterbus driver raises it;
'You're not a Moneymore girl yourself?' he asks,
deadpan. I make a cowardly retrogression,
slip ten years back. 'No, I'm from New Zealand.'
'Are you now? Well, that's a coincidence:
the priest at Moneymore's a New Zealander.'

And there's the second question, unspoken.
Unanswered.
          I go to Moneymore
anonymously, and stare at all three churches.
In Belfast, though, where sides have to be taken,
I stop compromising – not that you'd guess,
seeing me hatless there among the hatted,
neutral voyeur among the shining faces
in the glossy Martyrs' Memorial Free Church.
The man himself is cheerleader in the pulpit
for crusader choruses: we're laved in blood,
marshalled in ranks. I chant the nursery tunes
and mentally cross myself. You can't stir me
with evangelistic hymns, Dr Paisley:
I know them. Nor with your computer-planned
sermon – Babylon, Revelation, whispers
of popery, slams at the IRA, more blood.
I scrawl incredulous notes under my hymnbook
and burn with Catholicism.
          Later
hacking along the Lower Falls Road
against a gale, in my clerical black coat,
I meet a bright gust of tinselly children
in beads and lipstick and their mothers' dresses
for Hallowe'en; who chatter and surround me.
Overreacting once again (a custom
of the country, not mine alone) I give them
all my loose change for their rattling tin
and my blessing – little enough. But now
to my tough Presbyterian ancestors,
Brooks and Hamilton, lying in the graves
I couldn't find at Moneymore and Cookstown
among so many unlabelled bones, I say:
I embrace you also, my dears.

          FLEUR ADCOCK, *The Scenic Route*, 1974

THE STREET CHARACTERS OF OLD have their contemporaries today: Fonsie Conway, Neddie Doherty, Starrs Kelly and all those unknowns who enrich life in every generation – like the anonymous scribe who was moved to write in large gable-size letters 'F . . . 1690, WE WANT A REPLAY', or the woman who admonished a black British soldier with the words: 'To think I spent years giving the priest money for the black babies and now you have the cheek to come over here and torture the life out of us.' Or the lady who chided a British Army major for sending troops into a back entry after a group of youngsters. 'He hasn't enough sense to order his own dinner. Sending youse out to do his dirty work.' Then to the major: 'Come on out of that jeep and fight your own battles.' When he ignored her challenge telling her to 'F ... off', she retorted, 'Yiz are all the same, yiz think you know everything. I cudn't like ye even if I rared yeh. Hell's gates and somebody blows yiz up. Then youse'll get some sense. Annoying people with your oul carry on. Lads can't even stand at their own corner. Someday the shoe'll be on the other fut, then ye'll know what side your bread's buttered on. Go away on home and leave us in peace. And take lappy lugs (the major) with youse. God help his poor wife. My heart goes out to her. At least with my Paddy if I've nothing to eat I've something to luk at. Imagine that poor woman waking up in the morning with your big watery gub in the bed beside her. Ya big long drink of water, giving your orders there. You think you're the fellah in the big picture. If I was a man I'd go through you like a dose of salts. You cudn't fight your way out of a wet paper bag.' And then, as the Brits left without their intended captives, she concluded, 'God forgive youse for making me make an exhibition of myself in the street. Them wee bucks showed youse the road home. There's better men in the Children's Hospital. You cudn't catch the cold.'

GERRY ADAMS, *Falls Memories*, 1982

MAUREEN REMEMBERS ALL THE GIRLS SINGING, 'We are little Catholic girls and we come from West Belfast; We all go to Benediction and the wind blows up our ass.'

Some of the street traders and local characters brought colour and humour to Majorca Street and the neighbourhood with their eccentric ways. Jimmy Webb remembers Orny Boke dressed up in a long coat and in the company of Blind Dan knocked the doors, begging for coppers. 'Rapper Up' was a woman who rapped windows to get people out of bed in the early hours: for this service she received 3d a week. The rag men, fish sellers, coal men and newspaper boys all had their distinctive calls. One woman who sold wool and thread from a hand cart shouted, 'We're giving them away, with the price never up yet.' The ice cream woman drew attention by banging the tin lid of her wafer box and blowing a little tin horn. One other character whose visit to Majorca Street was always welcome was Maggie Marley. Maggie arrived pushing her well-decorated hand cart on which she had a colourful display of balloons and coloured paper hand streamers which she would give out in exchange for old rags, jam pots or bottles.

GEORGE FLEMING, *Magennis VC*, 1998

THE WOMEN OF THE DISTRICT who wore the traditional black crocheted shawl were nicknamed 'Shawlies'. This garment served many different purposes; for warmth, for carrying children and for concealing charitable offerings to a neighbour in need. It might sometimes be worn with a plaid scarf for extra heat.

The main garment was a heavy strip petticoat frock, worn buttoned to the neck, usually navy or black in colour and hanging in folds to the ankle. Around the waist was tied a crisp bleached apron which was meticulously pleated. Great care was taken to keep these aprons smart. They were regularly steeped in washing soda, then starched and carefully ironed. The women usually went barefoot, but had gusset boots for occasional wear.

CARMEL GALLAGHER, All Around the Loney-O, 1978

BY THE BLACK STREAM

Entries patent leather with sleet
Mirror gas and neon light . . .
A boy with a husky voice picks a fight
And kicks a tin down home in pain

To tram rattle and ship horn
In a fog from where fevers come
In at an East Wind's
Icy burst of black rain . . .

Here I was good and got and born

Cold, lost, not predictable
Poor, bare, crossed in grain
With a shudder no one can still

In the damp down by the half-dried river
Slimy at night on the mudflats in
The moon light gets an un-
earthly white Belfastman.

PADRAIC FIACC, By the Black Stream, 1969

WHEN THE QUARTER-TO-EIGHT BELLS WERE RINGING Colm and Jamesy went out to their Holy Family. At the bottom of the street Jamesy had to turn back as he had forgotten his prayer beads.

The streets were filled with a frosty October mist and the bells tolled loudly above the roofs of the houses. Boys came in groups from different streets and when they passed under a lamp-post the light glistened on their polished boots and water-plastered hair. They were all talking at once, and now and again two or three lingered behind to swap cigarette cards or play chestnuts.

Colm and Jamesy with their hands in their pockets took the short cut over the fields, past the dark brickyard, up a few narrow streets, and when they came to the Monastery Father Carthy was on the lighted porch, clapping his hands and urging the boys to hurry up. Colm and Jamesy went to their section – Our Lady of Sorrows. The prefect asked Jamesy why he was absent the last two meetings and he replied that he was sick.

The church was heated and boys were warming their hands on the hot pipes. Around the High Altar a misty incense had gathered from the October devotions just ended. Lights shone on the varnished seats and late boys raced to their places.

A priest ascended the pulpit and thumped it with his two fists. 'Silence!' he shouted. 'You'd think you were in a picture hall and not in the House of God! You wouldn't get boys from the Shankill Road to behave like you. The next boy I get talking, I'll run him out the door.'

MICHAEL McLAVERTY, *Call My Brother Back*, 1939

The Faubourg Malone

It was too rich and strange a diet: a few sentences or images were enough to bring on a reverie of speculation. Who were these people, what was Belfast? Was it the place I saw on the news or was it poets and 70 Eglantine Avenue? How could there be a street in Belfast called Eglantine Avenue? I began to infer there was more to Belfast than met the camera's eye.

CAROL RUMENS, Honest Ulsterman

'My' Belfast is a muse-city, a city of weather and un-certainty. If my settings are more likely to contain trees than barbed wire, this is because I am lucky enough to know first-hand the leafier aspect of Belfast. It is not the whole story, far from it, but it is not a lie. And I do not offer it to the reader in complete political innocence. I want to show a city where, in spite of everything, peace, love, friends and poems are sometimes made, and where a female imagination can find mirrors, because there is a widespread assumption elsewhere that these things do not exist, that there is only the endless, intolerable round of horror. At the same time, I don't want to minimise this horror or suggest that anyone is not touched by it.

CAROL RUMENS, Preface to Thinking of Skins

I BEGIN WITH AUNT LIZZIE (*arma virumque cano*) the way you begin with fabulous creatures in the corners of maps – the map in this instance of the *faubourg* Malone and the lower Lagan valley as unrolled in the golden reign of Edward. Not that Aunt Lizzie was any dragon; she was the kindliest creature in the world, and no reason to be anything else – smelling in winter of warm furs; at all seasons of port, plum cake, and violet scent. Nevertheless, driving to town with Aunt Lizzie was like driving to town with Catherine the Great; you were not only protected in cold weather by exuberant layers of fur rugs, you were encapsulated in 'the funds', ennobled by the divine right of whiskey dividends – let the serfs by the roadside shiver their acknowledgements. Even the lower Lagan valley, smoke clouds and all, looked different from Aunt Lizzie's landau. All those factory chimneys belching away under the Black Mountain were just a vulgar painted background as far as Aunt Lizzie was concerned; in behind them was a dark forest where the princess put in a furry paw, yanked out a husband–director, then retired again, wrapped in fur, to Belfast's outer belt of woodland, to the long green vistas of the Castlereagh hills, and everybody lived happily ever afterwards as if some magician had put a spell on them, with consols doing nicely and fairy prince Edward VII on the throne.

Talk about *la belle et la bête*. Not that, except for occasional shopping expeditions to Lindsay's or Robinson & Cleaver's (complete with fairytale coachman, top hat, cockade, and all, on the box seat), Aunt Lizzie made many descents to the dark forest of Belfast; her business was in the *faubourg* supported by the forest; enchanted woodland, and no black smokestacks for her. She had regular snowstorms of visiting cards (first and third Thursdays) to distribute right down the Malone Road, cards from an elaborate silver card-case chained to her fur-wrapped person with a silver chain. To get into this card-scattering act you rolled, violet-scented, right down into the Boulevard Saint-Germain of Edwardian Belfast, right in amongst the mansions of the linen manufacturers and the coal kings, almost as far as the slightly superfluous Queen's College and the ghastly little Victorian clock-tower-cum-*pissoir* at the entrance to the Botanic Gardens.

DENIS IRELAND, *From the Jungle of Belfast*, 1973

THE ONE DESIRE

The palm-house in Belfast's Botanic Gardens
Was built before Kew
In the spirit that means to outdo
The modern by the more modern,

That iron be beaten, and glass
Bent to our will,
That heaven be brought closer still
And we converse with the angels.

The palm-house has now run to seed;
Rusting girders, a missing pane
Through which some delicate tree
Led by kindly light
Would seem at last to have broken through.
We have excelled ourselves again.

PAUL MULDOON, Why Brownlee Left, 1980

THE BOTANICAL GARDEN OF BELFAST was established in the year 1830. A great many of the English botanical gardens are not twenty years old. I was much surprised at the youthfulness of almost all English scientific institutions, and at finding how much less has yet been done for science in the remote parts of England than in those of Germany. The Botanical Garden at Belfast is the finest in Ireland, next to that of Dublin, over which latter it has indeed many advantages. Although these two cities are scarcely twenty German miles apart, their climates are very different. Dublin has a much hotter summer and a much colder winter than Belfast. This fact the polite director of the botanical garden explained to me by saying that Belfast was sheltered by a chain of hills on the land side, while Dublin lay on the edge of a wide unsheltered plain. In the garden at Belfast, situated under the fifty-fifth degree of latitude, the cypress and arbutus grow very well in the open air, although they are not found wild, as in the south. The north of Ireland has however the yew-tree to make amends for this deficiency. The garden also contains a fine collection of all the heaths indigenous to the Irish bogs, among which are many large and fine specimens. I was particularly interested in a part of the garden called the British Garden, containing as perfect a collection as possible of all the plants found wild in the whole British dominions. There was also a very fine collection of grasses, which must always be interesting to British gardeners, since the English attach so much importance to large and fine lawns, or grass plots. I saw in this collection no less than 400 species of grass, which are all indigenous to English soil. There are gardeners in many of the great English cities who cultivate nothing but grasses, and make a distinct trade of dealing in the seed. The *Festuca ovina*, the *Poa trivialis*, and the *Poa nemoralis* are grasses which produce a very thick, soft, fresh verdure, and are consequently much sought after for lawns. Australian plants also thrive excellently well in the temperate atmosphere of Belfast, and indeed throughout Ireland. A rose, originally brought from China, has also become very general in Irish gardens, where it is left unprotected winter and summer.

J.G. KOHL, Ireland, 1843

I HAD ASKED OWEN TO MEET ME IN THE BOTANIC GARDENS, for I didn't
want to call at his house; and having arrived before the appointed time, I
began to pace up and down within sight of the front terrace, my head filled
with anxious thoughts. Two or three gardeners were raking the sidewalk,
and a man with a pair of clippers was trimming the edges of the grass. As
they pottered over their work they carried on a disjointed conversation,
principally about religion, or rather about the dangers of Roman Catholicism. The man with the clippers kept referring to something that he called
High Rosary, and the rakers from time to time interpolated suitable
grunts, or an occasional sentence. I moved farther along the main walk and
sat down . . .

Nurses passed, wheeling perambulators. At a distance of five or six yards
some little girls settled down stolidly to a mysterious game in which a great
deal of rhymed dialogue was the chief feature. An old pensioner, sucking an
empty pipe, hobbled up to my bench, seated himself in the corner, and
began, with much fumbling of trembling hands, to unfold a newspaper.
He did not read it, however, but turned his rheumy eyes upon me, and in a
husky wavering voice made a remark about the weather. I did not want to
talk, and pretended not to hear him: whereupon he repeated it more loudly,
and this time I had to answer. Then suddenly I saw Owen at the gate and
sprang up to meet him.

FORREST REID, *Peter Waring*, 1937

THAT SEPTEMBER was a painful and critical month for me. This was
partly due to depression caused by the outbreak of a war I had long
known to be inevitable and partly due to my own trauma at the time.
Irene, goddess of peace, had said 'No', and I felt as if my emotional
structure was crumbling. 'No' shouted the angry gods, as the leaves fell
heedlessly from a brooding sky. I wandered restless, apparently defeated
before the struggle had started, hurt and rebellious but drained of energy,
obsessed with futile sexual fantasies and doomed to non-conformist frustra-
tion. Under the shadow of Cave Hill and Divis, along the towpath to Shaw's
Bridge where hardy swimmers still plopped Adam-naked in the cool Lagan,
around the big tinsel-laden stores in the city centre, in the dusty second-hand
bookshops of Smithfield, back and forth from the Stranmillis Road to
Belgravia Avenue off the Lisburn Road (where my old school friend, Leslie
Baxter, lived), feverishly intent on long-forgotten enterprises of work and
play I hastened, while the world cocked its ear and waited for the crunch of
bombs and the moans of the injured. Or I would go up the Antrim Road to
Brookhill Avenue and glance at the dignified, if nondescript, brick house
inhabited by my beloved blonde Irene. I consulted a doctor who diagnosed
my complaint as 'nervous dyspepsia'. As for my chronic catarrh, he advised

me to emigrate to Canada as soon as I had the opportunity. O God!
O Montreal!

ROBERT GREACEN, The Sash My Father Wore, 1997

OUR AVENUE

Our avenue was long, a thoroughfare
for carts with coals, bread, milk, or passing through;
you'd risk no sprint across it, or but few,
so frequently those cartwheels trundled there.
Houses with tiny gardens set before –
some peopled with schoolteachers, ministers,
with civil servants, factory managers –
the largest with steep steps up to the door.

Yet faces, shapes, still fill the vivid frame,
the bearded doctor of divinity,
the huge bookmaker, the grey secretary,
for each had features, each had his own name;
but for romance, for mystery I'd choose
the Rosenfields, the Weiners, our own Jews.

JOHN HEWITT, Kites in Spring, 1980

GRETTON, SIR CHARLES BRETT'S HOME, remained quite unaltered for thirty years after his death. After his widow died in 1930, aged ninety-three, his three daughters lived on there. As a schoolboy, I was taken often to visit my great-aunts: they were kind, hospitable, and friendly, but no longer young. This, like Tennyson's Lotus-land, was a land where it was always afternoon; there was a constant tinkling of tea-cups, and an endless stream of lady visitors, some wearing fur tippets, almost all wearing hats with large hat-pins. There was an annual children's party in the garden, with a treasure hunt involving parcels hidden at the end of criss-crossing clues of coloured string (Aunt Nina's admirably labyrinthine invention). There was a raucous green parrot in the kitchen, and an elderly and itchy Airedale terrier called Barney. There were beautiful scrapbooks, and wooden bricks, and a china bird with its beak wide open, which could be fed an astonishing number of ivory counters; there were Chinese puzzles and painted boxes-within-boxes; I am glad to say that most of these enchanting Victorian toys are still in the family. When I grew older, I was sometimes allowed to read in my great-grandfather's sunny study. It was not quite a haunted room, but it had a definite and personal atmosphere of its own: very still and silent: faintly scented with the leather of chairs and book-bindings, and an elusive odour of long-ago tobacco. Everything in the room remained exactly as great-grandpapa had left it; except that Aunt Nina, who kept the books dusted and the furniture polished, tried to keep the library up to date with new books, and meticulously maintained the card-index catalogue.

C.E.B. BRETT, *Long Shadows Cast Before*, 1978

VARIANT READINGS

I expected bleachworks and burnt-out cars, not fuchsias:
Not cedar and sky-trickling larch, their remote massed shade,
Nor to hear my footsteps, lonely in streets of wet hedges
That tell me: here peace, and love, and money, are made.

Home was like this long ago, but can't be again.
I'll have chosen guilt and illusion, if I choose this
Most English of Irelands, our difference seemingly less
Than that between neighbourly hedges, depths of green.

CAROL RUMENS, *Thinking of Skins*, 1993

I SPENT SIX MONTHS IN BELFAST IN 1988 pretending that life was normal. I visited friends. I went to the Public Record Office, guarded by wardens and high railings which I no longer noticed after a while. I went to people's homes for dinner. I went to the cinema or to see a play at the Lyric. I drank in pubs and the next morning bought a local paper to read the news of the previous night's atrocities, which might have taken place anywhere in the world but had that strange added thrill attached to any piece of news which happens to take place around the corner. I was able to walk to the place where the explosion had taken place and feel the crunch of broken glass beneath my shoes. It was the least I could do, I thought, to give some credibility to the worries of my friends back in Paris. The closest I came to Belfast's everyday violence was when a bomb shattered my kitchen window; had I been washing up at the sink, a shard of glass could easily have sent me to the casualty ward of the Royal Victoria Hospital.

There is not a single person in Belfast who has not been touched by the violence in some way, who does not have a relative, a friend or a colleague who has been injured by a bomb, arrested for a while or intimidated by the paramilitaries. It is possible, of course, not to look and so to pretend that these things do not happen and that life in Belfast is like that in any other Western European city. It is possible but, in the long run, unsustainable. If a society is riven by intercommunal violence in the way that Belfast is, then that violence has to be looked into, analysed, discussed – and condemned and rejected.

MAURICE GOLDRING, *Belfast: From Loyalty to Rebellion*, 1991

W HEN NOT THE GUEST OF FRIENDS IN BELFAST I have stayed in a student lodging in one of the avenues off University Road. A pleasant and ingrowing way to lodge, as well as inexpensive. But not always possible, I imagine, during term. Here, as everywhere in Belfast, I had a sense of air and light; and the lady of the house sang so radiantly as she went about her work that first I thought we had perhaps *La Tebaldi* on the wireless. But no; our brilliant mornings of Verdi and Donizetti were all from one innocent, splendid Belfast throat; and the singer, though in fact she did look some-what Italian, was Ulster through and through, and a pious Methodist churchgoer, I gathered. I wonder if she sings as she can at Meeting?

The Belfast Museum and Gallery is near my happy lodging – but I would rather say nothing about the collection, for it illustrates, only to astound, the city's brutal indifference to fine art. Belfast is *not* a capital city, granted. Neither is Liverpool, neither is Manchester, yet they have pictures that can be considered and from which some beginnings of knowledge of art can be acquired. But Belfast, rich Belfast – I remember bicycles, and instructional exhibits in connection with Dunlop who made the pneumatic tyre – a favourite son, I think? There are stuffed animals too, and some mediocre watercolours of Belfast. There are Laverys, and young people's canvases. But – a gallery of painting? Ah well, having seen the College of Technology which the openhanded burghers raised to cut across the face of Sir John Soane's Royal Academical Institution in College Square, why should one expect to find a master, old or young, on a gallery wall?

KATE O'BRIEN, *My Ireland*, 1962

T HERE WAS HEAVY FOG LYING, like underdone air, the Monday morning Drew started to work. It was a twenty-minute walk from his flat into town. Malone Road, University Road, Bradbury Place, Shaftesbury Square . . . Buildings appeared to him one at a time, stripped of context, jutting into space, as though craning their necks. *Where the fuck are we?* . . . Dublin Road, Bedford Street, Donegall Square – West, North – Donegall Place. Turning a final corner, he followed for a time the course of the culverted Farset as it flowed, unseen, from its shrouded source to its ancient, city-christening union with the fog-bound Lagan, and then he was there. Belfast's Bookstore.

GLENN PATTERSON, *Fat Lad*, 1992

THE LINEN INDUSTRY

Pulling up flax after the blue flowers have fallen
And laying our handfuls in the peaty water
To rot those grasses to the bone, or building stooks
That recall the skirts of an invisible dancer,

We become a part of the linen industry
And follow its processes to the grubby town
Where fields are compacted into window-boxes
And there is little room among the big machines.

But even in our attic under the skylight
We make love on a bleach green, the whole meadow
Draped with material turning white in the sun
As though snow reluctant to melt were our attire.

What's passion but a battering of stubborn stalks,
Then a gentle combing out of fibres like hair
And a weaving of these into christening robes,
Into garments for a marriage or funeral?

Since it's like a bereavement once the labour's done
To find ourselves last workers in a dying trade,
Let flax be our matchmaker, our undertaker,
The provider of sheets for whatever the bed –

And be shy of your breasts in the presence of death,
Say that you look more beautiful in linen
Wearing white petticoats, the bow on your bodice
A butterfly attending the embroidered flowers.

MICHAEL LONGLEY, *The Echo Gate*, 1979

IT WOULD BE WRONG to suppose that father and I were always at enmity. Sometimes, when he was in a good mood, I would sit on his knee and comb the dark hair that was beginning to silver at the sides. Or we would go out together on placid, golden-tinted summer evenings, sauntering up the drab Short Strand and onwards to the leafy oasis of Ormeau Park, where decades earlier the young Forrest Reid used to listen to the strains of a German band. Mother talked about these German bands that had been a feature of Ulster life before the First World War. The only foreigners in Belfast in my time were a handful of Italians, who ran ice-cream shops and sold fish and chips. Nobody I knew would have touched *pasta*.

ROBERT GREACEN, *The Sash My Father Wore*, 1997

THE STREET OUTSIDE WAS A UNIVERSITY BYWATER, once a good residential area, which had lately been reduced to the level of taking in paying guests. Miss Hearne stared at the houses opposite and thought of her aunt's day when there were only private families in this street, at least one maid to every house, and dinner was at night, not at noon. All gone now, all those people dead and all the houses partitioned off into flats, the bedrooms cut in two, kitchenettes jammed into linen closets, linoleum on the floors and 'To Let' cards in the bay windows. Like this house, she thought. This bed-sitting-room must have been the master bedroom. Or even a drawing-room. And look at it now. She turned from the window to the photograph on the mantelpiece. All changed, she told it, all changed since your day. And I'm the one who has to put up with it.

But then she shook her head to chase the silly cobwebs from her mind. She walked across the room, inspecting the surface. The carpet wasn't bad at all, just a bit worn in the middle part, and a chair could be put there. The bed could be moved out an inch from the wall to hide that stain. And there on the bed was the Sacred Heart, lying face down, waiting to be put up in His proper place. Nothing for it, Miss Hearne said to herself, but to go down and ask the new landlady for the loan of a hammer.

BRIAN MOORE, *Judith Hearne*, 1955

IN THE LOST PROVINCE

As it comes back, brick by smoky brick,
I say to myself – strange I lived there
And walked those streets. It is the Ormeau Road
On a summer's evening, a haze of absence
Over the caked city, that slumped smell
From the blackened gasworks. Ah, those brick canyons
Where Brookeborough unsheathes a sabre,
Shouting 'No Surrender' from the back of a lorry.

And the sky is a dry purple, and men
Are talking politics in a back room.
Is it too early or too late for change?
Certainly the province is most peaceful.
Who would dream of necessity, the angers
Of Leviathan, or the years of judgement?

TOM PAULIN, The Strange Museum, 1980

THERE ARE STILL TO BE FOUND ABOUT BELFAST the remains of some of the old country houses: and we shall find that many have a story attached to them, that comes down to us from the twilight of the shadowy past.

Ballydrain is one of the most interesting. It belonged to – and was probably built by – a family named Stewart. They came from Scotland in the year 1605, and resided for many generations in the house, and they intermarried with many well-known families. The estate was afterwards bought by Mr Montgomery, whose descendants still live at Ballydrain.

Hospitality was always a striking characteristic of the Irish people, and in the early times people travelled slowly over very bad roads with no light, and there was but poor accommodation for travellers. Inns were a long distance apart, so some benevolent people received travellers and took them into their houses for rest and refreshment. There were many houses of this kind throughout the country. In the year 1675, we find there was a Free House at Ballydrain, where poor travellers could procure food and lodging. A stone is still to be seen, which was built into the wall of the house, with this inscription carved on it.

'A Free House 1675.'

One of the Stewart family built Macedon, another built Maryville and Myrtlefield, and also a house called Windsor in the Ballydrain grounds. Maryville on the Malone Road has belonged to the Wilson family for generations. Tradition says it was at Cranmore, beside Maryville, that King William rested when on his way to Belfast, and the tree where his horse was tied is still to be seen. Cranmore was formerly named Orange Grove, and was the residence of a family named Eccles. The jug which King William drank out of and the bed he slept in were for a long time treasured in the house.

Malone House is erected on the site of a very extensive fort, called Castle Cam, or Freeston Castle, but there are no remains of the ancient fort now to be seen. There was also an old Church on the top of the hill in Upper Malone called 'Capella de Crookmuck'. The trees in the grounds surrounding

Malone House are remarkable for their stately beauty and wide-spreading branches. There were several ancient forts in the same neighbourhood, but any history of them cannot now be found. On the left of the road leading to Shaw's Bridge, the foundations of a fort are still seen. There are remains of a third in the grounds near Lismoyne, and yet another was in Friar's Bush graveyard.

MARY LOWRY, The Story of Belfast and Its Surroundings, 1912

THOUGH WE ALL TALKED OF 'WOMEN' WE MEANT GIRLS; and by 'girls' most of us meant schoolgirls from Victoria College or Methodist College; girls studying for the same exams as ourselves and playing hockey instead of rugby. Nice, respectable girls who were willing to chat and giggle with us and who would stand on the touch-line at Osborne Park on Saturdays and cheer us whenever we scored a try or a goal, lingering around after the game, in twos or threes, so that they could gang up with us and go giggling along the Malone Road. I never had much luck with these girls, possibly because my attention had to be partly on my bicycle which always seemed to get in the way. Usually as soon as we reached the Old Stranmillis Road I gave up the pursuit, said 'Cheerio' to everybody, and proceeded up the hill alone. Unfortunately none of the girls lived in the same part of town as myself, so the only way to get near them was to meet them in the gods of the Opera House. And if you were lucky and cunning you might find a place behind a girl and when the lights went down you could make her comfortable by letting her sit between your legs, and later imperceptibly manoeuvre yourself so that she lay cradled against you. Such experiences were disappointingly few and never led to much more excitement other than a stroll up and down Great Victoria Street and an ice-cream in the Continental Café; which altogether constituted a fairly daring night out. There was little chance of anything serious following on these casual encounters. Even though you were sometimes given a promise that you could see her again the next Saturday night, your girl would call over her shoulder on departing, 'Perhaps'. And with the uncertainty of that 'perhaps' you lived in hope until Saturday at last came and the longed-for face was nowhere to be seen in the crowded gallery of the Opera House.

JOHN BOYD, Out of My Class, 1985

CHILDREN IN THOSE DAYS were forbidden to do anything likely to amuse them on Sundays and their reading was confined to the Bible or books dealing with it. Here again my father's practice was in advance of his time and surroundings. He even recommended the *Pilgrim's Progress* for Sunday reading, although I think that most people would have regarded it as too exciting for the sacred day.

GEORGE A. BIRMINGHAM, *Pleasant Places*, 1934

THE FORMER SHORELINE guided the plan of the town and provided vantage points where roads coming from the town centre could branch out freely on firm ground. To the west Peter's 'Hill' and Mill Street (so called from the watermills which utilised the last falls of the Farset River) where the Shankill and Falls roads had their starting points, diverging as they rose towards the hills. To the south firm ground was reached at Fountainville, where 'Sandy Row', the original road to the south and to Dublin, reached the heights of the Malone sands. As Denis Ireland put it, you passed here from the sloblands to the snoblands. I remember the appealing notice that formerly stood on the railway bridge at Bradbury Place, 'Drivers please let down the reins going uphill'. On the eastern County Down side the sloblands meet rising ground at another celebrated road junction, the Holywood Arches, and also at Mountpottinger and Ormeau.

E. ESTYN EVANS (1963), in *Ireland and the Atlantic Heritage, Selected Writings*, 1996

ON HYNDFORD STREET

Take me back, take me way, way, way back
On Hyndford Street
Where you could feel the silence at half past eleven
On long summer nights
As the wireless played Radio Luxembourg
And the voices whispered across Beechie River
In the quietness as we sank into restful slumber in the silence
And carried on dreaming, in God

And walks up Cherryvalley from North Road Bridge railway line
On sunny summer afternoons
Picking apples from the side of the tracks
That spilled over from the gardens of the houses on Cyprus Avenue
Watching the moth-catcher work the floodlights in the evenings
And meeting down by the pylons
Playing round Mrs Kelly's lamp
Going out to Holywood on the bus
And walking from the end of the lines to the seaside

Stopping at Fusco's for ice cream
In the days before rock 'n' roll

Hyndford Street, Abetta Parade
Orangefield, St Donard's Church
Sunday six bells
And in between the silence there was conversation, and laughter
And music and singing, and shivers up the back of the neck
And tuning in to Luxembourg late at night
And jazz and blues records during the day
Also Debussy on the third programme
Early mornings when contemplation was best

Going up the Castlereagh hills
And the Cregagh glens in summer and coming back
To Hyndford Street
Feeling wondrous and lit up inside
With a sense of everlasting life
And reading Mr Jellyroll and Big Bill Broonzy
And 'Really the Blues' by Mez Mezro
And 'Dharma Bums' by Jack Kerouac
Over and over again

And voices echoing late at night over Beechie River
And it's always being now
And it's always being now
It's always now
Can you feel the silence?

On Hyndford Street where you could feel the silence
At half past eleven on long summer nights
As the wireless played Radio Luxembourg
And the voices whispered across Beechie River
And in the quietness we sank into restful slumber in silence
And carried on dreaming in God.

VAN MORRISON, Hymns to the Silence (1991)

WHEN I HEAR OR READ Sam McAughtry's accounts of his boyhood in Belfast I feel deprived: deprived because sheltered. I cannot believe that even the children of the professional classes, even in Belfast, are now protected as we were protected, from the contagion of what for want of a better term I must call 'real life'. I doubt whether I should much have enjoyed the life lived by so many people only a mile or two away; but it is impossible to tell, because I am what my experiences have made me. That life was incomparably richer and more tumultuous than mine. Working-class children grew up much more quickly than we were allowed to do. Our existence was circumscribed, cloistered and colourless by comparison. Yet we were supposed to be the privileged ones. Every effort was being made to give us a better start in life than our fellow-citizens were getting.

How much of what Sam McAughtry recounts really happened to him, and how much of it is an imaginative recombination of things seen and heard about, I can only guess. But even if we suppose that one-quarter of what he tells is first-hand experience, it is still ten times more than what happened to me. It seems, also, that the rough-and-tumble of working-class street life, whether in Belfast or in Naples, stimulates the mythopoeic faculty, provided, of course, it is there to be stimulated. I repeat, it is impossible to tell. Perhaps I am naturally an unimaginative fellow.

Nothing in our house was ever done on the spur of the moment. Anything which was embarked upon had to be carefully prepared in advance, precautions taken, contingencies provided for. We never visited anyone else's house except by prior arrangement, and nobody ever came to ours. Present-day children stay overnight in the homes of their friends, and ring up their parents if they remember to do so. We never stayed overnight in anyone else's house, not even by arrangement, nor anyone else in ours. My brother and I were given one bicycle between the pair of us, which, even at the time, struck me as less than lavish. Yet it would not have occurred to us to question this dispensation.

There were not, even, many books in the house. There were two copies of Lord Macaulay's essays; one had been won as a school prize by my father, and the other had been won as a school prize by my mother. There was no copy of the works of Shakespeare. The copy I still possess was bought by me in 1934 at the age of fourteen.

Yet benefits were lavished upon us. We were packed off for three months at a time to expensive boarding-schools. There was no going home at weekends, not even at half-term as happens nowadays. We spent, once, a part of the holidays with a school-friend in Dublin, and the same friend spent, once, part of the holidays with us. We were led to believe ourselves privileged, as indeed we were. We had the best of everything, handmade boots and shoes, dancing-lessons and other such benefits. We hardly ever went to the cinema. If my memory were good enough I could still enumerate the three or four films I saw between the ages of ten and fifteen. We never went round the corner to buy sweets. We had not much taste for sweets. I am grateful for this: I still have quite a few teeth of my own.

MAURICE JAMES CRAIG, *The Elephant and the Polish Question*, 1990

SUCH OLDER BELFAST DISTRICTS AS THE FALLS AND THE SHANKILL, named after their main streets, have been identified with particular religions for over a hundred years – the Falls Catholic, the Shankill Protestant – but in the last eight years or so, streets between them that were roughly mixed have become one or the other. Even in more modern areas, such as Cliftonville, Ballymurphy, and Andersonstown, intimidation and fear have caused shifts of people; the planners of relatively new municipal housing estates have seen their hopes for a peaceful mixture dashed. The result is that Belfast is split into wedge-shaped slices that are Catholic or Protestant, virtual 'ghettos' – the term is used by the residents with a certain pride – in which those who belong feel a communal warmth and those who do not are aware of an almost tangible hatred. The exceptions to this are such areas of middle-class homes as those along the Malone and Antrim roads, where, at least on the surface, a more or less suburban privacy and tacit tolerance prevail. The move to the suburbs and to nearby towns like Bangor has caused the population of Belfast to fall from about 400,000 to roughly 360,000 in the last ten years, as people get away from decaying nineteenth-century slums and the contemporary violence that springs partly from such housing conditions.

ANTHONY BAILEY, *Acts of Union*, 1980

from BELFAST: A POEM

And nigh the Lagan's arched mouth
In corner towards the Bridge's south,
The works of EDWARDS boldly stand,
Like a strong bulwark on the strand.
And forward, as your course you bear,
To right of old MOUNT POTTINGER,
Sits SHAMROCK LODGE, and each chateau,
Sheltered from storms that rudely blow,
And close contiguous are laid
Those works of quick productive trade,
Where Chemistry's prolific art
The fruits of Science can impart –
Where COATES's Iron-works display
Their owner's ingenuity,
Whose perseverance, and whose skill
Their proper ends can well fulfil,
The stubborn mineral to produce
In all the various forms of use.

SAM LYONS, 1822

STRANDMILLIS WAS A FAVOURITE RESORT, and the canal bank was then, as at present, a popular route to Shaw's Bridge. To go round by Shaw's Bridge, as it is called, was then a more serious undertaking than at present. The Ormeau Road was not complete, so the only way back to town was by the Rookery, or Ballynafeigh Road, into Ballymacarrett. Ballymacarrett was in those days a centre of industry – the foundry, glass-blowing, watch-glass making, rope-making, weaving, lime-burning, vitriol and salt works were in operation. Ballymacarrett at that time could boast of having public gardens, an hotel, racket and ball courts, and all the roads leading out of it were paved in the centre ... The shore or strand, stretching from the site of the County Down Railway Station to Connswater, was the great sea bathing place for those who could not afford to go to Holywood. In addition to the expensiveness of public conveyances in those days, there were very few of them. I remember when Belfast could only boast of four outside cars. Of course there were boats to Holywood, but it was a tedious journey, especially when the tide was out – in fact, of all the approaches to the town, the most improved is the approach from the sea. At present we have magnificent channel and river steamers landing their passengers upon our streets at every condition of the tide by means of the deepened river and the new cut that has superseded the old and circuitous channel.

THOMAS GAFFIKEN, *Belfast Fifty Years Ago*, 1894

THE IMPORTANCE OF ELSEWHERE

Lonely in Ireland, since it was not home,
Strangeness made sense. The salt rebuff of speech,
Insisting so on difference, made me welcome:
Once that was recognised, we were in touch.

Their draughty streets, end-on to hills, the faint
Archaic smell of dockland, like a stable,
The herring-hawker's cry, dwindling, went
To prove me separate, not unworkable.

Living in England has no such excuse:
These are my customs and establishments
It would be much more serious to refuse.
Here no elsewhere underwrites my existence.

PHILIP LARKIN, *The Whitsun Weddings*, 1964

LOUIS MacNEICE AND BERTIE RODGERS were migrants who arrived in Belfast once or twice a year, either singly or together, stayed for a few days, and then went off on their travels to England or Europe or beyond. Some of us always made a fuss of them as soon as they landed in Ireland, and the celebrations lasted until they left. The flat of the artists George and Mercy MacCann off Shaftesbury Square was one of their bases, its walls lined with pictures, some painted by George and Mercy themselves. There was also a Russian icon of which Mercy was very proud. The centre of the flat was a long refectory-like table in the dining room where their guests sat on chairs, stools or a bench and the bottles would move backwards and forwards and across like chessmen, as a stream of visitors arrived with bottles or were ordered to go out and fetch a bottle – or two if they felt like it – at the convenient off-licence in Botanic Avenue.

Belfast takes itself seriously, so seriously indeed that it has never paid much attention to its writers and artists. The numerous churches – and 'chapels', as the Catholic places of worship are called – may suggest that the inhabitants are religious-minded, and this I suppose is true, for both Catholics and Protestants take their faiths very seriously. But seriousness without tolerance in religious matters can prove dangerous to civilised living, and Belfast has never been otherwise than a dangerous and explosive city, a city from which writers and artists have fled, given the opportunity to do so.

JOHN BOYD, *The Middle of My Journey*, 1990

WE DROVE BACK WITH THE SUN SINKING ON OUR LEFT. The country was extravagant with gorse as if a child had got loose with the paints. Gorse all over the fields and sprawling on the dykes. Rough stone walls dodged their way up the mountain. A hill-side under plough was deeply fluted with shadows. The pairs of fat white gateposts with cone tops showed the small fields of small farmers. Brown hens ran through a field, their combs like moving poppies. Then Belfast again, swans on the Lagan, and home towards the Black Mountain, now a battleship grey, by a road called Chlorine Gardens.

LOUIS MacNEICE, *Zoo*, 1938

CHLORINE GARDENS, BELFAST

Oh to live in Chlorine Gardens,
Where the brain leaps in the pan.
A hundred husbands' hundred hard-ons
Get it, as and when they can.

A myriad sins, a myriad pardons
Form the average Christian span.
Oh to live in Chlorine Gardens
Where a man can be a man!

Oh to live in Chlorine Gardens
Where a chap can read a book:
A bulging row of hard-back Ardens,
Both the Grigsons (how to cook
Spatch-cocked woodcock laced with lardons,
Fricassee of Lalla Rookh!)
Ah, the smells of Chlorine Gardens —
Lift the lid and take a look!

Lift the lid on Chlorine Gardens
Where the chess-buffs rise at dawn
To play old games of Leonard Barden's.
Their wives choose flip-sides with a yawn:
Their ears, and hearts, are Jack Teagarden's
While hubby touches up a pawn.
Oh what games in Chlorine Gardens!
No one ever mows the lawn.

No one mows those Chlorine Gardens
Where the sperm soars with the yeast.
Virginity like Dolly Varden's
Anticipates a midnight feast.
Each recondite position hardens
When the wind blows nor' nor' east.
Oh to sleep in Chlorine Gardens!
Few the sheets that stay uncreased.

Oh to sleep in Chlorine Gardens!
The minister is non-committal,
Murmuring, confidens et ardens:
'Wait while I slip into a little
Something of Teilhard de Chardin's.'
God! On Sunday morning it'll
Be grand to live in Chlorine Gardens:
More theology, less spittle.

Yes. To live in Chlorine Gardens
Where the spirit comes on strongly
Not as in your Berchtesgadens

Where things somehow turned out wrongly.
Forget your Spas, your Baden–Badens
(All along, down-and-out along-lea):
Come and live in Chlorine Gardens
With Paul Muldoon and Edna Longley –

Yes, come and live in Chlorine Gardens
With Paul, and us, and Edna Longley.

JAMES FENTON and JOHN FULLER, Partingtime Hall, 1987

Bloody Hand

Murders and assassinations are dreadful subjects,
but common here . . .

MRS McTIER TO WILLIAM DRENNAN

Down the hill of lies and horror
Belfast city slipped.

JAMES SIMMONS,
'The Ballad of Gerry Kelly: Newsagent'

BLOODY HAND

Your man, says the Man, *will walk into the bar like this* – here his
    fingers
Mimic a pair of legs, one stiff at the knee – *so you'll know exactly*
What to do. He sticks a finger to his head. Pretend it's child's
    play –
The hand might be a horse's mouth, a rabbit or a dog. Five
    handclaps.
Walls have ears: the shadows you throw are the shadows you
    try to throw off.

I snuffed out the candle between finger and thumb. Was it the
    left hand
Hacked off at the wrist and thrown to the shores of Ulster?
    Did Ulster
Exist? Or the Right Hand of God, saying *Stop* to this and *No*
    to that?
My thumb is the hammer of a gun. The thumb goes up. The
    thumb goes down.

CIARAN CARSON, *Belfast Confetti*, 1989

O N THE EVENING OF 13 JUNE 1974 I arrived home from work as usual around six o'clock. 'Home' was a comfortable foursquare former manse in the Malone Road area of Belfast. It was a very pleasant summer evening; the long avenue of lime trees was in full leaf. The children were away. My wife was waiting for me with the news: 'They say there's a car-bomb in the park behind us.' This was the parallel avenue some 75 yards away. Somebody had shouted a warning over the hedge; the ends of the avenue had been sealed off by the police, and the houses fronting it cleared. There had recently been a good many bombs in the city, mostly in commercial buildings, but there had also been a vast number of hoaxes and scares. 'I don't believe it,' I said; 'let's sit down and have a glass of sherry. But we'd better keep away from the windows.' (There is always a quandary in a bomb-scare: if windows and doors are opened, the damage is minimised, for the blastwave can travel freely till it spends itself: but anyone in the process of opening windows when the explosion comes may be dreadfully mutilated by flying glass.) We decided to leave the windows alone, poured ourselves sherry, and sat down in our usual chairs on either side of the fireplace in the sunny drawing-room.

Five minutes later, as we were sitting peaceably chatting and sipping, there was the loudest explosion I have (yet) heard; a sucking wave of blast; and all the glass in every window in the room fell shimmering and tinkling to the ground. By good fortune, it was the secondary inward wave, not the initial outward blast, that broke the windows; so that most of the fragments fell harmlessly onto the window-sill or into the rose-bed outside.

When we had collected ourselves – it took a little time – we went outside and joined our neighbours on their lawn; the police were afraid there might be another bomb, and had ordered everybody out of doors. We lay on the grass for three quarters of an hour before the all-clear was given. Then we dispersed to assess the damage. We were lucky. We had lost many window-panes; several doors and door-frames had been broken or displaced; a ceiling was cracked; a great many slates (as we were to discover next winter) had come loose. Our next-door neighbours had fared much worse: their roofs and ceilings were severely damaged. The house in the avenue behind us, outside which the car had been left, was almost completely destroyed: the owners (friends of ours) lost nearly everything they possessed.

That summer, each time I mowed my lawn, the blades of the motor mower would give a crunch and a shower of sparks when they struck some brown and mangled piece of metal hidden in the grass; these were fragments of the car that had been blown up.

C.E.B. BRETT, Long Shadows Cast Before, 1978

WHAT HAPPENED? Everyone asks this as they look at the rubbled streets of Belfast and Londonderrry on the television. The question never seems to be well answered, and only leads to more questions. If there had been no Catholics, would the Ulster Protestants have found it necessary to invent them? Certainly for years and years they provided the only spark of thrill and threat which could blast the monotony of the Ulster everyday. Month after month I remember listening to the same repeating rumours that the Catholics were marching up from Dublin – 'mustering' on the border – and infiltrating industry. Did all those interminable Ulster sermons seem less tedious when it was envisaged that iron-handed Papists might very soon try to put a stop to them? Did the polluted belch of Northern industry seem less hideous if it was felt that greedy Papal fingers were tentacling out to grasp the factories?

Can there be a boredom so powerful that it finally acts like an explosive?

CAROLINE BLACKWOOD, *For All That I Found There*, 1973

WHEN YOU CONSIDERED that it was the underpopulated capital of a minor province, the world seemed to know it excessively well. Nobody needed to be told the reasons for this needless fame. I didn't know much about Beirut until the artillery moved in. Who'd heard of Saigon before it blew its lid? Was Anzio a town, a village or just a stretch of beach? Where was Agincourt exactly?

Belfast shared the status of the battlefield. The place-names of the city and country had taken on the resonance and hard beauty of all history's slaughter venues. The Bogside, Crossmaglen, the Falls, the Shankill and Andersonstown. In the mental maps of those who had never been in Ireland, these places had tiny crossed swords after their names. People thought them deathfields – remote, televised knackers' yards. Belfast was only big because Belfast was bad.

And who would have thought it thirty years before? Little Belfast could be such a beautiful city. Squatting flat in the oxter of Belfast Lough, hazily level with the water, the city was ringed with mountains and nudged by the sea. When you looked up the length of most Belfast streets, there was some kind of mountain or hill staring back at you.

ROBERT McLIAM WILSON, *Eureka Street*, 1996

from AFTER SEYMOUR'S FUNERAL
SECTION VIII

Glaziers' hammers in Ann Street
After the patriots' bombs;

Emergency shutters of hardboard
Pre-emptively at hand;
Buses burned in the depots:
A population resigned
To follow the ruts that tumbrils
Have totted like debts on the streets.

Wherever – here or there –
Whenever – now or then –
War, you declared,
Is the inverted self
Of mirror-images –
MacTweedledum against McTweedledee –
Whose glib apologists
Make altar-room for flags
Amenably with hymns;
And walk the road with hard
Men clubbing calloused drums.

While patriots infiltrate,
Plain citizens lack language to prefer
A proper challenge at the barricades.
Who, they could say, *goes where?*

Today, they blocked the bridges, the
Traffic festered in the thoroughfares.
Old, abdicating buildings close
Their eyes, hands at their sides, aghast.

While dust recoils
From the smoke's uprising, wounds
Of aching absence let
In profiles of sky and a quizzical eyebrow of birds.
They have tidied bricks into cairns where a terrace died.
Staying is nowhere, Serafico, now.

ROY McFADDEN, *Collected Poems (1943–1995)*, 1996

THERE CAME MORE NIGHTS OF TERROR, but towards the end of that month of June a lull came as the King and Queen of England opened the Belfast Parliament and Ireland was partitioned.

Colm sat for exams in the College. Then came July and the summer holidays, but there was no peace. Houses were raided by police and auxiliaries during curfew; and in the poorer Catholic districts the people were organised to raise the cry of 'Murder! Murder!' if anyone entered their streets at night.

One night a lorry load of police and specials were ambushed by the Republicans in Raglan Street. One policeman was shot dead and some wounded.

Sitting up in their beds the MacNeills heard the volleys of shots crackling like breaking sticks. Colm was the only one who knew that Alec was out with the Republicans, for that evening he had told him as he gave him his pocketbook and asked him to pray. Now as he listened with cold fear to the air alive with shots he couldn't pray; he thought of Alec with a light rifle at his shoulder firing from the cover of an entry or from behind a lamp-post.

MICHAEL MCLAVERTY, *Call My Brother Back*, 1939

TROUBLE HAD STARTED IN THE SHIPYARDS; shootings and reprisals were a daily occurrence and the military had taken charge of the danger spots in the city. I was taken off the meter work and was told by the superintendent to keep the lamps in Seaforde Street and the Short Strand in repair. This area was one of the dangerous parts for shooting in the city. I asked why I was selected for this position and what had happened to the lamp maintenance man who did this district. I was told that this was a military order to keep this area lit up; I was issued with a permit and was told that I would have military protection if I applied to the officer in charge. I had the feeling that like Uriah of the bible I was being sent to the front line.

The people living in this area did not want the streets lit as they said they were a target when on the streets, and felt more secure from bullets in the dark, but the military who were patrolling this area insisted that the lamps be lit. This was in 1922, and anyone who lived in this area remembers the cross-firing that was kept up day and night. No one would venture out and trams passed this area at full speed empty, or with passengers lying flat on the floor. My first morning with a handcart full of lamps; when the boy who was with me came to the end of the bridge which led into this area he refused to go any further and left me and went back to the workshops. I don't blame the boy, but for the fact that I had a wife and family and was threatened with dismissal if I refused to do this work, I would have given it up.

I can't tell how I got the cart into this area. I ran with it and got safely into Madrid Street and into Seaforde Street with rifles cracking overhead. When I arrived with the lamps and fittings I was surrounded by a number of men and women who told me to clear out. I had to explain my position as a workman. It was the women who carried the day in my favour, but I was told that every lamp and fitting that I fitted up would be smashed when the lights were lit, and I want to say here and now that during these winter months that I kept the lights repaired the people in this area never interfered with me. But there was times when I had to clear out, when someone who lived in the district had been shot by a sniper. It was the snipers on the roofs and back windows who were the danger. Anyone seen on the streets within the range of their gun was their target, and they found out later through the press what side he belonged to. I had seen men who were going to work shot dead as a reprisal for some other victim. My only dread was when I was standing on the ladder putting up a lamp, bullets that I suppose were meant for me went through the lamp reflector. I brought some of these lamps back to the workshops and my workmates had many discussions on my narrow escapes.

ROBERT McELBOROUGH, The Autobiography of a Belfast Working Man, 1974

BELFAST WAS ONCE A TOWN OF DISTINGUISHED CHARACTER. In the eighteenth century it had for a while a reputation for radical, egalitarian thought. Now this city of 395,000 human beings is a place of memorials and landmarks. 'That's where McGurk's Bar stood . . .' 'That's where the Abercorn Restaurant blast occurred . . .' 'Down there is Farringdon Gardens, a whole street of houses burned out . . .' Reminders everywhere of loss, death, mutilation, blindness, pain, individual agony, and family grief, not easily wiped away. With so much flattened, burned out, or in ruins, it is a city perfectly ripe for planners, redevelopment, motorways, ring roads, giant housing projects. Many walls left standing are covered with the graffiti of violence. For new arrivals, it's a shock to halt at a street crossing and stare into the muzzle of a semiautomatic held by a soldier in a Land-Rover waiting for the light to change. Pairs of armed vehicles patrol the streets. Soldiers on foot patrol the sidewalks.

ANTHONY BAILEY, Acts of Union, 1980

THE ICE-CREAM MAN

Rum and raisin, vanilla, butter-scotch, walnut, peach:
You would rhyme off the flavours. That was before
They murdered the ice-cream man on the Lisburn Road
And you bought carnations to lay outside his shop.
I named for you all the wild flowers of the Burren
I had seen in one day: thyme, valerian, loosestrife,
Meadowsweet, tway blade, crowfoot, ling, angelica,
Herb robert, marjoram, cow parsley, sundew, vetch,

Mountain avens, wood sage, ragged robin, stitchwort,
Yarrow, lady's bedstraw, bindweed, bog pimpernel.

MICHAEL LONGLEY, Gorse Fires, 1991

ACCOUNT FROM THE 'BELFAST NEWSLETTER' OF A MILITARY RIOT IN
BELFAST, ON SATURDAY, 9TH OF MARCH, 1793.

'ABOUT THREE QUARTERS OF AN HOUR after six o'clock in the evening,
a body of the 17th Dragoons, intermixed with a few others of the
military, rushed out from their quarters, and drove furiously through most
of the principal streets, with their sabres drawn, cutting at any one that came
in their way, and attacking houses. This lasted near an hour, when, through
the interference of magistrates and some military officers, the party were
dispersed. In the course of this business, the windows of a number of the inhabitants were broken, and some signs torn down. A great number of
persons were slightly wounded, who had taken no part in the affray.
Charles Ranken, Esq., a justice of peace for the county of Antrim, in
endeavouring to take an artilleryman, and after commanding his Majesty's
peace by virtue of his office, was repeatedly stabbed at, and in a slight degree
wounded. Mr Campbell, surgeon, happening to be in a street through
which the party were driving, one of them ran across it, and made several
cuts at him, some of which penetrated through his clothes and slightly
wounded him. The windows of a milliner's shop were broken, in which
cockades were hung up for sale. A man had his ear and his hand cut with a
sword. Happily no lives were lost, and to the prudence and quiet demeanour
of the townspeople it was owing.

'The houses which suffered most were those of Mr M'Cabe, watchmaker;
Mr Orr, chandler; Mr Watson, on the Quay; Mr Johnson and Mr Sinclair,
public-house keepers in North Street: and the shop of Miss Wills, a milliner,
in High Street. Their malice seemed principally levelled at the Volunteers.
Two of the dragoons received ample punishment from the swords of their
officers. The consternation of the town may be easily supposed.

'Two causes have been assigned for this unprovoked disturbance: viz.,
that there was a sign of Dumurier at a small public-house in North Street;
and that a blind fiddler who plays through the streets at night, happened to
be playing Ca Ira, a French air. With respect to the sign, it was erected before
there was any prospect of a war with France, and the circumstance of its
being there could not be countenanced by the people, for few had ever
heard of it till the riot brought it into notice. As to the tune played by a
blind mendicant, it is too trifling a cause to be seriously mentioned, though
he deposed on oath that he never knew the tune in question.'

QUOTED IN RICHARD R. MADDEN, The United Irishmen: Their Lives and Times, 1857

O N THAT SUMMER AFTERNOON the street was thronged with . . . towns-folk from every walk of life: executions were a public occasion, and those who wished to watch the spectacle in greater comfort hired windows over-looking the scene. To shield herself somewhat from the staring crowds Mary had drawn the veil of her bonnet over her face; it was afterwards said that a soldier had lifted the veil with the point of his sword and cut it off.

But very many amongst the throng were there, not from idle curiosity, but from a desire to follow to the end the man whom they venerated as master, leader and friend. It was well known that Harry possessed to a remarkable degree the quality that commands devotion, and every precaution had been taken by the military against a demonstration in his favour, including a strong guard of dragoons.

It was a fearful scene. Three weeks previously James Dickey the attorney from Crumlin had been hanged, and his head cut off and placed on a spike on the Market House. Four days later the same sentence had been passed on John Storey the Belfast printer, who had been a fellow prisoner with Harry at Kilmainham. Both these men had fought at Antrim. In the beginning of July Hugh Grimes and Henry Byres, leaders at Ballynahinch, had suffered likewise. There they were – four heads with their sightless eyeballs staring down on the little procession making its way to yet another hanging. In the glare and heat of that exceptionally warm summer flies buzzed around the festering flesh, and the Town authorities issued a warning against the consumption of uncooked fruit.

When Mary Ann left him, Harry stood, tall and majestic, looking after her till she was out of sight. Later she heard from others of the calmness and composure with which he faced death and of the last minute intervention by Major Fox to save his life, moved this time perhaps more by admiration for his heroism than by the desire for information. Why, his uncomprehending mind may have wondered, must such incredible fortitude, such poise, such self-control, be so uselessly squandered, the fellow must be given one more chance to get away. Harry answered him with a smile.

There are good grounds for supposing that when all was over it was Mrs Burnside who received the body of Henry Joy McCracken from the hangman and performed the last ministrations, a poignant tribute to the abiding devotion and loyalty of his weaver friends.

MARY McNEILL, The Life and Times of Mary Ann McCracken, 1960

T HE RIOTS OF THIS YEAR [1864] were due to the importation the previous year of some hundreds – perhaps thousands – of navvies to dig a new dock, and it was found out that a large proportion of these men were Roman Catholics. The balance of fighting power among the belligerent classes was thereby disturbed; so when the illegal 'walking' of the

Protestants on the Twelfth of July was interfered with by the opposite party, the result was a series of encounters in many of the streets. It was, however, only when the Romanists tried to organise a party procession of their own a month later that the town was given over to civil war, which police and military found impossible to put down. I believe that it was when I was on my way to school that I saw the cars and waggonettes of the Catholic procession attacked by a body of men who seemed to have been in hiding in what was strategically the best point of attack on the projected route of the excursionists. This was at the junction of four streets in the very centre of the town. Two of the streets led from the Catholic quarters, and the moment the processional cars emerged from these, they were met with a volley not only of stones, but of bullets as well, and in another moment the central ground had become a battlefield. Of course, the constabulary came up at the double, but they had to be sent for: they were certainly not waiting in anticipation of the meeting of the rival factions.

From that morning for close upon a month the town was in the hands of two mobs. Shops were shut in the principal streets and business was practically suspended in all directions; for the mills and the foundries and the shipbuilding yard of Harland and Wolff – it had only been established a few years, but was turning out some good work – had closed. I remember saying to a boy who walked with me, under the convoy of one of my father's men, that Donegall Place looked as it usually did on Sunday, with all the shops closed, and no traffic to be seen.

Before we got to the end of the street we had to run for our lives. A large and nasty-looking mob came swaggering down the roadway, every man carrying a bludgeon of a very formidable type, if he had been strong enough to use it; but even now I am still of the opinion that it was quite too unwieldy for close fighting. It was a piece of wood fully four feet long, roughly squared, as if for a gate post, up to within about six inches from one end, where it was whittled away from the four inches of the square to two inches for the grip. A thick band of leather nailed loosely on this end allowed a hand to be thrust through, so giving firmness to the hold. But from the difficulty that some of these desperadoes had in brandishing this club I could see that it would be formidable only for men who were on the ground: a boy would have no difficulty in evading its stroke; but it was as terrifying in appearance as are the horns of Highland cattle to lowland visitors.

This day was, I afterwards learned, one of the most eventful in the whole history of the town. A regular pitched battle took place upon the navvies' own ground. I visited it a few days later as the burghers of Brussels visited Waterloo, and saw how the fighting had been conducted. The dock which was being dug extended over fifteen or twenty acres, and it was already ten feet below the embankment. The Protestant army had got possession of the bank, and drove the navvies into the mud before them with what is, I believe, termed by war correspondents, 'a withering fire' of guns and pistols. The navvies, however, seemed not to have been quite taken by surprise. They were able to respond to the fire, for they had gone to their work of excavation pretty much as the restorers of the walls of Jerusalem had done when working under the eyes of their enemies – with a sword in one hand and a trowel in the other, only the navvies had guns. For more than an hour the conflict lasted, and undoubtedly blood was shed on both sides, and there was no police interference until the navvies had been driven across the muddy basin which they had been digging.

F. FRANKFORT MOORE, *The Truth About Ulster*, 1914

IN BELFAST, ON MAY 31ST [1922], the shooting of two Special Constables brought a horde of Specials in armoured-cars into the Catholic streets, which they raked with machine-gun fire. Renewing the attack at night, they broke into houses and set fire to them, fired on fugitives and murdered, among others, a blind man and a bedridden woman who were too helpless to fly. Over eighty Catholic families were rendered homeless in that one night; three Catholic women and five Catholic men were killed. The blind man, who was killed by a bomb, proved to be a Protestant lodging in a Catholic house. Another Special Constable and another Protestant civilian were killed.

By the end of May, it was estimated, the total number of Protestants killed during the year in the Six Counties was 87; of Catholics 150. The first eighteen days of June added 6 Protestants and 21 Catholics killed.

The Catholic Hospital, the Mater Miseracordiae, in Belfast, was like a war hospital in the first week in June. The wards, even the children's wards, were filled with bullet-wound and shrapnel-wound cases; fifty children under sixteen years of age had been treated there for wounds since February, when the bombing and sniping of children had first become a part of the expulsion campaign, and there were boys lamed for life in the wards. On the night of June 4th the hospital was surrounded by an armed mob who fired through the windows with rifles and revolvers. Doctors and nurses rushed from ward to ward, lifting patients who could not roll or crawl from their beds and laying them on the floor under the windows where they were safe. Many patients, after that experience, were too unnerved to remain in the hospital and invalids on crutches and on stretchers joined the throng of fugitives fleeing to the South.

DOROTHY MacARDLE, *The Irish Republic*, 1937

THE COASTERS

You coasted along
to larger houses, gadgets, more machines,
to golf and weekend bungalows,
caravans when the children were small,
the Mediterranean, later, with the wife.

You did not go to church often,
weddings were special;
but you kept your name on the books
against eventualities;
and the parson called, or the curate.

You showed a sense of responsibility,
with subscriptions to worthwhile causes
and service in voluntary organisations;
and, anyhow, this did the business no harm,
no harm at all.
Relations were improving. A good
useful life. You coasted along.

You even had a friend or two of the other sort,
coasting too: your ways ran parallel.
Their children and yours seldom met, though,
being at different schools.
You visited each other, decent folk with a sense
of humour. Introduced, even, to
one of their clergy. And then you smiled
in the looking-glass, admiring, a
little moved by, your broadmindedness.
Your father would never have known
one of them. Come to think of it,
when you were young, your own home was never
visited by one of the other sort.

Relations were improving. The annual processions
began to look rather like folk-festivals.

When that noisy preacher started,
he seemed old-fashioned, a survival.
Later you remarked on his vehemence,
a bit on the rough side.

But you said, admit it, you said in the club,
'You know, there's something in what he says.'

And you who seldom had time to read a book,
what with reports and the colour-supplements,
denounced censorship.
And you who never had an adventurous thought
were positive that the church of the other sort
vetoes thought.
And you, who simply put up with marriage
for the children's sake, deplored
the attitude of the other sort
to divorce.
You coasted along.
And all the time, though you never noticed,
the old lies festered;
the ignorant became more thoroughly infected;
there were gains, of course;
you never saw any go barefoot.

The government permanent, sustained
by the regular plebiscites of loyalty.
You always voted but never
put a sticker on the car;
a card in the window
would not have been seen from the street.
Faces changed on the posters, names too, often,
but the same families, the same class of people.
A Minister once called you by your first name.
You coasted along
and the sores suppurated and spread.

Now the fever is high and raging;
who would have guessed it, coasting along?
The ignorant-sick thresh about in delirium
and tear at the scabs with dirty finger-nails.
The cloud of infection hangs over the city,
a quick change of wind and it
might spill over the leafy suburbs,
You coasted too long.

JOHN HEWITT, *An Ulster Reckoning*, 1971

ON THE NIGHT OF THURSDAY, August 14th 1969, this reporter was crouching beneath a Catholic block of flats in the Falls Road, Belfast, as a police armoured car roared past, turret traversing. Suddenly it screeched to a halt, and a long burst of fire from its heavy machine gun echoed the length of the street. Behind the corners half the way down the road lay police whose sub-machine guns and revolvers had been blazing intermittently for more than an hour. Two policemen wounded by snipers were being tended in the shelter of an armoured personnel carrier; flames were pouring from burning buildings higher up the street. A few minutes later, I was watching a nine-year-old Catholic boy dying where he lay, half his head blown away by a burst of automatic fire. Behind the police line, groups of Protestants armed with petrol bombs, dustbin lids and staves wandered with impunity.

Had this been Chicago, Washington or Detroit, the scene might have been made almost bearable by its awful familiarity. But Belfast is part of Northern Ireland, Northern Ireland is part of Britain [*sic*], and these were British policemen in a British city engaged in full-scale battle with British citizens. This melodrama had been played here before, it was to be played here again before 1969 was out, and New Year brought little guarantee against repetition. In London and Manchester, Plymouth and Hull – every city in England – people read their newspapers, were appalled, and yet totally bewildered.

MAX HASTINGS, *Ulster 1969*, 1970

THE BALLAD OF GERRY KELLY: NEWSAGENT
for Gus Martin

Here's a song for Gerry Kelly,
Listen carefully and see
what's the moral of the story.
It makes no sense to me.

Worked ten hours six days a week,
Sundays closed at three.
They say he made a decent living,
Rather him than me.

Social centre for the neighbours –
not much cash in that –
buying fags or blades or tissues,
waiting on to chat.

Sixty nine the nightmare started,
Loyalist anger rose:
sweet shops, butcher shops and pubs
were burned down, forced to close.

Who'd believe who never saw it . . .
the broken glass, the noise,
voices shouting 'Fenian bastard'
– little Ulster boys?

Down the hill of lies and horror
Belfast city slipped
Twice the Tartan thugs came for him,
robbed and pistol-whipped.

Standing in his shattered shop
and taking inventory
of loss and damage, Gerry Kelly
longed to get away.

Who would buy the ruined business
that he'd worked to build?
No one, so he waited, hoping
until he was killed.

One dark evening last November –
turn the lights on till we see –
Gerry Kelly still in business,
wife gone back to make the tea.

Sorting out the evening papers
while his son is selling sweets,
in our time, our town, two gunmen
walk in off the streets.

JAMES SIMMONS, *West Strand Visions*, 1974

THE HALL LIGHT CAME ON.

Facing him, a flashlight in one hand and a revolver in the other, was a hooded figure, its head masked in a woollen balaclava helmet, the eyeholes cut wide showing the cheekbones. The intruder wore woollen gloves, a cheap blue Western-style shirt with metal-clip buttons, faded jeans and running shoes. Behind him, standing by the light switch, was another, similarly dressed figure, also pointing a revolver.

He had seen them on the evening television news and in newspaper photographs, theatrical figures, firing revolver volleys over paramilitary graves, marching in parades with banners and flags. But like most people he kept well away from the events themselves so that now, for the first time in his life, he was looking at them, here in his house, real revolvers, faceless, staring eyes, scruffy boys in woollen masks. Who are they? Are they Protestants or Catholics – UDA or IRA? Is this one of those mistakes where they come in and shoot the wrong person?

'What do you want?' He heard the fear in his voice.

BRIAN MOORE, Lies of Silence, 1990

THERE ARE FEW ENOUGH PEOPLE ON THE ROADS AT NIGHT. Fear has begun to tingle through the place. Who's to know the next target on the Provisional list? Who's to know the reprisals won't strike where you are? The bars are quieter. If you're carrying a parcel you make sure it's close to you in case it's suspected of being about to detonate. In the Queen's University staff commonroom, recently, a bomb-disposal squad had defused a bundle of books before the owner had quite finished his drink in the room next door. Yet when you think of the corpses in the rubble of McGurk's Bar such caution is far from risible.

Then there are the perils of the department stores. Last Saturday a bomb scare just pipped me before I had my socks and pyjamas paid for in Marks and Spencer, although there were four people on the Shankill Road who got no warning. A security man cornered my wife in Robinson and Cleaver – not surprisingly, when she thought of it afterwards. She had a timing device, even though it was just an old clock from an auction, lying in the bottom of her shopping bag. A few days previously someone else's timing device had given her a scare when an office block in University Road exploded just as she got out of range.

SEAMUS HEANEY (1971), Preoccupations, 1980

THE CITY IS FULL OF NOISES. It shares with other places, of course, the constant roaring and rumbling of traffic, and the whine of passing aircraft. But for those with well-tuned ears, there are other things to be heard. Not just the resonant calling of muezzins from the minarets, the sounds of chimes and peals and single bells; not just the constant mewing of gulls, the twitter of birdsong, the baying of countless (and often ownerless) dogs; but more sinister noises too.

The sullen crash of a bomb. The crackling of flames, the collapse of roof-timbers and the downfall of slates, the tinkle of shattered glass. The sound of shots, near or far, and then perhaps the sound of answering shots. Repeater fire: occasionally heavy-machine-gun fire: the firing of so-called baton rounds. The clatter of a hovering helicopter. The shock of a rocket hitting a moving jeepful of men. Home-made mortar bombs, striking in over the netting screen surrounding a poste de gendarmerie. The sharp crack of nail-bomb, blast-bomb, pipe-bomb, booby-trap. The deep roar of a land-mine. And, by way of accompaniment to all these sounds, the clanging bells and screaming sirens of ambulances, fire engines, security vehicles; perhaps also the blowing of whistles, the confused sound of voices high-pitched with passionate abuse, the clashing of dustbin-lids.

Not all these sounds are to be heard every day; or even, very often; yet, too often.

There are other sounds characteristic of the City. At certain seasons, the brash music of military bands, pipe bands, brass bands, flute bands, silver bands, accordeon bands; the rattle of side-drums and snare-drums, the thunder of enormous bass drums lacerated with whippy drumsticks, to the time dictated by a conductor playing upon a penny whistle. Other sounds again are the shrill and barely intelligible street-cries of newsboys; the variegated music, much of it melancholy and despairing, of itinerant buskers; the plaintive and (as it seems) never-ending ringing of burglar-alarms.

ALBERT RECHTS, Handbook to a Hypothetical City, 1986

TWO SPECTRES HAUNT ME

Still from these years two incidents remain
which challenge yet my bland philosophy,
on this neat sheet leave dark corrosive stain,
which mars the dream of what I hope might be.
First, on the paved edge of our cinder field,
intent till dusk, upon our game, I ran
by accident against a striding man
and glimpsed the shotgun he had thought concealed.

Then, once, I saw a working man attack
a cycling sergeant. Whistle. Warning shout.
As if by magic plain-clothes men sprang out,
grappled the struggler, carried, rammed his head
against a garden wall. I watched the red
blood dribble down his brow, his limbs grow slack.

JOHN HEWITT, Kites in Spring, 1980

IN CROMAC STREET, Bonar paused and looked around as if in search of something. 'Did you see any of the Troubles?' he asked.

'Only a papish fruitshop burned out in the Dublin Road when I was a kid.'

'I saw a man shot dead – there.' Bonar pointed to the street corner opposite.

David was impressed. 'Where were you?'

'I was down a message for my mammy' – at the endearment David winced – 'and just as I was crossing here I heard the shots. I bunked for a doorway and when I looked out there was the man down on his hands and knees coughing and three fellas running away down Eliza Street. The man fell on his face and two ould shawlies came out of a house and pulled him onto the pavement. After a minute I thought about going across to have a look at him, but a peeler came running up and when he'd looked at him, he took off his jacket and threw it over the fella's face.'

'He was dead?' asked David, his eyes wide.

'Stiff. Look. I'll show you something.' He drew David across the street and at the low window-sill of a shop took his hand and ran his fingers over the ledge. 'Feel it? That's where one of the bullets struck. It went right through him.'

'How d'you know?'

'I saw it. I saw the peelers digging it out of the wood. The ould lady in the shop got fed up with people coming and looking at the hole. At first she thought it would bring custom to her place but she only sold cooked pigs' feet and not everybody eats them. So she had the hole puttied up and painted over. She mighta left it. It was a sorta historical thing, wasn't it?'

David agreed doubtfully. He hadn't known that murderous death had been so close to Colinvista Street. 'Who was the man?'

'They said he was a rebel that squealed. That's why the peeler covered up his face. He probably deserved it. They never caught the three fellas.'

SAM HANNA BELL, *The Hollow Ball*, 1961

IT MAY BE THOUGHT THAT with the troubles of 1798 the Rebellion ceased. It was scarcely so; vigilance was still needed, and military rule still prevailed, and continued more or less during these two years. The Court-Martial continued still to be held in Belfast, and prisoners with pikes were occasionally brought in for trial. General Nugent caused the names of all the inmates of every house living therein to be affixed in a conspicuous place on the houses, and if any be absent from sunset to sunrise, the owner shall be accountable, and be liable to such punishment as a Court-Martial shall inflict. The magistrates at the same time declared the whole County of Antrim to be in a state of disturbance. Our town participated in these stringent regulations. As an example of insubordination, Richmond Lodge, only two miles from Belfast, the seat of Charles Rankin, Esq., was attacked for arms by five men, whose faces were covered with green veils. Notwithstanding this and many similar outrages which took place, the people were still unwilling that the civil law should be superseded, and the military introduced in its stead.

GEORGE BENN, *A History of the Town of Belfast*, 1880

THE TRADE MARK OF THIS AGE OF COMMERCIALISM is stamped upon Belfast. Its physiognomy is eminently matter-of-fact. The city is neat, business-like, roomy. You can feel, before you are half an hour in it, that it looks upon time as money – although it still tolerates horse traction in its tramcars, due, I was told, to some hitch in the contract which prevents the corporation from forcing electric traction on the companies. Belfast hums with industry and calls itself progressive. And yet, underlying all this commercialism, all this thrift, and all this cult of the main chance, there is a cast iron bigotry – a cruel, corroding, unfathomable, ferocious sectarian rancour.

You feel this, too, before you are long in Belfast. It works its way into most fields of human activity. You see it in the stern features of shopmen, who actually make their business interests subservient to Orangeism. You read it in the Press. At the Custom House esplanade there is a fierce anti-Catholic open air, gutter-orator, propaganda going on nearly every Sunday. The high councils of fanatics and schemers, who direct the No-Popery campaigns, may be said to be in permanent session. Of the ten thousand operatives working in the ship-building yards, I was told that not ten are Catholics. A Catholic's life would not be safe there, according to my informants. The owners of the yards are not bigots by choice. They are the victims of circumstances. If they employ Catholics they would be in hot water the whole year round. To begin with, things would be constantly happening to the Catholics. Bolts and crowbars and hammers and packages of rivets, and sharp heavy pieces of scrap-iron would be falling on their heads, coming, to all seeming and appearance out of the sky. No one could be pointed to as the thrower of such missiles. It would all be put down to accident. There would be no hostile manifestation of a noisy character. There would be no howling. But, all the same, Catholic mechanics would be dropping off from day to day. One would be found lying under a girder at the bottom of a ship's hold; another would be found sprawling on a scaffolding with the point of a three-inch shackel-pin buried in his brains; later on another would be found under a lift with both legs broken.

It would all be seeming accident. The employers might or might not be obliged to pay damages, but, in any case, they would have no end of legal trouble on their hands. No one can control scrap-iron in Belfast when there is sectarian or political trouble in the wind. Odds and ends of boilers and girders and other projectiles disappear from the yards and reappear down town in showers, smashing heads and windows and the peace of the realm.

WILLIAM BULFIN, Rambles in Eirinn, 1907

THE RIDING SCHOOL

Dung, cobble, wall, cypress;
Delight in art whose end is peace;
No cold-eyed horseman of the Irish skies
Can compare with me
Leading out the Grey of the Blues.

I in my red blanket
Under the Cave Hill Mountain
Leading out the Grey of the Blues:
The blindness of history in my eyes;
The blindness of history in my hands.

To get up at four every morning
And to lead out the Grey of the Blues;
Delight in art whose end is peace;
Hold his reins with my eyes open;
His dappled hindquarters;
His summer coat;
His knotted mane;
His combed-out tail;
His swanface;
His bullneck;
His spineline;
His tiny, prancing grace-notes.

And I in my red blanket
Under the Cave Hill Mountain
Leading out the Grey of the Blues:
The blindness of history in my eyes;
The blindness of history in my hands.

I take pride in my work;
Delight in art whose end is peace;
The way I lead out a song;
The way I hold the reins of a song in my hands

Between my stubby fingers.
I talk to my song;

My song talks to me.
In the blackest weathers
We have our sunniest hours.
How many early mornings
In black rain I have talked my song
Round and round the pink paddock!

I in my red blanket
Under the Cave Hill Mountain
Leading out the Grey of the Blues:
The blindness of history in my eyes;
The blindness of history in my hands.

My song is nearing the end of its tether;
Lament in art whose end is war;
Opera glasses, helicopters, t.v. crews;
Our slayings are what's news.
We are taking our curtain call,
Our last encore.
True to our natures
We do not look into the camera lenses
But at one another.
In a gap of oblivion, gone.

I in my red blanket
Under the Cave Hill Mountain
Leading out the Grey of the Blues:
The blindness of history in my eyes;
The blindness of history in my hands.

PAUL DURCAN, *Crazy About Women*, 1991

BELFAST TODAY is a city of scaremongers; its inhabitants would be less (or more) than human if this were not so. People told me that on Sandy Row they like to take Catholics – or even suspected Catholics – around to the back of a pub and slit their throats. When I argued that such occurrences must be very infrequent the reply was that the arrival of a Catholic in a Sandy Row pub is very infrequent.

DERVLA MURPHY, *A Place Apart*, 1978

T HE WEEK OF 12–16 AUGUST 1969 was when the British public came face to face with the fact that there is a part of Britain where politics can kill. The physical savagery on the streets was brilliantly conveyed at the time by television and newspapers. What was harder to distinguish, let alone convey, in this bloodstained jumble of events, was the actual sequence which precipitated British power into Ulster.

For Northern Ireland, those five days were a watershed, not only because the British Government and its Army became inextricably and fatally involved, but because the clock was set back fifty years, finally disintegrating O'Neill's brittle reconciliations. The events have since entered the folk histories of both Protestants and Catholics. The Catholics, especially of Belfast, now see August 1969 as an attempted Protestant pogrom. The Protestants had their suspicions confirmed that the Civil Rights struggle was merely a 'front' for traditional IRA insurrection.

SUNDAY TIMES INSIGHT TEAM, *Ulster*, 1972

UNDER THE EYES

Its retributions work like clockwork
Along murdering miles of terrace-houses
Where someone is saying, 'I am angry,
I am frightened, I am justified.
Every favour, I must repay with interest,
Any slight against myself, the least slip,
Must be balanced out by an exact revenge.'

The city is built on mud and wrath.
Its weather is predicted; its streetlamps
Light up in the glowering, crowded evenings.
Time-switches, ripped from them, are clamped
To sticks of sweet, sweating explosive.
All the machinery of a state
Is a set of scales that squeezes out blood.

Memory is just, too. A complete system
Nothing can surprise. The dead are recalled
From schoolroom afternoons, the hill quarries
Echoing blasts over the secured city;
Or, in a private house, a Judge

Shot in his hallway before his daughter
By a boy who shut his eyes as his hand tightened.

A rain of turds; a pair of eyes; the sky and tears.

TOM PAULIN, *A State of Justice*, 1977

Bygone Canon, Bygone Spleen

Religion and politics combined to rouse the people of Belfast almost to a state of frenzy.

J.L. PORTER, *The Life and Times of Henry Cooke*

But I'll go down to Belfast
　　To see that seaport gay,
And tell my aged parents
　　In this country I can't stay:
O 'tis dark will be their sorrow
　　But no truer hearts I've seen,
And they'd rather see me dying
　　Than a traitor to the Green!

ANONYMOUS

from THE BATTLE OF AUGHRIM
ORANGE MARCH

In bowler hats and Sunday suits,
Orange sashes, polished boots,
Atavistic trainbands come
To blow the fife and beat the drum.

Apprentices uplift their banner
True-blue-dyed with 'No Surrender!'
Claiming Aughrim as if they'd won
Last year, not 1691.

On Belfast silk, Victoria gives
Bibles to kneeling Zulu chiefs.

Read the moral, note the date:
'The secret that made Britain great.'

Derry, oakwood of bright angels,
Londonderry, dingy walls
Chalked at night with 'Fuck the Queen!'
Bygone canon, bygone spleen.

RICHARD MURPHY, The Battle of Aughrim, 1968

D R HENRY COOKE, in the first half of the nineteenth century, was the framer of sectarianism in the politics of Ulster. Belfast, up to the Reform Act of 1832, was a fortress of Liberalism. Cooke's teachings changed this. The banns of a marriage which he proclaimed at Hillsborough, Co Down, on October 30, 1834, between the Established and the Presbyterian Churches heralded a politico-religious alliance between the two bodies. He urged the Presbyterians to make common cause with the Tories at a time when Sir Robert Peel, who carried Catholic Emancipation through dread of revolution in Ireland, laboured with all his might to make the Orange interest impregnable. Before Dr Cooke's day sectarian riots were unknown in Belfast. Since then riots have broken out with varying degrees of violence and duration in 1857, 1864, 1872, 1886, 1893, 1898, 1920–1922, and 1935.

T.J. CAMPBELL, Fifty Years of Ulster 1890–1940, 1941

I F I RENOUNCE MY POLITICS, I must renounce my religion. I have not learned them from Whig, or Tory, or Radical; I have got them from the Bible – I have got them from that mysterious warning revealed to us to be a guide to our feet in these latter days: – 'Babylon the great is fallen, is fallen, and is become the habitation of devils, and the hold of every foul spirit. Come out of her, my people, that ye be not partakers of her sins, and that ye receive not of her plagues.' My politics are inseparable from my religion. To my party I still adhere, because they are our best barrier against fierce democracy on the one hand, and more terrible Popery on the other. Between Protestantism and Popery there is still an impassable wall. But if we passively lie down in the ditch, our bodies will be the bridges for Popery to pass over; or, if we in anger forsake the garrison, it may soon be compelled to surrender to our common foe.

DR HENRY COOKE, quoted in J.L. Porter, The Life and Times of Henry Cooke, 1871

WHEN I WAS IN BELFAST, violent disputes were raging between Presbyterian and Episcopalian Conservatives with regard to the Marriage Bill; between Presbyterians and Catholics on the subject of the Home Missions; between the Liberals and Conservatives, of course. 'Thank God,' for instance, writes a Repeal journal, 'that the honour and power *of Ireland* are not involved in the disgraceful Afghan war!' – a sentiment insinuating Repeal and something more; disowning, not merely this or that ministry, but the sovereign and her jurisdiction altogether. But details of these quarrels, religious or political, can tend to edify but few readers out of the country. Even in it, as there are some nine shades of politico-religious differences, an observer pretending to impartiality must necessarily displease eight parties, and almost certainly the whole nine; and the reader who desires to judge the politics of Belfast must study for himself. Nine journals, publishing four hundred numbers in a year, each number containing about as much as an octavo volume: these and the back numbers of former years, sedulously read, will give the student a notion of the subject in question. And then, after having read the statements on either side, he must ascertain the truth of them, by which time more labour of the same kind will have grown upon him, and he will have attained a good old age.

WILLIAM MAKEPEACE THACKERAY, *The Irish Sketch Book*, 1842

POLICE BATON CHARGES were quite a common occurrence in the early 1900s. The police themselves were never popular with either Protestant or Catholic crowds and, often enough, they had to face either ways when a riot was proceeding. In those days, the old RIC only carried firearms on ceremonial parades. Today, the Royal Ulster Constabulary are armed to the teeth: rifle and bayonet, revolver and baton, and tommy gun when needed. My first collision with the police happened on the relief of Ladysmith celebrations.

When the news of the relief of Ladysmith was received in Belfast, the entire population downed tools and crowded the main thoroughfares to demonstrate. There was a continuous procession of cheering crowds along the principal streets. This continued hour after hour without cessation.

As the evening wore on, the procession was augmented with dozens of brass and fife-and-drum bands. I was following a brass band in the procession along Royal Avenue when a shower of stones dropped amongst the crowd, thrown from the direction of Kent Street. Kent Street, being a Catholic quarter, was naturally pro-Boer.

There was an immediate rush by the crowd in this direction, but the police were waiting for this eventuality. They knew the likely hot spots when Protestant crowds decided to demonstrate. So I record my first baton charge. There was a panic when the police charged and I came out of the scrimmage minus one canvas shoe and my cap. Still, I enjoyed the excitement and went over my adventure with great gusto when I finally arrived home, somewhere about two in the morning.

THOMAS CARNDUFF (1954), Life and Writings, 1994

I KNOW IT SOUNDS ALMOST INCREDIBLE, but at the first church I attended in Belfast in the early nineties urchins, hidden from observation in the back seats, used to while away the time by scribbling on the walls, or cutting with their pen-knives on the pews, such sentiments as 'Ulster will Fight', 'Morley, Murderer and Atheist' – the author of the *Compromise* had been Irish Chief Secretary during the '86 riots and his name at the time was an abomination to Orangemen – 'Blast John Dillon and Tim Healy', and remarks even more unfit for polite ears. This was simply a case of 'as the old cock crows the young ones cackle', for the parson was a famous Orange stalwart whose sermons were political tirades garnished with Scripture quotations, and who once offered me a book entitled *Mr Gladstone, or a Life Misspent*, which, to my eternal regret, I did not accept.

JAMES WINDER GOOD, Ulster and Ireland, 1919

DURING MY SCHOOL DAYS I had been obliged, much against the grain, to learn history. It was a task for which I had little aptitude because I never had any memory for dates, and when I left school I was still abysmally ignorant of even the outlines of Irish history.

This was not to be wondered at, because the whole trend of my education lay in ignoring the fact that we were Irish and not English, and the facts about Ireland as distinct from England were completely ignored. I joined lustily in singing 'God Save the Queen' without the words of the National Anthem meaning anything at all to me, and the unfurling of the Union Jack was just a part of the general hullabaloo. But as I grew up I began to ask questions, especially on the Twelfth of July and on Saint Patrick's Day when Orange and Green were knocking hell out of each other with gusto and kidney stones. I had heard with untouched feelings the story of the Battle of the Boyne. They were battles fought long ago and could have little interest for a youth in 1898. I had learnt a certain amount about the Irish political situation from Jimmy [James Winder Good] who had read much, and from what he told me I now gathered that a monster demonstration was being organised to commemorate the rebellion of 1798, and that any opposition could lead to very dirty work at the crossroads.

I knew enough about Belfast to know that a demonstration of any kind was meat and drink to hot heads on both sides. So completely immured had

I become in my own ivory tower of art that in 1898 I did not know what constituted the difference between Nationalist and Unionist. All I knew was that they were continually fighting bitterly and savagely about what seemed to me of quite minor importance. Jimmy gave me a brief account of what had led up to the present situation, saying that it looked pretty serious, that troops were being hurried to Belfast from all quarters.

People were coming from all over Ireland to take part, and a certain Maud Gonne, whom I had never heard of, was to lead the procession on a white horse. With these thoughts in my mind to help me forget the precariousness of my own situation, I took a walk through the poorer quarters of the town. I could not help noticing as I walked through the streets the great difference between the Unionist and the Nationalist quarters. On the one hand were the large houses with spacious lawns of the lords of industry and on the other the workers, men, women and children trudging through the ill lit streets to their cheerless homes. I knew that, roughly speaking, the well housed were Unionist and the poor Nationalist, and I wondered why. Then the thought of my father's championship of the under dog surged up in me and I decided that I would be a Nationalist.

Wandering aimlessly down a street which led to the School of Art, I met a girl called Mary McCracken who was a student there. I stopped and spoke to her and asked her how she was getting on with her work. As we strolled along together she told me she was very busy helping with the decorations for the great procession. She was a Catholic and an ardent Nationalist and was thrilled to be helping with the great work. We turned into King Street and crossed into Smithfield. Smithfield was unusually crowded with blousy, untidy women, and we learned that Maud Gonne was there somewhere in the jostling crowd. Everybody wanted to see her and speak to her, including Mary. I decided to wait with my friend and see this strange woman who appeared to have such an influence over the crowd. But there was so much noise and excitement that I came away.

PAUL HENRY, *Further Reminiscences*, 1973

THE FIRST INCIDENT OF MY LIFE of which I retain a vivid memory was of Ulster fighting, and the *casus belli* of more than fifty years ago has not been removed; on the contrary, it has been intensified during the latter half of this space of time, until Ulster to-day resembles one of those volcanic basins which only need a single stone to be flung into them to produce such an eruption as may change the whole face of the landscape.

Of course, there was no talk that I can recollect in the nursery of the possibility of a riot. I was not old enough to know what the word meant even if I had heard it spoken. But after our usual Sunday midday dinner we were taken for a walk among those streets of Belfast which were in close proximity to the quay-side – our nurse was a Presbyterian, and had connections in the mercantile marine of these localities. It must have been in the house of one of her relatives that some loud conversation was going on when we were brought in from the street. The names of some clergymen were, I remember, tossed about on the tumultuous waves of converse – 'Dr Cooke', 'Dr Drew', and, I think, 'Dr Gregg' – these were the names that I heard in connection with an important and much-used phrase 'cloddin' stones'. I was old enough to know what 'cloddin' stones' meant, but not old enough to be aware of the close connection there has ever been since the days of the martyr Stephen between theology and geology. But there had been 'cloddin''; I heard that the 'Papishes' had made a vow, the terms of which should never have reached the ears of a child, that they would treat certain divines as Stephen had been treated, only they did not mention the martyr's name, nor did they hint that it was to heaven they meant to 'clod' the clergymen. (I was at that time fully informed as to the direction in which Stephen had been sent, as I am sure every other Protestant child in the Province was also.)

But before our nurse's whispered protest – with a wink in our direction – against the bad word that had been spoken in quoting verbatim the terms of the awful vow that had been made, there was the sound of shouting in the street – shouting and cheers and the rush of many feet. Upstairs the children were sent amid the shrieks of our faithful nurse; but there were windows in the bedroom where we took refuge, and from one of them I saw a flying crowd of men and women, boys and girls of the mill-working order, and behind them were riding at the trot three dragoons with their sabres drawn and at the 'carry'.

I had never before seen a mounted soldier with a brass helmet and a real sword, and I recollect distinctly how I was thrilled by the sight. I had seen many pictures in bound copies of the *Illustrated London News* dealing with the recent war in the Crimea, and I had been to a panorama of the still more recent Indian Mutiny, so that my knowledge of warfare was more than superficial, and there before my eyes was warfare itself going on – warfare at the trot, to be sure, with nothing of 'the wild charge they made' in the illustration to Balaclava, but still warfare beyond pictures and panoramas, and the result was rather too much for me. I went down before the excitement of the moment; but so far as I could gather, when the nurse had shaken me together and silenced my yells, I was the only one who had been ridden down by the three dragoons. The crowds outside had rushed into a narrow side-street, and the three dragoons had continued trotting down the broader thoroughfare. They had disappeared before my eyes were dry, and I thought that the battle was over.

But before many minutes had passed there came shouts, as if the whole town of Belfast were being crushed into the mouth of the street. Beneath our eyes there surged such a crowd as I had never seen before, formed of the 'all sorts' that constitute a town crowd, and a town crowd is a town riot in the making; and with a clatter of hoofs on the large, kidney-shaped boulders that formed the ideal paving in that neighbourhood in that day, there came, also at the 'trot' with sabres at the 'carry', what seemed to me to be a whole army of cavalry – thousands more than the artist had been able to put into the picture of Balaclava, and he had done his best to suggest that there was a considerable crush there – down they trotted for nearly half-an-hour, five thousand men might have been in that street; and that was the rough estimate of the number of the soldiers made by our nurse, and I believed her until I was puzzled by recognising the faces of several of the men as those whom I had noticed riding past the window a few minutes earlier. Then it was I made my first acquaintance with the stage trick of causing a very small army to do duty for a very large one. The dragoons had simply trotted down the street, wheeled by their left into another that was parallel with the first, and so round to our window once more.

I am sure that they tired of this roundabout riding, making a demonstration, but doing nothing. I recollect that I asked our nurse why the soldiers did not fight. I do not remember that she gave me any ex-planation of their lapse; but I know that it was no more satisfactory to me than was the explanation of the trombone player in the orchestra of a theatre when the manager noticed him idling through eight or ten bars at a time, and demanded to know if the man expected to be paid for doing nothing. But after half-an-hour's trotting round, the dragoons were ordered to march; and now we all had more leisure to observe one another, and I saw that several of the men got on excellent terms with our nurse and her relations (female) who stood admiringly at the windows. We small fry had our faces glued to the lower panes.

Then all at once shouts were heard coming from the broad thoroughfare at the head of our street, and the dragoons ceased their game of marching and counter-marching. The street was clear of people, but it was plain that something exciting was going on on a more heroic scale a few hundred yards away. But we were old campaigners by now, and ridiculed the cau-tionary phrases of our nurse when someone suggested that we should be safer at home. We boldly walked forth, and up the street, and there I saw a white-haired, elderly gentleman on horseback, with dragoons on each side of him and a whole line of soldiers with rifles and bayonets fixed, standing at 'attention', while the old gentleman removed his hat as if he recognised a lady at a distance, and then began to read, very badly indeed, something from a paper which he tried to hold in a suitable position before his eyes, but which the nervousness of his horse rendered almost impossible. After a very poor display of elocution, and a deplorable one of horsemanship, we heard the words, 'God save the Queen', followed by a hoarse 'Present arms!' from a mounted officer wearing a shako with a little white ball poised at the top in front; while he gave his sword a twist and brought the hilt up to his face, and then lowered the point of the blade. There was a clash of rifles all down the long line of red-coated infantry, and before another word of command had been given, a policeman, who looked a very worm by the side of the glorious military, though he did wear a tall, glazed hat and a black coat with a leather belt, and though he carried a serviceable grazier's walking stick, spoke some uncivil words to our nurse, commanding her to 'take them childer out o' this or it'll not be tellin' ye. Don't ye see that he's read the Riot Act. Heth! you're a gierl bringin' them wee 'uns intill a crowd like thon!'

This was distinctly personal; and somehow we felt more dismayed by the broad Belfast staccato of a member of the most inefficient police force that ever existed since the days of Dogberry and Verges, than we were by the show of force in scarlet and gold; and there was nothing more for us in the way of riots that day. We had not far to go to reach our home, and we were greeted by father and mother with that show of emotion which is reserved for the fourth act of the opera when the hero returns from the wars.

But when we had been enfolded in loving arms, and that scene was over, the nurse received her scolding, and dissolved in tears.

At tea that evening I heard the situation of affairs in the town discussed between the grown-ups. It seemed that some of the more bellicose of the clergy, Episcopalian as well as Presbyterian, had taken to preaching *en plein air* some highly-seasoned Protestant doctrines, condemning in the emphatic way of those days the 'errors' of the Church of Rome. The *locale* of their mission was one that afforded many opportunities to passing members of the erroneous creed to hear some home-truths, and they had the bad taste to respond with stones and other missiles, which are really, in their own way, quite as irritating as any theological arguments. The supporters of the preachers found them so, and the old Ulster conflict – the old world conflict – was renewed. The most sensible nations have fought for years over a woman, others have fought over the possession of a worthless piece of land – over the honour of a contemptible ruffian, but we know that the most 'plaguy knocks' have been given by those who endeavour to 'prove their doctrines orthodox' by such means.

F. FRANKORT MOORE, *The Truth About Ulster*, 1914

DURING THE YEAR 1797, the town of Belfast exhibited a shocking scene of confusion and outrage – of assassinations, informations, arrests, and military violences; and to such a state of subjection were the conspirators reduced by the unremitting vigilance and exertions of the civil and military powers that while insurrection had burst out, in the following year, and was blazing forth in various parts of Ireland, not the slightest symptom of commotion betrayed itself here – and the editor clearly recollects the death-like silence which pervaded the streets when the counties of Down and Antrim resounded with the noise and tumult of battle. The usual consequence attendant on an unsuccessful insurrection now began to appear, multitudes of prisoners were brought in from the surrounding country, and of these several were devoted to an untimely end and by the summary mode of Court-martial. – Such was the unfortunate issue of this ill-fated conspiracy in the North of Ireland.

Historical Collections Relative to the Town of Belfast, 1817

PARTIES RUN VERY HIGH IN BELFAST; the Protestants being divided among themselves, while the Romish enemy, or rather enmity, is strong in bitterness, though weak in comparative numbers. Such life and bustle as the broad thoroughfares present would be highly amusing, did not some bodings of a violent conflict damp that feeling. Here you might behold a knot of gentlemen, most earnestly discussing the merits of respective cases, and balancing the probabilities of success; there a group of peasants, just arrived, receiving information from their city friends, and with looks of stern resolve, or fiery impatience, venting in their own language the sentiments of their hearts. Carelessly lounging by, you see now and then a Highland officer, his air of good-humoured unconcern neutralised by the keen quick glance that ever and anon takes in the general aspect of things around him; while at the windows of a large building, and probably at others which I did not observe, parties of private soldiers are to be seen, with the same quiet yet watchful expression of countenance. To complete the picture, numerous bodies of the armed police, in their dark-green uniform, are scattered in every direction, mingling among the people, conversing with some, admonishing others, menacing not a few, and evidently operating as a powerful check where such is greatly needed. It was through this assemblage that we wound our way, never impeded, nor falling in with anything like a crowd, to visit the institution where those afflicted classes, the blind, and the deaf and dumb, receive instruction. A day's sojourn would not allow of my seeing more than this of the interesting objects with which Belfast abounds; and I did not regret the selection.

CHARLOTTE ELIZABETH (Mrs Tonna), *Letters from Ireland*, 1838

from THE ORANGEMEN OF BELFAST

But when they drew near to the end of the town,
The Croppies of Belfast began for to frown;
Both hedges and ditches were lined along,
And with Courage they marched through the Rebel throng.

But as they were marching through Hercules Street,
A great opposition they happened to meet
From turn-coat Croppies, became Ribbonmen,
For to murder our Orangemen they did intend.

Belfast District Master, brave Woods is his name,
He bid them all return from whence they came
To their different Lodge Rooms, and have a due care,
If they were assaulted, no Rebel to spare.

So when he dismissed them they all marched away,
But two of those Lodges they met a sad fray;
When they entered North Street the Rebels did throng,
Both brick bats and stones upon them were thrown.

Brave Calwell and Lynas deserve great applause,
Like true sons of William they supported our cause;
Carrying the Colours, they were three times knocked down,
But they fought their way through and maintained their ground.

From every entry and from every lane,
The brick bats and stones in showers they came;
But the Lord still preserv'd them, their lives did secure,
Till they safe arrived at bold Thompson's door.

When they entered their Lodge Room, refreshment to take,
The Croppies another attack they did make;
Those cowardly Rebels to racking did fall,
Throwing stones thro' the windows to murder them all.

God prosper brave Carroll, and Morgan also,
And likewise M'Mullen, wherever they go,
For they fired out upon them, they loaded with ball,
And three of those Rebels before them did fall.

Those cowardly villains they scatter'd and fled
At the cries of the wounded and sight of the dead;
The valiant stout Lettens deserves great applause,
For they bravely supported the Protestant cause.

ANONYMOUS, c. 1813

ON THURSDAY EVENING DISTURBANCES WERE RENEWED in Sandy-row and Pound Loaning. Crowds collected in Durham-street, and several engagements with stones are recorded. The police separated the contending parties, and arrested some of the rioters. At midnight the belligerents grew weary, and retired. After a lapse of some hours, the denizens of the Pound again turned out, and they stole along Durham-street, armed with bludgeons and pistols. Roused by the police, and by their vigilant neigh-bours, men rose from their beds, and rushed into the street. Some of these poor fellows, who had left their wives and children behind them, were at once arrested, and sent to jail. Shots were exchanged between the two parties. A navvie was wounded, and several Sandy-row boys were cruelly beaten while passing through the Pound.

Thus the evil spirit of sectarian hatred was aroused. The Roman Catholic populace was penetrated with excitement, by a series of articles which appeared in the local organ of their party, tending to provoke a feeling of hostility. The Orange Institution was described as an 'infernal confeder-ation'. The character of Orangemen was assailed as brutal, cruel, and barbarous. The Catholics of Belfast were represented as lying down like dogs under the heel of a base-born tyranny, and were called to defend themselves against the leaders of the Orange lodges, who were said to be *thirsting for their extermination!* The Magistrates were charged with screening criminals, and delighting in the prevalence of disorder. The Town Council of Belfast was denounced upon the allegation, that they filled the ranks of the Police force with persons known to be Protestants or Orangemen, systematically excluding Catholics; and the members of the force were scouted as a partizan body, and stigmatised under the denomination of 'blue-coated scoundrels', in league with the denizens of Sandy-row.

THOMAS HENRY, *A History of the Belfast Riots*, 1864

WHEN TELEVISION DOES A RESTROSPECTIVE ON THE TROUBLES, or when people talk about their experiences in those years, even read-ing the history of former troubles in Belfast in the nineteenth century, pictures in the collective memory light up. A friend talks of how she had to leave her home and I see again the families clambering onto the backs of open lorries along with all their possessions, jumbled up like rags and bones. An account of rioting in 1935 or 1872 brings back the confused and novel soldiery throwing up another peace line or accepting cups of tea from local women. How quickly that changed, how quickly the denominations sorted themselves out, and how quickly communities adapted to the strange new world.

ROBERT JOHNSTONE, *Images of Belfast*, 1983

THE TROUBLES, 1922

The Troubles came; by Nineteen-twenty-two
we knew of and accepted violence
in the small streets at hand. With Curfew tense,
each evening when that quiet hour was due,
I never ventured far from where I knew
I could reach home in safety. At the door
I'd sometimes stand, till with oncoming roar,
the wire-cage Crossley tenders swept in view.

Once, from front bedroom window, I could mark
black shapes, flat-capped, across the shadowed street,
two policemen on patrol. With crack and spark
fierce bullets struck the kerb beneath their feet;
below the shattered street-lamp in the dark
blurred shadow crouched, then pattered quick retreat.

JOHN HEWITT, *Kites in Spring*, 1980

T HE NEW PARLIAMENT INITIALLY held its meetings in the Presbyterian College behind Queen's University before moving to the Robing Room in the Belfast City Hall. Victory in the Civil War left the pro-Treaty party in control of the Free State. However, Belfast at this time was a hotbed of sectarian tension; there were many riots and disturbances in which a number of people from both sides died.

Michael Collins wrote on 6 March 1922 to Winston Churchill:

The total death toll from 11th Feb amounted to 48 and 198 wounded while total casualties once the Orange pogrom began in July 1920 numbered 257. The forces doing the work should be at least impartial and attention paid to the haunts of Orange gunmen and aggressors. (Quoted *Irish News*, 4 Oct. 1996)

A report was also sent to Churchill from Sir James Craig on 11 March 1922:

The total death toll in Belfast from July 1st 1920 till March 8, 1922 is 123 Catholics and 112 Protestants. There had been peace for a considerable period in Belfast before the original murders by Sinn Féin gunmen took place.

Despite all this, in predominantly Catholic places like Majorca Street, Mulhouse Street and the surrounding area, a number of Protestants lived and got on very well with their neighbours. In between periods of unrest their differences would be seen with humour. Many local writers, actors and artists would bring this out in a creative form in books and on the stage. Their ideas came from everyday life. Belfast people developed a form of black humour without which they would have been unable to survive in such a religiously and politically divided environment. This humour would have emerged among the people who frequented many of Belfast's pubs and bars, especially in working-class areas like west Belfast.

There were four pubs, three bookies, two pawnshops, three fish'n'chip shops and a number of corner shops in this little area of Belfast. The favourite pub was Kelly's in Granville Street.

GEORGE FLEMING, *Magennis VC*, 1998

SITTING WITH THE PAPER ON HIS KNEES Colm saw the twisted life of the city: the fightings at football matches between Catholics and Protestants; the paintings on the gable-ends of King William on a white horse, his sword raised to the sky, and printed underneath: REMEMBER 1690 ... NO POPE HERE. And in the Catholic quarters, the green-white-and-gold flag of Ireland painted on the walls with UP THE REPUBLIC. It was a strange city, he thought, to be living two lives, whereas on Rathlin Catholics and Protestants mixed and talked and danced together. It was all a terrible mix-up. He threw down the paper and went into the scullery. Shamrock floated in a bowl and he picked a spray of it for his cap because tomorrow was St Patrick's Day.

MICHAEL McLAVERTY, *Call My Brother Back*, 1939

WITH MEMORIES OF THE REGULAR SECTARIAN POGROMS and incursions by unionist mobs that littered Belfast's history still kept alive by the reminiscences of the older members of the community, you were always ready to spring to the defence of the church and the area. We heard stories of the conduct of the Orangemen towards the church and the priests and of an attack on the bishop's house at Bankmore Street which filled me with dread throughout my childhood days. Each summer the stories from the old people seemed to be proved right when the Orange bands and their thunderous Lambeg drums were heard coming from the direction of the nearby Grosvenor Road. I can well remember experiencing such a sense of terror in my body that I ran to hide under the bed.

PADDY DEVLIN, *Straight Left*, 1993

THE ULSTER WAR has shown yet again that, irrespective of the political aims of those who resort to violence, the conflict has developed along lines determined by the cumulative experience of earlier clashes. When we turn to the nineteenth-century riot reports we find some of the familiar features of today: the setting up of barricades in Protestant areas of Belfast, the extinction of street lighting, the manufacture of home-made pistols and ammunition, the accusation that the police joined the Protestant rioters, the use of 'snatch squads' by the army to drag ringleaders from the mob, police complaints at meeting 'a wall of silence'. In 1864 and 1872 Catholic gun clubs were formed, and a Protestant Defence Association came into being. In 1872 the army was caught in the middle while trying to establish a peace line between the Falls and the Shankill; there was widespread burning, looting and intimidation in the streets between the two roads, which was precisely re-enacted in 1969 in the very same streets. In 1886 what are now called 'no-go areas' appeared after the police had been driven from the Shankill Road; after nearly two months, during which there was little ordinary crime, and the men of the area did their own vigilante policing, authority cautiously returned in the form of joint army-police patrols.

A.T.Q. STEWART, *The Narrow Ground*, 1977

AT THIS TIME [1864] in spite of the efforts of the clergymen of both creeds, and in spite also of the efforts of six hundred constabulary and twelve hundred soldiers, infantry and cavalry, the town was practically in the hands of a mob for over a month. Then some hundreds of special constables were sworn in, most of them being well-set-up young men, and armed with batons, and they patrolled the streets in force every night for some time. Shortly afterwards the usual autumn monsoon set in, and everyone who has lived on the coast of Ulster knows what this means: the rains descended and the floods came. Experience shows that while rioters do not mind the hottest fire, they object strongly to a cold shower of rain. There was no show after the first deluge. The mills, the foundries, and the shipbuilding yard resumed work. A few of the rioters who had been taken red-handed were brought to trial at the next Assizes and received what were called 'exemplary sentences'. Later there was a Commission of Enquiry appointed by the Government – how long ago it seems when one remembers that Lord Palmerston was Prime Minister! – and there were, of course, several 'findings', the most important being the dissolution of the old Town Police and the substitution of the Irish Constabulary.

F. FRANKFORT MOORE, *The Truth About Ulster*, 1914

BELFAST ON A SUNDAY AFTERNOON

Visiting Belfast at the end of June,
We found the Orange Lodge behind a band:
Sashes and bearskins in the afternoon,
White cotton gloves upon a crippled hand.

Pastmasters pale, elaborately grim,
Marched each alone, beneath a bowler hat:
And, catapulted on a crumpled limb,
A lame man leapt the tram-lines like a bat.

And first of all we tried to laugh it off,
Acting bemusement in the grimy sun;
But stayed to worry where we came to scoff,
As loud contingents followed, one by one.

Pipe bands, flute bands, brass bands and silver bands,
Presbyter's pibroch and the deacon's serge,
Came stamping where the iron Maenad stands,
Victoria, glum upon a grassy verge.

Some brawny striplings sprawled upon the lawn;
No man is really crippled by his hates.
Yet I remembered with a sudden scorn
Those 'passionate intensities' of Yeats.

DONALD DAVIE (1955), *Selected Poems*, 1985

As THE EVENING WORE ON, it was evident that warlike preparations were being made. The streets of Bigotsborough at this time were paved with smooth kidney stones known as 'pavers'. The side-walks were paved with small 'pavers' about the size of an orange, which seemed to have been placed there for the purpose of supplying rioters with an abundant and deadly store of ammunition. In every street of the Orange quarter the women were busily engaged in collecting kidney 'pavers'. As the 'pavers' were embedded in sand, it was sufficient to loosen one, for the others could then be picked out as easily as almonds from a plum-pudding. The women filled their aprons with these round stones and carried them to various strategic points, where huge piles were formed.

JAMES DOUGLAS, *The Unpardonable Sin*, 1907

IN PUBLIC RESPECTABLE FOLK deplore outbreaks of disorder; in private it is rare to find any who do not back one side against the other. An Englishman, who in his first days in Belfast had the ill luck to get mixed up in a party scuffle, used to tell how in his innocence he turned next morning to the local papers for an explanation of this madness, and discovered to his amazement Nationalist and Unionist journals alike engaged in a hot discussion as to which faction had the best of it. On occasion even respectable folk forget their respectability. Thus a merchant entering his office one morning after a Nationalist procession had hacked its way through a Unionist district, found his foreman, ordinarily the primmest of Puritans, with his coat half torn from his back, and blood running down his face from an ugly wound. 'John,' he cried in horror, 'don't tell me you were in this disgraceful business?' 'I was, indeed, sir,' said John. 'Thank God, I'm no arm-chair politician.' In John's sense there are few arm-chair politicians in Belfast, and his spirit flashes out in strange places. Some years ago, after a bad outbreak of rioting, the City Council proposed to take steps which, it was claimed, would go a long way to prevent future troubles. In the fighting quarter, it should be known, the streets are mainly paved with cobble stones or 'kidneys', to give them their local name. At the first sign of hostilities these are prized up with pokers and stacked in heaps by the women to serve as ammunition dumps for the fighters. The Corporation scheme was to substitute macadam for the cobble stones, but when the motion came up for discussion it was discovered that the plan was to begin with the Nationalist area, whose representatives, not unnaturally, raised a storm of protest against the unfair advantage this method of disarmament would confer on their opponents. I believe there were some negotiations, but they came to nothing, and to this day the cobble-stones remain.

JAMES WINDER GOOD, *Ulster and Ireland*, 1919

AN EXPRESSION WHICH IS OFTEN USED EVEN TODAY by older Belfast people when unexpected visitors arrive: 'They're in on us and not a stone gathered.' It harks back to the days when cobblestones, locally known as kidney pavers or pickers, were used against British Army and RIC raiding parties.

GERRY ADAMS, *Falls Memories*, 1982

from THE BATTLE OF THE BRICKFIELDS

With guns and pistols, and blades like crystals,
And stick and bludgeon, and stone and sling,

And the police eyein' the brickbats flyin'
And the kilties dancin' the Highland Fling.

But for powder scanty, Och! not one in twenty
Would have survived, as each party owns,
And we were all stranded till the women banded
And politely handed round the paving stones.

ANONYMOUS, 1872

I HAVE OFTEN BEEN ASKED BY ENGLISHMEN why Belfast people are so quarrelsome amongst themselves. Normally, they are no more quarrelsome than similar communities. Politics alone would have a poor chance of creating civil strife in Belfast without a background of religious animosity to keep it alive. There wasn't a solitary head broken during the 1902 by-election in South Belfast because the two opposing parties were Protestant. In the West Division, where a Catholic usually faced a Protestant opponent, the place was in turmoil for weeks, during and after the election. There is very little changed, even to the present day.

The same vicious system which separates the children into religious groups to create suspicion and misunderstanding, splits the adult population into similar communities. There is always the inevitable demarcation line between a Catholic and Protestant quarter of the city. When trouble starts, it is there the police concentrate. In the suburbs, where the population is somewhat mixed, there is generally peace and orderliness. That is, if the people are left to themselves.

THOMAS CARNDUFF (1954), Life and Writings, 1994

BELFAST HATREDS WERE MULTIPLE BUT UNVARYING. I'd heard them all before, the details and the emphases never changed. You could sing along if you liked. These fulminations were faded and dog-eared with age.

The tragedy was that Northern Ireland (Scottish) Protestants thought themselves like the British. Northern Ireland (Irish) Catholics thought themselves like Eireans (proper Irish). The comedy was that any once-strong difference had long melted away and they resembled no one now as much as they resembled each other. The world saw this and mostly wondered, but round these parts folk were blind.

Interestingly enough, Protestant/Catholic hardmen would still routinely and joyfully beat the shit out of Catholics/Protestants even if those Catholics/Protestants didn't believe in God and had formally left their faith. It was intriguing to wonder what a bigot of one faith could object to in an atheist who was born into another. That was what I liked about Belfast hatred. It was a lumbering hatred that could survive comfortably on the memories of things that never existed in the first place. There was a certain admirable stamina in that.

ROBERT McLIAM WILSON, *Eureka Street*, 1996

A LONG A GREY BELFAST STREET battalion after battalion, dressed in khaki, swinging their right arms high, make a roaring noise of feet, as they beat the stone surface. Fife and brass bands play. One band strikes up a rattling Orange tune:

> *Slitter-slaughter*
> *Holy water*
> *Sprinkle the Papishes*
> *Ev-er-y-one . . .*

Another drones out the homesick songs of war:

> *Pack up your troubles in your old kitbag*
> *And smile, boys, smile.*

Such war songs neither exalt battle nor jeer at an enemy; they're meant to console unhappy soldiers.

Watching the procession, we stand in a patch of garden before a redbrick house. Dick and I climb a plane tree, whose bark is black with grime, whence we obtain a wide view. 'You won't miss much,' my father observes.

The spectators cheer; but my father, with his parish in mind, is filled with the excitement of dismay. These are men of our own province marching as a public spectacle through the city before sailing to a war. They're the former rebels, transformed into the Ulster Division. Their own suits, belts, rifles have been put aside; now they wear the uniform of the British Army; now they'll fight in France side by side with those whom, a few months ago, they were prepared to shoot. Their illegal German rifles have gone to the Belgians, to be turned against the German senders. Events have taken a twist.

GEORGE BUCHANAN, *Green Seacoast*, 1959

I T IS A MISTAKE TO ATTRIBUTE the lawlessness of Bigotsborough to religious animosities. Its roots strike down through the strata of religious hate into economic degradation. Poverty is the mother of anarchy, and it is poverty that is the matter with Bigotsborough. It is not surprising that half-starved and half-educated larrikins regard rioting as a purple patch in their dismal and desolate existence. It is the only amusement they have. The Bigotsborough roughs have no quarrel with the police. They are simply imbued with the spirit of the sportsman who stalks a tiger or a lion, an elephant or a hippopotamus. It is that spirit which makes Bigotsborough joyously eager for a riot. It is only in Bigotsborough that you may see a mob merrily pursuing a policeman who is running for his life, and jovially turning his helmet into a football. It does not really matter whether they kick the policeman or the helmet. Their temper is not essentially different from that of the ladies and gentlemen who hunt the stag on Exmoor. The ladies and gentlemen eat their sandwiches and drink from their flasks, while the huntsmen cut up the carcase of the beautiful beast. The ladies accept a tooth or a smoking hoof as a souvenir. The only difference between the one hunt and the other is that the quarry in the one case is a Royal Irish constable and in the other a royal Devonshire stag. If the Bigotsborough rioters were properly educated at a public school and a university they would hunt foxes and stags instead of policemen.

JAMES DOUGLAS, *The Unpardonable Sin*, 1907

THAT FRIDAY NIGHT, a reinforcement battalion, the Third Light Infantry, landed at Aldergrove airport outside the city and drove straight to positions along the Crumlin Road. They were too late. That evening, the Protestants burned an entire Catholic street to the ground.

What happened was, once again, unpremeditated, the product more of fear than of malice, and avoidable with adequate policing. The disturbances began in the Clonard area about 3 p.m. on Friday afternoon. They ended twelve hours later. Once again, the lethal factor was geography.

SUNDAY TIMES INSIGHT TEAM, *Ulster*, 1972

SHE WAS A SHANKILL GIRL, used to the yell and fury of the rioters, but the silence, the queer calm, the strange, deserted appearance of the streets unstrung her as no street-tussle could have done. She hurried on to Shankill. Shankill is a wide, hilly road which, under various names, leads from what was formerly one of the principal streets of the town, viz., North Street, right up to the big bare hills that loom over Belfast.

Where Molly entered it now the road was a wide, open thoroughfare, lined on either side with shops, every one of which was shut and dark, except those darker ones which had been wrecked and burned some nights agone – they gaped blacker and wilder than the rest. The same loneliness, the same awful calm was also upon the big wide, busy road. Not a soul seemed abroad, not a breath disturbed the silence or bedewed the brilliant moonlight. Silence; fierce silence! what so terrible, so palpable, so overwhelming.

Molly Bennett flew forward, keeping close by the houses; her knees were shaking under her, her feet seemed scarcely to touch the ground; fear drove her on. She would have given much to be at home, but back she could not face. She tore on down the road; in her excitement she passed the place of rendezvous. Through the stillness of the night hissed a whisper.

'Mol-lie!'

The girl staggered as if struck. A rude, strong arm was thrust out from round the corner of an opening alley, and drew her into the shadow. 'What kept you?' said the voice.

'I–I–I'm not going,' said Molly, panting.

'Not going? Why? We'll never get a chance like this.'

'I got a fright,' returned Molly, 'coming down the road. I feel as if it were full of ghosts.'

Her companion laughed scornfully. She was a worker in the next 'stand' to Molly in the mill, and had prevailed on her to make this appointment; now at its fulfilling Molly shrank.

As they stood in the alley discussing, a strange remote echo swung up the silence. They both paused, and, stepping out into the open road, looked up and down. Nothing could be seen, yet ever the nearing, regular, yet half-muffled sound could be heard. Suddenly rising over Peter's Hill appeared a batch of men, marching solid square.

'Look,' cried Maggie Reilly; 'it's the Catholics coming to wreck the Shankill.'

'No,' said Molly. 'No. It's the soldiers,' and every vestige of colour left her face.

'We'll be arrested,' said the other girl in horror. 'They'll say we were carrying messages between the two parties.' It was commonly reported that the women bore messages; whether it really took place is a question, but certainly the women played a part in these riots – shouting, digging stones, carrying drinks to the men, hiding them in their houses when justice dared to approach.

'What are we to do?' breathed Molly.

'We'll hide here. Perhaps they'll pass on.'

They squeezed themselves into a doorway of the court in which they stood. Here for a second they stood breathless, every instant bringing the thundering tread nearer and nearer. The very ground beneath their feet seemed to tremble as the soldiers advanced double quick. The girls held to one another. Suddenly, as the detachment covered the mouth of the court, a horseman galloped up, and in a thundering tone cried 'Halt!'

Every sound ceased. The officer in command ordered his men to file up the court, and hold themselves for any emergency.

318

In a moment Maggie Reilly took in the situation, and stooping down quickly, took off her shoes.

'Come,' she breathed, 'come, we must make a dash for it.'

Trembling, half-fainting, yet goaded by fear, Molly plunged after her into the dark dirty back streets that twist and turn into each other in a perfect labyrinth. Breathless, panting, trembling, they held on their way until, after many turns and doubles, they issued again on to the main road, a little nearer the city. Here the thoroughfare is narrow, old; the shops dingy, and the entire locality minus the go-ahead business look visible higher up the road. A little lower down there opens into the main road two streets, one on either side, facing each other – low localities – the regions of doss-houses, thimble riggers, thieves, even of murderers. One is Millfield, with her crimes. The other, Carrick Hill, with its filth, degradation and slums.

It was toward this latter the girls headed.

AGNES BOLES, *The Belfast Boy*, 1912

ONE NEVER KNEW IN WHAT DIRECTION an attack would be made. The chief streets were, of course, lined with troops. But an orderly would come galloping down Castle Street with a message to the commanding officer to bring his men up at the double to some locality where a fight was going briskly on; and once I was in conversation with a mounted officer of Constabulary when an ADC to Major-General Montgomery-Moore galloped up to ask for reinforcements for the Highlanders who were in difficulties in a locality fully a mile and a half away! I felt that that sort of thing was closely akin to actual warfare. At any rate, the scene in that very wide and long thoroughfare, York Street, one night, let me know more about the tactics of street fighting than any previous experience of mine had done. I had been through a very nasty Malay riot at Cape Town, and had been a spectator of 'riotous operations' in Trafalgar Square, as well as in some of the disturbed districts of Ireland, North and South, but none of the principals in these actions knew anything of strategy, compared with those who engineered the sacking of York Street upon that dark night in August, 1886. The lamps had nearly all been extinguished – perhaps they had not been lighted at all – but when I came to the mouth of the road, scarcely a light was to be seen; still I had no difficulty in making out the movements of the dense crowds surging in every direction, and shot after shot I heard above the shouts that suggested something very like Pandemonium. Once or twice I was carried along in the rush of people before a police charge, and I was taught in the most practical way how to avoid a casualty; for I was simply hurried through the street and into the nearest by-lane, where I was forced to stand with the rest of the fugitives until the projectile, in the form of a squad of police or soldiers, had charged past. Then I was allowed a leisurely return to the field of battle.

A little of this was quite enough to serve my purpose. I began to feel that if I remained much longer, I might not be able to write out my comments on the scene in a perfectly unprejudiced way, so I sneaked down a narrow side street and, after a time, emerged from the purlieus of the fighting area. I felt that I had learned something of the impotence of every arm except artillery in the case of street fighting.

F. FRANKFORT MOORE, The Truth About Ulster, 1914

THE LAST RIOTS OCCURRED IN BELFAST IN 1935. About 2,250 Catholics were evicted, a total of 514 families, during these riots. Of these 514 families, 431 were evicted violently by the mobs, often with police standing by; 73 were burned out; 10 were removed by threats. Not a single non-Catholic was evicted. And this occurred in a city where the police, always armed with revolvers, and sometimes with rifles, constitute the largest police force in the world, proportionate to area!

All that cannot be done without two things – inflammation, which the leaders of the Government, and the Orange Order supply *ad libitum*, and the fear and ignorance of uneducated mobs played upon by these educated men. The industrial system of Belfast supplies both – privilege and its tools. It is an irresponsible privilege whose face may be seen in the ugliness of this city, in its great contrasts between rich and poor, its anomalies of wealth and poverty, its endless strife, for all of which the blame must rest on the wealthy who, for their own ends, have made it so and keep it so.

SEAN O'FAOLAIN, An Irish Journey, 1940

HE DROVE INTO THE ROUNDABOUT AT CARLISLE CIRCUS. In its centre was a stone plinth which had once supported the statue of a Protestant divine, a statue like many of the city's monuments, toppled in the war and never replaced. The white Ford came circling around behind him as he entered Clifton Street and drove past the headquarters of the Orange Order, that fount of Protestant prejudice against the third of Ulster's people who are Catholics. Above the ugly grey stone building was a statue which had not been toppled by war or civil strife, a Dutch prince on horseback, waving a sword, staring out over the damaged city at ancient unchanging Irish hills, a statue commemorating a battle three hundred years ago in which the forces of the Protestant House of Orange defeated, on Irish soil, the forces of a Papist English king. At the bottom of Clifton Street he turned right, driving along the edge of those Protestant and

Catholic ghettos which were the true and lasting legacy of this British Province founded on inequality and sectarian hate.

BRIAN MOORE, *Lies of Silence*, 1990

THE MOST FRIGHTENING THING is the extent to which one becomes hardened. This is neither insensitivity nor cynicism; it is a necessary mechanism of self-defence. In the first year of the Troubles, one listened intently to every news bulletin, and to the broadcasts of the Orange and Republican free-lance radio stations. One's heart turned over at the account of each new horror. One rushed to look at each new wall-poster – some of them, derived from the Paris student uprisings of 1968, were brilliant – I have still an illicitly obtained copy of the poster that read 'Malone Road fiddles while Falls Road burns'. One stood in the garden on summer evenings listening to fusillades of shots a mere mile away, wondering whose bullet had found what billet this time; watching the palls of smoke and sometimes the glare of flames from burning buildings, and wondering whose; listening to the windows rattle at the sound of unidentifiable explosions.

But after a year, still more after eight years, one no longer responds in the same way. The extraordinary has come, inevitably, to seem almost ordinary. When the morning news bulletin reports no bombs, no fires, no murders, no riots, no hijackings, then it has been a quiet night, and it is that that seems extraordinary (and in a depressing way, a little flat). The illegal radio stations have long since closed down: no more Free Belfast, no more Orange Lily at the record turntable. Such posters as now appear, and they are few, are dreary and uninteresting. Even the graffiti are uninspired, and rarely raise even a tired smile: as did the sudden rash of 'F.T.P.', which appeared all over the Protestant districts in 1970. (As Lord Hailsham remarked at the time, to Fuck the Pope remains an anatomical impossibility.) Today, when there is a bomb alarm, one evacuates briskly but with resignation, and tries to get on with one's work elsewhere till it is over. There is a traffic bollard near the City Hall that has often served me for an open-air desk. When there comes the crump of an explosion – unless it is very close – one perhaps looks at one's watch, so as to find out later which particular bang that had been; but work is not interrupted for more than a moment or two. And one comes almost to ignore the sinister bells and sirens, heard many times on most working days, which indicate that police cars, ambulances, fire engines, and the armoured cars of the bomb squad are galloping to an alarm.

As I have said, this is a necessary mechanism of self-defence: the protective scab that grows over even a deep wound. But I acknowledge, with distress, that it is inevitably accompanied by a coarsening of sensibility; a lessening of anguish; a deadening of humanity. One has heard now a thousand times the words of condemnation, certainly sincere and heartfelt, employed by politicians, clergymen, and other public figures when something particularly revolting has happened. They have become almost meaningless: the vocabulary has been exhausted. 'Terrorist', 'murderer', 'diabolical', 'dastardly outrage', 'cowardly crime': what other words can the poor men use? But the currency has been devalued; not just the currency of the words; the currency of the concepts, too. I am sure this is so of the individuals who commit the murders, who plant the bombs; otherwise no degree of idealism, whether in the cause of 'a Free Ireland' or in the cause of 'our Protestant heritage', could allow them to persevere without falling victims themselves to nausea, hysteria, and collapse. There is a protective mechanism for them too. Unhappily, if the rest of us are to survive without losing our reason, we must allow our own emotional reactions to be devalued. It is possible that all those who survive the Ulster Troubles of the 1970s will be morally or emotionally crippled for the rest of their lives. But I hope, and choose to believe, otherwise; just as a whole generation could return from the slaughter of each of the world wars without (as it seems to me) any perceptible loss of humanity, so (it seems to me) when this plague has passed by – and sooner or later, somehow, it must – the survivors will return to a more human level of sensibility.

C.E.B. BRETT, *Long Shadows Cast Before*, 1978

LIFE, FOR YOUNG WORKING-CLASS PEOPLE IN 1900, was somewhat empty of entertainment. There were no cinemas, few organised playing fields and, with the exception of religious societies, no attempt to induce the youth of the city to fit themselves into healthy and useful citizens. So we grouped ourselves into 'clans'.

In my youth, the 'clan' system in Belfast grew out of a code built up on mutual protection. It was dangerous for a youth between the ages of twelve and eighteen to wander out of his own district alone. He would be set upon and beaten up by young boys of his own age. To be quite fair, these youths were by no means of the criminal type; but, oh gosh, were they tough!

These 'clans' had their own particular hunting ground, and had a rendezvous in some back street in their own district, which made it difficult for the police to locate them.

My brother, Wilfred, had some connection with a clan from York Street, 'The Forty Thieves'. These 'Forty Thieves' would invade the centre thoroughfares of the city on Saturday night, and every clan within sight would disappear until the 'all clear' was sounded.

The 'Cronji Clan' were recognisable by their black-and-white check caps, and foregathered somewhere in the neighbourhood of the Falls Road. The 'Cronji Clan' and 'Forty Thieves' were bitter enemies and their battle cries were often the signal for some of the fiercest sectarian riots in the city.

The 'Bushrangers' held sway in what was once the red lamp district of the city, behind the present St Anne's Cathedral. How they came by the name I don't remember. I only know that we smaller fry kept a weather eye open for their appearance in the streets.

Another crowd of hooligans of local repute went by the title of 'The Bogey Clan'. There was a row on the Crumlin Road, one evening, when knives were used. A youth died from his injuries. The police swooped down on the 'Bogey Clan', a few days later, and a number of them were placed behind iron bars for the good of their souls and the peace of the city.

About this time, I was developing into a pretty wild sample of budding manhood myself. The fault was all my own. There were nine of us grouped together who made up 'The Pass Clan'. I joined the clan as much for protection as devilment. We were as tough a crowd of young bucks as could be found in the city. Our particular aversion was 'Catholics'. We ambushed them, jibed them, slaughtered them when opportunity came our way. Yet many of these 'corner boys' became useful citizens in after years.

My own chum, who was as ignorant of education as any illiterate, is now a full-blown Presbyterian minister in western Canada. Another set up business, a few years ago, on a leading thoroughfare of the city and, by all accounts, he is building up a promising concern. Two others, who were the mischief for getting us all into trouble, are foremen in their respective trades, while yet another occupies a position as Timekeeper in the shipyards. During the first Great War, five of the 'clan' joined the services, two reaching the rank of sergeant.

This picture of Belfast in the early 1900s may be lapped up by some of my readers who have no great love for the city's history or reputation. Yet Belfast in those days was no better or worse than any other seaport in the British Isles. In fact, what I saw of Glasgow, Liverpool, Cardiff, Sunderland, fails to cause me any grief in regard to the social life of my own city in the early days of this century. Even Dublin had little to be proud of when I knew it best. It's just that I was born and brought up here and poked my nose into places I had been taught to side step, but didn't.

THOMAS CARNDUFF (1954), *Life and Writings*, 1994

A S THE PROCESSION TURNED into the Pound Loney, a barefooted old woman, with dishevelled grey locks, a ragged green petticoat, and a tattered green Paisley shawl, appeared in the middle of the road, dancing a riotous jig.

'Three cheers for Jane the Nailer!' yelled the laughing crowd.

'To hell with King William!' screamed the old woman, her black eyes blazing with insane passion. Her yellow face was furrowed with a thousand wrinkles, her gums were toothless, and her bare feet were twisted and deformed. Tearing off her shawl, she threw it in the dust, and danced with frenzied vigour, shrieking horrible oaths, and tearing out handfuls of grey hair.

JAMES DOUGLAS, The Unpardonable Sin, 1907

O N 2 AUGUST [1969] the Junior Orangemen marched down the Shankill – once more, past Unity Walk flats, scene of the 13 July trouble. Once more, the residents turned out to protest. When, after a few stones had been thrown, the BBC's local news bulletin at 12.55 flashed the 'news' that the marchers had been attacked at Unity Walk, it was inevitable that there would be a confrontation on the return of the parade that evening.

Early in the afternoon, a Protestant crowd, led by the Chairman of the Shankill Defence Association, Mr John McKeague, rushed towards the flats demanding the arrest of a Republican leader, Jim Sullivan, who was seen in the courtyard. The presence of Sullivan was for many Protestants proof of a Republican plot justifying the attacks to come. From 4.30 p.m. an enormous hostile Shankill crowd gathered behind Unity Walk. The waving of a tricolour at the window of one flat provoked a massive attack. All the windows down one side of the block were smashed. The police, short of men, had to devote their energies to preventing an invasion of the flats by the returning Orange parade. Then they baton–charged the stone-throwing Protestant crowd and drove them up the Shankill.

It was too late. The Unity Walk flats complex occupies a large area, and to forestall a Protestant invasion through a side-entrance a police unit drove into an outer courtyard of the flats themselves. But just as they arrived, so did a section of the Protestant mob. To the besieged residents, it seemed that the police were leading the Protestant onslaught. Rioting broke out between the police and the inhabitants. When another police unit, guarding another entrance to the flats, rushed to the assistance of their colleagues, the Protestants invaded there too. Which confirmed the residents' fears. To the police, however, the incident looked very different: they thought they had been ambushed by the residents.

SUNDAY TIMES INSIGHT TEAM, Ulster, 1972

I N MAY, 1798, the insurrectionary movement having spread over the entire of the counties of Antrim and Down, martial law was proclaimed in the principal streets of Belfast, and four companies of yeomanry which had been formed here commenced permanent duty. The brass field-pieces which belonged to the Volunteers were all delivered up to General Nugent, military commander of the district, with the exception of one, which was soon after captured from the insurgents on their defeat at Antrim. On the intelligence that the insurgents had assembled in great force at Larne, every effort was made, by the proper authorities, to frustrate their intentions of opening a communication with their disaffected associates in Belfast. Sentinels were placed at the different outlets from the town, with rigid orders to permit no person to pass, except those going to and coming from market. A number of the inhabitants were, at the same time, formed into supplementary corps of yeomanry. When the insurrection broke out in the county of Down, many persons fled hither for security, from different parts of the country. While the troops were engaged with the insurgents at Ballynahinch, on the 12th and 13th of June, the shops were closed, and the inhabitants compelled to remain within doors. The cannonading was distinctly heard here, and after the defeat of the insurgents, in that quarter, the Belfast troop of yeoman cavalry published a declaration of loyalty.

Notwithstanding the powerful excitement which prevailed towards the close of the eighteenth century, Belfast, although the centre of motion to the Northern Union, was preserved in peaceable subjection, by the precaution of government in placing in it a strong military force; but the spirit of disaffection had diffused itself considerably, and seven individuals were executed here for treason. On the 17th of May, 1799, the last execution for high treason took place, soon after which the martial law was abolished. The Marquis of Cornwallis, Lord Lieutenant of Ireland, arrived in Belfast on the 7th of October, upon which occasion he was presented by the sovereign and burgesses with an address in favour of the Union, which was then under the consideration of parliament. On the 1st of January, 1801, the Union Flag was hoisted at the Market-house, and a royal salute fired by the artillery in garrison, in consequence of the Legislative Union between Great Britain and Ireland.

With the exception of commercial difficulties, from which, however, Belfast suffered less than any other town of equal importance in the kingdom, few circumstances have occurred in modern times to retard its progress; and it is now the most flourishing town in Ireland, being the first in trade, and the fourth in extent and population, celebrated alike for its manufactures and commerce, and for the public spirit of its inhabitants in the pursuit of literature and science, and in the support of charitable and other benevolent institutions.

JAMES ADAIR PILSON, History of the Rise and Progress of Belfast, 1846

THE CITY WAS IN PEACE. Outward hostilities had ceased, and the autumn lolled away. The military had been withdrawn; the up-country police, who, swelled with conscious majesty, and armed to the teeth, and with the law of the land at their back, had taken a cruel advantage of the undisciplined mob and shot them down like dogs, they too were out of town. So excessive was their savagery that to this day the people gnash their teeth at the memory of it; the old local and loved police were back to their beats, and things were settling into their normal working lines. Never since has the authorities drafted such numbers of strange police into the city; plenty of wise people say this act made the trouble worse. There is no doubt the people resented it, and in the end chased them, rifles and all, off the streets. 'The will of the people is the supreme Law.' But although the streets were calm and there was no fighting in the Brickfields, or up Springfield, or down York Street, or upon the Falls, or Shankill, the two sections of the people were struggling hard.

AGNES BOLES, *The Belfast Boy*, 1912

THE POLITICAL ATMOSPHERE IN BELFAST DURING 1912 was growing in intensity. Hundreds of Unionist Clubs were in formation all over Ulster. On April 9th, Sir Edward Carson watched a parade of a hundred thousand men in the Balmoral Show Grounds. It took the force, marching in massed column, three hours to pass the saluting base. On September 28th of the same year, almost half a million Ulstermen signed a solemn league and covenant.

I went along to the City Hall with another Young Citizen, Willie Baxter, who was afterwards killed in France, to sign the Covenant. Baxter was, like myself, a shipyardman, and I am afraid neither of the two of us were keen politicians at the time, but we didn't want to miss any of the fun. Carson arrived with his staff at the City Hall early in the day and was the first to sign. A flag was borne into the chamber supposed to have been carried by the Inniskillen regiment at the Battle of the Boyne. The flag was woven of silk with a crimson five-pointed star in the centre of its Orange folds and the cross of St George of England in the top left hand corner. No one had ever heard of the existence of this standard previous to the demonstration. It was handed back to its owners and has never been heard of since.

Sir Edward Carson, a southerner, was by this time hailed as the saviour of Ulster and the defender of the Protestant religion. Undoubtedly, he had won the admiration and loyalty of every Ulster Unionist. A small minority had their doubts regarding his sincerity but it did not reduce their hostility to Home Rule.

As the tense atmosphere increased, the Unionist Clubs were disbanded and formed into a new body, the Ulster Volunteer Force, to defend Ulster by force of arms if necessary. The military aspect of this force was soon apparent. Companies, battalions and divisions were organised on a elaborate scale. Ex-NCOs and officers of the regular army were given commands. The men were keen to learn rifle and company drill. There was no need to enforce discipline. It was already an established fact.

Both my brothers, Arthur and Wilfred, were members of the South Belfast Regiment. When there were no service rifles to train the men, dummy guns were used for this purpose rather than waste valuable time once company drill had been mastered. But the men were losing patience with their leaders because of their ludicrous position in playing at soldiers. The cross channel newspapers were poking fun at the Ulster Volunteers, the nationalists voiced their ridicule.

Baxter and I were invited by one of the instructors to visit a drill hall where the men were being put through their paces. It was a comic-opera sight to watch the men, with stern, determined faces slipping supposed cartridge clips into the magazines of wooden rifles.

Major Fred Crawford was doing his best to smuggle as many rifles into the country as would arm, at least, the border volunteers. But many of the more timid unionists were lukewarm when it came to armed resistance. Crawford went on with his work until the government sat up and considered it time to intervene. Many cases of guns and ammunition were lost in transportation.

The temper of the people had been tested to breaking point on the occasion of Mr Winston Churchill's visit to Belfast in February, when he addressed a meeting of Home Rulers in the grounds of Celtic Park. The nationalists had rented the Ulster Hall for the meeting but the unionist council managed to gain possession the previous evening and placed a heavy guard in the building and refused to move out. The nationalists were compelled to abandon the meeting in the hall and arrange another meeting place in Celtic Park.

Churchill, who was a member of the Liberal cabinet, arrived in Belfast as the principal speaker at the Celtic Park meeting. His reception, as he and Mrs Churchill left the Grand Central Hotel to enter their car, was almost a riot. I was employed on the staff of the *Ulster Echo* at the time and was on my way home for luncheon. I noticed the large crowd gathered round the waiting car.

As the Churchills appeared, the crowd surged forward with an angry growl. For a moment, it seemed the car would be thrown bodily over on top of the Liberal leader and his wife. The police, who were trying to humour the crowd up till now, realised the imminent danger and drove into the mob with fists and sticks, holding them off long enough to give the driver sufficient time to start the engine. It was an ugly situation and, but for the driver's quick thoughtfulness in swerving into the first side street, Churchill would never have reached Celtic Park, where a battalion of infantry guarded the approaches in case the unionists of nearby Sandy Row might start trouble in that direction.

As Churchill's car disappeared in the direction of the Falls Road, a strong nationalist quarter, I could hear loud and prolonged cheering further along Royal Avenue, at Castle Place. The angry crowd outside the Grand Central entrance immediately drifted towards that centre of trouble.

When I arrived at the corner of Castle Place, traffic was at a standstill owing to the mass of cheering people who blocked the entire street. From the balcony of the Ulster Club, Sir Edward Carson and his staff were haranguing the crowd with fiery speeches. It was some time before I could battle my way homewards. It had been a day of high tension.

THOMAS CARNDUFF (1954), Life and Writings, 1994

THAT NIGHT WHEN GOING TO BED I stood for some time at an open window and heard the report of shot after shot coming from the north of the town during several minutes, and I learned afterwards that firing had gone on all the night. The newspapers contained a full account of the carnage, and an ample account of the looting that had taken place.

F. FRANKFORT MOORE, The Truth About Ulster, 1914

from AUTUMN JOURNAL: XVI

And I remember, when I was little, the fear
    Bandied among the servants
That Casement would land at the pier
    With a sword and a horde of rebels;
And how we used to expect, at a later date,
    When the wind blew from the west, the noise of shooting
Starting in the evening at eight
    In Belfast in the York Street district;
And the voodoo of the Orange bands
    Drawing an iron net through darkest Ulster,
Flailing the limbo lands –
    The linen mills, the long wet grass, the ragged hawthorn.
And one read black where the other read white, his hope
    The other man's damnation:
Up the Rebels, To Hell with the Pope,
    And God Save – as you prefer – the King or Ireland.
The land of scholars and saints:
    Scholars and saints my eye, the land of ambush,
Purblind manifestoes, never-ending complaints,
    The born martyr and the gallant ninny;

The grocer drunk with the drum,
   The land-owner shot in his bed, the angry voices
Piercing the broken fanlight in the slum,
   The shawled woman weeping at the garish altar.

LOUIS MacNEICE (1938), Collected Poems, 1966

THIS LATEST IRISH CRISIS has very little to do with the twentieth century. It is the face of the ghost of history, four hundred years of insoluble hoplessness risen to haunt a new generation of politicians and priests.

MAX HASTINGS, Ulster 1969, 1970

Queen of Towns

Thanks to thy stars, thou Queen of Towns,
Confirmed success thy labour crowns,
Thy present Genius favours pours,
And Fame proclaims the day is yours.

SAM LYONS, 'Belfast: A Poem'

I declare I cannot read two pages without thinking of
Belfast. I am the continual joke of the lads here for making
Belfast the eternal subject of my conversation. I dream of
Belfast . . .

WILLIAM DRENNAN

THE PURPLE HILLS stood still like hoardings at the end of the streets, and
the slow sky crowded its golden colours into one last blush. At the
edge of the die-lightly day the silver pigeons wheeled, and, over all,
the grey hair-lines of rain, hours long, began to fall, rippling the puddles and
stippling the walls, and filling the pearly pubs, and wrinkling the pavement
like a cabbage leaf. No wonder that Ezekiel Knight wept over the beauty of
the drowned city as he listened to my father reading from the Book.

W.R. RODGERS, *The Return Room*, 1955

BELFAST IS REALLY A WONDER. It has been growing within the past
seventy years as few towns in the world have been, but it has not
outgrown its strength. It has been well looked after, morally as well as
physically, and the result is that to-day it can do what few other cities can

do. It can launch the largest ships that the world has ever seen; it can spend nearly a quarter of a million making a dock that will enable the biggest ships in the world to be repaired; it has the largest rope works in existence, and the largest spinning mill. For the production of such luxuries as whisky and tobacco in marketable form Belfast stands pre-eminent in the Customs list. For a variety of industries, and for every one of them all being a world's record in production, there is no city in the kingdom that can compete with Belfast. One spinning mill alone employs over eight thousand hands, and the great foundries quite as many. And then for special articles of world-wide fame, having no connection with the staple trade, one finds such intensely interesting works as the Sirocco on the County Down side of the river Lagan. Here have been manufactured for the past thirty-five years the Sirocco tea-drying machines which have revolutionised the tea trade and brought the Indian leaf into the market. The inventor of this, and perhaps of another hundred equally valuable contrivances, is Mr S.C. Davidson, the most brilliant and certainly the most fertile brain in the North of Ireland. On the other side of the river are the works of Messrs McCaw, Stevenson and Orr, the inventors of transparent printing, of Seccotine, and other articles in daily use all the world over. But no matter in what direction one goes in Belfast, one is brought face to face with stupendous statistics.

'Is it possible that we are in Ireland?' a distinguished stranger exclaimed, when I had shown him some of the wonders of this city.

And that is just what everyone is ready to ask on arriving in Belfast from Dublin. Of course, the only answer is:

'No; we are in Ulster now.'

F. FRANKFORT MOORE, The Truth About Ulster, 1914

WHAT SHOULD MOST CONCERN all Ulstermen and all Irishmen is the future of Belfast – for with it is inextricably bound up, for good or for evil, the whole future of the Irish nation.

STEPHEN GWYNN, The Famous Cities of Ireland, 1915

BELFAST IS REALLY IMPROVING VERY FAST, and though its landlord cannot do much for it at his own expense, yet want of money may operate to its advantage. May is a smart fellow, has taken ground opposite my mother's to build, he says, a faultless house. Haliday has proposed for the lot next to my mother's. The centre ground is to be railed in, and ornamented on both sides, fronting the L[inen] Hall, and a walk round it 81 feet wide. Government granted £1,600 for repairs, 6 of which only was laid out. The rest is to be given for the above purpose, which probably would not have been done but for the Donegalls, who now live in a corner house in L[inen] H[all] Street [*now Donegall Place*], to which this will be a great improvement, and here they *must* remain. . .

My mother says her house will be now more valuable, and when she dies perhaps you may come to it. The McCleans purchased Dr Haliday's. . . These same McCs have also got the old Market House, where shops are to be built that are now really elegant in *all* that street, even in Banks' and Hyde's house. The Town Hall is to be where there is at present a good 2d. market, the north gate. Our streets are well lighted, paved and perfectly clean, the sides raised.

MRS McTIER TO WILLAM DRENNAN (1803), Drennan Letters, 1931

F OR A PROVINCIAL CAPITAL in an under-populated country, Belfast is very famous indeed. It is famous for the violent political conflict of the last twenty-odd years. Little else is famous about Belfast. It has bred no famous painters; no great novels are set in Belfast. It has no great orchestra, its university is not celebrated. The 'troubles' have made Belfast a celebrity.

Few people who do not live in Northern Ireland know much about Belfast apart from its roster of political deaths and maimings. Few people realise how beautiful Belfast can be – a low-lying city at the mouth of a great bay ringed and nudged by mountains. Few people have heard of the city's dynamism and warmth. Few imagine the emotional substance necessary for a city to survive traumas like those Belfast has survived. Few are aware of the extent and prevalence of social deprivation in this televised town.

ROBERT McLIAM WILSON, The Dispossessed, 1992

D URING THE LAST TEN YEARS, Belfast has been progressively advancing in importance, not only as a commercial, but as a literary town. That spirit of liberal inquiry and literary improvement, which characterises the present age, could not fail to exercise a marked degree of influence on a part of Ireland, the inhabitants of which have ever been distinguished for their intelligence and public spirit. The most opulent cities in this country, not-withstanding their immense population and wealth, have not surpassed Belfast in their efforts to diffuse the benefits of knowledge.

The inhabitants of Belfast have, from the earliest period, been justly applauded for their enterprise, their liberality, and their independence. It is a circumstance highly creditable to their taste and benevolence, that, as their commerce has enlarged its boundaries, – as prosperity and distinction have rewarded their toil and perseverance, – so has there been a corresponding improvement in their intellectual character.

'Belfast,' says an eloquent writer, 'exhibits a picture of increasing improvement, which every man of taste and liberal education must contemplate with mingled emotions of pride and exultation; – the man of letters, the merchant, and the artizan, mutually engaged in the grand work of extending and improving the domains of knowledge; zealously co-operating with each other in reclaiming from wildness every sterile spot on the barren waste of ignorance, that promises to repay, by the richness of its produce, the expense and labour of its cultivation. It is a delightful prospect to behold, what may be denominated the leaders of the various classes of which society is composed in this town, scattering over a wide extent of the mental soil, the seed of some favourite plant or flower, in the growth of which they are peculiarly interested; watching its gradual development with incessant anxiety, until it arrives at maturity, unfolds its blossoms, and "dedicates its beauties to the sun".'

JAMES ADAIR PILSON, *History of the Rise and Progress of Belfast*, 1846

FROM HENCE WE WENT ON MILES TO BELFAST, thro' a Countrey, all the way from Ardmagh, Extreamly pleasant, well Improved, and Inhabited by English. Belfast is a very handsome, thriving, well-peopled Town; a great many new houses and good Shops in't. The Folks seemed all very busy and employed in trade, the Inhabitants being for the most part merchants, or employ'd under 'em, in this Sea Port, which stands, conveniently enough, at the very inner part of Carrickfergus. Thro' the Town there Runns a small Rivulet, not much better than that they call the Glibb in Dublin, which, however, is of great use for bringing their goods to the Key when the Tide serves. Here we saw as Dismall Effects of another Fire as that at Lisbon [sic], which here, in the night, had Lately burnt a house belonging to the Lord Donnegall's Family (whose Town this is), with three Young Ladys, sisters to the present Earl. It stands separate from the Rest of the Houses, which as it prevented the Flames going further, so it cut of timely Relief in the midst of courts and gardens, which are an Extreamly noble old Improvement, made by old Sir Arthur Chichester, who was, about 100 years ago, the Establisher of this Family, and Indeed of the whole Kingdome, Especially the North, by planting English Colonies and civilising the Irish. These Improvements are all Inclosed in a kind of Fortification, being Designed for a place of Strength as well as Pleasure, and is a lasting Monument of this kind of the greatness of its founder. Here we saw a very Good Manufacture of Earthen Ware, which comes nearest Delft of any made in Ireland, and really is not much short of it. 'Tis very clean and pretty, and universally used in the North, and I think not so much owing to any Peculiar happiness in their clay, but rather to the manner of beating and mixing it up. Here they have Barracks for we lay here this night, And the next day –

Dined with the Soveraign, Mr McCartney, where we were made free of the Town. After Dinner we went on towards Carrickfergus, about two or three mile from Town. We struck off from the Road, which runs all Long the Sea, to view a Park here belonging to the Lords of Donnegal. Here they carried us up a pretty high Hill, where is a very pleasant Fountain, well shaded with Trees, and from whence you have a very fine Prospect of Carrickfergus, the Bay, and Belfast, which from hence makes a very good shew. Returning to the Road, about half way to Belfast, we parted with Mr Chichester, and continued our journey to Carrickfergus.

DR THOMAS MOLYNEUX, *Journey to the North*, 1708

E XTRACT FROM THE *Manuscript Journal* of an *English gentleman*, who travelled through part of Ireland, in June 1635.

'From Carrickfergus to Belfast you ride all upon the Lough side, it is a most bare way, and deep in winter and wet weather, though it is hard and dry. At Belfast my Lord Chichester hath another dainty stately palace, which is indeed the glory and beauty of that town also, where he is mostly resident, and is now building another brick wall beside his gates. This is not so vast and large as the other, but more convenient and commodious; the very end of the lough toucheth upon his garden and *backside*; there are also dainty orchards, gardens, and walks planted.'

Historical Collections Relative to the Town of Belfast, 1817

I HAVE NOW BEEN A WEEK IN BELFAST, which has rolled not unpleasantly away. In the morning I walk the streets, and frequent the libraries; and in the evening I go to card parties and concerts. I am, therefore, in some degree competent to speak of the place and people. I do it without reluctance, for I can say little of either but what is good.

Belfast is a large and well-built town. The streets are broad and straight. The houses neat and comfortable, mostly built of brick. The population, in a random way, may be estimated at thirty thousand, of which probably four thousand are Catholics. These are almost entirely working people. A few years ago there was scarcely a Catholic in the place. How much Presbyterians out-number the members of the Established Church, appears from the circumstance of there being five meeting-houses and only one church. Three of these meeting-houses are in a cluster, and are neat little buildings. Neat and trimness, indeed, rather than magnificence, are the characteristics of all the public buildings. A large mass-house, however, to the building of which, with their accustomed liberality, the inhabitants largely contributed, is an exception.

The new college, when finished, if like the Edinburgh college, and, for the same reason, it is not doomed to remain for ever unfinished; will, I should suppose, be another.

JOHN GAMBLE, A View of Society and Manners in the North of Ireland, 1813

W E HAVE AT LENGTH conducted our readers, through a great variety of scenes, to this grand mart of the commerce of the north of Ireland, which is situated in the latitude of 54° 35' 43" north, and longitude 5° 58' 14", west of London; and, whether we regard this town, in relation to its trade, its shipping, its public buildings and institutions, the magnificence of the bay, on whose shore it stands, or the symmetry and beauty of its streets, and its open and elegant communication with the inland country, we are equally compelled by all those features of its history, to acknowledge, that it approaches nearer to perfection than any other town in that province; and, in point of commercial eminence, may justly be denominated 'the Liverpool of Ulster'.

A. ATKINSON, Ireland Exhibited to England, 1823

T HE CLERGY AND THE PARENTS make no attempt to teach sexual commonsense to the young. Among the middle classes in Belfast, hundreds of youths fling their arms round girls with an undesirable promiscuity, and, indeed, consider the girls rather dull – 'chilblains' is an expressive word I have heard them described by – if they object to the business. The curious thing is that practically all this amorousness which goes on within the middle classes themselves is quite moral from a conventional point of view. It is none the less demoralising on this account, for, where it exists, there can of course be no intelligent friendship between the sexes. The young male amorists, too, frequently end by going forth on adventures among women outside their own class.

I think, nevertheless, there is a good deal of respect shown to women in Ireland. A youth does not take a girl into public-houses for drink in any part of Ireland as you will see youths doing in London and in Manchester. Neither will you see him embracing her on tram-cars, and in all sorts of public places, with the frequency which is so odd a feature of the social phantasmagoria in cities like London. In London these public embraces seem to pass without notice. In Belfast, in the daylight hours, hugging couples would, I am afraid, be figures of satire for small boys.

ROBERT LYND, Home Life in Ireland, 1908

WHEN IN THE COURSE OF OUR PEREGRINATION we pass Black Head, we come within the sphere of influence of Belfast – that great busy place, not quite a *mushroom* city – there is nothing fungoid about it – but one of growth so fast and vigorous that the more deliberate higher races of plants supply no suitable parallel. How far the rapid extension of Belfast (*Béal feirste*, the ford of the sand-bank) is due to natural advantages, and how far to the vigorous blend in the blood of its inhabitants, I am not qualified to enquire: but if we glance at local geological history we unearth some facts which, if they afford no clue to this riddle, at least explain some of the natural aids and also difficulties which have accompanied its development. Belfast Lough, a fine harbour of refuge, twelve miles long and three to four wide, at the head of which the city stands, represents the long-sunken termination of the valley of the Lagan. It is also a marked geological boundary, for the elevated basaltic area ceases abruptly on its northern shore, though the underlying red sandstones of the Trias edge the lough on both sides, giving way on the County Down coast almost at once to the much older Ordovician and Silurian slaty rocks which cover most of the latter county.

ROBERT LLOYD PRAEGER, The Way That I Went, 1937

WHAT SHALL I SAY OF BELFAST? First of all it is a beautifully set city, the best in the British Isles. What other British city has for a park a 1100-foot mountain with primeval forest on its lower slopes, and 300-foot precipices for its summit? What city the size of Belfast has good sea-bathing within eight miles of its centre, and could with a little enterprise have it within five miles? Where can you wander in bluebell woods and hear the roar of riveting and see the flash of acetylene welders? As for its citizens, they are perhaps the best looking in the British Isles. Its women too are well-dressed, though perhaps not with the same amount of originality as those of some European capitals.

Belfast might be called a male city, and male cities are rarely so interesting as female ones, for a male city does not completely understand afternoon tea or morning coffee, and it has not fully forged the links that bind frocks, flowers, art, beautiful women, polished men, theatres, dining out, and good architecture together. But Belfast is alert, efficient and dependable.

What Belfast sets its hand to it will ultimately do well, for we are an ambitious people, and our problem is to find and follow the right sort of ambitions.

DENIS O'D. HANNA, *The Face of Ulster*, 1952

TO THE LINEN HALL

After extremity
art turns social
and it's more than fashion
to voice the word *we*.
The epic yawp
hangs like an echo
of the big bang,
though now we tell children
to shun that original –
primal light, soaked green,
the slob mud
and a salt tang.
There is a ban
on philosophies of blood,
a terse demand
for arts and skills
to be understood,
and a common flow
into the new academy
which rules with a chill,
strenuous and insistent,
enforced formality.
Here we have a form
and a control
that is our own,
and on the stone steps
of that eighteenth-century,
reasoned library
we catch the classic spore
of Gibbon and new *ceps*,
the busts and statues
that might be stored
under the squares.
Our shaping brightness
is a style and discipline
that finds its tongue
in the woody desk-dawns

of fretting scholars
who pray, invisibly,
to taste the true vine
and hum gently
in holy sweetness.

TOM PAULIN, *Liberty Tree*, 1983

S TRONG AND WEALTHY, the city came to feel more and more that it was
the capital of a self-contained region, the Protestant industrial North. It
had been raised to the status of a city in 1888 and its leaders wanted to show
that they were wealthy and powerful. Unfortunately, not a great deal
survives architecturally from Belfast's nineteenth-century heyday, but one
or two gems are left. Foremost amongst these is a magnificent pub, the
Crown on Great Victoria Street, a model of intricate decoration described
as 'indisputably the crown of Victorian pubs in Ireland, and many would
say in the British Isles'. Robinson and Cleaver, the department store,
provides another fine example of Victorian gothic. The City Hall was built
in 1905; massive and dignified with its Portland stone, corner towers and
soaring domes, it says to the world: 'We are rich and powerful and we are
here to stay.' How was it possible, one can ask with the benefit of hindsight,
that nationalist political leaders could ignore the political statement implicit
in the City Hall's architecture and think nothing of dismantling it as if it
were just another Martello tower built to keep the French at bay?

At the beginning of the twentieth century Belfast was at the height of its
commercial and industrial power, and proud of it; the spirit of the town at
the time can be caught in a guide published in 1902. Pride in industry rears its
head again and again: 'Belfast as a town has no ancient history and does not
lay claim to remote origin like so many towns in Ireland. Its record is simply
one of industrial progress.'

Belfast was proud to be young in much the same way that American cities
like Chicago also developed a patronising attitude to old-fashioned Europe,
which was seen as pleasant but backward. The guide claims that Belfast, with
the requisite number of success stories of self-made men, could be compared
with an American city, and one feels the author thought that, like an
American city, it also had a hinterland of wilderness where dangerous
natives roamed in frontier territory.

MAURICE GOLDRING, *Belfast: From Loyalty to Rebellion*, 1991

T HERE ARE NO FEWER THAN FOURTEEN BOOKSELLERS IN BELFAST; and
all of them enjoy a fair share of business. Nor are libraries wanting. The
Linen-hall library contains about 9000 volumes; the town contains four

circulating libraries, and more than one private book society; and several others are established in the neighbouring villages. Reading clubs are indeed numerous, among the country people of Down, Antrim, and Armagh, – I mean, among the lower classes; and are well and liberally conducted. I ascertained that the number of Tory periodicals sold in Belfast does not amount to half the number sold of a Liberal character. Of the monthly periodicals, Tait's Magazine enjoys the largest circulation; and next to it, comes the Dublin University Magazine.

HENRY D. INGLIS, *A Journey Throughout Ireland in 1834*, 1835

BELFAST STOOD FOREMOST in the early struggle with intolerance and corruption, in the bold discussion of political subjects, and in the dissemination of reform principles. The latter were embodied, in 1793, in a series of papers written by several persons, called *Thoughts on the British Constitution*. This collection of pieces is one of the earliest and the ablest expositions of arguments in detail in favour of reform that is to be met with. Another admirable series of letters on the same subject, under the signature of 'Orellana', were written at this time by Dr Drennan. The subversion of the government was disclaimed by the leaders of the people, and there can be little doubt on the mind of any one who reads the discussions of the Belfast politicians, that, although many of them entertained views that went much farther than reform, it was long before they acted on them, or extended their projects beyond the attempt to strengthen the democratic principle, and to combine the monarchical form of government with republican institutions. They were content to see the constitution restored and perpetuated, though, in the abstract, the predilections of such men as Tone, Neilson, Russell, Emerson, Kelburn, Joy, Simms, M'Cracken, etc., might be in favour of republicanism; but they could not overlook difficulties that lay in the way of any efforts for obtaining that object, and the probability of so far assimilating existing institutions to the latter, by means of reform, as to prevent the evils which had arisen from the monarchical form of government having become (in Ireland at least) an oligarchical one.

RICHARD R. MADDEN, *The United Irishman: Their Lives and Times*, 1857

MANY LAUDABLE PROJECTS were now set on foot by James I for the civilisation and settlement of Ulster, the greater part of which had been forfeited to the crown by the rebellion of the northern clans. No one contributed more successfully to the carrying on of these measures than Sir Arthur Chichester, Lord Deputy, with whose wise and prudent conduct the king was so well satisfied, that he 'conferred on him very considerable grants of lands in the province, and as a lasting mark of his favour, did by letters patent, bearing date at Westminster 23rd February, 1612, create him Baron Chichester of Belfast, entailing the honour on his issue male'. Among his other possessions, the grant makes mention of 'the castle or mansion-house, town and manor of Belfast; the territories of Tuognefall [the Falls,] Tuoghmoylone, [Malone,] Tuoghcinament, Carnemoney, Carntall, and Monks-land; the rectory of Sankill, [Shankil,] and all other rectories, &c. within the said territories; the entire fishing of the river Lagan, &c.'

Historical Collections Relative to the Town of Belfast, 1817

THE LAGAN TOWPATH. Beyond a humpback bridge, a church spire, rising from tree-tops. A resolutely Protestant spire, outlined against winter sunset, witness to Ulster history. Rooks threshed noisily in the plantation by the churchyard; below the humpback bridge the canal reflected lemon-yellow sunset. Overhead, masses of grey cloud sailed in from the Atlantic, passengers across the green wastes of Ireland, threatening rain in the night.

Beyond the canal, the moon hung like a lantern over the dark woods of Ballydrain. Not just an ordinary moon. A pale green moon, like an enormous green cheese. We walked on, pretending not to have seen it. But there it was. Somebody, perhaps for a joke, had hung a moon like an unsmiling green cheese over the canal and the thick black woods round Ballydrain House.

Then, as if a theatrical green moon wasn't enough, there was a wild, clanging burst of melody from the sky. It was the carillon in the church tower playing a well-known Christmas hymn: jerkily, with one of its notes about a quarter tone flat. Flat or not, with the green moon and the lemon-yellow water under the bridge, it was magic.

It stopped. Silence. Even the rooks in the plantation stopped cawing. Then it started again. Another wild burst of melody, clanging away over the woods, the Lagan valley. We set out for the churchyard, round by the hump-backed bridge. What genius had chosen this moment of December sunset, of lemon-coloured sky and water, of unsmiling green moon hung over the winter purple of the woods, to broadcast melody from a church tower?

DENIS IRELAND, *From the Jungle of Belfast*, 1973

YOU WOULD BE SURPRISED AT THE CLOSE, the perfect resemblance that the road to Belfast from Armagh bears to England. I could hardly persuade myself that Lisburn was west of St George's Channel: there is nothing Irish about it. The immediate approach to Belfast is splendid: a fine road, high cultivation, beautiful villas, substantial brick houses surrounded by bleaching grounds, the look of prosperity, and total absence of every thing opposed to it, might have prepared me for the aspect of the town itself, which, nevertheless, struck me with astonishment. The streets are wide, straight, and admirably paved; the buildings capacious, uniform, and equal to some of the best commercial parts of London; particularly the High Street, with its broad flagstones, its lofty houses, spacious hotels, and very handsome shops. The situation of this noble city is enchanting: it stands on a broad lough, with a mountainous back ground, plentifully interspersed with gardens about the environs, and altogether it rejoiced my heart to find such a spot in Ireland; so free from the distressing drawbacks that abound even in Dublin. But this is the north, the 'black north', the PROTESTANT north!

CHARLOTTE ELIZABETH (Mrs Tonna), *Letters from Ireland*, 1838

As O'CONNELL LEFT BELFAST, escorted by four cars full of police and a body of police cavalry, Dr Cooke addressed a massive open-air demonstration against Repeal:

I would show Mr O'Connell what he did not yet see – that is, the wonders of Belfast. It is true, that within only a comparatively recent period, our town was merely a village. But what a glorious sight does it now present! Turn in what direction we will, our eyes meet new streets and public buildings – numbers of new manufactories rise up on every side – and look where we may, we see signs of increasing prosperity. . . And to what cause is all this prosperity owing? Is it not to the free intercourse which the Union enables us to enjoy with England and Scotland – to that extension of our general commerce which we derive through that channel? I can fancy I see the genius of industry seated upon the hills which look down upon our lovely town . . . while, accompanied by the genius of Protestantism, her influence is shed, from that point, over the length and breadth of Ulster (Hear, hear and loud cheers) . . . Can there be any religious liberty, I would ask him, in a community. . . where freedom of conscience is unknown?

QUOTED IN JONATHAN BARDON, *Belfast: An Illustrated History*, 1982

A SHORT DISTANCE FROM THE QUEEN'S COLLEGE are the Botanical Gardens, a fashionable resort for the better classes of Belfast, though there seemed no restriction on entering beyond the payment of sixpence and entering your name in a book. These gardens are well worth seeing. They are of some extent, with greenhouses containing beautiful flowers, and a small sheet of water. A party were playing croquêt, and I observed that this game possesses the singular advantage of placing all on a perfect equality. A little girl was playing in company with some boys, and though at many other games she might have been snubbed, she was here treated with as much deference when it came to her turn as if she had been a grown-up person.

Among the public buildings which attracted my attention at Belfast were the Bank, the Commercial Rooms, the Custom House, and the Ulster Hall. The Queen's Bridge should also be seen particularly, as from the centre the stranger has a fine view of the quays and shipping.

Before leaving Belfast I should say a word or two on that, to the traveller, all-important subject, hotel accommodation. I do not of course contemplate making this work a guide in the ordinary sense, but as I observed, during my wanderings round Ireland, that many travellers were not using the usual guide-books, but some book of travels which had attracted their notice, so I think it may prove useful if from time to time, or perhaps from day to day, I set down some of that information which the reader would otherwise have to seek in an ordinary guide-book. At the Queen's Hotel the looking-glass in my bedroom was constantly spinning round, in a way as if it intended to go smash; and at dinner, the first potatoes I partook of in Ireland were hard-boiled; and at breakfast, the first egg I opened was a bad one, but beyond these small inconveniences, which might not happen to another traveller, this hotel was comfortable enough. There is also another hotel near here, called the Albion, which seems much frequented. Without doubt, how-ever, the Imperial and Royal must be the best hotels in Belfast, and to the former, at least to judge from the visitors' lists in the newspapers, people of rank and fashion do most resort. Before quitting Belfast I must also bear my humble testimony to the courtesy and politeness of the inhabitants, whom the stranger accosted during his walks through their streets. It seems strange to contemplate that, about this time last year, Belfast was the scene of a disgraceful riot, such as happily rarely occurs in any civilised country. All is so quiet and orderly now. I am told, however, by the waiter at the Queen's, that the disturbances were exclusively confined to the quarter of the town where they broke out, and that I might with perfect safety have come to that hotel.

AN ENGLISHMAN [W .W. BARRY], *A Walking Tour Round Ireland in 1865*, 1867

REVISITING BELFAST

Revisiting Belfast I recall most vividly
The startling red of the trams of childhood –
No red will ever be so red again –

And the torn posters, half-hinged on hoardings,
Behind which we played our hide-and-seek
Till the grey-lead dusk had called us home
After the realities in practice's sharp school.
The very air was different then
(Since I was different then).
Childhood preferred the artistic vision,
Vision without performance, without satiety,
Transmuting the stones to all rare minerals.
The air was brittle then, like glass
You saw through; that kindly was opaque to one's own skeleton.
I remember at school the trouble with masters
Frowning: cutting the key to fit the normal lock.
But stirring ashes kindles no fire
And one isn't yet sufficiently old
To lament the quick change of Act –
There is only another scene.
Belfast is a film of rapid memories –
Loitering homewards from school, discussing heroes
Or cycling for adventure past scarlet traffic lights
Or mitching to Bellevue to view the smoke-tossed lough.
And then the first whisper of desire,
The shamefaced, timid overture,
The quick rebuff – and sawdust in the mouth.
I think of those forgotten seaside trips
We called excitement: the liquid sand,
Caves to explore, tall cliffs to strut on
Far from industrial fog and fug.
But, most vividly of all,
I see the barbarous, shrieking red
Of Belfast's trams of childhood.

ROBERT GREACEN, Collected Poems 1944–1994, 1995

REJOICINGS FOR THE RECENT VICTORIES OF THE FRENCH

'THE TOWN OF BELFAST was almost universally illuminated. Everything de-monstrated sincere pleasure in the disgrace of two tyrannical courts, that attempted to dragoon an united nation into that deplorable state of spiritual as well as political bondage, from which it was just recovering, and that dared to tell twenty-five millions of men – YE SHALL NOT BE FREE.

'In the windows of six or seven houses a number of transparencies presented themselves: – A few of the mottoes are subjoined, as trifling circumstances sometimes mark the disposition of the times.

'Perfect union and equal liberty to the men of Ireland. – Vive la Republique: Vive la Nation. – Church and State divorced. – Liberty triumphant. – The Rights of Man established. – Despotism prostrate. – The Tyrants are fled; let the People rejoice. – Heaven beheld their glorious efforts and crowned their deeds with success. – France is free; so may we: let us will it. – Awake, O ye that sleep. – A gallows suspending an inverted Crown, with these words: "May the fate of every tyrant be that of Capet". – A check to Despots. – The cause of Mankind triumphant. – Irishmen! rejoice. – Union among Irishmen. – Rights of Man. – Irishmen! look at France. Liberty and Equality.'

QUOTED IN RICHARD R. MADDEN, *The United Irishmen: Their Lives and Times*, 1857

JOHN BROWN, SOVEREIGN EIGHTY YEARS SINCE, did not go very far from the town. Still, let it not be thought he retired to the rural beauties of Peter's Hill when he assumed the Sovereignty. He must have been there at a much earlier period, as we have seen a letter dated 1770, in which Miss Brown of Peter's Hill is mentioned. This John Brown practised a custom which may have been general with others; he carried his own quart pot from his house in Peter's Hill to the corner of North Street, and, after getting it filled from a little brewery which then stood there, sat down to enjoy his beer in the open air. The social condition of the community has greatly changed since that era. There seems to have been less animosity, more gaiety, amusement, and sight-seeing, than there is now – always taking into account the vast disproportion in size between the town then and now. In July, 1805, the Orangemen of the town paraded, without riot or molestation, in Donegall Place; they then marched to church to hear a sermon, and were afterwards dismissed to their lodges. At the very same time, Mrs Siddons was performing in the town. The Donegall family was then generally resident; the Marchioness gave entertainments to the townspeople and the gentry around in Donegall House and the Exchange Rooms; besides which, the coteries, balls, and suppers were periodical institutions. There were no religious assemblies on week-days in places different from the Established houses of worship, no temperance assemblies nor huge bazaars. The people of the present time are perhaps wiser and better in their day and generation, and aim at more ennobling objects. Some of the old inhabitants, whose youth had been spent in the former century, still wore, in the beginning of the present, powder and queues. They strongly affected top boots and smooth faces, and would have quite condemned modern costumes, and been utterly horrified at the unshaven appearance of almost all the men of all classes in the town.

344

The in-door costumes of these bewigged and top-booted inhabitants presented nothing very remarkable. They assembled, when the dews of evening fell, in some of the old-established hostelries in Sugar House Entry, Caddel's Entry, or some other equally quiet corner, and considered it a sort of duty there to imbibe a certain number of tumblers of old rum punch. The phrase 'total abstainers' was unknown in those days, and it is certain there were no coffee-stands in the town, in the modern sense of the term.

GEORGE BENN, A History of the Town of Belfast, 1880

MANY OF THE MERCHANTS' COUNTING-HOUSES are crowded in little old-fashioned 'entries', or courts, such as one sees about the Bank in London. In and about these, and in the principal streets in the daytime, is a great activity, and homely unpretending bustle. The men have a business look, too, and one sees very few flaunting dandies, as in Dublin. The shopkeepers do not brag upon their signboards, or keep 'emporiums', as elsewhere, – their places of business being for the most part homely; though one may see some splendid shops, which are not to be surpassed by London. The docks and quays are busy with their craft and shipping, upon the beautiful borders of the Lough; – the large red warehouses stretching along the shores, with ships loading, or unloading, or building, hammers clanging, pitch-pots flaming and boiling, seamen cheering in the ships, or lolling lazily on the shore. The life and movement of a port here give the stranger plenty to admire and observe. And nature has likewise done everything for the place – surrounding it with picturesque hills and water; – for which latter I must confess I was not very sorry to leave the town behind me, and its mills, and its meeting-houses, and its commerce, and its theologians, and its politicians.

WILLIAM MAKEPEACE THACKERAY, The Irish Sketch Book, 1842

ADDRESS TO BELFAST
I have been there, and still would go;
'Tis like a little Heav'n below.
WATTS

FAR-FAM'D Belfast! most justly stil'd
The guide and glory of the North,
Wilt thou attend a songster wild,
Who simply celebrates thy worth?
Tho' prejudice that worth may slight,
Deceiv'd by tales of party-spite,

Story's true page shall carry down
To time's late sons, thy high renown.

Nature, fair imag'd, walks thy *Stage*;
Thy *Fanes* Morality befriend;
While youths, by Discipline made sage,
Thy throng'd *Academy* attend;
Thy *House of Alms* – asylum bless'd! –
Receives the Poor, and gives 'em rest;
Thy *Sunday-Schools* humanely train
Th' unhappy babes of Want and Pain.

The friends of Liberty and Law,
Brave men and bright, in thee remain;
Whom Demagogue shall never draw
To wild misrule – nor despot chain:
Th' expressive Look – the faultless Form,
Is not thy Daughters only charm;
Good sense, Good-nature, *mental Health*,
Are theirs – a nobler dowr' than Wealth.

While Zeal, elsewhere, directs his Shafts
At the pure Heart that Truth would find;
Free as the gale, that gently wafts
Thy Commerce o'er, thou leav'st the mind:
Thy *Churchman* scorns to smite the meek
And passive *Quaker's* modest cheek:
Thy *Cath'lick* yields her willing hand
To *Calvin's* friend, in Hymen's band.

Ah! ne'er may Ignorance, allied
To Superstition, humble thee!
Nor Opulence engender Pride,
The parent of Misanthropy!
So Emulation shall inflame
Genius to write, that Taste may fame,
And Kindness soothe poor Merit's pains.
And Valour guard what Virtue gains.

Far-fam'd Belfast! O long may stand
Thy domes and spires, that long have stood!
Protected by thy Angel's hand
From Flame, from Tempest, and from flood!
And when old Time, who ruins all,

Shall doom thy splendid streets to fall,
May their exalted Natives rise
To nobler Mansions in thy Skies!

JAMES ORR, *Poems on Various Subjects*, 1804

A RAILWAY DID NOT MAKE ITS APPEARANCE IN BELFAST UNTIL 1839. There was, of course, a good system of mail coaches connecting the town with other parts of the country. As early as 1742 a stage coach ran between Dublin and Belfast, leaving Dublin every Monday and Belfast every Thursday, and occupying in winter three days and in summer two days to make the journey. The first mail coach between those two places commenced running in July 1790. In due time public conveyances by road were established from the town to all the important centres; there were four coaches to Dublin, three to Armagh, one to Ballynahinch, two to Ballymena, one to Carrickfergus, three or four to Londonderry, one to Comber, two to Dongahadee, two to Downpatrick, one to Dungannon, one to Enniskillen, one to Killyleagh, one to Kilrea, two to Larne, one to Magherafelt and Cookstown, three to Portaferry, one to Portglenone and six to Bangor. The services and roads were gradually so improved that the journey to Dublin came to be accomplished in twelve hours, and that to Londonderry in from eleven to twelve hours. In these early days and down to about the year 1842, Sedan chairs were in use in the town.

D.J. OWEN, *History of Belfast*, 1921

IT WAS NOT ... TILL 1789 that Belfast obtained the regular communication which towns of less importance already enjoyed with Dublin by stage coach, a fact which is to be explained by the badness of the roads and the steepness of the hills between Newry and Belfast. Belfast Lough is exceedingly picturesque, whether entered by the Antrim or by the Down side of the channel. The outer harbour is one of the safest in the kingdom. Great improvements were made about seventy years ago on the more immediate entrance to the port. The course of the Lagan, which runs past the quays down to Garmoyle, was originally most tortuous and somewhat difficult to navigate, but about 1840 the late William Dargan was employed to make a straight cut from the lower part of the harbour, and to deepen the channel so that ships of large draughts can be brought to the quays, which extend for about a mile below Queen's Bridge.

From such small beginnings – through the industry, grit, and perseverance of her citizens – the city of Belfast has become to-day one of the first commercial cities of the Empire, and the capital of Northern Ireland.

THE REVEREND CANON FORDE, *Sketches of Olden Days in Northern Ireland*, 1926

THE CITY BUILT AND GREW, of course, in some measure during the eighteenth century; but in a small way and spasmodically. It had little sense of destiny then, one imagines; and there appears to have been no cohesion or civic unity in its random developments – for many of its best plans – for instance College Square, Royal Terrace, the Crescent – were never completed. But many isolated buildings of beauty did rise between 1700 and 1820, and some of these, or fragments of them, are still about, to take us with surprised pleasure amid a too-much of commercial ugliness. Moreover, a city in which one can still every morning put down coppers at any newstand for a copy of the *Northern Whig* has assuredly had an eighteenth century! Indeed to be able to buy the *Northern Whig* daily on the way to work is one very good reason for liking to live in Belfast. And there is also the *Belfast Newsletter*, founded in 1737, and printed now where it was printed then, and owned now by the family that founded it. I have been told the *Belfast Newsletter* had somewhat in its time the character and repute of the present-day *Guardian*, and that it ran itself into sharp disfavour in the 1770s by upholding the American Revolution.

KATE O'BRIEN, *My Ireland*, 1962

THE KENDY MAN
All wore away tae one side, like a Kendy's Man's hammer.
Belfast saying

Rosy's Lumps, Peggy's Leg,
Taffy Lick an' Yellow Man –
Draw up, decent folk,
Eat them hot out o' the pan.
    (Sung)   Hokey, pokey,
                Penny a whack,
                Taste afore ye buy.
                O, what a happy land is Ireland!

Rock Kendy wi' thread strings,
Sugarstick in glass jars,
An' for cutties shy o' love
Conversation Lozengers.

Bull's Eyes, Roman Wheels,
Marchpane, as red as Cain,
Jujubes an' Farden Dips –
All that's boiled, sweet an' clean.

Sherbet an' Turkish Delight,
Easy on a body's weasand,
Tart bitin' Lemon Drops,
Gelantines, small an' pleasant.

Or, if ye chuse tae walk
An' sit awhile in Molly Ward's,
An' bide until the tide comes in,
I've slow goin' Tailors' Yards.

Licorice, Paregoric,
Tae cure a felon or a cold,
Peppermints for drunkards' breaths –
Sovereign as the King's gold.

Vintners o' the High Street,
Schoolmasters, ladies smart,
Entry birds, mothers' weans
Gather round my handcart.
    (Sung)   Hokey, pokey,
                  Penny a whack,
                  Taste afore ye buy.
                  O, what a happy land is Ireland!

JOSEPH CAMPBELL, *The Poems of Joseph Campbell*, 1963

THE HORSE'S STRIDE LENGTHENED ON THE THAWING ROAD and soon they were passing through the little clachan of Moneyrea, and the haze of Belfast rose before them, above the tree tops. They wound carefully down the long hill into the city, the people on the road became more numerous, and the hedges gave way to the heavy grey walls of an estate. Then came a row of white-washed cottages, once the village of Castlereagh but now chained to the city by row upon row of red-brick houses. Hamilton reined the horse down to walking pace as they joined the long jolting cavalcade of carts arriving in from the townlands lying to the south and east. Towering among them the horse-trams lurched towards the city centre.

SAM HANNA BELL, *December Bride*, 1951

from THE BELFAST POOR-HOUSE
AN HISTORICAL AND DESCRIPTIVE POEM

Here all the children, dress'd in Sunday clothes,
   Stood for inspection, plac'd in comely rows.
The female children, rang'd on the right hand,
   And on the left, the males in order stand;
There charms of modesty throughout appear,
   And uncorrupted innocence is here;
Admiring both with infinite delight
   He said, and gracefully 'a pretty sight'.
But true religion hath more fruit than sounds,
   Here read his gift, one hundred British pounds.

Unto the schoolrooms now I pass along,
   These little nurseries demand my song; . . .
In the first room, we fifty females find
   Taught by a mistress, careful, good and kind,
To spell, to read, to sew, to knit, and these
   Join'd with good breeding, in a female, please.
The second room holds near one hundred boys,
   Clean, healthy, young, and fond of playful toys;
To spell, to read, to sypher, and to write,
   They learn with ease – the master with delight,
Forms them in classes, and here 'skill'd to rule',
   Instructs and loves his noisy 'little school'.

Delight it must, the lovers of mankind,
   So many orphans in one place to find;
To see those children once depress'd and poor,
   Whose mean support was begg'd from door to door,
Now in becoming decency appear,
   And kept from vice and ev'ry hurtful snare,
Taught wisdom's ways, and fitted, when of age,
   To act a part respectful on life's slipp'ry stage.

Once these poor orphans were of friends bereft,
   And to support them no relation left;
Now in this house they find paternal care,
   And ev'ry child receives an equal share;
When they are taught, and of a proper age,
   (This might a scribe's decyph'ring pen engage)
The gentlemen, to persons fit and kind,
   To learn employments, these fine children bind;

And tradesmen wish to have in their employ
A well-instructed, healthful, poor-house boy.

DAVID BOYD, 1806

THE BELFAST LADIES' ASSOCIATION embraced an object which *lives* and *tells*, and will continue to do so, when they who formed it shall be no more on earth. It was on January 1st, 1847, that the first meeting was held in the Commercial Buildings by ladies of all religious denominations; and they there resolved to form a Society for the purpose of raising a fund to be appropriated to afflicted localities without any regard to religious distinctions . . .

I loved to linger in Belfast. All seemed to be life, and life to some purpose. All hearts seemed to be awakened to one and the same object, to do good most efficiently; and one peculiar trait was here perceivable – none of that desire for who should be *greatest* seemed prevalent. A mutual confidence prevailed. One would tell me enthusiastically that she did not know how the association could manage without Maria Webb; her judgment was always the turning point in all difficulties. Maria Webb would expatiate on the efficiency of Mary Ireland as a visitor and manager. A third would regret that the indefatigable Miss McCracken, she feared, would soon leave us, as her age had passed the line of three-score years and ten. Another expatiated on the faithful Miss —, who was a Roman Catholic, but whose labours of love had been untiring; and she was quite sorry that difference in religious profession had so long kept so many useful members at a distance, &c. This to a stranger could probably be viewed with a sober, impartial eye, that those moving in the machinery could not; and to me it looked like a heavenly influence distilling unperceived into the hearts of all, like the dew, which falls alike on the garden flower or mountain weed.

ASENATH NICHOLSON, *Annals of the Famine in Ireland*, 1851

THE ROMANTIC GROWTH OF THE CITY really *is* the Thing: the manner in which it keeps on doubling its population and increasing its riches. The frightening part of all this is that no man can tell what Belfast will produce in the way of ideologies. Founded in 1603, this city still seems to say: 'Give me time and I will let you know what I think about all that matter of Ireland a Nation.' It is heart-free of ideals, but these, like love, come as suddenly as a stitch in the side or a fall of soot from a chimney. One day Belfast is going to surprise the world and fall in love with an ideal. Life and perhaps national leadership are still before this dynamic place.

STEPHEN RYNNE, *All Ireland*, 1956

No CITIZEN OF BELFAST, no one who has breathed from his birth the atmosphere of that city, can ever feel himself uncomfortably inferior to anybody else in the world. We may perhaps be arrogant and disagreeable, though I think we try to conceal our pride, but we never suffer, as many other people appear to suffer, from the misery of self-distrust.

GEORGE A. BIRMINGHAM, Pleasant Places, 1934

Like Errigal, like a wave-top,
   Save for the snow of the crest,
Is the fairy mountain of Munster
   Where the Bandon flows from the West:
Owen I love and Errigal,
   But I love another best.

And it is not high Lurig Edain
   That looks from the Antrim shore,
Nor thy wooded slopes, Slieve Donard,
   Nor thy gates, O Barnes Mór.
Dear is each peak of Donegal,
   But there's one that I love more.

Look up from the streets of the city,
   Look high beyond tower and mast,
What hand of what Titan sculptor
   Smote the crags on the mountain vast?
Made when the world was fashioned,
   Meant with the world to last,
The glorious face of the sleeper
   That slumbers above Belfast.

ALICE MILLIGAN, Collected Poems, 1954

NARRATOR:

And in I would jump, into the skipping rope. In those days four flagstones from the garden gate was foreign ground, and the other side of the street was a newfoundland. At the bottom of the hill the world went by. Three main roads met here, and three corner-pubs supplied the bottle-neck for the belly of traffic. There was a cab-rank for jaunting cars and the skinny three-cornered horses stood sleeping with one limp leg all day long, while the jarveys collogued in the pubs.

W.R. RODGERS, *The Return Room*, 1955

BALLOONS AND WOODEN GUNS

O it was lovely round that other house
where I was born and lived for thirty years.
Life surged about us. So that time appears,
dull intervals suppressed, in happy shows:
Italian organ-grinders, parrots, bears;
that blind old Happy Jimmy by himself;
the German bands; the Ulster Volunteers
with wooden guns; the women selling delph;
carts with balloons; great horses galloping,
their huge fire engine brass and funnelled flames;
strung chestnuts every autumn; kites in spring;
girls skipping; slides and snowballs in the snow;
all those activities which bore the names
of May Queen, Kick-the-Tin, and Rally-O.

JOHN HEWITT, *Kites in Spring*, 1980

TWO YEARS BEFORE MY HOMECOMING, on one of my country pub-crawls with Dylan Thomas, I had met a BBC producer from Belfast, John Boyd. He asked me to look him up on my return; when I did so, I found that my experience with Radiodiffusion Française could be put to good use in Belfast. As a result of a number of 'talks' programmes, I obtained the entry to a quite different world within Belfast: that of the arts. This was of unexpected richness. Not, to be truthful, in terms of creative production; apart from expatriate Ulstermen such as Louis MacNeice, Tyrone Guthrie, and Bertie Rodgers, there were then few if any local practitioners of any of the arts who aspired to the first rank. But the talk was good. There were intersecting intellectual circles, each informed, witty, and amusing in its own way, centred on rival public-houses, semi-professional theatres, and clubs. These drew both strength and vigour from the contrasting strands of Catholic and Protestant culture running through the community. (This same interaction of traditions has contributed largely to the surprising artistic flowering that has accompanied the most recent Troubles.) The worlds of the arts, and of trade unionism – the two fields in which I sought and found most of my friends – were, as it happened, the only two fields of Ulster life from which sectarianism was wholly absent; in each, Catholic and Protestant could mix quite naturally and unself-consciously as they could do almost nowhere else.

C.E.B. BRETT, Long Shadows Cast Before, 1978

IT WAS SOME TIME AGO very much the fashion to abuse this unfortunate town, and indeed this propensity still continues amongst the very vile and ignorant, who always take their cue from those above them, and who are incapable of speaking at all without a prompter. Now, as there is perhaps, no spot on earth, where better morals, more decent conduct, more real virtue, or more of the light of reason prevails, it is curious to weigh the accusers against the accused.

Who then is it that dislikes Belfast?

A gang of corrupt courtiers, who build their fortunes upon the ignorance, vice, degradation, and religious disunion of this country – they dislike Belfast!

A gang of prostitute and base mercenaries, dependent upon these courtiers, who raise themselves to their favour by all manner of villany – such as persuading simple people to perjure themselves at elections, by laughing at conscience and integrity as a state joke – they dislike Belfast!

A gang of dissolute Bishops, who enjoy a great portion of the lands of the country, and a great share in the legislature of it, – who, instead of taking any tender or affectionate interest in the welfare of the poor, are no further known to them, than as they corrupt them by their example, or oppress them by their avarice – they, and their clergy hate Belfast! – *There are several laudable exceptions here.*

The whole gang of tax-gatherers, pensioners, and sycophants – cry out against Belfast!

The *gentlemen* of the standing army, whose duty it is to think, speak, and act – *as they are commanded*, even when their own lives are in question – and who are often slaughtered before they are quite fattened – *they swear, most bloodily, that they'll burn Belfast ! ! !*

Booby 'Squires, who are the dupes of subtle courtiers, and who have not sagacity to see that by making common cause with them, they are running headlong into the consequences of their vices – *'Lives and fortune men'*, and *'Protestant ascendancy boys'* – they are contemptible enough to spit their little venom at Belfast!

Guzzling corporations, jealous of their absurd monopolies, and mock dignity; they drink – *'Damnation to Belfast ! ! !'*

Old, idle, card-playing tabbies, who complain that the *mob* have raised the price of chair-hire, and of butcher's meat – they are at a loss to account for the wicked disturbances in Belfast!

And the *disinterested* tribe of the law, *take no fees* for railing against Belfast!

Northern Star, 1794

I REMEMBER STANDING at the top of a tall building in Belfast and looking out across a great part of the industrial portion of the city. It was a grey winter day, with an occasional light, cold drizzle of rain. Industrial Belfast lay in front of me, grey and dim and smoky, spread up the great amphitheatre towards the hills, which were just very faintly visible. All around and below me, thousands of curt, preoccupied, cautiously friendly people were at work at bleak industrial jobs. I felt that I was at the real heart of Belfast then, and I had no wish to be anywhere else.

HUGH SHEARMAN, *Ulster*, 1949

PRAYER FOR BELFAST

Night, be starry-sensed for her,
Your bitter frost be fleece to her.
Comb the vale, slow mist, for her.
Lough, be a muscle, tensed for her.

And coals, the only fire in her,
And rain, the only news of her.
Small hills, keep sister's eyes on her.
Be reticent, desire for her.

Go, stories, leave the breath in her,
The last word to be said by her,
And leave no heart for dead in her.
Steer this ship of dread from her.

No husband lift a hand to her,
No daughter shut the blind on her.
May sails be sewn, seeds grown, for her.
May every kiss be kind to her.

CAROL RUMENS, *Best China Sky*, 1995

Intent on
Jaunt and Enterprise

Looking upwards he saw Ellen at the top of the cliff, and raised his hat with a pleasant smile of greeting. It was Godfrey Martin, and he hastened to reach the higher level, when they found much to discuss.

'I am most happy to meet you here,' he said. 'It recalls to my mind our pleasant times in Belfast. How did you leave your friend, Miss Lydia Walcot?'

'She was getting all the amount of enjoyment possible from our provincial gaieties, and making the best of life in general, as is her way.'

ARCHIBALD W.M. KERR, *By the Pool of Garmoyle*

When I had scrubbed my face and got my eyes to stop watering for a moment, I saw that the evening's entertainment had begun to resemble one of Belfast's livelier nights. The air was thick with shrieks and fruit.

P.G. WODEHOUSE, *The Inimitable Jeeves*

from THE NORTHERN ATHENS: A SATIRICAL POEM

In EASTER times, and all the town let loose,
What prancing, rattling, driving it along!
When tailors' prentices deny their goose,
To cut a dash, and thread the mazy throng –
Cars, tandems, noddies, curricles, in use –
NORTH-STREET and ANN-STREET wedg'd with old and young;
Best bibs and tuckers flaunting in the sun –
Men full of whiskey, maidens full of fun.

The Long Bridge rattles, and the LAGAN quivers
Beneath the car-borne multitudes that pass,
Threatening to dash each vehicle to shivers,
And drown the unsuspecting souls *en masse* –
A bridge the vilest o'er the first of rivers –
Unworthy cities of *Athenian* class:
But folks will brave it; as of old, the ocean,
And Egypt's plagues, some sought the land of Goshen.

To HOLYWWOD th' elated wanderers bend,
The *el dorado* of each bounding hope,
The too short day's too fleeting hours to spend,
And give to pleasure, pleasure's liveliest scope:
To PEGGY BARCLAY'S, troops of travellers wend,
Or straight to CARRICK for the day elope,
The lithe of limb the CAVE HILL's steep ascending,
And brains of such as have them sent a-mending.

Bang up the rattling cars and tandems fly,
Through rut or dust, in sunshine or in showers,
Hearts taking hue and colour from the sky –
Gloom'd with the cloud, or sunn'd with all the flowers;
Smart girls, with love and laughter in each eye,
Like Houri peeping forth from GIEL's bowers,
Whose air, fine forms, and elegance outvie
Venus de Medici, although, to-morrow,
Unseen, without all MILL-FIELD's houffs ye harrow.

Fashion, a name abus'd when maggots speak,
Disdains to view the wriggling of the mites,
That once a-year, or sometimes once a-week,
Crawl forth when Nature's genial warmth invites;
Then HOLYWOOD or NEWTONBREDA seek,
To bask, and put their insect-forms to rights;
That, like their kindred spawn of sunny weather,
Flock in gregarious multitudes together . . .

All round the classic City, glad souls rush
To clasp the hem of harmony; intent
To flee dull toil: from FALLS to FRIAR'S BUSH,
From SHANKHILL to the SHORE, all air is rent,
Glad hearts surrender'd to their joys' full gush –
Full many a naggin quaff'd, and last groat spent,
In making holiday so gay as their's,
All heedless of their sins as of their prayers.

I loath each Orange Club, and dark Cabal,
Distracting Order, and confounding Peace;
I hate Associations, one and all –
KING WILLIAM's myrmidons, or those of Nice –
The direst woes that hapless lands befall,
That ne'er their victim from their fangs release, –
Yet, still, I like discussion's devious range,
For wit and widows prosper best by change.

ANONYMOUS, 1826

NARRATOR:

That was the resurrection-sound which wakened me each morning –
the Island horn. And in the dark of a winter's morning I could hear
the tramp of hundreds of feet going past to their lives in the shipyard.

Mrs Mulligan, a mile away, crossed herself uneasily as the
Protestant feet tramped past her house. And her twelve unruly
children fell quiet under the bedclothes, as they always did, for fear
the feet might quicken and break into a run.

Nothing was humdrum in those long away and far-ago days. The
morning rose up early for me, and the world went out of its way to
call me. I could hardly wait to finish my porridge. Not that I liked
porridge –

MOTHER:

You can either like it or lump it. There's many as wee bare-foot fella
would be glad of it.

NARRATOR:

The wee bare-footed fellows lived in the low-down streets at the back
of our house. But our front road was a high-up and respectable one.
All the boys in it wore boots. I could hear them now, running after
Barney Cusack's breadcart – a long kite-tail of mockery.

CHILDREN:

Barney Cusack's bread
Sticks to the belly like lead.
Not a bit of wonder
That you belch like thunder
When you eat Barney Cusack's bread.

W.R. RODGERS, *The Return Room*, 1955

THE CAR WAS STANDING AT THE DOOR in the clear grey and gold
afternoon, the horse's breath congealing as it blew out into the frosty

air, the jarvey, in a heavy coat, slapping his arms vigorously across his chest and stamping on the ground.

'But —' she murmured doubtfully, as Richard held out his hand to help her up.

'But what?' he smiled. 'We don't so often have weather like this that we can afford to waste it. There has been nothing like it since the year we all learned to skate.'

'You mean the year you and Martin learned. I never did and never shall.'

'I'm going to teach you this afternoon.'

He laughed again at her timidity, and there was something in his vitality, his high spirits, that overbore her feeble resistance. She submitted half reluctantly, yet with an intense pleasure, and next moment he had pulled the rug over her knees and climbed up himself.

They drove rapidly along the smooth road, the steps of the trotting horse ringing out with a metallic clearness in the still air. She wore a thick veil, and warm furs wrapped her throat, so that, in the absence of wind, she did not even find the drive too cold. On the contrary, she felt stimulated by it, and when they turned in at Ballydrain gate the last shadow of her scruples had disappeared.

The scene that met their eyes was bright, gay, animated. Overhead, the cold grey sky was already streaked with the scarlet of an early sunset, against which the leafless trees stood out black and naked. The lake stretched from its wooded banks, white, with a thin crisp coating of snow, which crackled like powdered crystals under the steel blades of the skates. A low continuous hum rose from the ice, growing rapidly louder as they approached the bank. Everybody seemed happy and amused. Beginners flapped about like large ungainly birds with clipped wings; the more proficient glided along in rhythmic, effortless curves. Boys, with lowered heads and arms waving like windmills, dashed recklessly in all directions, to the terror of the nervous.

He knelt beside her and secured her skates: then he put on his own and she stood timidly watching him for a minute or two while he made a preliminary trial of his skill. How easily he did everything like this! His beauty had never appeared to her to be more wonderful than at that moment. The wintry background threw into relief his warm brown colouring, and the grace of his movements was delightful to watch. She blundered to him as he held out his hands, not trusting herself, frightened to strike out, and he laughed softly. Then he grasped her hands firmly and they started.

She let herself go, losing all fear in the consciousness of his strength and skill, though a dozen times she would have fallen had she been alone. On every side came the murmur of voices and laughter. Bright spots of colour

— the hats, the dresses of girls — took on a strange brilliance against the background of dark trees and frost-bound woodland.

FORREST REID, *At the Door of the Gate*, 1915

'TIS PRETTY TAE BE IN BAILE-LIOSAN

'Tis pretty tae be in Baile-liosan,
'Tis pretty tae be in green Magh-luan;
'Tis prettier tae be in Newtownbreda,
Beeking under the eaves in June.
The cummers are out wi' their knitting and spinning,
The thrush sings frae his crib on the wa',
And o'er the white road the clachan caddies
Play at their marlies and goaling-ba'.

O, fair are the fields o' Baile-liosan,
And fair are the faes of green Magh-luan;
But fairer the flowers o' Newtownbreda,
Wet wi' dew in the eves o' June.
'Tis pleasant tae saunter the clachan thro'
When day sinks mellow o'er Dubhais hill,
And feel their fragrance sae softly breathing
Frae croft and causey and window-sill.

O, brave are the haughs o' Baile-liosan,
And brave are the halds o' green Magh-luan;
But braver the hames o' Newtownbreda,
Twined about wi' the pinks o' June.
And just as the face is sae kindly withouten,
The heart within is as guid as gold —
Wi' new fair ballants and merry music,
And cracks cam' down frae the days of old.

'Tis pretty tae be in Baile-liosan,
'Tis pretty tae be in green Magh-luan;
'Tis prettier tae be in Newtownbreda,
Beeking under the eaves in June.
The cummers are out wi' their knitting and spinning,
The thrush sings frae his crib on the wa',
And o'er the white road the clachan caddies
Play at their marlies and goaling-ba'.

JOSEPH CAMPBELL (1919), *The Poems of Joseph Campbell*, 1963

SOME OF THE MOST INTERESTING GAMES are the less usual ones. For example, Belfast has surely been unusual in having had so many grown men playing marbles. This practice probably arose as a convenient form of amusement at lunch hour in places too restricted for kicking a ball about. Latterly I have seen very little of this game, but at one time it was very usual to see men playing marbles in Belfast, and at least one of the public parks had a special piece of tarmacadam laid down for them. Of course the really exciting places to play were on cobbled pavements where there were really interesting hazards calling for much skill and judgement; but cobbled pavements are gone from Belfast. I am informed that there is a revival of the game in one district of Belfast just as I write. People who were unused to the spectacle of men playing a game which is generally played only by little boys were rather surprised and sometimes a bit scornful when they saw this fashion at its height in Belfast. But the obvious answer to critics is, why not? It is every bit as grown-up as billiards or horse racing. Marbles in Belfast are called marleys, so you will know what is meant if a Belfast mill girl looks at you quizzically and says rather pityingly: 'Honest to God, your head's like a marley.'

Another game played in the past in the Belfast district was bullet throwing, a dangerous game forbidden by law. It is not very long, however, since I had to jump for the ditch to avoid one of these iron bullets on a road on the outskirts of Belfast. The bullets are a little smaller than a cricket ball and, when hurled with great force along a road, could easily inflict a serious injury. When Professor Evans, of Queen's University, Belfast, had remarked in his book, *Irish Heritage* (which, incidentally, is very largely about Ulster), that he had not come across bullet throwing nearer than Cork, I suggested to him that he must look more like a policeman than I do. However, he had since discovered the sport near Belfast and had even a collection of bullets to show me.

HUGH SHEARMAN, *Ulster*, 1949

TO GIVE OUR PRESENT YOUNG BLOODS an idea of how we old fellows spent our wasted lives forty years ago, here are a few extracts from an old diary of mine dated 1905:

Sunday —th March – Spent the afternoon walking round the Custom House steps. Immense crowds assembled to listen to half a dozen orators, quack doctors and lay preachers. Vendors of 'welks', 'bulls eyes', and 'yellow man' doing a great trade. Afterwards, Jim and I stroll along the quayside watching the sailors aboard the cross channel steamers and admiring the sailing ships at York Dock. We travel as far as 'The Twin Islands' then turn back home.

Monday – Went to political meeting at Shaftesbury Square 7.30. About 2,000 people gathered.

Tuesday – It's painful rising out of bed at 5 a.m. in the morning to reach the shipyard for 6 am. I wonder will our dreams of an 8 a.m. start ever come true. 8 p.m., I meet Maud at Shaw's Clock, at the corner of Sandy Row and Lisburn Road. Bought a penny packet of pop corns. Maud was all delighted. Kept us chewing the whole evening. We had a lovely walk along Stranmillis. Very few houses after we pass Friar's Bush Cemetery. Ditches on both sides of the road after you pass Stranmillis House.

Wednesday – Went to Theatre Royal in Arthur Square. Paid threepence and managed a fine seat in the gallery. Saw a few of the town's big-wigs in the grand circle. The seats are very expensive in the circle – one shilling each. I suppose the big-wigs have pots of money to spend. The upper circle cost sixpence and the pit fourpence. The play this week is *The Face at the Window*. We were held spellbound with three murders, and the detective brought back to life through some electric contraption, long enough to write down the name of the murderer before he returns to his Heavenly abode. I should enjoy a grisly nightmare tonight.

Thursday – Went to the 'Cornhill, Tailors', Upper North Street, to pick up my new suit. They're easily the best tailors in Belfast. It was a perfect fit. I don't begrudge the cost – nineteen shillings and sixpence, although it's a lot of money for a tailored suit. I meet Maud at Pim's Clock corner of Donegall Pass and Dublin Road. We walk along Botanic Avenue only to spot her father and mother on opposite side. We had to fly for our lives. Thank goodness they didn't notice Maud.

She would have received a fair hiding. Maud is just past seventeen, and her parents are very respectable.

Friday – We are very busy down at the shipyards just at present. Immediately after a ship is launched they are preparing to lay a new keel. I met the rest of the boys for football practice on 'The Plains', at Rugby Avenue. There were four or five other teams scattered about the fields. The treasurer collected our membership dues – one penny per week per member. We have a satisfactory balance in hand, nine shillings and sixpence. That sum may be sufficient to pay for our football rigs next week.

Saturday – The boys are in great form. We played Shankill Rovers on the football pitch at Peter's Hill, in front of Brown Square Police Barracks, and won 4–2. There was a big crowd of spectators, but the police had an easy time keeping order. They did draw their batons three times to clear the pitch when we looked like winning, but with the exception of the referee having to be carried off the field, I don't think there were many serious casualties.

THOMAS CARNDUFF (1954), *Life and Writings*, 1994

PLAYING 'MAY QUEENS' WAS POPULAR WITH GIRLS, who dressed up their queen in clothes resembling wedding dresses. They would dance her along the streets with a shrill vocal accompaniment. Groups of children and teenagers in high-heeled shoes and old lace curtains would escort their queen and one girl would collect money in an old tin can. If they met a rival queen with her attendants, the air would be filled with angry cries. Part of the May Queen song went something like this:

> Our Queen up the river
> with your yah-yah-yah
> Your Queen down the river
> with your yah-yah-yah
> Our Queen up the river
> And we'll keep her there for ever
> with your yah-yah-yah-yah.

At Hallowe'en, we used to wear false faces and try to frighten old ladies. Our toy guns would emit loud bangs and we would let off rockets and Catherine wheels, and hold sparklers in our hands. If we had collected enough empty boxes from shops, we would then start a bonfire. Toffee apples on sticks would make their appearance in shops and I think these usually sold for a halfpenny each.

ROBERT GREACEN, *The Sash My Father Wore*, 1997

IT IS ODD TO FIND THE CUSTOM OF THE MAY QUEEN observed in Belfast and not, so far as I know, in any rural area of Ulster. In nearly every working-class district of the city, little girls dress up in all kinds of fantastic finery and, from shortly after Easter to well on in May, they parade about the streets followed by their courts, singing, dancing and entertaining generally, and begging with shameless persistence from every passer-by. On May Eve they light bonfires in the side streets and dance around them. Last year I asked one of the queens what they did with the proceeds of their begging, and I was told that they had a magnificent party, 'cake and buns and ice-cream and oranges'.

JEANNE COOPER FOSTER, *Ulster Folklore*, 1951

ALTHOUGH LIVING ONLY TWENTY MILES FROM BELFAST, Sarah had never been in the city before. Now she sat high in the cart, turning her head from side to side as she watched the teeming crowds of oil-stained men crossing the road, some under the horse's very nose, and some waiting impatiently until the traffic slackened.

'Where would they be coming from?' she asked, her eyes wide with surprise. 'They're shipyard workers,' Hamilton explained, pointing with his whip to where a mass of slender gantries like a piece of jagged lace stood at the bottom of a hill with a sliver of grey water at their feet, 'and this is their dinner-hour.'

She stared in wonder at a woman who shot out of a low doorway, like a cork out of a bottle, with a rabble of laughing dirty children tumbling behind her on to the pavement. A man in a tweed cap stood in the doorway shouting and shaking his fist. As the woman passed close to the cart Sarah saw that she was weeping.

They passed over the bridges leading into the town and Hamilton left the horse and cart in Cromac Square. He led Sarah to the variety market where old women, surrounded by piles of bedsteads, clothes, pictures, boxes of fruit and tottering columns of books, paused only in their monotonous cries to blow on their numbed fingers. Sarah bought a lustre jug and a worn paisley shawl for her mother. When Hamilton saw her eyeing two highly glazed and warty figures of a highland girl and her lover on whose delph plaid a tartan was daubed, he fished with finger and thumb in the slit pocket close to his waistband.

They carried their purchases back to the Square and laid the figures, wrapped in straw, at the bottom of the cart. When Hamilton had shaken up the horse's nosebag they went to a little eating-house close to the markets. The warm steaming air of the place was filled with the noise of voices and the clatter of knives and forks. The heat of the food and the rank smoke of their husbands' pipes had brought a dew on the faces of the women, as they sat with their dresses open at the neck, and their thick flushed wrists, toiling away at their plates.

SAM HANNA BELL, December Bride, 1951

I CANNOT NOW ADMIT to a feeling of nostalgia for Ballymacarrett, even though when I was growing up it satisfied all my needs. For then I was hardly aware of its ugliness, its air of squalor and staleness, the sour stench from the River Lagan at low tide in summer, the acrid stench from the fertiliser factory on the Mountpottinger Road, the nauseating slime of the Connswater river meandering its way past the ropewalks towards the shipyards and Belfast Lough. I suppose a boy accepts his environment as he accepts nature; his aesthetic sense lies dormant until he is capable of making comparisons: ugliness is not ugliness until beauty has been experienced. Anyway, I felt lucky to be living in such a lively and crowded place, with contortionists and ventriloquists and knife-throwers in the Popular cinema, and cowboy films in the New Princess; even the drab Willowfield cinema on the Woodstock Road had its attraction: its one-armed guardian who waved his stick if you dared to climb out of your seat or yell at the frightening episodes of the big picture.

JOHN BOYD, The Middle of My Journey, 1990

FOR MILES ALONG THE LISBURN ROAD, thousands waited to see the Orangemen walk in procession behind elaborate banners painted with symbols of their secret society. To us Belfast boys, the Black men we looked for in the procession were not negroes, but the most respected holders of the higher rank within the hierarchy of the Order. Purple men followed them in precedence and lastly the ordinary Orangemen, all three wearing sashes coloured after their rank and bordered with a heavy gold fringe.

Everywhere orange colour flamed in sash and banner, and in the lily which people wore. They twined in bunches with sweet-williams on top of the standards, for the orange-lily was as sacred to us as the shamrock was to the Mickeys or Fenians.

> *Do you think that I would let*
> *A dirty Fenian cat*
> *Destroy the leaf of a lily-o,*
> *For there's not a flower in Ireland,*
> *Like King Billy's orange-lily-o.*

Such sights! Such music, churning the Protestant blood in our veins! For my first eight Twelfths I had needs be content with trailing through the crowds, craning for a glimpse of glory, straining to see the cymbals flashing as zing-zing-zing they crashed in a flash of sun, pushing my way through a forest of arms and legs to catch the dozens of pipe-bands, the flutists, and the drummers. The drummers came between each Lodge, flaying the hides of the big bass drums from Lambeg, where, naturally, they made the finest drums in the world. The huge cylinders were painted and decorated in gold, red, and orange with figures and patterns, crests and royal coats-of-arms in a whirligig of colour and line. It was considered a point of honour by some Lambeggers to beat the great drums so hard, and for so long, that wrists chafed the drum's edge until the skin became sore or even until cuts and bleeding resulted.

As expression of loyalty to a Protestant throne it would have been hard to find anything finer. But as music the effect was open to question. Whether of pipes or flutes or brass, or simply four of the gigantic Lambeg drums, each band felt that responsibility for the day's music rested solely, and by no means lightly, on their shoulders. Consequently they blew, blasted, and banged as heartily as wind and muscle knew how. For a single band in isolation this would have been admirable, but since one band succeeded another long before the first one was out of earshot, closely followed by yet more, and all playing different music, the total effect was overwhelming.

ROBERT HARBINSON, *No Surrender*, 1960

S HE LAY BACK, SIGHED, AND SHUT HER EYES. Now or never, said the Black Angel. He leaned over her and kissed her on the lips. Her lips parted a little and he tried to put his tongue in her mouth.

'Who taught you that?'

'Nobody. Are you going to let me kiss you, or aren't you?'

She sat up and looked around. 'Not in front of those kids.'

The two little boys had followed them down the slope. They stood about fifty yards away, silently tossing the ball to each other. Murder rose in Gavin. He jumped up and ran toward them. 'Bugger off,' he shouted. 'Bugger off, or I'll call a policeman.'

'Look who wants a polis-man,' said the bigger child. 'It's you and yon doll of yours the polis will be after.'

Riposte delivered, the boys began to retreat, throwing the ball on a longer arc, spreading out, going over the crest of the hill. They might sneak back, but he would have to risk it. He walked down toward Sally, wondering how he could begin all over again.

'I heard that,' she said. 'You shouldn't use language like that in front of kids.'

'It's the only language that sort of kid understands.'

'I still don't like it.'

He sat down beside her on the raincoat. 'I was telling you,' he said, 'that I love you.'

'So you were.'

'What's that supposed to mean?'

'Oh, nothing. You talk a lot.'

Do you hear that, said the Black Angel. All talk and no action, she means. Go on. Kiss her again. Lie on top of her.

He held her shoulders and tried to kiss her mouth, but missed and kissed the tip of her nose instead. She smiled, lay back on the raincoat, and closed her eyes. What more do you want, the Black Angel asked. He bent over, kissing her, and she kissed back, and this time she let him put his tongue in her mouth. Her suit jacket was unbuttoned and, astonished at his boldness, he put his hand inside her blouse and felt her breasts inside their brassiere. There was no resistance. Jesus, said the Black Angel, maybe this is it, this afternoon, here on Cave Hill.

She was kissing him and her hands ran up and down his spine, inside his jacket. He began to inch her skirt up over her hips and, suddenly, in a clutch of desire, saw her legs above her stocking tops and put his fingers on her soft, bare inner thigh. His heart thumped. Dizzy, he began to feel for, and find, the waistband of her knickers.

'No, Gavin.'

Pay no attention, the Black Angel advised. All girls say that, at first.

'Gavin, please.'

Go on, get them off her, the Black Angel ordered.

She pushed him. Hard. She rolled out from under him and stood, pulling down her skirt. 'What do you think I am, Gavin Burke?'

'I love you,' he said, hoarsely.

'Well, we can't. It's a mortal sin.'

'Christ.'

'You're developing a very dirty tongue in that A.R.P. job.'

'I'm sorry. I just don't think it's a sin for a person to desire another person.'

'Who said it was?'

'You did.'

'I didn't. I said it was a sin for us to do it.'

'But not a sin to feel each other up and nearly drive each other loony?'

'You started that stuff, not me. Besides, that's a sin too.'

'Oh, yes, necking's only a venial sin. Well, let me tell you something, Miss Shannon. I'm fed up with this Catholic logic of yours. I've given all that up.'

'Don't be silly, you can't give it up, you were born a Catholic and you'll die one.'

'Want to bet?'

'Yes, I do. When the time comes you'll be no different from the rest of them, you'll be calling for a priest, screaming for one. Oh, I've seen these hard chaws in the wards, they're all the same, when their time comes, it's confession and extreme unction they want, just like anyone else.'

'I won't.'

'Gavin, how do you know, you're only a boy. And speaking of sins, it's a mortal sin to deny your religion.'

'Everything's a sin to you. Do you know what you are? You're a repressed Child of Mary, that's what you are.'

'Is that so?'

You thick, said the Black Angel, now, you've done it. Insulting her, that's no way to get what you want. Kiss her at once.

'Take your hands off me.'

'I'm sorry.'

'*Sorry.* So you've given up your religion, have you? You make me laugh.'

'Tell me, Sally. Would you go on going to Mass and the sacraments if you didn't believe in them? Would that be honest?'

'I'd go and see my confessor, if I were you,' she said.

'Oh, great. What confessor? Why should I go and see a priest, when I don't believe what the priest stands for?'

'Because the priest is older than you. Because he would show you where you're wrong. Although, in your case he'd have a hard job, you're so stupid and stuck-up.'

'Thank you, Nurse Shannon.'

'Not at all. I'm going home now.'

'Ah, wait a minute, Sally, let's not fight. I love you, you know. That's what counts.'

'Yes, you love me. And when I stop you pulling my pants down, you get as cross as two sticks and start blaspheming and cursing.'

'I'm sorry. But I *don't* believe in the Church. I'm fed up with the hypocrisy of the whole damn thing.'

'Well, Gavin, *I* happen to believe in the Church. That means I don't have any common ground with would-be atheists. And I don't suppose an atheist would want to go out with the likes of me.'

'I don't suppose he would.'

'Very well then,' she said. 'That ends it, doesn't it?'

'I suppose so.'

She began to walk away, going back up the slope. Over on his left, he saw a pair of legs in short trousers sticking out from behind a whin bush. Little bastards, they came back. Forget them, White Angel counselled. Run after her, tell her you were only joking. You're not an atheist. Tell her that. Make up. Make another date.

Let her go, the little tease, the Black Angel said. Child of Mary, you were right.

She turned and looked back as she reached the stile. He began to walk toward her. He wouldn't speak to her all the way home. Blast her.

BRIAN MOORE, The Emperor of Ice-Cream, 1966

from THE LAMMAS FAIR (BELFAST)

In Smithfield as I toddled through,
The dread uproar was deavin';
Wi' tinsel'd frock, an' painted brow,
The pappit show seemed lievin'.
A bulk o' fo'k aroun' was clad,
O' a' kin's you could mention;
Tae see aul' Jerry wi' the wig,
An miter'd frocks a' dancin',
          For pense that day.

Wi' tassel'd caps an' gleamin' blades,
Wi' fifein' an' wi' drummin';
The red coat boys now on parade,
They shake the grun they're gaun on:
An' clout the sheepskin yet extends,
An' wheeper's louder blawin';
Till after them fu' mony wend,
An' some's up tae them jawin'
                   Right glib that day.

The music quats – the serjeant cries,
Big bounty don't resist it;
A jug o' punch boys, don't despise,
A soger's life's the best o't.
An' see how many blackguard rogues,
An' strappin' billies listenin';
Wi' courage bauld charm'd ower their sads,
An' cagy shillin's fistin'.
                   Wha'll rue't some day.

There sits a tinker wi' his tins,
A turner wi' his ladles;
A gleg tongu'd spunkie's cryin' spoons,
Anither's at her fables.
Billowre! a singer's come tae han',
The crowd is geather'd roun' her;
A pick-pocket them slips amang,
His booty there to plun'er
                   Wi' craft that day.

Yeir Chaeny-mem is dinglin' loud,
Her bonnie cup an' saucer;
But presently there tak's her lug,
A fist that is a fasher.
'Wad ye sell a' the day yeirsel',
An' no gie me a share o't?'
Whan turns about aul' fisty Nell,
The offender's ower wi' bare hip,
                   Clean felt that day.

On this side sits a ging'-bread Joe,
The tither a grozet barrow;
The plumbs are here – ilk black's a sloe,
Melts in yeir mouth like marrow.

This way sit barley-sugar Jones,
Across there apple factors;
The cutler wi' his wheel an' hone's,
Beside the man an' pictures;
At wark that day.

Here's yellow-man, an' tuffy sweet,
Girls will ye taste or pree it;
An aul' wife crys gaun through the street,
'Boys treat yeir sweethearts tae it.'
'Och, here's the better stuff for them,
Teetotal sure's the cordial' –
Na, na, quo' Frank, a glass o' rum
'Fore soda water's preferable
On onnie day.

ROBERT HUDDLESTON, A Collection of Poems and Songs on Rural Subjects, 1844

WHAT IRISH CAPITOL CITY (a dea o dea!) of two syllables and six letters, with a deltic origin and a nuinous end, (ah dust oh dust!) can boost of having *a*) the most extensive public park in the world, *b*) the most expensive brewing industry in the world, *c*) the most expansive peopling thoroughfare in the world, *d*) the most phillohippuc theobibbous paùpulation in the world: and harmonise your abecedeed responses?

Answer: *a*) Delfas. And when ye'll hear the gould hommers of my heart, my floxy loss, bingbanging again the ribs of yer resistance and the tender-bolts of my rivets working to your destraction ye'll be sheverin wi' all yer dinful sobs when *we'll* go riding acope-acurly, you with yer orange garland and me with my conny cordial, down the greaseways of rollicking into the waters of wetted life.

JAMES JOYCE, Finnegans Wake, 1939

GEORGE R. SIMS'S MELODRAMAS came to Belfast . . . as regularly as Benson's Shakespearean Company. I must have seen *The Lights o' London* half a dozen times, and *Two Little Vagabonds* as often. In those days, theatre-managers were generous with advertising matter. The town hoardings and shop-windows were full of coloured pictures of scenes from the plays.

My face almost went through the window of Mr Chambers's tobacconist shop at the corner of Prim Street and Albertbridge Road every Friday, the day on which the posters were changed, as I gazed intently on the vivid pictures of exciting careers that were to be seen every week at the Theatre Royal.

ST JOHN ERVINE, *Belfast Telegraph*, 1946

THE THEATRE IN BELFAST was frowned on when I was a boy, and to see a play there was regarded as a sin. My father was liberal-minded beyond most of his fellow clergy and he never objected to my going to the theatre, though he asked me to do so as unostentatiously as possible, lest I should create a scandal.

GEORGE A. BIRMINGHAM, *Pleasant Places*, 1934

IF I AM LOYAL TO THE SCHOOL and to its old blue cap, it is not only for the sake of the hours that I spent within its walls. I loved it best of all, perhaps, as a school to stay away from – a school out of which it was possible for a discreet small boy to slip between one class and another – to wander among the streets of the town or climb up to the gallery of the Theatre Royal at the Friday matinée. If it is true that the quiet blue cap has been changed to a conspicuous and tell-tale yellow-and-black cap, it will clearly be more dif-ficult in the future for youth in the grip of the *wanderlust* to go out and see the world during school hours. I have heard, however, that, for a good many years past, a guardian has stood at the gates to prevent the egress of lovers of the open air and the arts without a permit. I am myself no advocate of miching, as we used to call it. If I had a son I should be grieved to hear that he had the habit of miching. But, in fairness, I cannot speak ill of those happy occasions on which, a frightened back turned towards the school, I crept along the path towards the gates of liberty. Sometimes a boarder, with a kindred passion for the theatre, accompanied me. How conscious I was of the blazing yellowness of Billy S—'s large boots – for Billy was a dude – as we hastened to the gates, fearing every instant that a schoolmaster might look out of a window and hale us back with a shout. It was the only oc-casion of the kind on which I ran. Billy insisted on running. And, as he ran, his boots spun through the air like two dazzling suns that I was sure must be conspicuous to the neighbourhood and must send their rays reverberating through every window in the school. It was in such circumstances that I first saw 'Hamlet' and 'The Second Mrs Tanqueray' and 'The Gaiety Girl'. Had I been wearing a yellow-and-black cap, instead of that cap of modest and retiring blue, I am sure my trepidations would have been increased tenfold, and, indeed, I might scarcely have dared to approach the gates at all. Hence – if the rumour about the change of cap is true – I would appeal to the new headmaster, if it is not already too late, to spare that ancient symbol of liberty out of consideration for the feelings of the young and idle. There have been enough changes in the world recently without this. The Inst. cap should have been among the eternal things.

ROBERT LYND, *The Orange Tree*, 1926

BALLADS WERE LARGELY INVESTED IN BY THE COUNTRY PEOPLE on fair and market days. These compositions were sung or bawled out in every thoroughfare, and any important news or extraordinary event, either foreign, local, or political, was communicated to the whole country in that way. It was the custom fifty years ago for the newspapers to be carried about and left at the houses and offices for an hour's reading on payment of one penny. M'Keown, who sometimes carried them, although a man of no education, had the gift of rhyming, and he could improvise four lines or so caricaturing any person in a style that was most amusing. He had a decided squint, and would keep scanning the person from head to foot while he composed the verses. Whilst we had our street celebrities, we had, in addition, a number of distinguished eccentric characters. Wm Dalway would distribute cakes and oranges, whilst 'Dr' M'Donald cleared the footway with his stick. Count Mahogany and P. M'Brennan attracted attention at all times. The former was a most foppishly dressed cabinetmaker, who wrought only three days in the week, and the latter kept a public house in Caddles Entry. He was extremely peculiar in his habits, so much so that if he had only to go to Mr Stewart's, in Legg's Lane – the next entry – he must dress in his best for the occasion, from shining castor hat to polished top boots; while, full of self complacency, he must salute every person he met.

THOMAS GAFFIKEN, *Belfast Fifty Years Ago*, 1894

from THE NORTHERN ATHENS: A SATIRICAL POEM

O rare delight, and *iligant* as rare,
As e'er distinguish'd land or featur'd age,
The motley wonders of a SMITHFIELD FAIR,
Where lions, bears, and hideous monsters rage,
Howling loud serenades from cage to cage:
Its laughter-scenes are more than Mirth can bear,
Infusing joy in devil, saint, or sage,
Who scratch their wigs, and fling to winds their care:
Here PAT, with cudgel tuck'd beneath his arm,
Halloos, and pulls his SHEELAH thro' the throng,
His sapling ready on the least alarm,
Love in his heart, and brogue upon his tongue –

Och! PAT or BARNEY are the broths of boys
To brain a PEELER, and to screech their joys.

VANITY FAIR, of which JOHN BUNYAN tells,
Ne'er equall'd jovial SMITHFIELD'S ranting sight,
Where matchless Folly shakes his cap and bells,
And every right is wrong, and wrong is right; –
Poteen each heart to fire and fury swells,
And Reason fuddles out her senses quite,
Whilst Caution mutinies, and Grace rebels,
And roar through all the *Fair* with all their might.
Here meets the Parliament of motley wares
E'er heard, nor never heard of, in one spot –
Tripe, nightcaps, poultry, grindstones, *easy* chairs,
Pigs, pincers, and canaries sold or bought;
Heartsease for hen-peck'd husbands; for their dears,
Rings for their tongues as well as for their ears.

Old metal, and much older rags are rang'd,
For tinkers', prigs, and Gemmen's gemmen's use,
Brimstone for naughty curs and pedlars mang'd
Gridirons, too, to *do* WILL COBBET'S *goose*,
New china vended, or for crack'd exchang'd,
Loose habits for *old rogues* on town let loose,
A horse to *find*, and eke to *find* – a noose.
Crowds pass on crowds, and vanish as they pass,
Whether of human shapes, or shapes of swine,
Like MIRZA'S wanderers, in far, lengthening line –
Or group'd – as in kaleidoscopic glass
We view the motly, varying figures shine; –
All, all in SMITHFIELD be, from West or East,
Like HELIOGABALUS' seventy-dished feast.

ANONYMOUS, 1826

CHILDREN SECRETLY LOVE the man who comes roaring up the street,
with his handcart of cast-off clothes and bones and bottles and empty
jam-pots. They adore him because of the cord cage, suspended from a pole
above the cart, in which glistening balloons in bondage sway and flutter and
rush all of a heap to one side, as though they were determined to free
themselves.

He is willing to exchange these air-balls for the horrible things with which
he likes to fill his cart; or if offered a penny he will yield a balloon without

demanding a boiled bone or a jam-pot. He is very obliging and very noisy, and altogether a very wonderful person.

HERBERT MOORE PIM, *Unknown Immortals*, 1917

THE RAGMAN

Rattle, rattle over the stones,
Rags and bones, rags and bones;
Blue balloons, and a dirty old man
Who never was washed since time began.

Round and round, and to and fro,
And up and down the whirligigs go;
And the blue-skinned bubbles fuss and fret
For lack of room in the ragman's net.

JOSEPH CAMPBELL, *The Poems of Joseph Campbell*, 1963

OLD BELFAST STREET CRIES have no echo to-day. Once the air resounded with 'Fresh cockles'; 'Any wash-tub hoops' on washing-day when housewives plied wash-tubs and scrubbing-boards, and 'Knives-scissors-razors to grind' from the itinerant who plied his whirring wheel, with its flying sparks.

T.J. CAMPBELL, *Fifty Years of Ulster 1890–1940*, 1941

'ANY OUL' REGS, BONES or battles,' he shouted hoarsely, as he led his donkey along the street. His small cart was piled with old clothes of all varieties and colours. Bones and bottles rested in a box at the back of the cart, partly covered by some of the rags. The little cart with its metal-rimmed wheels rattled over the street, lending a characteristic background noise to that hoarse voice. The rags, I was told, were used to make paper, the glass, naturally, was melted down, and the bones were used to make glue. Recycling in the twenties!

In another street, a man with a steamy cart would be shouting 'Fresh coal breek! Coal breek! Fresh coal breek!' The bricks – steaming cubes of compressed coal dust about six inches square – were a popular cheap form of heating at the time.

'Any oul' raws! Any oul' raws! Any oul' raws!' – that was the skin man, or refuse collector. Usually this character would be pushing a handcart, and his quest was for potato peelings and kitchen waste to be used for feeding pigs.

'Herns alive! Herns alive!' shouted the fish man. The herrings, in fact, were not alive. He was merely trying to emphasise the freshness of his 'Ardglass herns'.

'Sharpen yer knives! Sharpen yer knives! Any scissors, any scissors!' – that was the knife grinder on his bicycle-cum-grinding-machine, a Heath Robinson contraption which he pushed around. The bicycle had a wooden framework that housed sandstones, and once he propped the machine up, he would take to his saddle and pedal furiously, setting the sandstones in motion. Sparks would fly as he expertly ground the housewives' tired equipment into keen and potentially lethal weapons.

There was one character who wheeled a handcart with a superstructure in the form of a roof and four uprights, one at each corner of his cart. Balloons, red and white striped sticks with coloured paper streamers attached, and windmills – star-shaped pieces of celluloid on sticks – decorated his cart. It was generally well filled with jam jars at the end of the journey, and its adornments were depleted or completely gone, having been handed over to children in exchange for jars.

ROWEL FRIERS, *Drawn from Life*, 1994

NARRATOR:

Our house stood on a sandy ridge overlooking the river valley. High up in the back gable, at the end of the corridor, there was the 'Return Room'. It led nowhere but back again; a dead-end room, kept for visitors. But from the window I could see across the city. Goat's tow of a city that leaped from gutters to gantries at one go. City with the brick-red face and the bowler hat of smoke. City of ships and shawlies, doles and doyleys –

BELFAST MAN:

Ah sure, isn't it all a jar of worms anyway . . .

NARRATOR:

From the backstreet far below me came the grasshopper chirp of the blacksmith's anvil. I could see Mary Marley, the ragwoman, pushing her handcart of crockery.

MARY MARLEY

(*on echo*) New delph! New delph! Any ould rags? New delph!

NARRATOR:

Behind her walked the black man with his brush –

SWEEP:

Sweep! Sweep! Sweep!

(Empty tin kicked across cobbles.)

And shining like a shilling in a sweep's hand the empty tin went clattering across the cobblestones, scandalising my mother.

MOTHER:

I'll warrant you it's that hooligan Mickey Clark. If he's not cloddin' things he's kickin' them. It's a wonder his people wouldn't think shame, and him scouring the streets from dawn till dark. Never in the house for a minute.

W.R. RODGERS, The Return Room, 1955

THERE IS NO DOUBT that the great attraction to the Easter Monday crowd of visitors was the Mummy, which they seemed never tired of inspecting. Some history of a specimen so famous among the Belfast artisans and their families may not be out of place here.

The first mummy received by the Society for the Museum was presented by Thomas Gregg (of Ballymenoch), and was procured by him during a visit to Egypt, whence he paid the cost of its transit to Belfast. There was considerable excitement among the members when it was known that the mummy had reached Liverpool

The mummy was unrolled on 27th January, 1835, at a special meeting in the upper room of the Museum. Campbell, the teacher of painting, who had a studio in Fountain Street, made a colour sketch of the mummy when the lid of the coffin was removed, and during the unrolling members of the Society took notes of the observations made at each successive step. The hieroglyphic characters were deciphered and interpreted by the Rev Dr Edward Hincks, who was a brilliant Orientalist. Indeed, recent scholars have recognised him as the first to employ the true method for decipherment of the cuneiform inscription.

From the history of the deceased, as inscribed upon the case, it appears that it was the mummy of a woman, named 'Kabooti', and that she was a daughter of a priest of Ammon. The date was considered to be about 500 BC. On Friday, 30th January, 1835, an advertisement appeared in the local newspapers as follows: – 'The Egyptian mummy unrolled in the Belfast Museum on Tuesday last may be seen in its present state to-morrow, Saturday, the 31st, and on Monday the 2nd, Wednesday the 4th, and Friday the 6th February. The bandages will then be replaced with the exception of the head and feet, and the mummy will remain for exhibition in the large room in which the collection is at present arranged. Admittance to non-subscribers, one shilling'. (Signed by) R.S. MacAdam, James D. Marshal, M.D., Secretaries.

A series of papers dealing with the various questions raised by the discoveries made during the unrolling were read on 4th March, 1835.

William Webb dealt with the 'cloth enveloping the mummy', for which investigation he was singularly well qualified. Robert Patterson and George C. Hyndman spoke on the 'Insects discovered in unrolling'; Edmund Getty, 'Introductory remarks and description of the Hieroglyphics', William Thompson and Dr J.D. Marshall on the 'Dentition and anatomical state of the body'; Professor Stevely on 'Aromatics and mode of embalming'; William Patterson on the 'Colours used in the case of the mummy'; while Connery dealt with the 'Workmanship of the case'.

Other mummies were at later dates added to the collection. In 1841 John Charley was bringing home a mummy to present to the Museum, when the boat carrying it was upset on the Nile. The mummy was so injured that it was useless, but the case was brought to Belfast and presented to the society.

Belfast Natural History and Philisophical Society Centenary Volume 1821–1921, 1924

L ONG AGO, IN THE STREETS AT HOME, we had thrashed out the complete process of reproduction, and by now were on familiar terms with it. We used our talk about it simply because we knew, for unimaginable reasons, that grown-ups became embarrassed whenever sex was mentioned. In our own house, we were forbidden to raise the topic even though grass-widows, 'big diddies', hairy chests, and the forms of Mae West, entwined themselves in ordinary conversation. When tempers frayed, the coarse words making references to fornication or sexual organs were freely bandied and reverberated in no uncertain manner between the walls overloaded with sacred writings. Still, we might not raise the serpent's head in the normal course of speaking.

ROBERT HARBINSON, *No Surrender*, 1960

S EX PLAYED A SUBTERRANEAN PART IN THE LIFE OF INST. during the years I was there. Emotional friendships between younger and older boys were common but these affairs were, I imagine, nearly all natural to adolescence. At thirteen or fourteen I experienced two emotional affairs. For some months I worshipped from afar a dark-haired pudgy boy called Savage who spent his early mornings playing handball but not, alas, with me. My role was that of a morose spectator, too shy to participate in the game. Morning after morning I rose early and cycled to school for the sole purpose of mutely admiring my favourite at play. To my fervid imagination he possessed all sorts of virtues, and my joy would have been immeasurable if he had recognised my presence and invited me to become his partner and his friend. But I'd no such good fortune: I was ignored. Not a single glance from him fell in my direction, until a year later when he sat beside me in an English class and began chatting to me. My delight turned out to be short-lived. To my dismay I became aware that Savage had a pimply complexion, a rasping voice and ugly fat knees. When he begged me to help him with his homework I discovered he was both lazy and stupid. In short, he bored me and I changed my desk to get away from him.

My second affair was equally disastrous and even more mawkish. I was attracted to a slightly younger boy appropriately enough called Kidd who, because we lived in the same direction of the city, cycled across the Albert Bridge with me. For some reason I've forgotten, I nicknamed him 'Tinkerbell' and those journeys homewards with the wind in our hair and our caps stuffed in our pockets were, for me, pure bliss. Then, after a couple of ecstatic months, these same journeys turned dull and I no longer looked forward to them. Instead girls began to attract me. The problem was of course getting to know them at close hand as it were; to explore the mystery.

There was no mystery about boys; for after rugby games we all stood naked, flipping wet towels at one another, comparing our genitals and laughing at obscene jokes which we all thought to be excruciatingly funny. I remember one pale-faced youth with an aquiline nose and a sly manner who boasted of the sexual conquests he made every Friday evening. He played centre threequarters in the first fifteen, and when he performed poorly during the Saturday game we attributed his failure to his debilitating exertions of the evening before. But as he usually played well – else he wouldn't have retained his place – we always cast doubt on his tales. 'Oh well, you needn't believe me,' he would remark, with a wink and sly look. 'But if I didn't go out with women on a Friday night I'd play like an international. Instead I turn up like a wet rag – no spunk in me at all.' We half-believed him, we envied him, and we implored him to keep off his wild women before any of our important Schools' Cup matches. Probably he was a virgin, but certainly he had a good imagination.

JOHN BOYD, Out of My Class, 1985

THE EARLIEST RECORD I CAN FIND of cricket being played in Belfast is 1840, when the Belfast Cricket Club occupied a pitch somewhere convenient to what is now the Corporation Electricity Offices, at Laganbank Road.

The club was established 'for the purpose of affording young men an opportunity of partaking in the healthful, noble game of cricket'. The club consisted of ordinary and honorary members, who met 'for exercise' on Monday, Wednesday, Thursday and Friday evenings, and on Tuesday, Thursday and Saturday mornings – at 6 a.m.

Among the patrons were the Marquis of Donegall, Lord Lurgan, and R.B. Blakiston-Houston. Members wore flat-topped hats at practice and top-hats at matches.

Nearest record to the above, so far as I can discover, is a cricket club established at Ormeau in 1858. The members possessed a clubhouse at that time, and the pitch was probably that on which North of Ireland Cricket Club began to function, because in 1861 there is no doubt that North had commenced a career which continues till the present day.

Later – I think round about the '70s – Cliftonville Cricket Club secured a pitch in that district and the game really began to take root in Belfast.

THOMAS CARNDUFF (1954), *Life and Writings*, 1994

IN THE 70S, AGAIN, THERE WAS A RAGE FOR LAWN TENNIS, which was, perhaps, the first active game in which girls met men on equal terms, and if it has done nought else, it has added considerably to the average girl's height, and in due time fitted her to take advantage of the bicycle. When a Belfast man invented the pneumatic tyre, the bicycle became a necessity to woman as well as to man; and the two-wheeled carriage has created quite a revolution! How many it has allowed to view the country, and get a sniff of the sea! The simply-driven 'bike' was the forerunner of the modern motor, which can do its mile a minute, and requires legislation to limit its speed to 20 miles an hour. Pioneers of Railways (in their evidence before the House of Commons early in the last century) only asked for leave to run a train at five miles an hour, and thought that perhaps it might even go twelve with little danger on a well-laid railway line.

Not very many years ago the News Room was the centre of business activity in Belfast, and many thought, from its position at the junction of Donegall Street, Waring Street, Rosemary Street and Bridge Street, that it would retain its premier position for all time. Indeed, so rooted was that opinion that the three local banks built their head offices in the district.

The change of centre came with the trams. On their first introduction they ran from the Botanic Gardens to High Street, and thence through the then crowded Bridge Street to the Antrim Road. It was when the old Hercules Street was wiped out by the opening of Royal Avenue, and the trams were run through the new route and in other directions, that the centre moved at once to Castle Junction and Donegall Place, and now the old business part of the town is neglected. The removal of the municipal offices, and the building of bank and insurance offices around the City Hall, all point to non-disturbance of the present centre for many years to come.

Time was when many merchants lived right in the heart of the town, and within walking distance of their places of business. The trams have changed it all and have killed the old town life and the enjoyable sociable evenings of 30 years ago. Over Wellington Place, Fisherwick Place, College Square

North, Great Victoria Street and many other residential quarters of the 70s, 'Ichabod' is written, for the inhabitants have migrated to the suburbs.

ROBERT YOUNG, *Belfast and the Province of Ulster in the Twentieth Century*, 1909

THE GREAT SPORT IN BELFAST is, of course, association football. Every year the football season seems to end later and begin earlier, and one wonders if it may not presently catch up on its own tail. Cricket does not get very much chance in Ulster, the climate not suiting it quite so well as in southern England; and in Ulster it is an amateur game, for players rather than spectators. Nevertheless, when Ulstermen get down to a game of cricket they play it with determination. I remember passing Cliftonville Cricket Ground one late summer evening and finding that a match was in progress between Woodvale and North Down for the final of the Senior Cup. For six weeks after that I continued to pass at intervals and found that the same match was still being fought out. Rugby football is also popular as a middle-class game and is played in the secondary schools. Since it is a game which gives its victories mainly to those with weight and muscles, the matches are usually won by the schools which have the largest numbers of big and brawny boys on their rolls; and when I was at school I used to propound the black but not wholly unacceptable heresy that the lighter and more open association game was better suited to young people, particularly for competitive purposes among schools of different sizes. Some good hockey is also played in the province, and tennis in due season. Golf, too, has a wide appeal, for it is not the costly game that it is in the London area where links are available only at a high rent, and it can be enjoyed in Ulster as generally as it is in parts of Scotland. On the other hand, the game was introduced to Ulster relatively late, the first course being laid out at the Kinnegar, near Holywood, in the early 1880s.

HUGH SHEARMAN, *Ulster*, 1949

IT WAS IN THE UNITED KINGDOM, during the preparation of his division for the Overlord invasion, that Owen discovered the value of his new-found beauty in the exchange of sexual pleasures. Having reached his twenty-first birthday, which occurred on shipboard, without having had as much as a social engagement alone with a girl, he learned in Northern Ireland that it was possible for an eager student to master the preliminary curriculum in a single lesson. Not even his first instructress, the daintily aggressive daughter of a Queen's University theologian, suspected his inexperience; she mistook his diffident approach for an unwonted fastidiousness and accepted his final capitulation as a high tribute to her charms.

This initial relationship was the longest and, toward the end, the most troublesome of his amatory adventures on foreign soil. Confusing novelty with uniqueness, he was heavily committed by the time the reaction against premature monogyny set in. Fortunately, in the course of an ominously formal visit to the young lady's home, he was able to stimulate a current of doctrinal dispute with her father regarding the function of the Holy Ghost in the Trinity. It was not an issue on which Owen had any profound conviction but he chose to disagree so doggedly that the theologian ordered him from the house.

RING LARDNER JR, *The Ecstasy of Owen Muir*, 1954

DRUMMOND ALLISON 1921–43
Killed in action on the Garigliano, 2nd December 1943

Your voice is with me now.
Its confident Home Counties tone
Sounds across a fifty-year divide.
Your khaki figure walks a Belfast street
Intent on jaunt and enterprise.
We weave among the statues round the City Hall
Then ride east across the Albert Bridge.
Laughs fall like coins into the Lagan.
You talk of Keyes and John Heath-Stubbs,
Your Oxford friends – Keyes marked for death –
Of girls you lusted for in vain.
We spend an evening at the Opera House
Then sink young men's despair in pints
Of collared Guinness at 'The Crown'.

ROBERT GREACEN, *Collected Poems 1944–1994*, 1995

HE WAS TO TAKE HER UP MALONE; she had never been there, and it would be all new and beautiful. They were to drive to Shaw's Bridge, then walk back by the edge of the River Lagan; it was the prettiest outskirt of the city, the water was so limpid and calm, the little sculls and canoes floated by without a quiver. Then they could have curds and cream at Molly Ward's Locks, the car meeting them again at Stranmillis, and it would be a delightful, happy time.

AGNES BOLES, *The Belfast Boy*, 1912

W HEN THEY BUILT THE RITZ CINEMA, on the corner of the Grosvenor
Road and Fisherwick Place, it was acclaimed as the last word in
super-cinemas. It was big but I would never have considered it super. I
think Belfast's greatest cinema was the Classic in Castle Lane. To go to the
Classic was to feel you were doing yourself proud; it had all the hallmarks of
class. Its deep carpeting and classical design were richly extravagant, from
bas-reliefs to the heavily ornamental double curtains. It seemed to ooze
opulence, and a blissful contentment automatically followed.

ROWEL FRIERS, *Drawn from Life*, 1994

T HE BOYS OF BIGOTSBOROUGH were sorely beset by the irresistible
temptations of the docks, which were always crowded with ships of all
shapes and sizes from all parts of the world, great four-masters, brigs, and
barques, and barquentines, with strange figure-heads, and innumerable
tarry smells. There were to be seen sailors of every race from every port in
the seven seas – real sailors with real clasp-knives at their waists, real earrings
in their ears, and real quids in their mouths, negroes with shiny black faces,
Chinese cooks, mahogany-faced Lascars, fair-headed Swedes, and Scotch
engineers. What boy could hold out against these delights? Gaby felt the
dreadful bliss of temptation when Bob proposed to him one morning that
they should 'mitch'. The pleasure of 'mitching' was too sweet to be rejected,
and so Gaby, with the thrill of fear which is the chief grace of wrong-doing,
went a-mitching. The boys found the sailors very companionable, and they
were pale with rapture when one of Bob's briny friends showed them the
wonderful sight of a real fo'c'sle. They gazed on real sea-chests and real
bunks. They watched the cook peeling potatoes in the galley, and they
trembled with ecstasy when the bo'sun allowed them to blow his brass
whistle. It was a great moment when Gaby felt his feet on the ratlins and
actually touched a yard-arm, while the salt wind sang in the shrouds and
the sea-gulls whirred past his head.

Then there was a deliciously rickety bridge over the entrance to a dock,
which consisted of two frail planks with a perilous hand-rope. Here the boys
tasted the dainty of danger until a dock constable in a blue coat with brass
buttons drove them away. Then they went to the Hailing-house, and
watched the ships coming in, and heard the customs officer's challenge and
the captain's reply. There was a large timber dock containing hundreds of
logs chained together. It was pleasant to court death by drowning on these
slimy and slippery balks and beams. When these excitements palled, the boys
found a new delight at 'The Twins', two islands on which were established
two great shipbuilding yards, sonorous from dawn till dusk with
multitudinous clangings of steel and iron. Against the sky rose gigantic
gantries like aerial bridges, and the huge hulls of vessels in every stage of

growth. White Star leviathans lay like reticulated mountains, with hundreds of workmen crawling over their ribs like flies, and a tumult of industry rising out of their intestines. The boys watched the busy steam ferry darting to and fro, the pilots sailing out to meet an incoming ship, the steam dredger with its endless chain of buckets that came up from the bottom of the Channel full of liquid mud, emptied it into the hold, and went down again in quest of more mire with an insatiable appetite. By this time the sun had grown very hot, and Bob suggested that they should go to The Point and bathe. Gaby welcomed the proposal, and the boys hastened past the whitewashed fever huts to the end of the long narrow tongue of land. There they stripped and plunged into the sea that was breaking into spray against the shelving stony beach. After the bathe they ate their slices of bread and jam, and began to wonder whether it was near the end of school time. A man who was spearing eels told them that it was nearly three, so they hurried home – reluctantly leaving the enchanted shore. On the road Bob declared that he intended to try his luck as a stowaway.

JAMES DOUGLAS, *The Unpardonable Sin*, 1907

I WAS ONE OF A FAMILY OF THIRTEEN, and after I had spent a few years in Matilda Street we removed to 24 Gaffikin Street, I suppose to get close to the tram depot and to [my father's] work. It was during the time we lived here that I spent my time amongst the horses and the strappers who looked after the horses who were taken to Shaftesbury Square to be changed. I spent my happy years until I reached the age of seven [in 1891] when my father got me engaged as a point-shifter. My elder brother had been taken on as a trace-boy. Ma Black's pub in Gaffikin Street was the local for tram men. There was a large room at the back with a fire and tram men finishing at night were admitted even after closing time which was 11 p.m. I collected many pennies from the tram men and I used to be scared when I heard a tram man who had taken one over the eight cursing the manager because he had received a sentence from Nance for something he had done during his working hours. When I told my mother she used to tell me not to repeat it as the man was drunk.

We moved from Gaffikin to Teutonic Street which was being built with a water closet, something new to the working class, and it was during the time I was living here that the education act was passed. Up to this children were free to attend school or stay away. This act meant that my job as point-shifter was finished. I had made up my mind with other boys not to go as we had been told how masters used the cane for punishment. My father who could not read or write selected the Blackstaff National School, Ennis Place, for me, and the night before a number of us agreed to meet in the Bog Meadows instead. We carried out our intentions but each day our numbers dwindled until I and another boy were the only two left. I was always in bed every night when my father finished work but the School Inspector stopped my career of freedom. When I arrived home one evening he was waiting for me, and the threat of telling my father if I did not enrol the following day was sufficient.

The master of this school put fear into every scholar. We were all boys and he certainly taught us, for he used his cane. I remember pleading with my mother to allow me to stay at home on one occasion. She went out as I thought to do her shopping but she arrived back with the master. I felt the weight of his cane when I got to school. He would make the strongest boy carry the defaulter on his back whilst he followed up with the cane.

Scholars were compelled to bring a large piece of coal every Monday morning for the purpose of warming the school during the week. The master had to see each piece before you placed it with the rest. If it was a small piece you were sent back home for a larger piece. Many plans were adopted to get a larger piece. A boy would follow a bellman until he stopped at a house to deliver a bag. As soon as he entered the house with his bag of coal the boy jumped the cart or van and exchanged his small piece of coal for a larger one.

ROBERT MCELBOROUGH, *The Autobiography of a Belfast Working Man*, 1974

THE CRUISE OF THE CALIBAR

Come all ye dry-land sailors and listen to me song,
'Tis only forty verses so I won't detain yis long.
'Tis all about the adventiures of this here Lisburn tar
And how I sailed before the mast on board the *Calibar*.

The *Calibar* was a bonny ship, well-fastened fore and aft,
Her bow stuck out a mile in front and the tiller was a bloody great shaft;
With half a gale to fill her sail she did one knot per hour –
She was the fastest ship on the Lagan Canal and only the one horse-power.

The Captain to me says he to me says he to me says he,
'So you want to be a sailor and sail the ragin' sea?
You want to be a sailor, the ragin' seas to roll?
Well we're under orders for Portadown with half a ton of coal.'

On Monday morning we set sail, the weather being sublime,
And passing under the ould Queen's Bridge we heard the Albert chime,
But going through the Gasworks Strait, a very dangerous part,
We ran head on to a lump of coal that wasn't marked down in the chart.

Then all became confusion, the stormy winds did blow,
The mate slipped on a banana peel and fell into the hould below.
'More steam, more steam,' the Captain cried, 'for we are sorely pressed!'
But the Engineer on the bank replied, 'Sure the ould horse is doin' his best!'

We all fell into the water and let out a terrible roar.
A farmer threw us his galluses and hauled us in to shore.
No more I'll be a sailor to sail the raging main,
And if ever I go to Portadown, bejasus I'll go by train.

ANONYMOUS

TOWARDS THE END OF THAT SUMMER when the holidays were nearly over Colm, Jamesy, and Clare went with their mother on the last excursion of the season to Bangor. It, too, was on a Sunday. Crowds of people waved the boat off as she swung out from the wooden pier, and sailed down the lough. Behind, the boat left a suddy path in the water; gulls' shadows skimmed across the deck; and far away now, tiny trams were sliding over Queen's Bridge.

The city lay spread out in a loop, Cave Hill and the Divis range at one side, and the field-patterned Castlereagh Hills at the other; and because it was Sunday there was little smoke from the tall factory chimneys, but below in a blue haze stretched parallel rows of red-bricked houses choking each other for space. High up on the slope of the Black Mountain Colm pointed out to Jamesy where Toneroy lay; and then as the boat passed the shipyards with the skeletons of ships seen through a net of scaffolding, they began to play hide-and-go-seek with Clare, and sometimes for devilment shouted down the ventilators. Then they lifted Clare in their arms to see the terrifying splendour of the ship's engine, but the stuffy smell of heat and oil dizzied her head and she went and sat beside her mother, running a finger over her plush coat, making dark wavy lines on the velvety surface, and smoothing them out again to see the lines mysteriously vanish.

MICHAEL McLAVERTY, Call My Brother Back, 1939

THE FREQUENTERS OF THE SPINNERS HALL, it seemed, were well known here. The boss, polishing a glass behind the counter, nodded affably. A daft lot of characters, he agreed with the wife, but not to be sneezed at when it came to the custom of a back-street pub. And well behaved. They spent that much time arguing and drinking they had no breath left for singing and that kept the peelers away. 'And some good heads there. Educated men, if you cared to listen. I could go a bit of the way with some of those fellas,' he told the wife. So as Mr McFall led his friends into a snug the boss came round personally to take their order.

The air was full of the smells of cheap wines, greyhounds, porter, working clothes, whiskey, varnished timber. One sniff and Mr McFall was exhilarated. He ran a glowing eye round the snug table. 'Catholic, Jew and Protestant met in sociable intercourse. In our banausic society a refinement permitted only to minorities – the moneyed and the emancipated.' He waved a hand to the boss. 'Three pints, a black spool and a ball o' malt, Edmund, at your kind convenience.' The little man sobered. 'B'God, I'm glad that fella of mine didn't get bashed tonight!'

'Yah,' said Brendan examining his fist, 'and who would bash him? Sure there's nobody in that lot fit to punch his way out of a wet paper bag.'

SAM HANNA BELL, *The Hollow Ball*, 1961

M ANY A TIME I RODE TO THE LOUGH OVER THE MOUNTAINS, pushing slowly up the long winding slope overlooking Belfast Lough – a marvellous view – then rushing down the long road to the lough. One night – it was during 'the troubles' – my friend and I miscalculated the time necessary for the return journey and found ourselves coming down the road into Belfast after 'curfew'. This curfew order made it an offence to be out of doors within the city boundaries after eleven o'clock. Anybody found in the streets was liable to be picked up in an armoured car and kept for the night, if not longer, in the cells. Indeed, there was always the danger of the police shooting at sight. Hot and tired as we were after our long uphill grind we debated anxiously whether we should take the risk of riding two miles through the forbidden streets in order to get home. As the alternative was a very unpleasant night out on the hill-side we took the chance and managed to reach home unseen. The suspense of that stealthy ride is fresh in my memory still. Amidst such prohibitions, excitements, and difficulties did I gain my acquaintance with the birds and flowers of the lough.

EDWARD ALLWORTHY ARMSTRONG, *Birds of the Grey Wind*, 1940

W HEN I RETURN FROM TIME TO TIME to the damp Belfast streets of childhood, youth and early manhood, they no longer glitter like patent leather. They are sleazier, more littered. The lights are less bright. All changed, if not changed utterly. And not just because of the 'Troubles', which have brought destruction and tragedies too frequent to record to Belfast and the north of Ireland. Even before the latest outbreak of civil strife, the process of change was well under way – flyovers, blocks of flats, new hotels, high rises, fast food, Chinese restaurants. Even so, many of the old buildings still remain intact if put to different uses. My aunts' newsagent's shop on the Stranmillis Road is still a newsagency.

The vivid faces of the generation before mine have all gone – Mother, Father, Aunt Tillie, Uncle George, Tommy Gibson. All dead as, indeed, are some of my contemporaries, one or two of them younger than myself. I walk, a kind of exile, in a city of ghosts. As my late friend, the poet and writer, Clifford Dyment, put it:

> The end is death!
> I cry in terror.
> In the end, death,
> Agrees the mirror.

Ghosts – and memories. An image that comes to mind is of a doorway in Royal Avenue, a short distance from the Grand Central Hotel. It was a war-time evening, with army officers and their girlfriends coming and going to and from the hotel. I had been bored and depressed. Life seemed to consist wholly of blackout and drizzle. I went into a scruffy, ill-lit café somewhere around Rosemary Street. There I got into a bantering conversation with a buxom, dark-skinned girl called Peggy who wore gypsy earrings and had been unsparing in the use of powder and rouge. She spoke in that harsh type of local accent that lends itself to easy mimicry and laughter. I felt we could continue our conversation in a less oppressive atmosphere.

'Would you like a drink?' I asked, a trifle apprehensively, for I carried in my mind the idea of the Demon Drink.

'Well, I've never had one before, but I don't mind if you don't mind.' We went out into the drizzle and searched for a bar.

For a girl who had never had a drink before, Peggy showed a remarkable capacity as a learner. She consumed several gin-and-limes with consummate ease. I drank a couple of bottles of Guinness and felt well on the way down the slippery path. The dark brew went slightly to my head. Peggy told me about her dear old granny up the Crumlin Road and how careful she had to be 'with all them Yank soldiers about'. She surprised me by telling me she hated the police. This, in our small, in-grown community, signalled the fact that Peggy did not belong to my own tribe.

After our drinks we went out and, without speaking, looked for a door-way around Smithfield. The streets were unpeopled in the black night, all solid citizens were at home listening to the radio and drinking cocoa. Peggy kissed me with abandon and pulled me vigorously towards her.

ROBERT GREACEN, *The Sash My Father Wore*, 1997

from THE BELFAST COCKABENDY

You lads and lasses brisk and gay
I pray you pay attention
And listen now to what I'll say
Perhaps some things I'll mention
Which may your jealousy provoke
Or else 'twill please your fancy
We will pass it over as a joke
And I will kiss my Nancy.

When you come to Belfast town
Come not without some shillings
And you had better bring a pound
To make the lasses willing
Then if you wish a bit of fish
Go take a drop of brandy
And if you choose they'll not refuse
To play up cockabendy.

As I was walking up North Street
I being in good apparel
I on the way did chance to meet
A smiling pretty girl
Straight to a dram shop then we went
To take a drop of brandy
And home we went with one consent
To play up cockabendy.

ANONYMOUS

THE BASEMENT FLAT WAS dark and silent as the house above it. He put the hall light on and hurried ahead of her, wondering if the place was tidy. What a fool he had been to bring her; the flat was shabby, disgraceful, it gave the lie to his new clothes, to the wine he had ordered with dinner, to all his efforts to be gay and smart. Once he put the lights on in his den, he would lose her respect. It was like an old pensioner's place: a disgrace. He was too ashamed even to make an excuse for it. He took her coat and hung it on the hall stand. He heard her go into his den. Where the hell were the glasses? And how much gin was left in that bottle he bought last Christmas? He found the bottle and two small glasses and hurried in after her. She was standing by the dying fire, looking at his photograph collection.

'Is that you?' she asked, pointing to a dark young man with a tennis racket.

'No, Mick Hanratty his name is. That's me over there.'

'Oh, with the glasses. Yes.'

There was one decent chair and, God knows, it was not decent either. He swept it clear of magazines and newspapers before offering it. The place was filthy, filthy, he realised. But she did not seem to notice. She refused the armchair and sat on the rug by the fire. As she settled, her skirt lifted with a soft puff, rising above her knees. Mr Devine looked away. He had some orange crush somewhere, sticky, unused and warm. He put some gin in the glasses and made two gin and orange drinks.

BRIAN MOORE, The Feast of Lupercal, 1958

THEY WALKED DOWN THE ROAD AGAIN and entered the narrower channel of Sandy Row, a twin line of red houses undulating inexorably as a sine-curve traced in brick. A short way down it, to the right, Harbinson led the way through an anonymous door into a concrete-floored room with a solid wood partition down one side; the wood was pierced by three small windows with apron counters, along which a couple of shuffling men in cloth caps were even now sliding their silver and coppers. Half-hidden clerks passed them betting slips in exchange. The other walls were covered with sporting papers: the racing page from every publication imaginable, all giving volumes of advice as to what to back that day. 'THERSITES AT SANDOWN' claimed one. Another announced: 'THE SCOUT SAYS PILLOW TALK'. A third 'TWINKLE TOES FOR KEMPTON'. Colin thought: The astonishing names that men give horses!

Most of the papers had complicated tables, in which several tipsters gave their selections. In this way the reader could see at a glance what the experts, singly and collectively, thought of the prospects for each event. In some races all said the same, but in most there was wild disagreement. It was clear why the bookmaker, not the punter, was in business.

'What a place!' he said. 'I didn't even know it was here. There's only that boarded-up shop front outside.'

Harbinson, from one of the small windows where he was waiting to receive his docket, said: 'That's the beauty of this city. You can get anything you want or do anything you want. Only you have to be in the know.'

'What have you put your money on?'

'Nothing the tipsters give, you can bet. A nag called April Shower. I know a man who's married to the jockey's sister. It had better win. I'm down over a quid today already.'

Colin looked at his watch: three minutes to five. The beer sang gently in him. 'When will you know?'

'Straight away. They have a line through to most of the courses. Anyway this one is being televised.'

While they waited, Colin looked round at some of the people in the shop. There were perhaps ten or twelve of them now, all men. Some were young and yellow-faced, with pimply chins and slicked-down hair; they were discontented and shifty-looking, members of that depressed class of small clerks and counter-hoppers that clings to the underside of the bourgeoisie. Others were big, florid-faced men with fat cheeks and loud laughs, who had an air of black dustiness about them as though they were all coal-heavers: perhaps they *were* all coalheavers. And beside these were the hangers-on, the old broken-down men, their ancient clothes green with age and dirt, their whole bodies radiating senility and grime. They had battered hats and bleary eyes, their hands trembled as they turned the pages of the sporting papers, and they had no money to bet with. They were destitute, utterly destitute; they came here because they had nowhere else to go, nowhere else they knew well enough, not even the public park. God alone knew how they ate or where they found a bed.

'There it goes!' said Harbinson suddenly. A wave of cloth-capped men came bursting through the door brandishing pieces of paper and laughing their pleasure. 'They've seen the race in the pub down the Row. It's got a TV lounge.' He grabbed one man by the sleeve and said: 'What won it?'

'April Shower.'

'What price?'

'Hundred to six.'

Harbinson took his triumph coolly. 'In this game you have to have connections,' he said. 'I had five bob on that pony, and I'm getting over fourteen to one for it. A bloody good day.'

Colin said: 'And I owe you a drink.'

VICTOR PRICE, *The Other Kingdom*, 1964

THEY CAME ALONG ROYAL AVENUE AND DONEGALL PLACE, and at a restaurant looking out at the City Hall, Gwilym stopped and said: 'I think we'll go in here and have some tea.'

He led the way to the upstair part and they sat at a table near one of the windows. The people and the traffic moved below him as Peter sat looking down at them, while the quiet, efficient waitress set the table. The statues round the City Hall gazed solemnly over at them, and the domed roof of the building, with its pillar supports, gained in impressiveness from the more intimate view which Peter obtained of it here. The rush hour was in progress, and the trams came in a long line, stopping and starting from the stage below him. What a lot of people there were, and they all seemed to be in a hurry! The cries of the newspaper boys selling the evening paper were borne up to him, and the sizzling noise, too, of the trolley arm of the tramcars running along the wires overhead, and the irregular clatter of them as they passed over the different joinings, merged into a symphony of sound, and back of all this was the deep steady hum of the other activities of the City.

On the table before him the returned waitress set down a plate of golden-brown fish, and silver salver full of finger-length fried potatoes, rivalling the fish in mellow colouring, toast that was succulent with butter, hot scones in a covered dish, pastries rich with foamy cream and other fillings, bread in variety, and the amber tea flowing into the cups from the tea-pot out of which Gwilym was pouring it.

'Now dig in and take a good tea,' Gwilym said cheerfully, as he handed over a cup to Peter.

HUBERT QUINN, *Hold Back the Shadows*, *c*. 1940

THE RIVER STREETS

The side streets of my world in order ran
from Roe Street, Avonbeg, and Annalee
to Dargle, outer limit of my span,
whose lads about its corners taunted me.
Roe Street was quiet, swept, its pavements clean,
most children's fathers warders there, you'd say;
its doors had a shut look; at Halloween,
here were the bells to ring and run away.

But it was Avonbeg Street and its twin
where my chums swarmed; the closest then therein
were Walter, widow's son, who once displayed
such courage, when a tumble snapped his arm,
and John, the coachman's son, blonde English lad –
that coach Miss Bruce's, pride of Thorndale Farm.

JOHN HEWITT, *Kites in Spring*, 1980

THE BELFAST ACADEMY WAS OPENED IN THE YEAR 1786, and it has had a long and honourable history. Many of our finest public men have been educated within the old walls of the school in Academy Street, and for many years it was considered to be the first school in Ulster. The original building became too small for the increasing number of scholars, and, in the year

1876, the school was removed to the present very fine building at Cliftonville, where the Belfast Academy still holds a high place among the educational establishments of the city.

The story of the Academy cannot be complete without a brief notice of an event which is detailed at great length in one of the old books of the school records. Some real or fancied grievance roused the wrath of the boys and they took the law into their own hands. On the morning of the 12th of April, 1792, eight boarders and two day-scholars shut themselves into the mathematical schoolroom, and declared war against the masters until their requests should be granted. In anticipation of a prolonged siege, they had liberally helped themselves to a large quantity of provisions from the kitchen. They had also procured five pistols, and an unlimited supply of powder and shot, and were fully prepared for serious operations. They sent a written despatch headed 'Liberty Hall' stating fully their demands and refusing to surrender until their requests were granted. Smiths were brought to break open the door. Slaters were sent up to the roof to pour water down the chimney, but all had to retire before the reckless firing of the boys.

At last the Sovereign was sent for to recite the terrors of the law, but the uproar of the battle continued all day, until late at night the unruly boys capitulated. We have no distinct record of the after events, and one would like to know if the boys were 'disciplined with the rod' or were forgiven.

MARY LOWRY, *The Story of Belfast and Its Surroundings*, 1912

DENIS McCULLOUGH AND I started the Dungannon Club in Belfast in March 1905. The name revived the memory of the Irish Volunteer movement of 1782. The Dungannon Club was in many ways a remarkable body. It consisted of thirty or forty young men at a white heat of enthusiasm. They undertook anti-recruiting activities on a large scale, and, as it was easier to print illegal literature in Belfast than in other parts of Ireland, we printed anti–enlistment leaflets wholesale and retailed them at so much a thousand to people all over the country. The Club published many postcards and pamphlets, and in 1906 I founded and edited a weekly paper called *The Republic*. After six months *The Republic* was overwhelmed by its financial difficulties and was merged with *The Peasant* in Dublin. The principal writers in *The Republic* were James W. Good, the notable Belfast journalist; Robert Lynd, the essayist; P.S. O'Hegarty and myself . . .

In the early days of the Dungannon Club we found the utmost difficulty in getting people to come to our meetings, so McCullough, McDermott and I decided that if the people did not come into our hall, we would go out into their streets, and we organised a series of meetings at street corners, mostly on the Falls Road. I remember the three of us going for a walk just before the first meeting, and it must be admitted that we were frightened out of our lives. We borrowed a four-wheel cart from a small coal merchant called John Quigley, who had been a Fenian all his life. He was willing to lend us the cart but not the horse, for fear it should receive an injury. Consequently we had to pull the cart ourselves down the Falls Road to the place of meeting. Denis McCullough and I went up and persuaded Francis Joseph Biggar, the noted Belfast antiquarian, to part with his magic lantern and we prepared a number of slides containing statistics about emigration and the general decline of Ireland, and some made from cartoons drawn by Jack Morrow, a well-known local artist, and other artists among our friends. We put up the lantern at one end of the cart and a screen at the other, and, putting statistics and cartoons alternately on the screen, we spoke on these subjects. The lantern was often battered with stones thrown by hostile crowds, but was never put out of action. When one has learned how to handle a hostile mob in Belfast, other audiences seem pretty easy.

BULMER HOBSON, *Ireland Yesterday and Tomorrow*, 1968

IF I WERE TO GO BACK FIFTY YEARS, when, as a child, I began to discover Belfast, there still remains a yearning in my heart for the excitement and adventure of those days. Little remains of the historic buildings which were scattered in and around the city centre. Even the lay-out of many familiar streets have changed.

For instance, the *Ulster Echo* and *Witness* office in Royal Avenue has disappeared. So have the small lock-up shops on the opposite side, where one could purchase an ounce of Irish-grown tobacco. 'The Century Bar', where Sinclairs now stands, and 'The Palace Bar', at the corner of North Street, were by no means ornaments to the city's architecture, compared to the present structures. Still, they were landmarks.

The south side of Castle Place retained a number of original town buildings – two-storied residential houses. Carter's Waxworks occupied one of these. One room at the back of the building was set aside as 'The Chamber of Horrors'. If my memory holds good, there was a tableau re-presenting the murder of Terry, the actor, outside the stage door of a London theatre. Another was the gruesome spectacle of a murderer push-ing his victim into the mouth of a furnace.

A circus of 'Flea Performers' held us spellbound, indulging in spectacular jumps and hauling tiny carts about. 'The Bearded Lady' and 'The Head without a body', were periodical visitors. I believe the admittance fee for children was twopence or threepence.

In my boyhood days, Donegall Road was always referred to as 'The Blackstaff'. Durham Street was 'Pound Loney'. 'Bower's Hill', now the Shankill Road. Ballynafeigh was known to us as 'The Brickfields'. The streets between Agincourt Avenue and Rugby Avenue was 'Holyland'; and stretching from there to Botanic Avenue was a wide expanse of grassland called 'The Plains', where many rising stars of future soccer fame made their debut.

'The Chapel Fields', stretching from Linenhall Street to Joy Street, was also a venue for football fans and, during the festive seasons, was crammed with roundabouts, circuses, wild beast shows and boxing booths. I remember some wild scenes here when the crowds got out of hand and the showmen had to defend their property with whatever weapons they could fashion.

Sunday afternoons in Summer, the old Bangor boat plied happily from Queen's Bridge jetty to Bangor and back. But the fare was beyond the pockets of us youngsters. So we 'bunched up' and chartered a rowing boat at the Sand Quay and sculled away to the Twin Islands for something like threepence a head.

Further up the Lagan, opposite the Ormeau Park, Tom Boyce ran a ferry across the river as well as letting out row-boats. We often rented a boat from Boyce's and rowed as far as Stranmillis weirs. There were few houses within sight of the river in those days, and the trip was a pleasant change from the streets.

After I left school and graduated into 'longs', I travelled further afield in my search for Greater Belfast. Ben Madigan, a name which is rarely applied to the Cave Hill these days, was an adventurous trip. The Cavehill Road was a narrow thoroughfare, flanked on the left side by bogey lines which served the mountain limestone quarries, long out of use even then.

There had been a love tragedy at the foot of the quarry whilst I was still at school, when two youthful sweethearts sought spiritual union in death which was forbidden them in life. For many years some kindly passers-by would commemorate the sad event by drawing in limestone the initials of the two victims at the place of the tragedy. We youngsters always referred to the spot as 'Norah's Grave'.

On the summit of McArt's Fort, we discovered a seat hewn out of the solid rock, and overlooking Belfast Lough and the lovely Holywood hills. As children, it was known to us only as 'The Wearyman's Rest'. Many years later, when in conversation with the grand old Irish historian, the late F.J. Bigger, I mentioned this find, and was shocked at my own ignorance in not recognising it as the crowning chair of the chiefs of one of the Antrim branches of the O'Neills. The seat was practically demolished when I last stood on McArt's Fort.

One of our greatest discoveries was the 'Big Stone' at the top of the Glencairn Road. We filled our haversacks with buns and lemonade bottles and hiked it up the Ballygomartin. At the end of the Glencairn, we crossed the fields to the foot of the Gilbert Mountain where, in the centre of one of the fields, we reached our objective. It was many years later I discovered I

had chalked my initials on the face of an ancient standing stone, which had
been hoary with age long before the Gaels brought culture to pagan Ireland.

THOMAS CARNDUFF (1954), *Life and Writings*, 1994

WITH HIS SCHOOLBAG UNDER HIS ARM he went out on to the street
again and didn't wait for his brother. He ran round the back of the
houses, over the cindery waste ground, down the steep river bank, and
stood under the arch. The river swirled round him in a clayey flood, making his head dizzy. There was a cold suck of air under the arch and water
dripped in a steady stream from the roof, and before it had time to make
ripples it was carried off by the flood. Far off was the bright cave of light
that marked the end of the arch. Factory horns blew intermittently, and in
his mind he saw the boys in school standing in their yellow desks. The horns
ceased and a great hollowness filled the air. It would be geography now and
the glossy map would be unrolled and hung over the blackboard. He could
see the master calling Frankie and saying: 'Where is Peter?' The master,
perhaps, would disbelieve him and send a boy down to the house. Peter
came out quickly from under the arch, and hid his schoolbag under a
clump of stones. He clambered up the wet slope of the bank, ran up a few
streets, and came on to the Falls Road.

Outside the library he saw three bicycles. He stood beside the smallest of
them. He looked around and with casual pretence examined the maker's
name which was designed on the frame. Slowly his hand slid over the silver
handle-bars and in a few minutes he had it down the steps, his leg was over
the saddle, and he was pedalling wildly. He never looked behind. Up the
Antrim Road he raced, and twice the wheels caught in the tram-lines,
nearly throwing him. The rain still fell and it trickled down his hair and
into his mouth. But he enjoyed it. His mind stretched forward to his
granny's and already he was framing lies to tell to her. She'd be glad to see
him and she'd take off his clothes, wrap him in a blanket, and let him sleep at
the foot of her bed. She had done that when he had stayed three days with
her and had fallen into a river while trying to stab trout with a fork.

When he reached the end of the tram-lines a gush of freedom surged
through him. In front lay open country with trees shedding their leaves.
The telegraph poles were glossy with rain and overhead the wires trembled
as a flock of starlings settled upon them and then took off again wing-
rushing through the air. Dead leaves lay in drifts along the edges of the
road and their smell warmed the air. The wheels of the bicycle hissed in the
rain and Peter began to sing:

'Oh, it's nice to get up in the morning,
But it's nicer to stay in bed . . .'

MICHAEL McLAVERTY, *Lost Fields*, 1942

RAINEY SLIPPED A REVOLVER OUT OF A DRAWER. 'Have one?' he offered. 'These men will be ugly customers. That's all, I think. If you're ready, we'll get along.'

The train was due at 6.15 and they had just time to meet it. The weather had fulfilled all Rainey's evil prophecies, and now the rain was falling heavily on the glistening pavements while a squally wind howled and eddied round the corners of the buildings. The shops and offices were just disgorging their staffs and the streets were full of hurrying figures trying to balance dripping umbrellas and to keep dainty shoes out of pools. Trams packed to the steps clattered past while buses and cars sent the water flying in sheets from their spinning wheels.

'A dirty night for us, but a good one for our friends,' said Rainey as their car ran into the cab rank between the main arrival platforms at the Great Northern station. 'We'll stay in the car and as soon as you pick up Mallace you can get in. M'Clung will take over and keep him in view.' . . .

Mallace boarded a tram outside the station and M'Clung, dropping behind, was picked up by the car. They kept the tram in view and at Castle Junction, the City Centre, watched the quarry alight and walk to the tramway halt at the beginning of Royal Avenue. This was the point at which trams bound for the Antrim Road started, and French and Rainey exchanged satisfied glances. Once again M'Clung slipped out of the car, and mingling with the crowds waiting for trams, kept Mallace in view.

FREEMAN WILLS CROFTS, *Sir John Magill's Last Journey*, 1930

WHENEVER THE BALLROOM DANCING comes on to the TV my wife sometimes gives a bit of a sigh, and talks about the days when she went dancing as a girl in Belfast, with her dancing shoes wrapped up in brown paper under her arm. And her worrying about whether her father would find out. He thought she was out for a quiet stroll with her chum, the one sitting beside her in the tram, heading for the ballroom.

Up to the end of the fifties Belfast was a city of ballroom dancers. The Plaza, in Chichester Street, was the biggest dance hall. The top suburban spot was the Floral Hall, at Bellevue, right under the brow of Ben Madigan. Three thousand dancers could have been accommodated in these two places. Another ten thousand could have found a floor to suit their needs among the dozens of smaller halls in the city.

SAM McAUGHTRY, *from* 'Slow, Slow, Quick Quick Slow', *Belfast Stories*, 1981

MANY OF THE OLD CUSTOMS in small matters have faded away. Fifty years ago, the Cave Hill sports on Easter Monday were in full vigour. The Christmas rhymers or mummers followed their sports with equally strict observance. Now-a-days the latter is kept up in a feeble way in the suburbs of the town, but we are not aware that it is so in the town itself. Oliver Cromwell and his copper nose – whose history and ludicrous adventures were all printed in a little book, and may still be so, printers and performers being alike ignorant of the persons and events they endeavoured to commemorate – are among the amusing performances of a past age. Then, again, the bakers in their generosity sent a Christmas present to each of their good customers – a large loaf, plentifully stuffed with currants – and other tradesmen followed a like custom. Now it is abandoned, as the town has got too large for such customs. But everything is changed as well as these, and with regard to these a reverse has taken place – the servants who deliver their masters' goods to us now expect the gratuities, and our houses are besieged at Christmas by their looking for *douceurs* in money. The accent also of Belfast has much altered with 50 or 60 years. This was to be expected, so many of the young people of means being educated in England or the Continent.

GEORGE BENN, *A History of the Town of Belfast*, 1880

CHILDREN:
>Our queen can birl her leg, birl her leg, birl her leg,
>Our queen can birl her leg, birl her leg.

NARRATOR:
>Belfast was like that – a criss-cross place. We ignored Good Friday as being too near to Rome, but Easter was a high day in our calendar. Every Easter morning we would take a tram to the end of the lines. We would walk outside the city till we reached the Dundonald cemetery, and there we would roll our coloured eggs down a grassy slope till they broke. What possessed my mother I don't know, but it was something as old as the hills, and older than the hymn itself. For if our eggs failed to break, we would take them to a great tumulus, or prehistoric burial-ground, which topped the distant fields, and there we would finish the job. Then after surveying the family grave (and pocketing two white flint stones from it to strike sparks with) I would walk back through the broken egg-shells of light and shadow to the dusty terminus, with its litter of old tram-tickets and its squalling crowd of youngsters.

BELFAST WOMAN:
>If yous don't behave yourselves I'll never bring yous out again!

W.R. RODGERS, *The Return Room*, 1955

I HOPE THE ORMEAU PARK is as much fun to the children to-day as it was to children when I was young. We spent a lot of our time in it, all through the year. Do you recall those crowns and things we made with that grass – I forget its name – which can be wound furrily round stalks? We used to take three or four stalks of the grass, and then twine other stalks round them until we had made enough furry stuff to be bent into a crown or some other emblem. One could spend an entire afternoon in that pastime. Cricket, football, and, in the winter, skating and sliding on the little pond – all that and more in the Park.

Did you ever trundle your Easter egg in the Ormeau Park? Ah, but did you do the thing properly? Did you first go out and gather whin blossoms with which to dye the egg, or were you idle enough to dye it with tea leaves or weak and degenerate enough to buy an egg that had been coloured with chemical dyes? I was a well-reared child. I gathered the yellow blossoms to dye my egg, and was not one of your idlers who used tea leaves, or one of your weaklings who bought eggs already dyed. I was forbidden, even if I had had any desire, to touch an egg dyed with chemical stuff. Who knew what poison would penetrate the meat of the egg if the shell should have cracked while it was being dyed with chemicals? A boy might die in terrible contortions if he let that dark, purple stuff get anywhere near his inside. My egg was ritually dyed and ritually eaten. On Easter Monday morning I went to a mound in the Ormeau Park, where I solemnly trundled the egg until the shell broke. Then I sat down and ate the egg.

ST JOHN ERVINE, *Belfast Telegraph*, 1944

Labyrinthine Alleyways, Obliterated Streets

Shortly afterwards I jacked in school, and from then on *mar a deirtear, is é sin scéal eile* (as they say, that's another story). In the meantime, by some unnoticed, the Loney, Leeson Street and all that they meant have been erased and, the likes of it, as Tomás Ó Criomtháin wrote in *An tOileánach*, will never be seen again.

GERRY ADAMS, Falls Memories

Once more they came back for the names, and I began: 'Abyssinia, Alma, Balaclava, Balkan, Belgrade, Bosnia', naming the names: empty and broken and beaten places. I know no others.

Gone and going all the time.

Redevelopment. Nothing more dramatic than that; the planners are our bombers now. There is no heart in the Falls these days.

ANNE DEVLIN, 'Naming the Names'

Smithfield's old structure was burnt down in 1974 and has been replaced with unremarkable separate buildings, and the markets have gone, leaving a five-day hole in the city. None of these, and few of the many other changes in the look and character of Belfast over the past twenty years, are wholly attributable to the troubles.

ROBERT JOHNSTONE, Images of Belfast

There is a map of the city which shows the bridge that was
    never built.
A map which shows the bridge that collapsed; the streets that
    never existed.
Ireland's Entry, Elbow Lane, Weigh-House Lane, Back Lane,
    Stone-Cutter's Entry –
Today's plan is already yesterday's – the streets that were there
    are gone.
And the shape of the jails cannot be shown for security reasons.

The linen backing is falling apart – the Falls Road hangs by a
    thread.
When someone asks me where I live, I remember where I
    used to live.
Someone asks me for directions, and I think again. I turn into
A side-street to try to throw off my shadow, and history is
    changed.

CIARAN CARSON, *Belfast Confetti*, 1989

A S A SHY FOUR-YEAR-OLD, I trudged into the Holy Family school for the
first time on my 'fallen arches' (flat feet), too young to be much upset
by events beyond the neighbourhood: not least among them, the war in
Europe. Not many Belfast people were well off then, and it was not
uncommon to see small schoolboys wearing their sister's hand-me-down
skirts, pinned in the middle to provide a slim, pathetic illusion of trousers.

I thought of this dreadful poverty – it diminished Catholic and Protestant
lives alike – a few years ago on revisiting the docks area of the city. Pile-
drivers snorted and thudded, drowning the cries of seabirds which drifted
and dawdled over the quays of the Lagan river's lower reaches. When I was
a child, the snorts and thuds were on behalf of Britain, hugely reliant on
Belfast's shipbuilding capacity. Now, as I stared into the river, the clangour
behind me was for Belfast itself, a recreative surge in the midst of mayhem
by terrorist gangs. One memory swirled in the water below me. It was, I
think, just before the outbreak of war, when I had my first encounter with
this waterway. Belfast's skyline was soon to change under German
bombardment, but in general the city looked as it would continue to look
until I abandoned it in my twenties, before a very different kind of war
altered the skyline further. The Grand Central Hotel dominated Royal
Avenue, the main thoroughfare; the fruit and vegetable markets occupying
much of Oxford Street bustled; the Gaumont and Imperial picture houses

competed for audiences, and oysters were to be washed down with porter and stout at Mooney's in Cornmarket. All these landmarks have disappeared, or shrunk, or otherwise changed shape in the past quarter-century, their sites currently occupied by smart red brick, totemic atria and other modern delights. A stroll on Royal Avenue, Donegall Place, High Street and Great Victoria Street revealed a shopper's Belfast that was unfamiliar to me: miracles of glazing that reflected the sky; bright-red brick façades, free of the grime of ages; broad pavements with fresh tiles; ornate doors that breathed exotic essences into the street air each time they swung open. Yet beneath that grand exterior I felt little had changed. Chatting to wee, hard men in bars and youths with dead-fish eyes on street corners, I quickly formed the impression that Belfast's modernity is not much more than skin-deep, and that the pulse of sectarian hatred beats as enduringly as ever.

CAL McCRYSTAL, *Reflections on a Quiet Rebel*, 1997

A MAP OF BELFAST MADE IN 1685 shows that the essential features of the partly walled town of that time are bases of the modern nucleus. Eastward from the castle, which stood near the present Castle Junction, ran High Street, on either side of the Farset River, at the mouth of which were various quays. Near the castle was a market, the site of the 'Cornmarket' of to-day. Until the latter part of the last century High Street was still the main shopping centre, though Ann Street, parallel with it to the south, and leading from the bridgehead, retained a special interest in the provisions trade. Parallel with High Street to the north was Broad Street, the modern Waring Street, which became primarily associated with commercial activities: later the Exchange and many insurance offices were built here. Outside the wall to the west was Mill Street, leading to the corn mill on the Farset. It was decreed that the native people should live outside the wall, so that it is highly probable that Mill Street was the nucleus of the Irish population. This point to-day forms the apex of the Roman Catholic – i.e., Irish – population in west Belfast. So the main elements in the town's structure, physical and social, were laid in the first stages of its development. The Farset was eventually covered in, but High Street retained its width. Larger buildings eliminated the gardens which formerly backed it, but the narrow communicating lanes remained, and are to-day preserved as the 'entries' which, in particular, connect High Street and Ann Street.

EMRYS JONES, *Belfast in Its Regional Setting*, 1952

PERHAPS IN FEW OTHER STREETS is there so much left in width, and here and there in style of buildings, to remind us of the past, as in the lower portion of North Street. True, for the most part the old buildings have been replaced by new, and in places the new have been set further back than the old, thus leaving in places a wider roadway. Yet, notwithstanding these changes, the street retains much of the appearance it presented on a dark October evening somewhere about seventy years ago. The day had been stormy and wet, and the heavy clouds were chasing each other across the sky, allowing the watery-looking moon to obtain but fitful glimpses of the earth. Gas had for some time been introduced into the principal streets, but North Street had not yet been included in this progressive step, and its inhabitants had to be satisfied with the old oil lamps. And the few stragglers who gathered round the door of Gordon's 'North Star Inn', watching the cars from Derry, Coleraine, and Portglenone depositing their loads of stiff-limbed, weary passengers, looked strange and weird in the combination of fitful light shed by the moon's rays and the oil lamps. Under the light of one of the lamps a little old man had just finished closing his shop, situated about half-way up the street. After taking a look at the fast-driving clouds, he turned into the shop, and, putting on a white chimney-pot hat which had seen better days, he drew round him a wide cloak of blue cloth – an article of dress much worn at this period.

JOHN SHAW, *The Diamond Merchant*, 1898

HIS FIRST FREE DAY when the boarders were allowed out he made his way to the docks to see the ships. Their huge red funnels, white paint-work and varnished masts filled him with delight. At the other side of the harbour were the coal-boats, the crane buckets descending into their bowels and disgorging shining pyramids of coal on the quay. Over the Queen's Bridge lines of coal-carts rattled; trams mumbled; and once a donkey passed drawing a cart of steaming coal-brick. Colm stood on the bridge counting the big cross-channel boats, looking at the Lagan water swirling round the quoins of the bridge, holding captive in one corner, orange peel, straw; and empty cigarette packets. From the opposite side of the bridge he saw coming down the river barges laden with turf-mould and going to dock under a black shed which had on the roof big white letters – PEAT, MOSS, LITTER. He wished with all his heart that Jamesy was with him.

On his way back to the College he wandered about the city learning the names of the streets: Oxford Street, Victoria Street, Cromac Street, Durham Street, Townsend Street, Carlisle Circus, and he thought of the island names – Lagavristeevore, Killaney, Crocnacreeva, Carnasheeran, Crocaharna – words full of music, and he said them aloud to himself as he went along.

MICHAEL McLAVERTY, *Call My Brother Back*, 1939

NEARLY EVERY DAY immediately after lunch I used to wander about the Belfast streets – the docks, the bookshops in Smithfield, the back streets of the Lower Falls and Shankill, the Belfast and County Down railway station into which my father shunted his trains many thousands of times from early morning to late at night, returning home pale from weariness, his face streaked with oil. Sometimes I went into a pub, deserted in the early afternoon, to leaf over a second-hand book I had bought or just to sit for half an hour in silence. Occasionally I would go into St George's Church at the Albert Clock or the Catholic church in Chapel Lane, find a pew and rest. I had no religious faith, no belief in prayer, felt no need to worship a God or accept a creed. I suppose this should have cut me off, in some vital way, from many of my friends and acquaintances, but I do not think it did. I very seldom discussed religion with anyone except those whose attitude more or less coincided with my own – and that made for dullness – while to discuss it with fervent believers I always found a waste of time, like two people trying to conduct a debate but unable to understand each other's language. Long ago I reached the conclusion that a great many people who believe themselves to be, for example, Christians, give only lip service to their belief and lead lives of self-delusion. Neither the people of the Catholic South nor those of mainly Protestant Northern Ireland seem to me much different from the people of agnostic England in the spiritual quality of their daily existence, at least to judge from the quality of their press, television or radio, to which they devote more concentration than they do to their faiths.

JOHN BOYD, *The Middle of My Journey*, 1990

A GREAT VARIETY OF TYPES can be expected among those houses which are over a century old. The ones most likely to have survived are the upper-class villas, and those substantial terrace houses which were once the town residences of the same class. They were well-built, their upkeep has not been ignored, and their roominess ensured their use long after the contemporary workers' houses were condemned in theory and gradually replaced. Both in the terrace houses and in the villas of this period there is a pleasant survival of Georgian planning and façades. One of the best examples of a terrace of such houses is University Square, although the addition of bay windows to some of the houses in later Victorian times has somewhat destroyed an impressive dignity. In the centre of the city one can still detect a similar dignity beneath the hoardings and advertisements of Chichester Street, or, rather better preserved, in College Square North, where the fanlights are a faint reminder of another age. A terrace which exemplified the unified plan at the expense of individual houses is Lower Crescent, the boldest attempt at a belated copying of the terraces of Bath and Georgian

London. A similar attempt was made in Royal Terrace, on the Lisburn Road. All these examples link the centre of the old town with the most select of the suburbs, Malone, where many fine villas of this period were built.

Very little industrial housing of this early period now remains. One remnant is Rowland Street, Sandy Row. Here the houses, with their small windows and whitewashed walls, are subtly different from the standard bye-law housing which characterises industrial Belfast. These also are small houses and have inadequate amenities: brick-built and single-fronted, they could be described by the minimum requirements set out in the series of bye-laws under which they were built. There is little to relieve the monotonous brickwork in these houses apart from the custom of painting around the windows and doorways in yellow or orange. The restriction of this practice to certain sectors of the city, and the freshness of the paint in July of each year, indicate a sectarian bias, but it does serve to relieve a general drabness. On the whole it is more pleasant than the yellow brickwork, simulating firestone, which is often found around doors and windows and which, in larger houses, is patterned into diaper work; the bigger the terrace the more complicated becomes the yellow diaper, giving rise to what has been called 'bacon and egg architecture'. Bay windows are not a common feature of the smaller houses, but they become an essential feature of most of the larger terrace houses in streets which link the main thoroughfares. These often have an attic storey in addition, sometimes with dormer windows and often embellishments of pseudo-Gothic ornament around the doors and windows. Most of the smaller houses open directly on to the street, and usually they have no other open space apart from a small enclosed yard, often backing on to the next row of yards and having no rear access.

EMRYS JONES, *A Social Geography of Belfast*, 1960

NEWTOWNBREDA is now so changed from the time that Robert and Sarah first went there, that it would be almost unrecognisable to the inhabitants of 1862. At the start of his ministry, Robert was living in his mother's house at Queen's Elms. To get to Newtownbreda he had to go down by Donegall Pass and cross the river on the Coffer Dam within which the New Bridge (presumably the Ormeau Bridge) was being built. There was no road across the Plains, that piece of land lying roughly between the Malone Road and the Lagan, and often on dark wintry nights he would feel lonely and nervous on the long up hill road to his little church. When they eventually settled in the Manse, they were delighted with it, remote and secluded as it was then. In describing it Robert said, 'I remember the extraordinary stillness that surrounded us the first evening we retired to rest. After the stir of Belfast, it was awesome to look out through the uncurtained windows to the starry sky, no cart or traveller moved upon the road, and all was silence. When we looked westward there was nothing to hide the view of the Black Mountain, Rosetta House nestling in its woods and shrubberies hid the town, Knockbreda Rectory was the only house visible southwards.'

MARGARET A.K. GARNER, *Robert Workman of Newtownbreda 1835–1921*, 1969

A S HE DROVE HOME, a late northern summer's light cloaked the city's Victorian monuments and buildings in a ghostly, golden glow. Shopping areas were deserted. For years, people had been unwilling to walk the streets at night. He turned up towards Millfield, driving through those parts of Belfast which had become the image of the city to the outside world; graffiti-fouled barricaded slums where the city's Protestant and Catholic poor confronted each other, year in and year out, in a stasis of hatred, fear and mistrust.

'But it was the Germans who destroyed Belfast,' his father used to say. 'It wasn't these Troubles, it was the bombing during the last war. After the war they cleared the bombsites, but they never rebuilt.' It was true, he supposed, for he had seen photographs of the pre-war city, orderly, ugly, Victorian. But what the war had begun, a quarter of a century of civil strife had worsened, so that now, beneath the new motorways which crossed the city like slash marks on a map, the old heart of Belfast, those thousands of small dwellings which housed people whose highest ambition was a job in a shipyard or a mill, lay in a continuing plague of poverty, decaying, without hope.

BRIAN MOORE, *Lies of Silence*, 1990

S MITHFIELD AND CASTLE LANE accommodated Belfast's old bookshops. Castle Lane forty years ago was different from the Castle Lane of to-day. The old Theatre Royal ran along one side, and the centuries-old Corn Market opened off the other side. One or two of these shops had a retiring appearance, as if unwilling that customers should ferret them out, in the tradition of a famous bookshop in the Haymarket, London, where the windows were kept uncleaned and a simple-minded assistant, who cleaned them when the principal was on holiday, was dismissed for his pains. Eminent citizens were customers in Smithfield. Men prominent in the public eye were seen absorbed in tomes there. Book collectors found rare bargains there. Nearby Castle Lane, in William Street South, was the restaurant and oyster-saloon, in the windows of which was seen in a glass jar in spirits an arm of Donnelly, the Irish bruiser, the hero of the great fight with Cooper at the Curragh in 1814. A hundred yards away in Victoria Square was the old Morgue, where, through chinks in the window-glass curious idlers could see on a mortuary slab corpses which had met a violent end.

Smithfield, probably opened in 1780, accommodated early in the last century the cattle market, the grass market, the marshalsea or prison for debtors, the House of Industry or jail, and the one hospital and dispensary of the town. Show booths with clowns were there. Recruiting sergeants accompanied by detachments of soldiers with fifes and drums playing 'British Grenadiers', waited there for youths willing to take the King's shilling.

Till near the beginning of this century part of Millfield was tenanted by nail-makers in one-storey houses with thatched roofs. Cobblers were studded over the Falls. Clay pipe-makers favoured Winetavern Street. A craftsman had his own house, where he lived and plied his calling. Mass production was rare outside the mills and factories, foundries and shipyards.

Up to 1897 Frederick Street had a number of thatched houses. The old Royal Hospital was situated in this street from 1815 to 1903. Facing the Hospital was a tenement respecting which a tradition ran that Lord Edward Fitzgerald sought and found shelter when 'out' in '98.

T.J. CAMPBELL, *Fifty Years of Ulster 1890–1940*, 1941

LEAVING THE INFANTRY BARRACKS, a few thatched houses on one side of the road bring us to the gate of the old Poorhouse, which then opened at the head of Donegall Street. The new Roman Catholic chapel on one side of Donegall Street, and Boyd's Belfast Foundry on the other, then seemed more prominent than at present. From this point we had no road westwards except a narrow and crooked lane past the new burying-ground. This was the only enclosed burying-place we had, and the demand for ground soon obliged the committee to extend the grave-yard to double its original dimensions. This narrow lane leading to Pebble Lodge and Buttermilk Loaning has been widened, and in the main it is now embraced by our Clifton Street, but one or two old cottages still exist, and show the course of the lane. The entrance to the Poorhouse has been changed to opposite Frederick Street. Continuing our course round the boundaries of the town, we pass Carrick Hill and Lodge Road, Peter's Hill, Brown's Square, Millfield, and Barrack Street, till we arrive at the Pound. Then we must follow Sandy Row, which ... was part of the old Dublin Road; but you must not suppose that we had a compact town inside the limits I have named. In all towns and villages the main roads are first lined with houses, and Sandy Row stretched in this way as far from the town as to be an outlying district. It was the boundary of the town in that direction, but all between it and the Linen Hall was grass land. This ground lay low; the Blackstaff River ran through it; and in winter much of it was covered with water. At such times the Mall Ditch was a great convenience for the people living about Tea Lane. This Mall Ditch was a mound or bank of considerable dimensions, extending from the front enclosure of the Academical Institution to the Saltwater Bridge, where Sandy Row crosses the Blackstaff. The town ran inland to this bridge. It may be worth noticing that the course of the river between this point and the Dublin Bridge at Bedford Street has been considerably altered. It had more windings then. One bend that seems entirely effaced brought it close under the rere wall of the old 'House of Correction' in Howard Street.

THOMAS GAFFIKEN, *Belfast Fifty Years Ago*, 1894

BELFAST, BY COMPARISON WITH BALLYMACARRETT, was oblong. It had squares, too, but most of it was oblong. The additions that have been made to Ballymacarrett since I left it are, I regret to say, far from triangular. The passion for oblongs has spread through Bloomfield, Strandtown, The Knock, and beyond, though there was an opportunity to start a really magnificent triangle at Gelston's Corner if only somebody had had the sense to start it. Notice, by the way, how often a friendly pub forms the apex of a triangle. When you cross the Lagan into Ballymacarrett's chief suburb, which is Belfast, Bangor being the second, you find yourself in a confusion of characterless oblongs and even of rhomboids, though heaven knows a rhomboid is nothing to boast about. Chesterton wrote a poem in which he declared that the rolling English drunkard made the rolling English road. A chap with D.T.'s must have made some of the streets and roads on the wrong side of the Lagan. Some of them wamble about as if they had been brought up on Red Biddy.

But there are triangles in Belfast, too. I used to know them all, but now I can recall only several. There's a very good one with its apex where University Road meets Lisburn Road, and its base in Wellington Park, though the base is removable to Malone Avenue if you feel like going that far. I used to think that Great Victoria Street and the Dublin Road had started life as the sides of a triangle, but that the Dublin Road had taken to loose ways in Bedford Street and lost all control of itself before it reached Wellington Place, which was built to be a perfect base.

The oddest shaped tract of Belfast is one that was intended by heaven to be a triangle, but went off its head and made a lozenge of itself. If you do not believe me, take out a map of Belfast and look at the Old Lodge Road where it joins the Crumlin Road. Now, glance back to Carlisle Circus. You will agree with me, will you not, that if that area had ended, as it ought to have done, at Eglinton Street or even at Carlisle Street, as nice a triangle as a man could wish to see in a day's march would have been built. But those who started off well, could not let well alone, and had to go galumping down Clifton Street and Peter's Hill, with lamentable results to everybody.

You could, if you were as fond of triangles as I am, use Upper Library Street as the base for the triangle that begins where the Crumlin Road and the Old Lodge Road meet, but most of us have not heart enough for that. You can, of course, console yourself for the loss of this triangle by treating Agnes Street as the base of one, and running the sides down the Old Lodge Road to the point at Peter's Hill where North Street begins. The other side gives you a nice Belfast mixture, the whole of Peter's Hill and a bit of the Shankill. I will maintain until my dying day that the Cavehill Road and the Oldpark Road and Cliftonville Road and the bit of the Antrim Road which runs from Cliftonville Road to the Waterworks were intended to form a perfect triangle. But, sure, the people in Belfast had not as much feeling for triangles as the people in Ballymacarrett, and although they would start off well enough, they had not the strength to keep up the pace. The result is a lot of roads and streets running round like mad things, trying to remember how you make a triangle.

Every time I go home I find myself, sooner or later, in College Square, cursing heartily and at great length the bemused ass who ruined that fine site. What was the man thinking of when he stuck the Technical School in front of Inst.? That part of Belfast was very charming in my boyhood. Fisherwick Place had a serene look, as it faced Fisherwick Place Presbyterian Church in its lovely green yard. But a mania for development took possession of some person and we now have what I call the Early Woolworth style of architecture prevailing in that pleasant place. Fisherwick Church has been removed from its green yard to somewhere near Shaftesbury Square, and the Assembly Hall stands on its site. There is a rash of cinemas where agreeable houses once stood; and I have no doubt that one of these days we shall see, replacing the Early Woolworth style of architecture, the brazen development of it, which I call the Marzipan style. There was a hint of good architecture in Belfast once. You can see some signs of it round about Bedford Street. But the hint was not taken. What a pity!

ST JOHN ERVINE, *Belfast Telegraph*, 1946

'COW LANE', NOW VICTORIA STREET, was where the cows were driven through when they were taken to graze on the Strand ground, and Goose Lane was named for a similar reason. Skipper Street was where the 'skippers' or captains of the vessels lived, and it was then close to the docks.

Bridge Street was the principal bridge over the river in High Street, and it was here that the 'May Pole' was a striking feature for many years. The last Maypole left remaining in Ireland is still to be seen in the High Street in

Holywood. Church Street was so called from the old Corporation Church. It was formerly known as School-house Lane.

Bank Lane was once known as the 'Bank of the River'. Fountain Street was once called 'Water Street', as it was there that the fountains were, that at one time supplied the town with water.

Hercules Street was named after Sir Hercules Langford, and Sugar House Entry from the sugar-refining industry which was carried on there. It was to No. 13 in this entry that the dead body of poor, ill-fated Henry Joy McCracken was carried by his friends, after he was hanged at the Market House in the year 1798.

MARY LOWRY, *The Story of Belfast and Its Surroundings*, 1912

THERE ARE EXTREMELY FEW OLD HOUSES IN BELFAST; all have gone with the wigs, cocked hats, and the queues. Even at that time, small and rude as the town then was, its antiquated appearance must have been diminishing in 1799, as the writer of a letter of that date thus speaks of its general appearance after a considerable absence, and remarks 'how forcibly he is struck with the appearance it exhibited contrasted with that which it formerly presented, when so many hanging signs, pent-houses, street obstructions were allowed to remain; and in particular the numbering of the houses and labelling of the streets and lanes, giving a neatness and city-like appearance which was both useful and ornamental'. Doubts may be very reasonably expressed as to the city-like appearance of Belfast at this date, notwithstanding the removal of the obstacles referred to, and the substitution of more modern arrangements.

GEORGE BENN, *A History of the Town of Belfast*, 1880

WE ADVANCED ALONG DURHAM-STREET, peering, according to our wont, into all manner of courts and entries. In Victoria-court, we marked the flower-pot with its greenness adorning the windows, a sure sign of the taste and comparative refinement of the inmates. Allowing for its narrowness, we found cottage neatness, cleanness, and comfort in Davison's-court. The proprietor of this place, who lives at the entrance of it, and of whom I know nothing unless what I learned by the inspection of this little alley, deserves the highest eulogy; and his tenantry deserve to be joined with him in the praise, for they vie with each other in keeping their houses in the most perfect order. It did our hearts good to look at these cottages – the outside whitewashed, without a soil upon the pathway – and within, little palaces for cleanliness and beauty. In this court, there are twenty-eight houses, and fourteen of them are furnished with neat clocks –

a token of superiority of mind and habit. Nor let it be supposed that these cottages are beyond the reach of the poor. One shilling per week is the rent for each, and the people are, in general, in the humblest circumstances. We entered one, and learned that the husband is a porter, earning only 9s a week; yet he and his wife continue to live upon this, and the most refined individual in Belfast might sit at their hearth, while their little rooms are furnished with as much neatness as it is possible for the most fastidious to desire. We were delighted with the whole scene. It was like a vision of Dante's Paradise, after wandering through his Inferno. We lingered in the court, walking up and down with a feeling of perfect luxury. 'How is it,' said I, in a sort of ecstasy, to a woman whose furniture was white as the driven snow, 'that you are all so clean and orderly in this place?' 'Oh,' said she, 'Mr Davison likes to see us so.' Landlords, here is a great moral! This Mr Davison, whoever he be, has learned effectually, I think, one grand lesson much trumpeted in high places, but, I fear, little practised in any place, touching the duties of property. His is a sort of feudalism within that little pleasant domain, and his power is exercised in the most salutary form. His family of twenty-eight households all bless him. Their pride is to please him, and his pleasure is to see them happy. There they are, Protestants and Roman Catholics, living in perfect harmony, while their dwellings literally enjoy what Horace beautifully styles, *apertis otia portis*. I must not forget to mention, either, that not a single instance of cholera occurred within this entry (although so narrow), during the awful visitations of that scourge. The pestilence was rebuked at the threshold; it looked down, but, finding no encouragement to enter there, it turned aside to scenes where it could riot at its pleasure.

THE REVEREND W.M. O'HANLON, Walks Among the Poor of Belfast, 1853

LITTLE PALACES
for Gerard Fanning

Donkey's Lane:
an orchard and allotments,
broken window-frames, pigeon-huts
on stilts, corrugated iron;
and blankets hung out
on the line to air.

A woman dusts the living room.
The Queen on horseback
smiles down upon tongues
of sprouting ivy. Everything

is right with the world;
even the kerbstones are painted.

GERALD DAWE, Sunday School, 1991

MRS BITTERCUP:

Ach, God help the wee man! Sure if he was any smaller you'd have to cut the grass to see him. Well, it wouldn't do if we was all the same.

NARRATOR:

Nothing was ever the same in Belfast, for the place had character. The very stones in the street exerted themselves and rose up in cobbles – 'pavers' we called them – and the great roads grumbled along on granite setts.

Many's a time my knees would be dangling with blood-and-iodine ribbons, for I was born very close to the ground and I knew the flagstones like the palm of my hand.

You had to know what crack in the pavement not to walk on, for this one was lucky and that one unlucky; this stone was good for spinning tops and that one for skipping-games.

W.R. RODGERS, The Return Room, 1955

SOME OF THE SIGNBOARDS were rather grotesque. In Ann Street we had 'A bird in the hand is worth two in the bush'; in Corn Market there were 'The fruit girl', 'The mail coach passing through Dromore Square', where the proprietor (Maxwell Halliday) came from, and 'The Turk's head'. In Donegall Street, 'The saddle-horse and groom'; in Long Lane, 'The monkey shaving the goat', in Castle Lane, 'Roy's race on the Maze between Sharper and Swindler' (Roy was a retired jockey, and this race was considered one of his great triumphs); in High Street we had 'The black bear' and 'The spinning wheel'. Some dealers had no sign-boards, but hung out specimens of the goods they had for sale. Tinware, earthenware, and cast-metal goods were exposed upon the sidepath in Ann Street, and at a shop door next to where Grattan & Company are now placed (and where I often invested in balls and marbles) a turf, a piece of coal, and a scrubber indicated a very general store of small wares.

THOMAS GAFFIKEN, Belfast Fifty Years Ago, 1894

ONE OF THE MOST CURIOUS NAMES remains with us in 'The Donegall Pass'. There was no road at one time between the Dublin and Ormeau Roads, but Lord Donegall opened six wide avenues through the woods, and they were known as the passes. Donegall Pass alone keeps the old name, and people were allowed to use the footpath through the trees 'to pass' from one road to the other. Ormeau was built after the Castle in Castle Place was destroyed by fire. It was once a fine house beautifully situated on the bank of the Lagan, with spacious grounds and gardens, and some of the old trees now in the Ormeau Park may then have been the 'young elms' that gave it the name of Ormeau.

MARY LOWRY, *The Story of Belfast and Its Surroundings*, 1912

A FTER LEAVING HIS SHOP, the old man proceeded down North Street, through Bridge Street, and turned up High Street, his destination being the Ormeau Road, where at that time lived many of the aristocracy.

JOHN SHAW, *The Diamond Merchant*, 1898

WE ... MOTOR DOWN INTO BELFAST TO SEE THE SIGHTS, a long swift rush down the mountain-side, past the City Cemetery, down the Falls Road, the area which in the extraordinary history of this extra-ordinary city has so often resounded to the rattle of rifle fire, past the stark chimneys of the silent factories, and out into Castle Junction, the centre of the web of light which we have just seen from above. It is after midnight, but Donegall Place is still jammed with sightseers, a slow black tide surging past the lighted shop windows. There is electricity in the air, and no one in this usually sober city seems to think of going to bed. At the upper end of Donegall Place the City Hall, flood-lit in layers of red, white and blue, towers like a gigantic tier cake – the reward of the good Victorian ... At one o'clock the black tides are still surging past the lighted shop windows and the trams are still running, nosing their way through the crowds that occupy the roadway. What a strange world it is! a world full of flood-lighting, cheap electricity, new clothes, cigarettes, silk stockings, sixpenny seats at the cinema, and apparently endless leisure. I think of my dead father, now three years in his grave on the mountain-side above the city: how he toiled and moiled through the gas-lit decades of the Victorian era, and now we are all walking about through brilliant clean-swept streets, wearing new flannel trousers and smoking endless cigarettes, criticising European pictures, listening to wireless bands from the ends of the earth – a bright, clean, hard world in which gifts are showered on us in endless profusion, in which everything behind the illuminated plate-glass windows of the shops steadily cheapens, but in which one has only to step out of main street in order to see the grey, pinched faces of men, women, and children starving in the back alleys. A mad world, for all its concealed lighting, flood-lighting, and electric profusion. And leaving the thronged streets about the city centre and the three-tiered cake of a City Hall behind me, I walk home at one-thirty in the morning through the deserted commercial quarter, past rows of linen warehouses every third one of which bears a to-let notice, past the building that was my dead father's life-work and eventually the mauso-leum of his worldly hopes, and out into quiet suburban avenues where the only sign of the junketings at the centre of the city is an ominous-looking glare in the lofty summer sky.

DENIS IRELAND, From the Irish Shore, 1936

THE RAG TRADE

You walk around Smithfield in my dream
On christian name terms with the owners
Of old clothes stalls, second-hand bookshops,

Drifting between thrift and nostalgia,
That ache to reach home before the dust's
Final version of your school stories,

Before moths flit out like a nightmare
From the sweaty arm-holes in dresses
Worn by a mother or grandmother.

I am the man wiping his windscreen
With a rag you recognise as silk
Or chiffon, perfect material,

A stray to be taken in by you,
Washed, cared for, taught the secrets
Of covering and revealing your body.

When you ask for it, I give because
My books will always be second-hand,
Your underclothes never out of fashion.

MICHAEL LONGLEY, The Echo Gate, 1979

SMITHFIELD IS ANOTHER PLACE OF NOTE, topographically. We cannot ascertain the exact time when it was opened as a public market, but, from incidental notices, it was probably about the year 1780; it may have been then a grassy field. Previously to that time, all the markets, except the linen, were held in High Street. In whatever year, however, Smithfield was opened, the Cattle Market at least was settled in it. The cattle, in the year 1806, and probably many years before, and certainly many years after, were confined by strong, coarse wooden railings; the pedlars' stalls were in rows on the east side, out of the range of the cattle. This was on the Friday only. On all other days of the week, Smithfield, which contains several acres, was an utterly miserable-looking and deserted place, though several of the public institutions of the town were in it, and some of the cotton mills partly in the square, or in the streets adjoining. Besides the cattle dealers and the pedlars, there was also in Smithfield the market for grain, which was sold at a covered shed in the centre of the square, where the brewers, distillers, and corn merchants attended to purchase the small quantity of grain with which our market was then supplied; this began in 1804. A dozen of these gave notice in that year, in pressing terms, to all farmers to bring their grain to the public market-house in Smithfield, where they will find purchasers who will pay for the same in gold.

Smithfield, though desolate and quiet on all days except on those here mentioned, became yearly more popular as the town increased. There were many public-houses in it, with emblematical signs, these houses, no doubt, depending chiefly on their custom during the market-day. Its situation, and the numerous streets leading into it, made it a place well adapted for amusement, either for the inhabitants, or for the showmen who often visited the town.

The only emblematical sign which we remember was one on the east side of the square; this was after 1806, but it was perhaps to be seen in that year also. The inscription was –

> 'Ye Gentlemen and Archers good,
> Come in, and drink with Robin Hood:
> If Robin Hood be dead and gone,
> Come in, and drink with Little John.'

The archers good were depicted, in Lincoln green, with bows and arrows chasing the wild deer in sylvan scenery, and the little John who invited the cattle drovers and idlers of Smithfield to come in and partake of his hospitality, 'for a consideration', was a man above six feet high, and large in proportion.

The Marshalsea Prison, to confine the debtors who had been worsted in the Seneschal's Court, was likewise in Smithfield, and the iron bars which kept the prisoners in confinement are still to be seen in the room of a house on the north side of the square.

There was also in Smithfield the Hospital and Dispensary on the same side of the square, or rather in West Street, and the House of Industry, when it was established a few years after, on the south side. This square was really an important locality in the beginning of the century, and a very lively spot on Fridays.

GEORGE BENN, *A History of the Town of Belfast*, 1880

P ASSING FROM A FAIR GROUND, Smithfield developed into a market place where pedlars and dealers displayed their wares. One can visualise half of the population of the town congregating here for a bargain, with gamesters and toughs seeking an easy method making an odd shilling at the expense of their more simple townsfolk. When Smithfield was eventually roofed into a Corporation market, the hobby-horse, side-shows and boxing booth found another happy hunting ground in McCleans fields, at Ormeau Avenue which, in later years, received the popular title of the 'Chapel Fields'.

Round about the middle of last century, there was something like ten clothes dealers and eight auctioneers doing business in the Square. By this time, the new Town Council had taken over from the Sovereign and ruling Burgess, who were actually delegated to their positions by the Lord of the Manor, and Smithfield was, at last, a covered-in market. Previous to this, part of the square had been used as cattle pens. Tin smiths, coopers and booksellers also occupied stalls in the market.

Most of the public houses in the square were 'free and easies', supplying their customers with a song and dance as well as with pints. In opposition to the publicans was a 'Teetotal Hall', with a Pat McShane as superintendent. I think McShane eventually retired from the unequal contest as the hall disappears from the local directory, to give place to the Royal Hibernian Concert Hall which was, in fact, a typical Victorian music hall, under the management of Robert Calvert.

The cultural outlook of the Smithfield people expressed itself during the same period in the support of a 'National Theatre', controlled by Tom Armstrong. The type of play produced was, naturally, inspired according to the charge of admission. The prices ranged from a penny to threepence, which must be considered quite moderate for a Shakespearean session. About 1864, a National School was established, to be followed shortly afterwards by a lending library.

Much could be added to this brief outline of the history of Smithfield and its square. It has outlived many of Belfast's older institutions. With the exception of Clifton House (1774) and the Linen Hall Library (1788), it is all that is left of old-time Belfast.

THOMAS CARNDUFF (1954), *Life and Writings*, 1994

THERE IS NO DOUBT THAT SMITHFIELD is the rendezvous of a gang of youthful miscreants – candidates for the hulks and the gallows – who find a market there for their booty, and skulking-places in its vicinage where they may escape the eye and hand of justice. I should suppose that the very worst grade of our population will be found heaped together, corrupting and being corrupted, in this quarter. It is a sort of tumour, a morbid ganglion in the heart of our city; and, by a well-known law of disease, the vitiated humours of the system find their way to the diseased part – it draws to itself and assimilates even a portion of the wholesome succulence which would, otherwise, nourish and strengthen the body.

THE REVEREND W.M. O'HANLON, *Walks Among the Poor of Belfast*, 1853

IN SMITHFIELD, AMID THE WRECKAGE OF CASTLE AND COTTAGE, there sit stout ladies of noble lineage, disguised in print garments. Patiently they sit as they have sat for centuries, while little children come in and stare at them, and escape down those cross-passages which were made for such sudden retreats.

Smithfield is cunning and subtle; for it sets a face to the world that speaks of novelty and brightness. To the waves of the city it offers a sea-wall of tinsmiths, and an unlicensed League-room, where the famished are filled, and rich simmering joys are given to the good. Behind the barrier there sits the Sphinx. Even the deceiving surface reveals the spirit which it covers.

In Smithfield it is a law that the only things which may change are those that are not for sale: the peep-show passed, and there came the revolving view, and now the Mutoscope remains for its little moment, ready to be dethroned . . .

Smithfield has its sentinels and skirmishers; it has its gates and its guard; it is as a walled city whose battlements are reared to heaven so that its virtue may remain inviolate. And to this day the Curfew chimes the closing of its gates and the extinction of its fires; and then, dark and full of slumbers, it spreads out beneath the Ulster skies . . .

Within the walls there are many mysterious bins; and it is said that they contain stores against a siege. But the wise ask no questions; for strange tales are whispered of how, when a bin was opened centuries ago, it was found to be full of curious skeletons.

One there is in Smithfield who gathers about him the scum of our sphere: crutches and corset-busts, turbines and teapots, sewing-machines and Salvation Army tambourines, weigh-bridges and whetstones, yard-rules, and Yule-logs, zithers and Zulu-shields. And beside him there are strange old men who stew before stoves, and draw about them tyres and tubes.

In Smithfield there are drawers that have drifted from their drawer-holes in cabinet and chest; and there are spoiled mirrors that are said to have reflected the features of faithless ones, for even as we look into them they lie!

Once in the grand days when Smithfield was strong, and the city that clusters about it small, players were drawn to its doors, and actors of note strutted and smiled. And though the theatres are no more, the actors, who should long since have died, remain like moths upon some ancient web, living while it lives. They were famous ones, some of these; and are to be found drifting in great solitude, struck to stone, as it were, while they played, and still abroad in the dresses of the stage.

In Smithfield, breathing as it does the majestic maxim, 'Man know thyself', we have a storehouse of splendours, for the loss of which nothing could compensate this city of success.

HERBERT MOORE PIM, *Unknown Immortals*, 1917

'I HAVE FORGOTTEN SOMETHING,' says Ciaran Carson's poem, 'I am/going back.' Smithfield might be an ecologist's paradise, where consumer goods are recycled for further use. It might be a ruminant stomach from which objects at the edges of our lives are regurgitated and chewed over. I prefer to think of it as a nexus of nerve-endings in some obscure corner of a collective geriatric brain, a tangle of memories that meant something to somebody once upon a time.

Smithfield Market used to be a single entity, a covered square with a warren of little shops that set out their goods so that you had to step round them, like the souk in an Hibernian Casablanca. You could pick up bargains in second-hand furniture or cheap clothes, but the special thing about Smithfield was its oddity, all the strange little shops that you saw nowhere else. Everything you never thought of was there.

ROBERT JOHNSTONE, *Images of Belfast*, 1983

A VISIT TO SMITHFIELD could become a pilgrimage, a sort of homage to the multifarious facets of the human mind. With no obligation to buy, you could wander round the glass-roofed aisles or in and out of the shops, bemused by mountains of books, antiques, paintings, shops with rows and heaps of keys or mechanical parts, others with stacks of music sheets or leaning towers of records, old clothes depots and furniture dealers, cameras and carpets, bicycles and all the bibelots in my room at home. The old collector of Chinese *objets d'art* had given me many things, and round this elegant core I had built up a collection of curios derived, through jumble sales, from the Arabian Nights Smithfield.

ROBERT HARBINSON, *No Surrender*, 1960

HE JUMPED UP, surprisingly sprightly, and said, 'I must get to Smithfield before it closes. Belfast would be nothing without a visit to Smithfield.'

BERNARD MacLAVERTY, *from* 'St Paul Could Hit the Nail on the Head',
Secrets and Other Stories, 1977

COLM TOOK NO INTEREST IN THE PIGEONS, and on Saturday night when Alec and Jamesy went down town to talk with the bird-fanciers who congregated in Gresham Street, Colm went off by himself around the stalls in Smithfield, looking at the second-hand books, listening to the gramophones and watching a man making keys while-you-wait. Then to the clothes stall where blankets, coloured quilts, women's coats, men's swallow-tails, hung from the rafters overhead making the place cool and dark.

A woman sits on a stool with her hat and coat on and holds up a shirt as people pass: 'Mister, a bargain for one-and-six! ... Here it is for a bob! He doesn't want it ... H'm, collar and tie and all included he wants! ... What have we here! Yes, that's the very I-T. A dress shirt, ready to wear, as stiff as a corpse! ... How much! Don't all rush. Ninepence to you, sir! You never know the day you are going to get married. He doesn't want it neither. Gold cuff links and all he wants ... The people nowadays want no one to live.'

At another stall two shawled women were bargaining over a roll of oil-cloth, and near them in a side passage were tables, old golf clubs, fire irons, coal-buckets, and a model yacht with its sails rolled up. Colm's heart went out to the yacht but when he asked the price, it was too dear, and his face got red as he told the stall owner that he would call back again. He passed out of Smithfield on to the street and stood to watch an old man with a monkey. The man had a handle-organ tied round his neck with pieces of cord. The monkey, dressed in a vest and trousers, held a cocoa tin with a slit cut in the lid and sometimes he shook it to let the spectators know that he wanted money.

A man with clogs on his feet and a tall hat on his head passed through the crowd selling 'Old Moore's Almanac', while his brother stood at the corner of Gresham Street selling corn plasters and people called him the Corn King. He, too, had a tall hat and round the sides of it were pieces of cardboard inscribed with red-inked letters REMOVE THAT CORN.

MICHAEL McLAVERTY, *Call My Brother Back*, 1939

SMITHFIELD MARKET

Sidelong to the arcade, the glassed-in April cloud – fleeting,
    pewter-edged –
Gets lost in shadowed aisles and inlets, branching into
    passages, into cul-de-sacs,
Stalls, compartments, alcoves. Everything unstitched,
    unravelled – mouldy fabric,
Rusted heaps of nuts and bolts, electrical spare parts: the
    ammunition dump
In miniature. Maggots seethe between the ribs and
    corrugations.

Since everything went up in smoke, no entrances, no exits.
But as the charred beams hissed and flickered, I glimpsed a
    map of Belfast
In the ruins: obliterated streets, the faint impression of a key
Something many-toothed, elaborate, stirred briefly in the
    labyrinth.

CIARAN CARSON, The Irish for No, 1987

FARMS ARE ADVERTISED NEAR THE MALONE TURNPIKE GATE. Few now remember where the Malone Turnpike was. It was on the crown of the hill, nearly opposite where Mount Charles now is, surrounded by a sort of little village of mean houses. When the Lisburn Road was made, the Turn-pike was brought lower down, to catch the travellers of both roads. Fine fields and gardens are announced to be let adjoining the Malone Turnpike, which, it was said, would greatly increase in value on the completion of the new road projected into the town, which would enter by Arthur Street. We remember, and it must have been several years after 1804, when a person from the County Armagh, coming to visit an old friend in Belfast, complained of the way into the town by which he had been induced to come, and which led him in at the back of the Linen Hall ditch. He said he would never travel that way again, as his horse was nearly up to the saddle-girths, but would travel in future by the good old path of Sandy Row, Mill Street, and Castle Street. But the changes about Malone Turnpike are quite indescribable. We remember looking at a splendid garden of white currants and other fruit where there is now a large and substantial educational establishment and the station of the Central Railway. Splendid nurseries and gardens were also in the vicinity of the Salt Water Bridge, where now all is smoke and bustle.

GEORGE BENN, A History of the Town of Belfast, 1880

THE SITE ON WHICH THE PRESENT BELFAST BANK STANDS WAS, prior to 1769, known as the FOUR CORNERS, on which converged North Street, Bridge Street, Broad (now Waring) Street, and Rosemary Lane – Donegall Street had not then been formed. This open space resembled in many respects the English Village Green – a place where matters of local interest were discussed and gossip held unbridled sway, whilst the redolent air from the herb-planted gardens attached to the houses in Castle Street (now Place) suggested the name ROSEMARY for the lane which formed the northern boundary to the gardens. Such a site was an ideal position for the EXCHANGE, which Arthur, 5th Earl of Donegall, afterwards 1st Marquis, erected in 1769 at a cost of £4,000. The one-storeyed building was almost square, having a frontage of 65 feet towards Bridge Street, and in each of the three sides were five doors or gateways. Within that building traders or merchants met daily to transact their business dealings – commercial, banking, shipping – and it continued as an Exchange for close on half a century, until the growing importance of the town as a commercial centre necessitated the erection, in 1820, of the more commodious COMMERCIAL BUILDINGS, situated on the south side of what had been in reality the FOUR CORNERS; and which, for a time, retained the name, after the formation of Donegall Street had added a fifth termination at the open space.

S. SHANNON MILLIN, *Sidelights on Belfast History*, 1932

THE FIRST CHURCH OF WHICH WE HAVE ANY RECORD was called the Church of St Patrick of the White Ford; later on it was known as Shankill, or the old church. It was a place of importance, for it had six altarages or small churches attached to it. There is not a vestige left now of the church, and an unsightly mound marks the spot where it once stood. The old graveyard is still very occasionally used by families who possess a right to bury there. The nearest church to Shankill was mentioned in 1306 as being one of the 'altarages'. It was the chapel of 'The Ford', afterwards known as the 'Corporation Church'. It was the church to which the Sovereign, or Mayor, and the Town Council went in state on Sundays. We know it now as St George's Church, in High Street. The old chapel of the ford was a small building close to the river. It was largely used by travellers, who entered the church to offer prayers for their safe journey before they attempted the dangerous crossing of the River Lagan, for it was a very hazardous undertaking in those days. Both of these buildings were standing in 1306, and probably long before that remote period.

THE REVEREND CANON FORDE, *Sketches of Olden Days in Northern Ireland*, 1926

IF YOU GO DOWN COSGRAVE STREET IN TIGER'S BAY, Belfast, and stop at the spot where Lilliput Street makes a junction you'd be in a brave desolate stretch of tundra today. The right hand side of Cosgrave Street has been nibbled and hoked away, and only the rats live now on the ground where four generations of lovely people were born, and played, and lived out their lives.

Lilliput Street took its name from a country house in the area once occupied by a well-known family named Thomson, and when I was a boy in the district fifty years ago the name Thomson had a special meaning.

But if you were at the corner of Lilliput Street today one thing you would notice amongst the surrounding decay would be the cracked concrete road at the point where it joins Cosgrave Street. And nobody would blame you for thinking that this was just part of the senility and wrinkles and bald spots that can be seen in the whole of the inner city. But no. We did that, our crowd in Tiger's Bay, one Eleventh of July – 1930, to be precise. We did it with the biggest bonfire North Belfast had ever seen. We cracked the concrete, and heated the walls of half a dozen houses till the families in them had to evacuate for two hours. They came from the streets around in their hundreds to see our bonfire. When it was at its height the police came to see it, too, out of curiosity, wondering how we got the half of the stuff we were burning, but they never found out, thank goodness.

SAM McAUGHTRY, *from* 'Galloper Thomson's Ghost', *Belfast Stories*, 1981

SANDY ROW MAY BE a somewhat common name for one of our most densely populated and thriving shopping centres, but the place it holds in the history of Belfast and the story of the city's expansion is far from commonplace. True, the name has no meaning when compared with other districts like the Shankill, Falls, Malone, Ligoniel or Ballynafeigh, nor can it claim the significance of thoroughfares like the Antrim, Crumlin, Newtownards or Lisburn roads. Yet it has an importance out of all proportion to its area.

The story of Sandy Row is the history of a small community which grew up on the outskirts of Belfast towards the middle of the eighteenth century. It was cut off from the town by the then broad waters of the Blackstaff River, but being on the main road to Dublin, and nestling on the south bank of the river immediately after crossing the Salt Water Bridge (now the Boyne Bridge), it increased in importance because of the traffic which flowed across the bridge into the town from Lambeg, Lisburn, Dromore, Newry and as far south as Dublin.

At first, it was a mere row of one-storied cottages a few yards distant from the main road, with the tidal waters of the Lagan meeting the fresh water of the Blackstaff, and thus forming a little sandy cove where the labourers' wives washed their linen, and the children paddled to their hearts' content.

The driver of the mail coach from Dublin, once he had passed the toll gates at Malone, speeded up his horses as he raced through Sandy Row, across the Salt Water Bridge into the Pound Loney, swerved right into Hamill Street and Castle Street, to pull up at the Donegall Arms in High Street.

When the new Lisburn Road was constructed early in the last century, the tollgates were moved back to the corner of Sandy Row and the new road, Sandy Row, by this time had extended almost to the toll house.

Half-way through the 1830s rumours swept into the quiet lives of the people that a great railroad was to be constructed as far as Lisburn, with an immense terminus to be erected beyond Sandy Row. The inhabitants couldn't believe their ears. To them it was the end of the world.

By the end of 1839, Sandy Row had this rail barrier added to the Blackstaff, separating the district from the town. More disastrous still was the construction of a new road running from Fisherwick Place to 'The Pass' – Great Victoria Street. Sandy Row had ceased to function as a main road.

Up till now the male population had been employed on railroad construction or shaping the new thoroughfare. With these finished, the inhabitants had a lean time until the advent of the Ulster Brewery and flax mills at Linfield Road and Tea Lane. Although Tea Lane had already lost its identity in Rowland Street, the mill was still referred to as 'Tay Lane' Mill when I was a child.

It was during the 50s and 60s of the last century that the inhabitants of the rural areas adjoining commenced their influx into the industrial centres. Streets of these small kitchen houses so familiar to Belfast were springing up like mushrooms in the Sandy Row area.

Families from the outlying districts would pile their belongings on to a country cart coming into the town – for rail transport was beyond the pockets of these country folk – and unload at the first working–class area they came to, hoping that all would be well with them. There was work in the mills, factories, and shipyards, and, to them, higher wages than the land could possibly offer.

Sandy Row was Eldorado to these folk from Lambeg, Lisburn, Hillsborough and Dromore. They would travel all night, and possibly land in Belfast on a bleak, frosty morning, before an empty house in one of the back streets of that district. All they could hope for was a kindly welcome.

It was in 1861 that my grandfather left his cottage in Drumbo, joined the stream and settled at No. 18 Sandy Row. In my early years in Sandy Row practically every family residing there had connections with the country.

Where previously the Blackstaff had separated the district from the town, the railway now added another barrier. The railway company constructed a branch forking from Utility Street to the foot of the Lisburn Road, thus isolating the community and enclosing the entire district in a 'band of steel', with only two outlets, a bridge over the river and railway at Durham Street, and a pedestrian bridge over the Railway at Utility Street. But Sandy Row continued to grow.

During the late 1870s, Sandy Row was destined to make history in the field of sport. At the top of Linfield Road was Linfield mill with an expanse of field attached. The hecklers and roughers of the mill who had been using the field in leisure hours approached the directors for permission to form a football team and the use of the ground as a playing field. The directors, not without misgivings, gave permission and this was the starting point of a club that has one of the finest records in Ulster sport – Linfield.

From its earliest days, Sandy Row has remained an exclusively working-class district, with a strong Protestant and Orange background. It has been the cockpit of many election battles. When the district was part of the South Belfast division, it was in the Sandy Row area that the parties fought it out. Now the same applies to the west division.

THOMAS CARNDUFF (1954), *Life and Writings*, 1994

'MEN ALL STOOD AT CORNERS. You would have been identified as what corner you stood at. They would have said: "Oh, sure you know him, he stands at the corner of Henry Street." Of course, they were all pubs too. They'd nothing else to do, nowhere else to go.'

FLORRIE ADDLEY, quoted in Ronnie Munck and Bill Rolston, *Belfast in the Thirties*, 1987

THE ONLY BUILDINGS BEYOND THE LINEN HALL were M'Clean's new houses in Donegall Square South, and a small mill, four stories high, with a belfry on top, where Mr Duffin's Clarence Street factory now stands, beside the Covenanting meeting-house. This belfry was often made to serve as a target for ball practice on the first establishment of the constabulary force here, under Major Darcy, who lived in M'Clean's Buildings. Bankmore House was in the country, outside the borough boundary, and so were a few cottages on the river side, close to the bridge, some of which, though altered, still exist. Taking the Blackstaff as our boundary, we soon come to Mr Joy's paper mill and the row of workers' houses, which, till recently, stood between the mill and the Cromac bridge. On the opposite, or town side, Joy's dam covered the space now occupied by Joy Street (the arches communicating between the river and the dam are still visible). From this point the embankment of the river downwards was much frequented by the inhabitants; it was then a pleasant walk, having the broad river on one hand, and grass land extending to Cromac Street on the other.

An approach to this land from Cromac Street was called Clabber Loney. On this embankment, opposite to where the Gas Works are built, there was a constant running spring, called the 'Cromac Spa'. It was much frequented by people carrying away the water, or drinking it, with a little adulteration, brought for the purpose. Continuing our walk along the river side, we come to May's Dock, which extended back into Poultry Square (what is now called Police Square). There were two bridges across this dock – one near the entrance leading to May's Fields, the other connecting Church Lane with Cromac Street and May's Market. Church Lane was then the continuation of Cromac Street. That wide and splendid thoroughfare now leading from Cromac Street to Corporation Street could then have scarcely been imagined.

THOMAS GAFFIKEN, *Belfast Fifty Years Ago*, 1894

IT IS WELL WORTH NOTING AS A TOPOGRAPHICAL FACT, though similar ones could be mentioned of all the swelling suburbs of the town, that not many years ago there was a large field immediately behind the Linen Hall, spreading in an unbroken expanse to the edge of the Blackstaff. This was called M'Clean's field or fields, though we are not certain that ownership by Mr Adam M'Clean extended over the whole space. But it is certain that the part adjoining the Malone Road, and in a line with the five very large houses in Donegall Square South, had a low brick wall enclosing the ground. In this wall was a turnstile to give admittance to the field, which was crossed by a footway to the Malone Road. In that field we have seen Dr Thomson lecturing to his pupils, and instructing them practically in the art of levelling and surveying. The low wall mentioned ran for a considerable distance from the corner, and there a large Presbyterian Meeting-house now stands. The old ditch extended from the back of the Linen Hall to the old Dublin Bridge. It was a high unsightly dike, and hedge suitable for sheltering the birds of the air, and producing the wild fruits of the earth. The change here is entirely indescribable. Immense linen factories, warehouses, offices, Ulster Hall, &c., now cover this once vacant space.

GEORGE BENN, *A History of the Town of Belfast*, 1880

IN 1957 I STARTED ASSEMBLING MATERIAL for a book on the buildings of Belfast, ultimately published ten years later. I had already a pretty intimate knowledge of the streets of the city through my activity as a Labour Party canvasser; and, by way of the various title-deeds that from time to time passed through my hands, I had more information about the history and development of the town than was available to most people. For two years I spent the greater part of each day's lunch-hour perambulating the streets and alleys of the city centre, looking closely at every single building, and recording my comments in a series of notebooks. These comments were often inane, for it was only in the process of writing that I taught myself the grammar and even the vocabulary of architecture (I still have lapses that scandalise the trained architectural historian). In the process, I came to have a warm and appreciative affection for the odd concatenations of buildings that gave Belfast its very individual character. They ranged from the seemly late-Georgian terraces of College Square, the University district, and Great George's Street, through the crowded but often gaily painted streets of parlour and kitchen houses, to the imposing extravagance of banks, merchant palaces, churches (classical, Italianate, Venetian, or Gothic Revival), and pubs. If ever a book was a labour of love, this was it: and if, as one reviewer remarked, some of my swans were geese, I have no regrets for that.

For, as it turned out, it was published only in the nick of time. A year after it appeared, the Troubles began; and soon after, the bombing campaign. Like other cities, Belfast was already suffering from the double destructive mania of roads engineers and property speculators. Today it is a conservationist's nightmare. There are still a few fine buildings undamaged, but for the most part they are shabby and neglected. Great swathes of desolation sweep through the city, where the planners and traffic engineers have laid out new and over-ambitious road-lines; but ten years later, the roads have still to be built. Gaunt and ugly office blocks, many of them standing unoccupied, have replaced fine stone Victorian warehouses. Steel barrels filled with concrete – mostly rusting – shatter-proof films of plastic glued to window-panes, concrete-block and wire-netting entanglements outside likely targets, and high iron security gates and fences, with metallic exit-only turnstiles, disfigure the streets of the city centre. Hardly a late-Georgian terrace still stands complete: almost every one is punctuated by gaps where bombed buildings have been demolished. The carcases of bombed-out shops and office blocks stand for years while the compensation authorities haggle and niggle with the owners. Churches have lost their stained glass, pubs have lost their etched glass, the windows of both are too often impartially boarded up. In street after street, the majority of the red-brick Victorian or Edwardian terrace houses have been closed, doors and windows crudely filled with concrete blocks. Thank goodness, there have been no more high-rise blocks of flats, or gallery-access blocks of maisonettes, since the Housing Executive took over from Belfast Corporation and the old Housing Trust; I have had some hand in trying to work out a new and acceptable vernacular for urban redevelopment. Another decade must pass before it is clear whether we have had some success, or whether our mistakes (and mistakes there must be) will prove as egregious as those of our predecessors. In the meanwhile, the demolition men rival the bombers in coarse heartlessness; fine stone-carvings, columnar door-cases, handsome mantel-pieces, ornate keystones, elegant staircases and balusters, even such simple materials as dressed ashlar and graded slates, all are swept away by bomb or steel ball, by fire or bulldozer, in lorry-loads of smoking rubble: all end up as filling in the Harbour Commissioners' reclamation of the muddy foreshores of Belfast Lough to create new industrial estates.

C.E.B. BRETT, *Long Shadows Cast Before*, 1978

WHAT REMAINS OF BELFAST'S industrial architecture has a strange marooned look to it. Similarly, the redbrick Gothic of insurance houses and banks, stores and churches, hotels and theatres which was once the city's Victorian legacy has all but vanished. Belfast underwent the fate of many cities in Britain and Ireland caught and mauled by the hectic redevelopment boom of the 1980s. What has taken over, inside out as it were, is the shopping mall, the steel-framed Centre and the masked façade. These changes belie another truth, however, of the profound, irrevocable change Belfast experienced as the site of sectarian violence which took possession of the city from the late 1960s – bombing campaigns in the name of Irish national liberation vied with bombing campaigns in the name of preserving the British way of life. Peace-lines of metal girders divided communities against themselves, security barriers defaced the cityscape and turned the centre into a police zone.

GERALD DAWE, *The Rest Is History*, 1998

THE ONLY SPACES ON THIS MAP are the prison exercise yard and the parade ground of the military barracks (which is half a barracks now, and half a high-rise urban complex, only the prison remains inviolate) – a sad reflection on what, on this ubiquitous dense graffiti of public houses, churches, urinals, bonding stores, graving docks, monuments, Sunday schools and Orange halls – terraces and terraces of kitchen houses, one-up-one-down houses, parlour houses, town houses, back-to-back and front-to-back and back-to-front houses – flour mills, swivel bridges, goods sheds, drinking fountains, laundries, spinning mills, foundries, coffee stalls, Gallaher's tobacco factory spewing smoke and snuff and gouts of steam over railways, tramways, coal-quays, and I see now through the time-warp something like the Belfast of *Odd Man Out* as the camera pans down from some aerial vision (the VTO craft pioneered by Shorts?) into a mass of chimney stacks and mill-stacks churning out this Titanic smoke over the spires and cupolas; suddenly,

I have just climbed the Whiterock Loney to Black Mountain, and my father and I are sitting in the Hatchet Field as he smokes a Gallaher's *Park Drive* and points out, down in the inferno, Clonard Monastery, the Falls Road, Leeson Street, the Clonard Picture-House, and the tiny blip of our house that we both pretend to see – down there, in the Beechmount brickfields, I can nearly see James Mason squatting in the catacomb of a brick kiln where I played Soldiers and Rebels, these derelict cloisters half-choked with broken brick and brick-dust, that are now gone, erased, levelled back into the clay, like all this brick-built demolition city, like this house we strain our eyes to see through the smog, homing in through the terraces and corner shops and spires and urinals to squat by the fire – coal-brick smouldering and hissing – while my father tells me a story . . .

CIARAN CARSON, *Belfast Confetti*, 1989

Acknowledgements

The editor and publisher gratefully acknowledge permission to include the following copyright material:

ADAMS, GERRY, from *Falls Memories* (Brandon Publications, 1982), by permission of Brandon Publications.

ADCOCK, FLEUR, 'Please Identify Yourself' from *The Scenic Route* (Oxford University Press, 1974), by permission of Oxford University Press.

ALYN, MARJORY, from *The Sound of Anthems* (Hodder & Stoughton, 1983), by permission of Hodder & Stoughton.

ARMSTRONG, EDWARD ALLWORTHY, from *Birds of the Grey Wind* (Oxford University Press, 1940), by permission of Oxford University Press.

ARTHURS, JOHN B., from *Belfast in Its Regional Setting* (British Association for the Advancement of Science, 1952), copyright holder not traced.

BAILEY, ANTHONY, from *Acts of Union* (Faber & Faber, 1980), by permission of Faber & Faber.

BARDON, JONATHAN, in the *Independent* (31 October 1993), by permission of the author and the *Independent*; from *Belfast: An Illustrated History* (Blackstaff Press, 1982), by permission of the Blackstaff Press.

BECKETT, MARY, from *Give Them Stones* (Bloomsbury Publishing, 1990), by permission of Bloomsbury Publishing.

BEHAN, BRENDAN, from *Brendan Behan's Island* (Hutchinson, 1962), by permission of the Tessa Sayle Agency.

BELFAST NATURAL HISTORY AND PHILOSOPHICAL SOCIETY, from *Belfast Natural History and Philosophical Society 1821–1921* (1924), by permission of John Gray, president.

BELL, SAM HANNA, from *December Bride* (Denis Dobson, 1951; reissued by Blackstaff Press, 1974); from *The Hollow Ball* (Cassell, 1961; reissued by Blackstaff Press, 1990), both by permission of the Blackstaff Press.

BIRMINGHAM, GEORGE A., from *The Red Hand of Ulster* (Smith, Elder, 1912; reissued by Irish Universities Press, 1972); from *Pleasant Places* (William Heinemann, 1934), both by permission of Susan Harper.

DE BLÁCAM, AODH, from *The Black North* (W.H. Gill & Son, 1938), by permission of Carl de Blácam.

BLACKWOOD, CAROLINE, from *For All That I Found There* (Duckworth, 1973), by permission of the Wylie Agency.

BOLES, AGNES, from *The Belfast Boy* (David Nutt, 1912), copyright holder not traced.

BOYD, JOHN, from *Out of My Class* (Blackstaff Press, 1985); from *The Middle of My Journey* (Blackstaff Press, 1990), both by permission of the Blackstaff Press.

BRETT, C.E.B., from *Long Shadows Cast Before* (John Bartholomew, 1978), by permission of the author.

BRYANS, ROBIN, from *Ulster: A Journey Through the Six Counties* (Faber & Faber, 1964; reissued by Blackstaff Press, 1989), by permission of the author.

BUCHANAN, GEORGE, from *Green Seacoast* (Gaberbocchus, 1959); from *Morning Papers* (Gaberbocchus, 1965), both by permission of Sandra Buchanan, literary executor to George Buchanan.

BULLOCK, SHAN F., from *Thomas Andrews, Shipbuilder* (Maunsel, 1912; reissued by Blackstaff Press, 1999), copyright holder not traced.

BYRNE, DONN, *Changeling and Other Stories* (Samson Low, 1931), copyright holder not traced.

CALVERT, RAYMOND, 'The Ballad of William Bloat', by permission of Irene Calvert.

CAMPBELL, JOSEPH, 'The Orangeman', 'The Ragman', ''Tis Pretty tae be in Baile-Liosan' from *The Poems of Joseph Campbell* (Allen Figgis, 1963), by permission of Simon D. Campbell.

CAMPBELL, T.J., from *Fifty Years of Ulster 1890–1940* (Irish News, 1941), by permission of the Irish News.

CARNDUFF, THOMAS, from *Thomas Carnduff: Life and Writings* (Lagan Press, 1994), by permission of Lagan Press.

CARSON, CIARAN, 'Patchwork', 'Slate Street School', 'August 1969', 'The Exiles' Club' and 'Smithfield Market' from *The Irish For No* (Gallery Press, 1987); 'Farset', 'Question Time', 'Hamlet', 'Bloody Hand', 'Turn Again' and 'Belfast Confetti' from *Belfast Confetti* (Gallery Press, 1989), all by kind permission of the author and the Gallery Press; from *The Star Factory*, copyright © 1997 by Ciaran Carson. Published by Granta Books.

CAULFIELD, MAX, from *The Black City* (Jonathan Cape, 1952), by permission of Jonathan Cape.

CHESTERTON, G.K., from *Irish Impressions* (Collins, 1919), by permission of A.P. Watt.

CONROY, JOHN, from *War as a Way of Life* (William Heinemann, 1988), by permission of William Heinemann.

COSTELLO, MARY, from *Titanic Town* (Methuen, 1992), by permission of Methuen.

CRAIG, MAURICE JAMES, 'Ballad to a Traditional Refrain', by permission of the author; from *The Elephant and the Polish Question* (Lilliput Press, 1990), by permission of the author and the Lilliput Press.

CROFTS, FREEMAN WILLS, from *Sir John Magill's Last Journey* (Collins, 1930), by permission of HarperCollins Publishers.

DAVIE, DONALD, 'Belfast on a Sunday Afternoon', from *Selected Poems* (Carcanet Press, 1985), by permission of Carcanet Press.

DAWE, GERALD, 'A Question of Covenants' and 'Little Palaces' from *The Lundys Letter* (Gallery Press, 1985), by kind permission of the author and the Gallery Press; from *The Rest Is History* (Abbey Press, 1998), by permission of Abbey Press.

DEVLIN, ANNE, from *The Way-Paver* (Faber & Faber, 1986), by permission of Faber & Faber.

DEVLIN, PADDY, from *Straight Left* (Blackstaff Press, 1993), by permission of the Blackstaff Press.

DIBDIN, MICHAEL, in the *London Review of Books* (April 1988), reprinted by permission of the Peters Fraser & Dunlop Group.

DOUGLAS, JAMES, from *The Unpardonable Sin* (1907), copyright holder not traced.

DURCAN, PAUL, 'The Riding School' from *Crazy About Women* (National Gallery of Ireland, 1991), by permission of the author.

ERVINE, ST JOHN, in the *Belfast Telegraph* (1944, 1945, 1946); from *Mrs Martin's Man* (Allen, 1913); from *The Wayward Man* (Collins, 1926), all by permission of the Society of Authors as the literary representative of the Estate of St John Ervine.

EVANS, E. ESTYN, from *Ireland and the Atlantic Heritage, Selected Writings* (Lilliput Press, 1995), by permission of Mrs Gwyneth Evans and the Lilliput Press; from *Northern Ireland* (Collins, 1951), by permission of HarperCollins Publishing.

EWART, WILFRED, from *A Journey in Ireland, 1921* (G.P. Putnam's Sons, 1922), copyright holder not traced.

FENTON, JAMES AND JOHN FULLER, 'Chlorine Gardens, Belfast' from *Partingtime Hall* (Penguin, 1987), reprinted by permission of the Peters Fraser & Dunlop Group.

FIACC, PADRAIC, 'First Movement' and 'By the Black Stream' from *By the Black Stream* (Dolmen Press, 1969), by permission of the author.

FLEMING, GEORGE, from *Magennis VC* (History Ireland, 1998), by permission of History Ireland.

FORDE, CANON, from *Sketches from Olden Days in Northern Ireland* (McCaw, Stevenson & Orr, 1926), copyright holder not traced.

FORSTER, E.M., from *Abinger Harvest* (Arnold, 1936), by permission of the Provost and Scholars of King's College, Cambridge, and the Society of Authors as the literary representatives of the E.M. Forster Estate.

FOSTER, JEANNE COOPER, from *Ulster Folklore* (H.R. Carter, 1951), copyright holder not traced.

FOSTER, JOHN WILSON, from *The Titanic Complex* (Belcouver Press, 1997), by permission of the Belcouver Press.

FRIERS, ROWEL, from *Drawn from Life* (Blackstaff Press, 1994), by permission of Yvonne Friers.

FULLER, JOHN AND JAMES FENTON, 'Chlorine Gardens, Belfast' from *Partingtime Hall* (Penguin, 1987), reprinted by permission of the Peters Fraser & Dunlop Group.

FULLER, ROY, 'In Belfast' from *Last Poems* (Sinclair-Stevenson, 1993), by permission of Sinclair-Stevenson.

GALLAGHER, CARMEL, from *All Around the Loney-O* (St Louise's Comprehensive College, 1978), by permission of St Louise's Comprehensive College and the author.

GARNER, MARGARET A.K., from *Robert Workman of Newtownbreda, 1835–1921* (William Mullan & Son, 1969), copyright holder not traced.

GOLDRING, MAURICE, from *Belfast: From Loyalty to Rebellion* (Lawrence & Wishart, 1991), by permission of Lawrence & Wishart.

GOOD, JAMES WINDER, from *Ulster and Ireland* (Maunsel, 1919), copyright holder not traced.

GREACEN, ROBERT, 'Drummond Allison, 1921–1953', 'John Hewitt' and 'Revisiting Belfast' from *Collected Poems 1944–1994* (Lagan Press, 1995); from *The Sash My Father Wore: An Autobiography* (Mainstream Publishing Company, 1997), all by permission of Jonathan Williams Literary Agency.

GREEN, F.L., from *Odd Man Out* (Michael Joseph, 1945), by permission of Michael Joseph.

GREENE, GRAHAM, 'Convoy to West Africa' from *The Mint: A Miscellany*, ed. Geoffrey Grigson (Routledge, 1946), by permission of David Higham Associates.

GWYNN, STEPHEN, from *The Famous Cities of Ireland* (Macmillan, 1915); from *Highways and Byways in Donegal and Antrim* (Macmillan, 1989), copyright holder not traced.

HAMILL, BRENDAN, in *Krino* (1985), by permission of the author.

HANNA, DENIS O'D, from *Ulster As It Is* (B.T. Batsford, 1956), by permission of B.T. Batsford.

HARBINSON, ROBERT, from *No Surrender: An Ulster Childhood* (Faber & Faber, 1969; reissued by Blackstaff Press, 1987), by permission of the author.

HASTINGS, MAX, from *Ulster 1969: The Fight for Civil Rights in Northern Ireland* (Victor Gollancz, 1970), reprinted by permission of the Peters Fraser & Dunlop Group.

HEANEY, SEAMUS, 'Linen Town' from *Wintering Out* (Faber & Faber, 1972); from *Preoccuptions* (Faber & Faber, 1980), both by permission of Faber & Faber.

HENRY, PAUL, from *Further Reminiscences* (Blackstaff Press, 1973), copyright holder not traced.

HEWITT, JOHN, 'The Double-Ended Tram', 'On Dunmore's Waste', 'A Happy Boy', 'Reading', 'Encounter 1920', 'After the Fire', 'Our Avenue', 'The Troubles 1922', 'Balloons and Wooden Guns', 'The River Streets', 'Two Spectres Haunt Me' from *Kites in Spring* (Blackstaff Press, 1982); 'The Coasters' from *An Ulster Reckoning* (Blackstaff Press, 1971), by permission of the Blackstaff Press on behalf of the Estate of John Hewitt.

HOBSON, BULMER, from *Ireland Yesterday and Tomorrow* (Anvil Press, 1968), copyright holder not traced.

INNES, MICHAEL, *The Journeying Boy* (Victor Gollancz, 1949), by permission of A.P. Watt.

IRELAND, DENIS, from *From the Irish Shore* (Rich & Cowan, 1936); from *From the Jungle of Belfast* (Blackstaff Press, 1973), both by permission of H.M. Ireland.

JOHNSTONE, ROBERT, from *Images of Belfast* (Blackstaff Press, 1983), by permission of the Blackstaff Press; from *Belfast: Portraits of a City* (Barrie & Jenkins, 1990), by permission of Barrie & Jenkins.

JONES, EMRYS, from *A Social Geography of Belfast* (Oxford University Press, 1960), copyright holder not traced; from *Belfast in Its Regional Setting* (British Association for the Advancement of Science, 1952), copyright holder not traced.

JOYCE, JAMES, from *Finnegans Wake* (Faber & Faber, 1939). Excerpt from page 140 of *Finnegans Wake* reproduced with the permission of the Estate of James Joyce; © copyright, Estate of James Joyce.

KANE, ALICE, from *Songs and Sayings of an Ulster Childhood* (McClelland & Stewart, Toronto/ Wolfhound Press, Dublin, 1983), by permission of Alice Kane and Wolfhound Press.

KERR, ARCHIBALD, W.M. from *By the Pool of Garmoyle* (Northern Whig, 1925), copyright holder not traced.

LARDNER, RING, JNR, from *The Ecstasy of Owen Muir* (Jonathan Cape, 1954), by permission of Jonathan Cape.

LARKIN, PHILIP, 'The Importance of Elsewhere' from *The Whitsun Weddings* (Faber & Faber, 1964), by permission of Faber & Faber.

LEITCH, MAURICE, from *Silver's City* (Secker & Warburg, 1981), by permission of Secker & Warburg.

LEPPER, JOHN HERON, from *The North-East Corner* (Richards, 1917), copyright holder not traced.

LEWIS, C.S., from *Surprised by Joy* (Bles, 1955), by permission of HarperCollins Publishers.

LOGAN, JAMES, from *Ulster in the X-Rays* (A.H. Stockwell, 1922), copyright holder not traced.

LONGLEY, MICHAEL, 'Letters' from *An Exploded View* (Victor Gollancz, 1973), by permission of the author; 'The Rag Trade' and 'The Linen Industry' from *The Echo Gate* (Secker & Warburg, 1979), by permission of the author; 'The Ice-Cream Man' from *Gorse Fires* (Secker & Warburg, 1991), by permission of Secker & Warburg; from *Tuppeny Stung* (Lagan Press, 1994), by permission of the author.

LOWRY, MARY, from *The Story of Belfast and Its Surroundings* (Headley, 1913), copyright holder not traced.

LYND, ROBERT, from *Home Life in Ireland* (Mills & Boon, 1909), copyright holder not traced; from *The Orange Tree* (Methuen, 1926), by permission of Methuen.

MACARDLE, DOROTHY, from *The Irish Republic* (Victor Gollancz, 1937; reissued by Wolfhound Press, 1999), by permission of Wolfhound Press.

MCAUGHTRY, SAM, from *The Sinking of the Kenbane Head* (Blackstaff Press, 1977); from *Belfast Stories* (Ward River Press, 1981; reissued by Blackstaff Press, 1993), both by permission of the author.

MCCRYSTAL, CAL, from *Reflections on a Quiet Rebel* (Michael Joseph, 1997), by permission of Michael Joseph.

MCELBOROUGH, ROBERT, from *The Autobiography of a Belfast Working Man* (Public Record Office of Northern Ireland, 1974), by permission of the Deputy Keeper of the Records, Public Record Office of Northern Ireland, and the Ulster Museum as depositor of the document.

MCFADDEN, ROY, 'Ballyhackamore', 'After Seymour's Funeral' and 'Old Style' from *Collected Poems (1943–1995)* (Lagan Press, 1996), by permission of the author.

MACLAVERTY, BERNARD, from *The Great Profundo and Other Stories* (Jonathan Cape, 1987), by permission of Jonathan Cape; from *Secrets and Other Stories* (Blackstaff Press, 1977), by permission of the Blackstaff Press.

MCLAVERTY, MICHAEL, from *Lost Fields* (Jonathan Cape, 1942), © the estate of Michael McLaverty; *Call My Brother Back* (Jonathan Cape, 1939; reissued by Poolbeg Press, 1979), © the estate of Michael McLaverty, both by permission of the Literary Executors.

MAC LIAMMÓIR, MICHEÁL, from *Put Money in Thy Purse* (Methuen, 1952), by permission of Methuen.

MACNEICE, LOUIS, from *Zoo* (Michael Joseph, 1938), by permission of Michael Joseph; 'Belfast', 'Valediction', 'Carrickfergus' and 'Autumn Journal' from *Collected Poems* (Faber & Faber, 1966), by permission of David Higham Associates.

MCNEILL, JANET, from *Tea at Four O'Clock* (Hodder & Stoughton, 1956; reissued by Virago, 1988); from *The Maiden Dinosaur* (Bles, 1964; reissued by Blackstaff Press, 1984), both by permission of A.P. Watt on behalf of David Alexander.

MCNEILL, MARY, *The Life and Times of Mary Ann McCracken 1770–1866: A Belfast Panorama* (Allen Figgis & Company, 1960; reissued by Blackstaff Press, 1988), copyright holder not traced.

MAHON, DEREK, 'Glengormley', 'In Belfast', 'Ecclesiastes', 'Afterlives' and 'Courtyards in Delft' from *Collected Poems* (Gallery Press, 1999), by kind permission of the author and the Gallery Press.

MAY, NAOMI, from *The Troubles* (Calder Publications, 1976), by permission of the Calder Educational Trust.

MESSENGER, BETTY, from *Picking Up the Linen Threads* (Blackstaff Press, 1975), by permission of the author.

MILLIGAN, ALICE, from *Collected Poems* (Gill & Macmillan, 1954), by permission of Gill & Macmillan.

MILLIN, S. SHANNON, from *Sidelights on Belfast History* (W. & G. Baird, 1932), copyright holder not traced.

MILROY, JAMES, from *Regional Accents of English: Belfast* (Blackstaff Press, 1981), by permission of the Blackstaff Press.

MONTAGUE, JOHN, 'The Rough Field' from *Collected Poems* (Gallery Press, 1995), by kind permission of the author and the Gallery Press.

MOORE, A., from *Belfast Today* (*c.* 1910), copyright holder not traced.

MOORE, BRIAN, from *Judith Hearne* (André Deutsch, 1955); from *The Feast of Lupercal* (André Deutsch, 1958); from *The Emperor of Ice-Cream* (André Deutsch, 1966), all © Brian Moore, reprinted by permission of Curtis Brown; from *Lies of Silence* (Bloomsbury Publishing, 1990), by permission of Bloomsbury Publishing.

MOORE, F. FRANKFORT, from *The Truth About Ulster* (Eveleigh Nash, 1914), copyright holder not traced.

MORRISON, VAN, lyrics from 'On Hyndford Street' (Morrison) © 1991 by kind permission of Exile Publishing Limited/PolyGram Music Publishing Limited.

MORROW, JOHN, from *Northern Myths* (Blackstaff Press, 1979); from *The Essex Factor* (Blackstaff Press, 1982), both by permission of the Blackstaff Press.

MORTON, MAY, from *Sung to the Spinning Wheel* (Quota Press, 1952), copyright holder not traced.

MOTION, ANDREW, 'Leaving Belfast' from *Dangerous Play: Poems 1974–84* (Penguin, 1985), reprinted by permission of the Peters Fraser & Dunlop Group.

MULDOON, PAUL, 'The One Desire' and 'History' from *Why Brownlee Left* (Faber & Faber, 1980); 'Gathering Mushrooms' from *Quoof* (Faber & Faber, 1983), both by permission of Faber & Faber.

MUNCK, RONNIE and BILL ROLSTON, from *Belfast in the Thirties* (Blackstaff Press, 1989), by permission of the authors.

MURPHY, DERVLA, from *A Place Apart* (John Murray, 1978), by permission of John Murray.

MURPHY, RICHARD, 'The Battle of Aughrim' from *Collected Poems* (Gallery Press, 2000), by kind permission of the author and the Gallery Press.

O'BRIEN, KATE, from *My Ireland* (B.T. Batsford, 1962), by permission of David Higham Associates.

O'BYRNE, CATHAL, from *As I Roved Out* (Irish News, 1946; reissued by Blackstaff Press, 1982), by permission of the Blackstaff Press.

O'FAOLAIN, SEAN, from *An Irish Journey* (Longman & Green, 1940) copyright © 1940 Sean O'Faolain. Reproduced by permission of the estate of Sean O'Faolain, c/o Rogers, Coleridge & White, 20 Powis Mews, London, W11 1JN

ORMSBY, FRANK, 'Amelia Street' from *Business as Usual* (Ulsterman Publications, 1973), by permission of the author; 'Floods' from *A Store of Candles* (Oxford University Press, 1977; reissued by Gallery Press, 1986); 'King William Park' from *A Northern Spring* (Gallery Press, 1986), both by kind permission of the author and the Gallery Press.

O'ROURKE, P.J., from *Holidays in Hell* (Macmillan Publishers, 1989), by permission of Macmillan Publishers.

OWEN, D.J., *History of Belfast* (W. & G. Baird, 1921), copyright holder not traced.

PATTERSON, GLENN, from *Burning Your Own* (Chatto & Windus, 1988); from *Fat Lad* (Chatto & Windus, 1992), by permission of Chatto & Windus.

PAULIN, TOM, 'Settlers' and 'Under the Eyes' from *A State of Justice* (Faber & Faber, 1977); 'In the Lost Province' and 'The Other Voice' from *The Strange Museum* (Faber & Faber, 1980); 'To the Linen Hall' from *Liberty Tree* (Faber & Faber, 1983), all by permission of Faber & Faber.

PIM, HERBERT MOORE, from *Unknown Immortals* (Talbot Press, 1917), copyright holder not traced.

PRAEGER, ROBERT LLOYD, from *The Way That I Went* (Hodges Figgis, 1937), copyright holder not traced.

PRICE, VICTOR, from *The Other Kingdom* (William Heinemann, 1964), by permission of William Heinemann.

PRITCHETT, V.S., from *Midnight Oil* (Chatto & Windus, 1971), by permission of Chatto & Windus.

QUINN, HUBERT, from *Hold Back the Shadows* (*c.* 1940), copyright holder not traced.

RECHTS, ALBERT, from *Handbook to a Hypothetical City* (Lilliput Press, 1986), by permission of the author and the Lilliput Press.

REID, FORREST, from *At the Door of the Gate* (Arnold, 1915); from *Apostate* (Constable, 1926); from *Peter Waring* (Faber & Faber, 1937; reissued by Blackstaff Press, 1976), all by permission of the John Johnson Agency.

RICE, ADRIAN, 'The Musicians' Union' from *Impediments* (Abbey Press, 1997), by permission of Abbey Press.

Index of Authors